MW00680329

World of Trouble

THE LEWIS WALPOLE SERIES IN

EIGHTEENTH-CENTURY CULTURE AND HISTORY

The Lewis Walpole Series, published by Yale University Press with the aid of the Annie Burr Lewis Fund, is dedicated to the culture and history of the long eighteenth century (from the Glorious Revolution to the accession of Queen Victoria). It welcomes work in a variety of fields, including literature and history, the visual arts, political philosophy, music, legal history, and the history of science. In addition to original scholarly work, the series publishes new editions and translations of writing from the period, as well as reprints of major books that are currently unavailable. Though the majority of books in the series will probably concentrate on Great Britain and the Continent, the range of our geographical interests is as wide as Horace Walpole's.

World of Trouble

A Philadelphia Quaker Family's Journey through the American Revolution

Richard Godbeer

Yale UNIVERSITY PRESS NEW HAVEN AND LONDON

Published with assistance from the Annie Burr Lewis Fund.

Yale University Press books may be purchased in quantity for educational, business, or promotional use. For information, please e-mail sales.press@yale.edu (U.S. office) or sales@yaleup.co.uk (U.K. office).

Set in Scala type by IDS Infotech Ltd., Chandigarh, India.
Printed in the United States of America.

Library of Congress Control Number: 2019938842
ISBN 978-0-300-21998-2 (hardcover : alk. paper)

A catalogue record for this book is available from the British Library.

This paper meets the requirements of ANSI/NISO Z39.48-1992 (Permanence of Paper).

10 9 8 7 6 5 4 3 2 1

To Margaret and Grace,
For believing in me, and the Drinkers

Contents

ACKNOWLEDGMENTS

It is only right that I begin by expressing my gratitude to Elizabeth Sandwith Drinker and Henry Drinker for all they have taught me about the world that they moved in. They cannot have anticipated that their diaries and letters would survive so far into the future, or that just over two centuries after their deaths a historian who was born in England but lives in the United States would spend the better part of a decade reconstructing their experience of the revolutionary period. I doubt that they would approve of everything I have written about them, but I hope they would recognize at least part of themselves in the pages that follow and even more that they would think I have done my best to tell their story with authenticity and respect. Their children, grandchildren, and descendants into the late twentieth century took good care of family papers that could so easily have been lost, and eventually handed them over to the care of modern archivists. This book would not have been possible without their commitment to preserving Elizabeth and Henry's writings for posterity.

One scholar in particular has played a crucial role in making Elizabeth Drinker's diary accessible to all students of the revolutionary period. Anyone with an interest in the Drinkers owes a huge debt to Elaine Forman Crane, whose meticulously edited edition of Elizabeth Drinker's diary contains a wealth of information about the Drinker family and Philadelphia in the late eighteenth century. While working on this book, I have often given silent thanks to Elaine Crane and her team for their herculean efforts, and it is a great pleasure now to recognize their work. During my research, I have also come to appreciate afresh the depth of knowledge that archivists accumulate as they sift through collections to compile readers guides and extract items requested by visiting scholars. Steve Smith, Sarah Heim, and David Haugaard at the Historical Society of Pennsylvania have been particularly generous of their time and expertise. I am also grateful to the staff at Swarthmore College's Friends Historical Library, the Quaker and Special Collections division at the Haverford College Libraries, the American Philosophical Society, the Library Company of Philadelphia, and the Library of Congress.

I first encountered the Drinkers when I served on my very first doctoral dissertation committee in the early 1990s. That gave me the opportunity to work with and learn from Debra O'Neal, who was writing a dissertation about the transformation of women's domestic labor in eighteenth-century Philadelphia. Debbie's subsequent illness and premature death prevented her turning that dissertation into a book, which was a great loss to the field. The chapter in this book on Elizabeth Drinker's relationship with her servants is much indebted to my conversations many years ago with Debbie. I remember at the time wondering what role, if any, Elizabeth's husband had in the management of the Drinkers' domestic staff. Elizabeth gives us occasional hints in her diary about Henry's involvement, but it was when I stumbled on Henry Drinker's letter books at the Pennsylvania Historical Society, while researching for a book on male friendship, that I realized I could write a book in which both Elizabeth and Henry had equal voices. So many books owe their inception to such moments of accidental discovery, but often we are sensitized to items that we happen upon by past conversations, and in this case it was Debbie whose voice I could hear egging me on as I flicked through the catalog cards with increasing excitement.

Several institutions gave generous financial support that enabled me to spend time in Philadelphia combing through archival material. I was fortunate to receive a Franklin Research Grant from the American Philosophical Society, a Society for Historians of the Early American Republic Fellowship to work at the Library Company of Philadelphia and the Historical Society of Pennsylvania, and a University of Miami Provost Research Award, alongside ongoing support from the Department of History and the College of Arts and Sciences at the University of Miami, and the College of Humanities and Sciences at Virginia Commonwealth University. A Research Fellowship at the University of Miami's Center for the Humanities gave me a semester away from teaching in fall 2013, during which I wrote my first draft chapter about the Drinkers. At Virginia Commonwealth University, Dean James Coleman, Senior Associate Dean Alison Baski, and Associate Dean for Research Scott Gronert made sure that I had time to continue writing alongside my work as founding Director of the Humanities Research Center. My first administrative coordinator at the center, Gail Bartee Cantor, did a fine job of protecting me from interruption during writing sessions, and her successor, Michael Means, has been equally understanding of my need to set aside time for the Drinkers. I am grateful to Michael as well as Tom Woodward and Matt Roberts at VCU's ALT Lab for their help in formatting the three family trees, and to Frankie Mastrangelo for her help in formatting the map of the Drinkers' neighborhood.

As always, colleagues and friends have been generous companions on my journey with the Drinkers, providing much-needed advice as well as support and good cheer. The Premodern Society and Culture research group at the Humanities Research Center here in Richmond has been a wonderful forum for discussion of work-in-progress that manages somehow to combine rigorous critique with unfailing good humor and generosity of spirit. I am also grateful to members of the Omohundro Institute of Early American History and Culture Colloquium, especially Karin Wulf, the Fall Line Early Americanists, especially Douglas Winiarski, and the Triangle Early American Seminar at the National Humanities Center, especially Kathleen DuVal, for their comments on draft chapters. Other helpful conversations took place at a session of the 2011 annual meeting of the American Society for Eighteenth-Century Studies in Boston, entitled "Religion, War, and Nation: Philadelphian Quakers in the Revolutionary Atlantic," at a session of the 2012 annual conference of the Omohundro Institute of Early American History and Culture in Pasadena, entitled "Inward Vision and Outward Struggle: Quaker Reflective Practice and Political Contest in the Early Modern Atlantic World," and at sessions on motherhood and the female body, romantic courtship, and microhistory at the 2014, 2015, and 2016 annual meetings of the Society for Historians of the Early American Republic in Philadelphia, Raleigh, and New Haven, respectively. My special thanks to Wendy Lucas, Donna Rilling, and Ned Donoghue for alerting me to sources that I might otherwise have missed.

Virginia Commonwealth University is fortunate to have an unusually large number of scholars working on Early America and the Atlantic World. Michael Dickinson, Carolyn Eastman, Catherine Ingrassia, Mary Caton Lingold, Sarah Meacham, and Ryan Smith gave generously of their time in reading and commenting on individual chapters. Brooke Newman and Gregory Smithers read the entire manuscript and gave me comments that were both practical and insightful. Brooke and Greg are among my favorite colleagues and friends here in Richmond: they are very funny, very kind, and very smart.

Wendy Lucas, many years ago one of my doctoral students in California and now a treasured friend, indulged me during many phone conversations as I tried to figure out how to balance and integrate Henry's and Elizabeth's accounts of their life together. Wendy not only read the entire manuscript but later read parts of it again, an act of generosity verging on insanity. Christine Heyrman, who oversaw my own dissertation many decades ago and has unaccountably never quite tired of me, also read the entire manuscript and gave me characteristically generous-spirited yet incisive comments that cut right to the heart of whatever was lacking in each chapter. Sarah Crabtree and Jane Calvert, the readers for Yale University Press, provided model reports on the manuscript that balanced a clear recognition of what I was trying to achieve in the book with a frank appraisal of what more I needed to do if I was to get there. Just as I entered the final phase of revisions, I had the good fortune to meet Ned Donoghue, a retired lawyer and independent scholar who writes about pacifists in the eighteenth-century mid-Atlantic. Ned's wealth of knowledge about the Quaker exiles has been an invaluable gift, and I appreciate his careful read of the chapters dealing with the revolutionary period. However, my greatest debt this time around is to Chris Rogers, the history editor at Yale University Press. He has believed in this project from the start, has recognized the challenge of maintaining a focus on the specific story I wanted to tell without losing sight of the big picture, and throughout has been as relentlessly challenging as he has been relentlessly supportive. I hope he knows how much I admire him and appreciate his faith in me and this project. My sincere thanks also to Laura Jones Dooley for her careful copyediting of the manuscript, and to Adina Berk and Susan Laity for shepherding the project through production at the press.

My nonacademic friends have been unfailingly supportive and indulgent in ways that I hope I never take for granted. One of the payoffs for heading through middle age, offsetting the curse of bleary eyes and occasionally creaky joints, is the presence of friends who have been around for many years and who understand our quirks in ways that recently acquired friends, however perceptive and caring, cannot. I hope that my many friends, near and far, old and new, know how much they mean to me. Turning from my adoptive family to my biological family, I want to acknowledge two very special pillars of support. My mother, Margaret, and my aunt Grace have always been steadfast in their encouragement of my work, but they have both taken a particular interest in this project ever since I first started talking about it and have read every chapter in draft. Neither has any connection to the academic world, but they have both responded to the intimate drama of the Drinkers' lives and have helped me not to lose sight of the place that individual stories play in larger histories. To them I dedicate this book with love and gratitude. I know that both will be happy to share this paragraph with my trusty Jack Russell terrier, Rufus, who has been my faithful companion throughout this venture, reminding me at regular intervals—very regular intervals—to set aside the keyboard and get some fresh air. His devotion, sense of humor, and wisdom about all things truly important are a daily inspiration.

Richmond, Virginia
March 2019

An East Prospect of the City of Philadelphia; taken by George Heap from the Jersey Shore, under the Direction of Nicholas Scull[,] Surveyor General of the Province of Pennsylvania, engraved by Thomas Jeffreys in 1771 (Library of Congress)

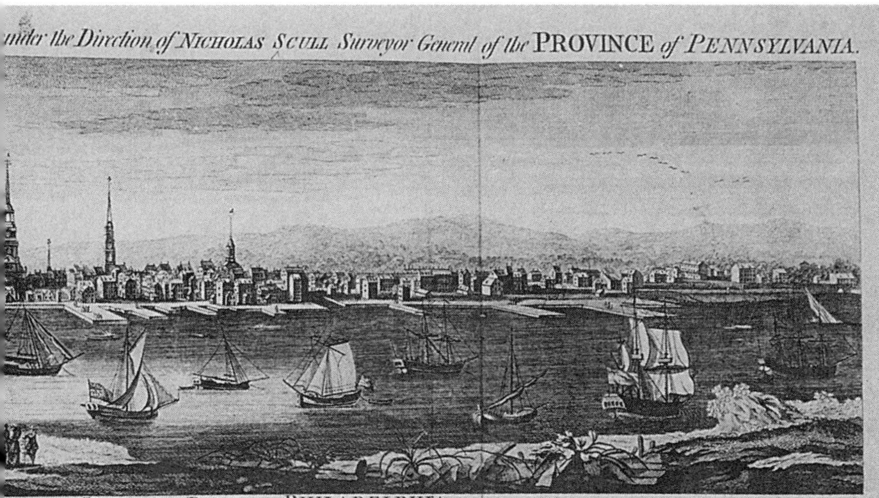
under the Direction of NICHOLAS SCULL Surveyor General of the PROVINCE of PENNSYLVANIA.
F THE CITY AND PORT OF PHILADELPHIA.

Introduction

It was September 11, 1777, and the moment that forty-two-year-old Elizabeth Drinker had been dreading was finally arrived. Elizabeth's husband, Henry, her senior by one year and a prosperous Quaker merchant, was among thirty men who had been arrested a week before on suspicion of treason. Pennsylvania's patriot government had brought no formal or specific charges against these individuals, but most were Quaker pacifists who refused to fight with or otherwise support either side in the War for Independence. The prisoners, locked up in a makeshift prison at the Masonic Lodge in Philadelphia, had written several letters of protest, denouncing their treatment and demanding a formal hearing. The Supreme Executive Council had informed them in turn that they must swear "allegiance to the Commonwealth of Pennsylvania, as a free and independent state," or suffer the consequences. Only a third of the prisoners took the oath and secured their freedom; twenty remained in prison, nineteen of them Quakers. Their families and friends, outraged by what Elizabeth called "the tyrannical conduct of the present wicked rulers," visited them daily, waiting anxiously to see what would happen next. The revolutionary government had decided to send the prisoners to Virginia as exiles, with their ultimate fate uncertain. Most of the detainees were men of property, and the council had promised that they would be allowed to depart in their own carriages, as befitted gentlemen, but that promise was now broken, and they were to leave instead in wagons commandeered for the occasion. The moment of departure turned out to be emotionally fraught and violent. Sarah Fisher, wife of prisoner Thomas Fisher, recorded in her diary that the prisoners were "dragged" outside into the wagons "by force" and then "drove off surrounded by guards and a mob." Yet not all of those who gathered to watch were hostile to the twenty men. When the time came for the prisoners' removal, wrote Thomas Gilpin, another of the exiles, the surrounding streets "were crowded by men, women, and children, who by their countenances sufficiently though silently expressed the grief they felt on the occasion."[1]

As wagons carried the exiles away, torn from their loved ones, gunfire resounded in the distance. Elizabeth noted in her diary that the town was "in great confusion" that day. Patriot soldiers were fighting a few miles distant at the Battle of Brandywine to halt the British advance toward Philadelphia, and now her husband had disappeared into a war-ravaged landscape from which he might never reemerge. Elizabeth could not find the words to describe the prisoners' departure, but she wrote that night that afterward she had gone "in great distress" to a friend's house before returning to her own home and her five small children. Over the coming days, she would assure Henry in a series of loving, anxious letters that he was "much talked of, and much felt for." In the meantime, Elizabeth faced an uncertain future as she assumed responsibility for protecting their home and young family against the horrors of war in a city held first by the patriots, then by the British, and then again by the patriots. By the time that Henry and the other prisoners returned eight months later amid growing controversy over their treatment, at no point formally charged with any crime, two of the exiles had died and Henry himself had endured serious illness. The "cruel separation" had proven a harrowing ordeal for him, Elizabeth, and their entire family.[2]

The fate of the Quaker community remained in peril throughout the War for Independence. Most Quakers, including Henry Drinker, condemned the British policies that led to protest, rebellion, and ultimately revolution. Yet Friends, as Quakers called themselves, were reluctant to reject outright the crown's authority, in part because the monarchy had defended them for many decades against persecution, but also and crucially because of their commitment to pacifism and to reform over revolution. Eighteenth-century Quakers believed that subjects had the right and duty to resist unjust policies through peaceful protest but should not seek to overthrow any government that God had placed over them. Quakers envisaged that constitutional change would take place gradually over time as people developed a clearer sense of what was right and sought to create just governments through debate, negotiation, and, when necessary, protest. Their insistence that change should occur through an ongoing process of peaceable reform, not violence or revolution, made them anathema to patriots who now wanted a complete break from Britain and what they saw as its hopelessly corrupt, oppressive system of government.

The outbreak of war made Quaker pacifism even more aggravating for patriots facing the might of the British army: when most Friends adopted a position of principled neutrality, patriots doubted their sincerity and accused them of having secret loyalist sympathies, thus the wave of arrests.[3]

Quakers had struck many people as dangerous ever since they first emerged as a radical dissenting movement during the English Revolution in the seventeenth century. Quakers rejected many beliefs central to mainstream Protestantism. Instead of seeing scripture as the sole and final source of divine truth, they believed each man and woman to have within them a spark of divinity that enabled them to discern and speak God's truth. That truth would emerge over time through revelation, which men and women of any social status might experience and then share. Their claim that apparently immutable truths were actually anything but stable appalled many contemporaries, as did the egalitarianism embedded within their theology. Quakers refused to bow, kneel, or remove their hats in the presence of social superiors, which outraged many contemporaries. Early Quakers were vilified, jailed, and martyred, but the Toleration Act of 1689 granted freedom of worship to all Protestants and obliged British subjects on both sides of the Atlantic to become more tolerant of religious minorities. Pennsylvania's founder, William Penn, was himself a Quaker and insisted on freedom of conscience for all Christians who settled in his colony. Whereas early Friends often adopted dramatic and confrontational tactics, in some instances even appearing naked in public as a form of prophetic expression, later Friends were much less disruptive and presented a calm, soberly dressed appearance to the world. Even so, the Society of Friends remained controversial and during the revolutionary era became once again vulnerable, even in Pennsylvania, targeted by patriots as a dangerous dissident voice.[4]

The arrests of September 1777 targeted Quakers in particular, but they aimed to intimidate into compliance anyone who questioned patriot principles or tactics as the Revolution pitted Americans against each other as well as against the British government. "All wars are dreadful," wrote Elizabeth, "but those called civil wars more particularly so." The American Revolution was, to be sure, nowhere near as bloody as the revolutions that erupted in France and Saint-Domingue a few years later. The uprising by slaves against French rule in Saint-Domingue that began in 1791 led to wholesale slaughter on both sides, and the revolutionary government in France sentenced more than sixteen thousand alleged counter-revolutionaries to death by guillotine during the infamous Reign of Terror in 1793–94. America had no guillotine, and the number of those hanged as traitors to the Revolution was modest when compared with the state-sponsored carnage in France. Yet many lost their lives in America's first civil war. Nearly five times as many Americans died in the War for Independence, relative to the size of population, as in World War II. Roughly one in five Americans remained loyal to the crown, and one in forty went into permanent exile as loyalists, the equivalent of almost eight million people today, their property confiscated by the patriots. Many who remained had their doubts about the Revolution. Those who spoke out often paid dearly for doing so: in Pennsylvania alone, the revolutionary government accused at least 638 individuals of high treason. Yet the new regime minimized overt dissent through a campaign of intimidation and violence. However noble its official founding ideals, the United States was born in blood, its midwife a campaign of terror.[5]

During the decade before Independence, patriots had proven ruthless and brutal in suppressing dissent. So-called committees of safety published the names of those who refused to support boycotts of British goods, denouncing them as enemies of American liberty and declaring, "Join or die!" That phrase was menacingly ambiguous: at whose hands would people perish if they failed to join the resistance movement, a tyrannical Parliament in London or local patriots determined to squash any views but their own? Printers who dared to criticize the patriots had their presses smashed and their publications burnt. Militant gangs known as the Sons of Liberty assaulted noncooperators, humiliated them, and tortured them. One of their favorite techniques was tarring and feathering. They stripped their victims in public and poured hot tar over their naked bodies, scalding and burning their flesh; they sometimes actually set them on fire. Next, they covered them in feathers and paraded them through the streets, beat them, whipped them, and often tied them to the local gallows. These ritualized assaults were not random or exceptional but key components in a strategy of intimidation. The circulation of accounts describing these attacks, in graphic detail, ensured that the victims served as examples of what lay in store for others who disagreed with the patriots, for whatever reason, and would have terrified all but the staunchest of souls.[6]

Many years later, as the war neared its end, the patriots were still wielding terror against those who questioned their principles or tactics. News of the British surrender at Yorktown on October 19, 1781, which effectively guaranteed Independence, reached Philadelphia three days later, and patriots immediately set about planning a victory celebration. They announced that in the evening of October 24 every household should put candles in its windows and so create a citywide latticework of flickering light as crowds made merry in the streets. Yet not all Philadelphians were eager to take part in this celebration, and many Quakers, including the Drinkers, refused to illuminate their homes. They soon found out that patriots were in no mood to tolerate noncompliance. That night a crowd made its way through the streets, threatening those who refused to cooperate and vandalizing their homes. However great the temptation may have been to appease the mob by lighting candles, some households had the courage to stick to principled refusal, regardless of the consequences. When John Drinker, Henry Drinker's brother, declined to illuminate his house, patriots gave him a beating and stole much of the inventory from his shop. Henry and Elizabeth Drinker escaped personal injury, but their home did not: the mob broke about seventy panes of glass in their windows, cracked the front door as they broke it open, and then threw stones into the house, smashing two panels in the front parlor. It was a terrifying night, Elizabeth wrote, and "scarcely one Friend's house escaped . . . many women and children were frightened into fits, and 'tis a mercy no lives were lost."[7]

World of Trouble tells the story of one Quaker couple, Elizabeth and Henry Drinker, who chose neutrality over patriotism or loyalism and paid dearly for that choice at the hands of those who had no patience for anything but unconditional support. That Elizabeth and Henry survived to tell their story was not a foregone conclusion, and their journey left deep scars that make them poignant characters with whom to travel through those turbulent revolutionary decades. Henry Drinker (1734–1809) and Elizabeth Sandwith (1735–1807) married in 1761, just before the first wave of protests against imperial policy. Henry was an upwardly mobile merchant and would soon become an influential member of the Philadelphia business community as well as a leading Friend in the city. When Elizabeth and Henry settled in Philadelphia's commercial district as a respectable young Quaker couple, they had no way of knowing that within a few years their world would come crashing down around them due to the rupture between Britain and its North American colonies. Economic boycotts followed by open rebellion had potentially ruinous consequences for merchants like Henry Drinker and placed them in a delicate situation as they tried to navigate between growing pressure to cooperate with boycotts, their own commercial interests, and their personal perspectives on the crisis. Henry and his trading partner, Abel James, made their own situation much more perilous in 1773 when they agreed to become local agents for the East India Company, which had secured from the British government a monopoly on tea imports to North America and soon became a reviled target for colonists who opposed imperial taxes on imported goods. That unfortunate decision, in combination with Henry's reputation as a leading Quaker, led to his arrest in 1777, on suspicion of treason against the new regime. During Henry's exile, the British forces occupied Philadelphia, and Elizabeth found that she had no choice but to take in one of the British officers and his retinue as billeted houseguests. The war quite literally invaded her home as the larger drama of revolution merged with the intimate drama playing out in the Drinker home. Even after Henry's return, neither he nor his family could take his survival for granted as patriots regained control of the city and resumed their persecution of anyone who refused them unconditional support.

Many Quakers, including Henry and Elizabeth Drinker, felt that the protest movement, though launched in support of liberty, had rapidly become another tyrannical regime with blood on its hands. As one of the exiles put it, "A people who had professedly risen up in opposition to what they called an arbitrary exercise of power, were in a little time so lost to every idea of liberty as to see, without dreading the consequences, the very foundation of freedom torn up." Elizabeth referred sarcastically to the "Guardians of Liberty," condemning them as "unfeeling men" and "cruel persecutors." Yet some contemporaries were equally harsh when commenting on Quakers and their claims to the moral high ground. Pennsylvania Friends were, in truth, partly to blame for a resurgence of hostility toward them. Over the preceding decades, they had played a prominent role in creating an increasingly toxic political environment. Eighteenth-century Friends turned out to be resourceful and ruthless in working to maintain a decisive influence over public affairs in Pennsylvania even as they became a minority within the colony, much to the irritation of non-Quakers who felt their views should have more sway. Their enemies also accused them of reinterpreting their religious principles from one occasion to the next as it served their own interests, so that an ethos of evolving truth became, or so it seemed to their adversaries, a convenient tool of cynical powerbrokers. Quaker commitment to pacifism seemed, moreover, both dangerous and callous as Native Americans threatened the lives of frontier settlers, so that their enemies depicted them as Indian lovers and traitors to fellow Pennsylvanians.[8]

Meanwhile, just as Elizabeth and Henry Drinker reached adulthood, the Society of Friends embarked on a program of internal reforms known as the Quaker Reformation. That movement aimed to close what reformers saw as a widening gap between values that Friends claimed to hold dear and their actual behavior. Reformers called for the stricter enforcement of codes regulating personal conduct and sought to instill a renewed sense of corporate identity. As colonial society became increasingly diverse and cosmopolitan, Friends should turn inward and become as far as possible a closed community, placing their trust in one another and avoiding the influences of a corrupt outside world. Yet when a group of prominent Friends resigned from political office in 1756, declaring that they now believed they could not reconcile their values with active involvement in public life, their neighbors noted that other Quakers continued in office, while yet others worked behind the scenes to shape public policy. Wealthy Quaker merchants in particular ensured that the assembly still protected their interests, sometimes at the direct expense of poorer Pennsylvanians. As the Society of Friends became increasingly introverted and tribal, so it became ever more vulnerable to accusations of separatism, self-interest, and hypocrisy.[9]

The climate of resentment and suspicion that Friends had helped to create over the preceding decades now came back to haunt them. When Quakers began to distance themselves from violent protests against British legislation and when they refused to fight in the Continental Army, not everyone was willing to assume that their motives were honorable. After all, merchants such as Henry Drinker stood to surrender significant profits because of the nonimportation agreements, to say nothing of open warfare, and poorer workers whose interests the merchant class had done little to protect over the years now figured prominently among the more radical protesters. Based on prior experience, some Philadelphians might well suspect, however unfairly, that the positions taken by affluent Friends were nothing but a flimsy camouflage for self-interest. As the colonies declared themselves states and fought in defense of their freedom, roughly one-fifth of Quakers broke with their brethren to side with the patriots, while a smaller number became loyalists, but the overwhelming majority of Friends adopted a position of neutrality. Their overriding loyalty lay neither with Britain nor with the new nation that patriots had determined to found but instead with their own Society of Friends, which they characterized as a holy nation in its own right, held together by moral principles to which they must remain loyal. Given the political and economic influence of Quakers in Philadelphia, their neutrality presented supporters of Independence with a significant problem. Instead of treating Quakers and loyalists as two distinct groups posing two distinct challenges, patriot pamphleteers such as Thomas Paine now exploited a cumulative reservoir of skepticism about Quaker sincerity and deliberately conflated them with the loyalists: anyone refusing to support their cause wholeheartedly was an enemy of the Revolution and should be treated as such.[10]

Living through the violence and intolerance of dissenting voices that marked the revolutionary era was a frightening ordeal for Americans in general and

Quakers in particular, yet the Drinkers lived through not one but several interconnected revolutions that make this period and their story even more gripping. Social, economic, and cultural transformation combined with political drama to create an era of unnerving upheaval and uncertainty. Changing attitudes toward sex, courtship, and marriage, across American society and specifically within the Quaker community, had profound implications for young people and older adults who wanted to protect or control them. Henry and Elizabeth were part of a pioneering generation that placed a much greater stress on romantic courtship than earlier couples had done. This romantic revolution had profound consequences, not least in creating expectations that sometimes went unfulfilled once couples settled into married life. As parents, Elizabeth and Henry worked hard to raise their children according to Quaker precepts and to ensure that their offspring entered adult relationships in accordance with strict requirements laid down by the Society of Friends. This proved no easy task as broader trends in American society gave young adults greater freedom in choosing sexual and marital partners. The Drinkers were among those who resisted this increasingly permissive environment, retreating into their heavily regulated community of faith, but that retrenchment created serious tensions within families and especially across generations. These cultural shifts and conflicts had just as seismic an impact on individual lives as political revolution. The same was true of a transformation in the lives and attitudes of free laborers, which shook the worlds of household mistresses and their domestics just as much as those of male employers and their workers. Affluent Friends such as the Drinkers faced the additional challenge of reconciling their faith's commitment to a simple way of life with their residence and participation in an urban world of gentility and conspicuous consumption. Ironically, Henry Drinker helped to adorn that world by selling exotic imported goods to local inhabitants.[11]

This book revisits the familiar story of the American Revolution from an unfamiliar perspective, that of Americans who felt unable to choose either side and paid a heavy price for acting in good conscience. It puts that unfamiliar version of a familiar story into the broader context of an era rocked by multiple and dramatic transformations for which few were prepared. Through the vivid personal accounts that Elizabeth and Henry left behind, we too can experience these multiple revolutions as they played out in Philadelphia and the Drinker household. Their own words, reflecting on the changes taking place around them, allow us to see and feel the impact of those changes, almost as if we were there with them. We witness the ways in which their public and private worlds overlapped as the political became painfully personal. Retracing their journey through this period gives us an intimate, human perspective on the revolutionary era that a more general narrative cannot hope to capture. Both Elizabeth and Henry left behind a massive body of writings, much of which has survived, telling us more about them than we know about almost any other couple of the period. That happenstance makes it possible to write a history of their life together in which we can listen to both their voices, sometimes as they commented on the same events or issues. They did not always see eye to eye, but for the most part they responded in harmony with a blend of anxiety, courage, and resignation to the many travails that they endured and survived. What follows is a reconstruction of their journey, as individuals and as a couple, through an era of turmoil and transformation as they tried as best they could to keep their family and their faith intact.[12]

This retelling of the revolutionary era also incorporates a layer of common experience that many books about this period minimize or ignore. The diaries and letters that Elizabeth and Henry left behind describe not only the extraordinary dangers of revolution but also more mundane day-to-day perils that they and other eighteenth-century Philadelphians faced. It is easy to forget that illness and accident posed a constant threat to life and limb in the world that the Drinkers inhabited. Most medical treatments available at the time simply did not work, and so the possibility of death hung constantly over every household, even if the wealth of its inhabitants gave access to the best physicians that money could buy. Women of childbearing age and their infants were especially vulnerable: Ann Swett, Henry's first wife, died in childbirth, along with their first baby, in 1758. He then almost lost his second wife, Elizabeth, to illness in early 1770, just as he was dealing with the second round of protests against British legislation; only five of his and Elizabeth's nine children survived infancy. It might be tempting to assume that in an era when mortality rates were high, people must have become accustomed to loss and felt the pain of bereavement less than we do, yet surviving evidence from the early republic does not support any such assumption. The Drinkers' loss of four children and several grandchildren tore at their heartstrings, however much they tried to accept such blows as the will of a just God. Fear of illness and the specter of death haunted Elizabeth's diary, with good reason.[13]

Elizabeth saw the experience of suffering as a great leveler, common to all humankind. "I believe," she wrote, "there are few so low who do not at times feel satisfaction and comfort, and none so high as not to experience anxiety, trouble, and distress." The Drinkers certainly endured a daunting succession of troubles. Though Elizabeth made occasional references to feeling happy, especially when at home surrounded by her family, and acknowledged from time to time that she should feel grateful for the blessings allotted her by Providence, she nevertheless saw herself as "not of a very sanguine disposition, but apt to fear the worst." Elizabeth wrote this in her early seventies as she watched her eldest daughter sink under what turned out to be a fatal illness. The family had survived earlier trials, but each left its mark, and this final blow would effectively kill Elizabeth as well as her daughter. She and Henry had learned through hard experience that commonplace perils could prove just as frightening and fatal as the ravages of war and revolution, even for well-to-do merchants and their families.[14]

~

A vast body of surviving material gives us unusually close access to Elizabeth and Henry's life together. Most revealing are Elizabeth's monumental diaries, which span almost half a century, from 1758 to 1807, over the course of almost three dozen volumes, along with several thousand letters that Henry and Elizabeth wrote to relatives, friends, business associates, and each other. Elizabeth's diaries and correspondence add up to a unique collection of female-authored prose, one of the largest and most significant from the colonial or revolutionary periods, addressing a wide range of domestic and public topics. Henry's business letters, account books, land records, and other papers enable us to reconstruct his day-to-day dealings as a merchant and investor. Henry's personal correspondence makes abundantly clear his devotion to Elizabeth, their family, and the Quaker community. Diaries and journals penned by friends and neighbors, official records kept by the Society of Friends, local newspapers, city records, and other contemporary accounts of the Revolution as it played out in and around Philadelphia help to fill out the already vivid and multilayered portrait left behind by the Drinkers themselves.[15]

The historical record is, of course, far from complete, and people writing in the past did not always discuss things that interest us or provide answers to the questions we want to ask.[16] Some material has been lost over time, including Elizabeth's diaries for 1787 and 1788. There are large and frustrating gaps in the diaries that cover the first half of her married life, some caused by illness, others most likely by her preoccupation with recurrent pregnancy and the business of parenting small children. Henry spent much of his time, especially in middle and later life, serving on dozens of Quaker committees and in positions of responsibility that included treasurer of the Philadelphia Yearly

Meeting and clerk for local and regional Meetings, consulting informally with other leading Friends, and providing support to neighbors who asked for his assistance. We occasionally glimpse this aspect of Henry's life in meeting records, in his correspondence, and in Elizabeth's diary entries, but much of it went unrecorded. The Drinkers had, moreover, little or nothing to say about events that loom large in most people's memory of this period. Elizabeth's diary made no mention in July 1776 of the Declaration of Independence: indeed, she wrote nothing on July 3, 4, or 5 of that historic year, a telling but frustrating silence. Henry's correspondence made no mention that I have found of the Constitutional Convention in 1787, perhaps because he found the prospect of another constitutional rupture amid bitter and toxic controversy so dismaying that he preferred not to comment. Elizabeth and Henry left behind many comments about their children's behavior and personalities. We know much less about what the children thought of their parents, though a handful of surviving letters give moving insight into the relationship between the two sons and their loving yet at times intimidating father.[17]

We have, unfortunately, only basic information about Elizabeth and Henry's family histories, their childhoods, and their teenage years. Henry's first marriage, along with his reaction to the death of his first wife and their only child, remains shrouded in obscurity. Other than a simple head portrait in silhouette, all we know of Elizabeth's physical appearance comes from two brief comments in her diary and a compliment in her obituary. In September 1776, at forty-one years of age, she weighed herself while visiting a mill and found that she was 130 pounds. In a much later entry, she mentioned that her hair was "black or dark." The obituary that appeared in *Poulson's American Daily Advertiser* following her death in November 1807 described her as having "possessed uncommon personal beauty." Even allowing for a degree of posthumous generosity, she appears to have been an attractive woman, and her portrait in silhouette gives an impression of gentle elegance, her clothing and hair a declaration of social status yet devoid of ostentation, as befitted a Quaker. Obituaries for men rarely commented on personal appearance. A year and a half into their marriage, Elizabeth rhapsodized about her husband's "sparkling eyes" and the "wavy ringlets" that "o'er his shoulders flow," but we have no visual rendering of Henry as a young man. There do survive a few drawings of him as a rather stolid middle-aged man, complete with the broad-brimmed hat characteristic of Quaker men, whose refusal to remove their headwear in deference to magistrates and other worthies became a notorious symbol of their egalitarian creed.[18]

Silhouettes of Elizabeth Drinker and Henry Drinker (Historical Society of Pennsylvania Portrait Collection [V88] and David McNeely Stauffer Collection on Westcott's *History of Philadelphia* [1095], Historical Society of Pennsylvania)

Yet despite these gaps in our knowledge, the thousands upon thousands of detailed letters and diary entries that have survived tell an unforgettable story about this couple's experience of the revolutionary period and of life in the late eighteenth century. Elizabeth's diary gives us access to many dimensions of her everyday life and her perspective on the world around her as it changed and convulsed. The diary begins on October 8, 1758, when Elizabeth was twenty-three and not yet married; it ends on November 18, 1807, six days before her death at the age of seventy-two. Elizabeth had her reasons for "scribbling something every night." She wrote that her main objective was not to be "amusing" or "instructive" but "to help the memory" by compiling a record of events that she might otherwise forget. Some of her neighbors shared their journals with friends, so that they became semipublic (a late eighteenth-century equivalent of our own online social media), but Elizabeth wrote mostly for her own "perusal and recollection." She declared in one entry that she had no intention of showing her diary to "anyone but some of my children" and so felt "more free" to include information on intimate topics such as her bowel movements, though even so she sometimes lapsed into French when writing about occurrences within the Drinker household that she found embarrassing or troublesome. The ability to write in another language demonstrated cosmopolitan polish, but it also enabled her to shroud and distance herself from, without actually denying, behavior that contradicted her notions of Quaker respectability.[19]

Elizabeth generally recorded events rather than feelings. She declared in one entry, "I can't describe how I have felt this day, [and] indeed it is what I do not at any time undertake to do." Yet her emotional responses to events did occasionally spill out onto the pages of her diary, increasingly so as the years passed by. Though her diary was not a spiritual autobiography, she did record her religious thoughts in moments of crisis, as well as Henry's constant engagements on behalf of local and regional Quaker corporate bodies. These included the Northern District Meeting to which he and Elizabeth belonged, the Philadelphia Quarterly Meeting, and the Philadelphia Yearly Meeting, which brought together Friends from Pennsylvania, New Jersey, and Delaware, as well as parts of Maryland and Virginia. The diary entries varied in length, depending on whether she had the time, energy, or inclination to write more than a few lines. Some are downright skeletal, others so rich in detail that they read almost like extracts from an eighteenth-century novel (surely not a coincidence, since Elizabeth enjoyed reading novels, albeit as a guilty pleasure). She mostly recorded aches and illnesses, the twists and turns of the weather, the comings and goings of her family, visits by neighbors and friends or business associates from out of town, and her latest frustrations with their household staff. Once her children no longer consumed most of her time, the entries grew longer and became more explicitly judgmental. Elizabeth wrote in her midsixties that she never intended "to say severe things," even if "with strict justice." This was, frankly, a stretch, as she did not hesitate to pass judgment, sometimes quite harshly, on servants whom she considered lazy or disobedient and the patriots whose hypocrisy and brutality she deplored.[20]

Though Elizabeth did occasionally mention political events on the national and international stage, she focused mostly on matters that affected her family's welfare, the Quaker community, and the city in which she lived. "I trouble not myself with other people's business," she declared in one entry. Although that claim was not entirely accurate, she generally paid attention to "other people's business" only insofar as it felt relevant to her immediate life and either affirmed or disregarded her values. Readers would go in vain to Elizabeth's diary for an overarching history of the American Revolution because what she cared about above all else was the Revolution's impact on her own personal world. Indeed, one of the diary's functions was to delimit that world through careful inventories of those whom she visited and those who called on her. Elizabeth recognized that many of the incidents she recorded might strike

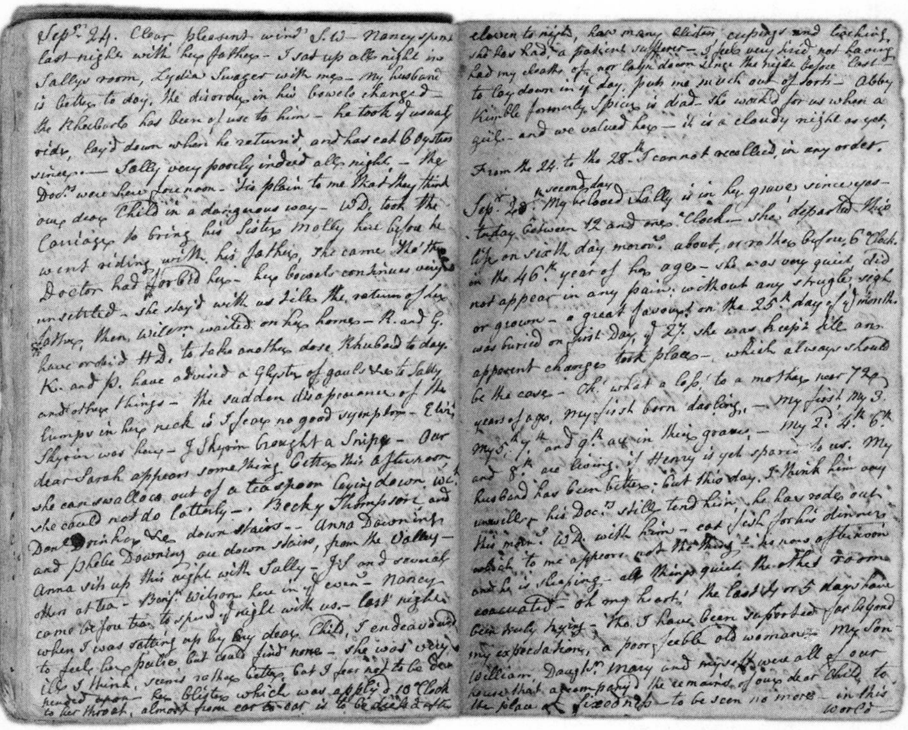

Diary of Elizabeth Drinker, September 24–28, 1807 (Elizabeth Sandwith Drinker Diaries [1760], Historical Society of Pennsylvania)

others as "trifling," but not so to her, and herein lies the value of the diary, as it takes us into her world as she lived and observed it. Elizabeth did not see public affairs as irrelevant to her life, but the intensity and particularity of her focus on matters that she cared about as a female Friend, wife, mother, and household mistress put that larger world in perspective. No experience is entirely typical. The domestic setting from which Elizabeth looked outward was materially comfortable and in many ways privileged. Undoubtedly, the Drinkers' wealth cushioned them from some of the worries that weighed on others; even during the wartime blockade, for example, they rarely had to fret about where their next meal would come from. Yet as the Drinkers watched warships firing on each other in the Delaware River from the upper windows of their home, as they worried about hostility toward them and other Quakers, and as they watched loved ones ail from illnesses they did not understand and could not cure, they clearly did not feel immune from danger.[21]

Henry did keep a diary during his journey across the Atlantic to England in 1759, but he speaks to us largely through his correspondence. His business letters survive for the most part in large and unwieldy letter books, in which his clerks wrote out full copies of his correspondence. The earlier letters chart the operations of an import-export firm in the mid-eighteenth century and show in vivid detail the mounting anxieties that merchants experienced during the pre-revolutionary period. They also testify to Henry's profound spiritual investment in a community of Friends that spanned the Atlantic, transcending earthly conceptions of nationhood. In the aftermath of Independence, Henry refocused his attention away from transatlantic trade to two grandiose ventures that he hoped would make money and at the same time infuse the new nation's economic development with Quaker values. Both of these ventures proceeded from an almost utopian vision of the new nation's future. Henry's correspondence takes us deep into the world of post-revolutionary entrepreneurship, at times verging on wild-eyed adventurism but routinely dragged down to a grimier reality. Unfortunately, these projects required skills that he simply did not possess and, to be fair, posed challenges that might have thwarted someone much better qualified. Henry's letters from these years radiate stress and frustration. Yet he continued to find fulfillment as a leader within his spiritual community. Always a man of business, he remained above all a man of faith.

Henry's commitment to his faith interwove with devotion to family as he and Elizabeth worked together to ensure that faith sustained their family and vice versa. For Henry, family was an emotional bedrock. His business correspondence rarely dwelt in any detail on his domestic life, but the letters that he and his wife wrote to each other during periods of separation allow us to see how much they relied on each other, emotionally and otherwise. Those letters and occasional comments in Elizabeth's diary reveal that Henry enjoyed spending time with his children and loved them dearly. He was, admittedly, often preoccupied with business matters and a seemingly endless train of Quaker committee meetings. Elizabeth also complained to her diary that she "many times experienced the great inconvenience of not understanding or fully knowing his mind," and he could at times be quite daunting as household head. Yet husband and wife knew that they could turn to each other in moments of crisis and did so. This was clearly a loving marriage and tightly knit family.[22]

~

Before we proceed, I should say a few words about my own journey with the Drinkers. Biographers often develop intimate connections with their subjects that are just as complicated and rocky as any real-life relationship. That has certainly been my experience in writing this book. Unless historians are to remain disengaged to the point of bloodlessness, it is perhaps inevitable that they will develop personal likes and dislikes for the people about whom they write. Because biographers focus so intently on one or a few subjects, their emotional responses often become correspondingly more intense. At times, I have felt deep sympathy for both Henry and Elizabeth, especially as they faced suspicion and danger during the Revolution, and as they lost five children, four in infancy and a fifth in adulthood. Only a reader with a heart of stone would remain unmoved by the letters and diary entries that they wrote as husband and wife, as mother and father, in response to those deaths. I have also come to admire deeply their principled refusal to support policies and actions that violated their beliefs, even when it must have been tempting to give lip service for safety's sake. Both endured significant hardship and anxiety because they held fast to those principles. At other times, they have seemed to me much less likable, especially when reading Elizabeth's condescending and sometimes heartless comments about her servants. Yet the Drinkers were products of their own time, and we need to understand them as such. I have tried as best I can to present them sympathetically without lionizing them and critically without demonizing them.[23]

As we prepare to join the Drinkers on the first stage of their journey together, we would do well to set aside some common misconceptions about early Quakers. The Society of Friends has become so firmly associated with egalitarian principles and social justice that we sometimes forget to adjust our expectations of what that would have meant in the past. Elizabeth and Henry Drinker were in some respects quite radical, by eighteenth-century standards, but their belief in spiritual equality did not translate into any comprehensive or consistent commitment to social egalitarianism: they were products of a hierarchical, racist society and by no means disavowed the attitudes that went along with membership in a privileged elite. The lack of titles and honorifics in Elizabeth's diary fits well with the Quakers' reputation for social leveling, but she rarely applied that principle when dealing with those less fortunate than she was. Elizabeth and her husband could be generous to "low people" (her words) when their behavior was appropriately deferential and met the moral standards that the Drinkers held to and expected everyone else to abide by, but those they considered less deserving did not fare so well. They both supported the emancipation of slaves, yet Elizabeth implied in one diary entry that blacks were "near" but "not quite the same species." Henry declared that he "sympathize[d] with the poor blacks" and wanted "to wipe away the ill-founded prejudices which have prevailed respecting that oppressed part of the human species," yet that did not stop him from trading with the sugar islands and so helping to sustain its slave-based economy.[24] Henry was also sensitive to the plight of Native Americans and served on a committee that worked to secure peace with Indian nations, "that the natives of the land might be justly dealt with and that they and the white people might live together in amity and friendship as becomes brethren." Yet this did not mean that Henry respected Indian cultures or wanted to preserve them. Indeed, he hoped that Friends could help lead Indians "out of their old habits to a more civilized state." What follows will not always please those who wish to preserve an idealized view of the Quakers, or indeed of the Drinkers. I can only respond that I have tried to present my subjects as authentically as possible, never expecting them to satisfy modern ideals any more than we would satisfy theirs.[25]

We would also do well to avoid making assumptions about the fervor and commitment of people who identified as Quakers. In this as in other faith communities, there was a range of piety and observance: not all Friends embraced their religion with equal rigor and consistency. The Society of Friends accorded women a much greater degree of independent agency than did most eighteenth-century Christian denominations and even encouraged them to testify in public as ministers of Christ, but that does not mean that all Quaker women wanted to become public speakers or even embraced an active, committed piety. In terms of attendance at public worship, service on committees, and the assumption of leadership roles, Henry was much more actively involved in the Society of Friends than was Elizabeth, though both husband and wife were deeply embedded within a social community that consisted largely, though not exclusively, of Quakers. Elizabeth attended meetings for worship regularly as a young unmarried woman, but in later years went very rarely, and bouts of ill health can only go so far in explaining her lengthy absences. The influence of Quaker beliefs on her worldview is clear in certain attitudes that she expressed, and she often turned to her faith for support in times of tribulation. Yet her public observance and involvement was much more intermittent than our stereotypes of Quaker women might lead us to expect.

Despite the respect accorded to Quaker women in spiritual matters, Friends had by no means abandoned a commitment to patriarchy. Late eighteenth-century writings about marriage often dwelt on the need for equality between husband and wife and depicted a close friendship between them as the essence of marriage. Yet most of these authors continued to assume that women and men would have different roles within a marriage and that ultimate power should remain in the hands of the husband. In this respect, Quakers were quite conventional: they generally understood their marital relationships in hierarchical terms, and the Drinkers were no exception. When Elizabeth read *A Vindication of the Rights of Woman* by the radical and unconventional Mary Wollstonecraft, she agreed with "many of her sentiments," but declared that she did not favor "quite so much independence" for women as the author called for. Elizabeth rarely challenged her husband's judgment and even more rarely to his face. Though she supervised their domestic servants and the day-to-day maintenance of their home as household mistress, final authority rested clearly and firmly in the hands of the patriarch. When Henry became a prisoner and exile during the War for Independence, Elizabeth had no choice but to take his place—temporarily, she hoped—as household head. She made significant, even momentous, decisions in that role and eventually joined several other women on a dangerous mission that they hoped would secure the release of their husbands; but she did so reluctantly and gave no sign of regret when she ceased to be the acting head of household on Henry's return. This should not surprise us, given her general worldview and how challenging, at times downright terrifying, her experience as a household head had been.[26]

~

Elizabeth and Henry's day-to-day lives were in some ways closely interwoven and in others quite separate. The structure of this book reflects that reality. The chapter describing Henry's struggle to protect his import and export business during the decade that preceded Independence has little to say about Elizabeth because she was not directly involved in such matters, though she was clearly watching and, as we will see, had strong opinions about some of the difficulties her husband faced. Likewise, Henry makes relatively few appearances in the chapter about Elizabeth's relationship with her domestic servants because this was largely her domain. Yet their spheres of activity and interest overlapped in significant ways, and though their priorities might at times seem to diverge, in times of crisis they braved whatever trials loomed before them together, even if physically separated. Their love for each other was never in doubt, and at the center of both their lives stood their children, their greatest source of joy and of worry.

The chapters of this book divide the lives of Elizabeth and Henry Drinker into three overlapping periods that preceded, spanned, and followed the

American Revolution. The first two chapters cover their courtship and early marriage, neither of which proved smooth sailing. The third follows Henry and his business partner Abel James as they navigated the stormy waters of pre-revolutionary protest. Chapters 4 and 5 chronicle Elizabeth and Henry's experience of the War for Independence as armed conflict and political intolerance threatened the well-being and even survival of their family. Chapter 6 joins Henry in the aftermath of Independence as he reinvented himself as a speculator and post-revolutionary visionary. Meanwhile, revolutionary principles percolated throughout American society, and chapter 7 follows Elizabeth as she dealt with a succession of domestic servants who showed an increasingly independent-minded and egalitarian spirit, contradicting her own expectations of deference and obedience. The final two chapters focus on the challenges that Henry and Elizabeth faced in later life as they tried to hold their family together as a bulwark of Quaker respectability amid the turbulence of the post-revolutionary era, even as they confronted their own mortality. While Henry struggled to meet his obligations as a church elder and to hold together his fraught business concerns, he and Elizabeth also faced wrenching personal losses: they had survived revolution and war, but now forces even more indomitable shadowed their closing years.

Yet those final trials were many decades away in the summer of 1759 as young Henry Drinker prepared to set sail for England. He had already lost his first wife and their child, but we now join him as he tried to put that loss behind him and embarked on two new journeys, one across the Atlantic and the other his courtship of a captivating young woman named Elizabeth Sandwith . . .

1 • "A Cornerstone to My Love-Fabric"
In Which Henry Drinker Woos Elizabeth Sandwith

Our story unfolds in the city of Philadelphia, which William Penn had envisaged as a commercial hub for the mid-Atlantic region of North America and as the capital for his brave new experiment in freedom of conscience. By the 1750s, Philadelphia had surpassed Boston as the largest city in North America. It was by eighteenth-century standards a massive metropolis with thirty-five thousand residents. The streets also teemed with a transient population of sailors eager to enjoy themselves in the city's taverns and brothels, newly arrived immigrants speaking a variety of languages, and farmers from the hinterland come to sell their crops at market. This must have been a bustling, rowdy, chaotic, and foul-smelling place to live in or visit. The breezes that swept up from the Delaware River through alleys that city planners had inserted to funnel fresh air into the city often carried instead the pungent smell from produce that lay abandoned and rotting on the wharves. Eighteenth-century Americans believed that diseases could travel through the air, and in 1793, when yellow fever crippled the city, many thought that the epidemic had originated in piles of waste on the docks, then wafting its deadly way up through those same alleys into the heart of the city. Seaport dwellers were in other ways vulnerable to the elements. Fires routinely burned homes, stores, and warehouses to the ground. In winter, freezing temperatures transformed the Delaware into a block of ice and brought trade to a halt; the subsequent melting of ice and snow produced rushes of water and flooding. In the spring of 1800, the river rose so high that shopkeepers on Water Street had to remove the goods from their stores. Beyond the coastline, merchants could lose their cargoes and crews just as easily to storms as to pirates and the ships of enemy nations.[1]

However troublesome the Delaware River might prove at times, the open sea was a good deal more dangerous, and so twenty-five-year-old Henry Drinker may well have felt both excited and nervous as he prepared in August 1759 to brave the Atlantic Ocean. Throughout the last week of that month, the young man worked diligently to put his personal and business affairs in order. Henry was about to leave Philadelphia for several months on a trip to Great Britain. The son of a Philadelphia "scrivener" or office clerk, Henry was doing remarkably well for himself. In 1744, George James, a successful shopkeeper in the city and a fellow Quaker, had taken Henry on as an apprentice, then aged ten. The indenture specified that over the coming four years James would teach him "shop-keeping or retailing goods and book-keeping," Henry working in return as an assistant in James's store. Young Drinker's master died the following year, but Henry completed his indenture with Abel James, George James's son. In the meantime, Henry lost both of his parents: his father died when he was twelve and his mother when he was sixteen. Henry stayed on to work with Abel well beyond the conclusion of his indenture, and by his early twenties they were business partners. James, who was nine years older than Drinker, had already become a successful import and export merchant, at first in partnership with Quaker merchant John Smith and then on his own. Together he and Henry would build one of Philadelphia's most prominent mercantile firms, James and Drinker. In addition to running an import and export business, they had a store on Water Street that sold a wide variety of goods from England, Ireland, the Caribbean, and other mainland North American colonies.[2]

The purpose of Henry's voyage across the Atlantic was to purchase goods for sale back in Philadelphia and to establish relationships with merchants, manufacturers, bankers, and influential Quakers in England. It was young Drinker's first trip across the Atlantic (also his last, as it turned out), and so the partners asked a business associate in England to introduce Henry among his friends there, trusting that they would welcome him as a "stranger" and provide any necessary assistance. Moral character mattered as much as business acumen within the Quaker community, and so it would have been advantageous that Anthony Benezet, a prominent Philadelphia Quaker, recommended Henry to a friend in Bristol as "worthy of thy notice, being a kind, well-disposed young man, esteemed among us." Abel was married with several children, whereas Henry was single and childless, which may have been the reason for his going on the lengthy trip instead of his senior partner. Though still a young man, Henry was already a widower: in the spring of 1757,

—1st of 11mo. 1744—

This Indenture Witnesseth, that
Henry Drinker junior, Son of Henry Drinker of
the City of Philadelphia, Scrivener, Doth By
Virtue of these Presents (with ye Advice & Consent of his Father)
put himself Apprentice to George James of sd City Shopkeeper,
With him (or his Assignee Provided it be his Son Abel James)
to Live & as an Apprentice to serve from the date hereof
Untill the Expiration of Four Years and one month During which
Time the sd Apprentice his Master, for the Time being,
Faithfully shall serve his Secrets Keep his Lawful
Commands readily obey. He shall not in any Wise
damage his said Master, nor Waste his Goods, nor
Lend them unlawfully to any. He shall not Buy
nor Sell, Nor absent himself at any Time from his
Masters Service without his Leave. But shall
diligently & Circumspectly attend ~~attend~~ his Masters
Business of Shopkeeping during the aforesaid
Term of Four Years & one Month And the said Master
shall Teach, or Cause his sd Apprentice to be Taught &
Instructed in the best Method he can of Shopkeeping or
Retailing Goods, & Bookkeeping. And Learn or
Cause him to Learn Arithmetick as far as the Rule
of 3 Direct & the Rule of Practice. And
shall find & provide for him sufficient Meat
Drink, Apparel, Lodging & Washing during the sd Term
And at ye End thereof give him One good new
Suit of Apparel besides ye rest of his Wearing Cloaths
In Witness whereof the said Parties have to
these Presents, interchangeably set their Hands
& Seals Dated ye first Day of the Eleventh Month
Anno Domini one thousand seven hundred & forty four

5

Sealed & Delivered in the Presence of
Henry Drinker
William Bennett

Geo James

Henry Drinker's indenture to George James, 1744 (Drinker Family Papers [1934A], Historical Society of Pennsylvania) at the age of twenty-three, he had married Ann Swett, whose Quaker family lived in Newcastle, some forty miles from Philadelphia. Ann had died just over a year later in May 1758, along with their newborn child, leaving Henry doubly bereaved at the age of twenty-four.[3]

The young man had more than business on his mind that summer. He was looking to remarry and had settled on Elizabeth Sandwith, a close friend of his first wife and his junior by one year. Many years later, Elizabeth would write that she and Ann Swett had "loved one another sincerely." Ann, lying "delirious" on her deathbed, had asked repeatedly for Elizabeth, and when she arrived, Ann apparently said, "Betsy, I want thee to go with me. Will thee?" Elizabeth had replied that she would, if Ann drank the medicine she had been refusing, but Henry now wanted his first wife's friend to go with him instead. Elizabeth was the second daughter of a deceased Quaker merchant and lived in Philadelphia with her older sister, Mary. Henry had been courting Elizabeth for several months, though they were not yet formally engaged. When the time came for him to say farewell to those he held "near and dear," one of them was Elizabeth Sandwith. Henry decided to keep a journal of his voyage, though he abandoned the venture soon after he arrived in England, probably because he was too busy. The entries that he wrote before his departure and during the voyage laid bare his feelings as he left his native land and faced the perils of a transatlantic voyage. Henry could feel welling up inside him "the most tender sentiments for a dear young woman who had been long the object of my love, respect, and esteem." Indeed, he felt "cemented" to Elizabeth "in the purity and nearness of tender affection." Henry described their parting as a "trial" of his emotional self-mastery, but he braced himself and managed to contain his feelings when he took his leave of her. At the same time, he was encouraged by the tears Elizabeth shed at their parting, "rising from the heart to the eyes of my dear girl" (he evidently saw no need for her to master her emotions), and he emerged from the interview feeling if anything "more cheerful than usual."[4]

Yet his mood soon changed when it transpired that the ship in which he was to sail for Bristol and that he co-owned with Abel James had developed a significant leak, taking in ten inches of water each hour. They would have to delay their departure until the leak had been fixed. This turn of events was, Henry wrote, "very discouraging": he had hoped for a brisk passage across the Atlantic and an equally swift return, so that he could wed Elizabeth as soon as possible and settle into married life. The delay he now faced was, he wrote, "truly a burden upon my spirits." Once repairs were complete, several carpenters whom Henry invited on board to inspect the work confirmed that the ship was now "far from dangerous," but the captain remained "uneasy," and when the passengers came aboard to proceed down the river toward open sea, the crew at first refused to set sail. Morale improved over the next few days as it became clear that the ship was now taking on only an inch or two of water per hour, and Drinker's gift of three young pigs helped to assuage the sailors' anxieties. Now all they needed were favorable winds to set sail. Meanwhile, Henry's devotion to Elizabeth had not blinded him to the beauty of other women. Before the vessel departed for the open sea, he went ashore one day with the pilot and wrote that night that nothing had happened worth writing about, "save the appearance of a fine, well-made country lass at the watering place. I think I scarcely ever set my eyes on a girl that seemed to have a greater flush of health, and a more smiling, contented countenance than this."[5]

Once they set out on their voyage, far removed from the company of other women, "well-made" or otherwise, Henry lay in his cabin contemplating the prospect of marriage to Elizabeth. "While I thus lay musing," he wrote, "free from all heavy corroding cares, such thoughts stole in upon me as filled my breast with treasures ineffable and led me through the luxuriant meanders of expected felicity. The dear object of my warmest wishes, her inward greatness, unaffected wisdom, sanctity of manners and amiable person poured in upon me a tide of love." The voyage itself proved something of a trial as he went through several bouts of seasickness and endured weeks of inactivity, time hanging heavy on his shoulders. Yet he relished "the pleasures of solitude" which he somehow found aboard a cramped ship and enjoyed feasting on a dolphin caught by the second mate (he failed in his attempts to harpoon one himself). Drinker was doubtless looking forward to spending time in a country he had never seen before and to establishing connections there that would serve him and his partner well in the coming years. Yet according to his journal entries, what he really looked forward to was the journey home. "Oh! propitious gale," he wrote, "still waft us forward, that I may the sooner bend my course back to my loved native shore, where hearts cemented in the lasting bands of virtuous love may know a closer union." These romantic and implicitly sexual yearnings did not fade over time. Several months later, when Henry found out that a ship docked in Bristol was about to depart for Philadelphia, he wrote to Elizabeth that he wished he could also leave for home and was jealous that the captain, known to both of them, would most likely see her long before he did. Henry repeatedly assured his Betsy of the ardor with which he anticipated their reunion. The delays keeping him in England, he declared, built up inside him a "torrent of anticipated bliss." Sometimes he convinced himself that their prolonged separation would lead to even greater "felicity" when they were eventually reunited, but this "philosophy" was "of short duration," he wrote, as he lacked "patience for such cold comfort."[6]

The effusive romantic language that Henry used in his journal and correspondence would not have surprised contemporaries, but it did represent a significant departure from the tone adopted by men of previous generations. Courtship on both sides of the Atlantic became increasingly romantic during the eighteenth century in its mode of expression and in its actual goals: potential partners and their families assessed their compatibility more and more in terms of mutual love, which now featured as prominently in the choice of a spouse as did social, economic, and spiritual suitability. Indeed, it would not be going too far to describe Henry and Elizabeth as part of a pioneering generation in the romanticization of courtship. No record survives of Henry's reading habits during these years, but he was clearly versed in the language that contemporary authors encouraged suitors to use as a demonstration of their feelings and he did his best to incorporate that style of address into the letters he wrote to Elizabeth. During his stay in England, Henry worried that he could not devote the time to romantic correspondence currently expected of absent lovers. He warned Elizabeth that because of his hectic schedule she would look in vain for "long epistles" of the sort that suitors were supposed to pen. Nonetheless, he assured her of his "tender" and "unalterable" attachment: "let me say little or much," he wrote, "believe this and bosom it up as an incontestable truth."[7]

The handful of letters that Henry wrote to Elizabeth from England was perhaps modest in volume, but their content cannot have left Elizabeth in any doubt about his passion and devotion. In a note to Elizabeth's sister, Mary, that enclosed a love letter to Elizabeth, Henry wrote that he had written the cover note in part to avoid attaching an outer seal to the letter for Elizabeth; had he done so, there would have been "some danger of losing a word" made illegible by the wax. That word might perchance be "a cornerstone to my love-fabric," the loss of which might "sap the foundation." Though this "structure" was only paper, yet it should be treated as "a small material (a mite in the treasury) towards the forming a copious work." Henry was well aware that he needed to lay a solid foundation for success as a merchant and as a well-connected Quaker if he was to impress and win a worthy bride. Yet the love-fabric crafted from words of romantic devotion was equally important, he declared, in building an emotional foundation for married life. Henry doubtless expected that Mary would pass on these words to her sister.[8]

Contemporaries expected suitors to share their feelings not only with their sweethearts but also with relatives and friends who helped to weigh the union's suitability. Whereas in the early nineteenth century the expression of romantic love would become a private matter, largely confined to the two parties concerned, eighteenth-century courtships on both sides of the Atlantic often played out in semipublic. Courting couples must demonstrate to relatives, friends, and neighbors that they were a good match romantically as well as in other regards. Parental control over the marital choices made by adult children had declined during the second half of the colonial period, and in any case, neither Elizabeth nor Henry had surviving parents. Yet relatives and other adults were still eager to influence such decisions as best they could, and the circulation of romantic correspondence by young people recognized the legitimacy of that larger community involvement. Once Henry returned to Philadelphia, he showed portions of his journal to friends and loved ones, including Elizabeth herself. Henry doubtless wanted to share with them the excitement of his transatlantic adventure, but he also needed to demonstrate his feelings for Elizabeth. His audience, which consisted largely of Quakers, would have been pleased to see that he stressed his regard for Elizabeth's "inward" qualities and her "sanctity of manners." This was, he assured all concerned, a spiritually inflected romance. Henry's romantic declarations were, then, partly a rhetorical performance for the benefit of his readers, including Elizabeth but also their social circle. (Given what he wrote about her in his journal, it is hardly surprising that Elizabeth found reading the journal "a pleasure," but we will turn to her feelings about him and his courtship shortly.)[9]

No one could simply take for granted the sincerity of Henry's commitment to Elizabeth, given the current cultural climate, which on both sides of the Atlantic encouraged, even celebrated, bawdy conversation and promiscuous behavior. Libertinism was all the rage in eighteenth-century England's fashionable society, overlapping uncomfortably with a rising ethos of romantic courtship. Those who fancied themselves part of the beau monde demonstrated their sophistication by extolling promiscuity and lionizing those who paraded their sexual escapades and infidelity for all to see. Affluent families in North America often sent sons across the Atlantic to complete their education and acquire social polish. Some of these aspiring gentlemen embraced libertinism à la mode with great enthusiasm, using their time in London, Bath, and other English cities to engage in sexual adventures. As they indulged in the carnal pleasures of what must have seemed to them a modern-day

Babylon, they proved at the same time their cosmopolitan sophistication to those who often dismissed North Americans as colonial bumpkins.[10]

Yet by no means all Anglo-Americans approved of this permissive environment. Those on both sides of the Atlantic who aspired to moral respectability rejected with indignation what seemed to them a culture of unbridled depravity. Contemporaries tended to depict libertinism as a primarily aristocratic impulse, and many middling gentry as well as merchants were eager to dissociate themselves from what they saw as aristocratic degeneracy. Southern planters in North America often identified with the English aristocracy (however implausibly), yet a growing number of colonists wished to distance themselves from what they saw as less worthy aspects of Englishness even as they continued to be proud of their English ancestry. Quakers would have no sympathy with a journey of sexual adventurism, and American Friends who traveled to England generally sought out like-minded company there; they may have traveled thousands of miles, but they still sought to live within the same morally upstanding Society of Friends, and Henry Drinker was no exception. During his time in England, Henry seems not even to have flirted with other women, let alone indulged in sexual dalliances, and he claimed in his letters to Elizabeth that people complimented him on his "constancy" to her. A cynic might scoff at such assurances, but given the dense network of transatlantic correspondence to which Henry and Elizabeth belonged, he would hardly have made such a claim had there been the possibility of contradiction from other sources.[11]

Just before Henry's departure from Philadelphia, his brother John had sent him a farewell letter in which he reminded him of the need to keep his guard up in the face of temptation. "I have no doubt but thou art well-armed against open vice or libertinism," he wrote. "But pray, brother, beware of being too secure; place not too great a dependence on thy own prudence, knowledge, and experience. In this there is danger; but in that fear which keeps the heart clean, there is abundant safety. I believe thou hast attained a good degree of steadfastness in thy religious sentiments, yet a vigilant watch is an indispensable necessary, for infidelity may assume specious forms and irreligion appear with angelic countenance." John need not have worried: Henry was apparently "well-armed" and determined to preserve himself in what he described as "the purity and nearness of tender affection" for Elizabeth. Indeed, the young merchant wrote in his journal that he was confident about his future prospects with Elizabeth primarily because they both "found[ed] their friendship on virtue's basis." Henry wanted to reassure his audience back home (including his sweetheart) that he was most assuredly not a libertine and that his feelings for Elizabeth were not those of transient infatuation: he understood that a lasting relationship depended on deeper bonds of loving friendship between morally upstanding individuals. This fit well with an emerging conception of marriage as a lifelong romantic friendship as well as with Quaker marital ideals that celebrated peaceable harmony and holy conversation between husband and wife. Henry did not frame his courtship in explicitly religious terms, but he was for the second time wooing a fellow Quaker and presented his romancing of Elizabeth as informed by moral goals and sensibilities. He envisaged that their life together would blend a cautious embrace of social fashion with the moral dictates of their faith.[12]

Yet Henry could not take it for granted that his courtship of Elizabeth would end successfully. Indeed, he was still working hard to convince Elizabeth and her friends of his worthiness as a suitor. In his correspondence, the young merchant sought to demonstrate his future prospects, both as a "man of business" and as a personage in the Society of Friends. He gave her brief accounts of his activities as he traveled from city to city and of the "very valuable" and "worthy" Quaker circles in which he was moving. "From this short sketch," he wrote, "my Betsy may be informed I get into some good company while abroad." Henry also deployed on his own behalf rumors of an explicit betrothal between him and his "dear Betsy." He told her that when he arrived in Norwich, he discovered that a report of his engagement had preceded him, which he heard "repeatedly" during his stay there "and not without a secret pleasure," even though such reports were premature. His host in Norwich was apparently eager for "my Betsy (when I have an indisputable right to call her so)" to correspond with his wife. Elizabeth, Henry predicted, might think such overtures "more seasonably communicated" once they were actually married. "Why indeed," he responded, "those ceremonials are very necessary things, but where there is a union of hearts, which I trust is the case, and only a little time wanting to reduce this mutual esteem into its proper economy, I hope a delay will not be thought essential in this point."[13]

Even though Henry recognized that Elizabeth had not yet agreed to marry him, he claimed that gossip had transformed the possibility of their engagement into a social fact, implying none too subtly that this placed her under an obligation to him. In one letter, he wrote that most of the people he spent time with in England knew of his "particular attachment" to her. He then added, "I have sometimes thought [that] if my Betsy should turn me off when I return, what a sad character would she have in this kingdom, where I have heard so

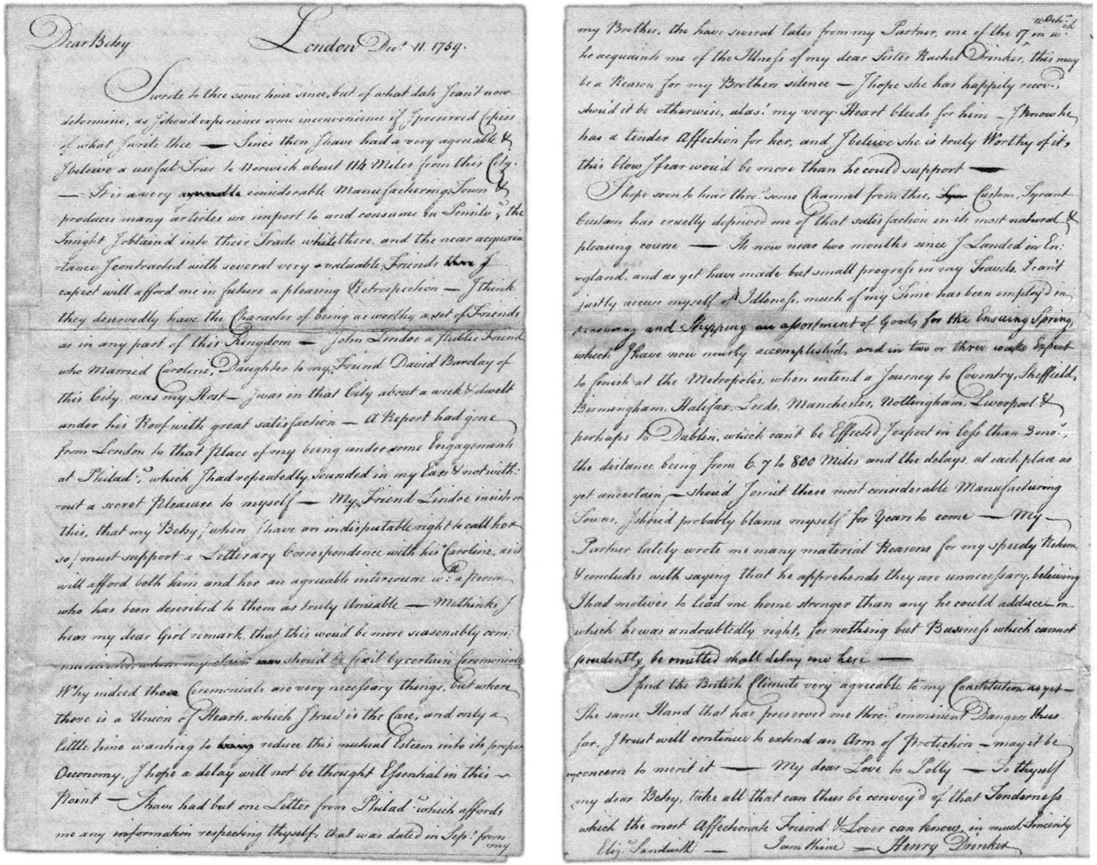

Henry Drinker to Elizabeth Sandwith, December 11, 1759 (Drinker Family Papers [1934A], Historical Society of Pennsylvania)

My dear Betsy — England — Bristol Jan. 1st 1760 —

From London I wrote thee a few lines about the 24th Ult°. the 28th I mounted Coach for Bath (107 Miles from London) ... I reach'd the 29th in the Evening, the 30th in the morning, being Sabbath Day, took a view of that noted City and drank two pints of its Salubrious Waters — in the Afternoon took Post Chaise for this Place about 14 Miles distance, which I reach'd before Evening.

And here I find my little Capt. Falconer just ready to depart for my Native Shore, with what Joy could I return with him! he'll visit that dear Western Clime perhaps before I leave this, and it is not improbable but may see my dear Betsy long before her Owner — sometimes my dear Creature when I am intently Thoughtful of my return, the Pleasure I propose to myself at that time, pours in upon me in such a Torrent of anticipated Bliss, that I am ready to conclude, the many protractions I meet with here, in fact seem to be Fostering up great Felicity for me in future, but this is a kind of Philosophy that is but of short duration, I want Patience for such cold Comfort —

I had a Letter from Daniel Mildred of the 29th Ult°. inclosing one from my Partner of an old Date — Sench Francis brought it and gave it Daniel, he says in his Letter to me, perhaps it may contain some agreeable Lines from thy Betsy — Another Letter I have from John Lindoe at Norwich which has a Postcript from his Wife, claiming a correspondence with my Betsy, as the Criterion of my Regard for herself and Spouse — Hence my dear Girl thee may form some Judgment how I am circumstanced in England — when I get into Comps. scarce any of my acquaintance but know via Certificate or otherwise of my particular attachment to a certain E. Sandwith — I have sometimes thought if my Betsy shou'd turn me off when I return, what a sad Character wou'd she have in this Kingdom, where I have heard so many Encomiums on my Constancy &c — and in Philada. I dare say many People believe that all is done to finishing — therefore if a Rival shou'd offer before my return, fail not to show him this Letter and tell him from me, that I don't believe he ever can or ever will Love thee with more Ardour and Sincerity than thy Henry — Here let me recommend thee to be plain simple Betsy (I don't mean silly) and receive the above in the simplicity it is offer'd, and avoid putting wrong constructions on the Words of a poor silly Fellow, who knows not to Indite better — I do declare what I say about Character, is not intended to tie thee to those Sentiments I with Pleasure saw rising from the Heart to the Eyes of my dear Girl before I left her, tho' in her I suspect not any variableness or change — Nor did I mention Encomiums out of meer Vanity — but hold, instead of mending I fear its making bad worse — This is Chit Chat between us who have spent many Hours (as I often remember) in that way —

I had a Piece of intelligence some time since which I must confess gave me Pleasure — Ellis Lewis Son of Robt. Lewis and a Relation of S. Pemberton's came to London from Philad. about two months since — he says before he left

left home he was pretty well convinced that S. Emlen had found
favour in the Sight of E. Moode, and that there was some hopes
neither he nor she would die old Batchelors — pray my kind Respects
to Betsy Emlen — my kind Love to Sister Polly & any other
of our Friends thee may think proper to use freedom with in the
Character of H. D's dear Betsy —

I came from Pill this Evening about 5 Miles from this City,
while there I accidentally met and spent sometime with a certain
John Jervis son to John Jervis and Cousin to John Jervis of Philad.a;
he was waiting a fair Wind to go on a Trading Voy.e to Guadeloupe,
I inform'd him of my Knowledge of his Relations at Philad.a &
he desires his Compliments may be sent them —

I yet remain in my story of getting Re-embark'd about two mo.s
hence, if I change for better or worse, shall make it a pretext for
the satisfaction of writing to thee again soon, now must leave thee
with my best wishes for thy Peace, Health and Well being every
way and rest unalterably thy

Affectionate

Henry Drinker

P.S.
If it should be convenient when
at Liverpool shall take a trip over
to see Uncle Samuel at Dublin

Eliz.a Sandwith —

Henry Drinker to Elizabeth Sandwith, January 1, 1760 (Drinker Family Papers [1934A], Historical Society of Pennsylvania) many encomiums on my constancy, etc. And in Philadelphia, I dare say, many people believe that all is done to finishing." Letters that Henry received during his absence from business associates and friends in Philadelphia confirm that his courtship of Elizabeth was a topic of conversation within his social circle on both sides of the Atlantic and that there was general approval of his choice. One correspondent wished him "such happiness . . . in possession of thy pretty Betsy" as "should crown the wish of an honorable lover." Yet the reference to Henry's taking possession of Elizabeth implied a degree of control over the situation that Henry himself does not seem to have felt at this stage of the courtship: "persuading a young woman out of her name" (as another of his correspondents put it) was proving far from straightforward. One of Henry's business partners did claim to have heard that Elizabeth was waiting "impatiently" for his return, but Henry was apparently not so sure about that.[14]

Even at a distance of three thousand miles, Henry was determined to apply whatever pressure he could. If a rival should materialize before his return, he wrote, Elizabeth should "show him this letter and tell him from me that I don't believe he ever can or ever will love thee with more ardor and sincerity than thy Henry." Realizing that Elizabeth might read his words as implying that she was in fact entertaining other suitors and so guilty of infidelity, Henry went on to ask that she "receive the above in the simplicity it is offered, and avoid putting wrong constructions on the words of a poor silly fellow, who knows not to indict better." He added that he was not trying to "tie" her to "those sentiments" which he had observed in her before his departure for England, though of course that is exactly what he was attempting. He assured Betsy that he "suspect[ed] not any variableness or change" in her, though clearly he was worried about that possibility. He also claimed that he did not mention "out of mere vanity" the tributes other people had made to his own "constancy," yet such tributes might imply that he had received attentions from other women, which might have tempted a less worthy fellow to stray. At this point he realized that he was digging himself deeper and deeper and had best leave off before he did further damage to his cause: "instead of mending," he wrote, "I fear it's making bad worse." Henry then added revealingly, "This is chit chat between us who have spent many hours (as I often remember) in that way." Elizabeth's refusal to commit herself had apparently prompted him on previous occasions to wrap himself up in knots of insecure protestations. The next paragraph, though allegedly a change in topic, relayed news of an engagement between two friends of theirs, ensuring that "neither he nor she would die old bachelors."[15]

Elizabeth's feelings on receiving these manipulative protestations of attachment and her general perspective on Henry's courtship are much more challenging to reconstruct for the simple reason that their transatlantic correspondence was completely one-sided. During his absence in England, Henry received no communications from Elizabeth with news of herself or any reassurance of her feelings for him. Elizabeth did braid watch strings for Henry before and after his trip as expressions of her affection, but messages of endearment were not forthcoming during his time abroad. There was nothing anomalous about this: though contemporaries expected men to pour their hearts out in letters to their sweethearts, there was no expectation that women would reciprocate. Hardly any love letters survive from young women in eighteenth-century Philadelphia to their male suitors. Nor did Elizabeth communicate with him indirectly by sending messages or news through friends or relatives. Henry wrote in December 1759 that since arriving in England he had received only one letter that included any information about Elizabeth, though he "hope[d] soon to hear through some channel" about her. He evidently had no expectation of hearing directly from Betsy herself: "Custom, Tyrant Custom," he declared, "has cruelly deprived me of that satisfaction."[16]

Reading those silences cannot have been easy for Henry. Had he seen Elizabeth's diary, what she wrote there would have offered little in the way of enlightenment. Indeed, one would not be able to tell from her entries before or during Henry's absence that she was either in love with him or about to accept an offer of marriage. She noted his visits during the months before his departure without any accompanying remarks, just as she did the visits of many other neighbors and friends. Elizabeth described his setting sail for England and the drama surrounding the ship's departure in a little more detail, though without any editorial comments suggesting regret at his departure or anxiety about the leak; she also noted the arrival of his various letters from England, but again without any accompanying remarks. Transatlantic journeys were always risky, even in times of peace, and England was currently at war with France. Henry's journal made clear his relief when he and his companions arrived on the southern coast of England "in these dangerous times" without "accident from the enemy or otherwise." Elizabeth had lived her entire life in a seaport and so must have been aware of the dangers, yet she made no mention of worrying that Henry might end up a prisoner of war. She did make a note in her diary when reports reached Philadelphia of several vessels sinking during a storm in March 1760, adding that the crew and passengers were safe. It is possible that Elizabeth took an interest in this mishap because she knew that Henry would soon be boarding a ship to return across the Atlantic, but she did not say so.[17]

Both men and women avowed that the period of courtship preceding marriage conferred on women a measure of power, albeit fleeting and heavily circumscribed. As young women prepared to pass from living under their parents' authority to a home in which they must defer to a husband's will, men had to woo them and must accept that potential wives had the right to accept or reject their advances. Henry's letters expressed both uncertainty and anxiety about his prospects with Elizabeth, and this was not unusual. Indeed, some men sank into frenzies of insecurity and even fury due to their unaccustomed dependency on what they saw as a woman's whim. The increasingly romantic tone of courtship during the eighteenth century must have intensified the sense of emotional vulnerability that men experienced as they sought to win the favor of prospective wives.[18] Young women, meanwhile, were well aware that the protocols of romantic courtship gave them an opportunity, however temporarily, to lord it over men. Ann Swett, before becoming Henry's first wife, referred to suitors in letters to her friend Elizabeth Sandwith with a cavalier assumption that the young men in question must accommodate her and not the other way around. None of these letters refer explicitly to Henry Drinker, though it is possible that he was the young man waiting "downstairs all alone" while she wrote on one occasion to Elizabeth. She wrote mischievously that the young man should be grateful to Elizabeth for making Ann absent herself for that purpose, since he would be "much the more welcome" once she had finished with her correspondence. Ann also declared that he "may as well stay away" if he brought no letter from Elizabeth. Was Henry bringing letters from the woman who would one day be his second spouse and delivering them to the current object of his affections, soon to become his first wife? Elizabeth suggested that Ann visit Philadelphia in order to spare "the poor lad the trouble" of traveling out to Newcastle, where Ann was living, to which Ann responded breezily, "Who desires him to come oftener than he has an inclination? And if he has an inclination, it must be a pleasure to him."[19]

The women in Ann's and Elizabeth's social circle clearly understood that in choosing a husband they were making a momentous decision that, if they were not careful, could turn out to be a disastrous mistake. After all, they were consigning themselves, permanently, to a man who might or might not treat them as they felt they deserved. Insofar as they had a choice, even if an entire clutch of eligible suitors lined up in supplication, they were each choosing their future patriarch. Before she married Henry Drinker, Ann told Elizabeth that her father had been "letting us know," or at least "endeavoring to convince us," that "a husband has a right to correct his wife when she deserves it." The young ladies of the household were apparently "determined not to be convinced of what might [at] some time or other be of disservice to us." At present, wrote Ann, this had no immediate or direct relevance for her because she was still unmarried, but Ann was "determined to plead for the liberties of [her] sex in every station," and so "I said what I could, which was very little." Whether her limited response was due to her father's unwillingness to tolerate contradiction from his daughters or her own reluctance to speak out against him is unclear. Other young women in their circle were also well aware that some men's perspectives on marriage should give them pause. Elizabeth Moode expressed her outrage that men might consider their wives as nothing more than practical helpmates, refusing to acknowledge their spiritual and intellectual capacities. Writing of an unnamed man, she declared, "Does he think that women were made for no other purpose than being slaves to men? . . . Does he think that all the business of our lives is only to learn how to make a sausage or roast a joint of meat and take care of a house and practice, in short, good economy? All that is necessary, I avow it, but can't we be that and take charge of our spirits at the same time? Must we neglect the most valuable part for fear of offending our masters?" After all, she wrote, "the most mediocre capacity is capable of learning."[20]

The stark reality was that suitors did become masters. Once a woman accepted a man's hand and became his wife, her ascendency ended and she must defer to her erstwhile suitor's authority. It is, then, hardly surprising that young women like Elizabeth Sandwith delayed committing themselves. Elizabeth, furthermore, may have resented that Henry had previously chosen her friend Ann over herself and now made him pay for that decision by keeping him in suspense. Yet that delay was risky. What guarantee was there that he would wait indefinitely, or that other eligible suitors would appear to take his place if she rejected him, or if he lost patience and took his attentions elsewhere? How much choice did she really have? Moreover, high-handed behavior before marriage might lead to retribution afterward, perhaps in the form of harsh discipline that Ann Swett had acknowledged as a grim possibility.

Elizabeth must have believed that taking so long to consider Henry's suit was justified, but at least one of her friends was afraid that Elizabeth might take this too far. Writing in February 1760, a little over halfway through Henry's absence, Elizabeth Moode echoed Henry's own words, only more bluntly, when she told Elizabeth Sandwith that their social circle already considered her "engaged for life" and that it was "in vain" for her "to hope to be looked upon in any other light." The involvement of relatives and friends in the courtship process meant not only that a man was open to scrutiny by an entire constellation of interested parties but also that he could use that larger community to pressure the woman he wanted to marry, and Henry clearly understood how to play that game. He had backed the object of his affections into a corner, and Moode now counseled that her friend reconcile herself to that fact. Moode advised that when Henry returned from England, Elizabeth should "grant him what he so earnestly wishes for," and sooner rather than later: "show thyself a generous conqueress, nor take pleasure in showing thy power, neither stretch it to its utmost extent, for thou knows most things are weakened when carried too far." Her so-called conquest, in other words, might prove futile if she either alienated her would-be husband or soured his devotion and temper even before they married. No surviving letter or diary entry suggests that Elizabeth Sandwith was worried about Henry's likely treatment of her following marriage, and given her close friendship with his first wife, she was in a position to know. Yet Moode was hinting that her friend misunderstood the rules of the game she was playing and her own best interest. She recommended that her friend give Henry what he wanted and so demonstrate her willingness to become a compliant wife even as she conquered his heart. Though Moode invoked the "power" that a woman wielded over her suitor, she also warned her friend that any such power was limited and easily squandered.[21]

Another possible explanation for Elizabeth's delay is that she may have wondered if she could secure a more socially advantageous and less risky match. Henry was, after all, only the son of a clerk and had committed to a hazardous occupation. He came from a long line of skilled artisans. Phillip Drinker, a potter, had emigrated from England with his wife, Elizabeth, and two sons in 1635. They had settled in Charlestown, Massachusetts, where Phillip continued to work as a potter and operated a ferry service on Mystic River. Their son John and his son Joseph were both shipwrights in Beverly, Massachusetts. Joseph and his wife Ruth's son, also named Joseph, became master carpenters in Beverly, but Joseph Jr. then migrated to Philadelphia.[22] There he joined the Society of Friends and married Mary Janney, an English-born Quaker. Joseph and Mary Drinker were our Henry Drinker's grandparents. In 1731, their eldest son, Henry, born in 1709, married Mary Gottier, the descendant of Huguenots who had fled France in the late seventeenth century and settled in Charleston, South Carolina.[23] Henry and Mary Drinker had five children, including our Henry, who was born on February 21, 1734. Unlike his father, grandfather, and great-grandfather, all of whom worked with wood, our Henry's father was a "scrivener," or office clerk.

In apprenticing his son to a successful shopkeeper, Henry Sr. presumably hoped that his son would flourish in the world of trade, and the young man's subsequent entry into partnership with Abel James did herald the possibility of a bright future. The Philadelphia tax list for 1756 included Abel among the top 5 percent of those assessed, so Henry had clearly aligned himself with an affluent man. But at present he was listed in the less impressive 59 percent to 80 percent of assessed Philadelphians, along with other individuals described in the tax records as tailors, saddlers, dyers, bakers, glove makers, shoemakers, tobacconists, carpenters, millers, sea captains, and boatmen—a mostly respectable yet hardly dazzling company.[24] At the time of his proposal to Elizabeth, Henry had already invested in land outside the city, which was also promising, but he could offer neither impressive lineage nor inherited wealth. There was, moreover, no guarantee that his success in trade would continue: mercantile ventures were notoriously risky. In wartime, they became especially "precarious" (to quote James and Drinker) because trading ships could fall victim to enemy attack. Henry returned from across the Atlantic in June 1760 to discover that the French had captured a ship filled with articles that he and Abel were relying on for "spring supplies." Because Henry did not know that this had happened at the time of his departure from England, he had not been able to place alternative orders, and so the firm found itself with a big hole in its inventory. Wartime prohibitions on trade with merchants in enemy territory posed an additional challenge as traders faced a sudden contraction in their scope of operation. Residents of a major seaport would have been well aware that even in times of peace, some firms flourished while others floundered, sometimes because of the owners' ineptitude or questionable judgment calls, at others because of bad luck that no one could foresee. Marrying into trade was by no means a safe bet.[25]

Elizabeth Sandwith would have been especially familiar with the hazards of trade, as she was the orphaned daughter of a Philadelphia merchant and shipowner. Elizabeth's great-grandfather John Jervis had emigrated from Ireland to North America in the late seventeenth century and brought with him his second son, Martin. John eventually returned to Ireland, but Martin, who became a shopkeeper, bought a house on the west side of Second Street between Market and Chestnut Streets, in which his daughter Sarah and her children, including our Elizabeth, were all born. Sarah Jervis married another Irishman, William Sandwith, in 1731. Elizabeth's father had migrated in 1727, bringing with him credentials from the Friends' Meeting in Dublin so that he could secure admission to the Society of Friends in Philadelphia. He traveled as commander of his own trading vessels and continued to do so for a decade after his marriage before settling in Philadelphia to ply his trade as a merchant on dry land. Elizabeth had two siblings: Mary, her sister, was three years her senior; William was born eleven years after Elizabeth and did not survive infancy. Their mother died in 1756 at the age of forty-eight, following a long illness, and their father followed two months later, at the age of fifty-six, after suffering an apoplectic fit.

At the time of their parents' deaths, Elizabeth and Mary were in their early twenties and unmarried. Their mother's brother, John Jervis, administered their affairs, but they went to live with Thomas Say, a Quaker pharmacist and philanthropist in the city who served as executor to many Philadelphian estates and as guardian to several orphans. The two young women stayed as boarders in his home for fourteen months. Many years later, Elizabeth remembered Say as "an inoffensive, well-minded, patient man."[26] The sisters then took up residence in the household of recently widowed Ann Warner, whose deceased husband had been a carpenter and merchant. They lived with Warner and her children in Front Street for almost four years, and it was to this house that Henry paid frequent visits as a suitor. When Elizabeth went to declare her "intentions of marriage" at the Northern District Monthly Meeting in November and December 1760, Ann Warner accompanied her in loco parentis. Her four years' stay in the Warner household seems to have been comfortable and contented. Many years later, when a new owner had much of the house demolished and then rebuilt according to the latest fashion, Elizabeth recalled nostalgically spending "many hours of moonlit night" on the porch that was now pulled down. She and Mary were fortunate in that they could afford to live comfortably on the inheritance their parents had left them, but it seems unlikely that they both intended to remain single. Unmarried women could and did survive on their own, more so in urban than in rural communities, yet marriage remained the norm and the two sisters were probably hoping that at least one of them would marry.[27]

Elizabeth Sandwith was a respectable but hardly stunning marital prospect, and as she considered Henry's advances, she could not be sure that another equally promising match would come her way. Yet she seems to have had a high opinion of herself and the circle in which she moved. In August 1759, she wrote in her diary that "eight women Friends" had dined together at Ann Warner's house, "which made fourteen of the best sort, ourselves included."

Whether Elizabeth was claiming that their status rested primarily on spiritual or social qualifications is unclear, and her remark may have been partly or even wholly playful. However, she does seem to have hoped to advance her prospects through marriage, and she was not yet entirely confident that Henry Drinker was her best option. Trade was not only risky but also carried with it a distinct social stigma across the Atlantic, and that stigma was not entirely absent from the North American colonies. Philadelphia derived most of its wealth from commerce, and Elizabeth's father had been a merchant; even so, she may have had reservations about marrying a merchant and so tying herself permanently to the mercantile world.[28]

Yet placing material prospects and social respectability above spiritual credentials was itself risky in terms of a young Friend's reputation, especially given that Pennsylvania Quakers were in the mid-eighteenth century reaffirming the centrality of shared religious identity and moral character in choosing a marriage partner. Shortly before Henry left on his trip to England, Elizabeth's close friend and namesake, Elizabeth Moode, wrote to express her concern that she might be using the wrong criteria in calculating her prospects for happiness. "My heart has been earnestly engaged on thy account," she wrote, "with desires that thou mayst be directed aright." She urged Elizabeth to consider spiritual as well as worldly factors, declaring, "Not only thy temporal but eternal interest in some measure depends on the choice thou makes." It was perhaps only reasonable that Elizabeth should want to be confident of her suitor's prospects as a successful and respectable member of Philadelphian society, but according to Moode, her first and foremost consideration should be his spiritual integrity and whether he cut a worthy figure in the Society of Friends. "Let me entreat thee, therefore," she wrote, "to endeavor to turn thy mind inward and wait upon the Lord to know what his mind and will is concerning thee . . . I doubt not but that if thou art truly submissive to the will of our heavenly father, thou'll be conducted aright." If Elizabeth responded to this doubtless well-intentioned advice, the letter does not survive.[29]

Soon after Henry's return in June 1760, Elizabeth's attitude toward Henry seems to have changed. Her diary entries became much more detailed in their descriptions of Henry's visits and somewhat more revealing of her feelings. Henry brought with him from England a gift of "locket buttons set in gold" with her name inscribed inside that perhaps assuaged any doubts she had about his ability to maintain her in the style to which she hoped to become accustomed; the buttons became treasured possessions. He resumed his suit with renewed determination, and those efforts soon bore fruit. Elizabeth had apparently decided that Henry was a good prospect and that she could not keep him waiting indefinitely. He now came to visit almost daily, sometimes staying late into the evening. On July 4, 1760, she wrote that he was there "till past eleven," which she considered "unseasonable," but her pleasure in his company overwhelmed her scruples. "My judgment don't coincide with my actions," she wrote, " 'tis a pity, but I hope to mend." Shortly after Elizabeth and her sister left the city to spend a fortnight at William Parr's house on the Delaware River, Henry rode out to the estate for afternoon tea, walked with them in the gardens, and stayed well into the evening. A few days later he was back in the company of several friends: "they all spent this day with us, took a walk after dinner to the summerhouse, round the bank as far as the boat-house." They then went out rowing, which Elizabeth thought inappropriate on a Sunday, though this did not prevent her from going along. After tea, all of the visitors left except for Henry, with whom Elizabeth took a long walk "in the gardens, to the summerhouse, round the meadow banks, etc." He did not leave until "between nine and ten." On his third visit, he stayed overnight, leaving the next morning "before we were up." The next day he returned and again slept over at her host's home.[30]

Once she was back in Philadelphia, Henry resumed his evening visits, sometimes staying "till after eleven" or even "near twelve o'clock." A week later, he arrived unexpectedly, Elizabeth being under the impression that he had just left on a brief trip to Burlington, New Jersey. "This evening I shall never forget," she wrote, "for 'tis a memorable one." Though she did not say so explicitly, this was when she finally agreed to marry him. The next morning Henry did leave town, though he was back the following day to resume his daily visits, now as her acknowledged husband-to-be. He had left Elizabeth in a state of perturbation that according to her journal entry matched the tempestuous weather ("there is a great similitude this day between the elements and my mind"). Henry's visits now became so habitual that one day when he did not come by the house she wrote, "I know not what's become of HD," and on another, "No Henry this evening." Elizabeth was beginning to realize just how hectic the life of an ambitious young merchant could be. She noted in several entries that Henry was "very busy," writing in one that he had been "dispatching the ship Friendship, Nathaniel Falkner master," on a voyage to London. Owning property also carried obligations as well as social prestige, and one morning he told her he was going that afternoon "to his place beyond Frankford to have it surveyed." It is unclear whether Elizabeth was at this stage impressed, resentful, or concerned by his being so preoccupied with business affairs, though once they were married her feelings on the subject would become much less opaque.[31]

The morning after his successful marriage proposal, before leaving town, Henry returned to Ann Warner's house before Elizabeth arose and had "a conference" with her sister, Mary. Elizabeth did not explain why Henry needed to meet with Mary, but he was in all likelihood inviting her to come and live with them once they were married. Providing a home for unmarried and widowed relatives was a generally recognized responsibility. Mary accepted the invitation. A few years later, Henry mentioned in a letter that his sister-in-law had a "sweetheart," but he did not name the fellow, the relationship came to nothing, and Mary remained unmarried. Even though she invested her inheritance in property and became a landlord in her own right, she stayed on as a permanent member of Henry and Elizabeth's household, actively involved in running their home and raising their children. It is not clear if Elizabeth consulted with Mary about her choice of husband, though given that they lived together in the same house and slept in the same bed, it is difficult to imagine that the subject did not come up. Nor is it clear whether Elizabeth and Mary saw themselves as close friends. The sisters often went together to visit neighbors, including John and Mary Armitt, but it was Elizabeth and her friend Elizabeth Moode who had their hair bound together in a wig for John Armitt, not Elizabeth and Mary.[32]

Yet whatever the tone of Elizabeth's relationship with her sister, Henry's offer of a home seems to have been much more than a routine expression of marital duty. Henry Drinker and Mary Sandwith were remarkably close. In January 1760, when he enclosed a letter to Elizabeth in a note to Mary, he informed his prospective sister-in-law that he did this for two reasons. One was so that the seal would not obliterate any portion of the inner love letter, but Henry wrote that he had another "more material" motive. This was the pleasure of writing to Mary, "a very particular favor," he declared, "since there is but one woman in the world beside [thee] that is so exalted in my esteem as to receive that mark of my great condescension." Henry evidently thought that his playful tone might lead Mary to dismiss his compliment because he added, "all joking apart, I do think upon a close scrutiny, that there is something of love, friendship, esteem, and all that abides in the recesses of my bosom for thee, and not a little neither." As we have already noted, suitors and their sweethearts often shared love letters they had written or received with relatives or friends, but Henry was especially eager to ensure that Mary felt incorporated into his romantic correspondence with Elizabeth. He asked Mary to "tell that girl that sleeps of the right or left side of thee, I know not which, that though she may have flattered herself that she has made a monopoly of my heart, which is condemned by all merchants an unfair traffic, yet assure her from me that thou hast a large apartment there." He then envisaged a striking physical intimacy that incorporated him and both sisters. "Let me commend thee," he declared, "to the arms of that dear sister of thine and she to mine in due time, and myself to you both in the month of May or thereabouts, when I hope I shall be favored to meet my dear Polly and Betsy in health and prosperity in my dear native city, which will be a pleasure beyond description to thy sincere and truly affectionate friend."[33]

It is possible that Henry's choice of one sister over the other had not always been a foregone conclusion. Indeed, Elizabeth may have delayed in giving herself fully to Henry because she wondered if his love for Mary might rival his devotion to herself. Yet if she delayed, Elizabeth might end up as the unmarried sister-in-law of a prosperous merchant instead of becoming his wife. This sobering possibility may perhaps have tipped the balance as Elizabeth considered whether finally to accept Henry's offer. If so, Henry's conversation with Mary the day after Elizabeth agreed to become his wife may well have involved some delicate diplomatic maneuvering. During the months that followed, Mary played a strikingly intimate role in the life of her brother-in-law-to-be and in the preparations for his marriage to her sister. When Henry fell ill with a fever in the early fall of 1760, it was she, not Elizabeth, who visited him during his convalescence. Elizabeth was also not feeling well, and neighbors might have considered it inappropriate for a bride-to-be to visit the sick young man, especially if he was bedridden, but Mary was also a young unmarried woman. Two months before the marriage, Henry was already describing himself in a letter to Mary as "thy loving brother." In early January 1761, Elizabeth noted that Mary was "busy down at the house in Water Street" that she and the married couple were about to move into. Elizabeth went over later that same day to help, but over the coming week, Mary toiled away at the house getting things ready while Elizabeth "stayed as usual at home," complaining that she had no company, nursing a sore throat, and knitting a pair of mittens. Henry would call sometimes at Ann Warner's home in Front Street to spend time with Elizabeth and sometimes at the house in Water Street where Mary was preparing for the new life that the three of them would soon settle into together. At this stage, Elizabeth's diary betrayed no resentment of the time that Henry spent with Mary over at their future home, but once the wedding took place and they moved in together, Mary's willingness to perform the role of household mistress whenever Elizabeth was ill or otherwise unavailable would test and occasionally fracture the young bride's equanimity.[34]

"All the Tenderness of a Sister"

Whatever the future held, neither Elizabeth nor Henry nor Mary had any reason to expect that they would face it in emotional isolation. As Quakers, they belonged to a tight-knit community that had always stressed the need for loving solidarity as they faced the enmity of people who neither understood nor respected their faith. During the first half of the eighteenth century, Pennsylvania Friends had become somewhat less isolated and isolationist, in large part because they lived in a colony that guaranteed freedom of worship for all Christians and wielded considerable power. Perhaps the most visible symptom of this relaxation was a trend toward marriage outside the faith, but greater integration could also mean a dilution of faith and community. That new threat gave rise to a groundswell of anxiety among Quakers in the mid-eighteenth century: just as Elizabeth, Mary, and Henry were entering adulthood, many Friends became convinced that immersion in a diverse and increasingly affluent society posed a fundamental threat to their principles and way of life. They worried especially that intermarriage endangered the future of their faith, as the children from such unions might not grow up in households committed to Quaker values. In response, the Society of Friends launched a determined campaign to reinvigorate their distinctive spiritual identity through a renewed stress on marriage within the faith, the careful religious education of children, and the avoidance as far as possible of outside influences. This transformed the Society of Friends with remarkable speed into an increasingly introverted and clannish community. Quakers could not cut themselves off completely from the rest of colonial society, and some were much more committed than others were to this isolationist impulse, but many Friends now committed to withdrawal from mainstream society.[35]

That renewed ethos of tribal solidarity expressed itself on the personal level as a web of loving, supportive relationships. Quakers were not alone in cultivating close friendships that bound men and women in affectionate, purposeful, and virtuous collaboration. Contemporaries did not think of society as an abstract, impersonal entity but as a latticework of personal connections that tied people together. Nor did they have much interest in autonomy or individualism: instead, they aspired to a dense interdependence, both practical and emotional, that would further their interests and sustain them as they navigated life's opportunities, challenges, triumphs, and tragedies. Young people in particular sought support from friends as they contemplated the choices and responsibilities that they faced as adults; as friends, they hoped to nurture in one another their capacity for virtue and piety as well as the knowledge or skills that they needed to fulfill their duties within and beyond the household. Their friendships would also make them happy. Elizabeth's namesake and fellow Quaker, Elizabeth Moode, wrote that a friendship devoted to "bright virtue" would bring "every human joy" to "the fair bosom of the blooming youth." Close friends often referred to each other as brothers and sisters, characterizing the bond between them as a form of kinship, and Moode wrote that she felt for Sandwith "all the tenderness of a sister." Yet Moode had in mind a distinctive version of sisterhood. Quakers thought of themselves as a spiritual family and as brothers and sisters in Christ. Though they envisioned themselves as Friends of all humankind, they preferred to form personal friendships with one another, united by their spiritual affinity.[36]

Elizabeth Sandwith lived her day-to-day life and pondered her future options, including her choice of husband, as part of an intimate social circle within the Society of Friends. Her relationships with Ann Swett and Elizabeth Moode were particularly close and affectionate. Even as Ann declared her unwillingness to visit Philadelphia so as to save her suitor the trouble of riding out to see her at Newcastle, she assured her "beloved" friend Elizabeth that she nonetheless intended to come into town soon so that she could visit her. Elizabeth Moode was downright effusive in her expressions of loving devotion. In a poem that she composed for Elizabeth on the subject of "sacred friendship," she paid homage to friendship's "celestial flame" as the "true source of bliss" and "a constant pleasure that can never cloy." In another piece, written while away on a trip, she conflated her love for Philadelphia with her longing to see and embrace "dear Betsy":

> Grant me once more to see my native home,
> No more I'll wander, never more I'll roam.
> If blest in your dear arms once more I rest,
> See that dear face and to thy breast be prest . . .

However much she loved the City of Friends, Moode assured her friend that "had there not been an ES" there, "very probably EM would not have had her thoughts that way."[37]

For young Quakers such as Elizabeth Moode, one of the principal appeals of friendship was that it provided them with moral reinforcement as they worked to become worthy members of society. That sense of ethical imperative, though not unique to Quakers, had a particular resonance for young Friends in the mid-eighteenth century, given that their community was currently reaffirming spiritual priorities, especially in the selection of a spouse. When Moode wrote to warn her friend against caring too much about social and economic prospects as Elizabeth pondered Henry's suit, she began by stressing her responsibility to speak out as a loving friend. Indeed, she felt "a perfect freedom to communicate some hints . . . which are the product of a true and unaffected friendship." Broader loyalties and imperatives underpinned these loving expressions of concern, for the Society of Friends would survive and prosper only if its members entered into spiritually committed marriages. Yet advice such as Moode gave her friend, however well intended, could easily cause offense and alienation, unless the recipient trusted her friend's honorable intentions and made "allowance for defects which proceed from the weakness of the head, not from the badness of the heart. Such is that friendship," Moode continued, "which I trust subsists betwixt us, and which I hope time instead of weakening will aid and strengthen." As it turned out, these two friends did not have the opportunity to test the longevity of their devotion to each other. Elizabeth Moode married in the same year that Elizabeth Sandwith became Henry Drinker's wife; she emigrated to England with her husband, Samuel Emlen, and their children in 1764 and died three years later. Several decades later, Elizabeth Drinker recalled in her diary the books that she and "Betsy Moode" had read together "with pleasure" in their youth, that memory resurrecting "old feelings" that Elizabeth clearly still treasured.[38]

When Elizabeth Moode suggested, however tactfully, that her friend refocus on Henry's religious qualifications, she was in effect recommending that Elizabeth Sandwith embrace the spirit of reformation that was sweeping through their religious community, forsaking worldly concerns in favor of spiritual purity. Elizabeth's diary entries for these years do not suggest a deeply religious sensibility, though at this point in her life the diary functioned for the most part as a record of activities, rarely including commentary of any sort, so that the absence of spiritual remarks does not necessarily indicate lack of religious faith. Elizabeth did eventually marry Henry, and she was at this point in her life an outwardly observant member of her religious community. She attended meetings for worship in company with her sister and the Warner family; she also went to "youth meetings" specifically designed to address the needs of young adults, as well as extraordinary gatherings such as a public meeting of the committee compiling a summary of Quaker belief and practice.

So routine was her attendance at meetings for worship that any absence called for special mention and explanation: "Stayed from meeting this evening," she wrote on January 20, 1760, "it being very dark and the streets dirty." A week later, she was "detained from meeting this evening by rain." Whether her regular presence at meetings for worship was due to pressure from Ann Warner is impossible to tell, but this was, for whatever reason, an important part of her day-to-day routine. In later years, Elizabeth's attendance at public worship dropped off, due in part to frequent illness. Yet the diary entries that she wrote in the latter part of her life contained more remarks of a spiritual nature. Elizabeth was now free from the burdens of childbirth and motherhood, leaving her more time to write. The worldview expressed in those entries was that of a steadfast though not zealous Friend, and the parameters of her social world continued to coincide with those of the local Quaker community, but her public involvement in Quaker affairs or worship was now minimal.[39]

Regardless of how devout Elizabeth may or may not have been as a young unmarried woman, her daily life was in many respects quite typical of someone at her stage of life from the middling or upper ranks of Philadelphia society. She spent much of her time visiting relatives, friends, and acquaintances, or receiving guests at the house where she and her sister lived. Elizabeth's social life was distinctive only in that most of the people she mixed with were Friends. Some of those who arrived at Ann Warner's front door had come specifically with the intention of spending time with one, some, or all of the residents there and settled in to drink tea or even share a meal; others called in on their way somewhere else and stayed for only a few minutes. Some visits were doubtless quite perfunctory, fulfilling social obligations; others expressed the cordiality or perhaps festering resentments of long acquaintance; much more intimate consultations took place when close friends and beloved relatives came by. October 6, 1759, was a typical day, unfolding as a succession of visits. Elizabeth "called in the morning at Joshua Howell's, at Francis Rawle's, and at Uncle Jervis's, went from thence to Betsy Moode's, dined and spent the afternoon there, took a walk in the evening with Betsy Moode, [and] called at William Brown's." Betsy Moode went home with our Elizabeth and stayed for supper. Elizabeth then "went part of the way home with her" and called again on the way back "at Joshua Howell's," where she found Ann Warner and her own sister on a visit of their own.[40]

Visiting played a crucial role in the everyday lives of men as well as women, so that once Elizabeth married Henry, a constant flow of callers passed back and forth through their front door. Her own social circle overlapped with his, and the two now merged to some degree. People passed in and out of their home each day to gossip, chat, confer, and offer words of support in times of illness or distress. They also came by to consult with Henry about the affairs of the local Quaker community in which he became a leading figure and about business matters in which Quaker merchants and investors concerned themselves. Some appeared only once in the lists of visitors that figured prominently in Elizabeth's diary, others in dozens upon dozens of entries. The comings and goings that gave shape to Elizabeth and Henry's daily routine identified them, on the one hand, as members of respectable Philadelphia society and, on the other, as a couple who belonged to and moved within a very specific segment of that urban world. Excepting marriage, declining health had the most impact on Elizabeth's social routine. Well before she reached old age, a series of illnesses prevented her from leaving the house for weeks or even months at a time, so that she socialized mostly as a recipient of visits rather than as a visitor. Elizabeth was not antisocial and complained when no one came to see her, but she became a largely passive member of her social and religious community.

Before her marriage, Elizabeth's day-to-day life blended the obligations of membership in the Society of Friends with interests and pursuits typical of a genteel resident in North America's largest city. Her identity as a Quaker did place limitations on her options for recreation. In November 1759, she attended a meeting at which a Friend read out a paper containing "advice against going to fairs" (often an occasion for drinking and gambling). Yet Elizabeth's parents and teachers raised her to become a fashionable as well as morally upstanding woman. On the one hand, she attended the school of Anthony Benezet, a renowned abolitionist Friend who doubtless inculcated his students with Quaker principles (the same Benezet who thought highly of young Henry Drinker). Elizabeth later described him as "our much valued friend and schoolmaster." On the other hand, she had a French master, Peter Pappin, and the French phrases that she occasionally inserted into her diary entries bespoke her claim to a transatlantic Francophone sophistication.[41] Urban and urbane gentlefolk, including Quakers, had to make themselves familiar with the classics and current trends in literature and science. Elizabeth was an enthusiastic reader of both printed and manuscript literary efforts, ranging from Alexander Pope's translation of Homer's *Iliad* to extracts from her suitor's journal of his transatlantic voyage. In February 1760, she spent an afternoon at a neighbor's home, "where we were entertained with diverse objects in a microscope, and with several experiments in electricity." Elizabeth took an interest in mortality rates from smallpox and in later years from the yellow fever, showing a numerate as well as literate mind at work.[42]

Elizabeth also took part in the popular pastime of visiting neighbors' gardens. These outside spaces were almost as important as parlors in the social lives of fashionable Philadelphians, especially in the warmer months. Elizabeth seems to have had a genuine appreciation for natural beauty, noting in one entry that she and her friends "picked some very beautiful wild flowers" in the woods near a home they were visiting. They were, she wrote, "much pleased with the vast number of fire-flies which appeared in the meadows after dark." While staying at William Parr's home on the Delaware northeast of Philadelphia, Elizabeth and her sister spent much of their time walking around the estate, admiring the garden beds, and enjoying the summerhouse. Henry also visited and wooed her there. Strolling through gardens was, however, as much about performance of gentility as it was a personal indulgence. Displaying a knowledge and an appreciation of the latest developments in horticulture was one of the ways in which men and women could demonstrate their sophistication in company with each other. In November 1759, she and several friends spent the afternoon at Andrew Hamilton's Bush Hill estate, which had a major art collection and extensive grounds, both open to the public.[43]

A considerable portion of Elizabeth's time was devoted to needlework, blending women's traditional labor with decorative skills that demonstrated leisured gentility. As a married woman, Elizabeth would make shirts for her husband and a range of garments for her servants, though she also employed women to make clothing for herself, Henry, their children, and other members of the household. Yet many of the projects that Elizabeth took on as a single young woman served to highlight her skill in genteel needlework as much as her practical domestic abilities. Her careful notation of the various stitches she used bore testimony to her pride in her work, and she would have exhibited these items to others in her social circle, proclaiming her membership in a community of women acquainted with the latest fashions in decoration and who had the time to engage in intricate needlework. Elizabeth's diary began with a list of more than eighty needlework projects that she completed between 1757 and 1760. These included "a screen in Irish stitch flowers," "a round pincushion in queen stitch and ten stitch," and watch strings for Henry Drinker (his watch a marker of gentility). She also took part in group projects, noting in several entries that she had "helped to quilt" at the homes of friends and neighbors, occasions that showed off the abilities of those involved as well as completing an essential household item.[44]

Alongside her participation in traditional feminine crafts, executed with a clearly genteel inflection, Elizabeth observed from the sidelines a community of marriage, childbearing, and motherhood in which she would soon take her place as a wife and mother. She attended Monthly Meetings at which couples applied for permission to wed and then in due course married.[45] She also visited the homes of friends who had recently given birth, joining in bedside celebrations now that the moment of greatest peril for mother and child had mercifully passed.[46] Those who attended at actual deliveries were mostly older women who had personal experience of giving birth. As a young unmarried woman who did not yet have skills that would make her useful at a birthing, Elizabeth became involved in less fraught moments. She helped Sally Wharton to "iron baby clothes," for example, but stayed at home when Ann Warner went to help her daughter Rebecca Rawle give birth.[47] Elizabeth seems to have been particularly interested in visiting infants after they had been inoculated for smallpox. This procedure, currently gaining favor among Philadelphians, involved taking the content of pustules on smallpox patients and inserting it into cuts made in the child's arm or leg. Inoculation was controversial and potentially fatal, but as Elizabeth noted, the mortality rate from inoculation was significantly lower than when people contracted it "in the natural way." Dr. John Redman, who would become Elizabeth's preferred physician, first came to her notice when she observed him inoculating her friends' children. In due course, Elizabeth had her own infants inoculated and would later take an interest in experiments with vaccination against smallpox; she became a staunch advocate for the new preventative treatment.[48]

"Brethren So Nearly United in Spirit"

Just as Elizabeth devoted much of her time to visiting, so the same was true of her future husband, though since he was a young man and a junior partner in a successful business concern, his world was considerably more expansive than hers. Henry seems to have maintained a hectic schedule. Most of his visits to Elizabeth took place in the evening, but he also called in at the Warner home during the day on his way to and from business engagements. Some of these appointments would have taken place in public places such as the London Coffee House, some at the store owned by James and Drinker on Water Street, some on the premises of other firms or retailers, and others in private residences where men of business often had offices. (Because Henry was not yet a homeowner, he could not yet provide hospitality in his own right.) When he was not busy down at the firm's wharf, supervising the loading and unloading of cargo, or at a desk piled high with the massive correspondence on which their business depended, Henry would have spent time conferring with other merchants, establishing new contacts, negotiating with suppliers or retailers, and gathering information. A trading firm such as James and Drinker needed constant updates about price fluctuations and exchange rates, their competitors' movements, the ability of potential buyers to meet their obligations, and their past record for paying up on time. Perhaps most important of all, Henry needed to maintain a visible presence among fellow merchants as a rising member of their community, worthy of notice and consideration. Henry did not keep a diary that recorded his movements in Philadelphia, and so we cannot know how much of his time, if any, he spent in purely social activities, or indeed how often he attended church meetings, but he had a reputation for being a devout, virtuous young man and was almost certainly a regular presence at meetings for worship. It seems unlikely that either his temperament or his frenetic schedule would have allowed for frivolous pastimes.[49]

There was a tight overlap between Henry's mercantile activities and his religious world. Eighteenth-century merchants tended to do business with people from the same religious background, so that for a young man in Henry's position, the building of contacts within the trading world would have overlapped with the establishment of relationships within the Quaker community, both locally and further afield. Henry stressed in the letters that he wrote to Elizabeth during his stay in England that he was busy cultivating "worthy" Quakers. These included men of business who could further his firm's interests, but they also had to meet his standards of integrity. Quaker merchants claimed to conduct their business in close alignment with their religious principles, including forbearance toward worthy debtors who had fallen on hard times. James and Drinker valued "principles of strict honor and good conscience . . . more than any profit in trade," and were determined to avoid "dishonorable" business dealings; otherwise, they declared, "we could not justify ourselves to God or the world." They assured John Lindoe, a Quaker merchant based across the Atlantic in Norwich, that they wanted to order goods from him "not only from motive of interest" but also because they wanted "to cultivate and preserve a correspondence with a person we have so true an esteem and friendship for." Henry had met Lindoe during his visit to England and warmed to him immediately. That Lindoe was a relative by marriage of their London friend and Quaker merchant David Barclay made the connection even more appealing, as it kept their mercantile activities within a network of shared faith and kinship.[50]

Such networks were much more than instrumental. Quakers had a long history of having to rely on one another for support in the face of hostility from outsiders, and the trading friendships that James and Drinker nurtured would prove crucial once they and other Friends faced renewed persecution during the revolutionary period. In early 1776, as the deepening conflict between Britain and its North American colonies made transatlantic correspondence more and more challenging, James and Drinker assured their friends and business associates Frederick Pigou and Benjamin Booth in London that even a complete severing of communication could not break the emotional bonds that tied them together. "The time seems very long," they wrote, "since we last heard from you, and as troubles and difficulties multiply in this part of the world, we fear we shall in a great measure be deprived of that satisfaction for a considerable time longer. Yet we trust you will throughout these melancholy and gloomy scenes continue to maintain and cherish those friendly and kind sentiments you have heretofore given us many proofs of." The personal relationships that Henry and Abel had developed with fellow merchants would sustain them even after they could no longer do business or even communicate with them. "On our parts," they wrote, "we shall remember and gratefully retain a sense of them and trust we may yet before the close of time convince you that we are with unalterable regard your faithful and affectionate friends."[51]

Shared faith and affection went together for men like Henry, who felt a particular closeness to his spiritual brother John Pemberton. When Pemberton left Philadelphia on a missionary trip to Europe in the 1780s, this gave Henry an opportunity to express on paper the "fellow feelings" he had developed for John over the preceding decades. He thought about his absent friend with "tenderness and near sympathy," hoping now to capture in words the affection that had for many years "cement[ed]" them together in "pure unity." (He had used the same verb to describe the bond developing between him and Elizabeth during their courtship.) He received John's words of advice and sympathy as "a balm to my spirit," recognizing with humble gratitude that Pemberton and his other friends looked past his many "frailties and deficiencies . . . veiled and as it were hid under the mantle of love." Whatever their tribulations over the years, even when separated for long periods, "brethren so nearly united in spirit" remained "dipped into each other's states and conditions," bound across the miles and oceans "in near brotherly sympathy." Their "near union" made them "as epistles written in each other's hearts."[52]

Friendship and kinship could converge in more than one direction. Just as close friends with a shared faith could become brothers and sisters in Christ, so particular relatives could develop a personal bond far deeper than the unchosen, sometimes perfunctory connection of kinship. In 1759, Henry's brother John Drinker reconstructed the evolution of their relationship from one of biological fraternity, devoid of any significant emotional connection, into a meaningful and loving friendship between two men who were spiritual as well as literal brothers. Writing shortly before Henry's departure for England, John wrote that although their "nearness of blood" and "the many kindnesses" Henry had conferred on him might seem "sufficient to excite not only the affection of a brother but the warmest returns of sincere and grateful friendship," yet his love for Henry had matured and deepened through his own spiritual odyssey. When John had gone through a phase that he characterized as moral "deformity" ("corrupted by evil communication, my mind empoisoned with vicious sentiments, when scarce one spark of love for virtue was left unextinguished"), he and Henry had been "in a manner strangers, not even maintaining a brotherly intercourse." It was when he "awoke" to his own spiritual depravity and the malign influence of his "companions in iniquity" that he became aware he was "destitute of a friend" (that is, a true friend with his spiritual interests at heart). It was at this point, he wrote, that he "longed for a nearer intimacy with my brother" and "our friendship began." That friendship, he wrote, was "implanted in virtue's grateful soil . . . thence supplied, it lives; and owes thereto, I trust, its present greenness."[53]

"Intentions of Marriage with My Friend HD"

John Drinker evidently saw his brother Henry as a good man and a good brother, but he also believed that Henry was ambitious. Several years before Henry's departure for England, John had declared,

> Henry, thou wishest an estate
> Of thousands tens, and country seat
> With every needful implement
> To serve each purpose and intent.

If Henry wished to become a respected member of his religious community and at the same time a prominent Philadelphian, complete with a country estate, in an era when Friends had become much more sensitive about appearing to value material over spiritual concerns, he would need a wife who could help him reconcile these potentially conflicting objectives. Was this, perhaps, one of the "needful implement[s]" to which John referred? For Henry as for

Elizabeth, building a successful and happy life would rest in no small measure on his choice of a spouse. Following the death of his first wife and their child, Henry became convinced that Elizabeth suited his needs, and she had finally agreed to take him on. In the morning of November 28, 1760, he once again visited Elizabeth at the home of Ann Warner. Henry ate breakfast with the family, and afterward he and Elizabeth went together to Meeting, accompanied by Warner and Mary Sandwith. Along with three other couples, they requested permission to wed. The Monthly Meeting determined whether young people who wished to marry had permission to do so from their parents or guardians (no longer an issue in this case), and whether each party was free from previous commitments. The committee also ascertained if the candidates' behavior together had been above reproach, which no one could take for granted in an era of skyrocketing premarital pregnancy rates. A committee appointed to investigate then submitted their report at a subsequent meeting.[54]

Why it took Henry and Elizabeth so long to approach the Monthly Meeting is unclear. To be sure, Henry had been quite unwell in the early fall. Yet Abel James wrote in late October that his young partner was now "recovered from his late indisposition, but not passed meeting yet," suggesting that more than illness was responsible for the delay. Perhaps Elizabeth still had lingering doubts about Henry's prospects or was still reluctant to end a period during which Henry was wooing her with considerable enthusiasm and she remained free of anyone else's authority, other than Ann Warner. Unmarried free women who did not live with their parents were independent in ways that she certainly would not be once she became a wife. In any case, Elizabeth's diary notation of this momentous step was characteristically succinct: "declared my intentions of marriage with my friend HD." Four weeks later, on December 26, she noted that they had "passed the second meeting." Henry returned to Warner's house that evening with the news that "our good old king" George II had "departed this life" and that his grandson had been proclaimed George III. Change was clearly in the air. A few days beforehand, Elizabeth's good friend Hannah Hicks, who had come into the city "on account of her father's being ill of the pleurisy," told Elizabeth over tea that she was going to stay in Philadelphia "till I have changed my name." Even the measurement of her feet for a new pair of shoes and a visit by her dressmaker for a fitting took on new significance as the young woman prepared her wedding trousseau.[55]

Once the bed that Elizabeth and Mary had slept on together at Ann Warner's home was moved to the house on Water Street where she, her husband, and her sister were to live, Mary had to sleep on the floor of Ann Warner's chamber while Elizabeth bunked in with Warner and her daughter Nancy. Elizabeth's nerves were by now understandably on edge. On January 9, 1761, she noted that five years prior she had also been "much agitated," though from a "very different" cause: January 9, 1756, was the date of her mother's death. Her sister and Ann Warner had spent "the greatest part of the day in Water Street preparing for the important day," but Elizabeth stayed behind in Front Street, focused on spiritual preparation for her coming life. "May I so conduct myself in this state of perpetual change," she wrote, "as to arrive at last to that state of bliss, never to be again separated from my dear parents." Over the coming years, Elizabeth would engage with her faith mostly in the context of her dedication to family, so it is not surprising that this moment of spiritual contemplation, unusual in the early portion of her diary, centered on the formation, loss, and reconstitution of loving familial bonds in this world and the next.[56]

Elizabeth and Henry finally married on January 13, 1761. Fifty-six witnesses signed the marriage certificate, along with the bride and bridegroom. Elizabeth wrote no diary entry for that day or any other until mid-May. Indeed, she penned only three entries for the remainder of 1761. It was just a few minutes' walk from the house on Front Street where she had lived for almost four years to her new home on Water Street, but she now passed from one mode of life to another. No longer would she be a single young woman, living in someone else's home but legally independent and receiving the constant attentions of her suitor, his addresses decked out in the language of romantic love. Instead, she would become the mistress of a hopefully prosperous home but subsumed legally within her husband's identity; that husband would now expect her to manage their home and bear their children while he focused on building his business partnership with Abel James. The transition would prove at times quite fraught.[57]

2 • "Tenderness, Care, and Anxiety" at Home and Abroad

In Which the Drinkers Embark on Married Life

The rented house that Elizabeth and Henry moved into as a newly married couple in January 1761 was located on Water Street, parallel to the street where Elizabeth and her sister had been living with the Warner family. Front and Water Streets were the two thoroughfares running closest to and alongside the Delaware River. This was a rambunctious neighborhood, peopled by merchants, tradesmen, artisans, and seafarers. Water Street provided direct access via a series of alleys—some sloped, others stepped—to the wharves where merchants such as James and Drinker loaded and unloaded their cargoes. Nearby were storage sheds, lumberyards, and shipbuilding facilities that crowded the embankment. Initially known as "the street under the bank," Water Street was significantly lower in elevation than Front Street. Built in the late seventeenth century as a dirt pathway alongside the river, it was later paved with cobblestones and after that with stone paving blocks.

By the time of the Drinkers' arrival, Water Street had become an amalgam of residential homes, offices, stores, and warehouses. A dancehall had opened on the street in 1748, and several years later, in 1754, a company of English actors performed for two months at a Water Street storehouse that they named the New Theater until it closed because of protests by Quakers. The neighborhood had a reputation for maritime rowdiness, and several of the more substantial houses on the street had barred windows to protect them from passing carousers and criminals. Despite efforts by Philadelphians such as Benjamin Franklin to clean up the city's streets and improve its standards of hygiene, the waterfront remained grimy and often unsanitary. The stench from rotting refuse on the docks often swept up into Water Street, which a late eighteenth-century visitor to the city described as strewn with "filth and dirt," so that walking along the street could prove a distasteful experience. The general atmosphere fit uneasily with the values of an upwardly mobile and self-consciously respectable Quaker household. To be sure, this was a convenient spot for a busy, ambitious young merchant such as Henry Drinker to hang his hat, but the location was far from ideal in other respects, and so it is not surprising that the Drinkers moved on once they could afford to do so.[1]

Ten years into their married life together, the Drinkers relocated from the house they rented on Water Street to a home that they owned themselves at 110 North Front Street. Their new residence was next door to where Elizabeth had lived before her marriage. It was only one block farther from the river, but at a much higher elevation than Water Street and more clearly separated from the docks and wharves, so it offered a less hectic and malodorous setting in which to raise their growing family. Yet this was hardly a quiet neighborhood. Front Street was eighteenth-century Philadelphia's principal thoroughfare, running along the top of the embankment that separated the river from the city. People traveled along this street when heading out of town toward Frankford and other settlements along the Delaware; it also led to the highway that linked Philadelphia to New York City. During the revolutionary war, it was along this street that troops headed in and out of the city to and from the north. From the windows of houses along Front Street, residents and their visitors could see out onto the river and into one of the city's busiest streets.

The Drinkers were still living in the midst of the city's trading community, and the street in which they had now settled was uneven in its respectability, though this was true of most neighborhoods in the city. Front Street was at first primarily residential, but by the time of the Drinkers' arrival, many commercial establishments had set up shop, creating a bustling environment in which people from different ranks of society mixed with one another, at least on the street if not inside their homes. During their residence of well over thirty years in this street, the Drinkers' neighbors included a biscuit maker, mustard and chocolate manufacturers, a grocer, tobacconist, ironmonger, apothecary, tallow-chandler, goldsmith and jeweler, barber, baker, fringe maker, milliner, sailmaker, feather merchant, wood merchant, cabinetmaker, and chair maker. Few of the buildings along Front Street were entirely residential or commercial: most of the stores had living quarters behind or above, and many homes included offices where merchants such as Henry could do some of their work and confer with business associates.[2]

Change, which in general did not sit well with Elizabeth, loomed constantly on the horizon as neighbors moved in and out of the surrounding homes, as

Detail from *An East Prospect of the City of Philadelphia; taken by George Heap from the Jersey Shore, under the Direction of Nicholas Scull[,] Surveyor General of the Province of Pennsylvania,* engraved by Thomas Jeffreys in 1771 (Library of Congress). The Drinkers' house at 110 North Front Street was in the neighborhood to the immediate right of the steeple at the left of this image.

tradesmen set up and dismantled stores, and as businesses flourished or crashed (often in rapid succession). The house next door was for many years the home of Elizabeth's former landlady, but in the late 1790s a new owner demolished much of the original building to make way for a "renovated, enlarged, and beautified" structure "in the modern style or taste." Elizabeth did not approve and thought the house "better as it was," though she did acknowledge that not everyone had to share her attachment to "old fashions and old things," and the improvements presumably made their block look much smarter. Nor did she welcome the arrival of commercial ventures that degraded her immediate surroundings. In 1784, one of their neighbors built a

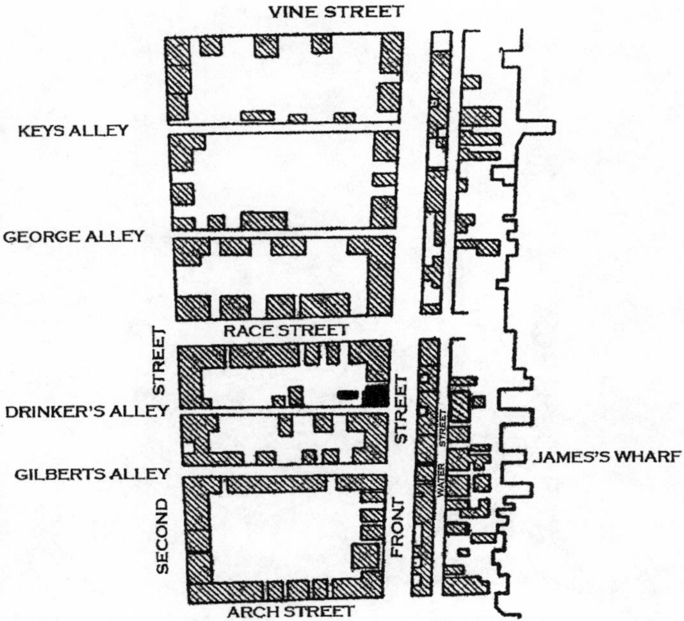

Street map of the Philadelphia neighborhood in which Henry and Elizabeth Drinker lived, showing their home at 110 North Front Street (marked in black) and Abel James's wharf, which became known as James and Drinker's wharf, based on the city map published by Matthew Clarkson and Mary Biddle in 1762 (Wikimedia Commons)

large soap-manufacturing facility directly opposite them, "a disagreeable circumstance," she wrote, presumably not least because of the smell. Yet the odors wafting from a chocolate manufactory down the street must have provided some compensation, and in the same month that the "Soap House" opened, Elizabeth noted the departure of "a very troublesome neighbor" named Pantlif after officials found a cache of stolen goods in his house. He and his family absconded once a friend had bailed him out of prison, and Elizabeth was relieved to see them go. Clearly, not all change was bad.[3]

The environment in which Henry and Elizabeth now settled was hardly the cloistered community of likeminded souls that Quakers envisioned for themselves as they worked to reform the Society of Friends from the 1750s onward. Philadelphia Friends must have realized that they would have to seek moral community within their own homes and through networks of devout families that transcended the bustle and unbridled behavior for which the city was renowned. Proximity did not necessarily imply intimacy, and Elizabeth seems to have been quite adept at insulating herself from neighbors whom she considered unsuitable. She regularly exchanged visits with respectable Friends who lived within walking distance, but most other people she simply ignored. In the summer of 1806, the chocolate maker's wife called on them to inquire about a physician she wanted to consult. The Hahns had lived for two decades "within three doors of us," Elizabeth wrote, yet she could not remember ever having seen her before, "so little notice I take of many around us." Elizabeth was doubtless not alone in responding to a mixed neighborhood by giving the cold shoulder to those with whom she did not wish to associate.[4]

The Drinkers' new home was an imposing three-story brick structure situated on the block between Arch and Race Streets. It was, by eighteenth-century Philadelphia's standards, a veritable mansion, standing on an impressive double lot that measured forty-one-and-a-half feet wide and two hundred and thirty feet deep. The main structure was thirty-six-and-a-half feet wide and fifty-two feet in depth. A flight of wide stone steps led up to a front door positioned in the center of the wall facing the street, with parlors on either side of the entrance hall. Ornate brackets, known as modillions, supported the eaves at the top of the house. Each of the three floors had four rooms and a passageway. The entryway on the ground floor had wainscot paneling and boasted two pairs of fluted Doric columns; another pair of fluted columns adorned one of the parlors. The rooms and passageways on all three floors had skirting boards at the base of the walls and cornices at the top; there was also a garret, simply finished with plaster. A separate two-story kitchen and washhouse, measuring fourteen feet by forty-two feet, provided sleeping quarters for some of the live-in servants. A third building, also with two stories, measuring twenty-five feet by thirty feet, functioned as a stable and coach house with its own cellar. The lot extended across half of a ten-foot-wide alley that led alongside the house from Front to Second Street. The Drinkers moved in on March 9, 1771, and four months later embarked on a major facelift, "new-jointing the front bricks and renewing the faces of the red bricks over the door and windows." Painters busied themselves inside, and Henry assured Elizabeth, who had fled the chaos to take the waters at Bath Springs, just north of Bristol, Pennsylvania, that the results would be well worth the effort. "It really makes the house look well," he wrote, "and very different from its former appearance."[5]

The Drinkers now owned a large garden that Elizabeth evidently treasured. She acknowledged in her diary how fortunate she was as a city-dweller "to have room enough" for a garden, and "such elegant room," whereas "many worthy persons" found themselves "pent up in small houses with little or no lots," doubtless "very trying in hot weather." Elizabeth could escape whenever she liked into their private haven and declared, "What a favor it is." In springtime she commented how beautiful the garden looked, "the trees in full bloom, the red and white blossoms intermixed with the green leaves," which were "just putting out," and "flowers of several sorts" blooming. Even when the weather was too cold, or she too unwell, to venture outside, Elizabeth could appreciate her garden from inside the house. One February she declared, "I think I never saw the trees look prettier, not even in the summer season, than they do this day, so beautifully bespangled with frost." Elizabeth was always saddened when inclement weather inflicted damage on her prized specimens, noting on one occasion that their fruit trees had been "stripped" overnight by a westerly wind, their plums and nectarines "almost all taken, none of them quite ripe." Weather was not the only threat: in 1793, when the family left for an extended stay in the countryside, she worried that their garden as well as the house itself, both "filled with valuables," would be vulnerable to thieves. Sure enough, "some naughty person or persons" broke into the garden, stole much of their fruit, and "broke the limbs" from a "beautiful tree," much to Elizabeth's irritation.[6]

This impressive new residence was not the Drinkers' only piece of real estate. They acquired a handful of other lots in the city as well as land outside Philadelphia, including several "plantations" or country estates. Many well-to-do Philadelphians left for rural destinations during the summer to escape the heat and stench of the city; country homes also provided a refuge when epidemics swept through the city. Quarry Bank, the Drinkers' principal getaway, was located on the outskirts of Frankford, just outside Philadelphia; it sat on nineteen acres of land and was set back at some distance from the main road leading northward to New York. Henry and Elizabeth made a number of improvements after buying the property, including the addition of a summerhouse. According to a visitor to the estate, "the beauty of the place consisted in the lovely view presented from the summerhouse of the pastures, streams, bridges, mills, the village, numberless roads winding through tall trees, luxuriant shade, and rising above all other objects was seen Christ Church steeple, five miles distant." In 1794, the Drinkers would purchase another property, Clearfield, which Elizabeth described as "a very beautiful and pleasant place," noting complacently "how delighted and pleased would many women be with such a retreat." On her first visit there, she discovered that it had a charming view of the surrounding countryside from the roof, which was almost flat and surrounded by railing. This property became not only a summer retreat but also a place of discreet refuge for one of their teenage servants when she became pregnant by the family's driver.[7]

In theory, Quakers such as Henry and Elizabeth Drinker were committed to simplicity in their personal clothing and home furnishings. Yet upwardly mobile Friends who wished to exhibit gentility through their material possessions rarely allowed religious scruples to get in the way. The Philadelphia Yearly Meeting had lamented in the 1730s that many members cared far too much about "needless, fantastical, and superfluous things, in dress and furniture." A decade later, the local Monthly Meeting enquired specifically as to whether Friends were maintaining an appropriate "plainness" in apparel and occasionally targeted specific individuals for their sumptuous clothing. By the time that Elizabeth and Henry were setting up home together, the reform movement within the Society of Friends had accentuated such concerns. In the face of mounting criticism, affluent Quakers generally avoided extreme ostentation without going so far as to embrace asceticism. They opted for a restrained refinement through which they could exhibit good taste without opening themselves up to accusations of gaudy exhibitionism or vapid worldliness. Elizabeth wrote in later life that she had never been "much taken up with the pomps and vanities of this world," a claim that would have raised some eyebrows. In common with most Quaker gentlefolk, she avoided ribbon or lace, yet she and her children dressed themselves in expensive fabrics. Elizabeth had a gown of dark green silk, and her nineteen-year-old son William acquired an outfit made of black velvet. The gold sleeve buttons that Henry brought back from England for Elizabeth before their formal engagement became valued possessions in part for sentimental reasons but also because they showed that she belonged to a world of genteel fashion. Each of the three Drinker daughters had a gold watch given by a family friend, and Mary Sandwith had Henry order on her behalf from England "a neat silver watch," specifying that the case should be made of green leather, with her name "in capital letters to be placed on the skirts of the dial plate." This was not a flashy item, but it did exhibit her status as a woman of means who could afford a custom-made timepiece.[8]

The Drinkers made similar compromises as they furnished their home, investing in handsomely crafted furniture but generally avoiding showy drapes or upholstery. When a man came by with some wallpaper samples at her request, Elizabeth considered all but one "too gay." Yet the Drinkers accumulated an impressive collection of furniture, much of it made from mahogany, walnut, and other fine woods. During the War of Independence, they had to surrender many of these items as payment for taxes and fines (the latter for Henry's refusal to serve in the Continental Army). Elizabeth noted indignantly in 1779 that they had to give up "one walnut dining table, one mahogany tea table, six handsome walnut chairs, [with] open backs, crow feet, and a shell on the back and on each knee," along with a looking glass and some pewter dishes, to pay the continental tax. Her detailed description of what the officials had carried away spoke volumes about the value she attached to these pieces and her bitterness at their removal. The Drinkers replenished their furnishings by importing pieces from their summer home in Frankford, maintaining their dignity and filling as far as possible the empty spaces that would otherwise remind them of their recent losses. They continued in later years to decorate their house in town as befitted a genteel family. Elizabeth was doubtless pleased in 1797 when her husband purchased a silver fluted tea service from one of the city's foremost silversmiths. A few years later, they had wallpaper hung in their entryway, following the fashion of the day, which had previously limited wallpapering to inner rooms.[9]

The Drinkers were also eager to keep up with the latest in bathing facilities. In summer 1794, their daughter Ann set up a primitive shower bath at her parents' house, probably in the backyard or washhouse, that relied on servants pouring water through a colander over the bather's head while he or she stood in a large tub. Four years later, the family acquired a more elaborate mechanism that the bather could operate by pulling on a string that released water from above the bath. Henry was the first to try it, followed by Ann "in a single gown and oilcloth cap." Several of their servants also tried the shower, which Elizabeth described as "a fine frolic for them," but it was not until the following summer that she ventured under the newfangled contraption. "I bore it better than I expected," she wrote that evening, "not having been wet all over at once for twenty-eight years past." In 1803, their son William purchased a sedentary bathtub for the household, made of wood and lined with tin, with casters on the bottom and "a brass lock" to let the water out. Bathtubs had caught on in Europe during the closing decades of the eighteenth century and soon after became the rage in affluent households across the Atlantic. Henry and William had in the past used public bathhouses and still did so occasionally because it was, Elizabeth wrote, "less trouble." It took considerable time and labor to fill the bath with hot water, and so several members of the family went into the tub one after the other. "We make the best of it," Elizabeth noted, adding that she did not mind going in "after my husband or son, etc.," but that William and Ann "chose to be the first, or not to go into it at all." Sometimes the servants followed them, at which point, Elizabeth acknowledged, "the water must have been foul enough." Meanwhile, the city had put into operation a new municipal water supply system that pumped water from wooden tanks into homes through a network of distribution pipes. In 1807, the Drinkers had a water hydrant installed in their washhouse, which must have made life a little easier for their servants.[10]

"In a Manner Forsaken"

The location of the Drinkers' home on Front Street, though not perhaps as tranquil or refined as Elizabeth and Henry might have wished, was certainly convenient for a merchant. Henry was constantly on the move between the wharves and warehouses, the store on Water Street in which he and his partner sold a wide array of goods, the coffeehouses in which men of trade met to discuss market conditions, and the offices or parlors in private homes where merchants often did business. Elizabeth had commented during their courtship that Henry was "very busy," and so she should not have been surprised that following their marriage he continued to devote most of his time to his and Abel's firm. He also became increasingly involved over the coming years in committee work for the Society of Friends; he served as an elder in his local Monthly Meeting, as clerk for the Meeting for Sufferings, as treasurer for the Philadelphia Yearly Meeting, and on several diplomatic embassies to local Indian nations. Henry's success as a merchant and his emergence as a leading member of the local Quaker community must have gratified his ambitious wife, vindicating her choice of Henry as a husband who would give her the status she craved.

Yet occasional remarks in Elizabeth's diary suggest that she sometimes resented his preoccupation with matters that took him away from their family. She wrote in one entry that she could not record every occasion on which Henry was "out again" because this would be "too frequently said." In another she described her husband as "always at home and never at home," capturing neatly his unavailability even when in the house because he was either working in the office he had set up there or receiving in the front parlor visitors who had come to discuss business. Even after Henry ended his partnership with Abel James and became less involved in the world of trade, his was hardly a life of leisure. "I am not acquainted with the extent of my husband's great variety of engagements," Elizabeth wrote in 1795, "but this I know, that he is perpetually and almost ever employed." She estimated that the time he spent away from "his own family or his own concerns" accounted for "ten twelfths of his time." On this particular occasion, Elizabeth chose to depict her husband's choices as an expression of his exemplary moral character: "if benevolence and beneficence will take a man to heaven, and no doubt it goes a great way towards it, HD stands as good, indeed a better, chance than any I know of."[11]

However, Elizabeth was not always so quiescent in the face of her husband's preoccupation, in part because she worried that his frenetic schedule would damage his health, especially as he grew older. On one occasion, she noted wistfully as he left to visit their son Henry Sandwith at his home some thirty miles from the city, "a little relaxation from business may be useful to HD." Elizabeth considered Henry too "venturous" and disapproved of his willingness to travel on business or church affairs even in bad weather: "scarcely any wind or weather stops him," she bemoaned. In 1796, when Henry put their Clearfield estate up for sale only two years after purchasing it, Elizabeth wrote, "Could my husband, like some other men, attend to and enjoy that pretty and healthful place, I would not wish it sold for twice as much as we shall get for it." This remark raised the question, at least implicitly, of what her life would have been like had she married one of those other men. However, she had not done so and Henry clearly did not resemble them; she had made her choice and now she had to live with the consequences. One can almost hear Elizabeth sigh as she wrote this entry, perhaps in resignation, perhaps in anxious exasperation, most likely a blend of the two. If her delay in marrying Henry had been due in part to concern about his material prospects, the decade that followed must have appeased any such concerns, but her husband's success had its price. During the months before her marriage, Elizabeth had been on the receiving end of almost daily attentions from Henry. She had grown up among a generation of young women who expected such attentions, and some of them may well have anticipated that these would continue once they tied the marital knot. The problem with such expectations was that they were not necessarily realistic and might end in disappointment.[12]

There is no hint in Elizabeth's diary or in the letters that she and Henry wrote to each other when occasionally separated during the first decade of their marriage that their love was fading, indeed quite the opposite. Elizabeth referred to her husband as "my dear Henry," "my sweetheart," "my best beloved," and "my HD." For his part, Henry declared in one letter, "The sight and company of my dear wife is a treasure nearer and dearer to me than anything else in this world." In another, he wrote "with a continued flow of that tenderness that has long abounded in my breast for the best of wives," signing off as "unalterably thy affectionate husband." When Elizabeth fell seriously ill in 1769 and remained in a precarious condition until the following spring, the letters of comfort written by Henry's friend John O'Kely leave no room for doubt that Henry's own letters to O'Kely (which unfortunately have not survived) laid bare what O'Kely called his "truly distressed situation." Elizabeth doubted that she could match her husband's "knack of expression" when writing about her feelings. "Could I methodize my thoughts," she wrote in a letter to him, "I should take up a great deal of my Henry's time in telling him how much I loved him." She also worried that "too much love may cloy" in a letter from her, perhaps because custom dictated that declarations of romantic devotion should come from a man, not a woman. Yet she assured Henry that she "would freely vent the feelings of my heart, was I capable."[13]

Nonetheless, however eloquently loving Henry proved when he turned his attention to their relationship, his frequent preoccupation with business frustrated Elizabeth, even as she enjoyed the fruits of his success. Lapses in communication made his absences from Philadelphia even "more tedious," as Elizabeth made abundantly clear. She was dismayed in February 1766 by news of an unexpected extension to one of his trips ("To think of two or three weeks longer is intolerable," she declared), but Henry could compensate by writing as often as possible. "As thee knows, my dear creature," she wrote, "how much pleasure it will give me to hear from thee, and how few opportunities there may be, I hope thee will not omit embracing such as may offer." On another occasion, Henry must have responded to a request of this sort in a way that she did not appreciate. Replying to two "precious" letters that had just arrived, she adopted a tone that should have given him pause for thought: "I am far from wishing," she wrote, "that my Henry should write merely to please me more often than 'tis quite agreeable and convenient to himself." In a letter written just seventeen months into their marriage, Henry made a joke of his absences. "As those ties and bonds of affinity subsist between us which seem to demand that at least an appearance of familiarity and near acquaintance should be kept up between us," he wrote, "I mean those links which are brought about by wedding, bedding, our little Sal included, these and other weighty reasons move me to desire that thou'll send John off this afternoon about 5 o'clock (at which time I intend to set off home) with the chaise to meet me on the road, intending still to support an acquaintance with thee." Henry may have hoped that this jocular tone would lighten what he guessed to be his wife's mood, but whether Elizabeth saw the humor in her situation as she sat at home with their infant daughter is open to question.[14]

Elizabeth became most resentful of Henry's absences when the family left Philadelphia in the summertime to spend several weeks at their country home on the outskirts of Frankford. Henry often rode back into town to take care of business and frequently stayed there overnight to reduce the amount of time that he spent riding back and forth. Either Elizabeth had expected that her husband would spend more time relaxing in the countryside with her and their children, or she had not realized how much his absences would affect her, especially when he stayed in town overnight. Their country retreat was much more isolated than their home in town, so that Elizabeth could not occupy herself with the constant coming and going of visitors. People did call on her, but not so many as she was used to, and there were days when she found herself without any company at all, other than her sister, the children, and servants. This might not have mattered if her own family had been complete, but to spend day after day "in the absence of my best friend" was not her idea of an enjoyable vacation. One evening she "took a run to the end of the lane at nine o'clock to look for my best beloved, but saw him not; as the moon shone bright, I was in hopes it would induce him to come, though late." On another occasion, after noting that she did not expect Henry that night, she inserted into her diary this touching couplet:

> Such quick regards his sparkling eyes bestow:
> Such wavy ringlets o'er his shoulders flow!

Her young husband was apparently a charming companion when actually there, and Elizabeth found life in the country "exceeding agreeable" when they were "all together." Yet this was a rare occurrence, and so Elizabeth felt "in a manner forsaken, my dear Henry engaged in town." Late eighteenth-century authors often depicted marriage in terms of loving companionship between husband and wife, but that was difficult to sustain if the husband was preoccupied or elsewhere. "Did it suit HD to be constantly here also," she wrote, "I think I could be very happy in the country." However, this did not suit Henry, and so she in turn was far from happy. Neither she nor Henry left behind any hint as to whether she communicated her unhappiness and frustration to him or, if so, how he reacted.[15]

To make matters worse, Elizabeth's sister, Mary, was also frequently absent, mostly in company with Henry. Very occasionally, Elizabeth herself would accompany Henry back into town, but she generally stayed put, either because she felt unwell or because she did not wish to leave her children behind. Mary often traveled back to Philadelphia with Henry and stayed overnight with him, assuming the role of household mistress. Elizabeth's diary entries contained no explicit expressions of jealousy toward her sister, nor did they hint at any suspicion on her part that anything untoward was going on between Mary and her husband; nor do there survive in other sources any reports or rumors about inappropriate intimacies between Henry and Mary. Yet Elizabeth's frequent references to "my Henry and sister" in the entries written during her stays at Frankford suggest that she felt it necessary to stress, at least in the privacy of her diary, that Henry belonged to her and not to Mary. In the summer of 1771, Elizabeth wrote in a letter to Mary that Henry had been "affectionately acknowledging" his sister-in-law's "tender care of him, and saying how clever it was to have two wives." He may simply have been expressing his gratitude for having two women, in addition to a handful of servants, who devoted themselves to taking care of him. Yet given the emotional intensity of Henry's letter to Mary from England during his courtship of Elizabeth and the amount of time they spent together away from Elizabeth, it is tempting to wonder if he and Mary had developed a rapport akin to emotional adultery, even if their relationship was completely nonsexual. Following Elizabeth's life-threatening illness a year before, Mary's presence may have provided Henry with the reassurance that if he became widowed a second time, he had someone on hand of whom he was very fond and who was already helping to raise their children and run the household. Elizabeth gave no hint of how she felt about Henry's boast, but she told Mary in that same letter that they were both hoping she would consent to spend a month in Bristol at the water springs, "free from care of us and ours." However sincerely grateful Elizabeth may have been for her sister's "many, many kindnesses," she might perhaps have welcomed the opportunity to send her away for a while.[16]

Elizabeth and Henry did occasionally travel together, leaving Mary behind with the children. They journeyed through rural Pennsylvania for a week in the fall of 1764 and embarked on a twelve-day trip to New York City in September 1770. They departed on another trip through the Pennsylvania countryside in the summer of 1771, visiting Ephrata, the site of a Dunker settlement, and Bethlehem, where they toured a Moravian community and the famous waterworks there. Elizabeth also accompanied Henry on a visit to the Atsion ironworks in New Jersey a week after he and Abel James became majority owners in 1773; the following year, she drove out with him on several occasions to see a new vessel under construction for James and Drinker at a shipyard just outside Philadelphia. Yet these were exceptions: Elizabeth usually stayed at home when her husband traveled on business and remained in their country residence when he returned to Philadelphia and his mercantile concerns, often accompanied by Mary.[17]

Though Elizabeth would clearly have preferred her husband to spend more time with her, the couple by no means lived completely separate lives, especially since he did some of his business at home. Elizabeth was far from ignorant of the ventures he embarked on or of the various worlds in which he moved. She evidently listened to and perhaps took part in conversations about trade, politics, and church affairs as her husband engaged with visitors in their parlor and sometimes at their dinner table. Henry often had Elizabeth sign deeds of property transfer, and she sometimes mentioned in diary entries her husband's negotiations with other landowners. In his letters to Elizabeth, Henry sometimes went into considerable detail about his business concerns and passed on news about trading conditions. He evidently assumed she would be interested to hear about such matters and that she would feel comfortable passing on instructions to employees in his and Abel's firm. On one occasion he asked her to remind his clerk that he should "keep minutes of every material occurrence relating to our business" during his employer's absence. Very occasionally, especially toward the end of her life, Elizabeth admitted that she was unsure exactly what her husband was doing. She wrote in one entry, "HD was summoned to court on some occasion, I don't understand what." Yet the very fact that she saw this as noteworthy suggests that she usually had some grasp of her husband's various concerns.[18]

Nonetheless, whereas most rural wives in the late eighteenth century would have been active partners in running the family farm, Elizabeth was not involved in the actual operation of her husband's business, other than passing on messages and providing an orderly, welcoming environment in which he could entertain and consult with fellow merchants and clients. Elizabeth's principal business was managing their household and raising their family. The latter enterprise turned out to be physically and emotionally grueling, bringing with it many trials and occasional tragedy, but she did not travel that journey alone, as her sister and, more intermittently, her husband were actively involved alongside Elizabeth and supportive when things went wrong. If Henry had two wives, she had a husband and wife. Her children had, in effect, three loving parents.

"The Tenderest of Mothers"

Elizabeth's situation as a household mistress was somewhat unusual in that she had a sister who lived with the family, never married, and by all accounts played a significant role in helping to run the Drinkers' home. One of their neighbors, Ann Warder, described Mary Sandwith as their "housekeeper," and in later years Elizabeth would acknowledge that she had time to sit, read, and write because her sister took on many tasks that would otherwise have fallen to her. Yet Elizabeth was throughout her married life actively involved in the supervision of her servants, and she seems also to have kept a close watch over the fiscal affairs of her domestic kingdom. Henry entered into his own accounts for 1776 a list of household expenses that he copied from "my wife's memorandum book." That book does not survive, but Elizabeth had made a detailed inventory of expenditures. These included the cost of food, washing, ironing, candles, oil, thread, buttons, ribbon, gloves, silk handkerchiefs, fabric, wood, shavings, shells, pamphlets, tobacco, a teapot and cruet, new spectacles, a pair of stays, the mending of a watch, payment to the fire company, schooling, a comb and case, medicine, brushes and a broom, chimney maintenance, a joiner's labor, servants' wages, contributions to poor relief and aid for prisoners, and expenses from various trips. The outside back cover of her diary for 1805 and the inside front cover of that for 1806 listed payments to the milkman and hired servants, along with the dates for each stage of the walnut pickling process that year. Elizabeth was evidently not out of touch with the practical operations of her household.[19]

Elizabeth devoted much of her time and energy during the first two decades of her married life to the demands of procreation and motherhood. Indeed, the lengthy gaps in her diary during those years were almost certainly due to her preoccupation with bearing and caring for her growing family. Elizabeth became pregnant on at least eleven occasions and gave birth to nine children, the first arriving nine months and ten days after her marriage to Henry, the last twenty years later. We do not know if a midwife or physician attended Elizabeth at these deliveries. William Shippen Jr. returned from studying anatomy and obstetrics in London to set up his own medical practice in Philadelphia just as Elizabeth and Henry were starting a family. Decades later, Elizabeth would encourage her own daughters to draw on Shippen's obstetric services, for which he was by then well known, but the presence of male physicians at deliveries was not yet a routine practice during the period when Elizabeth was giving birth. She may have been one of Shippen's first obstetric patients, but his surviving record books begin in 1775, and by then all but one of Elizabeth's children had been born, Elizabeth wrote, "with great difficulty."[20]

The only pregnancy of her own that Elizabeth described in detail was her last in 1781. During her second trimester, she wrote repeatedly that she was "very poorly," often "troubled with a vomiting, and otherwise unwell." Toward the end, Elizabeth was "confined" at home for several weeks. This did not bother her as much as she thought it might other women because she was "no great goer abroad at any time," but Elizabeth was less philosophical about being "often up in the night, tried with sickness." The delivery itself was not quite as agonizing as she had anticipated: Elizabeth wrote that she was "favored . . . beyond expectation." Yet she clearly considered childbirth a harrowing experience, describing it as "the time of distress." That she did not even mention giving birth to her other children, excepting a brief comment that Henry was away on a trip when she was "upstairs" in 1774, was doubtless due in part to her not having time or energy to write during or after her confinement, but perhaps also she chose not to recall the ordeal. When her daughters and daughter-in-law became pregnant, Elizabeth's comments on their sufferings were interlaced with grim reminiscences about her own "agonies bringing [them] into this world of troubles." Pregnancy, she wrote, had always been "attended with great difficulty to me and mine," and as for the actual births, "lingering tedious distressing times have always been our lots." Reacting to the death of a neighbor who died several days after giving birth to her seventh child at the age of forty-two, Elizabeth made it abundantly clear how relieved she was to be past her childbearing years. "I have often thought," she wrote, "that women who live to get over the time of childbearing, if other things are favorable to them, experience more comfort and satisfaction than at any other period of their lives."[21]

All of Elizabeth's nine deliveries were successful, but she had at least two miscarriages, in 1763 and 1768, and four of her children died during infancy. In other words, only five of Elizabeth's eleven known pregnancies resulted in the birth of children who survived into adulthood. Her third child, Mary, was born in 1765 and died the following year; her fifth, Henry, arrived in 1769 and expired that same year; her seventh, Elizabeth, arrived three years later and also died before the year was over; her ninth and final child, Charles, was born in 1781 and perished in 1784. Her eldest, Sarah (known as Sally), was born in 1761 and lived until 1807; she predeceased her mother by just under two months, a devastating blow that cast a dark shadow over the final weeks of Elizabeth's life. Ann (known as Nancy) was born in 1764 and lived until 1830. William (known as Billy) arrived in 1767 and lived until 1821, though he endured serious health problems for many years and was a source of deep anxiety to his parents. Another boy, Henry Sandwith, was born in 1770 and lived until 1824. Their eighth child, like their third named Mary (known as Molly), was born in 1774 and would live until 1856. Molly was the only one of these nine children to live longer than her parents, both of whom died in their seventies: Sally was almost forty-six at the time of her death, Nancy sixty-six, Billy fifty-four, Henry Sandwith also fifty-four, and Molly eighty-two.[22]

Of the four babies born to Elizabeth who died in infancy, their mother made no mention in her diary of little Henry's or of her namesake's death, but she did describe Mary's passing, one year old, in 1766 and that of Charles in 1784 at the age of two and a half. In a poignant string of entries, Elizabeth recorded that Mary had been "drooping for some time past," but was now "grown worse." The family was staying out at Frankford, and although it was late June, the weather had been dreadful, "which had great effect on my little lamb." In early July, they took her out for a ride, hoping the fresh air would do her good, but the baby reacted badly. They then summoned a doctor from Philadelphia, who brought two "blisters" (localized irritants designed to produce inflammation and then a discharge of fluid), which they applied to her ankles at night. The infant continued to get worse, and so Elizabeth took her back to Philadelphia, "not quite without hopes," but the illness "proved too much for her." Elizabeth's account of Charles's death in 1784 was equally touching. "Our dear little one" had been very frail at the time of his birth, but "after diligent nursing had outgrown most of his weakness and promised fair to be a fine boy." A week before his death, he was "fat, fresh, and hearty," but then he "became much oppressed with phlegm," and the doctor predicted that he would die "unless we could promote some evacuation," so prescribed a purgative that he thought would produce "a gentle vomit." It caused instead a dramatic convulsion that did not get rid of the phlegm, and the little boy expired some twenty minutes later. "Thus was I suddenly deprived," wrote Elizabeth, "of my dear little companion over whom I had almost constantly watched from the time of his birth, and his late thriving state seemed to promise a reward to all my pains."[23]

In addition to losing four of their own children, Elizabeth and Henry watched many of their nephews and nieces succumb to various illnesses. John Drinker lost his baby son Joseph in 1759 and four-year-old Ann in 1766. Joseph Drinker and his wife Hannah's infant son Thomas died in 1763; the same couple lost newborn twins Priscilla and Aquila in the summer of 1775, followed a week later by their one-year-old daughter Hannah. Another of Henry's brothers, Daniel, buried his little daughter Sarah in 1765, an infant son in 1767, and a baby girl named Elizabeth in 1768. Many of Elizabeth's neighbors had miscarriages, gave birth to stillborn infants, or lost their children soon after birth. One December, she ventured out to spend time with Margaret

Stocker, who was distressed "on account of her youngest daughter's suffering in a difficult and dangerous labor." The infant had been stillborn and the mother "in bad health since." Elizabeth repeatedly expressed empathy with the anguish that women went through as the promise of new life turned into bereavement. When Elizabeth's niece Mary Cope lost her child an hour after he was born, Elizabeth wrote, "Poor Polly, she must feel sad when she reflects on the contrasted situation of her babe, whom she felt last night, alive and warm, now inanimate and in its cold grave." One summer when she was staying out at Clearfield, the wife of their gardener there, Mary Courtney, gave birth to a dead infant. Elizabeth noted in her diary that six of Courtney's seven children so far had been stillborn. She wrote that Mary "suffered greatly," and poverty compounded the suffering. "I feel much for her," she wrote, "to be sick and poor is hard indeed." The next day a neighbor dug a grave for the infant in a nearby meadow and Elizabeth attended the burial, "desirous of seeing it properly done."[24]

Managing the emotional trauma that accompanied these losses must have been daunting, but Elizabeth's friend Hannah Haydock, writing soon after the death of her own infant child in 1764, wrote that bereaved mothers must submit to the "very pinching" trials of faith that God had ordained for them. Quakers laid great stress on the notion of resignation, an acceptance of God's will even when going through deeply painful ordeals. Despite their grief, Friends should acknowledge all that they had to be thankful for — in Elizabeth's case, wrote Hannah, "a loving husband" and "fine children for which I doubt not thou art thankful," blessings that Hannah hoped "may be continued." Elizabeth's diary entries about her own bereavements made no mention of any religious perspective through which she could make sense of or alleviate her suffering, but the letters that Henry wrote in response to illness and death in their family did so quite explicitly. Faithful parents, Henry reminded his wife, should focus "daily and hourly . . . on objects beyond this world" and strive to "look beyond the natural and immediate connection of parent and child." When their second son named Henry became gravely ill at the age of seven, his father sought to prepare himself and his wife for the possibility that this little boy might also not survive. Whatever happened, he wrote, they should defer to God's will: "although I think often about him, I give him up; and if restored to health and to his dear mother and me, it will be a favor, and if not it will all be in best wisdom, I doubt not for his and our real good."[25]

Henry's insistence that bereaved parents should defer to God's will did not reflect any lack of parental love on his part or any underestimation of his wife's grief. While Elizabeth wrote of *her* loss and the lack of "reward" *she* would receive for the trouble she had taken as a mother, Henry framed the tragedy of these infant deaths in terms of *their* loss and his anxiety about *her* emotional state. Henry's affection as a parent came through clearly in a letter that he wrote to one of his friends soon after little Mary's death in 1766. He described his daughter as "a most engaging sweet child . . . called hence in a state of perfect innocence." Until her illness, she had been "our most hearty child" and "raised till then with much the least trouble." Henry focused, however, not on his own grief but on his wife's. "It is not over yet," he wrote, "as she is one of the tenderest of mothers; she cannot forget the sweet infant, though she endeavors to be resigned." Perhaps he did not want to admit his own limited success at achieving resignation, but he also clearly cared and worried about his wife's emotional state.[26]

In addition to the possibility that babies might be stillborn or die in infancy, childbirth was a major cause of death among women of all social ranks. Elizabeth had experienced this grim reality within her own social circle a few years before her marriage when her close friend and Henry's first wife, Ann Swett, died during childbirth at the age of twenty-two, along with the infant. Over the course of her diary, Elizabeth noted nineteen deaths that were in all likelihood associated with pregnancy and delivery. In later life, she went to view the corpse of her twenty-six-year-old neighbor Elizabeth Fisher, who had died in childbirth and left behind four little children, including the newborn infant, who though tiny seemed to Elizabeth "healthy and likely to live." No wonder, then, that she described pregnancy as an illness. Like many other women of her generation, Elizabeth used lactation to prevent conception: after bearing five children in under eight years, she nursed that fifth child for more than two years and did the same with her eighth and ninth. Whether Henry was aware of this strategy or agreed with it is unclear. Women could have had many reasons for asserting greater control over their bodies and limiting family size, but in Elizabeth's case, the stark horror of pregnancy and childbirth seems to have figured prominently in her decision.[27]

Even if mother and infant survived delivery and its immediate aftermath, child mortality posed a constant threat. When John O'Kely congratulated Henry and Elizabeth on the birth of their son Henry Sandwith in 1770, he declared, "As the dear little heart is now partaker in this *dying*, may he also share with us in *eternal life!*" O'Kely's reference to the inevitability of death and the happier prospect of eternal life was surely well intentioned, but this rather ambiguous felicitation may well have reminded the Drinkers that joy following a child's arrival might soon give way to tragedy. Parents sometimes lost small children through accidents, but most commonly because of illnesses barely understood and for which there were no effective treatments. During the summer of 1763, Elizabeth noted the death of infant Joshua Emlen from "vomiting, purging, and cutting teeth," of a neighbor's "little servant boy" from drowning, and of two "little negro" children from dysentery, which was currently widespread "in country and town." Elizabeth admitted in a letter to one of her close friends that when her own children's "frequent indispositions" coincided with waves of infectious disease passing through the city, she became "greatly oppressed" by anxiety. "I believe it is the case of every tender mother," she wrote. In the summer of 1767, when Elizabeth was staying out at Frankford with all of her children except Sally, whooping cough began to spread throughout the neighborhood. Sally stayed put in the city, and when local children started to die, the entire family returned to Philadelphia. That winter, the Drinker children belatedly contracted whooping cough and remained sick for several weeks; given the recent fatalities, this must have been terrifying for them and their parents. Illness and mortality outside their own home always cast a dark shadow over their own children's ailments. Several years later, when Sally came down with "a rash and sore throat," her mother noted grimly that "great numbers" in the city were similarly "afflicted" and several recently "taken off with the putrid sore throat."[28]

Elizabeth kept watch for any signs of illness in herself, her husband, and their children, which she then noted assiduously in her diary. A modern reader thumbing through her diary entries might be tempted to conclude that she was a chronic hypochondriac, yet fearful responses to headaches, sore throats, and stomach pains that today would seem inconsequential were at the time well justified. Bouts of fever, vomiting, and loose bowels might portend serious illnesses that regularly killed people of all ages. Medical treatment was mostly ineffective and sometimes did more harm than good, based as it was on misconceptions of disease. Many people still believed that illness resulted from an imbalance of four bodily fluids, known as humors (yellow and black bile, blood, and phlegm), so that recovery depended on the restoration of humoral balance through bleeding, purging, sweating, and the raising of lesions that would fill with pus and so remove harmful matter from the body. Rival explanations for sickness focused on the harm inflicted by spasms in blood vessels or by unhealthy vapors on the humors, but the recommended solution was still removal of surplus blood. Recent medical innovations such as smallpox inoculation suggested that specific diseases had specific causes, and some contemporaries were turning away from bleeding as a cure-all, but this remained a central component of medical treatment in most households, including that of the Drinkers.[29]

In the absence of antibiotics and without anesthetics or antiseptics to protect the patient during surgery, even minor illnesses or injuries could become fatal. Alongside bleeding and purging, most households relied on a stock of medicinal plants and recipes passed down through the generations. The Drinkers used laudanum (concentrated juice from the opium poppy mixed with alcohol) to reduce pain and Peruvian cinchona bark (which contained quinine) to address a range of abdominal and other ailments. Households routinely consumed food well past its prime, and dental disease was endemic, so that people were often unable to adequately chew or digest their food, resulting in abdominal torment. Toothaches and stomach pains tormented Elizabeth, Henry, and their children throughout their lives. Two years before her marriage, a "tooth-drawer" had removed one of Elizabeth's teeth and then reinserted it, hoping it would self-implant. This was a common procedure, but the reinsertion did not take, and so the tooth had to come back out again. The dentist also tried to remove another tooth but could not get it out, and Elizabeth wrote that she "suffered much thereby." Four days later, she was in so much pain from a sore throat, perhaps brought on by her recent dental work, that they had to send for a doctor "after ten o'clock at night." She had meanwhile attended the burial of a neighbor who "died of a mortification in her mouth."[30]

New procedures such as smallpox inoculation were saving lives, yet they were also risky in their own right. Inserting infected pus into the arm or leg supposedly produced a milder version of the disease that would then provide immunity, but sometimes the results were fatal. The protective pills that doctors prescribed before inoculation could also cause significant side effects, even assuming that the apothecary did not make deadly mistakes. In December 1762, Elizabeth copied into her diary an account from the *Pennsylvania Gazette* of three local children having died after taking the wrong medicine as a preparatory for smallpox inoculation. "How careful aught the vendors of medicine to be," the newspaper warned, "that none but discreet and intelligent persons are suffered to attend and serve in their shops." Elizabeth and Henry had their firstborn child inoculated just two months later, and one can only imagine the anxiety they felt. Henry Sandwith did become ill after taking preparatory pills in 1773, as did Molly in 1779, though both survived the ordeal.[31]

If parents chose to entrust their infants to others for wet-nursing, they opened their loved ones to an additional danger, since nurses might bring infection with them into the family. The general expectation in the late eighteenth century was that mothers would breastfeed their own children unless prevented by serious illness. Quakers in particular condemned mothers who handed off their children for fear that breastfeeding would harm their figure; such women committed the sin of pride, they warned, while parents who worried that breastfeeding would interrupt marital relations should think more about their children's welfare and less about their own pleasure. Elizabeth nursed her infants whenever possible, but she farmed out Ann, her second child, once she realized she was pregnant again, fearful that continuing to feed her six-month-old might divert nourishment from the baby growing inside her. Ann Harper, whom they hired for this purpose, was apparently in good health at the time but succumbed to smallpox two years later, followed soon afterward by her little son Jessie. Though Harper was no longer working for them, the death of someone whose relationship to their child had been so intimate must have been alarming. Elizabeth's sister visited the ailing nurse, and one has to wonder what Elizabeth thought of her taking such a risk. Ann and her tiny sister Mary had just undergone inoculation, and both were "very fretful with their sores."[32]

Daddy and Aunt Mary

Elizabeth did not face alone the anxieties and recurrent tragedies of motherhood. Neighbors and relatives provided a dense network of support in times of trial, but even more importantly, her husband and sister were actively involved in caring for the Drinker children. Though often either away from home or preoccupied with business of one sort or another, Henry was by no means a constantly absentee husband and father. Henry's frequent use of his home office meant that he was much more of a presence in his children's day-to-day lives than if he had regularly left home to work from dawn to dusk. As he wrote in his office or received visitors in the parlor, he would have heard and seen his infant children as they ran around the house, cried in distress, and laughed in delight. They may at times have been an unwelcome distraction, but Henry was at least aware of their games and tantrums; their paths must have crossed, however briefly, many times throughout the day. In fact, Henry turned out to be a loving and devoted parent, clearly enjoying the time that he spent with his children, deeply concerned for their spiritual welfare, and conjoined with Elizabeth in worry and grief when their offspring ailed or died.[33]

Fathers were rarely present during childbirth, but Henry did participate in caring for his children from infancy onward. This included helping to arrange for wet nurses and then visiting his children while under the care of these women. The wet nurse whom the Drinkers hired to feed Ann in 1764 lived out in Frankford, and the baby stayed with her, but Elizabeth, Henry, and her sister rode out frequently in various combinations to visit Ann. Several years later, in the summer of 1771, Elizabeth had to abandon breastfeeding Henry Sandwith. The family was staying in Bristol for several weeks so that Elizabeth could take the waters there, and a local doctor insisted that she was too "weakly" to breastfeed "such a hearty, growing boy." Her husband and friends convinced her to follow the doctor's advice, and so they hired a local woman, Sally Oats. The parents went together to deliver their "little lamb" into Sally's care and returned later that same day to make sure that all was well. Because Oats lived nearby, Elizabeth was able to visit her infant son almost every day until her return to Philadelphia in mid-August. Henry accompanied her whenever he was in Bristol, and during that fall, they took several day-trips out from Philadelphia to see their infant son. It was Henry and Mary who visited Sally Oats with orders to begin weaning the infant. When little Henry Sandwith fell ill the following summer, his father and aunt took him out on several occasions in a carriage, hopeful that the fresh air and movement would do him good. Writing several years later, Henry referred to the many "laborious days and nights" he had spent alongside Mary caring for his "chicks" when Elizabeth was too "infirm and weakly" to do so, but for him this was clearly a labor of love.[34]

Both Henry and Mary had to juggle multiple roles when Elizabeth was indisposed. In October 1781, Elizabeth's delivery of her ninth child coincided with the Yearly Meeting. They had nine houseguests, and the nurse looking after Elizabeth had to leave unexpectedly. Though doubtless exhausted by the ordeal of delivery, Elizabeth did notice that Mary was also "much fatigued," and Henry clearly appreciated all that his sister-in-law did for them. Writing to his children while away on a trip with his wife, he urged them to obey and honor their aunt "as one of your earthly parents." From their infancy onward, she had behaved toward them as "an affectionate, tender parent." She was "under no obligation to disregard her own ease, and to give up her time, and even to injure her health" for their sakes, so they should always be looking out for opportunities "to make due returns for so much love, tenderness, care, and anxiety." The Drinker children were clearly very fond of their aunt, missing her sorely when she left for short periods to visit relatives or friends.

On one occasion, William threatened to nail her "frock" down if she tried to leave again.[35]

Henry had a strong paternal streak that also extended to his wife (he sometimes referred to her in his letters as "my baby"). He relished the time he spent with his children and in the summer of 1771 wrote his wife a lovingly detailed description of four-year-old Billy's behavior on a trip into the countryside. "Our son was particularly drowsy," he wrote, "but the novelty of crossing the little river and the many red-headed woodpeckers we disturbed from the old fences as we rode along amused him so much as to keep him awake and good company the rest of the journey." Once his children were old enough, he took them fishing, which according to their mother "much delighted" the youngsters, though on one occasion Sally fell in the creek. He took them out in their sleigh during the winter months and in warmer weather for drives in the family chaise (sometimes with their mother, sometimes with their aunt). In the spring of 1773, Henry accompanied his daughter Sally, now eleven and a half, as she rode to the city's racetrack on horseback, the first time she had ridden unassisted other than in the alley next to their house. They rode out together on many subsequent occasions, and he then took his other offspring out on horseback once they were old enough. In 1774, he took them in the family wagon, along with several other children in the neighborhood, to watch the launching of his and Abel James's new ship. There were also more somber family excursions. In July 1775, Henry and Elizabeth took thirteen-year-old Sally, eleven-year-old Nancy, eight-year-old Billy, and four-year-old Henry Sandwith to the funeral of their infant cousin, Hannah Drinker. When Henry was preoccupied with business, Elizabeth and Mary devised little expeditions of their own. In August 1774, they took Sally, Nancy, and Billy to see a waxworks exhibit, and that October they went to see the new jail under construction on Walnut Street before strolling through "the negroes' burying ground" and visiting the impressive new house built for prominent resident John Dickinson.[36]

Yet Henry would not have approved of all the activities that Mary and Elizabeth arranged for the family in his absence. One of his nephews recalled in later years that the entire family, "with the exception of Henry himself," were "extravagantly addicted to novel-reading." According to this nephew, "the practice was, when he was absent, for the rest to assemble, and the children to listen while the mother or aunt read." When they heard Henry entering the house, "the cry was, 'There comes your father!' and the book was forthwith secreted." Henry happily encouraged his children in innocent amusements such as sleighing or fishing, but he would not condone habits that he saw as morally problematic, such as reading novels. Parents must not fall into the trap, he reminded Elizabeth in one of his letters, of "indulg[ing] every forward humor and indolent habit." This would "promote the growth of such evil and destructive weeds, which too many sadly mistaken and fond parents are in the practice of." Though he welcomed opportunities to have fun with his children, Henry's foremost concern was their spiritual welfare. He wanted "it frequently revived and impressed on their minds that this world and its fading enjoyments and pleasures afford no real or substantial joy." He regularly took his children to worship and when away from home sent letters containing little homilies that he asked them to "soberly and diligently read over and attend to." Among his dearest wishes was to see his "beloved girls and boys advanced and improved in the knowledge of the blessed truth . . . that as they grow up in stature they may advance and increase in divine favor." Henry's determination that his children should embrace Quaker values and follow closely Quaker codes of conduct would create in later years significant tensions within their household as his growing children developed their own ways of thinking and plans for the future.[37]

Although Henry often wrote about and to his children collectively, he also thought and wrote in terms of their individual personalities and foibles. On one occasion, he sent specific messages for sixteen-year-old Sarah, thirteen-year-old Ann, ten-year-old William, and three-year-old Mary. He had written to seven-year-old Henry Sandwith separately and intended to do the same for each of his children, but ended up having time only to send brief messages for the others in a letter to his wife. He urged his oldest daughter Sally to be "exemplary" and to "promote a kind and loving disposition in [her] brothers and sisters." She was to avoid "all impertinent curiosity, gadding unnecessarily abroad, appearing at the front door unconcerned and thoughtless, or mixing with light and unprofitable company." His greatest wish for Nancy was her "preservation in innocence and simplicity, and growth in godliness." To that end, he recommended "a watchful care and guard over her own temper and natural disposition, so that nothing might escape her that might irritate or promote anger or resentment." He reminded Billy that he had labored hard "for his preservation and separation from the evils and corruptions which too much prevail amongst the giddy thoughtless youth." He would be distressed if he now found out that Billy had "given into temptations and wrong things, and lost that fear of displeasing his heavenly as well as earthly father." He should stay at home, "keep out of all rude and loose company," and focus his energy on the reading of "the holy scriptures and other religious books." To "dear little Molly" Henry sent "a kiss and much love, with a charge to be a good girl, and to think and talk of Daddy sometimes."[38]

Henry evidently had a particular affection for his youngest daughter. During one of his absences, he wrote that Molly, though not mentioned in his wife's most recent letter, must be "one of her mother's comforts": "the sweet prattler," he continued, "is not forgotten by her father, and when she has been mentioned, my feelings testify that she is near my heart." He asked Elizabeth to kiss her for him and to tell the little girl that he loved her. Elizabeth replied that when her sister read this passage aloud to Molly, the little girl "listened attentively, and when she had done, came to me without speaking, with her mouth held up, by way of demanding ye kiss thee sent her." Elizabeth told him in another letter that "dear little Molly . . . when first she awoke, called out, 'Mammy, I seed Daddy last night, Daddy's come home.'" Elizabeth asked where she had seen him. "I don't know," Molly replied, "he did not laugh at me, nor hug me, but he looked at me." Elizabeth concluded, "The dear little creature had been dreaming."[39]

"Keep a Good Lookout on Account of Enemies"

As Henry became a father and experienced, alongside Elizabeth and Mary, the heartaches as well as joys that came with parenthood, so the other part of his life, which focused on his business partnership with Abel James, also brought with it a plethora of practical challenges and anxieties. These were in their own way just as daunting, and just as difficult to anticipate or control. International trade was on many levels unpredictable and perilous. It involved juggling ventures and commitments that were mutually dependent and yet independently precarious. As merchants arranged for the transportation of cargoes and money, across the Atlantic and along the Eastern Seaboard, they had to contend with bad weather, leaky ships, the duplicity or incompetence of trading partners, and the constant threat of attack by pirates. Transatlantic communication was at the best of times slow and unreliable, making it difficult to gauge markets in other regions of the world and adjust consignments accordingly. In times of international conflict, much greater uncertainty and danger cast a shadow over commerce as hostile nations used trading restrictions as a weapon against one another and, in the event of actual war, attacked trading vessels, appropriating their contents and in some cases adapting them for military use. Merchants needed to be skilled and fleet of foot to navigate their way through such crises, but even in times of peace a misread of trading conditions or straightforward bad luck could lead to significant losses. Henry embarked upon his second courtship, married Elizabeth, and became a father during the French and Indian War, a major transatlantic conflict that posed an unprecedented threat to import and export firms such as James and Drinker. On both domestic and mercantile fronts, his immediate future would provide great fulfillment but also significant anxiety.

By the time of Henry's marriage, the firm of James and Drinker was emerging as one of the premier mercantile houses in Philadelphia. In recognition of his new status and responsibilities as a married man, Henry would henceforth receive an equal share of the profits, making him an equal partner with Abel James. At the beginning of 1776, he estimated that their trading ventures over the previous fifteen years had yielded a profit, even after deduction of unpaid debts, of more than £20,500 each. To put that lump sum in perspective, Henry valued his spacious house on Front Street, including furniture, horses, carriages, and other stable equipment, at under £4,000; the two new trading vessels that he and James had built in 1757 cost £2,256 and £2,500. The partners were doing very well. Much of their trade was with the West Indies, where they sent beef and pork, grains, deerskins, beeswax, tallow, and naval supplies; on their return journeys, the firms' trading vessels brought back sugar, coffee, rum, mahogany, and guaiacum wood. The two partners also shipped raw products across the Atlantic to Bristol and London as well as Lisbon and Madeira, importing dry goods and a wide variety of manufactured products from England. Once French Canada became British Canada following the successful siege of Quebec in 1759, the firm expanded its northward trading ventures. James and Drinker owned several vessels and were part owners of several more, so they could transport goods in their own ships rather than paying others to do so. In fact, carrying freight for other merchants and providing passage from one port to another became a major source of profit for the firm. James and Drinker also underwrote insurance for other merchants' ships and cargoes, though that particular component of their business operations could become troublesome, time-consuming, and costly when a ship or shipment went awry.[40]

One reason for their success was that the range of their ventures enabled them to switch back and forth between different components of the import and export trade in response to market conditions. At their store in Water Street, they sold a dazzling array of goods that varied according to the time of year and the shifting market. Meeting the multifarious and sometimes unpredictable demands of customers was no easy task. James and Drinker assured one correspondent that the inventory of goods they kept in stock was "as well assorted as any in the city." Yet they often had to purchase goods from other vendors to complete unexpected orders, and doing so was sometimes very difficult as particular articles they did not have on their own shelves were scarce throughout the city. Yet their advertisements in local newspapers presented Philadelphians with an impressive catalog of goods from exotic locations around the globe. Sometimes they announced the availability of just a few specific items, perhaps because these particular articles were newly arrived, or perhaps because they were eager to get rid of them. In January 1765, readers of the *Pennsylvania Gazette* were informed that James and Drinker's store had in stock "Barbados rum and Jamaica spirit, best Bohea and Hyson tea, French indigo, nails of most sorts, window glass, Durham pig iron, a new ten inch and a half cable, and a large variety of European and East India goods." In April 1764, a brief advertisement drew readers' attention to "a parcel of choice Muscovado sugars" as well as Jamaican molasses, French indigo, Carolina tallow, myrtle wax, and pitch. Other advertisements listed dozens upon dozens of articles for sale "on reasonable terms," including fabrics that ranged from "Venetian and corded poplins" that could be used for dresses and upholstery to "negro cottons and plains" (cheap and unadorned material for clothing slaves and black servants), "an assortment of India and English silk handkerchiefs," bed lacing, bootstraps, patterns for breeches and vests, threads, bobbins, and buttons; spelling books, primers, and psalters; sealing wax, slates, and pencils; spices, snuff, and assorted pills; horsewhips, gunpowder, scythes, and sickles; candlesticks, tea kettles, warming pans, and bellows; door knobs, locks, and carpentry tools; mugs, chamber pots, plates, dishes, and spoons; leather, pitch, tar, and turpentine. Their store was a veritable Aladdin's cave of serviceable treasures shipped in from far-flung destinations and now ready for purchase, by Philadelphians and long-distance customers who ordered by mail.[41]

Just as the Drinkers' personal attire and domestic furnishings represented a compromise between Quaker simplicity and the conspicuous consumption that befitted their genteel social status, so James and Drinker's business operations had to balance Quaker values with the practicalities and opportunities of international commerce. It was ironic that trade with the West Indies played such an important role in their business, given the increasingly vocal opposition to slavery voiced by Quakers in Philadelphia and elsewhere. Friends argued that the ownership of one human being by another violated their belief in the fundamental equality of all human beings. Yet it was easier for Quakers to condemn slavery in the abstract than it was for them to avoid its spoils, which lurked everywhere in stores and homes on both sides of the Atlantic, especially in trading hubs such as Philadelphia. Henry's success as a merchant and the material comfort enjoyed by his family depended heavily on trade with islands whose economies in turn depended on slave labor. James and Drinker assured their trading partners that they would have found participation in the buying and selling of slaves morally repugnant: they wrote that they were glad to have "other branches of trade to follow for a living" and hoped they would never "have a temptation to think of it." Yet they added that they were "not disposed to censure others for being engaged in the encouragement of the African trade" or sharing "immediately" in "the profits arising from it." Indeed, they could not have done so without breaking with many, if not most, of their business associates. Moreover, they themselves knowingly benefited from slavery, importing staple products that enslaved Africans produced and providing the means for that labor system to continue. In October 1758, the partners sent beef to a trading post on the coastline of present-day Honduras, apologizing for the inferior quality of the meat, but expressing the hope that "at this price we thought it would suit you for your slaves."[42]

The firm was in fact involved in human trade, albeit white indentured laborers rather than enslaved Africans. Strictly speaking, they were selling indentures that committed servants to work for several years as compensation for the cost of their passage across the Atlantic. Yet when Joseph Richardson advertised in 1760 for the return of a runaway servant whom he had "bought" from James and Drinker, his wording reflected a general sense that employers effectively owned their servants for the duration of their indentures, even though they were formally free and had legal rights. Merchants such as James and Drinker were, in truth, acquiring laborers in England and then selling them on to employers who could use them pretty much as they saw fit. Henry discussed the logistics and expenses involved in transporting "a load of servants" across the Atlantic alongside arrangements for the shipment of timber and Irish linens, as though indentured laborers figured in their calculations as just one more article of commerce. In 1774, they instructed the captain of their new ship, the *Chalkley*, to procure in Bristol "a number of likely sound young men and boys to come out as indentured servants . . . avoiding elderly persons or even younger that have been broken tradesmen or such as are not qualified for laborious work." They urged him to bear in mind "that hearty, likely boys" provided "the readiest sale." Their primary concern was clearly the acquisition of fit and profitable laboring bodies: indentured servants, like linen and timber, must be in good condition and suit their purpose.[43]

James and Drinker dedicated much time and energy to building and maintaining a vast network of connections to support their transatlantic trading enterprise, yet they were well aware that importing goods was not the only way to meet demand in North America. The colonies had been slow to develop a manufacturing base that would sidestep the need for constant shipments across the Atlantic, not least because skilled labor was scarce and expensive. However, given the high cost of shipping heavy items such as iron across the Atlantic, seventeenth-century colonists soon became eager to extract and manufacture locally. By the eighteenth century, with a growing demand for iron in Europe, it became clear that such ventures represented an opportunity not only to meet local demand at a comparatively low cost but also to export abroad. In 1764, James and Drinker became part owners of an ironworks at Brunswick in New Jersey, investing considerable sums in the construction of buildings and machinery to enable the production of stamped ore for local use and export across the Atlantic. Henry was confident that the Brunswick venture would bring in a healthy profit after sales had repaid the initial outlay. He wrote to a friend in 1764 that he had recently "made a descent of near one hundred and twenty feet below the surface into the bowels of the earth to view the treasure." He was clearly excited, though he also claimed to feel guilty about his own "relish" for this pursuit: "How infatuated is man," he declared, "so to pursue the root of all evil, as some say."[44]

Henry would come to regret his own infatuation with profit and material wealth. He and Abel James had built together a flexible and far-reaching mercantile enterprise. Theirs was an impressive success story, but international conflict, along with political tensions within Philadelphia, would endanger that narrative of expansion and prosperity, which eventually came to a dramatic end in the 1770s. James and Drinker had become partners in the mid-1750s, just as Britain and France embarked on a massive military conflict that spanned several continents and lasted almost a decade, effectively the first global war. North America became one of the major battlefields in this mighty struggle between competing imperial powers, and firms such as James and Drinker had to grapple with the practical implications as the trade routes that their ships traversed became contested territory and as both sides passed measures to restrict the flow of goods back and forth across the Atlantic World. Merchants, in common with artisans and farmers, benefited from the influx of cash to pay for the needs of British soldiers as they fought in North America. Yet firms such as James and Drinker also had to deal with the dangers and losses that went along with doing business in time of war.

One of the basic challenges merchants faced at any time, a lack of reliable information, became much more crippling when they were trying to do business in the midst of international conflict. Reliable news of a trade embargo or formal declaration of war could take weeks, if not months, to reach all those affected, whereas rumors, which could prove unfounded or distorted, often seemed to travel much faster. Merchants such as James and Drinker had no choice but to rely on flexible contingency planning or, in other words, their best guesswork. In the early months of 1756, as Philadelphians expected at any moment to receive news that England and France had declared war, Henry and Abel emphasized repeatedly in their correspondence that they were playing a waiting game. Merchants had no way of predicting whether vessels currently sailing across the Atlantic or down to the West Indies would have to travel through a war zone. In their instructions to Captain Daniel Rees, who was heading down to Jamaica, the partners acknowledged that if war broke out by the time of his arrival, he might have to disregard the orders that they had sent with him for a return shipment. There was no telling how soon the French would have privateers in action on the Eastern Seaboard, attacking vessels belonging to England or its colonies. The partners warned Rees to "keep a good lookout on account of enemies" and to avoid approaching "any vessel at sea." Captain Rees may well have rolled his eyes at this belaboring of the obvious, but it was their ship, and they had good reason to be worried.[45]

It was not until May 1756 that England and France formally declared war, and in late July the news had still not reached Philadelphia, though "imperfect accounts of a declaration" were now circulating. The price of many articles had risen in anticipation of shortages, and so the partners were happy to get hold of some relatively cheap salt before suppliers became reluctant to sell "at any reasonable price," in effect hoarding to maximize eventual profits. That fall, news reached the city of an imminent embargo on goods heading out of North American ports, to prevent the French from getting hold of them and to prevent shortages, which would in turn keep prices as low as possible for the English troops in North America. This prompted James and Drinker to prepare with "the greatest hurry imaginable" to dispatch their brig *Esther* before the embargo came into effect. Unfortunately, they were unable to get on board all the flour they had promised to one of their customers, "which you must excuse," they wrote in apology, "as there was no such thing as guarding against such a contingency." Predicting embargoes was now critical, especially when they could end up with consignments of food rotting away on their wharf instead of making their way to other markets. Yet they were also contending, as always, with the vagaries of the weather, which could overturn even careful planning and informed guesswork. In March 1759, their plans to dispatch across the Atlantic a vessel filled with naval stores before the expected announcement of another embargo came to nothing when the boats delivering those articles could not reach the city for the simple reason that the waterways froze up. In order to ensure a speedy departure, the partners had to fill the hold with logwood instead, which was not what their customers in London had requested and reduced their profit from the journey.[46]

The situation became much more problematic once the British began to assert control over the actual trading ships owned by firms such as James and Drinker. When the military command prohibited the departure of any vessels from North American ports in 1757, merchants suspected that the intention was to secure transportation for the royal troops, which indeed turned out to be the case. The embargo lasted four months, and those ships pressed into service included a vessel that James and Drinker had just refurbished at great expense following damage by large chunks of ice. When another embargo for the same purpose occurred a year later, two more of their ships, the *Concord* and the *Friendship,* were pressed into service. The British government promised to pay shipowners for use of their vessels and to provide compensation if the ships sank or ended up in enemy hands, but meanwhile firms such as James and Drinker lost significant freight capacity and therefore profits. They also had no way of knowing how long they would remain without the impressed vessels, making it difficult to plan future trading ventures.[47] Meanwhile, the threat posed by privateers operating on commission from the French government became a constant source of anxiety. Insurance rates were rocketing, and vessels often sold their goods at the first island port they came to, even if the deals they struck were disadvantageous, rather than risk proceeding onward and losing their cargo to the enemy. The partners instructed their captains to proceed southward in company with other vessels for mutual protection, sometimes suggesting routes that were reportedly less infested by privateers.[48]

For trading firms such as James and Drinker, war was not entirely bad news. During the midcentury conflict between Britain and France, they were able to demand higher freight fees because of the dangers involved. In addition, the influx of cash across from England into North America, to pay for goods and services needed by the king's military forces, fueled a consumer spree as inhabitants spent that cash on goods imported from Europe and India. However, this left merchants such as James and Drinker with a significantly reduced inventory that was difficult to replenish because of wartime disruptions, leaving them unable to fill future orders. Nor was there any immediate prospect of an end to the war and the massive practical headaches it was causing. The two partners went through a brief period of optimism about the prospects for peace after the fall of Montreal in 1760. The following year, they sought to capitalize on British victories in Canada, sending ships northward to Quebec, Halifax, and Montreal. Assuming that peace was now likely, they also approached a firm in the West Indies about the possibility of joining forces to build a new trading vessel that would travel back and forth between Philadelphia and Barbados, with occasional forays across the Atlantic to England and Ireland. They began to consult with colleagues about the likely impact of peace on the price of European goods as well as, crucially, insurance rates. Yet intransigence on both sides delayed the final cessation of hostilities by months and then years, so that the firm had to reconcile itself to continued losses. French privateers still posed a significant threat in the West Indies, and British officials continued to appropriate ships in North American ports for use by the imperial forces. Henry and his partner were doubly eager for peace: as Quakers, they opposed war on principle; as merchants, they abhorred the disruptions that came with war. "Our interest as well as inclination," they acknowledged, "leads us strongly to wish for it."[49]

~

Merchants on both sides of the Atlantic hoped that the Peace of Paris, signed after many delays in February 1763, would usher in a new era of unfettered trade and increased profits, but they were to be sorely disappointed. Soon afterward, the British government imposed new taxes on the colonies in North America to recoup some of the expenses incurred in protecting them against French incursions; it also determined to assert closer control over the colonies, which many British officials had come to see during the war as disunited, obstreperous, and generally unreliable. Growing colonial outrage in the face of new legislation to tax and more closely control them led to a series of economic boycotts against the importation and consumption of British goods. These developments had grim implications for trading firms still recovering from losses incurred during the previous decade. Not only did James and Drinker resent further disruptions to their business operations, but they also objected to the violence and intimidation that accompanied protests against British legislation. Some Philadelphians, noting that an end to the boycotts would benefit merchants, refused to take such objections at face value: Quakers might claim that their pacifist principles prevented them from endorsing or participating in anything but peaceful protest, but their enemies accused them of being disingenuous and self-interested. To make matters worse, James and Drinker made a series of stunningly inept decisions that made them extremely unpopular among those who supported resistance, then rebellion, and finally revolution. Those miscalculations placed them and their families in grave danger. Ever since going into partnership with Abel James, Henry Drinker had proven himself an astute man of business, but it now became clear that his and Abel's political instincts were woefully deficient.

3 • "Obliged to Wade through This Sea of Politics"
In Which the Firm of James and Drinker Flounders in Storms of Political Protest

In April 1764, Henry Drinker wrote to inform his friend and fellow merchant Frederick Pigou in London that Pennsylvania had plunged into political crisis. According to Henry, "great numbers" of the colony's inhabitants feared that their "just rights" were in danger. The villains in this crisis were the colony's proprietary owners, and salvation, Drinker believed, lay in the arms of the royal government. During the previous century, monarchs had granted vast tracts of land in North America to individuals who not only would own the land but also had extraordinary authority to govern these "proprietary" colonies. In 1681, Charles II handed over a territory north of Maryland to William Penn, a Quaker whose father had loaned the king a large sum of money. Penn envisioned a colony in which all Christians would enjoy freedom of conscience and worship, a radical concept in the seventeenth century on both sides of the Atlantic. The colony, named Pennsylvania after its proprietor, flourished economically, not least because Penn's promise of religious freedom proved a huge draw, but the relationship between Penn and the settlers was often testy, at times downright hostile, and matters did not improve under his sons. As Drinker told the story, successive proprietors had enriched themselves at the direct expense of the inhabitants and pursued policies "destructive of the just rights of the people" as guaranteed by their 1701 Charter of Privileges. Henry was convinced, based on the proprietors' "uniform conduct for many years," that they intended to reduce Pennsylvanians to "a state of slavery." People "throughout the province" were now signing addresses to George III, asking him to rescue them from the proprietors. The situation had become so dire that the only safe way forward, he believed, was for Pennsylvanians to come under the direct control and protection of the British government.[1]

At the same time that "great numbers" of Pennsylvanians were lobbying for this change in government, Parliament was passing a series of laws designed to tighten control over the colonies in North America and to raise money through new taxes that would help to pay for American defense. Henry Drinker and his business partner, Abel James, thought this legislation misguided, but they were convinced that careful arguments and peaceful protest would bring the British government to its senses. Throughout the fall of 1764, they passed information back and forth between their business associates in London, who kept abreast of the latest developments in Parliament, and their friends in the Pennsylvania assembly, which was planning to submit a letter of protest to Parliament. Several colonial assemblies, including that of Pennsylvania, asked Benjamin Franklin to cross the Atlantic and present their case in person at the next sitting of Parliament. Franklin agreed to do so, but he also accepted another ambassadorial role, as James and Drinker related in updates sent to friends across the Atlantic. As well as speaking for the colonies in general, Franklin would also advocate more specifically for Pennsylvanians who wished to be "put under the government of the crown," ridding them of the hated proprietors and securing "those inestimable liberties and privileges granted by charter and laws to [their] forefathers." Franklin, Drinker, and their allies in Philadelphia were worried about both of their formal transatlantic relationships, one with the British government and the other with British proprietors. Yet the former struck them as much more reliable than the latter, and they may well have hoped that placing their trust in the royal government would help their campaign to reverse the new taxes and other measures coming out of Parliament.[2]

Not all Pennsylvanians would have agreed with Henry Drinker's perspective on the political situation; nor would they necessarily have seen Quakers as natural allies in a struggle to defend the rights and liberties of colonists. Over the coming decade, a growing number of Americans became convinced that Parliament posed an even greater threat to their liberties than did the proprietors. They described that threat in similar language to that used by critics of the Penn family, accusing the British government of plotting to take away their freedom and of reducing them to "a state of slavery." Quakers who had argued that the crown would protect colonists' liberties against the Pennsylvania proprietors and who still believed that the British government would eventually see the error of its ways would find themselves in grave danger as radicals accused them of having betrayed their fellow Americans and of colluding with the British government. Crucially, this was not the first occasion on which Pennsylvania Quakers had found themselves accused of scheming against their neighbors. Indeed, some colonists had long considered the Quakers to be conniving powerbrokers who cared much more about their own power than the welfare of others, and Friends were far from blameless in the creation of that reputation.

To be sure, Quakers had been energetic throughout the colonial period in resisting what they saw as the dictatorial and exploitative behavior of the Penn family. Yet many Pennsylvanians saw Quakers as equally self-interested and high-handed. Friends dominated the colonial assembly and worked ruthlessly to retain a decisive influence over public affairs even as successive waves of immigration turned them into a minority. They exploited divisions among non-Friends and minimized political representation from western regions where Quakers were few in number. Despite the absence of an officially authorized church in Pennsylvania, the Society of Friends enjoyed unofficial precedence, and its leading members had disproportionate political influence. By the middle of the eighteenth century, power within the Society of Friends had concentrated in the hands of wealthy Philadelphians, including Quaker merchants who ensured that the colonial assembly passed laws serving their interests. The colony's overall prosperity reconciled many Pennsylvanians to Quaker dominance; the determination of Friends to defend the Charter of Privileges also proved popular; and many non-Quakers joined them in opposition to the establishment of a militia, for fear that it might serve as an instrument of repression. Nonetheless, their controversial religious beliefs, their tenacious grip on power, their silencing of other voices, and their clannish sensibility irked many neighbors. As reform swept through the Society of Friends at midcentury and Quakers turned inward, embracing an increasingly tribal sensibility, this deepened their reputation as a self-involved community unlikely to protect the welfare of all Pennsylvanians.[3]

Quaker leaders also displayed remarkable inconsistency in applying their religious principles to public policy, and their apparent willingness to deploy those principles in the service of political ends opened Friends to charges of cynicism and hypocrisy. Their commitment to pacifism caused the most trouble. Quakers had long refused to bear arms themselves, but at the same time held that governments were duty-bound to protect their subjects and expected their own government to shield them against their enemies. For many years, they were even willing to pay taxes that would fund warfare, obeying the scriptural command to render unto Caesar what was due to Caesar: not waging war themselves was a personal commitment, but many early Friends acknowledged a public responsibility to support civil government as it defended its subjects. Reconciling these dual positions, which to some outsiders seemed at best inconsistent and at worst hypocritical, became a good deal more challenging once Pennsylvania Quakers became part of the government and so, when the colony came under attack, more directly complicit in the waging of war.[4]

This was not a pressing dilemma so long as external threats remained remote and the colonial assembly could authorize taxation for use by the monarch without specifying that its purpose was to fund defense. However, when the crown requested in 1739 that Pennsylvania raise a militia to defend the colony against French and Spanish attacks along the coastline and the proprietor introduced a tax bill for that purpose, political crisis ensued. Leading Quakers were reluctant to let Thomas Penn take the lead, which would set a dangerous precedent for expansion of proprietary powers in the future, and so set out to defeat his bill. They justified their opposition by claiming that it would violate their commitment to peace, even though they had previously interpreted that commitment as only prohibiting Friends from taking up arms themselves. Their enemies now accused them of refashioning their principles to suit their own political ends. Two years later, when the Quaker-controlled assembly reversed its position and passed a bill to raise funds for defense, claiming that the governor and not the assembly would be taking military action, this struck even some Friends as mere sophistry.[5]

Over the coming decade, a growing number of Quakers would embrace quite sincerely a more comprehensive interpretation of their peace testimony, which it was difficult to reconcile with any direct involvement in government. When the French and Indian War got under way in the mid-1750s, the need to raise public funds in support of the war effort placed Quaker assemblymen who identified with this broader version of pacifism in an impossible position. In 1756, ten Friends resigned their seats in the assembly, declaring that public office was incompatible with adherence to their religious principles. Yet more than a dozen Quakers disagreed and remained in place, a significant number in a body of only three dozen; although now a minority, they formed the nucleus of a ruling coalition, and other prominent Quakers worked hard behind the scenes to protect the ascendency of that coalition. Many non-Friends either did not understand these divisions within the Quaker community or chose to ignore them, so that when remaining Quakers in the assembly passed legislation to support defense, their votes tarred all Quakers with the brush of hypocrisy.

As the war raged on, settlers along the western frontier of Pennsylvania became increasingly angry that the colonial assembly was not doing more to protect them against Indian attacks. Many of these settlers were Scotch Irish Presbyterians, and they directed their anger primarily against Quakers, in part because of the Friends' well-known sympathy for Indians, dating back to William Penn's utopian vision of peaceful coexistence between English settlers and native inhabitants. Scotch Irish settlers now accused Friends of refusing to defend fellow colonists against Indian raids. In December 1763, a vigilante band of about 50 farmers from Lancaster and Cumberland Counties (known to posterity as "the Paxton Boys" because many of them lived in and around Paxton Township) killed 20 Conestoga Indians in two separate raids. About 250 armed frontiersmen then marched on Philadelphia, demanding redress of their grievances. The marchers intended to extract a group of Indians taking refuge in the city and threatened to kill anyone who got in their way. A delegation led by Benjamin Franklin met with the marchers just outside Philadelphia in February 1764 and averted their entry into the city, but this did not end the crisis.[6]

A flood of pamphlets that swept through the streets of Philadelphia during the ensuing weeks placed blame for the vulnerability of frontier inhabitants squarely on the shoulders of Indian-loving Friends who were allegedly happy to profit from trade with neighboring Indian nations while leaving western settlers defenseless. Such claims deepened the unpopularity of Quakers among those already needled by the continued political influence of Friends even after they had supposedly withdrawn from public affairs to salve their consciences. The pamphleteers railed against "a certain faction" that had "the political reins in their hand" and used that power to "tyrannize over the other good subjects of the province," plotting even to "enslave the province to Indians." To make matters worse, about two hundred Quaker men took up arms and joined in the city's panic-stricken preparations to defend itself against the Paxton Boys, opening Quakers in general to accusations of rank hypocrisy and giving further credence to claims that they favored Indian lives over those of fellow colonists. Lutheran Henry Muhlenberg noted that "pious sheep" whose "tender conscience" had prevented them from raising "a hand for defense" during the war were now eager to "shoot and smite a small group of their poor, oppressed, driven, and suffering fellow inhabitants and citizens from the frontier."[7]

As Quakers faced a rising tide of hostility, they recognized that their history of antagonism toward the Penn family made the current proprietor an unlikely source of support. Some Friends now became convinced that they could rely only on the royal government to protect them against their enemies and so joined the campaign, led by Benjamin Franklin, to end proprietary government and turn Pennsylvania into a royal colony. Other Quakers worried that this proposed switch to a royal government might necessitate giving up the Charter of Privileges and so refused to support the campaign, but once again, Friends in general would end up associated with a position that only some of them supported, and the so-called Royal Government Controversy would cost Quakers dearly. Franklin stubbornly refused to abandon his campaign for a switch to royal governance until 1768, despite a wave of new taxes and restrictive measures suggesting that the British government was even more exploitative and dictatorial than the proprietors. Franklin subsequently managed to reinvent himself as a torchbearer for American freedom, but Quakers had a harder time shaking off their depiction of the royal government as the colonists' natural protector. When Quaker merchants such as James and Drinker joined in opposition to new taxes and other imperial measures but refused to endorse threats or violence against royal officials, they became vulnerable to inaccurate yet plausible claims that Quakers were once again siding with royal authority over the interests of fellow Americans. Nor was it difficult for radicals to stir up long-simmering resentment of the city's wealthier merchants and depict them as the enemies of poorer Philadelphians, exploiting popular antagonism toward the mercantile elite to gain support for an increasingly uncompromising stance toward new legislation and British authority.[8]

James and Drinker made no mention of the Paxton Boys in their correspondence with other merchants, nor did they allude to growing hostility toward Quakers. Perhaps the two partners considered the crisis a local matter with no broader significance. Perhaps they did not want to worry their associates elsewhere and put them off doing business with a city in meltdown. They may have been reluctant to recognize even between themselves that there was a crisis. To be sure, most of their letters focused exclusively on specific business deals; chatty they were not. In the letter that Henry wrote to Frederick Pigou about the campaign for a royal government in Pennsylvania, he predicted that his friend would wonder why he felt "obliged to wade through this sea of politics." That was, he continued, "a strange subject" for a merchant, whose interests and instincts were very different from those "of a statesman or politician." Henry explained that the mounting political crisis over proprietary behavior had become "the general topic" of conversation in Philadelphia, and he assumed that merchants in London with business connections in

Pennsylvania would wish to keep abreast of the situation. Apparently, he assumed that the Paxton Boys would not be of interest to them, or perhaps he thought it best that they remain unaware of the situation. Yet it was somewhat disingenuous for any Quaker merchant to claim that he rarely took any interest in politics, since Philadelphia's mercantile community had long been active in ensuring that the Pennsylvania assembly served its interests. Even if not directly involved in public affairs, merchants such as James and Drinker could not afford to remain aloof from politics because their business interests depended in part on public policy and transatlantic relations. Henry's London connections made him an important source of information as tensions deepened between the British government and its North American colonies, so that men of note in the city would surely consult with him.

During the coming months and years, Henry would "wade" repeatedly and ever more deeply into a "sea of politics" as the British government's policies aroused increasing anger, especially in commercial hubs such as Philadelphia. James and Drinker opposed those policies, but equally disapproved of the ways in which their fellow Philadelphians chose to express their outrage. At first, the principal concerns that Drinker and his partner voiced in their correspondence were largely self-serving. During the first half of the eighteenth century, Americans had become avid consumers of imported goods, and their purchases counted for a growing proportion of England's foreign trade; they now sought to flex their newly developed muscles as consumers in that transatlantic economy. A series of boycotts on the importation and consumption of British goods turned out to be an effective weapon, but politicizing the marketplace had profound implications for merchants who made their living from shipping and selling goods from across the Atlantic World. It is, then, hardly surprising that trading houses such as James and Drinker resented the boycotts and were eager to see the tensions that had caused them resolved as quickly as possible.[9]

Yet much more than business interests were at stake. As Quakers, James and Drinker were committed to the peaceful resolution of any disagreement, and so they condemned in all sincerity the intimidation and violence that accompanied colonial protests. Friends believed that subjects had the right to object when faced with government policies that they believed to be mistaken and unethical, but they advocated for change through peaceful reform, not violence and revolution, arguing that subjects had no right to overthrow a government that God had placed over them. Reasoned and respectful petitions for redress of specific grievances were acceptable and indeed called for in the present circumstances, but outright challenges to parliamentary or royal authority were quite another matter. Furthermore, while a growing number of their neighbors worried about the threat that recent parliamentary legislation posed to civil liberties, Friends were mindful of their own spiritual liberties. Early Quakers had suffered through waves of persecution on both sides of the Atlantic, but since then the British government had imposed freedom of conscience throughout its dominions and so enabled American Quakers to enjoy a relatively untroubled existence. Friends were understandably reluctant to forsake that protection. Yet their primary loyalty lay neither with the crown, nor with the proprietors, nor with their fellow colonists, but instead with their own Society of Friends, which they envisaged as a people or nation in its own right under God. That separatist worldview would also cost them dearly. Patriots frustrated by the principled neutrality of most Quakers following the Declaration of Independence would depict them as either loyal to the crown or loyal only to themselves.[10]

Friends such as Henry Drinker noted with increasing bitterness that the patriots' crusade for liberty left little or no room for alternative perspectives on the crisis, even if those other points of view were also critical of government measures. As radical agitators became increasingly intolerant of any dissent, they viewed Quakers in particular as likely traitors to the cause. Once Philadelphia became embroiled in outright rebellion and a War for Independence, Friends learned quickly that their businesses and their social standing were in grave danger. Indeed, those who refused on principle to support Independence, whatever those principles might be, might have to pay with their lives. Until recently, the life of an eighteenth-century Pennsylvania Friend had appeared far removed from the persecutions of the past, but that change in fortune now seemed illusory. A new era of persecution had dawned, and Friends made sense of their ordeal during the 1770s through a sensibility of suffering and resignation inherited from their seventeenth-century predecessors.

The crisis that now threatened to engulf Friends had profound implications for entire families, not just men who participated in public affairs. The wives of Quaker merchants like Henry Drinker and Abel James could not avoid becoming aware of the events unfolding around them. As their husbands struggled to keep their businesses afloat and defended their commitment to peaceful protest amid increasingly stormy political waters, they consulted regularly with fellow merchants, relatives, and other Quakers at places of business, at public venues such as coffeehouses, and in their own homes. Discussions about the state of trade or politics would sometimes have taken place over meals or tea, in the presence of their wives. We know from her diary that Elizabeth Drinker kept a close watch on her husband's movements, and she was doubtless present for some of the conversations about current events that occurred in their own home or at the houses of friends and neighbors. She may or may not have spoken, but she surely heard at least some of what the menfolk said. Whether Henry spoke privately with Elizabeth about the positions that he took during these years or sought her advice is unclear; her diary gives no indication that he did, but then she rarely described their conversations in diary entries even when we know from their letters that they were consulting about particular problems they were facing.

During the 1760s and early 1770s, women of all social ranks, especially those who lived in seaports, became increasingly conversant with political events and debates. The success of economic boycotts would depend in large part on household mistresses refusing to purchase or consume British goods, and so newspaper articles addressed women directly, stressing the importance of their contribution. "Ladies," declared one contributor, "You have it in your power, more than all your committees and congresses, to strike the stroke . . . your country will rise and call you blessed." Letters and journals written by women show not only their awareness of the political issues at stake but also the increasingly partisan and passionate positions that they took as debates raged in assemblies, newspapers, coffeehouses, the streets, and their own parlors. Women gathered, sometimes at formal public meetings, to express their support for the boycotts, and as one South Carolina woman put it, "none were greater politicians than the several knots of ladies who met together. All trifling discourse of fashions and such low chat was thrown by, and we commenced perfect statesmen." According to Elizabeth's neighbor and fellow Quaker Sarah Fisher, "politics" was "the prevailing topic of conversation, and indeed it seems at this interesting period to be so at all times and in all companies."[11]

Yet Elizabeth's diary entries give little sign of any interest in the political crisis until relatively late in the chain of events that led to Independence. Throughout the 1760s, she remained strikingly reticent about the mounting tensions between Britain and its colonies, nor did she mention the waves of protest that swept through the streets of her city, despite the serious implications for her husband's business and Quaker discomfort with the protesters' use of violence and intimidation. As the situation worsened in the early 1770s, Elizabeth did begin to describe attacks on those who spoke out against the resistance movement. She added little in the way of editorial comment, but her laconic remarks made it abundantly clear that Elizabeth shared her husband's contempt for the hypocrisy of those who claimed to stand for freedom while ruthlessly silencing any point of view other than their own. Yet Elizabeth's focus remained on her domestic world and those she loved. Only once the patriots targeted her own family did she immerse herself in what was happening around her.

"An Entire Stagnation to Our Trade"

During the fall of 1764, as protests against government measures to raise taxes and tighten control over the colonies gathered momentum, James and Drinker busied themselves maneuvering to benefit from a government grant that would support the extraction and transportation southward of coal from the island of Cape Breton in Nova Scotia. James and Drinker hoped to secure a commission to act as agents for the handling and sale of that coal in Philadelphia and were busy mobilizing their friends in London to lobby on their behalf. "Our succeeding in this application," they wrote in October 1764, "is a matter we shall be much pleased with." New business would be very welcome, given that the prospects for transatlantic trade that fall were "as discouraging as any . . . for a number of years past." Lumber and produce were in short supply and therefore expensive; merchants could not secure freight for outgoing vessels and faced the prospect of their ships remaining idle throughout the winter. It was also "generally agreed," the partners reported, that new taxes and legislation prohibiting the colonies from printing paper money would soon "damp . . . trade in general." To make matters worse, the British government had announced its intention to enforce customs duties more efficiently than in the past, instructing royal ships and custom house officials to keep what James and Drinker called a "sharp look out" for smugglers sneaking goods into North American ports. This would further inflame those opposed to the new taxes. The partners hoped that the coal venture would compensate for some of their other losses, apparently oblivious to the possibility that those who opposed the British government's actions might not react well to a local firm benefiting from a contract issued by that same government. This would not be the only occasion on which the partners displayed a remarkable lack of political sensitivity that would cost them dearly over the coming years.[12]

The winter of 1764–65 turned out to be bracing in many ways as severe cold descended on Pennsylvania and the ships that lay in port became encased in ice for several weeks. By the spring of 1765, the two partners were becoming more and more frustrated by "the present distressed situation." A slump in trade had combined with a shortage of hard currency to leave many of those indebted to James and Drinker unable to meet their obligations. When an unexpected hogshead of hats arrived from England in the summer of 1765, the partners had to inform the sender that such articles had "dull" prospects in the present economic climate. They also predicted that once new parliamentary regulations took effect, the colonists would most likely react by manufacturing for themselves many of the articles that they had previously imported from Great Britain. That hogshead of hats would then become even more difficult to sell.[13]

James and Drinker were well aware of the groundswell in Philadelphia and other seaports against the British government's new measures. Indeed, the two partners agreed that the measures were "ill-judged" and "insupportable." Public anger focused on the Stamp Act, which introduced a tax on all legal transactions, customs papers, publications, educational diplomas, and even playing cards; the document or article in question would have to be stamped as proof that the tax had been paid. James and Drinker considered this new tax an outrage and referred to stamped papers as "badges of slavery." Protest was clearly in order, but the partners had serious reservations about how other opponents of the legislation chose to express their anger. The opposition movement coalesced around a three-pronged strategy that combined economic boycotts, evasion of the customs officers, and violent demonstrations. Not surprisingly, James and Drinker were eager to minimize disruption to trade, as boycotts would damage their business; they disapproved of smuggling in part because it offended their commitment to law and order, but also because smuggled goods might undercut their own inventory; most straightforwardly principled was their opposition to violence. This put the partners increasingly at odds with protesters, even as they agreed with many of their complaints.[14]

During the spring and summer of 1765, extralegal resistance groups that called themselves the Sons of Liberty used intimidation and violence to ensure compliance with the boycotts. Local gangs terrified most of the newly appointed stamp distributers into resignation by heckling and threatening them in the streets, burning them in effigy, destroying their offices, and vandalizing their homes. In a letter to David Barclay and Sons in London, written that October, James and Drinker wrote that "many thoughtful Friends and other inhabitants" considered "the riotous proceedings" now engulfing seaports to be "a very injudicious method of obtaining the desired redress." Yet these tactics of intimidation were proving very effective, and calls for more restrained tactics by "the better disposed" went largely unheard. The phrase "better disposed" had a double connotation, referring not only to people who opposed violence but also to the upper ranks of Philadelphia society. Shockingly, they wrote, even some individuals "whose stations should have led them to a more circumspect conduct" had encouraged dockworkers and other laborers, artisans, apprentices, and servants to riot. James and Drinker strongly disapproved of "the people's rising in tumults and threatening mischief." Not only were the protests offensive to Quakers because of their violence, but "the people" were themselves potentially dangerous. Unrest of this sort had the potential, especially during an economic downturn, to redirect its anger away from royal officials to privileged city residents who were less obviously vulnerable to hard times, including affluent merchants such as James and Drinker.[15]

The two partners anticipated "an entire stop to business" once the Stamp Act came into effect on November 1, 1765. "We seem here very much at a loss to know how this matter will issue," they wrote to their business partners in Barbados, "and fear it will be the cause of much confusion among us." Meanwhile, the weather, as constant a cause of anxiety for merchants as for farmers, continued to prove unhelpful. The summer of 1765 was "uncommon dry," which incapacitated many of the region's water-powered mills; bread and flour prices in the Philadelphia market rose accordingly. The forges were also dependent on waterpower and so could produce little iron, making it impossible for companies such as James and Drinker to procure and ship most of their iron orders. In common with other import and export merchants, James and Drinker did their best to assemble cargoes and then spent a "much hurried" October trying to ensure that their outward-bound ships left port before the date on which the Stamp Act would take effect.[16] Early in November, James and Drinker reported that most of their ships had "cleared out" by the deadline, though in the rush many of them had set sail "not one tenth part loaded." The partners also busied themselves calling in old debts to provide themselves with cash that would offset the dramatic decline in trade expected during the coming weeks and months. This, of course, did not endear them to those who owed them money.[17] James and Drinker predicted that the political impasse would bring many "mischiefs" beyond "an entire stagnation to our trade." After November 1, any legal transaction would require a stamp. If these were not available because distributers had resigned under pressure, or if firms such as theirs declined to use stamps, whether on principle or because they were afraid to do so, they would not be able to proceed legally against debtors or to engage in any other business that required official validation. "In short," they declared, "we know not whose lot it may be to be ruined."[18]

James and Drinker reported to friends in London that a veritable reign of terror had settled over the city. "No person," they wrote, "dare attempt use a stamp paper or in the least degree propose anything short of the most fixed opposition to it." Government officials had stowed the stamp papers on board a royal ship, "to preserve them," as James and Drinker put it, "from any violence which it is apprehended they might suffer if in the power of the people." That November, Abel agreed to serve on a committee charged with enforcement of a nonimportation agreement that more than four hundred traders had signed. He may have hoped to exert a moderating influence over the methods used to pressure recalcitrant merchants into cooperation. James and Drinker intended to abide by the terms of the nonimportation agreement, perhaps in part because they worried that they might otherwise become the targets of intimidation and violence that the Sons of Liberty had recently used so effectively against the stamp distributers. As it turned out, compliance with nonimportation was so complete that at no point during the Stamp Act crisis did the committee need to act against any Philadelphia traders, but future events would show that agitators were ready and willing to terrorize noncompliant merchants.[19]

Alongside concern for their own interests and their dismay at the tactics used by protesters, James and Drinker also worried about the damage that the Stamp Act was inflicting on transatlantic relations and the impact of boycotts on those with no economic cushion to protect them in hard times. The political crisis, they wrote, had "really altered the face of things amongst us" and made it "impossible to carry on trade with our mother country as formerly." Their reference in several letters to "our mother country" and to Benjamin Franklin's going "home" in order to represent colonial interests in London (even though Franklin himself was born and raised in Boston) emphasized their sense of shared identity and interest with Britain, which the government in London and agitators in the colonies were now threatening. They had, in addition, basic humanitarian concerns, warning their correspondents across the Atlantic that if recent legislation remained in place and the colonies began to manufacture locally instead of importing from across the Atlantic, this would damage not only the owners of English manufacturing firms but also those who worked for them. As James and Drinker urged fellow merchants in England to lobby Parliament for repeal, they appealed to their common interest, their sense of fairness, and their compassion for "the distresses of thousands of your poor" currently out of work because of the boycott. Without "a change of measures," they wrote, "we have great reason to believe that many, both with you and us, must be reduced if not ruined."[20]

Merchants such as James and Drinker were stuck between a rock and a hard place. If they tried to send ships out of port without stamps, they risked having their vessels seized by British officials. Yet if they decided to abide by the new law, whether because their business interests trumped their principles or because they felt bound to obey the laws of the land, no matter how misguided, then they would have to brave the fury of opponents to the stamp tax; they would also have a hard time procuring stamps. Officials representing the government in North American ports were well aware that the impasse was likely to have a serious economic impact on everyone involved, including the government itself, which was eager to maximize tax receipts and would hardly benefit from a cessation of trade. A dose of informal pragmatism soon promised to soften the impact of the crisis. A few weeks after the Stamp Act came into effect, James and Drinker heard that customs officers had decided to let trading ships proceed out of port without stamped paperwork if "no stamp paper was to be had," providing them with written certification that such was the case. The officers issuing these certificates of clearance hoped to prevent "difficulties" when vessels that departed without stamps reached their destinations or crossed paths with royal ships while at sea. Their overarching intention was "to keep all things as quiet as they could." Merchants would be able to tell representatives of the crown that they had tried to comply with the law while assuring protesters that they were not using the hated stamps.[21]

This concession provided some reassurance for law-abiding merchants such as James and Drinker. The two partners were willing to use stamps if they could be procured somewhere other than Philadelphia; their neighbors would then, they hoped, remain unaware of their compliance with the government's demands. They now instructed the captains of their vessels currently anchored at other ports to make sure that they asked for stamped documentation before embarking on the next stage of their journey, requesting alternative authorization only if stamped papers were unavailable; they could then affirm later, if questioned, that they had tried to abide by the Stamp Act. If they could procure neither stamps nor alternative certification, they should stay put. They had heard that some royal officials would allow ships without stamped papers to enter ports where stamps were available, "upon paying ten pounds sterling fine and double stamps." Such penalties were, they noted, "highly unreasonable" when stamps had been unavailable at the port of origin, but this was much preferable to seizure and, they hoped, "the worst we can suffer."[22]

Yet whether all British officials would accept certification even from their counterparts in other ports that a ship's owner or captain had been unable to procure stamps was open to question. James and Drinker received reports that officials in Barbados intended to seize any vessel arriving without stamped papers, so that many merchants did not think it worth the risk to send ships southward without stamps. The two partners remained hopeful that a ship carrying an official certification that stamps were unavailable at the port of origin might avoid fines or at least seizure. "We know they ought," they declared, "as it is . . . quite out of our power to get stamped paper." As they dispatched ships to various destinations in the closing weeks of 1765, they gave their captains detailed instructions to cover a range of contingencies. They told Captain William Barnes, heading for Barbados, that he must "endeavor to learn" immediately on arrival whether there was "any danger of a seizure or detention . . . for want of stamped paper," or if officials would impose a fine on ships arriving with alternative certification. If he could not obtain entry with alternative certification, or if it seemed likely that officials would detain the ship, he should "quit the island with the greatest diligence" and seek a more welcoming port on a neighboring island. If it appeared that he could land his cargo on paying a fine, he should ascertain if the goods on board would fetch a price that would "leave a profit on the goods after deducting all charges." If he should be boarded by royal officials and the vessel or cargo seized because of not having stamped papers, he was to "take all the necessary steps for an appeal home," which his employers would "prosecute with all diligence and zeal, as we are not in the least to blame in the matter." Whatever the circumstances, he was "to make no breach of the acts of trade," though by sending him on his way without stamps they were in effect already making him complicit in a breach of the law.[23]

As the winter wore on, trade remained immobilized not only by ice in the Delaware River but also by the inability of trading firms to get reliable information about the likely treatment of ships traveling without stamped papers. "Different and contradictory accounts" from across the Atlantic World left merchants such as James and Drinker "in a state of suspense." Abel wrote in late February that their vessel *Friendship* had been given clearance to leave without stamps, "but was afraid to move, as several vessels had been seized by the men of war for want of stamped papers." The two partners were becoming increasingly cautious, and Henry, who was away on a trip to North Carolina when he heard this news, wrote that although he was eager for the ship to leave "if it could be done anyhow with safety," otherwise she must remain in port. One of their business associates sent stamps so that the vessel waiting to sail in his direction could depart with legally valid paperwork, but the captain "dare[d] not use them" for fear of retribution in Philadelphia. English warships had also seized many vessels midvoyage, and James and Drinker were understandably "afraid to risk our own or friends' property." They could only assure their clients that once "the present obstructions" no longer stymied their business operations, they would move swiftly to fulfill their orders.[24]

The partners were hopeful that pressure from the trading community in London would bring about repeal of the Stamp Act, but their inability to predict with certainty whether or when Parliament would see reason made it impossible to plan with any confidence for the coming season. Merchants now found themselves in the frustrating position of turning away customers because their store was so "thinly furnished with goods." Moreover, the stagnation of trade left trading firms with little hope of collecting debts owed them, which in turn would prevent them from forwarding payments that they had promised. James and Drinker could not "remember such distressing times . . . We find ourselves more pinched than we ever remember to have been."[25]

The partners' mood became much more optimistic that April when a ship from Ireland brought news that the House of Commons had voted for repeal by a sizable majority. Caution was still in order since neither the House of Lords nor the king had endorsed the repeal, but news that the Stamp Act was in fact no more reached Philadelphia on May 19. That evening, Elizabeth noted in her diary that a vessel arriving from England had brought news of the act's repeal, and the next day she wrote that Philadelphians had "illuminated" the city in celebration. These were her only mentions of the Stamp Act crisis, and seven years would pass before Elizabeth referred again to tensions between the English government and its colonies. No one living in Philadelphia could have remained oblivious to the protests that raged in the city streets, and Elizabeth must have been aware of her husband's anxiety about the crisis. Yet she had chosen not to let these events and concerns intrude into her diary, which proceeded as if nothing at all was amiss, until the moment of legal resolution, which she did see fit to mention.[26]

As James and Drinker looked back on the crisis in letters to friends and business associates, their focus remained on mercantile rather than political or constitutional issues, though they continued to describe the Stamp Act and other measures passed by Parliament as "mischievous" and "ill-judged burdens." They and other merchants could now sigh with relief, putting behind them this "most distressing season" and looking forward to the profits accruing from normalized trade. James and Drinker were confident that the "many difficulties" caused by the Stamp Act could "hardly be expected to happen again." Though they focused in these letters on the practical challenges they had faced as a trading firm, Henry did admit in his personal correspondence that another aspect of recent events concerned him. In a letter to Samuel Emlen, a Quaker minister, he noted the atmosphere of distrust that had prompted "rash spirits" in Philadelphia and elsewhere to question the motives of anyone who counseled "moderate and careful conduct." In particular, he deplored the treatment of Benjamin Franklin following his appearance before the House of Commons to argue the colonists' case. At first, there was broad consensus that Franklin "had done eminent service to the colonies," but a growing chorus of detractors subsequently accused him of "being like a snake in the grass" and claimed that he had "artfully reserved his assistance in the matter till he saw the act would be repealed, and then joined the strongest side." Not coincidentally, Franklin had also lobbied in London for an end to proprietary rule in Pennsylvania and its replacement by direct royal control. That position was quite compatible with opposition to specific measures passed by Parliament, but Franklin's enemies questioned the sincerity of his objections to that legislation. These attacks on Franklin's character suggested just how vulnerable individuals were in the current political climate to willful misinterpretation of their words and behavior. Others might be similarly vulnerable, and Henry could only hope that he and Abel were right in predicting that the recently ended crisis was unlikely to repeat itself.[27]

"Unnatural Dissensions"

That prediction turned out to be woefully naive. In repealing the Stamp Act, Parliament did not mean to concede the colonists' claim that it had no right to tax them. Not only did Parliament leave in place other recent laws that colonists found offensive, but it also passed a Declaratory Act, in which members asserted their right to legislate for the colonies "in all cases whatsoever." Whether that included the right to tax did not remain in doubt for long: one year later, in 1767, Parliament passed a new series of laws to tax lead, paint, paper, glass, and tea imported from Britain to the colonies. The prime minister, Charles Townshend, planned to use some of the proceeds from these new taxes to pay royal officials directly instead of having colonial legislatures foot the bill, which would free officials from any dependence on local representatives. He also augmented dramatically the army of customs officers responsible for enforcing the duties. This combination of measures infuriated many colonists and prompted a second wave of protests in North American seaports, along with demands for the resumption of consumer boycotts. The renewed violence that accompanied protests against the Townshend Acts prompted the Society of Friends to voice its explicit disapproval of any campaign to reverse government policy that did not restrict itself to peaceful tactics. This placed Quaker merchants in a very awkward position. If they distanced themselves from the protests, as their principles and the Yearly Meeting urged them to do, others might accuse them of using those principles to camouflage less exalted motives. After all, Quaker merchants would benefit from the resumed importation and sale of British goods, and cynics might suspect that Franklin's supporters in his quest to bring Pennsylvania under royal governance, including Quaker merchants such as James and Drinker, also sympathized in secret with the British government's claims to absolute sovereignty, whatever their claims to the contrary in public. Neighbors who had in the past accused Friends of self-interested chicanery might conclude that they were up to their old tricks once again.

James and Drinker made no secret of their dismay at the prospect of further disruptions to transatlantic trade and their own business operations, but they also lamented what they saw as a tragic breach in transatlantic friendship. "For certain it is," they wrote, "that the prosperity and happiness of this young colony is greatly broke in upon by the late unnatural dissensions which have subsisted between us and the parent country." Whereas a growing number of American commentators depicted the "mother country" across the Atlantic as abusive and demanded that their "parent" become more nurturing, James and Drinker paid much less attention to issues of right or wrong and focused instead on the need for mutual accommodation so as to bring about the restoration of harmony. "It is the sincere wish of the dispassionate, the cool, and the reasonable," they wrote, "that neither side would dwell upon punctilios and small points of honor, but rather sacrifice small matters for great and permanent good." That perspective owed much to the spirit of decision-making that informed interactions between Quakers, stressing the avoidance of confrontation, a calm working toward accommodation, and the need for all those involved in a particular dispute to accept what others believed to be the common good even if at variance with their own instincts or perceived interests.[28]

As each side refused to compromise, Quakers such as James and Drinker began to distance themselves from what they saw as an unnecessary and intemperate dispute. The partners identified explicitly with their "young colony" but referred repeatedly in their letters to those agitating against the Townshend Acts as "the Americans," effectively dissociating themselves from the protest movement. At the same time, though they clearly felt a deep connection to "the parent country," they had little sympathy with the government that had precipitated a renewed crisis in relations. As Quakers, their primary loyalty lay with neither the colony in which they lived nor the country from which they originated, but instead their own transatlantic religious community, the Society of Friends, along with its commitment to calm and peaceful resolution of differences. Yet combatants in the escalating war of words had increasingly limited patience for neutrality or calls for moderation, which did not augur well for the likes of James and Drinker.[29]

Most of Philadelphia's merchants opposed at first the resumption of a trade boycott, preferring to wait and see if petitions submitted by colonial assemblies or the lobbying efforts of British merchants and manufacturers would have any impact. Quakers in particular found this strategy appealing because they preferred peaceful objection to more confrontational methods. English Quakers were also warning Friends in North America that strident opposition to the new measures would rouse patriot sentiment on their side of the Atlantic and so have "fatal consequences." However, when neither petitions nor lobbying brought about a change in government policy, the city's mercantile community committed to an intercolonial nonimportation agreement. On March 10, 1769, both Henry and Abel were among those elected to a committee charged with enforcement of a new boycott on April 1. The two partners also agreed to sign a letter sent by "a committee of merchants in Philadelphia" to their counterparts in London, subsequently printed in newspapers on both sides of the Atlantic. That letter insisted that "American behavior" had been "grossly misrepresented" and that the increasingly confrontational position adopted by "the people of this province" was in response to the intransigence of the government in London. Yet the letter did not go so far as to endorse violence, which enabled Quakers to sign with a relatively clear conscience. Though they and most of their fellow merchants deplored the extreme tactics adopted by the Sons of Liberty, they were understandably reluctant to risk personal injury or damage to their property by opposing the agitators, who had again taken to the streets, threatening anyone who refused to cooperate with the boycott. They may also have figured that they could do more to contain the situation by participating than by withdrawing. At least for the time being, ambiguous wording saved the day.[30]

Within a few months, James and Drinker were again in crisis mode, doing their best to contain the damage inflicted by the boycott. The partners predicted that unless Parliament repealed the Townshend Acts soon, the boycott would leave Philadelphia "bare of many articles," and so it proved. They could try to obtain goods from other North American seaports, but the committee overseeing the boycott required that ships transporting supplies to Philadelphia from elsewhere on the Eastern Seaboard had to bring certification from the original port of entry proving that the cargo had reached North America before April 1, 1769. "Apologiz[ing] for the trouble," James and Drinker now had to ask business associates in other ports to procure the appropriate paperwork, preferably "certification from a patriot committee." They could not afford to be slipshod, in part because they were themselves members of the local enforcement committee, but also to avoid any doubts about their loyalty to the cause.[31]

In November 1769, Abel James sailed for England. He was far from well and had decided to visit northern England in the hope that its bracing weather would reinvigorate him, which it apparently did, but he was also planning to confer with merchants about the ongoing crisis and to join with them in lobbying Parliament for repeal of the controversial duties. Several months later, London merchant John Masterson wrote to Henry that Abel had proven invaluable as an expert on "all matters relating to America." Support for repeal in London had begun to gather momentum as it became increasingly clear that the decline in trade due to consumer boycotts in North America outweighed the revenue provided by the new duties. A new and more conciliatory prime minister, Lord North, took office in early 1770. He persuaded members of Parliament to repeal all the Townshend duties excepting that on tea, which was to remain in force not only as a source of revenue but also to show that the government had not backed down from the Declaratory Act.[32]

News that the duty on tea would remain in place did not reach Philadelphia until early May. Meanwhile, the city's merchants had become increasingly divided over whether to continue nonimportation. Henry had been predicting since the previous December that "interest, all powerful interest," would eventually triumph over "public spirit and patriotism." When subscribers to the nonimportation agreement organized a general meeting for May 1, 1770, a caucus of merchants who imported dry goods from across the Atlantic determined to meet a few days beforehand so that they could agree what position to take. Henry told Abel that he had intended to avoid both meetings, as he could not decide which course of action to support. On the one hand, he "pitied the situation of shopkeepers and others who were much distressed by being thus put out of the common course of their trade." Some were predicting that tradesmen with "small capitals" would "sink under it if continued another season," which Drinker did not think "wide of the mark." On the other, he "could not think of deserting a measure we had deliberately gone into for the securing and supporting our liberties and valuable rights." Doing so would incite "at once the contempt and indignation of the other colonies, not to say the exultation and derision of the mother country." Henry and two other Quakers, John Reynell and Jeremiah Warder, had already stopped going to meetings of the nonimportation enforcement committee, probably because they felt uncomfortable with the committee's aggressive tone and now recognized their inability to exert a moderating influence. The Philadelphia Yearly Meeting was urging its members not to serve on such bodies because of the threatening and violent tactics that radicals were using to get their way. In September 1769, it had exhorted "every member of our religious society" to "guard against promoting or joining in any measures" that were "inconsistent with our principles" and that their enemies might use to "represent us as a people departing from the principles we profess."[33]

Yet Reynell now visited Henry and asked him to attend the caucus of dry goods importers with him so that they could argue for postponing a general meeting until the city's trading community could reach consensus on how to proceed. Henry duly obliged and the caucus did secure a postponement of the general meeting, but the position in which moderates like Henry found themselves was increasingly perilous as radical protesters railed against anyone who opposed them. One of his Quaker friends, John O'Kely, wrote that he felt for Henry as he tried to "preserve his honor and conscience free from blemish in the midst of a crooked and perverse generation." It was "hard indeed to swim against the stream." Personal anxieties compounded a stressful situation: Elizabeth had been extremely ill in recent months, and Henry had been bracing himself for the possibility of her death. Though she did survive, her recovery was slow, and he was distracted with worry. He wrote to Abel that the present fraught state of affairs had reinforced his "natural disposition . . . to be drawn out into public life as little as may be, for in all my cool reflecting moments, it appears to me inconsistent with my love of peace and real happiness." Much to Henry's relief, his service on two local commissions, one for poor relief and the other for maintenance of the city streets, was now ending. Henceforth he would "steadily refuse . . . any other public office." Taking on even seemingly innocuous duties such as these had been "accompanied with too much pain to be long continued." Public affairs were, it seemed, intrinsically toxic, and he wanted no more of it.[34]

By the time the general meeting finally took place on May 15, news from London that the tax on tea would remain in place had dampened any euphoric claims to victory such as followed the repeal of the Stamp Act. The nonimportation subscribers now had to decide whether to end the boycott, leave it in place, or opt for a partial resumption of importation with specific items still banned. The meeting in mid-May produced no consensus. According to Henry, "a very great number of our respectable tradesmen, artificers, and mechanics" then urged the merchants to stand firm, and when they met again on June 5, they voted to leave the existing nonimportation agreement in place. However, the will behind that reaffirmation soon fractured: by early fall, the city's trading community was seething with resentment against merchants in other seaports who had abandoned their commitment to nonimportation, resumed the shipment of goods from England, and then, adding insult to injury, shipped them to Philadelphia for sale there. Merchants who stood firm would suffer for their own constancy, and as Henry pointed out, remaining loyal to the boycott under such circumstances "would be fighting the winds indeed." That September, he signed on behalf of James and Drinker a letter from seventeen Philadelphia merchants to the nonimportation committee, requesting a meeting of the subscribers to revisit their decision. They met on September 20 and voted by a large majority to end the boycott. Abel had remained in England until September, hoping to receive news that nonimportation had ended so that he could purchase goods to carry back with him across the Atlantic, but he finally lost patience and set sail for Philadelphia at about the same time that the merchants there were voting to reopen trade. He arrived back in Philadelphia two months later on November 22, 1770.[35]

The general boycott was due to end on January 15, 1771, but before then Henry was to get another foretaste of how easy it might be to get on the wrong side of the radicals. Several English merchants, anticipating the resumption of importation, had gone ahead and shipped consignments that would most likely reach Philadelphia before the formal date for resumption of trade. Strictly speaking, these goods were still illicit, and they might cause the recipients considerable embarrassment. James and Drinker were dismayed to learn that one of their business associates in New York had arranged to have articles recently arrived there and addressed to them sent on to Philadelphia by stage boat without waiting for instructions. They became aware of the consignment's imminent arrival only when they received a letter telling them it was on its way. "This matter has given us a good deal of thought and concern," the partners wrote, "lest it might be thought by our fellow traders and citizens a scheme laid by us to take an undue advantage of them." They managed to persuade their neighbors that such was not the case, but Henry and Abel would soon find themselves in a much more challenging situation as many Philadelphians became convinced that their firm was willing to place its own interests above those of the common good. Seduced by the prospect of a juicy profit and completely misjudging the public mood, they took on a commission that would identify them closely with the British government and its detested legislation. They then responded so ineptly to popular outrage against them that within months they found themselves labeled as enemies of their country, placing themselves and their families in serious danger.[36]

"Painted in Very Odious Colors"

Three years later, James and Drinker received promising news from one of their closest friends in London, Frederick Pigou. He and his partner in New York, Benjamin Booth, were lobbying for a commission to sell tea shipped to New York by the East India Company, and they hoped to secure a similar deal for James and Drinker in Philadelphia. The East India Company had been on the verge of bankruptcy, but the government in London moved to prevent this by granting it a monopoly on the sale of tea in North America via the Tea Act of 1773. Parliament authorized the East India Company to sell through its own agents instead of using intermediaries, which would reduce the price of taxed tea below the going rate for smuggled tea. Far from intending the monopoly as a provocation, government officials assumed that colonists would happily purchase legal and cheaper tea instead of illegal tea that cost more. They and those who agreed to serve as agents for the company failed to anticipate how many Americans would condemn the Tea Act as a tawdry attempt to bribe them into accepting Parliament's right to tax, or that other merchants would resent no longer being able to sell tea, at least not legally.

Pigou and Booth recognized from the outset that some Americans might oppose the landing and sale of the company's tea because they objected to paying the duty. Yet they predicted that those leading the charge would be smugglers and their associates, a criminal clique that resented the prospect of losing customers. They might claim to be standing on principle, but their political posturing was in reality nothing more than a smokescreen to hide "their own private, sinister purposes." Once consumers understood this, they would surely welcome the opportunity to enjoy cheaper tea without breaking the law, rejecting the arguments made by self-interested agitators; the tea agents would then reap considerable profits. When James and Drinker first heard about the possibility of this commission, they also assumed that "respectable people" who condemned smuggling would support "the sale of what comes agreeable to law" and so happily buy tea from them. They may also have believed that even those less fastidious about purchasing smuggled goods would welcome cheaper tea, and they doubtless saw the commission as a significant opportunity to make up some of the losses they had incurred over the past several years because of the boycotts.[37]

Yet what James and Drinker initially viewed as an "act of friendship and real regard" turned out to be an unintentionally poisoned chalice. In June of that year, Henry was one of a dozen Philadelphians who protested against unpopular new restrictions on the building of street stalls in a petition that urged the city council to follow Parliament's example in setting aside their prerogatives, "for the preservation of the public peace." This reading of recent political events was either breathtakingly naive or downright disingenuous because Parliament had not renounced its right to tax Americans and still asserted that prerogative in the form of a tax on tea. If Henry and his partner seriously thought that most of their neighbors would welcome the East India Company's cheaper tea as a gesture of goodwill from a chastened Parliament, they had completely misread the mood of the city. Over the past few years, public opinion in Philadelphia had become more rather than less sympathetic to radical positions, so that news of the monopoly and commissions prompted immediate outrage. Clearly shaken by the widespread and furious opposition, James and Drinker met on October 2, 1773, with the other prospective tea agents in Philadelphia, Isaac Wharton, Thomas Wharton Sr., and Jonathan Brown. The five men agreed to say as little as possible in public about their plans and to act in unison. Yet both commitments evaporated two weeks later when a public meeting on October 16, attended by some three hundred Philadelphians, condemned anyone who committed to "unloading, receiving, or vending the tea" as complicit in a "violent attack upon the liberties of America" and "an enemy to his country."[38]

A committee elected at that meeting proceeded the next day to visit the merchants reportedly selected as agents for the sale of the politically tainted tea and demanded that they resign their commissions. Thomas and Isaac Wharton yielded immediately; Jonathan Brown was out of town, but on his return, he also capitulated. James and Drinker were a good deal less compliant.

According to the committee's report, the two partners acknowledged having received "an intimation" that they would be appointed "to receive and sell the tea," but they were not yet in possession of any explicit commission. They assured their visitors that if the tea should ever arrive and with paperwork clearly appointing them as agents, they would then announce publicly whether they accepted that commission. For the time being, they refused to predict what their decision would be, though they added that "as honest men" they would feel an obligation to protect the tea if it had been committed to their care. They assured the committee that they had "the same ideas" about Parliament's latest attempt to impose taxes on the colonists as their "fellow citizens generally," but when pressed to be more specific, they "declined any further answer." The committee characterized these responses as "not so explicit and candid" as they might have wished, and as news of the interview spread like wildfire, the two men found themselves accused of deliberate evasion.[39]

The partners realized immediately that they had made a serious mistake and wrote an open letter of clarification. When they told the committee that their "ideas" about the tax on tea were "the same" as those of "our fellow citizens generally," what they meant was that "if the said act was enforced here, it would be an infringement of our common rights as Englishmen." Indeed, they wrote, "it never occurred to us that these words could mean or bear any other construction than this." It had been their intention "that the people should be left under no doubts or anxiety respecting our conduct." The committee thanked James and Drinker for resolving the "ambiguity" of their original response, which had, they averred, been "striking to every member of the committee" and "public opinion." Yet the committee rejected their claim that this had been a straightforward misunderstanding. According to the committee, James and Drinker had "insinuated" that resolutions against the landing and sale of the tea, endorsed by the public meeting on October 16, "might not speak the general sense of the inhabitants, which the partners had said 'was difficult to be known.'" The committee also pointed out that James and Drinker had still not stated clearly what they intended to do if offered a commission to sell the taxed tea. The committee members concluded by stating, somewhat ominously, that they were "*now*" confident (their emphasis) that James and Drinker would act "as their fellow citizens have a right to require of them," since doing otherwise after condemning the Tea Act "would be indeed doubly criminal."[40]

The evasive answers that James and Drinker had given when questioned by the committee were at the very least imprudent, but a few days later, in a letter to Pigou and Booth, they accused the committee of setting out quite deliberately "to make us obnoxious to the people." Calls for "cool and moderate measures" were now ineffective when pitted against "falsehoods circulated for the purpose of interesting and warming the passions of the people." James and Drinker claimed that they had conducted themselves "with great integrity of heart and, as far as our judgments could serve us, leading to peace." They had wanted "to avoid doing anything which might raise a disturbance." If this was true, their tactics had misfired, producing exactly the opposite result to that intended. The two men now became public and vilified symbols of the taxed tea and all that it stood for. An undated broadside that appeared that fall in Philadelphia made it abundantly clear how great a risk James and Drinker had taken in refusing to give way. "The eyes of all," the broadside declared, were "now fixed" on the commissioners as "men who have it in their power to ward off the most dangerous stroke that has ever been meditated against the liberties of America." The "unhappy" experience of those who had agreed several years before to act as stamp distributers, it reminded James and Drinker, should provide an example of "how foolish, how dangerous it is to undertake to force the loathsome pills of slavery and oppression down the throats of a free, independent, and determined people."[41]

For the moment at least, James and Drinker vowed not to surrender. They continued to believe that some of their critics had a personal stake in preventing the cheaper tea from coming to market and that, because they had initially welcomed the possibility of a commission, they now had a duty to protect the tea once it arrived, until the controversy could be resolved and the tea sold or removed peaceably. Much about that commission remained unclear: they had no idea what instructions they would receive from the East India Company or at which North American port the tea would first arrive. James and Drinker hoped that the tea heading for New York would reach its destination first and that New Yorkers would allow the tea to be unloaded, if not put on sale, setting a precedent for the same thing to happen in Philadelphia. There was also much confusion as to what the various clauses of the Tea Act actually meant in practice, including whether the duty would be due before departing England or on arrival at an American port. Some observers believed that this would make a significant difference to the tea's acceptability, though radicals opposed the landing of the tea even if the East India Company had paid the tax in England before the tea was shipped to North America. James and Drinker declared themselves ready and willing to discuss the Tea Act and their position as potential agents for the East India Company, but only in private and with "men of principle and candor" who were willing to talk "in a friendly manner as becoming fellow citizens, desirous of our and the public peace." The two partners claimed to be confident that once "sensible and judicious" Philadelphians considered their positions more carefully, "bustle and noise" would give way to "deliberate discussion."[42]

Yet James and Drinker were so nervous about the increasingly charged political atmosphere that they reminded Pigou and Booth to treat their correspondence as confidential. This was an absolute necessity, they wrote, as "very few" were willing to "listen to any reason" and might willfully misinterpret whatever they said. As the weeks passed by, the public furor escalated into character assassination and threats of violence. Henry complained that the broadsides and pamphlets circulating through North American seaports were full of allusions to "cursed tea, detested tea, rotten tea, etc., etc., with a torrent of abuse of the British Ministry, Parliament, India Company, American Tea Commissioners, etc., etc." In early November, the mayor of New York had to intervene to prevent the burning of Benjamin Booth in effigy. By the end of that month, a Committee of Tarring and Feathering had formed in Philadelphia and declared in print that the tea ship's captain and the Delaware River pilots would suffer dire consequences if they dared to bring the tea into port. When news arrived that a tea ship was on its way, a pamphlet came out threatening James and Drinker personally as agents of the East India Company. The partners reported to friends elsewhere that "the torrent [was] not likely to be stemmed," as even those Philadelphians who disapproved of such tactics were "unwilling to engage openly in opposition to the multitude, or even to press any less spirited measures." The radicals were in no mood to compromise and had effectively silenced all other voices.[43]

James and Drinker decided, nonetheless, to advocate for a compromise that they hoped would contain the increasingly volatile situation. They now proposed that their firm convey the tea, once it arrived, to "a place of safety," where it could be kept until Parliament repealed the duty on tea. The partners promised that they "would not move in the sale of the teas while the Revenue Act continued in force." Pigou and Booth were adopting a similar position in New York. Their proposal had no effect whatsoever. On December 2, the day on which written confirmation of the partners' appointment as agents for the East India Company finally arrived, "A Card" addressed to James and Drinker was printed and distributed in the city, declaring as follows:

> THE PUBLIC present their compliments to Messieurs JAMES AND DRINKER.—We are informed that you have this day received your

> commission to enslave your native country; and, as your frivolous plea of having received no advice relative to the scandalous part you were to act in the TEA-SCHEME, can no longer serve your purpose, nor divert our attention, we expect and desire you will immediately inform the PUBLIC, by a line or two to be left at the COFFEE HOUSE, whether you will or will not renounce all pretensions to execute that commission?—THAT WE MAY GOVERN OURSELVES ACCORDINGLY.

James and Drinker's resolve now finally crumbled, and they sent a statement for public display at a local coffeehouse, in which they confirmed that they had received formal letters of appointment from the East India Company but had decided to "decline acting under the said appointment" in deference to "the general opinion of the people." They claimed in their statement that throughout the crisis they had maintained "steadily and publicly" a "thorough regard for the security and preservation of the civil rights and true interests of their country." Back in October, they had assured the committee elected by opponents of the Tea Act that "they neither meant nor intended to do anything that should be disagreeable to their fellow citizens." They now thought it "seasonable" to reaffirm those "sentiments." Yet refusing to back down entirely, they still recommended that the tea be unloaded and "deposited in a place of safety," to remain untouched and unsold as long as the tax on tea remained in force. The East India Company should be informed of this arrangement and encouraged to lobby Parliament for repeal of the offensive tax "as the most certain mode of opening the way for a sale of their teas here." If the company declined to do so or failed to bring about repeal, Philadelphians should allow it to arrange for removal of the tea for sale in "some other part of the world."[44]

James and Drinker's decision to combine surrender with advice on how the city should act, along with renewed claims that the committee appointed in October had misinterpreted their statements, proved counterproductive. A few days later, they acknowledged in private correspondence that their attempt to "quiet the minds of the people" had instead "occasioned great wrath." Their statement had apparently come across as presumptuous and still somewhat disingenuous. When the partners claimed that they had declined the tea commission in accordance with "the general opinion of the people," some people read that statement as implying that they would have gladly accepted the commission if "supported by any considerable number of the inhabitants." The committee replied that it by no means agreed with James and Drinker's version of events, though it accepted grudgingly their refusal of "the said appointment."[45]

Until this point, Elizabeth's diary had been silent about the controversy swirling around her husband and his partner, but she now finally acknowledged what was happening, albeit only in passing. Writing late at night on December 2, she noted simply that her husband and Abel James had "sent a paper to the coffee-house this evening concerning the tea." Henry and Abel had written dozens of letters about the increasingly vicious attacks on them that led eventually to their making that public statement, but Elizabeth devoted just one sentence to their plight. We have no way of knowing if Henry discussed his and Abel's predicament with her, though it seems almost inconceivable that he would not have done so, given the frankness of the letters that went back and forth between them during the crises that lay ahead. Even if Henry had decided to shield Elizabeth from his anxiety, or perhaps did not wish to admit what a ghastly error of judgment he had made, she surely must have been aware of her husband's uneasiness. Her friend Rebecca James, wife of Henry's partner, was potentially an alternative or additional source of information, and the two women may well have discussed their husbands' plight along with their own perspectives on the situation. It is possible that Elizabeth quite deliberately banished such worries from the world she created for herself in the pages of her diary, maintaining an illusion of normality and safety, but if so, that emotional strategy would become increasingly difficult to maintain.[46]

As Philadelphians awaited the arrival of the tea ship, the *Polly,* James and Drinker heard that opponents of the tea tax were planning to prevent the ship even from reaching the city's harbor. The partners considered petitioning the governor in hope that he could be persuaded to step in and enable the tea to be landed for safe storage, but decided not to do so. "Such a step," they wrote, "would undoubtedly have made the town too hot for us." A few weeks later, news arrived that Bostonians had destroyed ninety thousand pounds of East India Company tea, worth ten thousand pounds sterling, by tipping it into their harbor. Elizabeth noted simply that news had arrived from Boston of "342 chests of tea being thrown into the sea." She did not record that Philadelphia's church bells rang in celebration. When the general mood turned out to be one of enthusiastic approval, James and Drinker expressed their "surprise and great concern" that even this massive destruction of private property had not prompted a backlash against the radicals. Few people, they observed, were willing to condemn those responsible or voice concern about possible reprisals from the British government. "Are these," they asked in consternation, "the guardians of our liberty? Are they to be patterns and waymarks for the other colonies?" When the *Polly* arrived at Gloucester Point, on the opposite side of the river from the city, a meeting convened at the statehouse on December 27, attended by eight thousand people, the largest gathering ever assembled in Philadelphia. The meeting resolved that the ship should be permitted neither to enter the harbor nor to unload the tea and that the captain should be told to take his cargo back to England. It also expressed its wholehearted approval of the Boston Tea Party. The *Polly* remained at Gloucester Point only long enough to take on supplies for the return journey and then set sail for England. Elizabeth noted succinctly that both ship and cargo had been "sent off."[47]

If James and Drinker had hoped that public hostility toward them would dissipate now that the tea ship and its reviled contents no longer hovered on the horizon, they were sorely disappointed. They complained to their friends elsewhere that they were still "painted in very odious colors by many warm spirits" and "a very bitter spirit . . . raised" against them. Respect for law and order seemed to be crumbling as leading opponents of the Tea Act condemned anyone who spoke up in defense of private property rights as "criminal" and silenced alternative views "by putting individuals in fear of their lives." James and Drinker held that these "mock patriots" were for the most part "a bad set of men . . . the outcasts of society . . . capable of fraud, bribery, and perjury," who had "ensnared" their neighbors into "rash and disorderly steps" that were "harmful to society and destructive of true patriotism." Contrary to accusations leveled by their critics, declared the two men, "none of them love their country or desire its real prosperity and the preservation of its liberties more than we do."[48]

What did James and Drinker mean by "true patriotism"? As the partners looked back over the past six months, they deplored an increasing tendency to depict Britain's interests and those of its colonies as distinct. Their critics accused them of joining a conspiracy to undermine "the liberties of America." Yet James and Drinker insisted in letters written to friends in England that they had been "regulated and directed by what we then conceived to be our duty to our country, considering your side and our side of the Atlantic as our country, and the general good of the whole is what we did wish and aim to promote." They understood their "country" to be neither Pennsylvania, nor the colonies in general, nor England, but rather a comprehensive transatlantic community. That expansive conception of loyalty was not yet inherently problematic. After all, opponents of the Stamp Act and Revenue Acts had based their opposition on the argument that colonists were Englishmen and so rightfully exempt from taxation without representation. Even the most obdurate of opponents to recent parliamentary legislation professed love of Britain while excoriating its government and indeed claimed to uphold principles embedded within the British constitution. However, a distinct, albeit inchoate, American identity was now threatening to eclipse older assumptions about an overarching, transatlantic commonality, and that transformation placed the two partners in grave danger. Because of their monumental blunder in allowing themselves to become associated in the public mind with the duty on tea and the official claims that underpinned it, their enemies could now depict them as pawns in a dastardly British plot to enslave Americans. Whatever happened next, they would have to tread very carefully.[49]

"Zeal of a Deluded People"

Subsequent events did not suggest that the political tide was likely to turn any time soon in favor of compromise and reconciliation. News reached Philadelphia in May 1774 that Parliament had responded to the Tea Party by giving orders for the closure of Boston's port and a series of other disciplinary measures known as the Coercive Acts. Henry and Abel were bitterly disappointed, as they had hoped that the government in London would respond in a more temperate manner, and they felt deep sympathy for Bostonians, "especially the moderate among them and those who have not been concerned in the late violent measures." The two men were well aware that many Philadelphians now connected them with the tea interest, and so they "avoided mixing with the crowd" as reports of the British response percolated through the city, prompting further popular outrage. James and Drinker worried that renewed protests would not only endanger them personally but also provoke the government in London into yet more repressive and restrictive measures with serious repercussions for trade and their own firm. They were awaiting the completion of a new 180-ton trading vessel, and the resumption of normal trade was crucial if they were to secure an adequate return on their investment, which had been under the circumstances quite optimistic. Yet as spring passed into summer, it seemed more and more unlikely that the "judicious" men with whom Henry and Abel identified would be able to contain the "fury" of "party rage." The partners were clearly unnerved when an anonymous essay urging restraint appeared in print early that summer and radicals demanded that the newspaper editor "give up the author." As those trumpeting the cause of liberty became increasingly intolerant of dissenting voices, the irony was not lost on James and Drinker. "We hope for more liberty ere long," they declared, "although at times we almost despair of seeing things settled to our liking." The two partners recognized that some of those "heating the minds of the people" were "not actuated by design or wicked and interested motives, but misled by the notion of liberty and service to their country." Yet whatever their motives, they were "urging the people on to what must in all human probability terminate in our own distress and ruin."[50]

James and Drinker believed that the only way out of the impasse was for the colonies "to meet the British ministry and Parliament in a friendly and cordial manner, and temperately and impartially seek a reconciliation." However, as plans got under way for the First Continental Congress in Philadelphia that September, charged with producing a united response to the Coercive Acts, the partners predicted that the congress would adopt a much more confrontational approach and express "the usual anathema against those individuals whose judgment may not approve of every resolution formed." Once the delegates convened and began to consider their options, James and Drinker deplored their apparent lack of concern for the widespread economic impact that retaliatory measures might have on both sides of the Atlantic. When they heard that the assembly was contemplating "a total stop to the exportation of flax seed and lumber to Ireland, that the poor may be distressed," intending quite deliberately to "drive things there to extremities," they asked indignantly, "how such measures can be reconciled to what may become us as men and Christians?" These were the same delegates whom their neighbors called "the saviors of America" and who were preparing a report "on the great object of American rights and grievances."[51]

Congress committed that fall to a Continental Association that would enforce a total shutdown of trade with Britain until Parliament repealed the Coercive Acts. Goods arriving from Britain after December 1, 1774, would go into storage, and any arriving after February 1, 1775, would have to return across the Atlantic. Exports to Britain and the West Indies would be banned effective September 1775. Mercantile firms such as James and Drinker worried that ships leaving England before news of the ban arrived there might not reach the Eastern Seaboard until after it came into effect, especially if they traveled to ports elsewhere in the Atlantic World before proceeding to their final destination. Although goods arriving after December 1 would supposedly be put in storage, the partners worried that the cargoes might be vulnerable to "such liberties" as had been taken with "private property in different parts of America" (referring, of course, to the destruction of the East India Company's tea in

Boston harbor). "We know not," they fretted, "what mad lengths some of the people may go." Abel and Henry waited impatiently for the arrival of the *Chalkley*, a ship belonging to their firm that was supposedly on its way from Bristol with a sizable cargo. They had written to the ship's captain in late September, urging him to set sail "as soon as it can be prudently done," but the vessel failed to arrive by December 1, and at the end of January it was still nowhere in sight. It turned out that a delay in the arrival of their letter had prevented the *Chalkley* from loading in time to beat the deadline. It would be galling to have their cargo refused entry, but the two partners had agreed that they would not challenge in any way the Committee of Observation and Inspection's instructions. "Those measures which will lead to peace," they declared, "will be our choice."[52]

Adding insult to injury, the ban on trade would damage law-abiding merchants such as themselves while allowing a market in smuggled goods to flourish with impunity. James and Drinker, echoing their earlier comments about opponents of the Tea Act, now complained in their private correspondence that some of the "modern patriots" who supported the ban were secretly profiting from illegal trade even as they paraded their "false pretensions to public virtue." The 1774 Yearly Meeting in Philadelphia had urged Friends to "keep clear" of smuggled goods, purchasing them neither for resale nor for private use, "that so we may not be any way instrumental in countenancing or promoting the iniquity, false swearing, and violence which are the common consequences of an unlawful and clandestine trade." James and Drinker were determined to abide by the principles reaffirmed in that statement, but such scruples were proving very costly, and however hypocritical some of the patriots might be, they dared not voice their disgust in public. "Let any man dare oppose or counteract the decrees of the Congress," they reported, "he ought to be forthwith, say they, treated as a traitor and hanged without judge or jury on the first high tree." Many considered it "almost treason . . . even to throw out a hint to curb the present heat and zeal of a deluded people, as we think numbers amongst us really are."[53]

As the situation continued to deteriorate, Elizabeth began to record in her diary ugly incidents in which the patriots vented their "heat and zeal" on those brave souls who dared to disagree with them. In May 1774, she noted that Philadelphians had made an effigy of Massachusetts governor Thomas Hutchinson, who refused to condemn the Coercive Acts, and carted the effigy around the town with a plaque that denounced him as a traitor, then hanging and finally burning it. In September 1775, she devoted an entry to the public humiliation of attorney Isaac Hunt and the violence that ensued. Hunt had represented a retailer accused of selling British goods in violation of the Continental Association; he had also challenged a patriot committee's right to regulate commercial activity. The crowd forced him to apologize for the positions he had taken and then paraded him around the city so that he could express his remorse repeatedly to those who gathered to watch. John Kearsley Jr., a physician who also opposed the Continental Association, fired on militiamen from his home as they led Hunt on a cart through the streets. Kearsley was apprehended and escorted under guard through the streets to be heckled and abused. His hand, Elizabeth noted, had been "much wounded with a bayonet." Elizabeth was not yet willing to acknowledge, at least in the pages of her diary, that Henry might also be in danger, but she could no longer ignore the patriots' intimidation and mistreatment of those who disagreed with them.[54]

In their more unguarded letters to friends far away from Philadelphia, Henry and Abel wrote that the world as they knew it seemed in danger of collapsing. A further "stoppage of trade" would lead to "deep losses and perhaps ruin" for firms such as theirs, all in service to what they described sarcastically as "the Grand American cause." This was serious enough, but the crisis posed a threat to much more than their balance sheets: it was shaking the foundations of social order. Leading Friends in Philadelphia declared that "those in superior stations" should set an example in the present crisis so that "those of inferior stations" would "pursue those measures which make for peace, and tend to the reconciliation of contending parties." Yet men in "superior stations" had opened a Pandora's Box by fanning the flames of discontent among poorer Philadelphians and mobilizing them in demonstrations and riots. As repeated disruptions of trade caused serious hardship among the less privileged inhabitants of seaports such as Philadelphia, and as their employers continued living quite comfortably, protests against royal policy showed signs of transforming into broader social unrest. Some of the leading agitators came from social backgrounds that would not previously have qualified them to play a prominent role in public affairs. Henry and Abel described these men as "new lords" exercising a "new species of power . . . set up and carried with so high a hand" that it amounted to "unlawful tyranny." Those who wielded that power were enemies to all that was "reasonable, orderly, and legal." It seemed to Henry and Abel that the natural order of things was disintegrating before their eyes. "Strange and indeed melancholy times are these," they wrote, "as they appear to us."[55]

Though a majority of delegates in the First Continental Congress rejected demands that they prepare for open war with Britain, armed conflict did seem increasingly likely, and that was equally horrifying to most Quakers. "Too many," wrote James and Drinker, had "got into a habit of speaking lightly of even war and bloodshed." They found it "astonishing" that people who claimed to follow Christianity, a religion "distinguished by its breathing peace on earth," were "so blind to its instructions as to harbor a thought of drawing the sword upon our brethren and natural friends." The Yearly Meeting in Philadelphia had warned repeatedly against "joining with or countenancing any measures . . . not consistent with our peaceable profession and principles." That refusal of Friends to support violent protests against British legislation had already led patriots to question where Quaker sympathies really lay. In the event of a war, Friends would find themselves in a much more perilous situation. James and Drinker knew well that their consciences might soon call on them to speak out in support of peace, and they promised Friends elsewhere that when that moment came they would do so, whatever the "popular clamor" against them. Yet for the time being, they remained as far as possible "quiet and retired." This was, they wrote, essential if they wished "to avoid insult and abuse," for in the current political climate even "the most innocent and best intended actions" could come across "as criminal and inimical to the prostituted word, liberty."[56]

Henry and Abel were reminded just how vulnerable they were in the spring of 1775, when Parliament prohibited colonists from trading with any foreign country, including Canada, effective that coming September. The two partners had been preparing to send supplies northward to Newfoundland aboard the *Princessa* and now urged the ship's captain to set sail before the restrictions came into effect, but the patriot committee charged with regulation of trade reacted to news of the parliamentary ban by suspending immediately all exports to Canada. James and Drinker now informed their business associates that any attempt to evade this patriot ban would result in "consequences more fatal than the mere destruction of vessel and cargo." What they did not mention was that a patriot delegation had called on them and pressured them into complying with this latest retaliation. According to Christopher Marshall, a retired pharmacist who lived in the city and who heard about the incident, James and Drinker had initially "equivocated," but once they realized that "the people" were "resolute," handed over the ship's papers and halted plans for its departure. A few weeks later, they secured permission to send their ship to England instead and moved quickly to get it dispatched, well aware that the

Continental Congress might decide to push forward the September date it had previously set for an end to all exports intended for England.[57]

"Every day seems to produce something disagreeable," the partners wrote in May 1775. They assured their correspondents across the Atlantic that the colonists were becoming "more united and determined than ever," especially after news spread southward of an unsuccessful attempt by the governor of Massachusetts to take control of the munitions stores there, which led to bloody and historic clashes between royal troops and American militiamen at Lexington and Concord. Once news arrived of the battle that took place that June at Bunker Hill in Massachusetts, lingering hopes of "peace and concord" seemed increasingly illusory. "Things look very melancholy," they wrote, "we fear much blood has been spilt." From their perspective, that bloodshed was a moral abomination and an affront to God: those who had "fomented and blown up this flame" would have much "to answer for in the great day of account."[58]

Meanwhile, the trade bans announced by Parliament and the Continental Congress were due to take effect that September. Activity on the wharves of Philadelphia became increasingly frantic as firms competed desperately for cargoes so that they could dispatch vessels before the deadline. When the *Chalkley* set sail for Bristol in early September, James and Drinker sent instructions that if the trading bans should remain in effect for long, their business partners there should try to sell the ship on their behalf. If they could not get a good price, they were "to guard against her being unemployed" by sending the vessel to Honduras Bay for a load of mahogany that could then be shipped back to Bristol. Soon afterward, Henry and Abel changed their minds. Since the boycotts had begun a decade before, many of their debtors had not been able to meet their obligations, which in turn had made it impossible for them to pay money that they owed, including to their friend and trading partner in London, Frederick Pigou. They now decided, "considering what it becomes us to do as honest men," to transfer ownership of the ship over to Pigou.[59] Over the coming months, James and Drinker put their inventory up for public sale and Henry withdrew from trade entirely, at least for the time being; James continued to trade on his own. As "business of many kinds" became "very slack," they predicted in letters to friends elsewhere that the collapse of transatlantic trade would put "great numbers of the poor" out of work, deepening "the distresses of this country" and quite possibly dooming many to starvation.[60]

Equally distressing was the "unnatural and cruel contention" that had caused these economic woes. In some of their letters, James and Drinker now referred to "Great Britain and these colonies" as "two countries," but they clearly did not see that "breach" as necessary or desirable. They still believed that "mutual interest" between "the subjects of England on this and the other side [of] the Atlantic" should have prevented the crisis in transatlantic relations from reaching such a "melancholy and distressing state." A growing number of Americans were now edging toward the conclusion that they could secure their rights as Englishmen only by separating from England and fighting for Independence. Henry and Abel still clung to the hope that "the God of peace and universal love" would "mercifully interpose, so that this once blessed and peaceful land may not be stained with further effusions of blood." Yet that eventuality seemed increasingly implausible, and even Elizabeth acknowledged in her diary that there was "much talk" about British warships gathering along the Eastern Seaboard. However, what mattered most to Elizabeth over the coming months and years was the civil war unfolding in her own city, especially as it targeted the Society of Friends and endangered her own family.[61]

"A Trying Time to Our Society"

The refusal of Friends such as James and Drinker to endorse violence had aroused deepening resentment and suspicion throughout the succession of colonial protests that now culminated in armed conflict. Quaker merchants might claim that the patriots' tactics offended their religious sensibilities, but some Philadelphians suspected that what really bothered these individuals was the impact of trade boycotts on their businesses. Such suspicions did not spring out of nowhere: leading Pennsylvania Friends had previously used their commitment to peace as a political weapon when jousting with the Penn family and their enemies in the assembly. Their reputation for deploying supposedly sacred truths selectively and in their own interest now came back to haunt them, as patriots refused to take their declarations of principle at face value. James and Drinker freely admitted that their perspective on the escalating crisis had blended principle and self-interest. Their firm was facing considerable losses, and they resented that trade boycotts were "robbing the honest trader of his substance." Yet the partners laid claim to principled concerns "independent of our interest" and vowed to act as their consciences dictated, even if that turned out to be at the expense of their own material interests and personal safety.[62]

Those concerns focused not only on the violence that now threatened to engulf the colonies but also on what they saw as an unnecessary rupture among natural friends who could and should have resolved their differences through calm and mutually respectful negotiation. Though Quakers had always believed in their right to protest against injustice, they considered governments to be God ordained, so that critics of government policy could advocate peaceably for reform but could not in good conscience justify open rebellion. Around a fifth of American male Quakers now decided in the present crisis that this position was no longer tenable and a misreading of God's will: they therefore joined the patriots and took up arms. The Society of Friends disowned most of these dissenters, who went on to incorporate as a distinct community of faith, calling themselves Free Quakers. A much smaller group of Friends identified as loyalists. The overwhelming majority of Quakers adopted a principled neutrality, refusing to support either side in the bloody war that now stained red the battlefields of North America.[63]

The enthusiastic support given by Friends such as Henry Drinker to Benjamin Franklin's campaign in the 1760s for the transformation of Pennsylvania into a royal colony made it all too easy for patriots to claim a decade later that Quaker claims to neutrality were insincere. Patriots were in no mood to tolerate dissent and could not afford to respect disengagement as they prepared to take on the British army, especially when those disengaging included such affluent and influential members of colonial society. The Society of Friends now urged its members to withdraw from public life and to refuse any governmental office. Yet leading Friends rewrote history when they declared in early 1776 that they had always been apolitical, not wanting to become "busy bodies in matters above our station" and preferring to "live a peaceable and quiet life." This claim, made in a published declaration of their foundational principles, was obviously false and did the Quaker cause no favors, reinforcing their reputation for untrustworthiness and mendacity. Even after some Quaker representatives had resigned from the colonial assembly in 1756, others had remained and Friends continued to exert influence behind the scenes. Their enemies had accused them of hypocrisy and double-dealing before, and now, patriots claimed, they were at it again.[64]

The public statements that Quaker delegates attending Philadelphia Yearly Meetings in the early 1770s put out to clarify and defend their position proved extremely vulnerable to misinterpretation, especially when read through a lens of suspicion and mistrust. Instead of pacifying their enemies, these statements added fuel to the fire of hostility now gathering around Quakers. Even as a growing number of Americans became convinced that the British government was plotting to take away their liberties and bleed them dry of their resources, the Yearly Meeting insisted that Friends in particular and Americans in general should be grateful for all that "the king and his royal ancestors" had done to protect them from their foes. Henry attended those Yearly Meetings from 1772 onward as a delegate from his local Meeting. He and other delegates who gathered at the 1773 Yearly Meeting reminded their brethren that they had long enjoyed "the blessings of liberty, peace, and plenty" because of the British government's insistence upon religious toleration for all Protestants. Those blessings, they insisted, should inspire a profound sense of obligation. In early 1776, the Yearly Meeting broadened that claim of indebtedness far beyond the Society of Friends to encapsulate colonial society as a whole. The delegates reminded "friends and fellow subjects of every denomination" in a declaration published that January that "the inhabitants of these provinces" had been "long signally favored with peace and plenty." Many of the original colonists had been "persecuted and subjected to severe suffering" until they arrived in North America and secured royal charters that gave them "very extensive powers and privileges." Yet the colonists had now apparently forgotten "the benefits, advantages, and favor" they had long received from the royal government. The delegates offered no defense whatsoever of recent legislation and they did not question the right of colonists to petition against what they saw as misguided policies, but they did urge Americans to shift their focus away from specific grievances to the long-term benefits of their membership within the empire. Given those advantages, Americans should surely "guard against every attempt to alter or subvert that dependence and connection."[65]

The Yearly Meeting also stressed repeatedly that Quakers objected on principle to the very idea of rebellion or revolution. Friends held that "the setting up and putting down [of] kings and governments" was "God's peculiar prerogative, for causes best known to himself," and that it was "not our business to have any hand or contrivance therein." They would "therefore firmly unite in the abhorrence of all such writings and measures" that expressed any "desire and design to break off the happy connection we have heretofore enjoyed with the Kingdom of Great Britain" or questioned "our just and necessary subordination to the king, and those who are lawfully placed in authority under him." The implication was that all Americans should follow their example, not because current imperial policies were justified, but because it was their duty as Christians. They could protest against specific policies, peacefully and respectfully, but they had no right to challenge the actual authority of the government.[66]

Friends insisted that their commitment to peace and their refusal to support rebellion against an established government, even when its specific policies seemed indefensible, rested on religious principle. Indeed, they were "actuated solely by a conscientious principle and Christian spirit." Any refusal to respect their principles was, in effect, a challenge to their faith and to religious freedom itself, a liberty as fundamental as any civil freedom such as the right to taxation by consent. In 1775, Pennsylvania Quakers reminded their neighbors of the principle enshrined in the 1701 Charter of Privileges, that "no people" could be "truly happy, though under the greatest enjoyment of civil liberties, if abridged of the freedom of their consciences." Friends remained committed to defending "the just rights of the people," but they reserved the right to do so in a manner consistent with their religious precepts, "as peaceable subjects" who spoke with both "Christian meekness and firmness." Those who condemned Quakers for their refusal to condone confrontation, violence, or any outright challenge to the authority of a government God had set over them were in effect denying one kind of liberty in the name of another. The solution to the crisis lay not in rebellion or revolution but instead in a forthright yet peaceable quest for reform within the British system.[67]

For those who read these declarations of principle as a roundabout endorsement of loyalism, the Quakers had a clear response that made good sense on its own terms, but in the present climate made matters even worse. Friends took the view that they had multiple loyalties on this earth to agencies charged with the enactment of God's will, but they owed paramount loyalty neither to local representatives, nor to Parliament, nor to royal officials, nor even to the crown itself, but to the Society of Friends. They demanded that others respect their right to spiritual and civil liberties as fellow subjects of the crown, as fellow Americans, and as residents of a specific colony built on the principle of spiritual liberty for all, but also and above all else as a nation in their own right. Quakers had often referred to themselves as a distinct "people" comparable to the Hebraic nation of Zion. Indeed, they conceived of themselves as "a holy nation" embedded within the colonies and Great Britain but not coexistent with either. "We are a people," they declared, and they had been throughout their history "a suffering people." As a spirit of reform spread through the Society of Friends in the middle of the eighteenth century, leading Friends encouraged the faithful to protect "the walls of Zion" against corrupting ideas and insisted that those among whom they lived respect their values as a separate people. It was as "the people called Quakers" that the

Yearly Meeting addressed their fellow Philadelphians. It was as "a distinct religious society" that they had crossed the Atlantic, had been promised freedom of conscience and other liberties in the charter signed by William Penn, and now demanded that the patriots who claimed to be defending liberty respect the Society of Friends' right to freedom of conscience. They were, they insisted, their own nation.[68]

That commitment to a distinct and deeply felt nationhood would become a source of comfort and sustenance in the trials ahead, but it also contributed to growing hostility toward Quakers. When their neighbors asked them to choose between continued deference to the royal government and allegiance to a new republic, Friends refused to do so. They now laid claim to righteous neutrality as a separate holy nation with its own history and identity that transcended their membership of any temporal principality. Unfortunately, others around them were committing to their own visions of exclusive nationhood. Non-Quaker ministers who sought to rally support for the patriots would increasingly equate the colonists' departure from the empire with the Israelites' exodus from Egypt, claiming that the new republic was itself a holy nation. Anyone who refused to identify wholly with that patriot cause was increasingly vulnerable to denunciation as a traitor.[69]

In the months leading up to the Declaration of Independence, revolutionary pamphleteers set out to vilify Friends as enemies of their country and as devious cowards who hid their loyalism behind a mask of pacifist neutrality. In the first edition of *Common Sense,* Thomas Paine characterized those who opposed Independence as "interested men who are not to be trusted; weak men who cannot see; and prejudiced men who will not see." Quakers were among his targets, though not mentioned by name, but in the third edition of that same pamphlet, Paine launched an explicit and malicious attack on Friends in particular, railing against their "professed quietude" and "pretended scruples." He claimed with particular relish that Friends had made nonsense of their claim to be apolitical by publishing that assertion in what was manifestly, according to Paine, a political pamphlet. Later that year, when Quakers expressed their concern that Pennsylvania's new state constitution did not protect freedom of conscience, their enemies deliberately misrepresented their reference to "the happy constitution" previously in place, claiming that they meant the British constitution when they were in fact referring to the colony's Charter of Liberties. "If this be not treason," declared the anonymous authors of a letter sent to the Council of Safety, "we know not what may properly be called by that name."[70]

Quakers in Philadelphia and elsewhere now braced themselves for renewed martyrdom. James and Drinker predicted that anyone who challenged the patriots would "be held up to the public in the most odious light as an enemy to the liberties of his country and be liable to insults and abuse." This was, they wrote, "a trying time to our Society and threaten[ed] to be more so." As in the past, Friends must "exert patience" and find reassurance in their own "uprightness of heart and rectitude of conduct," however others might detest their principles. "It ever was," the partners wrote, "and ever will be." Philadelphia Friends arranged for the reprinting and distribution of a letter written by William Penn in 1678, addressed to British Friends and entitled *To the Children of Light in This Generation*. Writing at a time of heavy persecution, Penn had urged Quakers to "stand as the heavenly seed of righteousness and shine unto others in these uneven and rough times that are to come." Though written a century before, it could not have been more apposite. Now that Friends faced another trial of their faith and integrity, they must once again stand firm, whatever the cost. The Philadelphia Yearly Meeting hoped that during this renewed "time of deep probation," Friends would stick to their resolve, make "manifest to the world the excellency of our peaceable principles," and embrace adversity as a spiritual opportunity to grow, individually and together. An antiwar poem that Henry kept among his papers urged those who faced persecution not to "bewail" their "momentary adverse doom" but to "kiss the rod" that would lead them through "deep tribulation" to "glorious recompense" and "immortal health."[71]

~

Elizabeth Drinker wrote nothing in her diary during the months leading up to Independence that would suggest she had resigned herself to a pilgrimage of affliction, but she was well aware that for her extended family the ordeal had already begun. In February 1776, her husband's brother, John Drinker, along with fellow merchants Thomas and Samuel Fisher, received a summons to appear before the Committee of Observation and Inspection for refusing to accept continental bills of credit. They had done so as a matter of conscience, arguing that the purpose of the new currency was to fund a war, but the committee denounced John Drinker and the Fishers as enemies of their country and instructed them to close down their businesses. Elizabeth noted that the committee "advertised" their offense in "handbills" distributed to the public and that later that month "Johnny Drinker's store" was "shut up by the committee." Elizabeth may well have wondered if this persecution of her brother-in-law was a dark omen for her own immediate family: it was entirely plausible that the threats directed against Henry over the past few years might now resume and intensify, should the patriots find any excuse, however flimsy, for acting against him.[72]

Elizabeth's husband doubtless felt he had good reason to lament the "commotions" that had brought his world to the brink of dissolution. His and Abel's firm had established itself as one of the premier trading houses in Philadelphia but had then suffered through repeated trade boycotts and had finally closed for business as transatlantic trade collapsed. Having worked so hard to achieve wealth, social status, and considerable influence, he and his partner now found themselves maligned and bullied by men whom they considered their inferiors, wielding "a new species of power." They and other Friends looked on in horror as the colonies plunged into war, renouncing loyalty to a government across the Atlantic that Quakers had long seen as their protector and abandoning a colonial charter that had guaranteed them freedom from persecution. From Henry's perspective, these were indeed "calamitous" and "distracted times," in which "unhappy confusions" and "miseries" showered down upon a "once happy land." Yet much worse lay in store for the Drinker family. The antiwar poem in Henry's possession promised a "glorious recompense" to those who suffered through persecution, yet it also acknowledged that in the meantime "grim adversity" was "grievous to sustain." Henry's entire family was about to discover just how true that was.[73]

4 • "Cruelty and Oppression"

In Which Henry Drinker Is Arrested and Sent into Exile

"Though we desire," wrote James and Drinker in the spring of 1776, "not to sit brooding over the evils of the present day as men in despair, yet are we in a serious situation." Philadelphia had become a dangerous place for those considered unsympathetic to the patriot cause and was likely to become more so over the coming months. Following the Declaration of Independence, Henry considered fleeing the city and wrote to Quaker friends in Thornbury, Chester County, asking if he and his family could take refuge with them, should that prove necessary. John Brinton wrote back, "Our hearts and house are open to receive you at any time when it suits you to come, and [we] shall be ready and willing to do the best we can for you." In early 1777, Henry's younger brother Joseph also offered refuge out at Kingwood, New Jersey, but Henry decided to stay put and brave whatever storm lay ahead. Joseph took comfort in knowing that his brother had left behind his life as a merchant, at least for the duration of the war, devoting his "time and talents" to defending the Society of Friends and so serving their God: "a wise choice, indeed, and a good paymaster thou wilt have if thou art faithful." Far better, Joseph wrote, that their faces be "turned zionwards" than to rely on "the friendship and grandeur of this fading world." As "the furnace of affliction" grew "hotter and hotter" in their "once favored city" that was "now become a babel of confusion and distress," Joseph prayed that Friends in Philadelphia would "stand faithful to the truth," that their behavior would inspire others, and that Quakers would then be respected for their integrity rather than "trampled underfoot." Unfortunately, for Henry and his family, Joseph's prediction that their God would first "suffer his people to pass through the furnace of affliction" turned out to be entirely accurate.[1]

The refusal of most Quakers to support the war effort placed them in an increasingly perilous position, as patriots now conflated them with loyalists. Philadelphian lawyer James Allen wrote in July 1777 that the term "Tory" was now used to describe "everyone disinclined to independence, though ever so warm a friend to constitutional liberty." Robert Proud, a Quaker schoolmaster who lived in the city, wrote that most of the Friends targeted by the new regime had been "entirely inactive either for or against" Independence, except for "occasionally using their persuasions to peace." Yet the Continental Army was facing the armed forces of a major imperial power and would need all the soldiers and financial resources it could muster; the prominent position that leading Quakers occupied within Philadelphian society and their considerable wealth made their refusal to contribute to the patriot cause particularly damaging. Local Quaker Meetings made no secret of their position, disowning Friends who served in the Continental Army or voluntarily supported the armed forces in other ways, such as providing food supplies, horses, or wagons. Because the state government was dedicating much of its time to the war effort, they also disowned individuals who assumed civic responsibilities under the new regime, along with those who agreed to take the oath of allegiance that patriots demanded in the aftermath of Independence. Quakers' continued insistence that they were not loyalists merely fed suspicions that they either were too cowardly to admit their true feelings or were trying to remain embedded in the community so that they could spy for the British. In March 1778, General George Washington instructed Brigadier General John Lacey Jr. to do all he could to prevent Quaker delegates from reaching a gathering of ministers and elders in Philadelphia. "The plans settled at these meetings," he wrote, "are of the most pernicious tendency." If any of the delegates had horses suitable for military use, the animals were to be "taken from them and sent over to the Quartermaster General." Lacey gave orders to shoot those who refused to stop when ordered to do so and to leave their bodies on the road as a warning to others. Edward Rutledge, who represented South Carolina in the Continental Congress, called for the hanging of Friends who refused to accept continental currency.[2]

Elizabeth had little sympathy for either side in the War for Independence. In her diary, she condemned both for their pillaging of her city and especially their brutal acts of repression. She referred to men fighting with the Continental Army as "the American soldiers" or "the Americans" and to their opponents as "the English" or "the British army," her choice of pronouns underlining her refusal to identify with either side (in contrast to "our dear friends," "our dear families," "my sisters in affliction," and "my dear Henry"). Her neighbor and fellow Quaker Sarah Fisher did not go quite so far, referring to the Continental Army as "our American army" and to supporters of Independence as "my countrymen," though she added in one diary entry, "I am sorry to call them mine." Elizabeth described those who refused to support the Revolution as "peaceable people," making abundantly clear that for her rejection of violence was the crucial issue. Her diary contained no exposition of Quaker thinking on the subject of political protest, and we have no way of knowing whether she took any interest in the detailed arguments that leading Quakers, including her husband, now articulated in public statements explaining their refusal to support Independence. Elizabeth was no politician, but she did care deeply about how political events affected her home city, her Quaker friends and neighbors, and her family. Over the coming months and years, she would catalog in her diary dozens of incidents in which patriots vented their spleen on "peaceable" Philadelphians, and once British forces occupied the city, she had much to say in condemnation of their behavior as well.[3]

Elizabeth's account of the revolutionary war provides a vivid counterpoint to narratives that focus on public affairs. Yet it would be a mistake to see this simply as a contrast between male and female worlds, or to claim that those worlds were utterly distinct. Her diary entries provide a richly detailed account of the war raging around her and its economic impact, though she focused on the availability and price of butter and beef rather than import duties or congressional resolutions. Her focus was always the impact of war on civilians and especially her own family. Henry's arrest in September 1777 and his subsequent exile in Virginia, two hundred miles away from Philadelphia, proved a harrowing ordeal for both husband and wife. Not surprisingly, Elizabeth worried constantly about her absent husband, but meanwhile she had little choice but to assume responsibility for the safety of her children and home, with the help of her sister, Mary. Though she often called on male neighbors for counsel or support, Elizabeth became, in effect, a temporary household head. Just as her diary focused above all else on the physical safety of her family, so the letters that Henry wrote during his exile showed him to be equally concerned about the threat that war posed to his wife and children. Henry was accustomed to exercising his rights and responsibilities as household head; he was a loving husband and father, and had been closely involved alongside his wife and her sister in caring for the Drinker children; his removal and consequent inability to protect or guide his family in person for eight long months was clearly and profoundly distressing to him. Henry seems to have been more committed than Elizabeth was to understanding their ordeal as a spiritual odyssey; for him that larger meaning of their troubles was always in plain view, for her, less so. Yet during their separation, Henry and Elizabeth reaffirmed in their correspondence how important they were to each other as a source of support and how similar in most respects were their priorities and anxieties.[4]

The Gathering Storm

Throughout the spring of 1776, Elizabeth made no mention in her diary of the campaign for Independence as it gained momentum throughout the colonies. She seems to have determined not to let the crisis intrude into her day-to-day life, at least as recorded in her diary. However, she could not ignore entirely the mounting hostility toward Quakers, especially when it targeted her relatives and her immediate family. In February, the patriots had shut down her brother-in-law John Drinker's store after he and his partners refused to accept continental currency, and it soon became clear to Elizabeth that much more than John's store was about to come under attack. On May 8, she noted that the town had been "in confusion" that afternoon when colonial forces fired from Station Island on two British ships trying unsuccessfully to sail up the Delaware River into Pennsylvania. Given that the Drinkers' home was just one block away from the Delaware, they must have realized that warships might soon reach the stretch of river visible from the upper windows of their house, which would place them in immediate danger. That June, she and Henry experienced the first of many direct assaults on their property when officials appointed by the Committee of Safety came to examine their window weights. The armed forces urgently needed lead, and so the committee had given orders for the appropriation of all lead weights used on windows and clocks. The inspectors found that the Drinkers' window weights were made of iron and so they departed empty-handed. Even if they had removed them, the Drinkers could have propped open their windows with rods or wooden planks; this was hardly a matter of life and death. Yet the intrusion made an impression, and worse was to come.[5]

Elizabeth's diary made no mention whatsoever of the Declaration of Independence, but on July 16 she wrote that "the American soldiers" had "broken open" the Friends' meetinghouse on Market Street and had "taken up their abode" there. The soldiers were on their way from Maryland to New York and needed somewhere to stay, but lodging them in a building owned by pacifists who were on record as opposing the war was, of course, a deliberate provocation. When local Friends protested, the officer in charge refused to surrender possession, though he did agree to let the Quakers continue using the building for worship. In January 1777, Elizabeth noted that five patriot soldiers had been "quartered" in her home "by order of the Council of Safety." As the barracks quickly filled with militia troops passing through the city, the patriots billeted surplus troops with families who refused to come out in support of the war. Elizabeth noted with relief that three of the soldiers "went off in an hour or two," but the remaining two lodged there for several days. Her neighbor Sarah Fisher objected in her diary to the patriots' foisting upon respectable households "men of very little principle, under no discipline, and so intolerably dirty that even in the cleanest of their houses the stench of their dirt is great enough to cause an infectious disease." Even had her houseguests been clean and well-behaved men of rank, Sarah doubtless would still have declared that the new regime was wielding "arbitrary power" in much the same spirit as "the Spanish Inquisition." Elizabeth was not so explicit in her condemnation of the billeting policy, but she probably would have agreed with Sarah. The soldiers were soon gone, and at least for the time being, her household had to deal only with occasional demands from the army for supplies. That June, men appeared at her front door to collect blankets for the patriot soldiers, but Elizabeth had no intention of equipping the Continental Army, and so they "went away without any, as others had three or four times before."[6]

When the new state governments, determined to ferret out potential enemies, announced that all citizens would be required to take an oath of loyalty, most Quakers refused to do so, and the situation became much tenser. In February 1777, Elizabeth noted that her husband had left the city with several other Friends to visit two Quakers recently jailed in New Jersey for refusing to take the oath. Friends read aloud at their local Monthly Meetings a letter from the Yearly Meeting reaffirming that Friends should neither take "the test" (as Quakers termed the oath) nor participate in the war effort. The letter urged brethren not "to submit to the arbitrary injunctions and ordinances of men who assume to themselves the power of compelling others, either in person or by other assistance, to join in carrying on war." It also condemned the newly mandated oaths as "tests not warranted by the precepts of Christ or the laws of the happy constitution, under which we and others long enjoyed tranquility and peace." The authors of this document were referring to Pennsylvania's 1701 Charter of Liberties, but their lack of specificity opened them to the charge that they were pledging their loyalty to the British. A new militia law passed by the state assembly in early 1777 reflected growing hostility toward Friends. Whereas previous versions had allowed conscientious objectors to make an alternative contribution instead of serving in person, this law allowed for no such exemptions and instead imposed fines on those who did not appear when summoned; it redefined pacifists as delinquents and traitors. At this point, Elizabeth began to include in her entries brief but cutting remarks about the new regime, questioning its legitimacy and condemning its suppression of dissent. When citizens elected Thomas Wharton Jr. as president of Pennsylvania's Supreme Executive Council in March 1777, she wrote sardonically, "Some call him governor." A few days later, she recorded that a soldier in Pennsylvania's Tenth Regiment was "shot upon the commons" for desertion and another for treason, on the orders of "our present ruling gentry." Philadelphia, she added, had "heretofore" been "clear of such business."[7]

Patriots were now eager to brand Friends as traitors who did not have the courage or integrity to declare their true loyalties, but they needed Quakers to speak and act in ways that exposed them, at least plausibly, as loyalists so that the new regime could justify treating them as such. John Lansing, who served as aide to one of the Continental Army's generals, Philip Schuyler, declared in the spring of 1777 that "Quakers in general" were "wolves in sheep's clothing" and "more dangerous" than open loyalists because they "shelter[ed] themselves under the pretext of conscientious scruples." That May, General Schuyler demanded a thousand blankets from Quaker households for use by his soldiers. He may have hoped to provoke Quakers into making provocative statements that would then make it easier to justify extreme measures against them, and if so, that strategy was remarkably effective. The Yearly Meeting in Philadelphia responded by sending the general a copy of Robert Barclay's *Apology for the True Christian Divinity* (first published in 1678), which explained the Friends' refusal to support war in any way whatsoever. Supporters of the Revolution saw this refusal to provide supplies as equivalent to opposing Independence and became increasingly blatant in their attacks on Friends as enemies of the republic. Elizabeth noted that on July 4, 1777, the town was "illuminated" by fireworks and "a great number of windows broke." These were the windows of Quaker shops and homes, vandalized in retaliation for their refusal to close their stores or light candles in their windows to mark what she described, in an entry dripping with sarcasm, as "the anniversary of Independence and Freedom." Sarah Fisher noted that patriots smashed fifteen of her windowpanes, "and all this for joy of having gained our liberty." Elizabeth did not mention whether any of her own windows were broken that day, though her careful record of all assaults on her household suggests that the house escaped damage.[8]

Though the Drinker home seems to have survived that first anniversary intact, growing hostility toward Friends was about to strike at Elizabeth's family in a very personal way. The Continental Congress gave orders in the summer of 1777 for the arrest of all persons "notoriously disaffected" from the patriot cause. Loyalists and other Philadelphians who feared that the new regime might label them as enemies of the people hoped that the British would march on Philadelphia and occupy the city before the patriots went further in their persecution of those who refused to support the war effort. General William Howe, commander of the British troops sent to quash the American rebels, had taken New York in the early fall of 1776. He then pursued Washington's army southward into New Jersey but did not cross the Delaware into Pennsylvania. It was not until the following summer that Howe finally set his sights on the rebel capital, Philadelphia, but he decided to travel by sea rather than land to avoid marching through New Jersey, and so his troops sailed from New York harbor on July 23, 1777. A week later, Elizabeth heard "an account of a large fleet" that people had sighted off the coast, but it "disappeared the next day." Though Philadelphians did not know this, Howe's forces were now heading toward the Chesapeake Bay, where they would disembark and then march northeast toward their city. The general had originally planned to land much closer, but reports of impressive defenses along the Delaware River prompted him to reconsider. The troops landed at the end of August and did not reach Philadelphia until September 26.[9]

The situation was becoming increasingly dangerous for "disaffected" Quakers. That August, Elizabeth wrote in her diary that Thomas Fisher had been "confined in the Jerseys." A new law stipulated that anyone who left the city without certification that they had taken the oath of loyalty would be imprisoned. Thomas Fisher had left the city without any such certificate, was stopped by a magistrate "who demanded to know if he had a pass," and then was arrested after it became clear that he had none. The magistrate released Fisher the following day, informing him "that they had considered his case and, nothing appearing against him, he was at liberty to return home." His wife, Sarah, wrote in her diary that she had spent the intervening time in "painful anxiety," though friends who came to visit assured her that the patriots had imprisoned him "merely to show their power and the badness of their hearts," predicting correctly that he would be released as soon as they had made their point. In the same diary entry that included a note of Fisher's arrest, Elizabeth wrote that her own husband had left on a trip to a Quaker gathering in New Jersey. She must surely have worried that Henry might also fall prey to examination and imprisonment as an alleged enemy of the revolutionary regime, but he was lucky and returned a week later without having suffered any harassment, at least none that he chose to share with his wife.[10]

Yet the situation was about to take a dramatic turn for the worse. Toward the end of August, in a letter addressed to the president of the Continental Congress, Major General John Sullivan accused Quakers of collecting information about the patriot forces and sending it on to the British. He described them as "the most dangerous enemies America knows." The document on which Sullivan based this allegation was almost certainly a forgery, but the war was not going well and any scapegoat was welcome. A congressional committee concluded that "persons of considerable wealth" among the Quakers, who were "with much rancor and bitterness disaffected to the American cause," had the means as well as "inclination to communicate intelligence to the enemy." Congress responded by passing a resolution for the arrest of eleven leading Quakers, including Henry Drinker and Abel James. Soon afterward, the Supreme Executive Council of Pennsylvania named more than forty men whom they considered "inimicably disposed towards the American states," again including James and Drinker. They arrested thirty over the next few days. When officials arrived to apprehend Abel at his estate outside the city, he asked that they allow him to remain there on grounds that his son Joseph was seriously ill. The visitors, after searching the premises and finding no papers to incriminate him, agreed to let Abel remain there, but he had to promise not to "give any intelligence to the enemies of the United States of America" and to appear before the patriot authorities on demand. Given Abel's implication in the Tea Act debacle and his close political alliance before the Revolution with Joseph Galloway, a leading figure in the colonial assembly who had now declared himself a loyalist, it is surprising that he eluded arrest. Perhaps his current location outside the city made him seem less immediately dangerous; his continued absence may have protected him from coming back into focus as a target of suspicion during the busy days that followed: out of sight, out of mind, at least for the time being. Whatever the reasons, Henry did not escape so lightly.[11]

Bidding Farewell to "My Dearest Husband"

It was at this point that Elizabeth's engagement with the Revolution through her diary transformed from a series of sporadic and brief entries into a detailed and moving narrative of personal tribulation. On the day that disaster struck,

Elizabeth was too distraught to write, and so it was two days later when she sat down to record the sequence of events. At around noon on September 2, 1777, three men appeared at the Drinkers' front door and demanded entry. Henry Sandwith Drinker, their seven-year-old son, was ill with a fever and "disordered bowels." Her husband was also feeling unwell and so had abandoned his original plan to walk over to the meetinghouse that morning. Instead, he was at his desk in the front parlor, making a copy of minutes from the Monthly Meeting, which he was currently serving as clerk. The three men came inside and presented Henry with "a parole" that committed the recipient to remain in the house until summoned by council. They demanded that Henry sign it, but he refused. The men then confiscated the book of minutes, searched his desk, removed "several papers," and took them away, telling Henry that he must stay at home until they came back the next morning. Because her husband was unwell, Elizabeth wrote, it was in any case necessary for him to stay indoors. She evidently did not want to give even her diary the impression that Henry remained at home in obedience to their visitors. Early the following day, the three men returned and "took my Henry to the Masons' lodge," which the patriots were using as a temporary prison, where they confined him along with the other alleged traitors "in an illegal, unprecedented manner."[12]

That evening, Henry wrote a brief letter to his wife, sister-in-law, and children back in Front Street. He and the other prisoners had no idea what their captors intended to do with them. Yet despite the temptation to sink into fear and foreboding, "through [God's] mercy" he had been "preserved in much inward quiet and resignation." Henry hoped that he would "be favored to continue in the same frame of mind," but that would depend in part on hearing from Elizabeth that she was also keeping to "the safe path of dependence" on God's "help and strength." He wrote to his children that they should show their love and concern for their father "by abiding at home out of noise and company in stillness and quietness." This first of many letters from Henry to Elizabeth, Mary, and their children during his absence set the pattern for those that would follow. Passing on practical information would play its part, but of paramount concern to Henry was his and Elizabeth's shared duty to meet the spiritual challenges of the coming ordeal and to ensure that their children did likewise. He finished this letter by declaring, "I love your eternal welfare above all—yours affectionately, Henry Drinker."[13]

The day after Henry's removal from his home, a flock of friends ("upwards of twenty") visited his family to give their support. That evening, Elizabeth walked over to the Masonic Lodge "to see my HD," where she also "met with the wives and children of our dear Friends and other visitors in great numbers." In her initial entry about Henry's arrest, Elizabeth limited herself to a recitation of events and their injustice, but in her next entry for September 5, she acknowledged her own "great distress." Yet her diary entries for the days following Henry's arrest made no mention of trusting in God or acknowledging her dependence on his "help and strength." Indeed, Elizabeth's account of her city's descent into the turmoil of civil war had throughout been remarkably lacking in any religious commentary. Her neighbor Sarah Fisher had wondered if the British army's delay in marching on Philadelphia was "some great design of Providence," intended to bring Philadelphians through "affliction and suffering" to "a sense of our ingratitude for the uninterrupted series of blessings" they had "enjoyed for so many years." Sarah would "endeavor patiently to bear that part of the trial . . . allotted to me and kiss the rod [so] that while it smotes it may heal." Elizabeth's diary made no mention of any need for self-examination. Whereas Sarah wrote in her entry for September 2 that God must have intended the wave of arrests "for our further refinement, as we are told it is through suffering we are to be made perfect," Elizabeth focused instead on her physical comings and goings, with occasional allusions to her anguish.[14]

Throughout the days that followed, Elizabeth, her sister, Mary, and the children went back and forth between their house and the Masonic Lodge to spend time with Henry. Little Henry Sandwith was still unwell, which doubtless added to their anxiety. Elizabeth did not yet know that the Executive Council had decided to send the prisoners far away to Staunton in Virginia, where they could not influence other Friends back in Philadelphia or spy on the revolutionary government. Once the prisoners were told of this plan, Henry wrote to one of his brothers, asking him to tell Elizabeth, Mary, and the children "in the most prudent and tender manner," and to reassure them that the prisoners had been promised treatment "consistent with their respective characters and the security of their persons." The authorities would even provide carriages to ensure their comfort and dignity, unless they chose to travel in their own vehicles. Henry wrote a brief note to Elizabeth, promising that he would give her "timely notice of every material movement." It was not yet clear when they would leave on their journey; the British were approaching the city, and the sound of cannon shots in the distance suggested that the armies had already engaged. "The clouds seem to gather," he wrote, "and all things seem to indicate great perplexity and confusion amongst our persecutors." He reminded his wife in closing that there could be only one legitimate response to their uncertain situation: "May we be resigned and given up is the continued wish of thy Henry Drinker."[15]

Yet inner resignation to God's will did not mean outward passivity in the face of mistreatment. Indeed, Quakers believed that God required the faithful to proclaim divine truth in the face of affliction. Immediately following the arrests, three of Henry's fellow prisoners wrote to the Supreme Executive Council, describing themselves as "peaceable" men who had "never bore arms" and declaring that the Council's actions were "arbitrary, unjust, and illegal," assuming an "authority not grounded in law or reason." The general warrant used to justify their arrest and imprisonment had not brought any specific charges against the prisoners; nor did it state which judicial body would preside over their cases or place any limit on the duration of their confinement. In "An Address to the Inhabitants of Pennsylvania," the prisoners characterized these proceedings as "gross enormities" carried out by an "engine of modern despotism" that if left unchecked would "establish a system of arbitrary power unknown but in the Inquisition, or the despotic courts of the East." They called for an immediate hearing and over a hundred Philadelphians signed a petition supporting their demand. The Continental Congress recommended that the Executive Council accede, but the council responded that it did not have time to hold hearings and requested permission from Congress to send the prisoners to Virginia for safekeeping. Congress responded that this was an internal matter for the state to handle as it saw fit. Neither body was willing at this point to take responsibility for the prisoners' ultimate fate, though both insisted that the arrests were justified. Over the coming weeks and months, one of the greatest obstacles to the prisoners' release turned out to be the eagerness of both Congress and council to deflect responsibility for what became an increasingly embarrassing situation. "They know not what they be at," declared Elizabeth. The council did offer to release any prisoner willing to swear or affirm that he would "be faithful and bear true allegiance to the Commonwealth of Pennsylvania as a free and independent state," but twenty of the prisoners, including Henry, refused because they believed that doing so would commit them to support the war.[16]

The remaining prisoners' families had no idea when their loved ones would depart, but meanwhile the patriot authorities did allow the detainees time away from their makeshift prison on condition that they promised to return as required. This relaxed arrangement allowed Elizabeth to provide her husband with an occasional meal at home and even the comfort of his own bed. She noted on September 6 that Henry had breakfasted at their house and on

September 7 that he was going to stay overnight. Earlier that day, the prisoners had asked their families to stay away from the lodge until late afternoon, "wishing to have this day more particularly to themselves in stillness." Alongside spiritual preparation for the ordeal that lay ahead, practical matters also needed attention. Henry drew up a list of articles to take with him on his journey. He sent instructions that his "great coat" should be "examined and repaired." He would need shaving equipment ("razor, strop, and soap box," and "coarse linen to wipe razor on"), towels, a hat cover, boots, shoes, "six good shirts and a like number of neck cloths," pocket handkerchiefs, nightclothes, underwear, and "herbs of different sorts" along with "elixir" and pills, tobacco, cigars, and a spoon, knife, and fork. He also stipulated that the prisoners would "jointly" need "coffee, chocolate, tea, loaf sugar, brown sugar, spirit, wine, biscuit, [and] tea pots." In addition, his "chain and harness" should be "examined and put in good order," in case his captors should allow him to travel in his own vehicle, as the original order from the Executive Council had indicated. Elizabeth, her sister, and their servants presumably set to work carrying out his instructions.[17]

Elizabeth wished to spend as many precious minutes as possible with her husband. The children also wanted to see their father, but on September 8 "little Henry" was so unwell that he "could not go to see his Daddy until the afternoon." Their daughter Nancy was also "unwell with disordered bowels" (her mother gave her some rhubarb), and the following morning Henry Sandwith was so "low" that Elizabeth stayed with him, sending their other son, William, "to enquire after his dear Daddy's health." Later on September 9, Elizabeth went herself and was present when news arrived that the prisoners would leave the next day. The Executive Council had instructed Samuel Caldwell and Alexander Nesbitt, officers in the Philadelphia City Cavalry, to escort the prisoners along with a city guard as far as Reading, some sixty miles northwest of Philadelphia. The guards could not be spared to accompany the exiles for their entire journey because reports indicated that the British were approaching the city, and so Caldwell had orders that at Reading he should hand the prisoners over to the lieutenant or sublieutenant of the county for the remainder of their journey. The prisoners, referred to in the council's instructions as "gentlemen," were to be "placed in light covered wagons, in such manner as not to be crowded." If any of them preferred to travel in their own carriages, they could do so. The officers were to provide the prisoners with "suitable accommodation" along the way and treat them with "politeness" but also "a proper degree of firmness and watchfulness." Elizabeth returned home "in great distress," and after settling "little Henry" she went back in the evening to find the prisoners writing a letter of protest against what she described as "the tyrannical conduct of the present wicked rulers." When she finally returned home to sleep, it was almost eleven o'clock, and as she sat down to write her diary, she "heard a cannon go off," a frightening conclusion to an upsetting day.[18]

Elizabeth arose on the following morning expecting to go and bid her husband farewell, but news arrived that the prisoners would now not depart until the next day because of difficulties in procuring wagons and men to accompany them. Henry was allowed to spend the afternoon, evening, and night at home. "Little Henry" still had "a constant fever" and Elizabeth was "apprehensive of his falling into a consumption." When the next morning came, there was another delay until that afternoon. Henry had breakfast with his family and then went to the lodge. Elizabeth went back and forth throughout the day. She and her neighbors could hear the sound of ammunition in the distance (General Washington was trying, unsuccessfully, to halt the British march toward Philadelphia at the Battle of Brandywine). Reports arrived of several armed vessels "up the river," and the town was, she wrote, "in great confusion." When news arrived that the wagons were finally ready and waiting at the lodge, Elizabeth rushed over with one of her daughters to "bid my dearest husband farewell" and "as quickly came away, finding a great number of people there, but few women." She seems to have felt out of place in mostly male company. Elizabeth wrote nothing about the prisoners' treatment on leaving the lodge, perhaps because she had already left and did not witness it herself, or perhaps because she could not bear to record what had happened, but her neighbor and friend Sarah Fisher, whose husband, Thomas, was among the exiles, was not so reticent. The promise that prisoners could use their own carriages had evaporated. Fisher wrote that the twenty men were "dragged into the wagons by force by soldiers employed for that purpose, and drove off surrounded by guards and a mob." Robert Morton, the sixteen-year-old stepson of James Pemberton, another of the prisoners, described bitterly this forced removal of the prisoners, "dragged by a licentious mob from their near and dear connections, and by the hand of lawless power banished . . . perhaps never more to return." Elizabeth went from the lodge "in great distress" to James Pemberton's house, got home at dusk, and immediately sat down to write a letter "to my dear." That letter does not survive, but in a subsequent note written on September 16, she assured Henry that he was "much talked of, and much felt for, not only by us who are nearly affected, but by a great many others." She concluded the letter with "Farewell for ye present, my dearest, thy faithful Elizabeth Drinker."[19]

Henry sat down at the end of his first day in transit to send his family "a salutation of love," assuring them that he was "bowed in reverent thankfulness" for having been "supported in a serene tranquil state of mind, almost uninterrupted from the first of my imprisonment until this time." Though their removal from the Masonic Lodge had involved "scenes" which to observers "might appear severely trying," he had been "wonderfully born up under them, or rather kept above them." Even as Henry acknowledged his dependence on God's guiding hand, he also allowed himself a moment of self-congratulation as he looked back over the past week. "My way seems clear and open, no material omission of duty in the late probation has occurred, but on the other hand a heartfelt satisfaction attends inasmuch as the blessed testimony has been supported and not baulked by me, a weakling." He clearly hoped that Elizabeth would follow his example and reminded her that "to be resigned and given up" to God's will was the best way to secure divine protection. "It will comfort my heart," he wrote, "to hear thou hast attained to this state."[20]

Back in Philadelphia, news of Washington's defeat at the Battle of Brandywine reached the city a day after the prisoners' departure. Elizabeth's son was still so sick that she had to give him "constant attention" throughout the day, but she did hear that American troops were entering the city "in great numbers" and that the dead were "said to be very numerous, hundreds of their muskets laying in the road." Not surprisingly, she was "a little fluttered" when she heard that afternoon "a drum stop at our door," followed by "a hard knocking." It turned out to be men with orders for her husband to report for military service. Elizabeth did not describe her feelings as she informed the men of her husband's removal from Philadelphia as a prisoner of the regime they represented. That afternoon, she noted, there was a meeting at the statehouse, "on what account I know not." More important to her was the arrival of news telling her that the prisoners had dined at the Black Horse on the road out of Philadelphia. Over the next few days, her little boy's condition fluctuated wildly, "a great weight upon my spirits," she confided to her diary, as she worried about both "little Henry" and the man after whom he had been named, her husband and the child's father. This was, she wrote, "a sickly season, many taken down with fevers. May it please kind Providence to preserve my dearest husband."[21]

Many of those who supported the Revolution were now leaving the city in anticipation of the British army's arrival. On September 14, Elizabeth moved her sick son to a room at the front of the house so that his bedroom could be aired, and they watched from the window as a seemingly endless procession of wagons and carriages passed by. "It took of that solemn appearance that this day ought to wear," she wrote. The next day, she heard that patriots had taken down the church bells, that one of the bridges over the Schuylkill River had been "taken up," and that they had cut "the ropes across the ferry." When Elizabeth heard that several of her neighbors' horses had disappeared from their stables, she gave orders for their own horse and cow to be hidden in the washhouse. This turned out to be a prudent decision because that night their stable cellar was "broke open" and several barrels of flour were stolen. On September 19, one of the Drinkers' servants woke Elizabeth with the news that the British forces were now nearing the city and that the Continental Congress, along with the state's Executive Council, had "flown" during the night. Elizabeth now discovered that "almost all the town" had been awake since one o'clock in the morning, boats and carriages "going off all night." Elizabeth and her family had somehow slept through the mayhem. By evening, the town was "much thinned of its inhabitants," including "most of our warm people," as she called the more ardent patriots. The Continental Army set to work seizing horses, blankets, and other supplies before finally evacuating, though for whatever reason they did not call on her.[22]

And so the town waited, "very quiet and still." On September 25, "little Henry" got dressed for the first time since falling ill, though he still could not walk without help. News reached the Drinkers that patriots had put bundles of tarred sticks in several outhouses "with mischievous intent" to burn the city and so deprive the British of shelter and supplies, though steady rain seemed likely to foil that plan, "a remarkable favor," she wrote in her diary that night. There was no way of predicting what else the patriots would do before the enemy's arrival or how the British would treat the inhabitants once they entered the city, and Elizabeth's entries finally began to acknowledge her family's dependence on God's favor as the city itself became a battlefield in the war. She could only hope that her family would be "strengthened and supported in the time of trial." On the following day, the British troops finally arrived. Though rumored to number around twenty thousand, only three thousand came into the city, while a much greater number remained encamped just outside the city at Germantown. Elizabeth noted that those who took possession of Philadelphia entered the city "without opposition or interruption, no plundering on the one side or the other." She focused in her diary entry on the "satisfaction" this would have given to "our dear absent friends, could they but be informed of it." Sarah Fisher's response was more overtly spiritual, noting that the lack of violence that day "called for great humility and deep gratitude" to God, who had spared the city from bloodshed as it changed hands.[23]

The Journey to Virginia and Life in Exile

As the exiles made their way northwest on the first leg of their journey to Reading, two of them soon became sick, which Henry blamed in part on the long days of travel that their guards insisted were necessary. He and his companions were also unhappy because their luggage had not yet caught up with them, and several of the prisoners had no change of clothes, rendering them both indecorous and malodorous. Many soldiers in the Continental Army were at this stage of the war much worse off for clothing, ill fed, and generally uncared for; the same was true of many prisoners of war. Nonetheless, these particular prisoners were eager to retain their distinct character as gentlemen. They had already lost one visible badge of social status when their captors reneged on their promise to let them travel in their own carriages: if others were to treat them with the respect they felt they deserved despite this setback, they needed to look the part. Yet as Henry wrote in a letter to his wife, it was "with much difficulty" that they persuaded the two officers accompanying them to wait even one day for the two sick men to rest before pressing forward, "with or without the clothes and stores" that they hoped were not far behind them. Caldwell and Nesbitt were anxious to complete their assignment and return to Philadelphia before the British reached the city, but in a letter to Elizabeth, Henry described Caldwell as "an unfeeling and inflexible man," Nesbitt "less so." The journey proved in other respects relatively uneventful until they reached Reading, three days after leaving Philadelphia. Locals threw stones at them as they entered the town, and two Friends who tried to visit them on the day of their arrival were, in the words of Thomas Gilpin, another of the prisoners, "violently pushed away, struck and stoned," one of them "considerably bruised and hurt." Whether this hostility was rooted in anti-Quaker sentiment or a belief that the prisoners were really loyalists is unclear, but whatever its cause, the violent reception must have been unnerving.[24]

The prisoners stayed in Reading for a week, partly because of torrential rain and partly because finding wagons to carry the prisoners and their baggage, which had now caught up with them, again proved challenging (their original transportation was returning to Philadelphia along with the officers who had brought them this far). In letters to his family, Henry complained that their "crowded situation" in local lodgings made it difficult to find "calm and recollection" for writing. On one occasion, he had to abandon a letter halfway through because the six other men who slept in the room where he was writing wanted him to put out the candle so that they could go to sleep. At any time of day, the "almost constant passing and re-passing" of other prisoners made it very difficult to concentrate, though Henry appreciated the "pleasing intercourse, exchange of good offices, and kind attention to each other's situation" that characterized their little community. The prisoners did not have to rely solely on one another for company and support. Henry reported that once they settled into their temporary lodgings, their captors allowed local Quakers to visit them, now unscathed by locals. This provided "solid comfort" in the form of "company and conversation" as well as "provisions and necessaries." The prisoners began to hold their own informal meetings for worship. One evening, they "sat down together, and after a time of religious quiet found the owning and overflowing presence of the rich Rewarder to be with us and amongst us, so that several of us could say it was a time of melting favor, affording strength and comfort to our minds." Despite the hostility of many locals toward them, Henry continued to feel "a tranquil serenity" which he trusted was "the reward for an unreserved resignation."[25]

During this pause in their journey, the prisoners obtained writs of habeas corpus from a justice of the Pennsylvania Supreme Court, ordering the officers guarding the exiles to bring them before a local magistrate so that a hearing into the grounds for their arrest could take place. The state assembly reacted by passing an act that explicitly denied the prisoners this right, and the Executive Council sent an order for the exiles to remain in custody and proceed to their destination as soon as possible. On September 20, the prisoners left Reading under a new guard. The county sheriff had instructions to escort them for the remainder of their journey into Virginia, but they were now going to Winchester instead of Staunton as originally intended. Unbeknownst to the prisoners, Isaac Zane Jr., the influential owner of an iron forge not far from Winchester who was contributing heavily to the war effort, had persuaded the Board of War to change the exiles' destination. Zane's father was the Friend who had sustained serious injuries from a hostile mob when visiting the exiles soon after their arrival in Reading. Outraged by this incident, Zane Jr. determined to do what he could on the prisoners' behalf. The Society of Friends had disowned Zane Jr. in 1774 after he stood for election as a burgess and took an oath of office in direct violation of Quaker principles, but even though Zane no longer attended Quaker worship, he understood why others would want to do so. There was a Monthly Meeting close to Winchester, but not Staunton, and Zane lobbied for the change so that the prisoners would have access to a supportive Quaker community. Winchester was also less distant but still, Henry estimated, around a hundred and eighty miles from Reading. That second and much longer leg of their journey, which took them in a southwestward arc into Virginia, took nine days. Henry and his fellow travelers now held out little hope of communicating regularly with their families back home: regardless of which side secured Philadelphia, the other would most likely establish a siege, cutting off the city's inhabitants from the outside world. They could write, but when or whether the letters would arrive was quite another matter. "We feel much for our wives and families in our separation from them," Henry wrote to Elizabeth. "I believe it may be said that our company generally are more affected under a sense of the difficulties of your situation than our own."[26]

The prisoners reached Winchester on September 29. Henry wrote soon afterward to assure his wife that he was "blessed with health of body," and this was true, he added, for most of the exiles. All twenty men were living in one house, "as commodious as this town affords." Their landlord and his wife, whom they had to pay for their board and lodging, were "kindly disposed" and provided most of their needs. Henry assured Elizabeth that their treatment by those whom they met on their way to Winchester had been very different from their rough reception in Reading. He claimed that "every man of principle and humanity," including many who supported the patriot cause, condemned their banishment as "the most unparalleled tyranny." There were "here and there" individuals "willfully blind to the apparent injustice of our case," but it seemed to him that "many of the people" were now convinced that the new government was inflicting "great evils" in the name of "true liberty," which, he added, was "an excellent thing when rightly understood." Henry may have presented a deliberately rose-tinted view of the situation to reassure his wife, or perhaps he was trying to persuade himself that the tide had turned in the exiles' favor, but not all of his companions were so optimistic. James Pemberton told his family that the Winchester townsfolk were "much enraged at them and declared that they should not stay there long."[27]

Henry and his fellow exiles were not the only wartime detainees in Winchester. Some 450 prisoners of war arrived in mid-October, and 300 Hessian prisoners were also being kept nearby, making it "a busy spot," as Henry commented wryly, but he and his "little society" of exiles were thankfully "separated from the noise and stir" that these other prisoners created. Before long, the twenty exiles secured permission to receive visitors; they could also move freely around the neighborhood, visiting and dining with new acquaintances in the vicinity. This was, then, an extremely relaxed version of imprisonment, based on a gentlemen's agreement that the exiles would not try to escape. Yet separated from their families and friends, removed from the comforts of home, deprived of their usual occupations, reliant on the sporadic arrival of letters and messages for news about the fate of their loved ones back in Philadelphia, and uncertain of their own future, the exiles' day-to-day existence must have been both monotonous and anxiety-ridden. Some of the prisoners soon moved out of the house to take up residence in other homes nearby. Henry remained where he was, and despite the departures, he still found his living conditions cramped. On one occasion, he wrote to his wife "in a crowd and much jogged," on another "in a room where much conversation passes—the candle light bad—and the time short." Compared to the privations suffered by other prisoners of war, these were modest sufferings, but for a gentleman accustomed to comfort and some degree of privacy, they were ample grounds for complaint.[28]

Pennsylvania's Supreme Executive Council was still eager to evade responsibility for the prisoners' eventual fate, and a letter arrived from that body about seven weeks after the exiles' arrival in Winchester, informing them that since they were no longer in Pennsylvania they should send any petitions or statements of grievance to the equivalent body in Virginia. The exiles did so, describing their "arbitrary, lawless, and tyrannical" treatment, again demanding a hearing, and requesting release from confinement until that hearing could take place. They also sent another address to Congress. Henry wrote to Elizabeth that he doubted whether either petition would have any effect: Congress had no desire to acknowledge its own culpability, and those officials in Virginia who had agreed to receive and imprison them were now accessories in an illegal, unjust, and un-Christian act. Henry imagined what his more outspoken brother John might say on the occasion, rather ingeniously giving voice to his own anger without having to own it as entirely his own; he was, after all, committed to a spirit of resignation, and there was besides no way of knowing into whose hands his letters might fall. "Surely," he declared, "these are not the men to let the oppressed go free and loose the bonds of wickedness; have they not for many years been wantoning in blood, and holding in a severe, merciless captivity thousands of their fellow men, whose cases are deplorable beyond description, and bear no comparison with that of my suffering brother and his companions?" What could anyone expect from people with a history of enslaving their fellow men and who now enjoyed supreme power? "Can righteousness be expected from men so depraved and corrupt? Verily, nay, mounted as they are in senates and in council chambers, in the seat of judgment and on the necks of men groaning under their cruelty and oppression."[29]

For over two months, the exiles lived in relative peace with little reason to complain beyond their cramped living conditions and forced separation from their families and friends. However, the situation changed dramatically in the morning of December 8 when one of the prisoners, a physician named William Drewet Smith, rode out on his horse and failed to return. Smith had made his escape and set off for Philadelphia. Earlier that year, the patriots had arrested Smith on suspicion of high treason, and although they subsequently discharged him owing to insufficient proof, officials pressured Smith before his release into signing the oath of allegiance. Even though he had done so, that did not save him from rearrest and exile in Virginia, which Henry included "among the jargon of inconsistencies" to which "malice and cruelty" had led their "persecutors." Yet Drinker did not condone Smith's decision to make his escape: the doctor had apparently been present when the exiles agreed among themselves that no one would try to get away without first telling the others, and yet Smith had left without warning anyone, so far as Henry could tell. Henry promised his wife that he would not "sneak home in a private manner" but would instead await an opportunity to return "as openly and publicly as may be."[30]

The prisoners worried that Smith's escape would have repercussions for the rest of them, and another piece of news that arrived soon afterward deepened their sense of foreboding. Congress had received information that one of the Quaker exiles, Owen Jones Jr., had been negotiating with friends in Lancaster to exchange two Portuguese gold pieces for continental currency, allegedly at a very advantageous exchange rate. The Board of War accused Jones of trying to inflate continental currency and did not believe it a coincidence that the value of that currency in the Winchester area had declined since the exiles' arrival. Jones denied that this was his intention and claimed he was merely trying to acquire currency to pay for his expenses. Board members also accused the prisoners of sending letters without showing them to their guards. In response, it now gave orders for the prisoners' removal to Staunton, their original destination and about a hundred miles farther from Philadelphia. Jones would no longer have access to paper, pen, and ink; the other prisoners must promise in writing that they would not "directly or indirectly do or say anything tending to the prejudice of these states," or else they also could no longer correspond with the outside world. The prisoners protested in new petitions to Congress and Pennsylvania's Executive Council that they were not responsible for the currency's decline in value and that they had offered, when they first arrived in Winchester, to show their correspondence to the county lieutenant, an offer he turned down. That officer now agreed to delay their removal until Congress and the council considered their petitions.[31]

Yet both of those bodies continued to claim that the other should decide what to do with them, so the situation seemed likely to remain at an impasse. The Executive Council had recently acknowledged that it doubted whether their exile "had answered any good end" or that their continuation in Virginia was "likely to serve the public cause." While Henry and his companions waited anxiously to hear how Congress would react to this admission, the governor of Virginia sent a letter to the county lieutenant instructing him to comply with the Board of War's order and take the prisoners to Staunton. It was uncertain whether the lieutenant would immediately act on the governor's instructions or delay until news came from Congress. When Henry wrote to his wife in mid-January, he had no idea whether he would soon "be moving homewards" or instead traveling further away to Staunton for "further trial" of their "faith and patience." Later that same month, the prisoners heard that the Board of War had suspended its order for their removal until Congress responded to the exiles' latest petition. There was apparently no consensus among members of Congress over how to respond. Some took the view that the orders for removal of the prisoners to Staunton were "grounded on weak frivolous pretexts," that their original arrest had been "altogether wrong," and that their continued confinement was "an increase of that wrong." Others, however, insisted that the exiles were "dangerous men and unfit to be entrusted with liberty."[32]

At the end of January, as Henry sat down again to write to Elizabeth, his frustration was all too evident. According to the latest reports, the Executive Council back in Pennsylvania had informed its delegates to Congress that it wanted the exiles freed and allowed to return home, but it was still insisting that the exiles were prisoners of Congress and that therefore the order must come from that body. This was, as Henry pointed out, hardly consistent with "the several warrants and orders" that the council had issued. He wanted the members of that body to give orders for the prisoners' release and to acknowledge "openly and candidly" that they had "done us wrong." Surely it was only "a spirit of pride" that held them back from doing so. Yet even if the tide of opinion was really turning in favor of the exiles, there was no guarantee that either Congress or the Executive Council would finally take responsibility for the situation. Henry assured his wife that he was trying not to dwell on the injustices of their situation and so avoid that "indignation and resentment which our unregenerate part is so prone to." His efforts were clearly not entirely successful.[33]

"From the Little Window in Our Loft"

Even as Henry tried to contain his frustration and anxiety about his own future, he was well aware that his loved ones back in Philadelphia faced immediate danger. "Surrounded and accompanied as we believe you are by thousands of armed men," he declared in a letter to Elizabeth that November, "frequently tried by the din of war and the alarms which they occasion, were I to go about describing my anxious feelings for my wife, children, and near and dear friends left in my native city, words would fail me . . . I know not what to add but love abundant." In her letters to Henry, Elizabeth said little about the "din" of war, perhaps because she did not want to distress him, but her diary entries were not so reticent. Throughout that fall and winter, she interwove updates about her children's health and the growing challenge of securing supplies for her household with descriptions of the conflict raging in and around Philadelphia. Elizabeth's interest in the war focused on her husband's situation, the safety of her own household, the fate of other Friends in and around the city, and outrage at the cruelties inflicted by both sides in the conflict. Neither her diary entries nor her letters to Henry showed any interest in the political or military events of the day other than as they impinged on these concerns. Yet Elizabeth now found herself immersed in a larger and dangerous world. During the coming months, she would find the personal strength to defend her home against intruders and to join with Quaker sisters in demanding the return of their husbands, though she neither sought nor embraced these opportunities to assert herself.[34]

That home was one block away from the waterfront. The location had been very convenient for Henry as he moved back and forth between his home office, the firm's store, and the docks; but now the family found itself right on the edge of an aquatic battlefield. Neither the British nor the continental forces could maintain control of Philadelphia without also securing the Delaware River, which ran past the city, connected its wharfs to the coastline, and provided access farther inland. Elizabeth and her family could see the river, the

Jersey shore opposite, and the outskirts of Philadelphia "from the little window in our loft." On September 27, a few days before Henry reached Winchester, patriot vessels sailed up the river and opened fire on the city; the British had already set up a battery and so were ready for them: one of the American frigates lost its foremast in the ensuing exchange of fire and ran aground. Elizabeth wrote that night that she and her family had watched part of this battle unfold from the top of their house. Another house nearby was struck during the battle, though Elizabeth noted that it was "not much damaged." As far as she knew, no one had been "hurt on shore," but a cook onboard one of the ships "had his head shot off." The next day, news arrived that the American troops were building batteries on the shore of the Delaware facing their neighborhood. A few days later, she wrote that they had sent "several fire rafts" down the river "to annoy the fleet," but the rafts "ran on shore" instead. The Drinkers were watching a war unfold quite literally before their eyes.[35]

For several weeks, Elizabeth and her family watched and listened as the British and Americans fought for control of the batteries positioned on islands in the Delaware River. The British needed to secure these batteries and two forts south of the city, one on each side of the river, so that their vessels could travel up the river with supplies for their troops and the city's inhabitants. The Drinkers now heard "cannon firing almost every day," and on October 21, they watched as Hessian mercenaries crossed the river in flat-bottomed boats to attack American batteries. Late the following day and into the next, the British forces tried unsuccessfully to take Fort Mercer, located on the Jersey shore. The sound of gunfire "seemed to be incessant," Elizabeth wrote, and when one of the warships positioned on the river blew up, it "appeared to some like an earthquake." Several neighbors went to the top of the Drinkers' house with a telescope to get a clearer sense of what was happening and that night the family could see campfires on the Jersey shore. The British suffered heavy losses during these various maneuvers and Elizabeth wrote that those who identified with them were "very much affected" by their defeat, whereas "those on the other side [of] the question" were "flushed and in spirits." Though she had clearly welcomed the patriots' departure, Elizabeth gave no indication that she identified with either "side" in the ongoing conflict.[36]

A month later, the British finally secured the island batteries, and they spent the next few days, amid falling snow and freezing temperatures, removing the barricade that patriots had installed in the Delaware River to obstruct a British attack on the city. As the American forces evacuated Fort Mercer on November 20, they destroyed the fort along with several U.S. ships. The

Drinkers had "a fair sight of the blazing fleet" from their upper windows and ten-year-old William counted eight vessels on fire at the same time. "We heard the explosion of four of them when they blew up," Elizabeth wrote, "which shook our windows greatly." Elizabeth did not record her own or her children's reactions to the sights and sounds of that day, but one of their neighbors, seven-year-old Molly Pemberton, wrote to her father, who was in exile alongside Henry, "I was so frightened with the roaring of cannon [that] I did not know what to do. Mamma told me not to be frightened but to lay abed." The following morning, the British burned another U.S. ship in full view of the Drinkers' house. Her family watched again a few days later as the British fleet arrived, consisting of "two or three twenty-gun ships and a great number of smaller vessels." Elizabeth thought it "an agreeable sight to see the wharfs lined with shipping," which promised at least some alleviation of the shortages that had made life additionally challenging for the city's inhabitants during the blockade. Yet across the river, they could still see "fire and smoke," reminders of the recent devastation.[37]

While battle raged on the Delaware, Philadelphia was also under attack by land, and reports of military action circulated daily among the city's residents. "We hear abundance of news," wrote Elizabeth, "but know not what to depend on." It did seem clear that "the Americans" were getting close to Philadelphia, which made travel between the city and neighboring communities such as Germantown and Frankford increasingly perilous. People traveling in and out of the city frequently fell victim to the continental forces, which eagerly seized vehicles, horses, and potential recruits. Elizabeth noted that a neighbor who had borrowed a horse and cart from her brother-in-law Daniel Drinker returned with the unwelcome news that continental soldiers had taken both, along with the neighbor's son. When Elizabeth lent a horse to another neighbor who wanted to visit her home out at Frankford, two patriot soldiers appropriated "her chaise and our horse." This particular neighbor's country residence had recently been "broke open" and "plundered." Other families were also reporting damage to their country homes, while desperate soldiers on both sides of the conflict were helping themselves to the crops grown on those estates. That November the British set fire to several houses outside the city where continental troops had taken shelter, and Elizabeth heard that the British were thinking about burning "all the houses etc. within four miles of the city" because they "serve[d] for skulking places." Not surprisingly, many residents of those outlying communities now moved into the city, including Abel James and his family.[38]

Moving back and forth became increasingly perilous as both sides in the conflict rounded up anyone suspected of supporting the enemy. Patriot soldiers arrested the brother of one of Elizabeth's neighbors as he was bringing provisions into town and took him to Washington's camp, where, Elizabeth wrote, he was "to be tried for his life." She also heard that two women traveling to Frankford "were stopped by the American Light Horse, and might perhaps have been detained" but for the intervention of an officer, who "after some apologies suffered 'em to return." Another neighbor's son had been "taken up" by British soldiers near Germantown, was "confined as a spy," and had to write to Abel James asking him to intercede on his behalf. The British commander, General Howe, had appointed loyalist Joseph Galloway as chief civil officer and superintendent of police in the city; Abel now used his prior association with Galloway in the colonial assembly to advocate for neighbors and friends in distress. If the patriots recaptured Philadelphia at some point, the British decision to put so much trust in a man who had previously allied closely with leading Quakers might come back to haunt Friends in general, who would now be even more vulnerable to accusations of clandestine loyalism. In the short term, Galloway's position of authority would benefit those who had personal connections to him, but for others not so fortunate the outlook was grim. British officers moved through the streets "numbering the houses with chalk on the doors" to identify patriot dwellings, and several of the Drinkers' neighbors were "taken up and imprisoned" because of their sympathy with "the Americans." Elizabeth noted with dismay that the British army was behaving much as its patriot counterpart had when it controlled the city.[39]

As travel in and out of the city became increasingly dangerous, farmers from the surrounding countryside were unable or unwilling to bring their goods into town. As a result, food became harder to get and more expensive: "if things don't change ere long," Elizabeth wrote, "we shall be in poor plight." She wrote in early November that they had not been able to purchase any butter "for three or four weeks past" and that all they had was from their own cow, which gave them "about two pounds a week." Her family was, she recognized, fortunate to have a supply of their own. In mid-October, butter had been selling at seven shillings and sixpence per pound; by late November, it was fetching twelve shillings. Because wealthier families had barely enough to feed themselves, they were in no position to provide food for those less fortunate. Elizabeth mentioned making monetary contributions for relief of the poor, but food was difficult to get even if one had the money to buy it. The situation improved to some degree after ships could again reach the city, but Elizabeth noted on December 11 that one trading vessel had run into a wooden barricade with iron spikes installed in the river before the British occupation. One of the spikes "made a hole in her bottom," and a cargo worth forty thousand pounds sank to the bottom of the river. When goods did reach the city, most tradesmen would accept only gold or silver as payment as paper money had depreciated so dramatically. Elizabeth lost one precious opportunity to buy "flour, butter, etc." because the seller wanted "hard money" and she had none to give. Sarah Fisher was contemplating the sale of her "best Wilton carpet" to raise some cash.[40]

The shortage of food and other provisions also posed a challenge for the British soldiers stationed in the city. Elizabeth's hostility toward the patriots by no means made her an automatic friend to their opponents. A week after the British entered the city, Elizabeth admitted that she had "not yet exchanged a word with anyone of the newcomers." She and her sister felt less endangered now that the British were in charge, and they decided that it was safe to remove their horse and cow from their hiding place in the washhouse, reinstating them in the stable. Yet the British forces proved no more scrupulous than their patriot counterparts in helping themselves to whatever they needed. They took "a quantity of hay" belonging to neighbor Samuel Emlen, and Elizabeth heard that Hessian mercenaries in particular were "plundering at a great rate such things as wood, potatoes, turnips, etc." In late October, soldiers came to the Drinker house demanding blankets, just as representatives of the Continental Army had done when it controlled the city. Elizabeth was out, and Mary put them off with the excuse that the mistress was not at home. A few weeks later, another soldier came for the same purpose. This time Elizabeth was at home and refused, but "notwithstanding" he entered the house, "went upstairs, and took one." She appreciated that the soldier at least behaved "with seeming good nature," asking that she "excuse his borrowing it, as it was General Howes orders." Henry's situation seems to have given Elizabeth and Mary some degree of protection from British demands. On that same day, another young man came to the house on a mission "to seize horses, but understanding to whom ours belong, said if we had ever so many, not one of them should be touched." The soldier apparently assumed that any enemy of the patriots must be a friend of the British.[41]

With growing shortages came an increase in "thieving and plundering," so that Elizabeth feared it was "hardly safe to leave the door open a minute." Early that December she went to drink tea with "neighbor Howell," whose family had been robbed the night before of a bed from one of their chambers. They were lucky not to lose more: the thief, "being surprised, got off without the rest of the booty, which he had laid out of the drawers ready to take away." Two days later, she heard that someone had removed the fence around the house her family owned in Water Street, in all likelihood for use as firewood. Elizabeth seems to have assumed that the British troops would move to impose law and order in the city, but as the weeks passed by, she came to realize that the British were themselves becoming part of the problem. "We daily hear of enormities of one kind or other," she wrote, "being committed by those from whom we ought to find protection." In mid-December at around eleven o'clock at night, as Elizabeth and Mary were going to bed, they saw "two soldiers in the alley, standing by the fence." They went downstairs and out into the yard, where they asked their servant Harry Catter if "John and Tom were yet in bed," though there was no John or Tom in the house, to which he answered on cue in the affirmative. Mary told him to "untie the dog," and they returned indoors, hopeful that "contriving in this manner" would dissuade the soldiers from trying to enter the property. The soldiers seemed to have left, and so they retired for the night, thinking that the scare was over, but an hour later, "a great noise in the alley" awoke them. Elizabeth's sister, Mary, and the children "ran to the window and saw the baker next door running up the alley" partially dressed, "the rest of his family with him." The next morning they learned that robbers had taken some of their neighbors' clothes, perhaps the same two soldiers whom they had seen off. As the cannons roared and windows shook, as criminals and soldiers burgled and pillaged, Elizabeth, her family, and her neighbors became increasingly skittish. "I often feel afraid to go to bed," Elizabeth wrote. "Every noise now seems alarming that happens in the night."[42]

Unwanted Guests

Elizabeth clearly felt besieged, and burglary was not the only form of intrusion that she feared her household might have to face. One afternoon in early October, a British officer had called to ask if the Drinkers "could take in a sick or wounded captain." Elizabeth told him that since her husband was absent she would appreciate his seeking "some other convenient place." The officer "hoped no offense and departed." Wounded soldiers were flooding the city, and a few days later, her sister, Mary, went with William and two neighbors to visit makeshift hospitals at the playhouse, the statehouse, and one of the Presbyterian churches. Over the coming days, Elizabeth and Mary sent servants back and forth across town with "a jug of wine-whey and a tea-kettle of coffee for the wounded men." Yet feeling compassion for wounded soldiers was an entirely different proposition from having them live under their own roof. Another officer called at the house later that same month to ask if General Grant "could have quarters" there: "I told him as my husband was from me, and a number of young children round me, I should be glad to be excused." The response was as gracious as before: "He replied, as I desired it, it should be so."[43]

Yet this turned out to be only a temporary reprieve. On the evening of November 13, Elizabeth's brother-in-law John Drinker arrived with the news that soldiers had taken possession of the house belonging to Henry and Elizabeth in Water Street. John had paid them a visit, and the soldiers promised not to damage the building or its contents. A week later, a Hessian officer who was lodging next door announced that he wanted to keep his horse in the Drinkers' stable. Elizabeth refused, but the following morning the unnamed Hessian marched into the house and asked to speak with Harry, their servant, perhaps because he preferred to speak with a man, perhaps because he already knew that he and Harry could communicate in Dutch. Elizabeth called the Hessian into the parlor. He "either could not, or pretended he could not, understand English," she wrote that night, "but told Harry in Dutch that he must and would put his horse in our stable." Abel James kindly intervened. He went to see Joseph Galloway and then, armed with "a few lines" from Galloway, went next door and "had some talk" that Elizabeth hoped would "settle the matter."[44]

This unpleasantness was the prelude to a much more alarming incident. Sitting at her desk late at night a few days later, Elizabeth wrote that her family had been "very much affrighted." There followed an unusually detailed account of what had happened. Their servant Jenny had gone outside just before nine o'clock in the evening and found Ann Kelly, another of the Drinker servants, in the backyard with a strange man. Jenny came indoors and told Mary Sandwith, who immediately went outside and discovered a young officer there with Ann. Mary "held the candle up to his face and asked him who he was," to which he replied, "What's that to you?" The young man followed Ann and Elizabeth's sister back into the kitchen. At first, he claimed that he had come to their house in error, but he did not leave. One of Abel James's sons, Chalkley, a young man in his early twenties, who happened to be in the house, "came into the kitchen, and asked him what business he had there," whereupon the officer "damned him" and "shook his sword" at him. Chalkley "with great resolution" wrenched the sword out of his hand and grabbed him by the collar. Mary, who was evidently no shrinking violet, took the sword from Chalkley and locked it in a drawer. The soldier demanded his sword and declared that he would not leave without it. Elizabeth, who until this moment had merely observed the proceedings, presumably with growing horror, now sent for Joshua Howell, a Quaker merchant who lived nearby. When he arrived, the officer declared that he knew "we were peaceable people" and claimed that he had surrendered his sword "on that account, out of pure good nature." This was presumably to save face; according to Elizabeth, he had told Chalkley "he would be the death of him." Howell got the officer out to the front door and gave him his sword, expecting that he would leave, but the officer remained there swearing, so Howell went to fetch Abel James.

After Howell left, the soldier stood "swearing in the entry [hall] with the sword in his hand." Mary had already locked Chalkley in a "middle room," probably to stop him from taking on the intruder again. She and Elizabeth now locked themselves and the children in the parlor. The officer banged on the door, still swearing away and demanding that they admit him. Not surprisingly, the children were terrified by this "enraged, drunken man" (Elizabeth was convinced that he must be inebriated). After striding about the entry hall several times, demanding that they "let him in to drink a glass of wine," he left the house. After Joshua Howell returned with Abel James, "they had some talk with him" out in the street and he departed, or so they thought. Elizabeth had the front and back doors bolted, along with the gate to the backyard, but about ten minutes later Harry came out of the kitchen and said the officer was in there. He had apparently reentered the premises over the fence and Ann had let him back into the house. Elizabeth then locked the parlor door again and Harry ran off to fetch Joshua Howell a second time, but he did not arrive until after the intruder had again left the house, this time accompanied by Ann. It was well after midnight by the time that Elizabeth sat down to record these events in her diary, and she had "not yet recovered" from "the fright." Chalkley James and one of her nephews spent the night there just in case the man returned.[45]

Elizabeth was "in a flutter" throughout the next day. It turned out that they heard nothing from Ann or "her gallant" until a week later, when Ann came to the back of the house, got Harry's attention when he was out in the stable, and asked him to fetch "her buckles etc." The following day, the young woman came again while her mistress was out and asked Mary how much it would cost her to buy out the remainder of her contract with the Drinkers as an indentured servant. Mary apparently "told her she did not know" but added that the mistress of the house had talked of "putting her in the workhouse," to which Ann replied, "If you talk so, you shall neither have me nor the money." Mary told her to come back later in the day, but she did not reappear until two days later. Elizabeth was again not at home. Mary informed her that they would take twenty shillings as compensation for her remaining time. Some three weeks later, in late December, Mary met Ann by chance in the street and the young woman "promised to pay," though Elizabeth never recorded any such payment in her diary.[46]

Almost two months after the intrusion, Elizabeth happened to catch sight of the officer who had caused them such a fright and "stopped him as he was passing the door." When she greeted him, the young man claimed he was "in a hurry," but she bade him "stand still till a noisy wagon which was going by had passed." She then berated him as follows: "If thee has no sense of religion or virtue, I should think that what you soldiers call honor would have dictated to thee what was thy duty after thy behavior some time ago in this house." "Who, me?" he replied. "Yes, I know thee very well," Elizabeth continued. "I have as yet been careful of exposing thee, but if thee don't very soon pay me for my servant's time, as there is officers quartered among numbers of my acquaintance, I will tell all I meet with." The officer apparently "stuttered" and then said, "I haven't got thy servant." "I don't care who has her," she retorted. "It was thee that stole her." "Well," he replied, "if you'll come up to my quarters in town." Elizabeth had no intention of running around town soliciting for the money: "I told him if he did not bring the money or send it soon, he should hear further from me." "Well, well, well," the man said, "and away he went, seemingly confused." Elizabeth had shown that when necessary she could confront and attempt to shame even an armed soldier, but neither he nor Ann reappeared with the money she owed the Drinkers for the breach of her indenture.[47]

Elizabeth was quite aware that episodes such as this were occurring all over town and that, had Mary not disarmed the soldier and separated him from young Chalkley, it could have ended in bloodshed. When a soldier burst into the Catherall family's home, "drew his bayonet on Isaac [Catherall], and behaved very disorderly," one of those present sustained a serious wound. Incidents such as these cannot have reassured local families as they faced the prospect of having British soldiers quartered in their homes, and not surprisingly, some resisted. Yet this was risky: Elizabeth wrote in her entry for December 15 that two of her neighbors were "in trouble" because officers had visited them seeking accommodation and became angry when the householders refused them. Three days later, another British officer, Major John Cramond, came to the door of Elizabeth's house looking for "quarters for some officer of distinction." When she gave the same excuse as before, he tried to persuade her "that it was a necessary protection at these times" to have a soldier on the premises. He said that she "must consider of it" and that he would return "in a day or two." Elizabeth was thankful that Cramond had "behaved with much politeness" since she knew that some soldiers had been "very rude and impudent" when making such requests, but she feared she would eventually have to give way. That night, the family's dog, Watch, began barking violently "as if someone was in the alley" and "put [her] in a flutter," giving further credence to the young officer's comment about their need for "protection."[48]

The next day, Elizabeth's sister went to consult with neighbors who had also received requests to take in soldiers, hoping to discover what strategies they had used to evade the imposition. While she was away, Major Cramond returned and Elizabeth told him that she and her sister were confident the authorities would exempt them because they were "at present lone women." He replied that he doubted this would be the case, and it now transpired that he was actually seeking accommodation for himself. Cramond was Scottish and a member of the Royal Highland Regiment. He told Elizabeth that "a great number of the foreign troops were to be quartered in this neighborhood" and that he believed some of them might prove "troublesome." She then told him how frightened she had been by "the officer that thief-like stole my servant girl over the fence" and related many other incidents of "bad conduct" by British officers that she had heard about. That behavior did not incline her to take one into her own home, she said, but Elizabeth had apparently told Cramond during their previous conversation "what sort of a man would suit" if she had no choice but to take in a lodger. He now assured her that "some of those qualities were his" (including "early hours and little company"), adding that he knew Joseph Galloway and assuring her that very few of the officers would suit her as well. The major then departed, saying that he would return the next day once she had thought the matter over. Elizabeth wrote in her diary that night that she was "straightened how to act." Cramond seemed to be a "gentleman" and she might "be troubled with others much worse." Elizabeth was also aware that some of her neighbors had "looked out for officers of reputation (if any such there be) to come into their families by way of protection."[49]

That same evening Enoch Story, a loyalist who claimed to have connections with the British command in Philadelphia, paid Elizabeth and Mary a visit. He was confident that he could keep those women whose husbands were absent "clear of the military gentlemen," though he also told them that the British officers were "much chagrined" by their difficulty "in getting quarters" and their "cool reception." Elizabeth wrote in her diary that night that the British could "in great measure thank themselves" for such difficulties; after all, stories were circulating about the ways in which officers mistreated the families hosting them. The soldiers living at widow Mary Eddy's house had reportedly forbidden her to use her own front door, so that she and her children were obliged "to go up and down the alley." One of them had brought with him a woman who he claimed was his wife, though Mary Eddy did not believe they were in fact married. He apparently "insulted" his hostess and "behaved very abusive." Another officer who wanted to lodge at the home of Quaker merchant Owen Jones "drew his sword, used very abusive language, and had the front door split in pieces." Elizabeth knew that her own family had "come off as yet wonderfully well." Would she best ensure that their run of luck continued by resisting Cramond's demands or by giving way in the hope that he was as respectable as he seemed?[50]

Cramond turned out to be a persistent fellow. On December 20, he came to the Drinker house a third time "with the same story over again," and when Elizabeth "put him off as before," he said he would return yet again the next day. After he had departed, Mary went to consult with Abel James, who in turn went to see Enoch Story. Abel returned with discouraging news: it now seemed likely that they would have to take in one of the officers. That evening they heard that the British had promised Mary Pemberton an exemption, but only because she was "an ancient woman" and allowed Friends to hold meetings in her home while the Fourth Street meetinghouse was providing shelter for the poor, who had been displaced from the almshouse to make way for wounded soldiers. It was now clear to Elizabeth that her family would most likely have to give way. "We must trust in Providence," she declared, "on that and all other accounts." Henry would have welcomed this acknowledgment: she had rarely made such declarations in her letters to him, or up to that point in her diary. Despite her consultations with neighbors, friends, and relatives, Elizabeth evidently felt alone and helpless. Her husband would normally have made decisions like this, but now Elizabeth had to act in his place. At this moment of crisis, she did what Henry had been advocating since his arrest: she explicitly placed her fate in God's hands.[51]

Yet even if guided by God's hand, she had to make a decision. As Elizabeth pondered whether to accept Major Cramond as a houseguest, events unfolding throughout the city tipped her hand. The family's property in Water Street was not faring well in the hands of British soldiers. On December 23, news arrived that they were demolishing the shed there. Mary went over "and desired them to desist." The soldiers refused on grounds that it was "a rebel's house," but when Mary "assured 'em it was not," they promised to stop if she allowed them to take the main gate, which she did. Once Mary had returned home, she and

Elizabeth sent Harry and one of their neighbors over there with a wagon to bring back the remaining wood. The two men brought back a wagonload, but "soldiers and the children in the neighborhood were pulling down the rest as fast as they could." Meanwhile, the Continental Army had launched another attack on the city, and the patriots were reportedly confident they would soon retake Philadelphia. On December 27, one of several clockwork explosives that the patriots had hidden in the Delaware River blew up near a warship and destroyed a smaller vessel, suspicious noises in the middle of the night continued to awaken members of the Drinker household, and everyone's nerves were on edge. In the morning of December 29, Cramond came back to the house, and Elizabeth finally, reluctantly, agreed to let him move in.[52]

On the following day, Cramond took up residence with the Drinker family. Elizabeth recorded in her diary that he brought with him three servants, "two white men and one negro boy named Damon." One would sleep in the house, the other two boarding with a neighbor. He also had three Hessian soldiers "to wait on him as messengers," so that the family had, as Elizabeth wrote, "enough of such sort of company." Outside in the stable, their lodger kept "three horses, three cows, two sheep, and two turkeys, with several fowls." Cramond took over a considerable portion of the house. He slept at first in one of the bedrooms, but three weeks after his arrival he moved "from the blue chamber to the little front parlor." Elizabeth noted with evident resentment that he now had "the two front parlors, a chamber up two pair of stairs for his baggage, and the stable wholly to himself, besides the use of the kitchen." The house was extremely congested. Going into the kitchen one night, Elizabeth collided with "the Hessian stable boy" and hurt her face, her cheek "much swelled and painful." By the next morning, blood had "settled" around her eye, and it looked "very ugly."[53]

Overall, Elizabeth and her family established a civil coexistence with the major and his retinue, but there were several points of contention between them. Elizabeth's initial impression of her houseguest, now "one of our family," was that he seemed "a thoughtful sober young man," which was, as she wrote, "a great favor." He had supper with them a few times soon after he moved in and during the weeks that followed, they occasionally had tea or coffee together. Cramond was quite sociable, despite his earlier promise that he kept "little company." Soon after his arrival, he had five officers over for dinner and then went out for the evening, but returned home before ten o'clock. Several days later, he invited a dozen officers to dine there with him, but Elizabeth noted approvingly that "they made very little noise" and left at a decent hour. Her neighbors and friends were "much taken with our major," and she hoped he would "continue to deserve their good opinion." However, a few days later she was becoming less sanguine. "J.C. had eight to dine with him," she wrote. "I have not seen him today but *en passant;* he has not yet come home and it is near eleven o'clock; I shall soon be tired of such doings." By mid-February, she was "all out of patience" and "gave him some hints," after which he "behaved better." Elizabeth was not happy to have her house used for schemes of pleasure that were inconsistent with Quaker notions of propriety. One evening he hosted a concert there: she conceded that the gathering took place "with as much quietness and good order as the nature of the thing admitted of," yet she clearly did not approve.[54]

Cramond was hardly a rake, but nor was he the kind of young man whom the Drinkers would have wanted as a member of their household or as a potential influence on their children. Elizabeth noted in one entry that the major had just attended an opening night at the playhouse on South Street. British officers had attended theatrical performances in New York the previous winter, and now they wanted to repeat the experience in Philadelphia. They set about organizing a season of improvised productions performed on Monday evenings at the Southwark Theater on South Street. Knowing that Quakers disapproved of such entertainments, they sent the proceeds to various charities, a canny move that doubtless softened opposition. Elizabeth refrained from any editorial comment in her diary, merely recording the fact of Cramond's attendance at the playhouse. She made no mention of his engaging in flirtations, or worse, with women in their neighborhood. Some of the city's womenfolk had leapt with grateful enthusiasm into the social whirl of concerts, balls, assemblies, and theatrical performances that accompanied the British occupation. "You can have no idea of the life of continued amusement I live in," one young woman wrote to a friend in Maryland, "I can scarcely have a moment to myself." Some worthy souls disapproved of such frolics and their possible consequences: there were, as Sarah Fisher noted, "very bad accounts of the licentiousness of the English officers in deluding young girls." Yet Cramond seemed to be a respectable fellow; or at least he never gave Elizabeth reason to think otherwise.[55]

" 'Tis Best to Make a Virtue of Necessity"

In letters to Henry that fall and winter, Elizabeth said nothing about the drunken soldier's intrusion into their home, or indeed any of the other scares that she and her family endured in the months following her husband's removal. She did mention briefly in early December that ever since the arrival of the British troops she had not been able to prevent their servant Ann from loitering at "ye gate and front door" to ogle and flirt with comely young redcoats. Now, she wrote, the young woman had departed with one of them, but the drama that preceded her departure went unmentioned. She wrote not a single word about Major Cramond until December 31, 1777, the day after he finally came to live in the Drinker house, perhaps because she did not wish to worry her husband. Nor did she ask his advice, in all likelihood because letters took so long to make their way back and forth that events would have superseded any advice he did give by the time it arrived. She turned instead to relatives and friends who were better acquainted with the immediate situation. When Elizabeth did finally broach the subject, she was remarkably vague, stating only that their family was now "somewhat increased" and that she had "made many efforts to be excused," but was "led to believe 'tis best to make a virtue of necessity." Either Elizabeth thought that she had mentioned the situation previously, or she assumed that Henry was aware from other sources of the pressure on families to take in British officers and would therefore understand her oblique remarks. After reassuring Henry that she was finding the situation "much easier than [she] expected," Elizabeth moved on to other topics. When she wrote again the following day, she mentioned only in passing that their "new guest" was behaving himself "much like a gentleman."[56]

Elizabeth's husband did not receive these two letters until late January, and his response made it very clear that these were the first indications he had received that anything of the sort was likely to happen. Henry was predictably angry about this invasion of his household and Elizabeth's failure to provide more information about the new lodger: "It would have been satisfactory," he wrote, "to have known who and how many have intruded themselves into the habitation of a banished man." Not only was Henry unable to protect his family while living in exile in Virginia, but another man, a soldier no less, who fought for the British army that patriots suspected Quakers such as Henry of secretly aiding, had taken up residence as the one adult male figure in the household. No wonder he was displeased. Yet despite his irritation with Elizabeth for neglecting to keep him fully informed and his outrage at the intrusion of another man into his home, he was also sympathetic to his wife's plight. This was "indeed hard measure," he declared. "My prayer is for thee and myself." A few days later, he wrote again and this time asked a series of pointed questions. "Who is it that could urge to be received into my house, after a proper representation of the situation the master was in? How many of such intruders are there and what part of the house do they occupy? And do they demand food, firing, etc., as well as house room?" As always, his children figured prominently in his thoughts. Henry hoped that Elizabeth and Mary were keeping them well away from "the company and conversation" of their lodger and his staff: "Did I not believe a religious and watchful care was kept up in this matter, my distress of mind would be great."[57]

Meanwhile, Elizabeth had again reassured Henry in a further letter, written on January 25, that "ye addition to our family" had brought with it no "real inconvenience . . . unless we are inclined to make trifles such." They had, she wrote, been "remarkably favored on many accounts." At the end of February, Elizabeth finally gave her husband a more detailed account of the British officer's arrival in their house and the living arrangements that they had worked out together. She assured Henry that she had tried to prevent his coming to lodge with them and would have persisted in her refusal had several of their friends not advised her to take him in. He was, she explained, "as far as we can learn, of a good character," and the size of their house made it very unlikely that she would be granted an exemption, so that she might end up with "one or more in his place that would be more disagreeable." He had now been in the house for eight weeks and had proven to be "a sober young man." She assured Henry that the Hessian soldiers who served under him were "inoffensive" and "behave[d] with decorum." She stressed that the major did not let the Hessians or his servants stray beyond the front rooms and the kitchen into other parts of the house. Cramond provided his own wood, hay, and food. He ate in his own room but occasionally had tea with his hosts, which was "not easily avoided" since he was evidently "a gentleman and a man of sense." Elizabeth was clearly eager to depict the situation as near normal and described their contact with the major as "but neighbors' fare." He sometimes had "company in ye front parlor," but she and the children could "see or hear but little of them." As far as she could tell, these gatherings featured "neither swearing nor gaming," and her lodger "always" broke up the party at a timely hour (a very different story from the one she recorded in her diary). Henry asked no further questions and Elizabeth offered no further information. Both of them seemed to prefer that they devote their correspondence to more pressing subjects, and it is to those that we now turn.[58]

5 • "Inward and Outward Trials"

Surviving the Revolution

As 1778 began, there was no end in sight to Henry's exile in Virginia, and it was now four months since the revolutionary regime had arrested him. Quakers back in Philadelphia saw the prisoners as potential martyrs following in the footsteps of earlier Friends who had given their lives in defense of their principles. Hannah Griffitts, a Quaker poet who had been fiercely critical of British policy before the Revolution but maintained an antiwar stance throughout the armed conflict that followed, wrote movingly about the sufferings inflicted by the War for Independence. In a poem addressed to her "Worthy Banish'd Friends," Griffitts drew a parallel between their ordeal and that of Christ: it was "the Christian's lot," she wrote, to "wear his master's cross as well as crown." She also compared their experience to that of the Israelites in the desert: just as God had ultimately led his children to "the promised land," so she trusted that he would restore her friends to "their native shore." The comparison to Israel reaffirmed Quakers' claim to nationhood in their own right. For patriots who also liked to equate their struggle for independence from Britain with the departure of the Israelites from Egypt, it would have been mortifying to know that their new government and its treatment of Quakers was being compared to "Egypt's yoke," from which another Chosen People hoped to be rescued by a righteous God.[1]

Henry Drinker also sought to understand the persecution that Quakers faced as a spiritual journey, though he focused on the personal dimensions of that journey and not the grandiose historical parallels that Griffitts invoked. Henry sought to embrace suffering as a trial of his faith, telling his wife that he was "ready to cry out, as David did formerly, 'It was good for me that I was afflicted.'" He remained optimistic, or so he claimed, that "a day of light and serenity" would succeed "this dark, gloomy time," a day when "faithful testimony-bearers" would find themselves safe once again and "sing praises on the banks of deliverance." Henry described himself as mostly "free from painful apprehensions or deep anxiety" and credited this equanimity to his resignation in the face of affliction. That spirit of resignation was a crucial component of Quaker theology: it arose, Friends believed, from an inner act of will as the faithful pledged their trust in God's wisdom and protection. When Henry wrote to Elizabeth that he hoped they would both "be supported under the present trial, and manifest that religious firmness and fortitude which the occasion calls for," he captured neatly the combination of passive dependence and active courage that lay at the heart of their faith. They must recognize their reliance upon God and draw from that an inner strength that would show itself in unwavering loyalty to their principles. No matter how repressive the revolutionary regime became, Quakers would find true freedom within themselves through trust in God, liberated from dependence on worldly comfort and security.[2]

Yet Henry recognized that maintaining that state of mind in the face of extreme suffering was a formidable challenge. He admitted to Elizabeth and his friends back in Philadelphia that his "greatest anxiety" was that he might falter in that equanimity, "flinching in the day of battle." This was an interesting choice of words from a pacifist, who now adopted the language of war to describe a spiritual struggle in defense of peace. While other men asserted their masculinity in donning military uniforms and fighting for one side or the other, Henry fought a different battle, with its own risks and tribulations. Prolonged separation from his wife, children, relatives, and friends had proven to be a testing emotional ordeal for Henry: "Such a separation," he wrote, "as I am neither a callous nor an unfeeling man, has at times assaulted me powerfully." He had, moreover, good reason to be anxious about his "worldly affairs, which in all probability may be much affected by the ruinous desolations and destructive consequences which attend the present evil day." A few weeks after his arrest, Henry asked Elizabeth to pray that her husband might be "preserved and favored in stability" and "willingly sacrifice everything, be it ever so near, to the manifestations of duty." This did not mean, he assured her, that she and their children were less "near and dear" to him than before. "Such an inference," he wrote, "would be injurious to the tender feelings of my heart, where I often find you, my beloved connections, sharing and possessing my warmest affections." His awareness of their situation back in Philadelphia was "forcible and affecting." Yet he and they should rely on a much more formidable protector. "What could I do," he asked, "if present with them? Are they not in the hands of an almighty and merciful director?" When Henry's anxiety for his family's welfare (which he referred to as his "weak spot") threatened his equanimity, he turned his mind toward "the watch tower, the sure rock and refuge," where he found reassurance and the strength to carry on. "All is given up," he declared, "even my Betsey and our beloved children, to the protecting and directing providence of best wisdom."[3]

Elizabeth was far from certain that she could follow her husband's example. The arrival from day to day of wildly inconsistent reports, some encouraging and others quite the opposite, consigned the exiles' wives to a constant emotional seesaw between hope and despair. Fortunately, she wrote, she was by temperament less "sanguine" than others and so "less raised" by "what is called good news," which meant that she had less distance to fall when discouraging rumors reached her. Yet Elizabeth was not immune to the emotional swings tugging at her neighbors' heartstrings. One evening she felt "a gleam of hope" on hearing that the prisoners might be released but "knew not whether to give way to the pleasing sensations"; the following day that "gleam" dispersed as contrary rumors plunged her into "depression of spirits." Elizabeth understood that the solution to her inner turmoil lay in setting aside her resentment of the power that "unfeeling men" seemed to wield over her husband and the other exiles: "Why do I talk of power? Are we not all in ye hands of an all wise disposer, in whom I hope to trust?" Yet as the months passed by, Henry began to worry that her spirits might be failing. "Watch against it, my dear Betsy," he urged. "Remember the distressing effects despondency may work on thy weak frame." This mattered, he wrote, not only for her sake but also because their children depended on her in his absence as "director and guide." As Henry considered this additional burden now placed on his wife, he came close to breaking down under the weight of his own anxiety: "I can't go on—seek for best help and I trust it will not be withheld."[4]

Elizabeth faced multiple challenges in the absence of her husband. Most fundamentally, she loved him, depended on him, and longed for his return. The misery she had felt when left alone on many occasions during the first decade and a half of their marriage was itself a testimony to how much she needed and missed him. Now she faced a much longer separation and could not rely on his safe return: the patriots might put her husband on trial as a traitor to the new republic, and the punishment for treason would be death. Meanwhile, she had to protect their family and make decisions that ordinarily would have been under Henry's purview. She also had to decide whether she should join other female Friends in trying to secure the exiles' release from captivity and exile. The prisoners had been petitioning various official bodies ever since their arrest, and leading male Friends in Philadelphia had lobbied unsuccessfully on their behalf, but in early 1778, the exiles' wives began to consider whether they should also speak out.

One of the ways in which Friends stood out from most other eighteenth-century Americans was their insistence that women as much as men had the right and duty to share God's truth in public. Women could stand and speak during Quaker worship whenever they felt moved to do so; they also held separate Meetings that operated in parallel with Men's Meetings, though how much independent authority Women's Meetings had varied from one locality to another. Friends actively encouraged the formal education of girls as well as boys, and female Friends figured prominently among the preachers who traveled, often for months or even years at a time, to share the Quakers' spiritual message. This was wildly controversial in a world that generally denied women any formal authority or public voice, whether in a religious or civil setting. The notion that women could and should speak out on spiritual matters held sway among Quakers as a logical consequence of their belief in the spiritual equality of all humankind. When the exiles' wives decided that they would protest their husbands' treatment, they did so in defense of their religious principles, which Quakers saw as the right and responsibility of women as much as men. Yet it was far from clear that patriot officials would take them seriously or even agree to meet with them, especially in a political climate so explicitly hostile toward the Society of Friends.[5]

Moreover, the empowerment of female Quakers even within their own community had its limits. For women to become actively involved in a political controversy, albeit with weighty religious implications, was a dramatic step even for Friends. Though radical in some respects, Quakers were much more conventional when it came to women's roles in contexts other than religious discernment. Though Quaker wives and mothers had a strong spiritual voice within their homes, their husbands were otherwise firmly in control, and Henry Drinker was every inch the patriarch, albeit a loving and devoted one. Following Henry's arrest and exile, Elizabeth grew into her new role as temporary household head and showed considerable backbone when dealing with threats to her family. Yet the dramatic step that her neighbors now proposed to take was quite another matter. Elizabeth agreed to join these other Quaker women in challenging the revolutionary government with much trepidation and only after several weeks of internal struggle. Though contemporaries often depicted Quaker women in general as outspoken firebrands, not all women who identified as Friends fit that stereotype, and Elizabeth was disinclined temperamentally to become an activist in behalf of her faith. She was, however, fiercely committed to her family. That devotion to "my beloved . . . my dear Henry . . . my lover" and their children sustained her throughout her husband's exile and drove her, albeit reluctantly, to join the embassy of wives that set out from Philadelphia in April 1778 to demand the return of their menfolk. If Elizabeth became an activist during those months, she did so primarily and self-consciously as a wife and mother.[6]

"Tokens of Love"

In the dozens of letters that Elizabeth and Henry wrote to each other during his exile, they discussed a wide range of topics, but the principal thread that ran through their correspondence was a mutual and passionate devotion to their family. Throughout the past decade, Henry had felt "obliged to wade" through a "sea of politics," and that did not change during his months in Virginia, as he and his fellow exiles kept anxious watch on a political landscape that they could not control and that sooner or later would determine their fate. Yet Henry was even more concerned about the fate of his loved ones back in Philadelphia, and the close attention he paid to his own situation arose very clearly from a deeply felt desire to reunite with them. The concern he expressed as a husband and father was partly practical, partly spiritual, and unabashedly emotional. He wanted to hear anything and everything about "our precious children," and Elizabeth responded with detailed updates about their health, activities, and behavior. She also wanted him to know how much they missed and loved him, confiding that "the long absence of their father appear[ed] strange to our two little ones," who could not understand "why their dear Daddy should be taken forcibly from them." She made sure to mention in one letter that she was writing late in the evening and the children were already asleep, or else "their love would be renewed to their dear Daddy, as mine hourly is." Despite their physical separation, Henry felt "daily and hourly" that he was "closely united" to his "beloved wife and children." In one of his letters, he imagined the scene that was doubtless unfolding as he wrote "round the well-known fireplace" back in Philadelphia:

> Mammy a sewing and sister a knitting, our precious Sal perhaps suddenly looks off from her employment to impart some fresh thought about Daddy, her dear sister finds some inconsistency and gravely sets

> the matter forth in other way, William innocently shows he is not an unconcerned person by entering also into the prattle, while Henry shoots his bolt artless and unpremeditated and from pure nature perhaps hits the mark. If snuff yet remains within reach, Mammy and Aunty, after many pauses over the box, winds up the whole with, "Well, I wish it may be so, I don't know how it will be."

Henry then excused himself by pointing out that since he could not risk discussing "politics and news" in letters that might be opened by his captors, he must fill them instead with less consequential matter, but he was clearly meeting his own needs through this flight of fancy, transporting himself home to the fireside with his loving and beloved family.[7]

Henry was determined to carry out his paternal duties as best he could even in exile and repeatedly asked Elizabeth to provide him with "minutia" about their "chicks," especially "their conduct, now while separated and from under the eye of their father." This was "a subject very near [his] heart," and he wanted his children "frequently to think so." He was concerned that they not allow the chaos of war to distract them from their religious routine and that their general behavior not deteriorate in his absence. To preserve "harmony" at home, they must "carefully watch" over their "tempers" and avoid "bickerings," along with any "undutiful conduct" to their mother or aunt, which he warned would make them less "lovely and endearing" in his eyes. Henry stressed in his letters that he wanted their children to appreciate the larger spiritual meaning of what was happening around them and to grow as souls through their family's suffering. They should understand that the cause of their father's arrest and exile was his adherence to "good conscience," not "any evil he has done or is justly chargeable with." They should "ponder deeply and seriously" their father's situation, "held in bonds and captivity by unrighteous and evil-minded men." He also wanted them to know that many others were suffering as war raged around them, "widows mourning the loss of their husbands and children lamenting and weeping for their fathers, while famine and want [were] staring many in the face who [had formerly] lived in affluence and plenty." As they contemplated this state of affairs, they should be "humbled deeply" and reaffirmed in their "thirst after righteousness . . . striving to outdo each other in acts of kindness and benevolence." Above all, like their parents, they should focus on their need of "divine help," without which they could "do nothing."[8]

Elizabeth's "chief satisfaction" now lay in hearing from her husband, but she sometimes went for weeks on end without receiving any word. The prisoners in Virginia and their families back home had to rely on friends or strangers traveling back and forth across dangerous territory to deliver their letters, which sometimes spent weeks in transit. "Our continuing so long," wrote Henry, "without any letters or intelligence from you is the most disagreeable part of our situation." Both husband and wife described their "suspense" while waiting to hear from each other as downright "painful." They seized any opportunity to send letters but had no way of knowing when or even if they would arrive. They were well aware that the patriots might intercept and open their correspondence, hoping to find evidence that the exiles were in fact passing on information to the British via their families and friends. Both Henry and Elizabeth resented this lack of privacy and the need to be careful even when giving "a plain relation of facts," for fear that the patriots might misread it as treasonous. Henry told his wife that he felt "limited and cramped" when he sat down to write. Elizabeth added a caustic note at the end of one letter for their unwelcome audience: "If anyone has ye curiosity to open and read this letter, it will be kind to forward it, as there is nothing in it that concerns anyone but the parties from whom it came and to whom directed."[9]

Elizabeth had another concern, that her letters failed to "express the feelings of my heart," especially when a sudden opportunity to send a letter demanded that she write quickly. The absence of any advance notice was fine "for those whose sentiments flow easily from their pen," but "it is not ye case with me, as thee knows." Yet her words, though simple and succinct, were expressive. "Being separated from my dearest husband in this cruel manner," she wrote a few days later, "is an affliction which is not one hour, while awake, out of ye mind of thy E. Drinker." Both of them clung to the comfort provided by those elusive, self-censored letters, and when rumors reached Elizabeth in January that the prisoners might be "deprived of ye means of writing," she declared that this would be "a fresh instance of ye cruelty and hardness of heart of our unjust persecutors." Henry referred to his wife's letters as "tokens of love" and was clearly jealous of his fellow prisoners when they received letters and he did not, even though their letters sometimes contained news of his own household. (One from Hannah Pemberton asked her husband to tell "our kind neighbor HD" that she saw "the younger part of his family daily, and the rest very often.") Henry complained on one occasion that Elizabeth seemed to be less diligent as a correspondent than were his comrades' wives. She wrote back with a hint of pique that she had written "by every opportunity" that she knew of and that if he received fewer letters from her than some of his companions did from their wives, this was not due to "want of industry or inclination" on her part.[10]

Spoken messages passed back and forth by travelers could also serve as a welcome balm to sore hearts. When Quakers journeyed that fall from Virginia to gather in Philadelphia for the Yearly Meeting, despite the dangers involved, some of them determined to carry back words of love and comfort for the Friends in exile. Elizabeth told her husband that two widows who lived not far from Winchester and were currently in town had called on her and the children so "that in case they should see our dear HD," they could tell him "they had been to his house." Several Quakers returning to Winchester from the Yearly Meeting in Philadelphia did indeed visit Henry and his fellow prisoners to share news about their families. Henry wrote to Elizabeth that October that although he was impatient for "a paper messenger from my beloved Betsy," the news he had received from these Friends provided in the meantime "much comfort and true satisfaction." Back in Philadelphia, neighbors flooded in and out of the Drinker house with letters, secondhand reports, and often-dubious rumors. "Many flying reports of various kinds today," she wrote in one diary entry, "but we know not what to depend on." Even reliably good news could prove bittersweet: a letter from Thomas Fisher, written that October on behalf of the prisoners, brought their wives in Philadelphia an "agreeable account of their all being well," but Elizabeth confided to her diary that overall it gave more "pain" than "pleasure."[11]

Henry's exile separated him not only from his immediate family but also from a broader network of brothers and sisters in Christ. He ended one letter by asking his wife to "tell all my friends that I love them" and wrote in another, "I desire to remember and to be had in remembrance by them." Fortunately, he could draw strength from "the sympathizing, tender, attentive care" that the exiles in Winchester gave one another. He and his "beloved friend" John Pemberton sometimes "retired from other company" to talk quietly together, "comparing our respective feelings and inward situation under our present allotment." The prisoners gathered regularly for religious worship, sometimes in the company of neighbors, including "some not of our Society." According to Henry, these observers "expressed their wonder" at how closely Friends were "bound together as a family of love."[12] Elizabeth was also grateful for the company and support of good friends. "When some of us get together," she wrote, "ye load at times seems taken off, and we are cheerful, not that those whom most we love are for ye shortest time forgotten by us, but Providence is kind." At one of these gatherings at the Drinker home, Samuel Emlen "mentioned how many comfortable seasons he had had in this parlor," and Elizabeth evidently felt the same way, describing the occasion as "comfortable and edifying." Yet neither the support provided by friends nor the solace of occasional letters could remove the strain of separation. Elizabeth noted repeatedly how many weeks had passed since Henry's departure. "I daily count the time," she admitted. At the end of October, she noted that his absence of almost seven weeks was already the longest separation they had endured as a married couple: "The Lord only knows how much longer it is to be." Elizabeth vacillated between painful awareness of their separation and hopeful anticipation of their reunion. If only she could have her "dearest friend" at her side again, she could "reconcile all ye other troubles" she had "yet met with."[13]

Henry was concerned about the practical as well as spiritual well-being of his family and urged Elizabeth to spare no expense in her efforts to obtain "necessaries and conveniences" for the household. He had heard that there were serious shortages of food and other provisions in Philadelphia, so was anxious to know how they were getting what they needed "in the present time of difficulty." His wife responded that they were managing quite well, not least because he had left them plenty of money on hand. Fresh meat was available most days, albeit "at a high price." They had salted pork laid by for the winter, "with flour and wood enough to last us three or four months." She also made sure to tell him that they had set up "a large stove" in the back parlor, which was "warm and comfortable." As fall turned into winter, Elizabeth "thought often" of the relatively thin garments that her husband had taken with him on leaving home in September and sent him several packages of clothing that she hoped would keep him warm. These included a pair of mohair gloves that his daughter Ann had knitted for him, though whether they would reach him safely was anyone's guess. She urged Henry to abandon his custom of drinking mostly water and instead to take each day "a glass or two of good old Madeira" to sustain him through "this cold season." Elizabeth also fretted that there was no one to perform for her husband minor tasks that she normally fulfilled and explained to Henry in a postscript "the method to clean thy steel pipe." No matter what else he had to contend with, she wanted to ensure that Henry could at least have a relaxing smoke.[14]

"In a Very Dangerous Way"

Yet Elizabeth's main concern in the early months of 1778 was her husband's health. Henry wrote in mid-February that "for some time past" he had felt sharp pains in his chest, accompanied by headaches and "other indications that bleeding was needful." A physician, Dr. Thomas Parke, visiting the exiles from Philadelphia, had accordingly bled him, which left Henry "weak and faint for a while." The doctor soon afterward returned to Philadelphia and called at the Drinkers' home to deliver by hand Henry's letter. He reassured Elizabeth that her husband's illness had not been truly alarming and that the patient was probably now on the mend. Elizabeth had been worried that something of the sort might happen, given that Henry was "subject to such attacks in the spring of the year." She wrote urging him to avoid "walking too far under the weight of heavy clothing" in cold weather and warned that any such clothing "must be thrown off with the greatest caution."[15]

Much worse was to follow. Henry wrote in early March to tell Elizabeth that his recent illness and the other prisoners' "bodily indispositions" had paved the way for greater "trials and afflictions" that were truly "solemn and awful." He had decided to be "explicit and candid." One of the other prisoners, Thomas Gilpin, was dead. Gilpin had ailed for several weeks in a "feverish state," and although he briefly seemed to rally, he then became steadily worse and eventually succumbed. John Hunt was also "in a very dangerous way," and his companions feared that unless he turned a corner soon he would also die. Several of the other prisoners remained ill, though not in mortal danger. Henry had been afflicted with "a slow sluggish fever" and an "old complaint" in the "kidney and loins," which "lay heavy" on him for several days. Thankfully, a combination of tree bark, asafetida pills, and "tender care" from John Pemberton had "soon afforded some relief."[16]

Henry and three of his fellow exiles were currently waiting to move from their present lodgings to a house about five miles away. Given his state of health and the coldness of the season, this was hardly good timing. The eleven prisoners still living in the original house assigned to the exiles had recently been at loggerheads with their landlord, who was charging them several times as much as their fellow prisoners paid elsewhere in town and had "taken offense" at what Henry considered "some trifling matters." Their other housemates were also leaving, so the "company of exiles" would soon be "very much scattered about the country." Winter weather was causing prolonged delays in the conveyance of letters back and forth between Winchester and Philadelphia, which left Elizabeth in "much distressed" suspense about Henry's health. Dark rumors of illness and death among the exiles reached the city long before Henry's letter announcing Gilpin's demise and Hunt's precarious condition, which doubtless intensified her anxiety. "It is whispered here that one of your company is no more," she had written, "and that several others are unwell. Oh! How much I fear on account of my dearest Henry."[17]

While Elizabeth was still waiting for the letter in which Henry broke the news of Gilpin's death and his own continued illness, he wrote an update that would provide scant comfort once it reached its destination. Following their move to new lodgings, Henry's health had seemed much better. He thought he was strong enough for a ride and so went out in company with John Pemberton, but the "sharp" winter air was "too much" for him, and he suffered a relapse. The following day he was "worse every way," the swelling "greatly increased," his head "disordered" with fever, and "a pain pretty constant a little above my left groin." After several sleepless nights, the symptoms began to abate. Henry had learned his lesson and now promised to stay in his chamber until it seemed "quite safe and proper to leave it." Though most of Henry's companions were also "much mended," John Hunt was still in a bad way, and the doctors were "very dubious of his recovery." Henry's mood was increasingly despondent, despite his gradual recovery. Much as he wanted to write something "that might tend to sooth and comfort," he found himself "little capable of affording any," even though he knew that "as true help-meets to each other, the smallest well-meant endeavors should not be with-held." He told his wife that he lay awake at night with "moistened eyes," thinking of his family. "In short," he wrote, "I retain you near my heart."[18]

Meanwhile, the seemingly endless wrangling over which official body should take charge of the prisoners had finally been resolved. Thomas Wharton Jr., who was serving as president of Pennsylvania's Supreme Executive Council, had become increasingly worried that growing sympathy for the exiles might undermine support for the patriots and determined to settle the prisoners' fate one way or the other. He therefore proposed that the council assume responsibility for deciding what to do with them, and Congress readily acceded. The exiles had no reason to mourn this abdication of authority by Congress, which in February had offered to release them, but only if they took an oath of allegiance. "How insulting," wrote Henry. "Did they not make the same offer in Philadelphia, when we protested against that ensnaring proposition and their tyranny?" Yet the council was no more sympathetic to the exiles, and according to one report that reached Winchester, it was planning to put the prisoners on trial, though as Henry wrote to his wife, they had no reliable information. Henry could at least assure his wife that he was feeling much better and would soon be "ready to go abroad." John Hunt, however, was fading fast.[19]

When news reached Elizabeth and the other prisoners' families that Gilpin had died, it sent a shock wave through the Quaker community. Given that

Hunt was in danger of following Gilpin and that several other prisoners had been seriously ill, including Henry, the lapse of time between the writing of letters in Winchester and their arrival in Philadelphia became ever more nerve-racking. "The thought of what may have happened in the interim," Elizabeth wrote in her diary, "distresses me much." She told Henry that she had gone to visit Rachel Hunt, who was "much afflicted," but had not yet felt "capable" of visiting Lydia Gilpin, though she "hope[d] to do it soon." A few days later, news reached Philadelphia that John Hunt had also died. "It affected me much," Elizabeth admitted in her next letter to Henry. What little she could do for her own husband she set about arranging: she sent him an ounce of rhubarb for his bowels and some other medicinal supplies, but advised him not to "make too free with purges." Their friend Richard Waln "advised ye burning of a small quantity of gun-powder now and then in ye room of any sick person, provided there is a chimney in it," and Elizabeth reminded Henry that the "method" they had used the previous fall when little Henry was so ill, "burning and sprinkling vinegar," had been "of great service." She would have liked to send much more, but the friends who had agreed to take a package were traveling on horseback and could take nothing bulky. She did enclose some "good paper" to ensure that he could carry on writing. Soon afterward, she found someone else who could take some "very sharp vinegar," and a "large phial of thieves' vinegar to prevent infection," along with a small almanac and some clothes. In return, she requested a letter telling her of his "restoration to health," which would be "an inexpressible comfort."[20]

"Perhaps It Might Be in My Power to Do Something"

What Henry did not know, because Elizabeth deliberately neglected to tell him, was that over the past month or so she had been struggling with a new source of anxiety. Susannah Jones, whose son Owen was also in exile at Winchester, had told Elizabeth in early February that she planned to visit General George Washington, currently based at Valley Forge, to plead for her son's release. Susannah "hinted" that Elizabeth might go with her to petition for all their exiled menfolk. Elizabeth wrote in her diary that night, "My heart is full of some such thing, but I don't see the way clear yet." Several of the prisoners' wives were already thinking about visiting their husbands that spring if the authorities had still not released them. Doing so would involve crossing a war zone, and Sarah Fisher, one of the women considering this possibility, had confided to her diary, "Nothing but an ardent affection and strong desire to see my beloved husband could induce me to think of undertaking such a journey, which will be attended with great difficulty, if not danger." What Susannah proposed was even more audacious: it involved traveling to the Continental Army's headquarters and plunging into the political mess surrounding their husbands' continued imprisonment. Quaker women had a long history of speaking out forthrightly, often at great personal risk, but that did not necessarily make the prospect any less intimidating, especially in wartime. A few days later, Susannah's proposition was still weighing on Elizabeth's mind: "I have been much distressed at times when I have thought of my still being here, when perhaps it might be in my power to do something for my dear husband." When she spoke about the possibility to Mary Pleasants, daughter of exile Israel Pemberton, Mary showed Elizabeth a letter from her father suggesting that she and her mother, also named Mary, might venture "something of the kind." "I hope," wrote Elizabeth, "it will please the Lord to direct us to do that which is right." It would be "a trial on us to leave our young families at this time," but if it was God's will, they "should leave and trust in kind Providence."[21]

A month passed by before Elizabeth made further mention in her diary of the proposed mission. On March 14, she noted that Susannah Jones was now thinking of "going to Congress," which had settled for the time being in York, Pennsylvania, and presenting a petition to that body. News had not yet reached Philadelphia that Congress was ceding authority over the prisoners to Pennsylvania's Executive Council. Susannah again dropped "several broad hints" that Elizabeth should join her, though Elizabeth still refused to commit herself. On March 25, Phoebe Pemberton and Mary Pleasants came by to discuss "drawing up something to present" on the prisoners' behalf. Elizabeth had already suggested that her brother-in-law John Drinker might be "a suitable person" to help them write a petition, and she accompanied her two neighbors over to his home that evening. John "appeared rather reluctant," Elizabeth wrote in her diary, "but 'tis likely he will think of it." She added that the women intended to deliver the petition themselves, "two or four of us," though they did not yet share this information with John, for any such journey would be perilous: Friends currently visiting from the Jerseys, she noted, had heard that patriots were "lying in wait to take them up on their return."[22]

Several of the prisoners' wives now determined to act, though others like Elizabeth still held back. There was constant "talk" about the proposed journey among her friends, and the pressure to make a decision left her "much distressed." Elizabeth's uneasiness about leaving her family intensified when "little Henry" accidentally swallowed a pin. Over the next few days, drafts of a petition circulated among wives, sisters, daughters, and female cousins of the exiles. Elizabeth noted that they refused to approve an alternative draft penned by Nicholas Waln: the prisoners' wives had clear ideas as to what the petition should say and did not intend to defer to men who might think otherwise. In the afternoon of March 31, Elizabeth joined "the rest of the women concerned," along with several men, at Mary and Israel Pemberton's house. Nicholas Waln read aloud the address on which they had settled; they may perhaps have given him this honor to salve his wounded pride after having rejected his proposed draft. All of the women present then signed it. That evening they decided that Susannah Jones, Phoebe Pemberton, Mary Pleasants, and Elizabeth Drinker would deliver the document on their behalf. Elizabeth did not share with her diary what had made her agree to join the "embassy," but she was still ambivalent about going. "I wish I felt better both in body and mind for such an undertaking," she wrote in her diary.[23]

In the meantime, Elizabeth worried that the prisoners had "no medicines, wine, sugar, vinegar, nor many other necessary articles" and had talked with the other wives "about sending necessaries to our dear husbands." What with wartime shortages and separation from the supplies that their families back in Philadelphia would have gathered and hoarded as best they could, the prisoners' day-to-day lives must have been austere. Some of the items that Elizabeth considered "necessary" may have seemed luxurious to people of lesser means, but the prisoners were used to a relatively high standard of living, and as several of them fell ill, the dwindling of their medical supplies was potentially very serious. Their wives back home decided to send a separate emissary to Washington's headquarters, requesting permission "for a wagon to pass with stores for our dear friends." That envoy took with him a letter written by Mary Pemberton on behalf of "the suffering and afflicted parents, wives, and near connections of our beloved husbands, now in banishment." The letter made no mention of the embassy that the women had formed and that was currently preparing to leave Philadelphia.

On April 1, Elizabeth went in search of new shoes, presumably for the journey she was about to embark on. Her expedition was unsuccessful, but she had a much more serious obstacle to overcome in the form of her sister. Elizabeth wrote in her diary that Mary had "declined taking the weight of the family on her" during Elizabeth's absence. Ever since Henry's arrest the previous September, Mary had worked valiantly alongside Elizabeth in running their household and protecting it from various threats, but she apparently drew the line at taking charge singlehandedly of the children and household, which currently included Major Cramond and his servants, while Elizabeth disappeared into the countryside. Whether she refused because she felt unequal to the task or because she thought her sister was taking her for granted is unclear. This domestic crisis prevented Elizabeth from attending a meeting "to settle matters" for the journey, and when she did go to speak with Mary Pleasants the following day, Elizabeth still "had reason to think that it would be no easy matter to get off." However, she finally concluded that she must leave her "dear little ones" to "the care of kind Providence," and her sister. Elizabeth acknowledged that this would be "a great care" to Mary, but she had taken the decision out of her sister's hands and could only trust that she would be "strengthened" once she knew she had no choice but to shoulder the burden. Tragic news had stiffened Elizabeth's resolve: news of John Hunt's death had finally reached the city, and as two neighbors went over "to break the sorrowful news" to Rachel Hunt, Elizabeth now knew that she could not hold back. That evening Nicholas Waln came over with a revised version of the petition. (Mary Pemberton had made a "small addition on hearing of the death of our dear friend J.H.") Elizabeth signed it amid "a storm of thunder and lightning, wind and rain."[24]

The women now had to find horses and drivers for their journey. Choosing the right men to go with them was no easy task: they needed individuals able to protect them if they ran into trouble and yet who would let the women take charge once they reached their destination. When Israel Morris offered to take them, they agreed only on condition that he accept their terms. They wanted him to "escort us and advise when we asked" but were adamant that he should not appear with them before Congress, which he evidently wanted to do. Morris eventually "acquiesced," although Elizabeth had her doubts that he would refrain from putting himself forward as their spokesman: "I hope that his going with us," she wrote in her diary, "may turn out more satisfactory than it at present appears to me." On the following day, Elizabeth went to visit Rachel Hunt, who was "composed, though in great affliction." She then went to see Mary Pleasants, and they agreed to be "bed-fellows" during the journey. A letter arrived from Henry that "much disconcerted" her: he claimed he was "much better," but "from the appearance of his writing, he is very poorly yet." This was, she wrote, "a day of great hurry and commotion . . . What with this letter, the preparing for our journey, the impossibility of my sending him such things as is necessary for him, with the number of Friends that are calling constantly, my heart is afflicted and fluttered very much . . . may the Almighty favor our undertaking." On April 5, the day of their departure, after eating dinner with her family, Elizabeth headed over to Mary Pleasants's house, where a crowd had gathered to bid the four women farewell. Susannah Jones, Phoebe Pemberton, Mary Pleasants, and Elizabeth set off at about two o'clock that afternoon, along with "two negroes who rode postilion" and Israel Morris.[25]

"Through Deep Ruts and Mud"

The four women and their companions stayed that night at the home of a Quaker miller, John Roberts, about ten miles outside Philadelphia, "kindly entertained by the woman of the house and her daughters." The risk they were taking in embarking on this journey became abundantly clear that evening when about a hundred soldiers belonging to the Continental Army arrived at the property and two of their officers "came into the house, saying that they had heard there were ladies from Philadelphia." Elizabeth and her companions wondered nervously why the soldiers were taking an interest in them, but much to their relief all the men wanted was to know how far away the town was. They "behaved civilly, and stayed but a short time." When the women went to bed, the troops were still outside, which gave them "some apprehension" as to whether the carriage and horses would still be there in the morning, though as it turned out all remained safe and sound.[26]

The four ambassadors had decided to visit both Lancaster, where Pennsylvania's Executive Council was sitting, and York, to petition Congress, but to do so they would need passes, and so they proceeded first to General Washington's headquarters at Valley Forge. This was only about twenty miles northwest of Philadelphia, and the women reached the headquarters early the following afternoon. They immediately requested an audience and sat down to wait with several officers. Martha Washington, the general's wife, joined them and seemed to Elizabeth "a sociable pretty kind of woman." By coincidence, they were visiting Valley Forge on a day of celebration: Major General Charles Lee had just returned after spending fifteen months as a prisoner of war. Washington was greeting Lee as the women arrived and was doubtless in good spirits. In due course, the great man left Lee and came to meet the four Quaker emissaries. He "discoursed" with them but, according to Elizabeth, "not so long as we could have wished." Washington had already received Mary Pemberton's letter and the day before their arrival had written to Thomas Wharton Jr., president of Pennsylvania's Executive Council. Wharton was namesake cousin to one of the exiles, but there was tension between the two men and Wharton Jr. was also a former Friend, disowned for marrying a non-Quaker, so the exiles and their wives could hardly rely on him for support. Washington recognized that because the exiles were now officially prisoners of the state, he had no authority to grant Mary Pemberton's request, but he recommended that Wharton grant passage for the supplies, "as far as may be requisite and consistent with propriety." Washington told the four women that he would give them a pass to Lancaster but could do no more than that. Whether he informed them that the Executive Council and not Congress would now determine their husbands' fate is unclear. If so, they evidently still wanted to visit Congress, perhaps hoping that it would find their arguments persuasive and pressure the council to release the prisoners.[27]

Washington and his wife then invited the four Friends to join them for dinner with his general staff, a celebratory meal at which Lee was to be the guest of honor, and they accepted. Given the reason for their visit, the atmosphere must have been somewhat awkward, perhaps even tense. Yet Washington was by no means a complete stranger to the exiles: he had previously met and dined with most of them in the fall of 1774 when he visited Philadelphia as a delegate to the First Continental Congress. He and his wife may have felt obliged to show courtesy toward women whose dress and manner showed them to be of some social standing, even though they were Quakers. They may also have been impressed that their visitors had dared to undertake such a journey and wished to get to know these redoubtable characters. Though the stance that Quakers had adopted toward the War for Independence and the problems this posed for the patriots often frustrated Washington, he had the previous October invited six delegates from the Philadelphia Yearly Meeting who were visiting Valley Forge on a peace mission to dine with him; civility could sometimes trump political tension even in wartime. Once the meal ended, which Elizabeth described succinctly as "elegant" (making no mention of the musical entertainment that accompanied the merriment and toasts, which she would not have approved of), the four women left the room with Martha Washington and sat for a while in her chamber. They saw no more of General Washington, but unbeknown to Elizabeth, he sent another letter to Wharton, asking that he give permission for the women, who seemed "much distressed," to proceed onward to York. "Humanity pleads in their behalf," he wrote, referring most obviously to the women but perhaps also to their husbands.[28]

No matter how cordial their reception at Valley Forge, Elizabeth and her companions soon received a chilling reminder that they were members of a suspect group that under other circumstances might receive a very different kind of treatment. As they left the house where the Washingtons and their entourage were staying, carrying with them the pass to Lancaster that the general had promised them, they came across fellow Quakers Isaac Pennington and Charles Logan, whom patriots had arrested on their way from Philadelphia to Winchester with letters and parcels. The women vouched for their honorable intentions and so the men went free, but Elizabeth had a dark feeling that Pennington and Logan might not have fared so well had she and the other women not been there. The two men secured a pass of their own back to Philadelphia and left their letters and parcels with the four women.[29]

Elizabeth and her companions spent the next three days making their way "through deep ruts and mud," frequently having to walk because the carriage became so unstable. As they crossed a river, Elizabeth related in her diary, water "came into the carriage, wet our feet, and frightened more than one of us." They stayed each night with Friends who did their best to make the women comfortable. On April 9, they arrived at the home of James Webb, about one and a half miles outside Lancaster, where they planned to stay "for a short season." There they heard the dramatic news that the council had just issued an order for the surviving prisoners to be brought to Shippensburg and there released. A rising tide of outrage about the prisoners' treatment had forced the council to reconsider its plans for them. Elizabeth's relation of this news was curiously matter-of-fact, accompanied by no exclamation of joy or relief. She and the other wives had heard so many unfounded rumors over the past several months that perhaps she was unwilling to place much faith in this latest report. Late that afternoon, they dried and tidied themselves, "wiped out the coach," and proceeded into town. They went straight to the house of the council's president, Thomas Wharton Jr., with whom they talked for half an hour. In the privacy of her diary, Elizabeth described that meeting as "not very satisfactory," though in a letter that she wrote the next day to friends back in Philadelphia she conceded that Wharton had "treated [them] with politeness" and was quite accommodating. When Wharton confirmed that the prisoners were to go free, the four women asked if he could arrange for the exiles' conveyance to Lancaster instead of Shippensburg, and he agreed. Wharton also promised to send a pass for Rachel Hunt to General Washington, who would forward it to Philadelphia, so that she could visit her husband's grave. The women then drank coffee with Wharton's wife before returning to the Webbs' home after dark.[30]

It was not until the day after arriving in Lancaster that Elizabeth finally wrote and revealed her whereabouts to Henry. She acknowledged that it must seem "strange" to him that neither she nor anyone else had made any mention of the expedition until now. She explained that they had not wanted to worry their husbands and so had asked their friends and neighbors not to say anything, but now that they had "come so far well," she trusted in "kind Providence" for safe completion of their mission. She admitted that the roads had been atrocious, but they had "four good horses and two experienced drivers," so had reached their destination "with no accident." After giving her husband the good news that his release was imminent, Elizabeth wrote that she hoped his health would allow him to make the journey from Winchester to Lancaster without any delay. To be reunited with him as soon as possible was, she wrote, "the wish next my heart," though she wanted him to "run no risk in endeavoring it."[31]

Henry, in the meantime, had no idea that his exile was about to end or that his wife was anywhere other than in Philadelphia. He was now feeling well enough to attend the Quaker Meeting that met about five miles from his lodging; he was also planning an excursion to visit his fellow prisoners at their various lodgings, which would involve in all a journey of about thirty miles. Henry was reconciling himself to the prospect of continuing in Winchester for some time and so asked his wife to request permission from their Monthly Meeting in Philadelphia for him to attend regularly the Monthly Meeting that met nearby. He assured her that although the swelling in his side was "not quite reduced," he could now ride "without inconvenience." Henry noted gratefully that a package sent by Elizabeth containing medicinal rhubarb had arrived just as his own supply was running out. He acknowledged in that same letter that it must have been distressing for Elizabeth to receive news of Gilpin's and Hunt's deaths, then to remain "in a very painful suspense" about his own state of health. He had also been thinking about his sister-in-law: "I have had it on my mind to write to our dear sister, and to express the sense I have of her affectionate, tender, and singularly obliging conduct towards me and mine, not only manifested in this time of trial and difficulty." He hoped that his children would "ever retain (with their father) a due and grateful sense of their aunt's tender care of them." Henry had no idea that Mary was now looking after their children on her own or that Elizabeth had left her in charge against her own wishes.[32]

Back in Lancaster, Elizabeth and her companions were still eager to present their petition to the Executive Council. The council's decision to free the prisoners had voided the main objective of their expedition, but the four women wanted the council to receive them and their written objection to their husbands' arrest and exile. On April 10, they handed over the address to Timothy

Matlack, one of the council's members and its secretary. The four women were then kept waiting over an hour before being informed that there was no need for them to appear in person before that body. Matlack, a brewer by trade, was another former Friend, disowned for inattention to his debts. Matlack wished to prevent or at least delay any meeting between the visitors and the council, but not, it would seem, from any personal hostility toward the women or their husbands: he was concerned that they might upset the delicate political balance that had led to the order for the exiles' release. "The zeal and tenderness of these good women," he wrote in a private letter, "are so great that it is with some difficulty and strong persuasion [that] they are restrained from making further solicitation before the arrival of their husbands, which would in my opinion be unfavorable for them rather than advantageous." Several days passed before the women were finally able, on April 14, to meet with council members. "They appeared kind" and made "a show of favor," wrote Elizabeth, "but I fear 'tis from teeth outwards."[33]

While waiting for their audience with the council, the four women met with the officer who was to take charge of the prisoners on their journey from Winchester to Lancaster. They were eager to send with him supplies they had brought with them so that their husbands could make use of them on their journey. Their host's son, William Webb, agreed to set off for Winchester the next day with letters and packages for the prisoners. However, the authorities denied Webb the pass he needed to make the trip because he had refused to take the oath of allegiance, "a great balk to us," as Elizabeth wrote in her diary, "all things being ready and William booted to set off." They now consulted with Friends in the neighborhood and learned that a local Mennonite named John Musser who had taken the oath was willing to go instead. He was, wrote Elizabeth, "as suitable as any we could find," so they packed letters and parcels into his saddlebags and off he went. Once they had met with the council, the four women departed to visit various Friends while awaiting their husbands' arrival. On April 19, they returned to the Webbs', and on the following day received letters from their husbands, "giving us expectation that they would be with us here the latter end of this week." They read the letters "over and over," rejoicing that their separation was finally ending and that the weather had now become "fine, clear, [and] windy, such as will dry the roads."[34]

It was not until April 15, when John Musser arrived in Winchester, that Henry and his fellow prisoners received the welcome news of their imminent release and heard that four of their wives were in Lancaster. Henry decided that he could not make the journey from Winchester to Lancaster on horseback without risking another relapse and so accepted an offer from a cousin who lived nearby to let him use the family's wagon. Henry sent a letter forewarning Elizabeth that his travel plans would put him "a day or two" behind his companions as he did not want her to worry when he failed to arrive with them. Henry was frustrated that John Musser had so little information about the mission that Elizabeth had joined: "he neither knows when you came from home, the motives which induced you at this time to undertake the journey, whether you came directly up from Philadelphia, or when you reached Lancaster." It was, however, "singularly pleasing" to Henry that his wife had "surmounted all difficulties" and joined the expedition. Yet now it was Henry's turn to worry about her health as he had heard that Lancaster was a sickly place. He urged his wife to stay away from the town whenever possible and suggested that she drink vinegar as a protectant. Above all else, he looked forward to "embracing" his wife with "unbounded affection."[35]

The four wives were expecting that their husbands would be formally released once they arrived in Lancaster, but in a final twist the Executive Council now announced that when the prisoners arrived they would be sent on to Pottsgrove, in Philadelphia County, and there set at liberty; they gave no reason for the last-minute change. Elizabeth wrote to Mary on April 22 that this was "far from satisfactory" to her and the other three women. "But whether we shall be able to do anything more to our wishes," she wrote, "ye Lord only knows, in whom we trust, and hope for the best." In the meantime, Elizabeth hoped that her children were "giving as little trouble to their dear aunt in my absence as possible." The following day she wrote again, asking if her sister had found the pin that Henry had swallowed ("I have thought of it often"). Waiting now became more and more excruciating. "Where," asked Elizabeth late in the evening of April 23, "are our dear husbands this night?" The following morning they went into town and pressed members of the council, unsuccessfully, to change their minds about the prisoners' diversion to Pottsgrove. Yet that evening such disappointments faded into insignificance when Phoebe Pemberton's husband, James, and Mary Pleasants's husband, Samuel, finally arrived. Elizabeth already knew that her own husband would be traveling more slowly and therefore was "not so much disappointed" when he was not with them. They all "sat chattering together till after ten o'clock." Henry made his appearance the following day. When Elizabeth sat down to write a brief diary entry that evening, she admitted that she could not remember anything that had happened before around one o'clock that afternoon, when "my Henry arrived at James Webb's, just in time to dine with us." He seemed "much heartier" than she had anticipated, indeed "fat and well." There were no more words that night, at least not for her diary.[36]

All eighteen of the surviving prisoners were now in Lancaster. Two days after their arrival, they submitted a petition to the Executive Council, repeating the request made by Elizabeth and her companions that they be released immediately instead of having to wait until they reached Pottsgrove. The council refused to meet them or to grant their request. It also made sure in the discharge papers not to absolve the exiles of any accusations brought against them; those charges of treason had never been specific or detailed but had lurked as vague allegations and would continue to do so. Most of the prisoners left that same day, but the four women and their husbands spent one more night at the home of James and Susannah Webb. They finally departed on April 28, though without Henry Drinker and John Pemberton, who stayed behind to speak one last time with Matlack in a vain attempt to change the council's mind and then took a different road. "I did not see my HD until evening," Elizabeth reported to her diary, with just a hint of reproach. On the following day, they reached Pottsgrove. Israel Morris had veered off to Washington's headquarters that morning and returned with passes for all of them: they were now officially free to go home.[37]

They proceeded on their journey that afternoon, and after "being frequently stopped" along the way by soldiers "posted on the road in different places," they spent the night with the wife of John Roberts, in whose home Elizabeth and her companions had stayed overnight just after leaving Philadelphia three and a half weeks before. The atmosphere there must have been tense since the patriots now suspected Roberts of having conspired with the British to rescue the exiles on their way to Virginia; he had left to seek protection with the British army in Philadelphia. The following morning, the last day of April, the guests had "a sitting" after breakfast at which John Pemberton addressed them, in all likelihood giving thanks for their release and expressing their concern for Roberts. Elizabeth referred to their traveling party as a "family," recognizing the bonds of affection and mutual suffering that bound these couples closely together. They then set off on the final stage of their journey. The four couples were "welcomed by many before and on our entrance into the city, where we arrived about eleven o'clock, and found our dear families all well." At this point, on April 30, 1778, Elizabeth paused briefly, as she had in several entries during her journey, to acknowledge a higher power: "for which favor and blessing," she wrote, "and the restoration of my dear husband, may I ever be thankful."[38]

"Fine Liberty"

The Drinkers had so many visitors over the coming few days that Elizabeth wrote it was impossible for her "to enumerate them" or "to particularize." There must have been much relief and rejoicing within their community of relatives and friends, but at the same time practical matters demanded their attention. A few days after her return, Elizabeth spent most of the day at various shops in the city, replenishing her supplies and buying some "Marseilles quilting" to make petticoats for her daughters. A week after their homecoming, Samuel and Mary Pleasants came over in the evening so that the two couples could at least "partly settle" what they had spent on their homeward journey and who owed what to whom. Not surprisingly, Henry's eight-month ordeal had taken its toll on him, physically and otherwise. He was suffering from "disordered bowels" and a fortnight after his return "was let blood." Yet he had survived, and Elizabeth would have been reminded of that blessing as she spent time with the widows of Thomas Gilpin and John Hunt. "Poor Lydia Gilpin," she wrote, was "under great affliction."[39]

Over the coming weeks, Henry recovered his strength and resumed his activities in and around the city. He and his former partner had shut down their import and export business, so Henry no longer spent his days overseeing cargoes as they came in and out of the city, consulting with fellow merchants in Philadelphia about shifting trading conditions, and responding to a steady flow of correspondence from trading associates on either side of the Atlantic. Back in 1773, Henry had become part owner of an ironworks at Atsion in New Jersey, and he did continue to play an active role in the management of that enterprise. Once the British abandoned Philadelphia a few months after Henry's return, traveling in and out of the city became much less dangerous. Elizabeth's lists of visitors to the Drinker home often included "people from the ironworks," and Henry made several trips out to Atsion, a journey of just over forty miles from Philadelphia, sometimes staying there for several days. The Drinkers were friends with the Saltar family, who co-owned and managed the ironworks, so that Henry's trips to the site served more than one purpose. Elizabeth accompanied Henry on two of these visits to spend time with Dorothy Saltar, who was dying of a "sore breast" (most likely cancer). Back in Philadelphia, Henry still owned and operated a store in the city's commercial district, though it now sold mostly iron products from Atsion. Business must have been good: Elizabeth noted in January 1782 that Henry had taken on three apprentices to work at the store. Yet iron was vulnerable to appropriation by the authorities, not least for use by the Continental Army; Elizabeth noted in one diary entry that some of their stock had been "seized for a tax." In addition to the ironworks, Henry owned and visited a sawmill at Maurice River (a tributary of Delaware Bay in New Jersey). These enterprises, along with income from rental properties, helped to support the Drinker family, though his partnership with Abel James had been so profitable that money was not a major concern.[40]

Business was no longer Henry's main occupation. He now devoted his time to sustaining morale among fellow Quakers as they faced the prospect of further persecution and to defending those who came under attack. During his exile in Virginia, Henry had drawn comfort from spiritual companionship, informal worship with fellow exiles, and attendance at local Meetings, but now he could resume and intensify his work as a leading Friend in Philadelphia. Henry was still clerk of the Northern District Monthly Meeting, and four weeks after he arrived back in Philadelphia, a Friend came by the Drinkers' home to deliver back into his hands the book in which successive clerks recorded the Monthly Meeting minutes. Patriot officials had confiscated that volume from Henry's desk on the day before his arrest, so its return must have been especially meaningful. During the coming months, Henry was often out of the house, which was nothing new, but whereas before the war he had spent much of that time taking care of mercantile business, now he was busy attending committee meetings and "visiting families" with other Friends. Friends routinely organized home visits to provide support in times of trial and to admonish those who were disregarding Quaker rules for conduct, but these visits took on new significance in a time of war and persecution. Sometimes they turned into "sittings" at which those present sat in silence (often "for some considerable time," as Elizabeth noted in her diary) until someone felt moved to offer a spiritual homily. Whether Henry spoke in that capacity is unclear, but others did so at the Drinker home. On one occasion, Elizabeth noted that a Friend spoke specifically "to the children." On another, several "Men Friends" who had spent the afternoon with Henry "on business" then stayed on for "a meeting in our parlor" at which two of them "had something to say to us."[41]

Henry was clearly in demand as a prominent Friend. He joined delegations that went to petition officials on behalf of Quakers accused of various offenses, visited imprisoned Friends, and spent time with their families. He was often away for several days as he traveled to Meetings outside the city or accompanied other Friends on the first leg of a journey to visit brethren in neighboring states; in 1779, he was absent for six weeks on a pastoral visit to Virginia with Quaker minister Samuel Emlen. Closer to home, when a consignment of goods that several Quaker merchants had ordered during his exile arrived at the waterfront, Elizabeth noted that he spent the next few days "busily employed on committees to settle properly this cargo of provisions." The city's population was still feeling the impact of wartime shortages, and these committees were probably working to ensure that the cargo's distribution did as much good as possible. Divisions within the Quaker community also claimed Henry's attention. Not all Friends agreed with their community's official position of neutrality, and this had led to a serious breach as some of them took up arms with the patriots. These renegades followed most Quaker principles other than the peace testimony, but their Monthly Meetings disowned most of them, and they responded by forming a separate Society, calling themselves Free Quakers. Henry now took part in negotiations with the disowned brethren, who wanted use of a meetinghouse for worship and access to the Friends' burial ground. In addition, he performed what may have seemed refreshingly mundane duties such as overseeing weddings and procuring a new cow for his family when they sent off the two old ones to fatten at pasture. Henry could now resume regular contact with neighbors and correspond with friends and relatives outside the city, a welcome return to some semblance of normality, though transatlantic communication remained impossible because of the ongoing war. There were also residual frustrations left over from his recent exile, including the disappearance of the trunk that had contained his clothes and other personal effects. When a wagon containing the prisoners' luggage reached Philadelphia, Henry's trunk was missing, and subsequent enquiries were fruitless.[42]

Henry's efforts to provide spiritual leadership extended even to the furnishings that adorned his home and the message they sent to visitors. He and his wife had accumulated an impressive collection of finely crafted furniture, but as he explained to a friend in late 1779, he now believed these trappings of wealth to be "inconsistent with ancient simplicity." In "this time of confusion and calamity," it was especially important for "real" Christians to keep themselves "unspotted from the world" as an example to those around them and to express their own "practical conformity" to God's will. He worried in particular that the luxurious surroundings in which his family lived might exert a bad influence on his children. That May, he read at a Northern District Meeting a public letter that Friends in Dublin had sent out the previous year, lamenting the worldliness and vanity of many who professed to be conscientious members of their Society. Determined to set an example, Henry accordingly tried to rid his own home of its "finery," but he "found it best to move gently forward to obtain the desired acquiescence and concurrence at home, so that my consort might appear united with me." Elizabeth was apparently not fully on board with this purge of their possessions, and they ended up storing in a spare room articles that they had not yet agreed to dispose of entirely.[43]

As well as setting an example of "ancient simplicity" for his children and other Friends, Henry may also have wanted to hide some of their belongings and so save them from appropriation by patriot officials once they retook Philadelphia. In a series of bitter diary entries, Elizabeth recorded the frequent plundering of their home by patriots collecting furniture and other possessions as payment for various new taxes and fines, many of which targeted conscientious objectors. The proceeds from sale of these articles would then support the war effort. On June 15, 1779, an agent of the government had come to collect the nonassociation fine levied on those who refused to serve in the militia. He took "a looking-glass worth between forty and fifty shillings, six new fashioned pewter plates, and a three quart pewter basin, little or nothing the worse for wear." A fortnight later, two other men came "to take an account of our property in order to lay the continental tax." Collectors subsequently took away with them in a cart "one walnut dining table, one mahogany tea table, six handsome walnut chairs, [with] open backs, crow feet, and a shell on the back and on each knee, a mahogany framed sconce looking glass, and two large pewter dishes." The Drinkers were fortunate in that they had more than one furnished home and so could restock their main residence on Front Street from their summer home at Frankford. Nonetheless, the government's constant demands continued to deplete the Drinkers' possessions throughout the remainder of the war. When a visiting Friend declared at a Meeting in Philadelphia that Pennsylvania, "once the flower of America," was now "a den of thieves," Elizabeth and Henry would doubtless have agreed.[44]

Elizabeth took her gentility very seriously, resisted her husband's efforts to purge their home of its more expensive trappings, and resented the patriots' seizure of their furniture to support the war effort. Yet she made a clear distinction between the restrained elegance that she tried to embody and the outbreak of shameless extravagance that accompanied the British occupation. On May 18, just a few weeks after her return to Philadelphia with Henry, officers in the British army organized a day of celebration in honor of General William Howe, who was about to leave the city and hand over the British command to General Henry Clinton. Not only did they spend a small fortune on the so-called Meschianza (after the Italian word for medley or assortment), but many Philadelphia ladies decked themselves out in showy outfits for the occasion, much to the disgust of those who considered such flamboyance problematic at any time but especially under the present circumstances. The hairdressers who had established themselves in town since the arrival of the British, advertising their ability to reproduce the latest fashions in London, now busied themselves providing local women with towering headdresses for this carefully coiffed, costumed, and choreographed occasion. Elizabeth roundly condemned "the scenes of folly and vanity" that would, she predicted, be "remembered by many" as a day of shame and disgrace. She described in uncharacteristic detail the "parade of coaches" through the streets to the Delaware, where "great numbers of the officers and several dozen women embarked in three galleys and a number of boats." They sailed down the river past the city with British flags flying, accompanied by "a large band of music" and a cannon salute. Once back on land, the officers and women made their way to a large property "decorated and fitted for this occasion in an expensive way for this company to feast, drink, and revel." After nightfall there was a display of "sky-rockets and other fireworks" over the river. Elizabeth would have condemned the extravagance and faux-aristocratic pretension of the daylong spectacle even if it had not occurred in the midst of death, misery, and privation, but the insensitivity of those who planned and participated in the parade to the circumstances in which it took place shocked her. "How insensible do these people appear," she lamented, "while our land is so greatly desolated, and death and sore destruction has overtaken and impends over so many."[45]

It was unclear at this point whether the British intended to stay in Philadelphia, and if so for how long. This would have a significant impact on the Drinkers' day-to-day domestic life since they were still hosting Major Cramond. Elizabeth's diary made no mention of her husband's first encounter with Cramond following their return from Virginia or of any conversation that she and her husband may have had on the subject. How long Cramond would remain their guest was uncertain. There were, she wrote in mid-May, "some movements in the army, which we do not rightly understand." A week later, they heard that the British officers, including their houseguest, had received orders to pack in preparation for departure, and over the next few days the Drinkers watched and listened to frantic activity on the docks nearby as the officers' luggage was loaded onto ships. Cramond told the Drinkers that he and his fellow officers had no idea when they were leaving, let alone what their superior officers were planning. The British command had, in fact, received instructions to evacuate Philadelphia and return to New York, but junior officers had either not yet been told of this or were under orders to keep quiet about the orders.[46]

Elizabeth noted that many Philadelphians were "in much affliction" as they faced the prospect of a British withdrawal, some because they had declared themselves loyalists during the British occupation, others because they had taken a position of neutrality and would again become vulnerable to accusations of disloyalty, perhaps even treason, once the patriots resumed control of the city. Though she did not say so explicitly, the latter group included her own family. The suspense ended on June 8, when orders went out for immediate evacuation and Cramond busied himself "sending the remainder of his things on board." He was not the only person leaving the Drinker home. Harry Catter, one of their servants, had agreed to become a wagon driver for the British army. "I wish," Elizabeth wrote, "the poor fellow may come to no harm." Cramond had supper with the Drinkers that evening and then went to bed; he was to leave at one o'clock in the morning, and Elizabeth decided to stay up until he had gone. When he departed, she and her sister stood at the door to watch the troops as they marched out of the city: "J.C. bid us adieu as they went by—and we saw no more of them."[47]

Elizabeth could now take back the part of her house that the young Scotsman had occupied for more than five months. One of his servants, Christopher, was still with them, waiting to accompany another part of the army with his master's horses. Elizabeth wrote "a few lines" for the major that Christopher agreed to take with him. It was six months before they heard any news of their former houseguest. They received a letter from him in December and then another almost two and a half years later, in April 1781. That September, Elizabeth noted in her diary that a third letter had arrived from New York, telling them that "John Cramond, a young officer who had lived six months with us while the British troops were in this city, and behaved so in our family as to gain our esteem," had died after a short illness. He had been an unwelcome guest, a uniformed military presence in their pacifist household, and yet not so disruptive a presence as she had feared when he first arrived at her front door and proposed himself as a lodger. The young man had won the "esteem," however grudging, of Elizabeth and her sister. What Henry thought of him remains a mystery.[48]

Over the coming few days, the Drinkers also parted with those of their neighbors and friends who had decided to leave with the British rather than brave the return of the Continental Army. During the British occupation, many patriots had found themselves under arrest, much of their property either seized or destroyed. Now the tables were about to be turned, and several thousand people who either identified with the British or feared they would be labeled as Tories fled the city. By the morning of June 18, Elizabeth wrote that there was "not one redcoat to be seen in town." No sooner had the British left but the continental forces reentered the city. They "had drawn swords in their hands" and "galloped about the streets in a great hurry," so it was hardly surprising that "many were much frightened." That evening an order circulated instructing the inhabitants to stay indoors after dark, warning "that if any were found in the street by the patrol, they should be punished." Her diary entry for June 19 began with a blunt and laconic statement: "The English have in reality left us, and the other party took possession."[49]

Elizabeth watched alongside the rest of her family and their friends as that "other party" proceeded to reimpose its will on the city's inhabitants. All shops and stores had to close temporarily and to "render an account of their goods," to prevent the removal or sale of any British articles that remained in the city. Because farmers coming into town to sell their produce could no longer buy goods with the money they received, consumers like Elizabeth worried that they would stop coming and so create a food shortage. The shops reopened a week later, but it was, Elizabeth reported, "very difficult to get anything." At the end of June, she had a nasty scare when a young patriot soldier, apparently "disordered in his senses," wandered into their house and went upstairs, where their servant Jenny was lying in bed unwell. Henry was out and there was at that moment "no man in the house," but one of their neighbors came in to lend a hand and found the intruder on the upstairs landing, "saying his prayers." The young man came back down with their neighbor and departed without any unpleasantness, but the incident must have reminded Elizabeth of the more violent intrusion that she and Mary had faced the previous November. Congress also returned to Philadelphia amid much patriot exultation, with "firing of cannon on the occasion," and there was "a great fuss," she wrote, on Independence Day, with "firing of guns, sky rockets, etc." Candles were currently "too scarce and too dear" for a citywide illumination such as had taken place the previous year. Elizabeth pointed out that the shortage "perhaps saved some of our windows," as the Drinkers would again have refused to participate and patriots might well have retaliated by again vandalizing Quaker homes. That same day, she noted, patriot soldiers led "a number of prisoners" into the city, a chilling sight for someone whose husband had left the city under guard the previous fall.[50]

With the return of patriot rule came the resumption of persecution and violence against those considered hostile to Independence, including conscientious objectors who refused to join the Continental Army or to pay taxes in support of the war. Sarah Fisher had predicted that the patriots would, if given the chance, ride roughshod over the rights they claimed to represent and become "a tyrannical government," led by "weak and wicked men." Both Sarah Fisher and Elizabeth Drinker must have been painfully aware that their husbands' return from exile by no means guaranteed future immunity. As a friend of the Drinkers warned, "ye may have to pass through a more trying dispensation than hitherto you have experienced." Over the coming months, Elizabeth would compile a grim catalog of Friends who came under attack. On July 14, their neighbor William Fisher appeared before the Executive Council, accused of "saying something inimical" to the revolutionary cause, and had to give security for his good behavior. A month later, Quaker Joseph Yerkes received a summons because he had failed to comply with a new law requiring all schoolmasters to take the oath of allegiance. The magistrate hearing his case gave orders for Yerkes's school to close. The Drinkers' son William had been a pupil there, but Yerkes was now unemployed and the children were without a teacher. "Sad doings," Elizabeth wrote. Others seemed likely to suffer a much worse fate. On August 1, Elizabeth noted that the authorities had arrested and imprisoned fellow Quaker Abraham Carlisle; he had taken a job issuing passes in and out of the city while the British were in control, and the patriots were now accusing him as a traitor, the penalty for which was death. There were occasional signs that those in charge might be susceptible to pleas for mercy. On August 11, Henry accompanied two other Friends to see General Benedict Arnold on behalf of several prisoners whom the authorities subsequently released; but three days later, Elizabeth noted that "one George Spangler was executed . . . for some assistance he had given to the British army," adding that he "left a wife and several children."[51]

That summer, patriot anger focused mainly on people who had actively collaborated with the British during their occupation of Philadelphia rather than those who claimed to be neutral. Elizabeth wrote in late July that officials had taken an inventory of property in the city belonging to Joseph Galloway (chief civil officer and superintendent of police in Philadelphia during the British occupation), Quaker Samuel Shoemaker (a former mayor of the city who had served as a magistrate under Galloway), "and several others." Earlier in the year, the Pennsylvania assembly had declared that Galloway and Shoemaker must either surrender and stand trial as traitors or face forfeiture of their estates. Both men left with the British in early June, but their wives stayed behind in Philadelphia to protect their property; they and their husbands apparently hoped that the families of those fleeing the city would remain unmolested. Yet the patriots now turned Grace Galloway and Rebecca Shoemaker out of their homes. Though Quakers were eager to differentiate their own position from that of loyalists, Friends such as Elizabeth sympathized with these loyalist women, at least partly from basic human compassion but also perhaps because they were well aware that some patriots saw Quakers as clandestine loyalists and might treat them the same way. When the day of Galloway's removal arrived on August 20, she refused to open the door, and so confiscation agents had to break into the house, forcing the kitchen door with a scrubbing brush lying in the backyard. She refused to leave and clung to the doorpost as the agents dragged her outside. Shoemaker's eviction took place on August 24, and Elizabeth went to visit her the day before her expulsion. On the day itself, Mary Pleasants escorted Rebecca to a relative's home, where she would stay for the time being with her three children.[52]

When Mary Pleasants went over to the Drinkers' home and told Elizabeth about Rebecca's eviction, she also shared another ominous piece of news. Officers had just been at her house and had taken away six mahogany chairs as a fine for the refusal of her husband, Samuel, to serve in the patriot army, a reminder that Quaker pacifists were still targets and might once again become a focus of the regime's enmity. A month later, Henry Drinker received his own summons to serve in the militia: he was to appear "with his arms and accoutrements" or pay a fine. Monetary penalties were not in themselves a major headache for the Drinkers, and their friends could survive without their mahogany chairs, but Henry Drinker and Samuel Pleasants had already suffered much worse for their principles, both having been among those arrested and exiled as suspected enemies of the state. Their families must have wondered what was coming next.[53]

Meanwhile, a wave of illness swept through the city and the Drinker household. Henry was again suffering from "disordered bowels," Sally from "vomiting and flux," Billy from "bloody stools," and Elizabeth herself "with a headache and vomiting and pained bowels." Elizabeth became so exhausted from having to stay up at night with her sick children that she eventually asked a neighbor to come and "sit up" with them so that she could get some sleep. Several of their neighbors had recently died of "the flux," so she was understandably worried. Elizabeth noted that August that her little son Billy "carried, or helped to carry, [former exile] Miers Fisher's child to the Burying

Ground . . . the first time of his officiating in that manner." Three weeks later, he assisted at the funeral of another child. That same month, one-year-old Joshua Howell died of the smallpox, and the Drinkers hosted a gathering after the funeral. Elizabeth noted that these children had at least been "taken in the natural way," which was more than could be said of Philadelphians who had already died in the war or would be "taken" during the coming months, either in battle or at the hands of the revolutionary authorities.[54]

Those who had left with the British rather than risk staying in Philadelphia under patriot rule now seemed remarkably prescient, and on September 6, Quaker minister Martha Harris predicted that "a very trying time was near at hand." A few weeks later, on September 25, Abraham Carlisle's treason trial began, and a jury found him guilty the next day. "It is hoped by many," Elizabeth wrote in her diary that night, "that he will not suffer what some others fear he will." Elizabeth's sister had already visited Carlisle's wife, Ann, but now Elizabeth went herself. On the last day of September, Carlisle's lawyers challenged the indictment on grounds that it was too vague to be legally supportable. Carlisle had sent for Henry a few days before, and he may well have been involved in the decision to appeal. The patriots had also arrested John Roberts, the Quaker miller in whose house Elizabeth and her fellow ambassadors had stayed. That same day, his trial began, and he was found guilty a few days later. Though Roberts also challenged his verdict, the court sentenced him and Carlisle to death. "Shocking doings!" wrote Elizabeth. Henry was among those who visited Roberts and Carlisle over the coming weeks. In the meantime, another prisoner charged with treason went on trial, though he was acquitted. Yet another was "taken up and put into jail for writing something they find fault with."[55]

Carlisle and Roberts were both due to die by the hanging noose on November 4. A week beforehand, Elizabeth accompanied her husband and several other Friends to visit the two men's wives, who had gone to speak with patriot officials and ask for mercy. Several petitions were also circulating the neighborhood. " 'Tis hoped and believed that their lives will be spared," wrote Elizabeth; "it would be terrible indeed should it happen otherwise." On November 3, Elizabeth was still hopeful, but the following day her diary entry read as follows:

> They have actually put to death, hanged on the commons, John Roberts and Abraham Carlisle this morning, or about noon. An awful solemn day it has been. I went this evening with my HD to neighbor Carlisle's. The body is brought home and laid out—looks placid and serene—no

> marks of agony or distortion. The poor afflicted widows are wonderfully upheld and supported under their very great trial. They have many sympathizing Friends.

As she sat with her grieving neighbors, Elizabeth must have remembered facing the prospect of widowhood herself earlier that year as her husband languished in exile and the authorities vacillated over whether the prisoners would face trial. Henry left town the next day to attend John Roberts's burial service in Merion, Pennsylvania. During his absence, Elizabeth and four of her children went to Carlisle's funeral in the city. It was "a solemn time," she wrote. "Our back parlor was filled this afternoon with company who came to the burial of our neighbor." Under these circumstances, it is hardly surprising that when two of Elizabeth's neighbors invited her to go with them a month later "to see G. Washington's wife" at "a grand entertainment" held in her honor, Elizabeth refused to go. She had met Martha Washington previously that spring when she and her fellow travelers petitioned General Washington on their husbands' behalf and they had met with polite treatment, but now that mission was over and Elizabeth had no intention of paying court to a woman so closely linked to a regime with blood on its hands.[56]

During the War for Independence, the revolutionary government accused at least 638 Pennsylvanians of high treason, of whom 43 went to trial; the patriots executed 7 of them, and 121 of those arrested lost their property. Two of the 7 executed were Quakers (Abraham Carlisle and John Roberts); of the remainder, 2 were tried and executed (Ralph Morden and George Spangler); 2 executed without trial (Hugh Jones and David Dawson); and 1 accused of treason but executed for burglary (Abijah Wright). Taken as a whole, this might seem quite restrained, especially when compared with the wholesale slaughter that took place in revolutionary France during the 1790s. However, potential targets in cities like Philadelphia did not know how many would end up dead, and for those who did lose loved ones, this relatively low death toll would have offered little consolation. Elizabeth took some comfort in the internal divisions that preoccupied "the men in power," surmising that their "differing much among themselves" was "one reason" why many "peaceable people" were "left quiet." Yet as the weeks passed by, more and more of the Drinkers' neighbors and friends came under attack. In March 1779, the patriots arrested former exile Samuel Fisher and tried him for allegedly passing on information to the British, an ominous sign that they had not given up on finding specific charges to bring against the returned men. "The jury," Elizabeth reported, "brought in verdicts to clear him twice, but being sent out a third time, they returned with an opposed verdict—fine liberty." The court spared Fisher's life but demanded that he forfeit half his estate and shut him up in prison for safekeeping. When he finally came home in July 1781, Elizabeth noted that he had been there two years and two days.[57]

During the years before Independence, Henry had been vulnerable both as a critic of violent protest and because of his ill-advised decision to become a tea agent. Now it seemed that his association with mercantile interests might again imperil their family. As food shortages and high prices took a heavy toll on the city's inhabitants, allegations began to circulate that merchants were exploiting the situation to line their pockets. In May 1779, Elizabeth wrote that many who belonged to the trading community were "apprehensive of a mob" that was to gather a few days hence "with a view of discovering monopolizers." On May 24, "threatening handbills" were "pasted at the [street] corners," a meeting at the statehouse was announced for the next day, and a muster of "a thousand or fifteen hundred men of the militia" took place. "A storm seems to be gathering," Elizabeth wrote, "happy for them that are prepared to meet it." At the public meeting, two committees formed to investigate the pricing and hoarding of goods, though with no authorization from the state government, and citizens were encouraged to seize anyone "inimical to the interests and independence of the United States." Afterward, men armed with clubs went to a number of stores and forced the owners to lower their prices. Over the next few days, another wave of arrests took place. One apprentice ended up in prison, Elizabeth reported, "for laughing as the regulators passed by." Henry was currently absent from the city on a trip to Virginia, and this was a mixed blessing for Elizabeth: on the one hand, he was safe from the "mob" in Philadelphia, but on the other, she could not be sure he was safe elsewhere. More than three weeks passed without any news of him.[58]

The Executive Council moved quickly to control the situation, releasing those against whom there seemed insufficient evidence to justify arrest and allowing others to post bail. Yet not surprisingly, people were very frightened. Toward the end of May, with Henry still in Virginia, two men arrived at the Drinkers' front door and announced that they had come to see what goods were stored in their house, citing as "their authority the populace." The men went ahead and searched the house, though Elizabeth conceded that they were at least civil. At first, she feared that the "inspectors" were singling out her family for investigation, but she later found out that they had searched most of the houses in her neighborhood. Several homes had also been "alarmed in the night by a mob." In early June, the hoarding committee summoned one of Elizabeth's brothers-in-law, John Drinker; Henry finally returned in mid-June. At the end of July, the committee on price fixing again included John on a list of those against whom the committee claimed to have incriminating evidence, and on August 30, the Drinkers found "an advertisement" affixed to their own front door, "mischievous and ridiculous in its kind, with a view to inflame the people." They now worried that Henry might also receive a summons.[59]

Just over a month later, on October 4, as John Drinker was leaving a religious gathering, a crowd consisting mostly of militiamen seized him and put him under arrest. Patriots had posted a broadside the night before, naming several men whose actions made them liable to removal from the city by force and exile, including John Drinker. According to Elizabeth's account of the day's events, the militiamen then allowed her brother-in-law to go home and have dinner with his family, a rather quaint gesture of respect and civility in the midst of a bitter and potentially violent situation. Afterward, however, they led him and several other men through the streets, "with the drum after 'em, beating the Rogues March." When they reached the home of lawyer James Wilson, who had defended several individuals accused of treason, the militiamen stopped with the intention of arresting him as well, but as Elizabeth put it, they "met with opposition." Wilson and several others had hastily barricaded themselves inside his house, and shortly afterward Joseph Reed, currently president of the Executive Council, arrived on the scene with a contingent from the city's Troop of Light Horse, determined to prevent the militiamen from taking the law into their own hands. In the street battle that ensued, several died and many more sustained wounds. The troopers arrested twenty-seven militiamen, rescued their prisoners, including John Drinker, and took them to the Old Jail, supposedly for their own safety. That evening, Henry and his family had "a sitting" in their parlor. One of their neighbors, as Elizabeth put it, spoke "in a very affectionate manner" and gave "good advice to the children." When she sat down later that night to record the day's events, the Light Horse was "patrolling the streets." Henry went to visit his brother the next day but could not get permission to see him until the day after that. The militiamen had allies in the state assembly, and a few days later Elizabeth heard that the assembly was planning "to send off all the disaffected" at their request, but John's family and friends refused to stand by and watch a repetition of what had happened to Henry and others two years before. On October 13, Elizabeth wrote that a group of Quakers had visited Joseph Reed on John's behalf and secured his release that afternoon.[60]

The Drinkers and their neighbors also faced the renewed prospect of having uniformed men placed in their homes. Just as the British authorities billeted soldiers in local households during its occupation of the city, so the Continental Army had done the same before surrendering Philadelphia and now resumed the practice; Elizabeth noted that most of the households targeted by patriots again belonged to Quakers. Not only patriot troops but also their European allies needed to find housing. In early 1781, two French officers came to her door "requiring decent quarters" for a lieutenant and his servant. They "behaved very respectfully," but when her husband refused, they replied, "They could not lie in the street, and would call again the next day." Those particular men did not reappear, and the lieutenant in question took up residence with a neighboring family, where he "behave[d] well." A few days later, the Drinkers received another similar request, and they again refused. Elizabeth acknowledged that the officers were having great difficulty finding quarters in the city, but she had no desire to share her house with another soldier. Nor did she want members of the patriot government as neighbors. When the family that had lived next door moved away in July 1781 and the Drinkers heard that a member of Congress was to move in, she wrote she was "not pleased with the change."[61]

More worrisome was the continued harassment of Quakers and merchants suspected of behavior contrary to the public interest. In August 1780, the *Pennsylvania Packet* published an article that once again accused Friends of active hostility to the new government and reprinted the letter that Major General John Sullivan had written to Congress in 1777, alleging that Quakers had provided the British with information about the Continental Army's movements. It was this allegation that had led to Henry's arrest and exile. A month later, the authorities imprisoned several merchants for trading with British-controlled New York. Elizabeth noted in her diary that a committee charged with addressing the depreciation of continental currency had established an official exchange rate for paying debts owed in British sterling and "appointed men to go round the city to the inhabitants with a paper to sign to the above effect." Anyone who refused to do so would be "held up to the populace as enemies to their country." The mood among the city's patriots that fall was not forgiving. In October, the *Pennsylvania Gazette* published an account of a plot by American General Benedict Arnold to help the British take a fort at West Point, New York. The plot was discovered and although Arnold escaped, the British officer to whom Arnold had given the fort plans, Major John André, was captured and hanged. Elizabeth described in detail the parade of Arnold's effigy through the city streets, accompanied by "several hundred men and boys with candles in their hands," many of them officers and infantrymen armed with guns and bayonets. They then burned the effigy. More executions followed, and two Quaker schoolmasters who refused to take the oath of loyalty spent several months in prison before their release in March 1781. They at least escaped with their lives.[62]

When news reached Philadelphia of the British surrender at Yorktown, many Quakers again refused to take part in citywide celebrations by lighting candles in their windows. This prompted another wave of abuse and vandalism. On October 24, Elizabeth wrote, "a mob assembled about seven o'clock or before, and continued their insults until near ten to those whose houses were not illuminated; scarcely one Friend's house escaped." Quaker Anna Rawle, a young woman in her early twenties, was living at the time with her grandmother on Arch Street. She wrote in her diary that a mob surrounded their house that night and started to break shutters and windowpanes. The terrified women took refuge in their backyard; two neighbors climbed over the fence, "called to us not to be frightened, and fixed lights up at the windows." This "pacified the mob, and after three huzzas they moved off." Anna recognized that her ordeal that evening was "slight compared to many others," especially those who stood firm. Elizabeth Drinker recorded that her home "had near seventy panes of glass broken, the sash lights and two panels of the front parlor broke in pieces, [and] the door cracked and violently burst open, when they threw stones into the house for some time but did not enter." Although clearly shaken, Elizabeth also acknowledged that it could have been worse. John Drinker was badly beaten, and the mob all but demolished the contents of some homes. "Many women and children," she added, "were frightened into fits, and 'tis a mercy no lives were lost."[63]

The widespread vandalism of October 24 was not the last scare that the Drinkers had to endure as the war wound down. Three months later, Elizabeth reported in her diary that two men came to the house when Henry happened to be absent, "with an order to search our house for British goods, which they accordingly did, examining drawers, trunks, and closets, presses, etc." They were almost finished with their search when Henry returned and demanded to see their order. It turned out that it referred to Henry's nephew and namesake, son of John Drinker, so that their house had been "rummaged by the mistake of the sheriff." Elizabeth's husband, doubtless outraged by this latest of many intrusions into his home, ordered them to leave. This mistake, Elizabeth commented wryly, would have given their nephew "time to hide his goods, if he had any," but the inspectors did not proceed to that other Henry's dwelling. Elizabeth "suppose[d]" they were "ashamed of the mistake they had made, as well they might, and afraid too." Elizabeth saw the incident as another indication of the new regime's character: " 'tis a bad government," she wrote, "under which we are liable to have our houses searched and everything laid open to ignorant fellows, perhaps thieves." In an outburst of pique, Elizabeth added that "HD, had he been so disposed, could have made them pay for their mistake."[64]

"Repairing of the Breaches in the Walls of Zion"

Elizabeth's claim that Henry could have held these officials accountable for their error was highly dubious, and in any case, her husband had continued to cultivate that same spirit of resignation that he aspired to during his exile. Shortly after leaving home on his 1779 pastoral trip to Virginia with Samuel Emlen, Henry wrote Elizabeth a letter in which he gave thanks for his inner "serenity," which remained his "prime object." He had been able to sustain that state of mind, despite "seasons of close trial and deep probation," because he had "a conscious sense, as holy Job did, of his own innocence," which provided "an anchor to the afflicted spirit." Henry reminded his wife that they both needed to trust in God's love and protection, whatever "inward and outward trials" they might have to endure. Toward the end of the war, Henry acknowledged in a letter to his close friend John Pemberton that he had from time to time experienced "weakness and discouragement, both inwardly and outwardly," as "a restless, persecuting spirit" continued "to rage and threaten." Yet at such moments, he reminded himself that such afflictions gave Friends an opportunity to demonstrate for themselves and others "the reality and measure of our faith." Indeed, his conviction that "the very deepest of our probations" would "work together for good" had, he claimed, grown stronger as the war wore on. Despite bouts of anger and despondency, he felt "secret confidence that all will be well in the end."[65]

If Elizabeth made an effort during those final years of the war to embrace a spirit of resignation and to contain her bitterness about the patriots' treatment of her family and other Quakers, it rarely showed in her diary entries. We do not know how blunt she was when talking with other Friends as they met in each other's homes, but at least in the privacy of her diary, she became increasingly outspoken about the injustices inflicted on her community by a regime that she saw as repressive and hypocritical. Yet her personal outrage remained entirely private: once Elizabeth returned from the embassy that she had joined, reluctantly, on behalf of her husband and his fellow exiles, and now that her family was reunited, she gave no sign of wanting to build on that experience by becoming a public figure either within or on behalf of her community. She visited friends to give her support when they fell afoul of the patriots and provided hospitality for mourners in the privacy of her parlor following Abraham Carlisle's execution for treason, but in public she held back even from undertaking duties within her Monthly Meeting that were quite normal for female Friends. In 1779, her neighbor Catherine Howell persuaded her to serve as an overseer for the marriage of her daughter, but Elizabeth wrote that she did not welcome "offices of this kind" and tried, unsuccessfully, to back out by going the next day to share with Howell her "scruples . . . respecting this (to me) new office." A few days later, she "felt a little comical on going into the Men's Meeting" to give her report. She and the other female overseer, Rebecca Waln, appeared at a subsequent Monthly Meeting to declare that the marriage had been "orderly accomplished." Waln spoke first and then Elizabeth had only to confirm what she had said, but this was nonetheless, she wrote, "something trying to me." She had not anticipated having to speak, thinking her presence beside Rebecca would suffice as "assent."[66]

Far from becoming emboldened to speak and act in public, Elizabeth now went for long periods without being seen, let alone heard, outside her home. To be sure, her physical frailty and her children's illnesses kept her confined for extended periods throughout the remainder of the war. In December 1779, she wrote that she had "stayed at home all day" for the last seven or eight weeks, except for attending worship "once or twice a week." On one occasion, she did agree to attend Quarterly Meeting as a representative from her Monthly Meeting but was then too "poorly" to go. In another entry, she admitted that it was only the third time "for upwards of eleven months past" that she had gone out to drink tea at a neighbor's home, and in October 1782 she attended worship for "the first time" in "many months." She did serve that fall as an overseer for the marriage of Rebecca James, daughter of Henry's former business partner, but Elizabeth was drifting into an increasingly housebound life, receiving many visits but paying very few, and rarely attending even public worship. Whether her retreat into a domestic cocoon was due in part to the horrors she had witnessed over the preceding decade is ultimately impossible to tell, though that may well have been a factor.[67]

In truth, Elizabeth had much for which to thank her God, as the Drinkers emerged from the revolutionary crisis scarred but intact. Yet she and her family had paid dearly for Henry's association with the East India Company and their principled objection to violent insurrection. If Elizabeth ever acknowledged the catastrophic mistake that her husband and his partner had made in agreeing to become tea agents, she certainly gave no hint of doing so in her diary or letters. She seems to have laid the blame for what followed at the door of those who fomented a blood-soaked revolution and then sought to silence anyone who disagreed with them. Though she reconciled herself, at least superficially, to the post-revolutionary order, Elizabeth made several scathing references to the "ridiculous doings" of "anniversary frolickers" on July 4. One year, she hoped that the anniversary would "pass without the commission of any enormity by those who pride themselves in their independence but know not how to prize or use it." A few years later, she noted that although there was much "rejoicing" when the anniversary came around again, "the most sensible part of the community" had "more reason to lament than rejoice." She also deplored the rowdy, drunken behavior that often broke out on that day, especially after nightfall: prayerful contemplation amid "peace and quietness would," in her opinion, have been "more commendable and consistent in a well-regulated government or state." Elizabeth was horrified when one of her own daughters went to observe the festivities on a hot summer's day in 1798. "My daughter Ann," she wrote, "like many other simpletons, are gone to look—I expect many will be taken sick, overheated, etc."[68]

Over the coming years, Elizabeth commented occasionally on the vicious and sometimes violent divisions that tainted politics in the new republic, but she rarely displayed any interest in public affairs unless they referred back in some way to her memories of the divisions between Americans during the revolutionary period, the violence that ensued, and her family's past suffering. Her diary for 1787 does not survive, so we do not know if she commented on the Constitutional Convention or the struggle over ratification. In her entries for the late 1790s, she criticized both the Federalist and Republican parties for their intemperate and divisive behavior, but she clearly identified more with the Federalists' commitment to order and hierarchy. From her perspective, the Democratic Republicans threatened to unleash once again the horrors of mob rule. Americans disagreed bitterly over whom they should support in the conflict now raging between monarchist Britain and republican France. Elizabeth's distrust of the Democrats may well have been due in part to their sympathy for the French Revolution, which had resulted in the murder of tens of thousands of citizens labeled as enemies of the people; during the War for Independence, France had supported the patriots. In the final year of her life, she fretted that the July 4 anniversary would bring renewed violence as Britain and the United States again teetered on the verge of war. People had been circulating handbills denouncing the British and a crowd (or, as she put it, "mob") had gathered outside the British consul's door a few evenings past, "beating the rogue's march, etc." These "inflammatory doings" must have reminded her of the threats directed against her own family and their friends some forty years past. Small wonder, then, that the elderly woman worried as to what would happen on the anniversary itself. As it turned out, the day passed by without serious incident. "So much the better," she declared.[69]

That Elizabeth remained embittered decades after the Revolution was understandable, given her own family's ordeal and the tragedies she had watched unfold around her. Many loyalist families had lost everything, and the legal doctrine of coverture that subsumed a woman's rights and property within those of her husband meant that the wives of men who opposed the Revolution participated fully in the material consequences, regardless of whether they shared their husbands' opinions. Quakers also suffered because of their refusal to support the war, not only through fines and confiscation of property but also as they endured intimidation, loss of personal liberty, imprisonment, and even death. The revolutionary government had executed Abraham Carlisle and John Roberts; Thomas Gilpin and John Hunt died while in exile. Israel Pemberton, another of Henry Drinker's companions in exile, never fully recovered his health after returning home and passed away a year later, six months after his wife, Mary, who had struggled to protect their family and its property during his absence. Others also proved unable to recover and move on: Hannah Griffitts described the decline of a friend who "died of a violent nervous disorder occasioned by the distress she suffered in the late distracted times," her mind reduced to "a wreck, tossed by tempestuous waves."[70]

Friends worried that their refusal to fight alongside the patriots might have a lasting impact on their reputation and treatment in the new republic. Following the British surrender, Anna Rawle wrote in her diary, "It seems universally agreed that Philadelphia will no longer be that happy asylum for the Quakers that it once was. Those joyful days when all was prosperity and peace are gone, never to return; and perhaps it is as necessary for our society to ask for terms as it was for Cornwallis." Yet such fears turned out to be unfounded. The Drinkers and many other Quaker families that had endured persecution and tragic losses during the war now returned to outwardly normal lives, reintegrating into post-revolutionary society with an apparent ease and speed that surprised some contemporaries. Rebecca Shoemaker wrote only months after the signing of the Peace of Paris that in Philadelphia "the general temper of the people" had "considerably changed with regard to the loyalists." Those who had opposed the Revolution now "walk[ed] daily and publicly about the streets without meeting with any kind of incivility or insult." Behind the facade of reconciliation lurked painful scars, but this postwar rapprochement was nonetheless quite remarkable.[71]

Several impulses drove this speedy reincorporation of families so recently humiliated and threatened by patriots into the social fabric of the new nation. Older associations and underlying interests rebound respectable Philadelphians to one another in solidarity, despite the different positions that they took during the war. Many elite Americans, including many of those who supported Independence, were not pleased that during the revolutionary period people from the lower ranks of society became visible and influential to a degree that seemed to them inappropriate and distasteful. From the perspective of wealthier Philadelphians, these were uncouth, unwashed, and insolent upstarts. The radicalism of Pennsylvania's state constitution, which gave the vote to all free male adults, may also have helped to reconcile privileged Philadelphians who, whatever their different perspectives on the British government's actions, or those of the patriots, saw eye to eye on the undesirability of social leveling. Furthermore, though some Americans sided unequivocally and persistently with either the patriots or the British, others came to deplore the behavior of both sides in the conflict. Even those Philadelphians who welcomed the British occupation of their city in late 1777, for whatever reason, found their presence a disillusioning experience, and there was much bitterness about the British withdrawal, which left their supporters at the mercy of the returning revolutionaries. Fear of continued reprisals against those who had refused to participate in the war effort must have been an additional and powerful incentive for Quakers to make peace with the new order, thus avoiding further acrimony, ostracism, and danger. Quakers had argued that patriots disobeyed God's ordinances by rebelling against an established ruler; they might now persuade themselves that they were duty-bound to obey the revolutionary government that God had, in his mysterious wisdom, allowed to triumph. No longer would Friends challenge the new nation's right to exist.[72]

Friends could now look back on the events of the past two decades and take measure of their own and others' responses to the trials and tribulations of those years. In a letter written in the summer of 1784, Henry Drinker expressed wonderment and relief that he had managed to survive without betraying the fundamental principles of his faith. "That I have so far got through without bringing a blemish on the testimony and precious cause," he declared, "is to me at times marvelous, knowing my own weakness and infirmities." Henry and other pacifist Quakers had watched in anguish as some of their brethren took up arms with the patriot forces, splitting their community of faith in two. Those who had stuck to their principles must now, wrote one of Henry's correspondents, "stand fast in the faith committed to us." That Friend's experience at a Yearly Meeting in 1783 convinced him that their brethren were "united in an ardent labor for the repairing of the breaches in the walls of Zion," which would "yet become the beauty of Nations and the joy of the whole Earth." While state-builders quarreled over the structure and goals of government in the emergent United States, Friends would focus on healing their own nation, the Society of Friends, with its integrity firmly in place as an example to the rest of humanity.[73]

Henry was determined not to forget the spiritual lessons of the war and decided that the suspension of his mercantile business, necessitated by transatlantic conflict, should now become permanent as part of a self-conscious decision to reorient his life. He believed that a combination of material deprivation and persecution during the war had prompted many Friends to acknowledge more fully their dependence on God, forcing a shift away from worldly toward spiritual concerns. Suffering had proven, once again, to be a purifying experience.[74] Yet he worried that the return of peace would bring with it the threat of spiritual backsliding and noticed that many of his Quaker neighbors were eager to revive businesses suspended during the war, including his former partner, who now formed a new import and export firm in partnership with his own sons. Many Philadelphians who had found themselves "turned out of their former occupations and course of living . . . mercifully shaken from their attachment to transitory things," had now become once again "involved and encrusted with earthly cares." Henry confided to John Pemberton that he had himself experienced "conflicts on this occasion." Several attractive business propositions had come from "distant parts," but having "examine[d] deeply wherein [his] solid peace might be preserved in this matter," he had decided to turn down these offers, "at least for the present or until my sons advance nearer to manhood." Henry was resolved "to walk wisely and circumspectly, striving to redeem the time" left him in this world and "to become more separated from worldly entanglements."[75]

6 • "The Cause of Humanity, as Well as Our Interest"

In Which Henry Drinker Reinvents Himself as a Moral Architect

Once the United States secured formal recognition of its Independence from Britain in the Treaty of Paris, a wave of euphoric optimism swept through the new nation as its citizens looked forward to an era of peace and opportunity. As transatlantic trade finally resumed and a new wave of migration into the backcountry gathered momentum, many Philadelphia merchants leapt back into the world of commerce, but Henry Drinker was not one of them. Trade had proven economically, politically, and personally perilous for Henry. Quaker firms like James and Drinker had come under increasing suspicion when they started objecting to the violent protests and intimidation that accompanied boycotts of British goods, and the partners' decision to accept a commission from the East India Company had left them dangerously exposed as targets of patriot wrath. When revolutionary officials started to round up leading Quakers in the fall of 1777, Henry found himself under arrest on suspicion of treason and sent into exile. Though he survived and eventually returned home, the war proved a grueling ordeal for Henry and his family. By the early 1780s, he had vowed not to revive his transatlantic business. Henry's decision resulted not primarily from any economic calculus but instead from a desire "to redeem the time" left him in this world by redirecting his energies toward more spiritually elevated goals. This turned out to be a fortuitous choice.[1]

Abel James was less chastened and shared in the general optimism that rising land prices and pent-up demand for imported goods would produce an economic boom. He therefore formed a new mercantile partnership with his sons, built two new ships, and placed substantial orders with firms across the Atlantic, the largest with Frederick Pigou in London, who had been one of

James and Drinker's closest business associates. He bought several expensive properties in Philadelphia and more than twenty thousand acres of land outside the city. Abel whipped himself up into a veritable tornado of activity or, as Elizabeth put it, "a great hurry of business." Unfortunately, property values did not continue to rise as predicted and the post-revolutionary appetite for imported goods proved to be short-lived, so that trading firms such as James and Sons soon found themselves with extensive inventories on their hands. Abel owed large sums for the land he had just purchased as well as for the European goods he had ordered, so this turn of events left him fatally overextended. In July 1784 he had no choice but to declare bankruptcy and put his affairs in the hands of four trustees, including Henry Drinker—a natural choice since the two men had remained close and were still collecting money owed by debtors to the defunct firm of James and Drinker. Abel was one of sixty-eight Philadelphia merchants to go under during the 1780s (13 percent of Philadelphian merchants operating in 1785). He owed a massive sum, and over half that debt was with Frederick Pigou, who also had to declare bankruptcy that fall, thanks in no small part to the credit he had extended to Abel, who as it turned out could not meet his obligations. The Drinkers were well aware by early 1784 that Abel was "in much trouble," as Elizabeth put it, but Henry was no longer immersed in the world of trade and so unaware of the extent to which Abel had overextended his assets. He wrote that summer that his former partner had recently become much less forthcoming about his "prospects and schemes," which Henry now assumed was because Abel had guessed he would disapprove and try to rein him in.[2]

When Abel finally revealed the disastrous state of his affairs, Henry was dismayed. He sympathized with his old partner's plight and convinced himself that recent illness had "clouded" Abel's formerly sound judgment, absolving Abel from any charge of willful irresponsibility or malfeasance. Yet Henry was also distressed that his friend Frederick Pigou had fallen victim to Abel's lapses in judgment and so readily assumed responsibility for collecting debts owed to Frederick by Abel and other American tradesmen. Henry admitted in private that he worried he might end up tainted by association with Abel, and he was determined to avoid blame for what were, after all, his friend's "deficiencies." Henry was now acting in three overlapping capacities: collecting debts owed to Abel and seeking to satisfy his former partner's creditors, acting on behalf of Frederick, and at the same time collecting debts still owed to James and Drinker. Henry had also partnered with Abel in purchasing land that signally failed to accrue value, though thankfully he was not involved in

Abel's mercantile ventures. Henry's efforts to balance these responsibilities and to demonstrate "religious rectitude in each department" would require "singular circumspection," as he wrote in frank and troubled letters to Frederick. These "entanglements" were "painful to dwell on," and yet constantly on his mind.[3]

Abel's erratic state of mind did not help matters. Henry confided to one of his correspondents that Abel had become "a good deal unhinged," careening back and forth between deep despondency and unrealistic optimism. A scanty paper trail made the challenge facing the bankrupt's trustees even more complicated. Abel had always been a slipshod record keeper, Henry noted, relying instead on "a tenacious memory." Now that his memory had deteriorated and he was, by his own admission, unable to recall in any detail many of the transactions he had handled over the years, his lack of formal recordkeeping turned into a massive headache for his trustees. Neighboring womenfolk were meanwhile concerned for Abel's wife, Rebecca, who was, in Rebecca Shoemaker's words, "a friendly, unambitious good woman, who wished for no more than domestic happiness." In 1785, Elizabeth Drinker spent a week with Rebecca at the Jameses' home in Frankford. She noted in her diary that Rebecca was often alone while Abel ran hither and thither hatching schemes to pay off his debts. Elizabeth doubtless empathized, given Henry's frequent absences over the years.[4]

Henry feared at times that the task of sorting through his former partner's affairs, "so encumbered with numerous difficulties," would drag on indefinitely. At first, the trustees hoped they could settle Abel's debts and leave his family with sufficient resources to live in comfort, but that turned out to be unduly optimistic. "It is improbable from present appearances," they wrote in 1786, "that much if anything will remain—a hard case indeed and much to be lamented." Abel's fraught relations with the Society of Friends during these years must have deepened Henry's distress. The Monthly Meeting for Philadelphia's Northern District censured and subsequently disowned James for his "great imprudence" in business, which had damaged many members of the trading community and also the reputation of Quakers. (Abel's lack of attendance at Meetings in recent years was also an issue.) They offered to readmit him if he paid his debts and exhibited a proper awareness of his "deviations," but Abel appealed the decision, and there followed a convoluted series of maneuvers and consultations that ended only with his death. As Abel's friend and a leading figure in the local Quaker community, Henry was placed in a very awkward position. He was determined to remain neutral, though he confided to John Pemberton that doing so took "abundant caution," and he admitted in private that Abel had given "much occasion" for offense.[5]

Despite being "greatly dejected and depressed in mind," Abel seemed to be in good physical health, so his death in October 1790 came as a surprise to everyone. Henry related in a letter to Frederick Pigou that his friend had been found midafternoon "at the head of the stairs leading to his bedchamber in a sitting posture, with his eyes and mouth closed, seeming in a sleep, but life was gone." Henry insisted that he would "ever esteem and love his memory," even as he lamented "the weakness and strange delusion which overtook him in his advanced age" and "cast a shadow on the brightness of his former character." Despite recent tensions with Abel, the local Meeting authorized his burial in the Quaker cemetery, and Elizabeth noted that "a numerous concourse of worthy citizens" attended the funeral. Rebecca James followed in April 1795, after spending the final years of her life in much reduced circumstances. At the time of Henry's death in 1809, the trustees were still selling off Abel's lands to meet his debts.[6]

Abel's descent into bankruptcy and subsequent public humiliation must have impressed upon Henry that he had been right to step back from the volatile world of commerce. In the same letter that announced Abel's death, Henry reassured Frederick Pigou in a tone that verged on the self-congratulatory that his own finances were in excellent order. In addition to accumulated assets from his earlier partnership with Abel James, he had income from the ironworks at Atsion, a sawmill, his store in Philadelphia, and several rental properties in the city. These considerable resources supported his family and paid for vast tracts of undeveloped land that Henry purchased following the end of the war across northern Pennsylvania and southern New York. At one point his landholdings amounted to half a million acres. Much of this property was close to the Delaware River, giving easy access to Philadelphia for the sale of crops and lumber. Farmers who settled in the Susquehanna Valley, where he also had land, could float produce down the Susquehanna River to Harmony, a settlement owned by Henry, and from there send shipments across to Stockport, a trading post on the Delaware that Henry also owned. The possibilities for future development in the region seemed extremely promising and because Henry had not become heavily indebted to acquire the land, he was less vulnerable than other speculators when land prices failed to rise as expected.[7]

Henry hoped to make money from these land investments and so secure his family's future, but his motives were not solely economic. Like many of his contemporaries, he believed that the nature of economic development had direct impact on a nation's moral character.[8] Henry sought to reinvent himself as an ethically driven entrepreneur who would bring both wealth and enlightenment to the post-revolutionary world unfolding around him. He was by no means the first Quaker to attempt such a combination: Pennsylvania's founder, William Penn, had envisaged his North American colony as a blend of grandiose moral vision and hardheaded economic planning that would, he hoped, enrich him and his descendants as well as the colonists who settled there. Henry wanted to shape backcountry settlement by encouraging respectable citizens, ideally Quakers, to move out into that region, where they would build orderly farming communities and treat local Indian nations with respect, resulting in a peaceful and morally upstanding westward expansion of the new nation. It was doubtless not a coincidence that settling Quakers on the frontier would offset the preponderance there of Scotch Irish Presbyterians, who had fomented so much hostility toward Quakers before the Revolution, accusing Friends of favoring Indians over white colonists in the backcountry; Henry would surely have been glad to dilute their influence. He also planned to deploy the sugar maples that grew in profusion across much of that land in an ambitious manufacturing initiative that would turn the production and marketing of maple sugar into a major component of the new nation's strategy for economic development. This alternative sweetener would supplant West Indies cane sugar in national and even international markets, striking a blow against African slavery in the Caribbean and so promoting a humanitarian cause close to the heart of Quakers such as the Drinkers.[9]

If Henry wished to influence the moral character of economic development and territorial expansion in the post-revolutionary era, he would have to engage and perhaps even collaborate with the representative bodies and other institutions that shaped public policy. Yet throughout their history, Quakers had frequently found themselves in conflict with political authority and enjoyed at best an ambiguous relationship to civil society. Recent events had underlined those tensions, and most conscientious Quakers avoided public office as they continued in their reformist quest to avoid as best they could the outside world and its corrupting influence. "I mix very little in politics," Henry declared in 1795, though he had made a brief foray into local public affairs in 1789 when he agreed to stand for election as a member of Philadelphia's Common Council. It is unclear why he did so, but fellow Quaker Isaac Hicks was horrified when he heard about the election. Hicks wrote Henry a forthright letter about the dangers into which he was falling by accepting a place in civil government, and Henry served only one term, most likely in response to this criticism. However, his subsequent avoidance of public office did not stop him from joining other Friends in lobbying state and federal bodies to promote causes that they considered ethically noteworthy. These included diplomatic relations with Indian nations and the abolition of slavery, along with less high-minded matters such as the location of county seats of justice in newly settled areas where Friends had invested in large tracts of land. Henry did still aspire to have a public impact, albeit from a position outside the public sphere. If all went according to plan, his land investments and the maple sugar venture would secure him both profit and public approbation, helping to restore his own reputation and that of Friends generally in the new republic.[10]

Yet the ambitious ventures into which Henry now sank the bulk of his capital turned out to be utterly fraught, bringing him disappointment, frustration, and financial worry at a time of his life when he felt his energy and taste for risk to be waning. William Penn's Pennsylvania pipe dream had landed him in debtor's prison, and now, almost a century later, many entrepreneurs in the early republic went broke. In the aftermath of the War for Independence, Henry could have followed through on his resolution to forsake "worldly entanglements" in favor of service to the Society of Friends. He decided instead to embark on a high-stakes venture that would, he hoped, promote principles held dear by Quakers and bring in handsome profits. He was to be sorely disappointed on both counts. To be sure, the logistical challenges involved were daunting, but Henry knew next to nothing about tilling the soil and spent little time out on the tracts he had purchased. Instead, he relied on agents, some of whom turned out to be quite unworthy of that trust. Others with whom he did business also turned out to be less than honorable. Elizabeth, watching with dismay the unraveling of Henry's plans, deplored such dishonesty, especially if carried out by "those who call themselves gentlemen." One can almost see her shaking her head as she added, "What times are these? Bad indeed!" The failure of some Quakers to fulfill their commitments particularly bothered Henry as this damaged the reputation of Friends generally as people of integrity. Meanwhile, many who bought land from him were unable to pay for it, while others who still owed him money from before the war went under, leaving Henry with few liquid assets. Henry did not go bankrupt and, at least on paper, had huge assets. Yet he had tied up much of that wealth in enterprises that proved intractable and financially draining, leaving him, as he put it, "starving in the midst of plenty." Henry and his family again survived, but his decisions again cost him dearly, casting a dark shadow over the rest of his life.[11]

"A More Contemptible Set of Beings Are Hardly to Be Found"

One of Henry's primary objectives in becoming a land magnate was to populate undeveloped land with "useful and reputable" settlers. He wanted as far as possible to avoid selling land to speculators, even though that might have proven more profitable in the short term, preferring instead respectable families looking to purchase small lots on which they would settle themselves. The "improvements" they made to the landscape as they cleared land for farming would then increase the value of surrounding lots when put on the market, while their reputation for sobriety and hard work would attract other desirable settlers. He was even willing to allow prospective buyers extra time before they started making payments for the land, if they were "clearly respectable, sober, and industrious." Immediate profit was clearly not the primary goal. Henry used the same language repeatedly in his correspondence to describe the people he wanted to attract. His ideal settler was "an honest, sober man, industrious, and a good farmer." He was particularly interested in "Friends or friendly peoples," that is, settlers who identified as Quakers or had values compatible with those of Quakers and were well disposed toward them. These upstanding and hardworking folk would draw after them into the backcountry "well approved neighbors and friends."[12]

Many contemporary thinkers believed that land ownership and an agricultural way of life would foster self-reliant, independent-minded, and morally upstanding individuals, essential qualities in the citizens of a well-functioning republic. Yet Henry clearly believed that at least some of those who bought land needed already to be people of character in order for this to work, and unfortunately, not all of those whom his land agents drew to these new settlements turned out to match their hopes and expectations. Henry complained that many buyers "never made a single movement" toward clearing or inhabiting their land. Some of those who did live on the tracts they had purchased led, in his estimation, "an idle dilatory life" that promoted neither economic development nor the moral character of the backcountry. Even those who did try to farm the land had a bracing time of it and could not turn a profit anywhere near as soon as they and Henry had hoped. That in turn made it difficult for land agents to extract mortgage payments, even from conscientious settlers who would happily have paid up, had they the cash to spare. While Henry lamented repeatedly his inability even to recover his outlay, let alone make a profit, some settlers may have regarded demands for payment by well-heeled investors, demands they had no hope of meeting, as callous and grasping.

European migrants and investors often had buyer's remorse once they or their agents saw the land they had rashly purchased. They had, Henry wrote, "strange and mistaken ideas of this country," expecting that the land would be ready for farming, only to discover it was "in a state of nature." He eventually concluded that unimproved tracts were better suited to native-born Americans or immigrants who had lived long enough in North America to understand "those difficulties which ever attend the subduing [of] a wilderness."[13]

Henry and his agents were eager to find men of social and moral stature who could provide leadership in these new communities and inspire reputable settlers to follow them into the region. Henry himself had no intention of relocating, and his agents out there did not have the standing to become magnets for settlement in their own right. But Samuel Preston, Henry's coinvestor and agent out at Stockport, thought that he had hit the jackpot in Quaker preacher David Sands, who had traveled extensively on both sides of the Atlantic and attracted crowds of enthusiastic listeners (as well as detractors) wherever he went. Sands approached Preston in 1792 with a proposition: he wanted to settle down in the Stockport area with a band of followers, bringing moral uplift to the region in exchange for a good deal on the purchase of three thousand acres. When Henry first heard about this proposal, his reaction was ambivalent: the establishment of a sizable Quaker community with a charismatic leader might justify preferential terms, yet Drinker doubted whether Sands was temperamentally suited to settling down and developing the land. The preacher was notoriously impractical and his material circumstances were so straitened that Henry did not see how he could pay for the land or maintain a household once settled there. "In the management of worldly concerns," he wrote, "David don't stand foremost."[14]

Despite these reservations, Henry took a risk and approved the deal. His association with David Sands turned out to be disastrous. Sands delayed for two years before finally concluding terms with Preston in 1794. He built a house on the land he had purchased near to Stockport and planted some apple trees but then stunned Preston by selling off part of the tract and announcing that he was leaving for Europe to continue preaching. Sands sailed for Liverpool in 1795, the land he had purchased from Drinker unsettled and unpaid for. Ten years would pass before Sands again showed his face out at Stockport. As Henry wrote to Preston, "the total failure on David's part in introducing a valuable settlement of friends" made "the bargain a bad one indeed." Henry proposed canceling the agreement, but Sands insisted that he would in due course meet his obligations, and Preston was inclined to trust him. Drinker respected Sands "as a pious man endowed with a precious gift" and insisted that he did not suspect him of "intentionally departing from moral rectitude." However, when Sands eventually returned to North America and visited northern Pennsylvania, Drinker instructed Preston to meet with him and insist that Sands either pay up and settle there or cancel the agreement. Sands still maintained that he intended "to lay his bones" at Stockport and promised to fulfill the terms of purchase as he understood them. However, the wording of the original agreement turned out to have been quite vague, and the three men now became embroiled in disagreement over exactly which plots of land Sands had purchased, what price he had agreed to pay, and whether he had really committed to bring settlers to live on the land. Henry claimed repeatedly that he wanted to avoid "any breach of that cordiality and harmony which has and ought to be maintained between us," but the dispute became increasingly bitter as it dragged on year after year. Preston now became convinced that Sands's behavior was underhanded ("There is something very mysterious, dark, and I expect wrong behind the curtain," he wrote in 1805), and Henry struggled to maintain any faith in his old friend's probity. In December 1806, Henry finally executed a deed to David Sands for roughly two and a half thousand acres, placing the deed in escrow until Sands paid up; the deed remained unrecorded until well after Henry's death. Sands did nothing to develop the land, and Henry's hopes for a Quaker settlement under David's leadership went unfulfilled.[15]

Meanwhile, investors could not expect to attract desirable farming families without providing a basic infrastructure for the region and so needed crews of skilled, hardworking laborers for clearing and construction work. Yet finding reliable workers to build homes and other structures, lay roads, and transport lumber proved challenging in a tight labor market. Henry's correspondence with his agents often referred to the problems they encountered in their efforts "to procure proper assistance." That phrase "proper assistance" referred to both practical skills and moral character: Henry instructed his agents to avoid recruiting "doubtful or forbidding characters" who might damage the "good name" of new settlements, but the shortage of labor often required that they overlook moral deficiencies as they vetted prospective laborers, especially if they had specific skills that were in demand. Henry also favored hiring married workers who would take their families with them, assuming rather naively that the presence of women and children would incline laborers to moral rectitude and sobriety. Yet Preston complained that laborers' wives often proved "difficult," "disagreeable," "discontented," and "a trouble to our concerns," so that if Henry did plan to hire married men he should make "strict enquiry" as to the "disposition" of their alleged better halves before making any final decisions. Preston's description of these "bad women" as "difficult" and "discontented" suggests that they challenged his authority, which would have upset him as much as any lack of work ethic or morals. He wanted deferential as well as respectable employees.[16]

Henry found that he had to be pragmatic. In 1793, when a fellow named John Hyson offered to join the workforce at Stockport as a cook, Henry was reluctant to turn him away, even though he had doubts about "his character and fitness" for the position. Henry sent Hyson out to the settlement, leaving the final decision to Preston. That same year he was willing to rehire a carpenter even after he decamped without permission and returned to Philadelphia, where he apparently busied himself buying "fine things" for another man's wife with whom he had "formed an acquaintance." Competent carpenters, like good cooks, were difficult to find, and as Henry conceded, with a heavy heart, "sobriety and fidelity" were "rare among that class of people." Yet he and his agents had their limits. They took a risk on Charles Bliss, hiring him to work out at Stockport despite his serious drinking problem. Bliss seemed to have reformed, but he then relapsed and ended up back in Philadelphia after Preston fired him. A few months later, Bliss provided Henry with written testimonials to his "clearness from intoxication," in the hope that he would override Preston's decision and give him another chance, but Henry demurred.[17]

Even though Henry recognized that there was no way to guarantee an entirely respectable workforce, he hoped that his agents would respond to "evil conduct" among their workers with initiatives designed to reform them. He was convinced that the rafters who brought lumber down from Stockport to Philadelphia were in particular need of such attentions: "a more contemptible set of beings are hardly to be found," he wrote to Preston. Henry wanted Samuel to wean these men from "their habits of drunkenness and profanity." In fact, he hoped to achieve a wholesale "Reformation of Manners" out in the backcountry. Eager to do his part, he promised to send some "good books" along with the next consignment of supplies. Morally improving books were in plentiful supply on both sides of the Atlantic, and back in Philadelphia Benjamin Franklin had established a circulating library so that even those unable to buy books could borrow them for the knowledge and lessons in virtue that they contained. Franklin had also set up "a club for mutual improvement" consisting of young men who met regularly to debate topics that they read about in advance. Henry seems to have been thinking along similar lines: he believed that what the rafters needed to redeem them was a supply of inspiring volumes that they could peruse and discuss in their spare moments. Whether a crew of rowdy workers living out on the frontier would welcome this opportunity or could even read was quite another matter.[18]

Sadly, Henry could not even rely on his own representatives to provide moral leadership. In the fall of 1795, Preston wrote to inform Drinker that he had just married his housekeeper, Marcia Jenkins. When Jenkins had arrived that summer, Preston described her as "a superior shining woman in words and deeds," a welcome exception to most of the women he encountered out in the backcountry. "She appears to have a capacity and disposition," he reported a few weeks later, "to manage and govern the difficulties of this place superior to my expectations of any woman . . . perhaps her equal will never again be found." Preston had also written that Jenkins preferred "a single life." He now assured Henry that their decision to marry had been neither "hasty" nor "inconsiderate," but he did acknowledge rather defensively that the marriage had taken place "without either priest, minister, or magistrate." Preston claimed that he had no other option because the Philadelphia Monthly Meeting had disowned him, which was not true, and because his bride had become rather jaundiced in her attitude toward the Society: after her father absconded to escape the demands of his creditors, their local Meeting had apparently been less than supportive. Henry declined to comment on Preston's claims concerning his membership status or his wife's alienation from the Quaker community, but a few weeks later the Monthly Meeting in Philadelphia recorded that Preston had married "not conformably to the order of our religious discipline" and did disown him. This was not the kind of moral example that Henry had hoped his agents would provide.[19]

"An Honest-Hearted Man Will Always Wear Well"

There was, of course, an alternative to relying on agents. Henry could have spent time in the region supervising matters himself. He did travel out to some of his tracts in the late 1780s, but he never visited Harmony or Stockport and for the most part managed his land investments from Philadelphia. One of the reasons for this was age: "My advanced time of life and increasing infirmities," he wrote in 1795, "render such undertakings much more difficult than in some years past." Henry's responsibilities as an elder within his faith community also made traveling difficult, especially following a spate of deaths in the early 1790s. As he explained to Preston, the local Meeting had been "stripped within a few years of many of its most useful and worthy members," leaving those left behind with little choice but to assume additional duties that trumped "all temporal concerns."[20] Both of his sons, William and Henry Sandwith, reached adulthood during the decade following the end of the War for Independence and so were old enough to represent him out in the backcountry. In the late 1780s, Henry Sandwith went to live with Thomas Lightfoot, a land surveyor in Reading, to learn skills that could then be deployed in the service of his family's land investments, and he traveled northward on several occasions to conduct business on his father's behalf. However, the young man then took up farming on a property some thirty miles west of Philadelphia and after his marriage in 1794 settled there, so that he was no longer available to provide regular assistance to his father. For his part, William had chronic health problems that prevented him from traveling great distances, though at home he often helped with paperwork relating to his father's business interests, especially toward the end of Henry Drinker's life.[21]

Given these circumstances, Henry had to depend on agents to whom he entrusted vast quantities of land. Along with the management of those tracts came a tangle of practical, legal, and financial challenges. He expected his agents to keep him informed and to seek his opinion, regularly at a great distance with no predictable or reliable means of communication. They had to be willing to live in conditions that were primitive even by eighteenth-century standards, far away from any established community, let alone the urban amenities of a city like Philadelphia. They also needed to have a wide range of skills as they negotiated land sales, oversaw the construction of buildings, roads, canals, bridges, and dams, compiled land surveys, kept accounts, and composed detailed reports for dispatch to Drinker back in Philadelphia. For the most part, Henry chose fellow Quakers, and some of these men became long-term business associates. John Hilborn, for example, founded the settlement at Harmony and worked for the Drinkers until his death in 1824. Samuel Law managed much of Henry's land across the border in New York and continued to do so for Henry's children long after the patriarch's death. Henry's priority when seeking men to represent him was "moral rectitude and firm attachment to my interest." Everyone had shortcomings, he admitted, but "an honest-hearted man" would "always wear well." He paid less attention to whether they had the practical skills required for the job, and in some cases, this had disastrous consequences. Not all of those he took on as agents turned out to have the stamina for life in the backcountry, or even the qualities of loyalty and moral integrity that he valued above all else. Samuel Preston in particular proved an increasingly irritating thorn in his side.[22]

Preston was, in theory, an ideal agent for Henry's purposes. A Quaker who had grown up in Bucks County, he had no wife or dependents when Henry first became acquainted with him and so could travel unencumbered around the backcountry as he conducted business on behalf of investors back in Philadelphia. Samuel had a reputation for keeping his employers fully informed; this appealed to Henry, whose hunger for detailed information was at times downright insatiable. Henry later recalled that Samuel had been "a promising young man, possessed of good natural qualities." Knowing that Samuel would have to deal with some shady characters, he was reassured by what he took to be the young man's character and principles, "which promised to bear him up through an evil world in a reputable and irreproachable train of conduct." Samuel started working for Henry in the late 1780s, locating and surveying land that Henry and Abel James had purchased in Northampton County. He made such a good impression that in 1789 Henry took him on as a partner in the purchase and development of multiple tracts on both sides of the border between Pennsylvania and New York. Samuel had no financial resources to contribute ("he never advanced a shilling," Henry wrote many years later), but in return for his management of the land he was to receive half of the profits. Samuel operated at first from Harmony, a new settlement on the Susquehanna River, but then moved to Stockport, another new settlement on the Delaware, where he lived at first in a modest log cabin. However, he then built a much more substantial house, the dimensions of which were slightly larger than Henry's impressive home in Philadelphia, along with a gristmill, a barn, a carpenter's shop, and three sawmills to prepare timber for transport on rafts down to Philadelphia.[23]

Samuel turned out to be an ambitious and, from Henry's perspective, extravagant developer. Year after year Henry sent "heavy sums" to pay for "improvements" at Stockport that seemed to yield little in the way of profits. When Samuel proposed that they open a store, Henry told him that he would prefer to reduce rather than increase his "entanglements" in the region, but Samuel went ahead anyway and opened the store in 1791. Samuel acquired a reputation for "grand plans" and "building castles," paying little attention to considerations of economy or more mundane managerial concerns. Henry did not appreciate this apparent profligacy: "I am really worn down," he declared in December 1791. "Our expenses and thy schemes extend beyond my capacity." Samuel was convinced that Henry would understand the need for these investments and the potential for future profit if he were to visit the settlement. He urged Henry repeatedly to travel out there so that he could inspect progress and give his advice, but Henry never did so and yet became increasingly critical of Samuel's decisions. Samuel had promised to provide regular and detailed accounts of his actions and expenses, but he became much less informative over time and Henry was predictably irritated, especially since so little money was flowing back to Philadelphia. He looked in vain for explanations as to how Samuel had spent the money or why he needed more, as was invariably the case, despite Henry's repeated pleas for "mercy to my exhausted purse."[24]

Henry was also worried about Samuel's volatile temper, which alienated settlers and other agents. Henry heard to his dismay in 1791 that a group of farmers was so eager to avoid doing business with Samuel that they were lobbying for the construction of a road that would give them an alternative point of access to the Delaware. Henry urged Samuel repeatedly to guard against "sudden starts of passion or anger" and to cultivate "a cool Christian temper of mind." Samuel's temper may have soured due to severe pain, about which Henry was remarkably callous. In November 1789, a large tree fell during a storm onto a cabin where Samuel was staying and injured him badly. His shoulder blade was broken, along with "all my ribs down to the hip," as he reported once able to write. Samuel suffered for the rest of his life from a bent back, spasms of arthritis, and palsy in the hand. Yet when he described these problems, Henry told him that he was "chicken-hearted under affliction and sickness."[25]

Henry's frustration over Samuel's extravagance, irascibility, and apparent lack of backbone deepened in the late 1790s because of the younger man's increasingly overt ambition to become a leading figure in northern Pennsylvania. This threatened the relationship of dependency that Henry had anticipated, and to make matters worse, his junior partner was now neglecting the management of Stockport in favor of his own self-aggrandizement. In 1798, the governor of Pennsylvania appointed Samuel as the principal associate judge in newly formed Wayne County. Samuel decided to mark his first public appearance in that position with a lengthy speech on the recently enacted federal Sedition Laws and the threat allegedly posed by French conspirators living in the United States, which he then had printed as a twenty-two-page pamphlet and distributed to everyone he knew of any consequence, including the Drinkers. When the pamphlet arrived at Front Street and Henry read it aloud to his family, Elizabeth commented sarcastically, "Had it been shorter, and less aiming at popularity, I should have liked it better, but I am no *Judge*." Elizabeth had never appreciated Samuel's assertive manner ("I can hear him amplifying below as I sit alone upstairs," she wrote during one of his visits), but Henry and his wife now became convinced that Samuel had delusions of grandeur and was seeking to rise above his rightful station in life. Depending on his mood, Henry reacted to the tone of self-importance that had crept into Samuel's letters with either friendly concern or satirical mockery. "With all due deference and respect for the Great Man I am now addressing," he wrote on one occasion, "I conclude his Humble Friend." Henry also felt that he could no longer rely on his partner for "candor or veracity," and he was clearly not alone in having reached that conclusion. When Samuel's behavior as judge proved so high-handed and legally problematic that he lost his seat on the bench in 1804, his partner urged him to set aside his "great schemes and plans." Samuel had paid the price for unrealistic ambition and must now trim his sails: "Cease to be the pompous vain Judge Preston," wrote Henry, "and mind thy proper business. Keep within the bounds of thy capacity, which be assured is a limited one." Anticipating that Samuel might not appreciate these bracing home truths, Henry ended the letter by declaring, "I am, whatever thou mayst think, thy real friend."[26]

Their relationship deteriorated further in the fall of 1805 when Samuel dispatched to Philadelphia a series of letters describing rumors about the state of Henry's finances that he claimed were circulating among the settlers. According to these alleged rumors, Henry's son-in-law, John Skyrin, had recently suffered dramatic losses in his trading ventures, and because Henry had also invested in these projects, he would have to sell off his lands for whatever he could get, reducing land values throughout the region. Potential land buyers were now reluctant to go ahead with purchases because they hoped that land prices would plummet following a Drinker bankruptcy. Samuel claimed that he was suffering from the ripple effect of these setbacks and wanted Henry to send a certificate of credit from a leading banker to reassure those shaken in their confidence. Elizabeth described these claims as "extraordinary" even by Preston's hyperbolic standards. Henry wrote back that his son-in-law's losses were real but not as great as some claimed, and that in any case he was completely uninvolved and so unaffected. Quite reasonably, he wanted to know who the "whisperers" were. Later that fall, several men from the region visited Philadelphia and told Henry that Samuel was himself spreading the rumors, but when presented with these counterclaims, Samuel responded that Henry was being "duped" by the visitors, who were among those responsible for the reports. He repeated his request for proof of credit, but by this point Henry had little faith in Samuel's claims. "As they deserve little notice," he declared, "[I] shall say but little."[27]

Henry had become convinced that Samuel's management of the estate served "no good purpose, but quite the contrary," and wanted out of the partnership. He complained that none of the proceeds from crops grown at Stockport or from lumber cut there had ever reached him. He insisted that large sums of money remained unaccounted for, that Samuel owed Henry interest for the many advances that Henry had made over the years, and that Samuel had no right to his half of the proceeds from the land, as promised in their articles of partnership, until he recompensed Henry for those advances. When Henry heard that Samuel was sending wood to a lumberyard in Bucks County operated by one of Samuel's brothers, he demanded detailed information about all shipments and sales of lumber. When Samuel assured his partner that he had been keeping "a full account of the proceeds of lumber sent down the river, the expenses, losses, etc.," Henry shot back, "I want something more than talk. I want to see those accounts."[28]

The two men would quarrel for years over those accounts and the terms under which their partnership should end. Samuel visited Philadelphia and spent many hours in Henry's home office as they tried to reach agreement, but "to little purpose" according to Elizabeth, who predicted it would be "a long settlement." Henry accused Samuel of "base and dishonest" behavior, while Samuel accused Henry of listening all too willingly to malicious gossip provided by "designing people" eager to "create mischief." Each condemned the other for "rank ingratitude." Henry dwelt repeatedly on his having taken Samuel "by the hand, poor and in that day little and humble," advancing him "with a liberality seldom to be equaled." Yet instead of managing diligently the estate entrusted to him, Samuel had sought to aggrandize himself and had cheated his benefactor. "Such is the business of the man who owes all he possesses in the world to me." Samuel pointed out that he had, at Henry's suggestion, "forsook all his other friends" to serve Henry "with fidelity" in the middle of nowhere. "Let thee blame me or not," he declared, "I am doing the best I can." He wrote that he was shocked and hurt by the abusive tone of Henry's letters and urged him to use "such language as gentlemen use or have been accustomed to expect." The estranged partners were still quarreling over the terms under which their partnership would end when Henry died in 1809.[29]

Alongside Samuel Preston, the other persistent thorn in Henry's side was William Cooper, an ambitious land speculator who also played a central role in Henry's ill-fated maple sugar project and, like Samuel, turned out to be a good deal less reliable than Henry thought when he first encountered him in the late 1780s. Henry and a fellow investor named Richard Wells were eager to work with Cooper, not only because he was a fellow Quaker and had a reputation for "experience and judgment in such improvements," but also because of his "influence with a class of people in New England . . . said to be sober and respectable." Drinker and Wells hoped that Cooper would persuade these godly folk to purchase and then travel south to settle on the tracts Drinker and Wells had acquired in northern Pennsylvania. This would surely prove "beneficial to the community at large, to the emigrants that may become purchasers, and at [the] same time our own views and interest." Cooper agreed to sell land on their behalf just so long as he could do so with a free hand and had their authorization to offer deeds without any initial deposit: the purchasers would have ten years to pay for their purchase, in the meantime making annual interest payments. Drinker and Wells entrusted him with sixteen thousand acres, insisting only that the buyers be willing to settle on the land immediately. By the summer of 1789, Cooper claimed to have sold most of the lots to "men of character" who were already present and working on the land. Other landowners based in Philadelphia had also engaged Cooper, and all seemed "well satisfied with the manner of his executing their business." Henry was confident that "two hundred families or upwards" would have settled in the region by early the following year, "most of them persons of good moral conduct, sober and reputable."[30]

Yet Henry had never seen the land in question and was placing a great deal of trust in Cooper's salesmanship as well as his integrity. That trust turned out to be woefully misplaced. By early 1790, Cooper was admitting that at least some of the buyers he had described as settlers were in fact speculators. He reassured his employers that the purchasers would soon either settle on the land or sell to others who wanted to do so, "generally answering the purpose expected," but several years later Henry heard that none of those who had bought the tracts entrusted to Cooper were living on the land. Some of them had sold their lots to actual settlers, but those settlers were in no position to make payments. Cooper now claimed that the region was "a very difficult country to settle, remote from mills, settlements, or markets," so that many people were "prejudiced against it," a far cry from the cheery tone he had previously taken. The land that Cooper had agreed to sell was, in reality, far less attractive to farmers than Henry had believed: the topsoil, exposed by deforestation, was soon bare of nutrients and eroded, leaving behind a much less fertile underlay; buyers soon realized that land such as this could not sustain farming beyond a few years. Most of those who had planned to settle moved on, and those who stayed were barely able to support themselves, let alone pay interest or principal on their mortgages. In 1800, Henry had received no payments from any of the contracts negotiated by Cooper. He determined to track down the buyers and recover the deeds, but that turned out to be difficult and expensive. Adding insult to injury, Cooper owed Henry a significant sum of money for goods that Henry had provided on credit and became increasingly evasive about payment of that debt. Henry eventually accepted land in lieu of cash, though he considered this "no small hardship" and determined to sell the land quickly. It then transpired that some of that land was completely unsuitable for farming, "a deception so gross and dishonorable" that he could scarcely believe any man who valued "honor and reputation" would have treated him in this way.[31]

Another aspect of Cooper's behavior also shocked Drinker. One of Cooper's sisters, Letitia Cooper Woodruff, an impoverished widow with several children who was living in Philadelphia, began to call at the Drinker home in the early 1790s, asking for money that she may have assumed Henry could recover from her brother William. Cooper instructed Henry not to hand over any cash and to tell Letitia that he would personally take care of her needs when he next visited Philadelphia, but Henry felt that he could not refuse assistance to someone "in such deep distress," and the amount Cooper owed him for these handouts grew steadily over the coming few years. Letitia may have hoped that approaching the Drinkers would embarrass her brother into action on her behalf, and indeed Henry told Cooper that leaving his sister and her children without any means of support would not reflect well on him. Cooper eventually arranged for Letitia to join him in Cooperstown. This sequence of events left Henry with a sour taste in his mouth as he came to realize that the man in whom he had placed so much faith could not be trusted even to treat his own relatives with proper care, let alone business associates.[32]

"A Remote Corner of the Country"

Even if all of the agents representing Drinker out on his "wilderness" tracts had been models of probity and tireless in their efforts on his behalf, the challenges facing them and their employer would still have been formidable. This was a daunting venture for all concerned. Given the lack of any reliable transportation infrastructure, the moving back and forth of people, supplies, information, and legal paperwork proved difficult even when the weather cooperated, but rain and snow could wreak havoc on plans to transport anything or anyone along the crude roads that reached into the backcountry, while drought, floods, or ice could stymie travel by river. Those entrusted with the delivery of documents or much-needed supplies were often unable to reach their destinations because of impassable roads or waterways and had to leave whatever they were carrying with someone else, often a complete stranger, who would, at least in theory, forward the goods or documents once conditions permitted. Even when weather did not sabotage a journey, primitive roads could inflict serious damage on goods or livestock.[33]

Improving the network of roads across the region involved raising money, exploring feasible routes, finding reliable contractors to do the work, leveling land, building bridges across rivers, and digging through hills. Henry sank large sums from his own coffers into road construction, though he became increasingly bitter about the money he was committing to such ventures while others refused to do so, even though they would benefit. Investors and settlers who were willing to contribute often lobbied aggressively for routes that would benefit them over their neighbors; negotiations over the routing of new arteries frequently turned into vicious struggles, with interested parties withdrawing if they did not get their way. Henry sought, whenever possible, to place the construction of roads in the hands of men he already knew or who came recommended by those he trusted. In 1807, he recommended Chalkley James, son of his former partner Abel James, for appointment as superintendent of a turnpike currently under construction. Chalkley was the young fellow who had defended Henry's wife and children against the British officer who broke into their home in 1777. He had gone into business with his father in the 1780s but was now in "straitened circumstances." Chalkley had prior experience in supervising road construction and a reputation for "judgment and fidelity," so that Henry could do a favor to the son of his deceased friend, repay his earlier heroism, and at the same time "prevent deception and unfaithfulness in the construction of said road." More often than not, however, he was dealing with strangers who either turned out to be unreliable or confronted logistical challenges that slowed or overwhelmed them.[34]

Deciding where seats of government and justice should be located in these new regions of settlement had an equally dramatic impact on the value and sale of land, so that landowners and their agents lobbied energetically in the state assembly for the location of county towns in close proximity to their own property. It remained unclear for several years whether Milford or Bethany would become the seat of justice for Wayne County, where much of Henry's land in northern Pennsylvania was located. Henry, relying entirely on information supplied by his agents, argued that Bethany's fertile soil, "elegance of situation," and accessibility made it the logical choice. He insisted that he was advocating for Bethany based on his impressions of the general interest and a desire to maximize access to the county's seat of justice. That he had significant land interests around that settlement and had already granted a thousand acres for the construction of public buildings was, he claimed, immaterial. According to Henry, Milford was a "barren spot in a remote corner of the country," and he seems to have convinced himself that his competitors were guilty of downright "knavery." The representatives eventually settled in favor of Bethany and Henry's interests, but it took several years of backroom politicking to get there as rival interests maneuvered to influence vacillating members of the state assembly.[35]

Confusion and disagreement over who owned which plots of land and where exactly the boundaries lay between them further complicated backcountry development. The maps used by landowners and their agents as they negotiated with prospective buyers were often inaccurate and sometimes drawn up by people who had never even visited the region. When Henry heard that there were potential buyers for his lands alongside Clearfield Creek, he provided a map of his forty lots there, which his son Henry Sandwith had compiled using information in the land patents. He freely admitted that the information in the patents might be unreliable: "surveyors of late years have been in the habit of hurrying over their work," he wrote, so that "frequent errors and blunders" occurred. Henry also enclosed a larger map that purported to show the location of those lots relative to "other lands in that country," but "for its correctness," he wrote, "I will not answer." He had to tell another potential buyer that he was "at a loss to know" if he actually owned the land the correspondent was enquiring about. Because surveys were often approximate, bitter disputes could arise between buyers of contiguous lots. Some settlers took advantage of confusion over where tract boundaries lay or the absence of settlers on adjoining lands to cut and sell lumber that did not rightfully belong to them. When that happened on the edge of one of Henry's tracts, he urged his agent in the area to prosecute the culprits in hope of discouraging "future pillage," but defending rights of ownership was not easy in far-flung regions where boundaries were hazy, the recording of titles was often haphazard, and the machinery of justice was often ineffective.[36]

Though some disputes over ownership focused on a particular copse or field that straddled two properties, others involved large tracts of land worth considerable sums. Dueling land claims were not unusual during this period and sometimes resulted from genuine confusion as buyers applied for land titles from officials who had no way of coordinating effectively and so might issue duplicate warrants for the same tract. Contiguous states often claimed sovereignty over the same territory along a border between them, and each sold the land to would-be settlers. Some disputes involved deliberate deception as shady speculators knowingly sold land to which they had no compelling claim. An absentee owner might not even notice that someone else had sold his land, whether fraudulently or in ignorance, until the new purchasers had already settled there and were understandably reluctant to leave. Landowners might find it impossible to remove occupants whom they believed to be trespassing without protracted legal action or resort to physical force. Henry recognized that confusion was likely to arise from time to time in situations where reliable information was hard to come by, especially given that the administrative infrastructure for granting land titles was, to put it mildly, incoherent. When rival claims to land that he thought he owned did arise, he favored engaging "in the most liberal and friendly manner" to ascertain who had the prior claim, hoping to avoid "strife or contention." Yet confusion over land boundaries and title records did frequently lead to bitter disputes, even when all parties were acting in good faith, and Henry recognized that not everyone was behaving honorably, so that he and his agents had to keep an eagle eye out for shifty behavior.[37]

Perhaps the biggest of the many obstacles facing Henry as he worked away to realize the potential of his backcountry investments was the so-called Connecticut intrusion. Rival claimants from Pennsylvania and Connecticut had argued for decades over who rightfully owned land along the boundary between the two states, but the situation escalated in the 1790s when scores of migrants from Connecticut arrived in northern Pennsylvania after purchasing land there from the Susquehanna and Delaware Connecticut Companies. These companies claimed ownership of vast tracts that Pennsylvania investors, including Henry Drinker, believed to be their property. Additional sales of land along the boundary by individual Connecticut speculators made the situation even more complicated and an attempt by the Pennsylvania legislature to settle the disputes through compromise legislation proved ineffective. At first, many Pennsylvanian landowners failed to take the situation seriously, much to the dismay of more attentive investors such as Henry Drinker. But as the insurgents from Connecticut became more numerous and increasingly "insolent in their conduct," as Henry put it, even the most somnolent of investors roused themselves and began to organize a joint response. Henry considered the Connecticut speculators and their agents to be criminals and con artists, so refused to negotiate with them. Yet he wrote that he felt "no small degree of sympathy" for "those deluded and misled people" who had bought from the speculators and then traveled to settle on land to which, he believed, they had no legal right. Henry was willing to sell his land to these settlers, assuming they were respectable folk, and dispatched agents on a series of tours to broker deals on-site. That the settlers had already purchased the land once from someone else was, of course, unfortunate for them, but that, he noted, was hardly his fault. Yet the settlers themselves most likely had little or no understanding of the larger struggle into which they had stumbled and would have resented new demands for payment by itinerant troublemakers claiming to speak for great men who presumably did not need the money. They might as well sit tight, hoping that these unwelcome strangers would soon give up and never darken their doors again.[38]

Henry was, at least initially, optimistic that his agents would persuade the intruders to repurchase their land on what he considered "reasonable and just terms." He also wanted his representatives to trace the borders of his tracts and record who was living there, demonstrating his prerogative as legitimate owner and none-too-subtly hinting at the possibility of legal action. Henry hoped that some of the "intruders" would buckle under and that others would follow their example "as is the way of a flock of sheep," but his agents repeatedly found their way obstructed by the Connecticut settlers as they tried to make their way through the region. At least in theory, Pennsylvania investors had the might of their state government behind them. The courts judged repeatedly in favor of those who had bought the land under Pennsylvanian titles and a spate of legislation known as the Intrusion Laws declared void all sales and claims to title that did not recognize Pennsylvanian ownership of the lands in question, imposing stiff penalties on those who engaged in any such sales. The state government also threatened to remove the insurgents by force if they refused either to repurchase or leave voluntarily. As a pacifist, Henry hoped fervently for "a quiet and peaceable adjustment of this matter" and considered it his "religious duty" to work tirelessly to that end. Yet he acknowledged that the prospect of Connecticut settlers simply giving up and leaving without a fight was far-fetched, and whether the governor would really authorize the deployment of troops was uncertain. Henry began to suspect that this was mere "vapouring" or "puff" and feared that threats of this sort followed by inaction would undermine their chances of victory.[39]

The reports that Henry received from his agents depicted an increasingly volatile situation that threatened to degenerate into physical violence, between not only Connecticut settlers and the agents of Pennsylvania landholders but also those Connecticut settlers who were willing to repurchase and those who became more determined than ever to defend their presence. When it became known that Bartlett Hinds, one of the settlers from New England, supported the legitimacy of the Pennsylvanian land claims, others denounced him as a traitor, dragged him through Wyalusing Creek tied to a horse's tail, and then thrust his hands into a burning effigy of himself. Not surprisingly, Hinds was afraid to go back to his homestead and spent several months separated from his family; Henry offered him refuge in Bethany, suggesting that he might resettle there, and when Hinds visited Philadelphia that May the Drinkers received him at their home. Henry believed that some local magistrates and sheriffs were reluctant to take action against "these lawless outrages" for fear of reprisals against them; but others, he suspected, were colluding with those he termed "the aggressors." Adding another twist to an already convoluted state of affairs, rumors began to circulate that some of the agents sent out by the Pennsylvania government to initiate prosecutions against illicit settlers were secretly in league with those defying Pennsylvanian law and land titles. "Thus," wrote Henry, "is the state degraded and its laws brought into contempt by the departments and offices in government being committed to unprincipled men."[40]

Even when Connecticut settlers were willing to repurchase land under Pennsylvanian title, negotiations often sank into a quagmire of confusion over which Pennsylvanian investors owned which tracts and where exactly their boundaries ran. Reliable information of any sort was hard to come by. Henry, for example, did not even know exactly how many intruders were living on his land. In 1801, the Pennsylvania landowners formed an association to defend their interests, and the committee that they authorized to coordinate efforts on their behalf, on which Henry served, hired an agent named Robert Rose to negotiate directly with those Connecticut settlers willing to settle. Rose turned out to be an energetic and determined agent, traveling considerable distances throughout the backcountry to negotiate with settlers. Yet Rose was working with multiple handicaps. He often had no surveys or maps of the lots in question. It was often unclear which Pennsylvanian investors owned particular lots, and even when he was certain on whose behalf he was acting, he rarely had explicit instructions or powers of attorney from the owners that he could use to legitimize land sales. The committee members were supposed to work with Rose in identifying and contacting Pennsylvania owners, but as Henry pointed out, the people they needed to consult with were "numerous and scattered over this and other states," making their task both challenging and time-consuming. According to Elizabeth's diary, Henry attended more than sixty meetings of this committee before her death in 1807, hosting some of the meetings in their home. "How often have they met," she wrote, "I fear to little purpose!" She was not alone in her skepticism, and eventually most of the committee members stopped coming: "all exertion and attention is at a stand," wrote Henry in 1806.[41]

Though Henry never accompanied Robert Rose to meet with the so-called intruders, Rose called at the Drinkers' home on dozens of occasions to discuss the latest developments and examine maps and papers with Henry and his son William. Other agents and many settlers also visited to give reports or negotiate purchases. Elizabeth's diary entries often referred to various aspects of the ongoing dispute, and the "back settlements" (as she called them) were clearly a part of everyday conversation in the Drinker household.[42] Though Henry sometimes convinced himself that the situation was improving, Elizabeth's description of one progress report as "not very favorable" captured accurately, albeit rather politely, the overall prospect. While Rose gathered information about the tracts in contention, the settlers living on them, and the terms that might end the impasse, Henry and other investors initiated prosecutions against some of the intruders who refused to cooperate. Yet many sheriffs and jurymen in the region were themselves immigrants from Connecticut whose titles were also vulnerable to prosecution under the Intrusion Laws, and so they not surprisingly refused to cooperate. The Pennsylvania state assembly responded with legislation "slicing off" (as Henry put it) large parts of Luzerne County, which was dominated by hostile officials, then adding that land to Lycoming County, where most officials were friendly to the Pennsylvanian interest. However, the reallocation of land from one county to another required the running of new lines. Some of the bloodier-minded Connecticut settlers now declared that they would oppose any such attempts to survey the land by disguising themselves as Indians and driving off the surveyors. Henry worried about Rose's safety and urged him to avoid "the haunts of men bent on murder," though how Rose was supposed to do that was unclear.[43]

Henry was by this point eager, if not desperate, to sell off his land in northern Pennsylvania. He was still optimistic that an expanding network of roads connecting backcountry tracts to rivers and via them to commercial hubs would eventually attract settlers. In the meantime, however, continued disputes over land titles made it very difficult for him to sell land and so secure a return on his massive investment in the region. Other speculators had borrowed large sums of money to purchase their tracts and then, unable to repay the loans, went into bankruptcy. This further depressed land prices in the region, putting off investors who might otherwise have been interested in Henry's land. Fellow land speculator Benjamin Rush wrote in 1801 that those who had purchased backcountry tracts must "accommodate to the present state of things" and do whatever they could "to relieve themselves without loss of what they once deemed valuable." Henry would have agreed. Though not in any immediate danger of bankruptcy, whatever rumormongers might claim to the contrary, he was overextended and needed to secure income from his land investments. "My reputation and credit is at stake," he wrote in 1805. A venture that had seemed so promising and honorable was now the source of nothing but "distress and uneasiness of mind."[44]

"The Diamonds of America"

Henry's disillusionment about his land investments was exacerbated by the failure of a parallel project that aimed to turn natural resources on that land into a marketable product. The ultimate objective was again to provide not only profit but also moral uplift to the new nation. The key to this grandiose scheme was the maple tree. Henry envisaged that the same hardworking and virtuous settlers who would turn the backcountry into a network of productive farming communities could, in their spare time, extract the sap from maples on their land. The transformation of that sap into sugar for commercial sale would free citizens of the United States from dependence on cane sugar imported from British and French slave plantations in the West Indies. By flooding the domestic and then international market with a competitive alternative to sugar from the Caribbean, promoters of maple sugar hoped to undermine the profitability of slave labor in that region and thus persuade the planters there to abandon slavery. This was the ultimate in ethical investment schemes: those involved would line their pockets with gold and, in the words of one maple sugar booster, "destroy negro slavery" in the Caribbean.[45]

The maple sugar scheme captured the imagination of many forward-looking Philadelphians at the end of the 1780s. Part of the venture's appeal was its apparent practicality. Because maple sugar came from trees well established in the region, its manufacture required no new clearing or planting and so promised immediate income for newcomers to the region. The process for manufacturing maple sugar seemed relatively straightforward and required no significant investment in equipment. Farmers could tap each tree from a V cut made with an ax, the sap flowing via a wooden spout into hardwood troughs. They would carry the sap in pails to kettles for boiling until it coagulated into molasses, which they would then strain and dry to produce brown sugar. Promotional literature stressed that a mere handful of laborers could produce large quantities of maple sugar year after year without damaging the trees. Nor would this interfere with regular farming duties: the tapping and manufacturing season occurred in March and April, a time of year when farmers were not particularly busy. Because the required labor was not arduous, it could be carried out by children as well as adults and so reduced or eliminated any need to hire extra hands. The *Federal Gazette* declared, furthermore, that the sugar maple was "a beautiful stately tree, extremely ornamental as well as useful on every farm." Beauty, utility, and profit—what more could one ask![46]

Farming families had long produced maple sugar for their own use and for bartering in their neighborhoods, but this plan envisaged an entirely different scale of production that would benefit settlers, land investors, and the new nation's economy. While individual farming families could augment their income by producing the sweetener, larger commercial ventures stood to make a fortune, or so the promoters claimed. Because cane sugar was such a costly import, the substitution of maple sugar would make a significant difference in the nation's trade balance. It would also free the new republic from reliance on the European powers that still controlled the West Indies, making Americans economically as well as politically independent: boosters therefore characterized the production of this "American sugar" as a new expression of patriotism. The scarcity and rising price of sugar in the early 1790s, following the revolution in Saint-Domingue, provided an additional incentive for farmers to become involved, affording them an opportunity to benefit themselves and their country. William Cooper, a passionate advocate for maple sugar, estimated that the maples in New York and Pennsylvania alone could meet the entire demand for sugar within the United States three times over; maple sugar had the potential not only to satisfy domestic demand but also to become a major export for the United States. In time, it might exceed even tobacco and wheat as a source of income for the new nation. Maple sugar trees were, declared supporters of this scheme, "the diamonds of America" and "gifts of Heaven," potentially "more valuable to the United States than the mines of Peru."[47]

This domestic sweetener was also, promoters stressed, free of the literal and metaphorical pollution that tainted Caribbean cane sugar. Island sugar contained not only juice from the cane itself but also "the juices or excretions of ants—pissmires—cockroaches—borers—fleas—mosquitos—spiders—

bugs—grasshoppers—flies—lizards—and twenty other West India insects," as well as "the sweat of the negroes and when they are angry, nobody knows *what* else." Whereas American sugar was made by farmers "accustomed to cleanliness" and so "particularly careful to keep it free of everything which can affect its purity," the "poor oppressed sugar boiler of the West Indies, perhaps a slave, and if not a miserable hireling," would not care about such considerations. The labor used to produce cane sugar left it tainted figuratively as well as literally. According to Benjamin Franklin, the violence inflicted on West Indies slave laborers, along with the wars fought to defend the islands, left cane sugar "dyed scarlet" with "spots of human blood." Yet Americans consuming maple sugar need not worry about any such affronts to their ethical palates: its sweet flavor, declared the *Pennsylvania Mercury*, "ought to be enhanced by the reflection that it is not stained with the sweat and blood of Negro slaves." Providence had covered "millions of acres in our country" with maple trees, and the benefits of maple sugar would extend beyond the United States to "the interests of humanity in the West-Indies," making "the commerce and slavery of our African brethren in the sugar Islands as unnecessary, as it has always been inhuman and unjust."[48]

Such concerns played a crucial role in attracting Quaker investors and other social reformers to the maple sugar initiative. "The cause of humanity, as well as our interest," declared one newspaper, "are both deeply involved in this fortunate discovery." Citizens of the United States who switched to maple sugar would strike a blow against the vicious plantation regime in the West Indies and simultaneously express their pride in American virtue, as embodied in "the prosperity and happiness" of free laborers. The *Pennsylvania Mercury* claimed that "the idea of freedom" wafted from "every dish of tea" sweetened with maple sugar. Fraught negotiations over the issue of slavery at the Constitutional Convention in 1787 had made it abundantly clear that legislating an end to chattel labor within the United States was going to be extremely difficult. Yet the maple sugar venture seemed to promise an end to slavery on the sugar islands, though not within the United States, without any need for legislation that attacked slavery directly. As production of maple sugar increased and demand for cane sugar fell, declining profits would drive the owners of plantations in the West Indies to abandon the production of cane sugar and the slave labor system that supported its production, or else they would go bankrupt. The transatlantic slave trade would, according to one newspaper columnist, "in all likelihood gradually cease of itself," a prediction that coincided nicely with the conviction expressed by American commentators such as

Thomas Jefferson that slavery would eventually disappear as a natural consequence of economic and social development, without any recourse to painful and divisive governmental measures. As another newspaper article declared, maple sugar production within the United States would "root out slavery" in the sugar islands by simply "speaking to the interests of the slaveholders."[49]

Antislavery activists were well aware that many potential allies were disinclined to support even the noblest of causes if it involved personal sacrifice, and so it was fortuitous that the availability of maple sugar would enable consumers to take a stand against slave labor without having to abstain from sugar consumption. Calls for Americans to boycott goods produced by slave labor met with limited success even among Quakers as sweet teeth and fashion trumped moral imperatives. There were advocates for straightforward abstention. An essay published in 1791 suggested that Americans could surely forego the "gratification afforded once or twice a day by the taste of sugar in our tea" if that were to serve such a noble cause, and news reached Philadelphia of a growing movement in England for the nonconsumption of West Indies sugar and rum, its members known as "anti-Saccharites." Thousands of families and even entire communities in England were apparently pledging nonconsumption. Yet the maple sugar scheme promised a happy alternative to self-denial: Americans could support a domestic product, strike another blow against the British Empire, and undermine slavery in the West Indies, all without making any sacrifice at the tea table. Maple sugar promoters hoped that support in England for abstaining from cane sugar might grow significantly once a morally preferable alternative became widely available.[50]

Benjamin Rush, an eminent Philadelphian physician and avid social reformer, added his own twist to maple sugar boosterism in a paper that he read to the American Philosophical Society in 1791 and then published the following year. Rush made all the standard arguments in favor of the alternative sweetener. He also pointed out the range of products that maple sap could be used to produce: "a most agreeable molasses," "an excellent vinegar," "a pleasant summer beer," and even hard liquor, though Rush hoped that maple sugar would never be "prostituted by our citizens" to the latter "ignoble purpose." In addition, Rush noted that those who used large quantities of sugar in their diet did not generally have "a love for strong drink." Abstemious Quakers in the audience when Rush gave his lecture were doubtless pleased by such assurances. Speaking as a leading medical expert, he assured his audience that sugar provided "the greatest quantity of nourishment . . . of any substance in nature." It defended the body against "malignant fevers of all kinds" and helped to cure an impressive range of physical disorders. As for the old wives' tale that sugar was bad for the teeth, such nonsense now had "so few advocates" that it did not warrant "serious refutation."[51]

Henry Drinker had been elected to the American Philosophical Society in 1786 and may well have heard Rush's address. He had at that point been considering the economic and humanitarian potential of maple sugar for at least a few years. In 1789 he corresponded at length with William Cooper about Cooper's plan to promote backcountry settlement by stressing the potential gains, economic and ethical, offered by maple sugar production. According to Cooper, densely forested and stony tracts that were not readily convertible into farmland could nonetheless become lucrative if developers rethought their use of the land: instead of indiscriminately deforesting, he advocated turning the maple sugar trees that were interspersed with beeches throughout the region into a source of profit. Cooper was particularly interested in getting Henry involved because as co-owner of the Atsion ironworks he could supply the kettles needed to boil the extracted maple sap. For his part, Henry was immediately attracted to a scheme that promised considerable profit, would promote settlement in the backcountry, and had clear humanitarian implications. This was before Henry began to doubt Cooper's trustworthiness, and so he agreed to provide on credit three hundred kettles for distribution to farmers who would pay for them in kind with maple sugar. Cooper was well aware how much he owed Drinker for this sizable credit. "I fully believe," he wrote, "thee hath gone greater lengths to serve me than I have ever before experienced."[52]

In mid-August 1789, Henry was stopped in the street by Benjamin Rush and Tench Coxe, a leading economist who was about to become Alexander Hamilton's second in command at the U.S. Treasury. The two men told him about a plan to promote the sale of maple sugar once it reached the city. Rush, Coxe, and their allies were asking households to promise in advance that they would purchase specific quantities of maple sugar, which would provide a guaranteed market and reduce the risk for those who were thinking of venturing into maple sugar production. Many families in the city had already committed themselves, and the promoters of the plan were hoping that five hundred households would subscribe. Henry was delighted and promised to subscribe.[53] That fall, as Cooper predicted a harvest of one hundred thousand pounds, Henry decided that in addition to purchasing the sweetener and supplying sugar kettles, both wholesale to Cooper and individually at his store in Philadelphia, he would experiment with sugar production on his own lands. Toward the end of 1789, he instructed Samuel Preston to start manufacturing maple sugar out at Stockport, setting an example that he hoped other settlers in the region would follow. Cooper and Drinker would then stand together at the forefront of a potentially transformative economic and moral enterprise. "The whole depends on the contrivance and industry of HD and WC," declared an ebullient Cooper in December 1789. "Some will talk and others write, but we must be doing in fact."[54]

Yet most of those involved in the maple sugar scheme—whether talking, writing, or doing—were shooting blind. They had little knowledge of the manufacturing process or the skills needed to produce the sweetener on a commercial scale. When Henry wrote to tell his friend Robert Morris about his plans, Morris sounded a rare skeptical note. He warned that the venture's success would depend on the maple sugar's quality, price, and dependability of supply. "Subscriptions don't hold long," he wrote, "unless supported by convenience or interest." That warning, which Henry chose to ignore, proved remarkably prescient. The first attempt to produce maple sugar on a commercial scale in early 1790 was little short of disastrous, due in part to unfavorable weather but also to lack of expertise. Cooper's efforts resulted in only twenty thousand pounds of sugar, a mere fifth of what he had predicted, and even he admitted that its quality was "the poorest that hath been known for this twenty years." The modest yield made its way to Albany for transportation onward to Philadelphia amid torrential rain that slowed the convoy of carts and soaked the casks; it was possible, even likely, that the sugar inside had been seriously damaged. Fortunately, the weather improved by the time that the convoy completed its journey by river, and Cooper arranged for his sugar to enter Albany in a blaze of triumph. He even persuaded the city mayor to host a maple sugar and tea party at his home and arranged for reports of this glittering social event to reach Philadelphia's newspapers. By the time that Cooper's sugar set off for Philadelphia, disappointment about its quantity and the possibility of water damage had been eclipsed in a carefully orchestrated publicity blitz that focused on the sugar's quality and taste, apparently far superior to that of the West Indies alternative.[55]

Henry's plan for a manufacturing venture at Stockport had its first setback when a falling tree injured Samuel Preston in November 1789, forcing him to return to Philadelphia for several months while he recovered. Another of Henry's agents, John Hilborn, stepped in to take charge of the project, but neither he nor Preston had any particular knowledge of sugar manufacturing. Henry was apparently convinced that the sweetener was easy to produce and so assumed that any of his agents could manage such a venture, but this proved to be unduly optimistic, and a lack of skilled hands with experience of sugar production combined with unusually frigid weather to result in a much lower yield than expected. Nevertheless, Henry professed himself happy with the quality, if not the quantity, of sugar that arrived from Stockport and sent a box for presentation to President Washington, hoping that the great man would endorse "what promises to become a subject of great national importance." The president's note of thanks and polite encouragement further buoyed Henry's spirits, and he set about dispatching samples to contacts across the Atlantic. Henry predicted that the parcel of sugar wending its way from Albany to Philadelphia would convert even "unbelievers" to the great cause, that maple sugar production could in short order "be brought to great perfection," and that his lands in the region would before long increase in value fivefold. The Atsion ironworks was producing vast numbers of sugar kettles for distribution across the region, and the prospects for future demand seemed extremely rosy.[56]

The excitement that accompanied the triumphal entry of Cooper's maple sugar into Philadelphia on September 8, 1790, did not last long. Cooper's reputation took a severe beating when Edward Pennington, a sugar refiner whom Henry had asked to inspect the hogsheads, broke the news that rain had penetrated every cask, leaving most of the sugar unmarketable. Once news spread that the supposed "diamonds of America" were almost worthless, not a single refiner in Philadelphia was willing to accept Cooper's sugar.[57] Henry now began to do some hard thinking about the disappointing yields from their first season of production. He had entrusted his venture out at Stockport to agents who had no more experience or knowledge of sugar manufacturing than he did. Cooper, though present in the region, had many other projects demanding his attention as well as a bloated sense of his own abilities. Many of the families that had previously produced maple sugar for their own consumption settled for a relatively coarse version of the sweetener that would not satisfy the discerning palate of Philadelphian society. Cooper insisted that a few simple improvements in manufacturing technique, such as preventing the collection troughs from filling with dirt or rainwater and keeping cattle out of the troughs by tacking shingles over the trough, would bring about a more consistent quality, and several newspapers had recently printed articles that contained guidelines for maple sugar production. Henry worried, however, that some of those articles were downright wrong and most of them too brief to be useful. At this point he would have been well advised to hire experienced sugar boilers who could travel through his backcountry tracts and give practical advice, but instead he set about publishing and distributing across the region a pamphlet giving "plain directions and information" about the techniques and equipment required for the production of high-quality maple sugar. Although it was officially penned by "a Society of Gentlemen," Henry's influence was evident in its practical tone, its emphasis on the pioneering efforts by settlers at Stockport, and its list of "Necessary Utensils," which began with exactly the size and design of boiling kettle conveniently available from the Atsion ironworks and Henry's own store in Philadelphia.[58]

Henry trusted that the second season of production would prove more successful and in that spirit sent additional kettles to Cooperstown, despite his not having received payment for those he had sent the previous year. (Henry had long been accustomed as a merchant to waiting significant periods for payment by middlemen, and so he would not as yet have been concerned.) He was also hopeful that the state assembly in New York would encourage maple sugar production by offering bounties to those who became involved, setting a precedent for similar measures in Pennsylvania. Though investors such as Drinker and Cooper stood to profit from such bounties, they insisted that the benefits would extend throughout the United States and beyond. Maple sugar boosters believed that they were still making headway with public opinion despite recent disappointments. Tench Coxe claimed in a letter to Benjamin Rush that he had "electrified" (or as he put it, "electerized") a dinner party in Philadelphia with his effusive description of maple sugar and all that it promised.[59]

Unfortunately, the winter of 1790–91 brought with it another round of exceptionally harsh weather, which prevented Preston, who had traveled to Philadelphia and New York in order to promote the maple sugar venture, from getting back to Stockport. This was a grave disappointment to Henry, though how much Preston actually knew about sugar production was open to question.[60] Hilborn was again in charge, and Henry hoped that his common sense and managerial competence, combined with the knowledge he had acquired the previous year, would ensure a successful season. Yet Hilborn was suffering so badly from lameness, a legacy of frostbite "when formerly a prisoner with the Indians," that he could not even get outside to supervise the laborers, and in March the snow lay so deep that it was impossible to collect the sap. Meanwhile, the government in New York had not passed legislation encouraging sugar production. That spring Henry ran out of promotional samples but could get no more from Stockport and so asked Cooper to send a parcel, but "the extreme failure" of that second season had left his partner's supplies equally depleted. The two men now engaged in a spate of mutual recrimination. Drinker criticized Cooper for not employing a sugar boiler with the requisite "skill and experience," though he had himself failed to do so out at Stockport. Cooper complained about the collapse of enthusiasm for his sugar among Philadelphians, whose "boasted spunk" had turned out to be ephemeral. "The patriotism of Philadelphia spends itself in air," he fumed. Drinker dismissed these fulminations, reminding him that as men of faith they should submit with humility to "the dispensations of Providence as to the seasons," in the meantime "persevering in a good thing and holding out to the end."[61]

However acrimonious their private correspondence, both men took steps to restore the positive buzz that had initially surrounded maple sugar production and to secure public support for their project. That involved some degree of collaboration with the civil government. Once branded as an enemy of the people, Henry was now meeting and consulting with the new nation's political leaders. In May 1791, Henry had breakfast with Benjamin Rush and Thomas Jefferson, the U.S. secretary of state. They discussed the prospects "for acquiring of wealth out of our wilderness," and Henry had a similar conversation with Hamilton. He was delighted to learn that Jefferson and James Madison were about to leave on "a long excursion into and through an extensive sugar maple country." Yet Henry was quite defensive about his association with these prominent public figures. When one of Henry's correspondents congratulated him on becoming a close confidant of such powerful men, he stressed in response that he had never been "on a footing of intimacy" with Hamilton, Jefferson, or Madison: though he had received "overtures" from them, he had held aloof. Henry was determined to salvage the maple sugar scheme and had great faith in its ethical as well as economic value to the new nation. If that involved working with the civil state, so be it. Yet he was well aware that most Quakers now shunned any direct involvement in politics, and after his recent dusting down by Isaac Hicks, he did not want to be accused of ambitions in that direction, thus his insistence that he was working with political leaders at arm's length, not hand in hand. "My path in life," he wrote, "don't naturally lead to an assimilation with great men, or at least with those so held in worldly estimation."[62]

Drinker and his project were attracting a great deal of attention. Many requests arrived for maple tree seeds, and he asked Preston to send a parcel of young trees down to Philadelphia so that "persons disposed to promote their culture" could examine them. Contacts in England were also voicing interest. Cooper sent samples of his own to President Washington, just as Henry had done the previous year, and to Jefferson. Both men sent encouraging replies and planted maples on their estates in Virginia. Washington's message of thanks appeared in the public press.[63] However, attempts to develop maple sugar production on a commercial scale had so far proven very disappointing. Cooper was heavily indebted to Drinker for the two consignments of sugar kettles, and when the next winter produced weather even less favorable than the previous two, he decided to cut his losses and abandon the venture. Local settlers who had expanded their production of maple sugar to meet commercial demand now reverted to producing for domestic use and local bartering. The demand for sugar kettles collapsed, and Cooper began to cut down the very maple trees that he had previously wished to protect from deforestation: he now wanted to turn them into potash with which to pay the debt he owed to Henry. To do that he needed potash kettles, which Henry duly provided, still optimistic that his partner would find a way to turn a profit from their land investments. Yet by the summer of 1792, Cooper owed him over a thousand pounds for ironware, and although Henry claimed that his primary motive in providing the kettles had been the "general benefit" that would result, he found Cooper's failure to pay up increasingly disturbing.[64]

Henry decided to persist, but after a third disappointing season at Stockport he committed to a fundamental shift in strategy that would, at least in theory, spread the financial burden and risk. Instead of proceeding as a single and singularly exposed investor, he set about recruiting subscribers for a company that would invest in a new production facility to be located several miles away from Stockport, on a three-thousand-acre tract alongside Little Equinunk Creek (now Manchester Township in Wayne County), which became known as Union Farm. In September 1792, thirty investors joined with Henry to form the Society for Promoting the Manufacture of Sugar from the Sugar Maple Tree and Furthering the Interest of Agriculture in Pennsylvania. Henry was one of the largest shareholders and became treasurer. Preston was to supervise construction on-site and the opening of a road that would connect the new settlement to the Delaware River. Henry invited John Kinsey, a Quaker from Bucks County, to become the site manager. Kinsey doubted that he had the specific knowledge or skills to superintend maple sugar manufacturing, but he gave way once Henry assured him that Hilborn would be on hand for the first season to share his experience in sugar production at Stockport.[65]

The 1793 sugar season proved to be an almost complete failure. That winter was again severe, and Kinsey did not even leave for Union Farm until early February because his children had come down with "the Scarletina" and could not travel. Despite Hilborn's presence on-site, the meager quantity of sugar sent down to Philadelphia was worth nowhere near what the company had spent on wages and supplies. "It was mortifying," wrote Henry, "to find so little had been done," and he found himself "at a loss" to explain the failure when questioned by dismayed shareholders. Meanwhile, several rafts carrying lumber from Stockport down to Philadelphia drifted off course and their retrieval proved expensive. To make matters even worse, the company's plan to supplement its income by selling off small lots of land to settlers floundered because many of the families who wished to settle there simply could not afford to buy. In desperation, the board agreed to lease some of the land, on condition that the tenants were "the right kind of people" and that they promised to plant sugar maples on the land. The rapid income from sugar and land sales that Henry and his fellow investors had banked on was nowhere in sight. Then, in the late summer of 1793, a yellow fever epidemic struck Philadelphia, killing several thousand residents and driving others to take refuge in the countryside. This made consultation between the company shareholders next to impossible, and not until that December did the governing board finally reconvene at Drinker's home.[66]

Kinsey was doing his best to cut costs and wanted to turn Union Farm into a self-sustaining community. At the end of 1793, he asked the subscribers for permission to clear land along the Little Equinunk Creek so that he could grow crops to feed "man and beast" instead of having to purchase food and convey it from elsewhere "at a heavy expense." They agreed to this sensible proposal but apparently suspected that he wanted to abandon sugar production altogether and so stipulated that he must make an effort to produce sugar next season, "so far as thou canst procure hands to aid thee therein." Kinsey now shared with Henry that he and his wife were unhappy living at the settlement and that both were suffering from bouts of ill health. The relationship between Drinker and Kinsey became somewhat strained as Henry, writing from the comfort of his home in Philadelphia, counseled perseverance and submission to God's will in the face of affliction. Indeed, Henry declared that his manager's "domestic affairs" were none of his business and warned against "improper discontent with the allotments of Providence." In June 1794, Preston wrote to inform Henry that Kinsey had become "so ill as his life is despaired of." Henry now adopted a warmer tone, claiming that he felt "real uneasiness" and "tender sympathy" for Kinsey and his family. Nonetheless, he informed Kinsey that November that the shareholders were increasingly concerned about how much they were paying him to oversee a venture that now seemed a dubious investment. They intended to replace him, not because he deserved "any censure," but because they needed someone with "a more robust constitution" who would also accept a more modest remuneration.[67]

Henry was now ready to admit that choosing managers based on their general competence and integrity rather than for any specific knowledge of maple sugar production had been misguided and that he had underestimated the challenge of training local settlers in the necessary skills to manufacture sugar on a commercial scale. The other investors had lost interest in the venture. "Few of the concerned give themselves any trouble or thought about the matter," Henry complained, and they were certainly not interested in making any further financial contributions, so that Henry's own "oppressed purse must bear all." Though he had originally refused to serve as company president, he was now in charge by default. To make matters worse, a fire on-site destroyed all buildings near the furnace and "numerous valuable materials." At a meeting in January 1795, only four shareholders turned up, including Henry. He suspected that the low turnout was due to "a prevailing sentiment" that the venture was doomed.[68]

Such turned out to be the case. When Kinsey identified a promising candidate to succeed him as manager but proposed that this individual have the same salary that he had received, Henry's response was indignant: "Can it be supposed that the managers would be so stupid as to go on in such enormous expenses?" Kinsey finally left in May 1795, at which time Preston stepped in temporarily, urged by Henry to avoid any but the most necessary expenses. Late that fall, the company's governing board decided to abandon the venture altogether and proposed that the land and equipment be sold as soon as possible, which the subscribers agreed to on November 9, on condition that no offer be accepted unless it would reimburse them for their "contributions to the society's stock" and pay off the company's debts. No one stepped forward to purchase Union Farm, despite Henry's hope that a new road under construction just south of the estate would stimulate interest. The title was in Henry's name, and he continued to pay the real estate taxes until his death, at which point his executors took over the payments. In 1833, the state assembly gave permission for the tract's sale at auction to recompense Henry's heirs for the many debts that he and they had incurred (with any remaining balance to be shared among the other shareholders). A family agent bought the property at the auction for a nominal sum, reconveyed it to the estate, and then resold it for a much higher sum. Yet the final proceeds amounted to less than a third of what the family was owed by time of sale.[69]

~

Henry had resolved at the end of the War for Independence "to become more separated from worldly entanglements." In 1787, he wrote that he had "for years past determined that no prospect of profit or advantage shall induce me to encumber myself with engagements that shall interfere with my settled plan of reducing my affairs into a narrow compass." Yet the entrepreneurial projects in which he subsequently took a leading role consumed much of his time and energy during the last quarter-century of his life. "HD as usual writing in the office," wrote his wife in 1798. "He is one of the greatest slaves in Philadelphia." Elizabeth's equation of her husband's situation with slavery might seem in hindsight stunningly insensitive for any number of reasons. Yet the comparison did capture both her and his sense that Henry was shackled to these twin ventures, neither of which yielded the returns he had hoped for. The increasingly emotive language that Henry used in his own correspondence when writing about his land investments and the maple sugar project made abundantly clear how stressful and demoralizing he found them. They also shattered his assumptions about the basic trustworthiness of fellow Quakers and humankind in general. His repeated encounters with knavery and betrayal appalled Elizabeth: "If HD had men as honest as himself to deal with," she lamented, "he would not meet with the many perplexities that he does." When Henry wrote in 1796 to impress on a friend how necessary it was "to guard against the Grand Discourager," he may have been trying to bolster his own as well as his friend's spirits. By the end of his life, Henry was much chastened and eager to warn his friends against committing to similarly risky ventures. In 1808, when Jason Torrey, Henry's agent out at Bethany and a landowner in his own right, decided to set up a general store to service the fledgling settlement, Henry advised him to beware of "aiming at great things and risking thy credit and reputation." He recommended that his friend be "especially guarded against selling on credit." Henry was doubtless aware that if he had followed that advice himself, he would not have been so strapped for cash toward the end of his life.[70]

Like many speculators in the early republic, Henry had made a series of wildly optimistic assumptions that one by one turned out to be unfounded and potentially ruinous. Despite many years of experience in the business world, he proved to be remarkably gullible, entrusting massive sums of money and his reputation to people who turned out to be inept, untrustworthy, or both. Yet perhaps the most fundamental deficit that Henry brought to these projects was that he knew next to nothing about agriculture. He was "so little of a farmer," he wrote to one of his agents in northern Pennsylvania, that he could give no "particular" advice and would have to rely on his correspondent's "own knowledge, added to that of some judicious farmer" in the region. This was surely the nub of the problem: successful extraction of wealth from these lands involved practical knowledge of the soil and the natural resources on hand, the skills required to turn those resources into marketable products, and either his direct supervision or a team of trusted and consistently trustworthy managers. Henry had none of these and yet somehow persuaded himself that his backcountry ventures would flourish.[71]

Henry had hoped to carve out for himself a second career in which he proved his worth to the new republic and showed that Quaker values could enrich the nation morally while also turning a handsome financial profit. If the frontier settlements that his agents managed for him had developed into well-functioning, godly, and peaceful communities, or if maple sugar had eclipsed its cane counterpart, shutting down slave plantations in the Caribbean, he would no doubt have celebrated these outcomes as landmarks on his journey as a man of faith. Yet as his dreams of moral uplift came crashing down and submerged in a nightmarish quagmire of frustration and anxiety, Henry resented more and more the time he spent on those wretched tracts and the treacherous maple trees that stubbornly refused to deliver on their promise. As Henry advanced into his sixties and seventies, and as bouts of ill health accentuated his awareness of growing physical frailty, he wanted to preserve his energies for those commitments closest to his heart, including service to his religious community and his own spiritual growth. However, much as Henry would have liked to focus on that religious estate "wherein consists the true felicity," his "earthly cares . . . beclouded and obscured" his way forward. Meanwhile, Henry's wife was also grappling with the challenges of a post-revolutionary world. She did so in response to a democratizing spirit that had made its way, unsolicited, into her own home. One of her principal duties as household mistress was to hire, supervise, and when necessary fire their servants. Domestics now expected very different treatment following Independence, and Elizabeth, who despite her Quaker values was no social leveler, did not respond kindly to such expectations.[72]

7 • "Times Are Much Changed, and Maids Are Become Mistresses"

In Which Elizabeth Drinker Tries to Fend Off a Domestic Revolution

"Jacob Turner and Sarah Needham, negro and negress, went to a wedding this evening," wrote Elizabeth Drinker late one night in January 1799. Turner and Needham were free black servants who lived and worked in the Drinker household, and they were courting. Elizabeth gave an unusually detailed description of their physical appearance that evening and of their departure from the house. Jacob was dressed for this festive outing in "a light cloth coat, white cassimere vest and britches, white silk stockings, and new hat." Sarah wore "white muslin, dizened off with white ribbons from head to foot, yellow morocco shoes with white bows, etc." Elizabeth clearly found their attire noteworthy: as a respectable Quaker matron, she would have disapproved of such ostentatious fripperies regardless of who was wearing them, but these elaborate outfits would have seemed particularly inappropriate when worn by servants, perhaps especially because the individuals in question were a "negro and negress." On a previous occasion, Elizabeth had noted sarcastically that Jacob and Sarah were out in the evening with "some other black gentry." They now left for the wedding in a carriage they had hired for the occasion, driven by a man whom their mistress specifically categorized as "white." At the time of her writing this diary entry, it was almost eleven o'clock and the couple had not yet returned. Elizabeth was describing a world turned upside-down, in which servants felt free to stay out late, blacks assumed the appearance and prerogatives of white "gentry," and a white man chauffeured a black couple to a party. "Times," Elizabeth concluded, "is much altered with the black folk."[1]

In March 1799, a few months after attending this wedding, Jacob informed his master and mistress that he and Sarah were themselves going to marry. "We have had a hint of the kind before," Elizabeth wrote. As free adults, Jacob and Sarah could make this decision without seeking the Drinkers' permission, but Jacob gave them only a week's notice of the impending nuptials, and a few days later Sarah went to stay with her mother until the wedding. She promised to return afterward, but only to stay for a few weeks until after the Yearly Meeting, at which time she would "go to room-keeping," settling into married life with Jacob in a rented room. Elizabeth often complained that reliable servants were hard to come by, so the prospect of replacing Sarah was far from welcome, but at the same time, she was glad to see one of her female servants find a reliable husband. "We may lose a good servant by it," wrote her mistress, "but if it is for her benefit, I shall be satisfied." Elizabeth and Henry offered to pay for a wedding supper, on condition that it took place at the Drinker home "in a sober way," but the couple turned down their offer in favor of a party at the home of Jacob's brother. The reason seems to have been Henry and Elizabeth's insistence on a "sober" celebration: "a wedding without a frolic," Elizabeth wrote, "would be no wedding, I believe, in their view." Jacob and Sarah were determined to celebrate on their own territory and on their own terms. The Drinkers did not attend (whether they were invited is not clear). Sarah did return as promised after her wedding but then left earlier than expected and without consulting her mistress. "Such conduct will not answer," Elizabeth wrote with exasperation. Jacob continued with the Drinkers for a year after his marriage, his master procured medicine for Sarah and Jacob's sick baby, born that fall, and when Sarah asked for a reference in July 1800, her former mistress gave her "a good one." Yet Elizabeth's comments about Jacob and Sarah during their employment in her home make clear her resentment of their independent-minded and, from her perspective, inconsiderate behavior.[2]

There was nothing unique about this chain of events. Following Independence, many domestic workers, and not just "the black folk," asserted themselves in ways that shocked and irritated employers like Elizabeth Drinker. These were, she complained, "high times with servants." Revolution took many forms in late eighteenth-century Philadelphia. The political upheaval that had brought Elizabeth's family to the brink of tragedy also gave rise to a revolution in the expectations and behavior of domestic servants. During the 1770s, Philadelphia experienced a populist upsurge that resulted in one of the most democratic state constitutions ratified in the aftermath of Independence. The egalitarian tone and substance of that constitution percolated through the city's wharves, artisanal workshops, and kitchens. Employers expected deference and obedience from their workers but now discovered, to their dismay, that servants and other laborers insisted on the freedom to choose for themselves how and with whom they should spend their free time, how they should dress, and whether to abide by the moral codes that their masters and mistresses expected them to follow. An English visitor to Philadelphia in 1794 made an explicit connection between political change and the behavior of domestics there: "a republic," he wrote, "is not the place to find good servants." Philadelphia's householders often complained of increasing "impertinence and irregular conduct" among domestic laborers, and Elizabeth Drinker was no exception. In September 1777, when Nancy Oat, a former indentured servant, came "to demand her freedom dues" (usually clothes and some cash), Elizabeth found the young woman's manner "very impertinent and saucy." Nancy's father then called on the Drinkers and "behaved with so much impudence" that Elizabeth refused to hand over the dues. Elizabeth clearly expected deference and gratitude but could no longer count on either. A year later, after complaining in her diary that another servant had invited a female friend to stay the night "without asking leave," she declared, "Times are much changed, and maids are become mistresses."[3]

A gradual shift from indentured servitude to wage labor accentuated that trend toward greater assertiveness among servants. White indentured servants were usually recent migrants from across the Atlantic who worked for a specified number of years in exchange for the cost of transportation from their point of origin, food, clothes, lodging, medical care, and whatever education or training their employers thought appropriate. Black indentured domestics were mostly children or teenagers who had fled slavery in the South; those who had helped them to travel northward, often Quakers, then placed them in white households as servants; once their indentures ended, they joined the city's free adult population. As the labor shortages that had plagued Philadelphia in its early decades faded, hiring servants by the day, week, or month became much more appealing to employers than committing for several years to a bound servant. The acquisition of black indentured servants continued as part of an ongoing strategy for supporting flight from slavery, whereas taking on white indentured servants was a more straightforward economic choice that became less attractive over time. From a servant's point of view, wage labor carried with it less security but greater personal freedom. Indentured servants became part of the family in which they lived, but they were in a subordinate position and always subject to close supervision. Free waged domestics worked and might also live in a family home, but they were not part of that family to anything like the same degree and they expected to do as they pleased during the hours when not actually laboring for their employers.[4]

There was no sudden transition within the Drinker household from a reliance on indentured servants to a system of wage labor. At any given time, the Drinkers had working for them a combination of indentured servants; free full-time domestics who mostly lived in but who had no contract and might leave at any time, either because they quit or because they had been fired; and casual employees who came to perform specific tasks such as sewing or whitewashing. These different categories of worker interacted with one another, and employers might well worry that the spirit of independence exhibited by wage laborers would influence the behavior of indentured domestics. Indentured laborers became free in due course and so embodied within their own lives the larger economic transition under way from bound to wage labor. When bound servants reached the end of their contracts and stayed on as free laborers in the same household, they expected different treatment, and that transition could prove troublesome for all concerned. Some young adults in this position were, not surprisingly, eager to move out and find new employers with whom they would establish a relationship unaffected by their former status.

Masters and mistresses who cared about the moral character of their servants found it increasingly difficult to guide or restrain them. One Philadelphian moralist urged employers to keep a close eye on servants at all hours, especially in "the evening, when they cease[d] to be subject to government" and so were "in the most danger of corruption." Yet employers might well have asked how they were supposed to keep a close eye on hired servants at times when they were not "subject to government." Elizabeth worried, moreover, that laborers coming to the end of their indentures might not be ready to exercise their new freedom responsibly, and she often seemed to doubt that they would ever be capable of functioning successfully without her guiding hand. Elizabeth felt this most intensely when dealing with domestics who had arrived in her home as small children and grew up under her tutelage; but it showed also in her treatment of servants who arrived as adults. George Fox, founder of the Society of Friends, had urged his followers to treat servants as if they were their children, which implied a good deal more than nurturing love. That attitude was alive and well among Quakers in late eighteenth-century Philadelphia. When Sarah Fisher's servant Betty, a widow with two grown daughters, left in 1786 to remarry, Fisher described her decision as "inconsiderate" and "girlish." Elizabeth treated employees who met her expectations with kindness and compassion, but she never entirely respected them as autonomous adults. The persona that she adopted as household mistress—

benevolent yet explicitly hierarchical, often condescending, and none-too-subtly infantilizing those under her authority—must have grated on the nerves of servants, especially given the rhetoric of liberty and equality percolating through the city. Domestic laborers might also have had unrealistic expectations after hearing Quaker employers use egalitarian language that servants might have thought applied to them. Despite their belief in spiritual equality, Friends rarely advocated comprehensive social leveling, but eavesdropping servants may not always have grasped such distinctions.[5]

The rowdy street culture of seaports such as Philadelphia posed an additional challenge for employers who wished to maintain a well-ordered household. Free servants made no secret of their eagerness to escape the restrictive surveillance of their employers once their work hours ended. The boisterous and bawdy venues for pleasure into which these workers disappeared at night were very much at odds with the moral code that respectable Quaker householders such as the Drinkers wished to impose on their dependents. Single, married, and widowed men and women, genteel and otherwise, servants of both sexes, casual laborers, apprentices, artisans, sailors, and other transients filled the streets and taverns, drank, made merry, flirted, and joined in sexual congress. Prostitutes were, according to one account, "so numerous that they flood the streets at night," and unemployed female servants sometimes turned to the sex trade as a way to feed themselves; others augmented their wages as domestics by working as prostitutes during their off hours. Philadelphia's vibrant street culture may well have been liberating and exciting for servants escaping the drudgery of their workaday lives and the sanctimonious attentions of their employers, but it posed many practical dangers, not least sexually transmitted diseases and pregnancy. Employers were not oblivious to these practical hazards, yet their primary concern was that servants under their charge might become morally corrupt and then taint their own homes.[6]

The presence in Philadelphia of a large and growing free black population further complicated the situation. Following passage of the state's emancipation law in 1780, slavery declined rapidly in Pennsylvania, by almost 80 percent between 1790 and 1810. Philadelphia became a haven for African Americans either freed from or escaping slavery, and the number of free blacks living in the city tripled during the 1790s alone. Many of these men and women worked as servants in the homes of wealthy Philadelphians like the Drinkers, some of them free laborers, others indentured as children or teenagers. By the late eighteenth century, Quakers identified closely with the antislavery movement on both sides of the Atlantic, but in earlier years they had figured prominently among slave owners and slave traders. Despite scattered calls for emancipation, not until the mid-eighteenth century did persistent lobbying by determined activists such as John Woolman and Elizabeth's schoolmaster Anthony Benezet finally bring about a change of heart among Quakers in general. That coincided with a broader transformation as the Society of Friends committed to a multifaceted program of reform. In 1758, Philadelphia's Yearly Meeting prohibited its members from buying or selling slaves; it also established committees to visit Friends who owned slaves, urging them to free all chattel laborers, but it was not until 1776 that the Yearly Meeting explicitly banned slaveholding.[7]

Henry and Elizabeth actively supported the antislavery movement, but in common with many other Friends, they retained the racial prejudices that pervaded Anglo-American society even as they advocated for emancipation. In the 1790s, Henry held antislavery meetings at their home, hosted a deputation of Friends from Rhode Island who had come to present Congress with a declaration against the slave trade, and three years later went himself with several other Friends to protest the kidnapping and reenslavement of freed blacks. Elizabeth commented that the Society of Friends had "done much in this business with good effect, but not so much as could have been desired." Indeed, it was not until 1796 that the Philadelphia Yearly Meeting finally removed color as an obstacle to full membership in the Society of Friends. The year before that change in policy, the Drinkers hosted a meeting of several Friends with Hannah Burrows, a woman of mixed race who had been preaching in the city and was seeking full membership. They also worked closely with antislavery activist Warner Mifflin to find shelter and employment for blacks fleeing northward from slavery, including in their own home. Skin color was not the primary determinant in Elizabeth's treatment of servants: whether the servant was indentured or a wage laborer seems to have made a greater difference, and black as well as white laborers worked for the Drinkers in both capacities. However, theirs was not a colorblind household: Elizabeth often labeled black employees explicitly as black, whereas for her whiteness was normal and generally went unremarked unless she was making a specific point about appropriate racial hierarchies, as in her description of a "white" coachman driving "negro and negress" Jacob and Sarah to a wedding. She condemned the system of slavery, and her heart went out to enslaved people; yet she clearly saw her black servants as a distinct group, and occasional comments in her diary betrayed deeply ingrained racism.[8]

Responsibility for domestic staff fell primarily on the shoulders of household mistresses, though Elizabeth did occasionally turn to her husband for support, deferring to or deploying his authority as household head. Henry hardly ever mentioned their servants in his letters, and so we glimpse his occasional involvement only through Elizabeth's diary. He often hosted meetings in their home or worked in his office there and so was doubtless aware of any significant problems his wife was having with their domestics. Both he and Elizabeth cared about the orderliness of their home, their family's reputation, and the welfare, moral and otherwise, of their servants. Yet the hiring, firing, and day-to-day supervision of the household staff lay mostly within her orbit. The one notable exception to this was their driver, a position that Henry saw as his purview. He also hired the clerks who worked for him in his home office, along with the younger lads who ran errands. They did not count as part of the domestic staff, and Elizabeth mentioned them only when she became aware that their work was unsatisfactory, presumably because Henry was complaining about them, or when he needed to replace them because they had quit or been fired.[9]

Elizabeth's diary laid bare the domestic tensions created by the emergence of a new social order in urban centers such as Philadelphia. She noted in entry after entry how servants' behavior had transformed and recorded her own responses, which combined outrage, frustration, and discomfort with the unfamiliar world unfolding around her. Elizabeth and Henry doubtless believed that they were fair-minded and compassionate employers, yet they demonstrated in their dealings with servants the class-related and racial assumptions that permeated the eighteenth-century Anglo-American white elite. Henry had started life as an apprentice, but he now had a clear sense of his prerogatives as employer and household head; Elizabeth also expected their dependents to treat her with the deference she thought appropriate. The expectations of householders in post-revolutionary Philadelphia had not changed at anything like the same pace as those of their employees. Whatever the rhetoric of equality and fraternal love that accompanied the Revolution, an older and explicitly hierarchical model remained firmly in place when it came to the running of most homes. The atmosphere within the Drinker household was complicated, multilayered, and ambiguous in ways that must have been confusing, uncomfortable, and occasionally maddening for all concerned. Elizabeth made no secret of her discomfort with changing "customs and manners," especially if those demanding change were employees. Ultimately, she had the upper hand, but the transformed expectations and behavior of her servants created tension on an almost daily basis.[10]

"That Necessary Branch of Housekeeping"

The Drinkers lived in a large house and most of the time had several full-time servants as well as casual laborers to keep their home in good working order. A constant flow of social callers, business associates, and Quaker committee members came by the house to see Henry, Elizabeth, her sister, and in later years their children, along with the houseguests who stayed with them during the Yearly Meeting that drew into the city Friends from across Pennsylvania and New Jersey. These visitors brought considerable dirt and disruption into the house (" 'tis a great work to clean this house thoroughly," Elizabeth declared), and they often stayed for tea or a meal. Servants cooked, cleaned, and ironed, carried messages back and forth between households, and accompanied members of the family on social visits. Elizabeth did not record systematically how many servants they had working in the house at any given time, but it would seem that there were generally between four and six in residence. These ranged in age from children whom they took in as indentured servants to mature adults of both sexes, which seems to have been typical of similar households in late eighteenth-century Philadelphia. Those who came to live in the house as free laborers tended to stay for weeks or months rather than years, in part because of frequent arguments between Elizabeth and her servants over their work performance and general behavior. The challenge of finding servants who would meet the family's requirements, compounded in the late 1770s by wartime disruption, made it difficult to find satisfactory replacements. In the fall of 1778, Elizabeth complained that her household staff had fallen from five to one: "It is the case with many at present," she wrote, "good servants are hard to be had, [and] such a time was never known here, I believe, in that respect."[11]

Those members of Philadelphia's elite who aspired to a European-style aristocratic mode of life had domestic staff with specific titles and responsibilities such as doorkeeper, coachman, and chef. Some of those families also had a male steward or female housekeeper who oversaw the other servants. Yet these self-consciously grandiose households were few in number and proved controversial in a republican city. Neither Elizabeth nor her sister considered herself above day-to-day supervision of servants, and there was no rigid differentiation of responsibilities among the Drinkers' servants, most of whom performed a variety of tasks depending on the needs of the moment. Even their coachman had to carry out other duties when not occupied in driving family members hither and thither. This lack of strict distinction in roles and status among the servants made for greater flexibility and expressed the family's repudiation of aristocratic parade. Theirs was an affluent, fashionably furnished, and (whenever possible) well-staffed household, but not an ostentatious one.[12]

The business of running a household had changed dramatically during the closing decades of the colonial period and would continue to do so during the early years of the republic. Seventeenth-century families had made on-site most of the products that they used and consumed, or they acquired them from neighbors in exchange for surplus produce or homemade articles such as soap or candles. Even household mistresses who employed servants participated actively in household labor, inheriting domestic skills from older female relatives and then passing them on to daughters, granddaughters, and servants; they were, in effect, the female equivalents of master craftsmen. This began to change in the decades preceding the Revolution, as households in larger towns and seaports could now purchase goods from stores that imported food, clothing, furniture, and other supplies from England, Europe, and the West Indies as well as other mainland colonies and local markets. In addition to becoming consumers in a transatlantic marketplace, householders who could afford to do so increasingly hired domestic workers to distinguish themselves from those who had to participate in physical labor. Affluent household mistresses such as Elizabeth Drinker now spent much more of their time managing servants than in carrying out tasks that even leading colonial goodwives and their daughters would sometimes have handled themselves.[13]

This did not mean that Elizabeth was incapable of performing such tasks. In one entry, she noted that she and her daughter Ann had spent the entire morning ironing, and she often spent time in the kitchen bottling ale, preserving walnuts, making jam, and baking pies. She and her contemporaries would have supervised their servants in part by being present and participating to some degree in household labor, but for the most part, they would have left menial tasks to their subordinates. Elizabeth had learned needlework as a girl and in later life spent time darning socks or knitting as well as taking on more demanding and largely decorative sewing projects. She employed seamstresses to make clothes for her husband, children, and servants but also did some of this work herself and expected to be closely involved; on one occasion she sent a seamstress away because she was too busy with other matters to keep an eye on what the hired woman was doing. Elizabeth noted that the work done by these women was less delicate than hers was, but they also got the job done more quickly: "poor girls," she declared, "they earn their money."

The sacrifice in terms of quality was worthwhile, she thought, especially when the clothing was for servants and so did not have to be "nicely done."[14]

The key to maintaining an elegant and efficient home was now effective management of its domestic workforce, which Elizabeth described as "that necessary branch of housekeeping." Contemporary guides for young married women stressed that household mistresses should be "ever watchful" over their servants. They should aim "to unite authority with kindness" and even "courtesy," which would "heighten their respect as well as their affection." Even in homes where deputies supervised the staff, mistresses were "ultimately answerable for the conduct of the whole." Most mistresses supervised their servants directly: Elizabeth's friend Nancy Shippen wrote that she devoted two hours each day to "domestic management," inspecting the work that had been completed and giving out instructions for the work to be done that day. According to another of Elizabeth's neighbors, Sarah Fisher, keeping an "attentive eye" on servants was "a weighty task." Sarah began to instruct her daughter Hannah in "family affairs" at the age of ten so that she would grow up to be "a good housewife and active mistress." The Drinker household was unusual in that Elizabeth's unmarried sister, Mary, shared these duties and took over entirely when Elizabeth was away or immobilized by illness. Nonetheless, Elizabeth was actively involved in the hiring, supervision, disciplining, and firing of the household workforce.[15]

The careful management of domestics was important not only to ensure efficiency but also for the maintenance of social distinctions and the moral fiber of the home. Post-revolutionary writings stressed the importance of the family home as an incubator for personal and public virtue, nurturing virtuous offspring who would become upstanding citizens. As Quakers and as an upwardly mobile couple eager to embody respectability, Elizabeth and Henry would have had particular reason to protect the moral integrity of their household. No one could hope to keep servants entirely separate from the family for which they worked; and given that some of the servants who came to live in these households were themselves children, they would most likely develop close relationships with the children of their employers, however carefully differentiated by status. Although domestics increasingly had their own sleeping quarters, often on a separate floor or even in a separate structure, families and their domestics nonetheless still lived in close proximity. The symbolic separation between "parlor" and "kitchen"—one the domain of the family, the other assigned to household staff—was in practice somewhat artificial as servants were constantly coming in and out of the parlor and household mistresses spent at least some time in the kitchen supervising and working with their servants. Domestics were ever present as they cleaned the home, washed the clothes, cooked the meals, and waited at table. Disorderly or immoral servants could easily contaminate the entire household, and so, declared one commentator, "None who pretend to be friends of religion and virtue should ever keep a domestic, however expert in business, whom they know to be guilty of immorality." Yet dismissal was the last resort, given the inconvenience of having to find a replacement. The working assumption was that mistresses could discipline and redeem most servants if they exercised an appropriate combination of kindness and firmness in nurturing, rewarding, admonishing, and punishing. "Those who continually change their servants," warned that same guide, "and complain of perpetual ill usage, have good reason to believe that the fault is in themselves, and that they do not know how to govern."[16]

Some employers were notoriously inept in managing their workforce, and Elizabeth's grown daughter, Ann Skyrin, was one of them. Elizabeth commented in her diary that Ann "could not keep order in the house—far from it," and when "heads of families are unsteady, servants take the advantage." Elizabeth acknowledged that "many others at this time" were experiencing difficulties in dealing with unreliable and impertinent servants, but her descriptions of the periodic crises in her daughter's household often laid the ultimate blame on those in charge, and especially ongoing tensions between Ann and her husband, John. "When man and wife do not live in unison," she wrote, "what latitude it gives to servants." As a result, the Skyrins were "much harassed by bad servants," and many a "rumpus" in their household resulted in domestics quitting or finding themselves out of a job. On several occasions, Ann had to call on her father for help in getting rid of problematic servants because neither she nor her husband were capable of dealing effectively with the situation. Henry was no more impressed than his wife was by their daughter's managerial skills and on one of these occasions "far from advocating for her . . . highly disapproved her conduct." Elizabeth also criticized her daughter Sarah and son-in-law Jacob Downing for their handling of domestics. In their case, marital discord does not seem to have been a factor, and yet, she declared, "their servants do much as they please."[17]

Disagreements between Elizabeth and Henry over the handling of unruly servants seem to have been rare, but the couple certainly had their share of problems with the domestic staff.[18] This was due in part to lack of reliable information about the abilities and character of prospective employees. Unless those who arrived looking for work brought a written recommendation or could give the name of a local householder as a reference, Elizabeth had little choice but to "judge by appearances." She hired one woman simply because she seemed "handy and capable," rejecting two others as "worse than indifferent in their appearance." If applicants had worked before in the city, Elizabeth or her sister could go and consult with prior employers. On one such occasion, "she will not do" was the verdict. Sometimes a current servant had worked with the applicant and could share information about her or his skills and reliability. Yet neither written nor spoken testimonials were always trustworthy. Elizabeth commented with perhaps justifiable resentment, "if everyone would give the true state of those matters as near as they could with propriety, neither worse nor better than they deserve, I believe they would be better served."[19]

Henry had a long run of bad luck in his efforts to find and keep a reliable coachman for the household. In 1796, he hired a new driver, Jacob Turner (the young bridegroom-to-be whom we met at the start of this chapter), only to have him leave a week later, at least temporarily, "on account of his lameness." Jacob recommended a replacement, Thomas Batt, who turned out to have a serious drinking problem. On one occasion, Batt was driving his master out of the city when Henry realized that he was sozzled almost to the point of senselessness, "leaning back or almost lying down, paying little regard to the horses or his driving," so that Henry had to take over and drive. After a few months, they had to get rid of Thomas, and Jacob returned, "still a little lame." He left almost five years later, following a "rumpus" with his master, and the following year they had to dismiss another driver, despite his being sober and competent, because he "stayed out as often at night as he came in, which was not the thing." As for his replacement, "we know little of him," wrote Elizabeth, "but must take the chance." That fellow also turned out to be unsatisfactory, and so they sent him on his way. His successor left a few days after starting work when news reached him that his mother had died. They lost their next coachman in the summer of 1802 when they left the city to escape the yellow fever; Elizabeth thought very highly of this latest fellow, but he could not afford to wait without pay until they felt safe to return and so took another position, leaving them once again without a driver. This time Henry promoted to the position a young servant already living with them. When that man left in 1806 to go to sea, they borrowed one of their son-in-law Jacob's servants, John Moore, until they found yet another driver named John Thomas. He seems to have sunk into liquor soon after marrying a woman whom the Drinkers had thought would prove unsuitable; he became increasingly problematic in his behavior and eventually quit, claiming illness ("it will be no loss to us," declared his mistress), forcing them to borrow Moore for a second time.[20]

The language that Elizabeth used to express her approval or condemnation of servants' behavior spoke volumes about her expectations as a household mistress. Not surprisingly, she wanted servants to be "industrious," "capable," and "steady." Those who proved to be "clever" or "smart" at their tasks earned her particular approbation. Yet that was not enough: when Elizabeth described employees as "serviceable," she referred not only to their competence but also to their moral character, their deference to her authority, and their gratitude for what she saw as her benevolence toward them. Those who were "well-minded," "well-disposed," "contented," and "humble" would set "a good example" for others working in the household, especially impressionable children who came to live with the Drinkers as indentured servants. Those who showed themselves to be "impudent," "saucy," "bold," "naughty," "sulky," "troublesome," "deceitful," or "ungrateful" were not only problematic in themselves but might infect others with their "high and independent spirit." Elizabeth did not appreciate servants such as Jacob Turner and Sarah Needham making decisions about their future without consulting her first, partly because in doing so they were claiming personal autonomy, but also because she doubted their ability to make prudent decisions without her guidance. Servants who "wanted more liberty" were always worrisome, not least because they might prove disorderly in other respects, especially in their moral conduct. A "giddy" young woman who kept bad company and turned out to have loose morals would not be welcome in the home of a respectable Quaker family; nor would a young man who threatened the virtue of innocent maids or coupled with promiscuous wenches. Elizabeth much preferred that servants spend most of their time at home under her protective surveillance and worried when they attended "frolics" at which anything might happen. There was also the question of appropriate dress and deportment. As the mistress of an affluent household, she was pleased when servants had "pretty manners," yet she did not want them to have "airs" and disapproved when they spent their earnings on "finery" and went out "clothed for fashion's sake." Above all, Elizabeth wanted an orderly and calm domestic environment. Any quarrel, disturbance, or uproar (what she referred to as a "rumpus") upset and irritated Elizabeth. Her managerial calculus focused, then, on the preservation of peace, order, and moral propriety (as she defined them).

Elizabeth envisioned herself as the mistress of an efficient household in which skilled and well-behaved servants worked hard, accepted her authority, and helped to maintain a morally elevated atmosphere, a haven from the chaos and depravity of the world outside. Her attitude toward domestics reflected a blend of maternal benevolence and distrustful condescension. She could be generous and compassionate to current and former employees when they found themselves in need of assistance, but refused to tolerate any behavior that deviated from her own values and expectations. Elizabeth had trouble understanding why servants did not always appreciate her attempts to protect them from what she saw as problematic behavior. "There is great trouble with servants sometimes," she declared, "more especially with some when we are thoughtful for their welfare." She would doubtless have empathized with another affluent Philadelphian, Elizabeth Fergusson, who wrote that she had "set out in life with an imagination that every creature was to be wrought upon by good usage." Yet dealing with servants had proven "a very great trial to the temper" as "daily observations" contradicted these "favorable sentiments of human nature." Indeed, she had come to "hate housekeep[ing]."[21]

"A Bold Hussy"

Of all the troublesome servants that Elizabeth had to deal with, Sally Brant was perhaps the most vexatious. Sally came to live with the Drinkers as an indentured servant when she was nine years old. She became, wrote Elizabeth, "one of the most handy" maidservants they ever employed and also had "very pretty manners," but in one respect she proved deeply problematic: Sally had a "vile propensity" toward flirtation and worse; indeed, she turned out to be "a bold hussy." At least in theory, employers had more control over indentured servants because their contracts gave masters and mistresses a quasi-parental authority that they did not have over free employees. However, just as children might resist parental authority, so too could bound servants prove disobedient and disruptive, especially as they became young adults. At the age of sixteen, Sally bore an illegitimate child, fathered by Joe Gibbs, the family's latest driver. Gibbs was black, so their affair was doubly illicit: not only were they unmarried, but their relationship crossed racial lines. Elizabeth's diary entries about Sally and Joe included no explicit remarks about the interracial aspect of their relationship, but her repeated references to their child as "yellow" or "very yellow" showed how much the infant's skin color weighed on her mind. On one occasion, she referred to Sally as "the white party concerned." Yet however dismayed the Drinkers were by Sally's behavior, they could not simply fire her because she was an indentured servant. They also had to shoulder the cost of her pregnancy, including loss of the young woman's labor, the child's delivery, and postnatal care, though in return they could apply for an extension of her indenture.[22]

Elizabeth first suspected that Sally Brant was pregnant in early August 1794. She questioned Sally "very closely and pointedly" but could extract little information from her. It is impossible to tell from Elizabeth's diary entry whether she focused simply on determining if Sally was pregnant or if she also tried to find out who the father might be, but whatever her questions, Sally was not forthcoming. Two days later, Elizabeth and her daughter Ann had "another conference with poor Sall," but this also yielded "nothing clear or candid." Elizabeth lay awake that night worrying: not least of her concerns was that Sally seemed remarkably unconcerned about her situation. On the following day, Henry and Elizabeth tackled Sally together, but this proved to be another "trying conversation, if a conversation it could be called," as their servant still said little in response to interrogation. Elizabeth found herself torn between compassion for Sally ("poor, poor girl, who could have thought it?") and growing frustration about the young woman's failure to exhibit any shame or regret. "I could not have thought," she wrote, "that a girl brought up from her tenth year with the care and kindness that SB has experienced from our family could be so thoughtless and hardened as she appears to be on such a melancholy occasion." Sally's pregnancy, for such it turned out to be, was going to involve the Drinkers in considerable inconvenience and expense, but it was also highly embarrassing: after all, she had become pregnant whilst living in their home under their moral guidance. Elizabeth was currently staying out at Clearfield, the family's country home, and Sally was there with her. In late September, as many Friends arrived in Philadelphia for the Yearly Meeting and visited their home on Front Street, the household mistress was clearly relieved not to be there. "What could I do," she wrote, "with SB in her present appearance with a crowd of company?"[23]

Although the Drinkers had little choice but to support Sally through her pregnancy, they could at least put an end to the relationship that had produced this unwelcome addition to their household. They were confident that Joe Gibbs had fathered the child, though Elizabeth never explained in any of her diary entries how they came to this conclusion. Most likely, someone had seen him and Sally flirting, kissing, or fondling each other. Because Gibbs was a waged employee, they could get rid of him more easily: they dismissed him a mere week after Elizabeth first voiced her suspicion that Sally was pregnant. Joe immediately left town, but a few months later he reappeared and was seen loitering around their stables. News of Joe's return soon reached Elizabeth, who thought his reappearance "audacious" and worried that he would make his way out to Clearfield: "we must endeavor," she declared, "to keep a good look out." The Drinkers were particularly anxious to keep Joe away from Sally, who was still displaying "very little apparent contrition." Indeed, she seemed "as full of glee as if nothing ailed her but what was right." Elizabeth wrote that she "would not wish to see her miserable" but opined, "Rather more steady thoughtfulness would become her better."[24]

In the meantime, Elizabeth and her sister received several visits from Sally's mother, Sarah Johnson. On the first of these occasions, Johnson seemed very upset: "Poor woman," wrote Elizabeth that night, "my heart aches for her." Johnson returned soon afterward to discuss her daughter's situation, bringing with her several relatives, perhaps for support as she discussed with her daughter's employers how they planned to care for Sally over the coming months. Later that fall, she visited again with herbs to make a tea that she claimed would facilitate childbirth when the time came. At first, Elizabeth played an active role in caring for Sally and helped to make baby clothes in preparation for the infant's arrival, but in early November, she handed the "grievous business" over to other hands. Elizabeth was now returning to Philadelphia and decided to leave Sally in seclusion at Clearfield in the care of Mary Courtney, the wife of their gardener there. Sally was at first quite distraught when told that she was to be left behind, but "seemed reconciled" by the time of their departure.[25]

The baby, a little girl, was born on December 2, 1794. A few days later, Elizabeth's sister and son William visited Clearfield, where they found mother and child well. Sally apparently burst into tears when she saw Mary Sandwith and "covered her head with the bedclothes." Perhaps the young woman was embarrassed or ashamed; or perhaps she wanted to block out another moral lecture. A week later, Sally's mother came by the house to ask that the Drinkers bring Sally back to town as soon as possible: she was worried that her daughter would become "too fond" of the infant if she was left long with her. Sarah Johnson was assuming that the Drinkers would farm the baby out when Sally returned to resume her duties in the Drinker household, but the Drinkers had not yet determined what to do with Sally. They could petition city officials to lengthen her indenture, as compensation for the expenses they had incurred on her behalf, but that would prolong the young woman's presence in their home. They could try to rid themselves of her immediately by selling the remainder of her indenture. Yet persuading a respectable employer to take on a young woman who had just borne an illegitimate child of mixed race would not be easy, and it seems unlikely that the Drinkers would have passed her on to anyone less than respectable, since they felt responsible for her moral welfare. In every other respect, Sally had proven to be highly satisfactory, and so they might want to keep her if she showed a willingness to mend her ways. Elizabeth hinted that there was some disagreement between herself and Henry over whether to bring the young woman back into their home: "we have not yet come to a conclusion how to do in that matter, though my opinion is that she would be better here than anywhere else." On December 23, Elizabeth visited Clearfield to see for herself how Sally was behaving and wrote afterward that she was "in rather too good spirits, everything considered."[26]

Not only did Sally Brant still exhibit what Elizabeth considered insufficient remorse for her behavior, but the young woman also assumed an independent parental authority over the baby that her mistress thought inappropriate, given Sally's bound status, the child's illegitimacy, and the infant's skin color. Sally had named the little girl Hannah Gibbs, acknowledging the paternity of Joe Gibbs, but Elizabeth had no intention of conceding either Sally's right to do as she pleased or Joe's status as a parent. She vetoed the name that Sally had chosen and renamed the baby as Catherine Clearfield, her last name indicating the estate on which she was born, a long-established tradition on slave plantations farther south. Given the Drinker household's opposition to slavery, this was (to put it mildly) ironic: Elizabeth was affirming her own mastery over the child and linking the baby permanently to her birthplace, whatever her eventual life journey. She might be "yellow" in terms of her skin color, but Anglo-American culture tended to conflate "negroes" and people of mixed race within one category; Elizabeth was effectively labeling the infant as black in a way that would be obvious to anyone who looked into her personal history. Elizabeth had no intention of legitimizing the ties that Sally laid claim to as the sexual partner of a black man and as mother of a mixed-race child. Instead, Elizabeth categorized the child as racially marked even as she and her husband denied the black father any involvement in his daughter's life. No wonder that Sally "appeared displeased," as Elizabeth wrote in her diary that night.[27]

Sally returned to the Drinkers' Philadelphia home in late January, but her baby stayed behind with the Courtneys. Elizabeth later wrote that she had decided on this course of action because she worried that admitting the baby into their home at Front Street would increase the likelihood of a reunion between the parents, but this strategy turned out to be ineffective, as Joe still tried to reestablish contact with Sally and was clearly interested in the baby. In February, Elizabeth intercepted a letter that Joe wrote to Sally, and a week later, her husband ran into him "a few doors from our house." Elizabeth recorded that Henry "laid his cane over [Joe's] back, and told him, if he found him skulking about our neighborhood he would lay him by the heels." Henry rarely resorted to violence, but his commitment to peaceable persuasion evidently had its limits. Joe apparently "looked sheepish, and walked off without reply." In early March, Henry went out to Clearfield with Mary and again encountered Joe about a mile from the family's estate. Once they arrived, Mary Courtney told them that Joe had been inside the house and made his way up to her room, where the baby was kept. When she asked him why he was there, he replied, "to see something you have got here," and "looked into the cradle." Yet when Courtney asked if he acknowledged the baby as his own, he "said no," though as Elizabeth noted, "he had all reason to believe it was his" and "had frequently boasted of it, but was fearful of the expenses that might accrue." If there was any doubt of his paternity, she added, "the color was convincing." Joe Gibbs made no further appearance in Elizabeth's diary and seems to have disappeared from all their lives.[28]

However eager the Drinkers may have been to keep Joe away from Sally, Elizabeth did not believe their ex-driver to be solely responsible for Sally's situation. Contemporary moralists warned that respectable young women faced constant danger from rakish men who would try to rob them of their innocence, seduce them into illicit intimacies, and then abandon them to unwed motherhood and ostracism from polite society. Yet according to these eighteenth-century writers, women of humbler origin lacked the innocence of their more refined sisters and were naturally lustful. Elizabeth feared that Sally was by temperament a "hussy." That April, she learned that the young woman had been "ogling" and "kissing" another man in the Drinkers' backyard: "S.B.," she wrote, "begins to show herself in her true colors." A week later, when Sally's mother came to visit, Elizabeth informed her of this latest incident and asked if she would take both Sally and Catherine away, adding that if she did so the Drinkers would pay for all costs incurred up to that point. Elizabeth was worried about the "bad example" that Sally was giving to other servants in the Drinker home and her own children, so was willing to sacrifice the year of service that Sally still owed the Drinkers. Much to her astonishment, Sally's mother "appeared more angry than grieved," declaring that "she should not care if the child's brains were beat out" and that "she would never have anything to do with it." Johnson said that she would take her daughter, but only if little Catherine stayed behind and if she had assurances that neither she nor Sally would have "anything to do with the child" in the future. She then "went away rather out of humor." When Henry came home, Elizabeth related what had happened, and they agreed that if they let Sally leave without having to take responsibility for her situation, "she would be in the high road to further ruin." That evening, Henry summoned Sally into the parlor. He told her "he had a right to send her to the workhouse and sell her for a servant," assuring the young woman that "if she did not mend her conduct she should not stay much longer" in the house. Sally apparently "cried but said nothing." "How it will end," Elizabeth wrote in her diary that night, "or what we shall do with her, I know not."[29]

The baby, meanwhile, was still out at the Drinkers' country estate. That April, the Courtneys left Clearfield and handed the infant over to their successors, George Fry and his wife. The Frys soon tired of having to care for little Catherine, and so a few weeks later the Drinkers arranged for Sally Morris, "a negro woman in the neighborhood," to nurse the infant until they could find a more permanent arrangement. At first entrusted to white caretakers, Catherine was now in the charge of a black nurse, reaffirming her removal from a white community. In late June, news reached Elizabeth that the infant was "very unwell, her bowels much disordered," and she sent medicine for "the poor little child." A few days later, the nurse's son arrived with a note informing the Drinkers that "poor little Caty was dead" and asking for a burial shroud. Soon after this, Elizabeth removed to Clearfield for the summer and visited the infant's grave, which was, she judged, "decently done up." Before leaving town, she told Sally that her daughter had died, "and took that opportunity to talk to her on that and some other subjects." Sally was at first upset but, according to her mistress, recovered very quickly. Elizabeth was convinced that Sally Morris had done her best to look after the infant: her family was "very fond of it," she wrote. Nonetheless, she concluded with breathtaking complacency, " 'tis gone, and no doubt but all's for the best."[30]

The Drinkers kept Sally on until her eighteenth birthday and the end of her indenture in April 1796. Perhaps they were unwilling to give up on her, perhaps her problematic behavior never quite overshadowed her abilities as a servant, or perhaps they thought it would be impossible to persuade someone else to take her on without deliberately withholding information—most likely a combination of all three. On the day after Sally's eighteenth birthday, her mother paid the Drinkers another visit and agreed to Sally's staying on to work for two months more as compensation for the expenses that the Drinkers had incurred "on her and [the] child's account." Elizabeth felt that she and her husband were being quite generous: they could legally have demanded up to a year. Yet the mother appeared again several weeks later and tried, unsuccessfully, to secure Sally's release two weeks earlier than agreed: "she was rather impertinent," wrote Elizabeth, "and all things considered very thoughtless and ungrateful." Sally had "promised amendment," and her behavior had improved dramatically, though Elizabeth was uncertain whether this was a sincere attempt to reform or merely a ruse "to get the more from us." She determined to "hope the best," and when Sally came to visit a month after her final departure, her former mistress gave her a Bible.[31]

Over the coming few years, Sally Brant called from time to time on her former employers, and Elizabeth noted in January 1798 that the young woman had now married a barber. Given that she did not mention his race, he was probably white. In April 1798, Sally came to collect some baby clothes that Elizabeth's daughters had laid by for her: she was now expecting another child, this time as a married woman. That December, Sally's mother died, and Henry Drinker gave permission for her burial in the Friends' graveyard, even though she was not a Quaker. Sally continued to visit until the end of Elizabeth's life, and her former mistress noted how well turned out her children were, "considering the little means to do it with." The Drinkers were now willing to be magnanimous as the former "hussy" had reformed, embracing marital respectability and so deserving their support. They clearly resented the embarrassment, inconvenience, and cost that accompanied Sally's pregnancy, but they had nonetheless fulfilled their contractual and moral obligations. The final disappearance of Joe Gibbs, Sally's subsequent marriage to a respectable artisan, and her ascension to wedded motherhood may have suggested to Elizabeth, Henry, and Mary in their more generous and probably self-congratulatory moments that the disruption, anxiety, expense, and mortification had ultimately proven worthwhile.[32]

"Get Rid of Her"

Sally Brant's dependency as an indentured servant had its price, not least in her being denied the right to name her own child, but pregnant servants who were not indentured might have thought Sally fortunate in that she was at least taken care of during her pregnancy and not thrown out onto the streets. Polly Moore also became pregnant while working as a servant in the Drinker household, but Polly was a wage laborer, and so the Drinkers simply dismissed her once pregnancy began to interfere with her productivity. Elizabeth noted that Polly was "now near lying in," and she was therefore "glad to get rid of her." It was mid-February, and the river nearby was iced up, but Elizabeth made no mention of whether Polly had anywhere to go for shelter or alternative employment once she left Front Street. Pregnant women seeking work as salaried servants may have hoped that their employers would take pity on them, providing them with shelter and support through the final stages of their pregnancy. Some of these women may have seen indentured servants such as Sally Brant being cared for and assumed that they would receive similar treatment, not understanding that employers did not have the same obligation to wage laborers. They soon found out otherwise. When one of Elizabeth's daughters discovered that a woman she had just hired was pregnant, Elizabeth's advice was blunt: "get rid of her as soon as possible."[33]

Wage laborers were in general much less secure in their positions than indentured servants. A bound domestic could grow into her position over time, especially if taken on as a child, whereas a salaried servant who could not do the job her employer had hired her for would soon be out on the street. If an indentured servant misbehaved in some way, her mistress would have words with her, perhaps punish her, and then hope for improvement, but Elizabeth had no qualms about getting rid of salaried servants who annoyed her. When Catherine Patterson vanished without any warning for "two or three days frolicking," Elizabeth summarily fired her. Her daughter Ann dismissed a new servant the day after her arrival because she had "stayed out all night" and then on her return informed Ann that she had to leave again to attend the burial of a cousin. Ann told her not to come back from the funeral service. Elizabeth felt obliged to give servants time off if they had a legitimate excuse, but she sometimes suspected them of exploiting her generosity and worried about the bad influences they might come under when removed from her protective surveillance. When fourteen-year-old indentured servant Sally Dawson went home to be with her dying father, Elizabeth did not want her to stay for the funeral. "It might appear hard to bring her away," she wrote, "but I like not the company she is in." Sally stayed anyway, risking the ire of her mistress. Because Dawson was indentured, her mistress could not fire her, but "black Jane" had no such security. One Christmas Eve, Elizabeth allowed Jane to attend a Methodist service, but late that evening she had still not returned. "If Jane don't come home by the time I have looked over the house," her mistress wrote, "I shall lock her out." Elizabeth suspected that Jane would have liked to go to church every day, had she been allowed to do so, and she clearly resented the loss of labor, even if for the sake of religious exercise. Jane's constant requests for time off, combined with her habit of smoking in bed, led to their parting company. "It is difficult to get suitable help," Elizabeth complained, yet she did not hesitate to fire salaried domestics like Jane who turned out to be unsatisfactory. "Some say a bad one is better than none," she wrote, "but I think in some cases none is better than a bad one."[34]

Even more vulnerable were those who hired themselves out as dailies to perform specific tasks such as whitewashing, upholstering, or sewing. Some casual laborers were married women who could not commit to full-time service because of their own domestic responsibilities. Working as dailies gave these women more flexibility, and employers sometimes allowed mothers to bring their children with them to work, but that flexibility operated in both directions, and dailies had to deal with the unpredictability of demand for their services. In April 1801, Elizabeth decided to send whitewasher Caty Roberts away until the Yearly Meeting ended because it was inconvenient to have her working there with so many visitors coming in and out of the house, but meanwhile Roberts was out of a job.[35] Anna Webb first came to work for the Drinkers as a seamstress in the summer of 1797 and returned intermittently throughout the last decade of Elizabeth's life. During her stays, some of which lasted several weeks, Webb became part of the household, attending meetings for worship with members of the family and even trying out the Drinkers' new shower bath, but Elizabeth could send her away at her own convenience. In May 1803, five days after Webb arrived to undertake a series of jobs that had piled up in the Drinker home, Elizabeth found that she did not have time to supervise her work and so dismissed her "until it suits better." Webb returned a month later, but again Elizabeth sent her away after several days with the work unfinished: Elizabeth was busy with a major housecleaning, and her daughter Ann was about to move house, so she "thought it was best to part with her at present."[36]

The least vulnerable of Elizabeth's wage laborers were domestics who had lived with the family as indentured servants and stayed on after they became free. In theory, she could dismiss them too whenever she liked, but Elizabeth had invested considerable time and energy in educating and training them. She also had a personal history with these young adults: she had known some of them since they were small children, was clearly fond of them, and responded to what she saw as problematic behavior with a blend of anxiety and resentment instead of straightforward irritation followed speedily by dismissal. Elizabeth was well aware that previously bound servants were often reluctant to remain in the same household once out of their indentures: "some giddy girls," she wrote, "think they can't be free while they continue where they served their time." Just over two years after Sally Dawson reached the end of her indenture, having lived with the Drinkers since she was nine years old, her mistress heard that Sally had applied for a position in a neighbor's home. "Poor girl," she declared, "she don't know what she is about." When the neighbor came to "ask S. Dawson's character," Elizabeth praised her as "honest, sober, and capable" but added disapprovingly that the young woman was eager for "more liberty." Elizabeth doubted that Sally was ready for life outside the protective environment that Elizabeth thought she provided and so must have been relieved when Sally ended up staying on in the Drinker household.[37]

Elizabeth fretted and occasionally fumed as Sally Dawson insisted on exercising her new rights as a free adult. One evening, Elizabeth noted with a mixture of irritation and concern that Sally had gone to see a play, did not return until after midnight, and had "a beaux after her." This provided a respectable Quaker mistress with ample cause for concern. Elizabeth also worried that Sally had become "very fond of dress and fashions." Instead of saving her salary, she spent most of it "to purchase finery." Moreau de St. Méry, a refugee from the French Caribbean who had settled in Philadelphia, wrote that many of the city's servants "love[d] to dress up for their evening promenade" and that sometimes it was "difficult to distinguish mistresses from servants." For young women such as Sally, that may well have been part of the appeal. Elizabeth, however, objected to servants dressing above their station and worried that "going out too thinly clothed for fashion's sake" was perilous in chilly weather. "No wonder they get sick," she declared. Sally also mimicked the hospitality displayed by her master and mistress, on one occasion hosting a tea party in the kitchen, to which she invited several friends from the neighborhood, both male and female. "It won't do often," her mistress wrote. Elizabeth feared that Sally might fall into bad company and was not pleased when she invited a female friend whom Elizabeth considered undesirable to stay overnight, yet Elizabeth "did not like to refuse." Sally had long since become part of the family, and it does not seem to have occurred to Elizabeth that she could simply get rid of her.[38]

"Pity and Compassion"

Elizabeth Drinker's own convenience and the practical needs of her household loomed large in her treatment of domestics, but a sense of responsibility toward those under her care also played a crucial role. Elizabeth expected dedication, deference, and gratitude from her employees; in return, she would show them and also their relations kindness, compassion, and generosity, both during and after their time in her service. She saw her household as a family and explicitly included her servants in that unit. On one occasion, Elizabeth referred to the servants currently living in as "the family of our kitchen." That phrase suggested a distinct group that gathered in a space clearly removed from the family parlor and yet part of her world; "our" implied possession and yet at the same time a connection that was both practical and emotional. Numerous entries in Elizabeth's diary recounted acts of kindness toward current and former employees, including not only indentured servants but also waged domestics and even casual laborers. In January 1796, she and her sister received a visit from Molly Hensel, "an industrious, ignorant, poor woman" who had worked for them many years before. They invited her into the kitchen for a simple meal and gave her some money and clothing, for which she was appropriately thankful. Elizabeth suspected that their guest was a drunkard but wrote that she "looked upon her with pity and compassion, as I believed her one of the many beings from whom much was not required." Her attitude toward the woman was utterly condescending yet at the same time kindly and hospitable.[39]

Not surprisingly, Elizabeth developed a particular attachment to those who stayed in her household for extended periods, especially children who grew up under her care as indentured servants. Elizabeth's heart went out to minors separated from their parents in this way. "I feel much for the poor little fellows," she wrote of three boys who came to live with them in 1794. In cases where the parents lived nearby and were of suitable character, she happily allowed them to visit. When dealing with relatives whom she considered less worthy, however, she discouraged any more than minimal contact: her own judgment superseded these other ties. Child domestics occupied an ambiguous position within the Drinker household. Having small children around was convenient, Elizabeth wrote, since they could "fetch and carry anything, and go about house on trifling errands," leaving older servants free for more skilled and physically demanding tasks. "Little Ned Fifer" was sent home a few weeks after his arrival on trial because he proved "too small" to suit their purposes. Elizabeth saw these children as an economic investment and trusted that the time she devoted to their care would prove worthwhile: "those small folk ought to be of service when they grow bigger," she wrote, "for they are very troublesome when young." Yet indentured children meant much more to Elizabeth than their current and potential worth as laborers. In one entry,

Elizabeth noted that Sally Dawson and Peter Woodward, both of whom grew up in the Drinker household, had been building a model house in the backyard, supposedly for her grandchildren but more, she suspected, "to please themselves and show their ingenuity." The house was an elaborate structure, "three stories high, built with brick and hung with paper hangings, furnished with beds, chairs, looking glasses, etc." It had "a garden, palisades, gate pump, [and] weather cock." The two youngsters devoted many hours to this project, including time when they should have been "otherwise employed." Yet Elizabeth said nothing about admonishing them for this distraction or redirecting them to their regular duties, and not only because the project would please her own grandchildren. Sally and Peter, though servants under her charge, were also part of the family and recipients of her not-quite-but-almost maternal care and affection.[40]

Sally Dawson arrived on the Drinkers' doorstep in December 1793 at the age of nine. Her mother had recently died, and her father, a carpenter, had decided to place her with a respectable family, which would relieve him from the burden of having to house, clothe, feed, and educate the little girl. Over the coming years, the Drinkers sent Sally to school and the Friends' Youth Meeting, ensuring her moral as well as practical education. There were also occasional excursions of pleasure, as when Elizabeth sent her in the company of an older servant to see an elephant that was currently on show in the city. Elizabeth herself cared for the little girl when she was ill, on one occasion "bathing my little maid Sally Dawson's face for a swelling and dressing her knee for a sore." The same doctors who came to examine the Drinkers when they were ill also cared for Sally and the other servants. Elizabeth worried intermittently that they would have "some trouble with her disposition," which she described as "naughty," "sulky when sick," "deceitful," and sometimes "consummately impudent." Yet Elizabeth clearly saw potential in her young charge and noted with pleasure that once Sally was old enough to become involved in kitchen work she proved "a handy cook." In the meantime, Elizabeth did what she could to protect the girl from bad influences, minimizing Sally's contact with her relatives, some of whom Elizabeth considered shady characters. Theirs was an intimate and affectionate relationship. Elizabeth noted that she often sat late at night "by the fire, she sleeping in a chair by me." In another entry, she wrote that she had just made a cloak for Sally, "the first I ever made unless for a doll." Perhaps she saw Sally, whom she described as "a pretty looking child," as her own little poppet, albeit useful as well as ornamental.[41]

Just how attached Elizabeth was to Sally Dawson became clear in 1803 when the young woman, now almost nineteen and living with the Drinkers as a free servant, fell seriously ill. That September, Sally began to complain of pain in her head and stomach. The city was currently in the midst of a yellow fever epidemic, and although Adam Kuhn, the doctor summoned to examine Sally, hoped that this would turn out to be a less serious malady, it became clear the next day that she did indeed have the dreaded infection. Kuhn now recommended that the Drinkers send her to the hospital, "unless her mistress could attend constantly on her." Elizabeth felt that neither her own fragile health nor her other responsibilities would permit her to give Sally the attention she needed, and keeping her in the house would run the risk of infecting others. Accordingly, the doctor wrote to the Board of Health, and a carriage arrived for Sally that afternoon. Elizabeth noted in a poignant entry that the fashion-conscious Sally took care of her appearance even as an invalid and waited, "dressed rather smartly," at the kitchen door while attendants packed her bed and linen into the carriage for the short journey. Elizabeth had written "a little letter to keep up her spirits," and her husband wrote a note to the attending physician at the hospital, asking that he take "particular care" of Sally. Elizabeth hoped that it might "please Providence to restore her" but went to bed that night with little "expectation of sleeping."[42]

Over the coming few days, Elizabeth questioned whether sending the young woman off to the hospital had been the right thing to do. Sally was not her own child, but Elizabeth had raised her since she was nine and was clearly racked by guilt as she described her family "sitting this evening, apparently at our ease, while our poor Sally may be vomiting her life away, or in the agony of death!" Sally died three days after her removal to the hospital. As Elizabeth wrote in her diary, "a pretty girl in the bloom of youth" had been "taken off the stage of life in no more than five days' illness—a lesson for the young and old." Henry described the young woman's death in letters to his friends as an "affecting" and "distressing event to us." Over the coming days and weeks, Elizabeth noted repeatedly how long it had been since Sally died. She had many questions about her final days but especially wanted to know in what frame of mind she had faced death. Her son William eventually brought back a report from the attending physician that Sally had made "very little complaint or moaning." Equally welcome was the doctor's reassurance that even if Sally had received "the best of nursing at home," she still would have died. "All this," Elizabeth confided to her diary, "is rather satisfactory than otherwise."[43]

The affectionate concern that the Drinkers showed toward Sally Dawson was also evident in their treatment of James Denning, their Irish coachman. In the spring of 1795, James became, as Elizabeth put it, "strange in his behavior." Physically James was a strapping fellow, almost six feet tall, yet emotionally he seemed increasingly fragile. At times, he became quite distraught and wept profusely. James told his master that he felt guilty because "he had sometimes overfed the horses, at another time suffered them to run away," but Elizabeth did not believe that this could be the underlying cause of his distress and suspected that something else was to blame. In early May, James declared that he was leaving, gathered his belongings in a bundle, handed over the keys to the coach house and stables, and came into the parlor "to bid us farewell with tears in his eyes." James was a wage laborer, and so the Drinkers could not prevent him from leaving, but they were upset that he would depart so suddenly and in evident distress. They became even more concerned when they asked him where he was going and he replied anywhere where no one knew him. He started crying again, telling his mistress that he had just "acquainted his master with the crime that lay heavy at his heart." Elizabeth went into her husband's office to ask for details, but Henry told her that what James had said was "unintelligible." She returned to the parlor and gave James some bread along with a glass of wine and water, to which her son William added thirteen drops of laudanum. James now revealed that he had recently been "at the Swedes' church, where the minister said something that pierced his heart." It would seem, then, that James was experiencing some sort of religious crisis. The family insisted that he rest for a few hours in his chamber, after which he had some dinner and then went outside to take care of the horses, apparently calmer and at least for the moment resigned to staying. "Poor fellow," Elizabeth wrote that night, "his nerves appear to be much affected . . . I feel much for the poor young man in a strange land." The coachman's parents still lived in Ireland, and James had told his master "he was afraid he should break their hearts," which clearly moved Elizabeth.[44]

A few days later, when James drove some of the family out to Clearfield for the day, he disappeared into the woods and was gone so long that they had to delay their return home. That evening he was very despondent and again wanted to leave ("he knows not where," Elizabeth wrote). He told the family that he was "a great sinner" and did not deserve the kind treatment he had received in the Drinkers' home. William gave him another dose of laudanum. After James went to bed, a neighbor and close friend of James came over and told them that the young man condemned himself for misdeeds that, had they been real, were "very bad, but he could not believe it, he looked on it as the effect of his low state of mind, which made the worst of everything." The neighbor added that the young man had "talked of hanging or shooting himself." On the following day, James reappeared with his bundle of belongings and this time actually left. A week later, Elizabeth noted that they had "no intelligence yet of poor James," and it was not until the middle of June that he reappeared in town, apparently in much better spirits. "We are pleased," wrote Elizabeth, "to see him in the land of the living." That November he again visited them, seemingly fully recovered and talking of "going home" to Ireland. Elizabeth noted that they would have welcomed him back into service had he not been planning to leave the country.[45]

Denning briefly reentered their lives a year and a half later, following his return from Ireland. In January 1797, they heard that he was going to stand trial for murder. He had been found asleep next to his current master's dead son, who had apparently been drinking heavily and whose body was badly bruised. According to one of several accounts they heard, James had also been drinking and had scraped his knuckles, suggesting that the two young men had got into a fight. The Drinkers were skeptical. Elizabeth wrote in her diary that she had never seen James drunk and that he had never expressed hostility to anyone other than himself. If he had committed the murder, the only possible explanation she could produce was that he must have been "deranged" at the time. Henry gave evidence at the trial in support of Denning, and the jury acquitted him, according to Elizabeth because "his general good character was much in his favor." Well over two years later, in August 1799, Denning came to pay the Drinkers a visit, the first time Elizabeth had seen him since the trial and, as it turned out, the last occasion on which they would cross paths. He told the Drinkers that he now had "a cancer in his leg." This was, she wrote, "an unfortunate man." Elizabeth and Henry doubtless felt that they had done all they could for him, but James was, after all, a free adult, and they could not protect him from his own demons.[46]

The Drinkers kept in touch with many of their former employees and often gave them money, medicine, or other assistance. When another of their coachmen, Benjamin Oliver, left to set up his own business, hiring out a carriage, Henry lent him forty pounds toward purchase of the horses he would need. Mary Brookhouse worked on and off for the Drinkers as a daily for two decades, cleaning and assisting in the kitchen when the household was understaffed. But in 1783 she injured her hand and it was left lame; Elizabeth made no further reference to her working at the house, and Brookhouse, who was then forty-seven, disappeared from the Drinkers' lives until the summer of 1797, when they heard that she was unwell. Elizabeth's sister went to visit her, and over the coming few years they sent food and medicine. In the fall of 1799, they heard that she had fallen into a fire, badly burning her back, and so Elizabeth sent "an old soft sheet" as well as some money. A few weeks later, Brookhouse finally died, and Henry attended the funeral at the Friends' burial ground. Elizabeth wrote that she had "always thought her a good-hearted woman," which was presumably why she so readily helped her. Her good opinion of Mary wavered when another daily told her that Mary had "latterly given way to strong drink," but Elizabeth noted that the gossip could not confirm whether Mary was drunk when she fell into the fire. When another of their former dailies, washerwoman Alice Wright, fell gravely ill in early 1803, the Drinkers sent one of their servants over to her home with supplies. Following her death, they provided a funeral shroud. "Poor Alice Wright," Elizabeth wrote, "has been one of our humble servants," and that was the key to Elizabeth's involvement: Alice had proven a worthy recipient of her patronage.[47]

If a former employee was less deserving, Elizabeth often implied, at least in the privacy of her diary, that the individual was getting her just deserts. Betty Burrage worked in the Drinker household on two separate occasions. She was apparently "an ill-natured old woman" and rarely stayed long in any position, though what Elizabeth characterized as "a disagreeable temper" may well have been an unwillingness on Burrage's part to show the deference and obedience that Elizabeth and other household mistresses expected from their employees. Drinker felt "pity" for Burrage despite her flaws and so gave her a second chance, but she fretted that the old woman set "no good example to our little folks in the kitchen," and Burrage quit six months later after yet another "rumpus" with her mistress. "Her absence not to be regretted," declared Elizabeth. When Burrage reappeared several months later "in a poor state of health," assuring the Drinkers that "the worst day's work she ever did was leaving this house," they declined to take her back. Yet when she visited again a few years later after falling out of a wagon and injuring herself, her former employers gave her food and money. After some hesitation, they also gave her a lukewarm letter of recommendation addressed to the Overseers of the Poor so that she could gain admission to the almshouse, where she had already spent time several years before.[48]

Burrage's plight as an aging and increasingly infirm widow with no family on hand to provide support was far from exceptional in late eighteenth-century Philadelphia. Poverty brought with it higher mortality rates, so that poorer women were more likely to lose their husbands than wealthier women, and most never remarried. By no means all widows had relatives nearby to provide support when they could no longer support themselves, especially in large cities like Philadelphia where many poor residents had migrated from overseas or rural communities to find work, leaving behind family networks. Even those who arrived with other family members might lose them to disease or misadventure.[49] As householders came to rely more on waged domestics, they often preferred to hire women who were mature, experienced, and skilled, but older women were also more likely to have health problems and would lose their jobs if they proved unable to fulfill their duties. Some domestics managed to set aside money to get themselves through periods of unemployment or even to set up independent business ventures. Anna Duffey, whom Elizabeth described approvingly as "a saving managing body," spent under a quarter of her wages while employed by the Drinkers over an eighteen-month period and had her mistress keep the bulk of her earnings until she was ready to leave and rent a house, in which she planned to "keep shop and take lodgers." Yet Drinker doubted that the money Duffey had saved would be sufficient for that purpose, and later that year a woman came by to inquire about Duffey's "character," most likely because she was thinking of taking her on as a domestic. Duffey had apparently gone back into service.[50]

Many women who worked as servants found themselves without resources or support when they reached old age, and Betty Burrage was no exception. As Elizabeth Drinker aged and ailed, but in comfortable security and surrounded by her family, Burrage reappeared intermittently at the Drinkers' door asking either for money or for work. "I thought she was gone," Elizabeth wrote after one of these visits, "but she is still here, an infirm old woman—has not lost her spirit." Burrage came to their home for the last time in August 1803, "wet to the skin" after walking a long way in the rain; she had fallen down and "hurt her face badly." The Drinkers offered her money for lodging, but Betty said that no one would take her in, and so Elizabeth let her come inside. She gave her a dry shift to wear while her clothes dried and told Sally Dawson to find Betty somewhere to sleep for the night. Elizabeth wrote that night that she thought Betty had "not long to stay in this world" but added that she had been "intemperate," implying that Betty's misfortunes were partly of her own making. Betty left the following morning, and Elizabeth made no further mention of her in the diary. We know from the almshouse records that Burrage returned there for the last time in April 1811, having outlived her former employer by more than three years; she died as an inmate two months later at the age of seventy-eight.[51]

"Our Blacks and Whites"

Elizabeth's attitude toward her domestic staff blended self-interest, condescension, and distrust with loyalty, compassion, and sometimes affection. That applied to all her domestics regardless of their skin color. The Drinker household was remarkably diverse, not only in its configuration of labor (which combined indentured and waged live-in servants as well as occasional dailies) but also in its multiracial makeup. Indeed, the establishment at 110 North Front Street represented in microcosm the racial melting pot that was Philadelphia. Black and mixed-race children, women, and men worked in the house alongside white servants and the Drinkers themselves. Free blacks had rapidly become a visible and even normalized component of the city's social landscape and workforce. Elizabeth's diary suggests that in many respects she and her family treated black and white laborers similarly, and she seems to have grown fond of black indentured servants who grew up in her household much as she did the white children and teenagers under her care. She and her husband condemned the system of slavery, gave active assistance to blacks escaping northward from slave plantations, and had deep sympathy for these souls in flight. Yet neither Elizabeth nor her husband was immune to the racial prejudices of late eighteenth-century North American society. Sally Brant's interracial relationship with Joe Gibbs and the child that resulted clearly made them very uncomfortable, and Elizabeth made occasional comments about Africans and African Americans that were explicitly racist, though she did not aim these barbs against her own servants. Her disposition toward people of color was as complicated and ambiguous as were those of other Americans who opposed slavery and yet still harbored racial prejudice. That attitude was humanitarian and mostly benign but also colored by racial preconceptions, an additional layer to the class-based condescension that framed her interactions with all people, of whatever skin color, from the lower ranks of society.

Elizabeth's parents owned at least one enslaved person. A nine-year-old whom Elizabeth referred to as "Black Judey" was living with the family at the time that Sarah and William Sandwith died. Quakers had not yet committed as a community to the antislavery cause, and as Elizabeth later recalled, "there was nothing said against keeping or selling negroes." She and her sister "loved the child," but because they were about to become boarders they did not think it practical to keep her and so sold her for twenty-five pounds. They soon regretted their decision, even though the purchaser had promised "to use her very kindly," and so a few weeks later they rode out to the property where

Judey now lived, offering her new mistress forty pounds to get the child back. Judey's new owner told Elizabeth and Mary that "she would not part with her for a hundred pounds," though she subsequently sold Judey to someone else. Years later, when there was "much talk" among Quakers on the issue of slavery and its immorality, Henry Drinker visited Judey's current owner, presumably at his wife's request, in an attempt to persuade him "of the inequity of holding [Judey] in bondage." Elizabeth wrote in her diary that Judey's owner refused to free her but did leave provision for her emancipation at his death. Elizabeth related this story twice in her diary toward the end of her life, each entry prompted by a visit from Judey, now a free woman. Elizabeth recalled that she and Mary "had formerly some uneasy hours on her behalf" because they "loved" her and "knew not what would be her fate." The money they had offered to repurchase "Black Judey" was a significant sum. They had wanted her back, apparently because they cared for her as a member (albeit a subordinate member) of their depleted and parentless family.[52]

As a young girl, Elizabeth attended antislavery activist Anthony Benezet's school, and in later years she became, alongside her husband, a committed ally in the antislavery struggle. Elizabeth was determined to lend a hand whenever she saw an opportunity, her principles perhaps reinforced by residual guilt from her earlier treatment of Judey. Elizabeth understood that even after African Americans fleeing slavery in the South reached the North, they were not necessarily safe. She referred in her diary to a report that kidnappers who were currently in the Philadelphia area had "attempted to take negroes away and put them on board a vessel." The Drinkers became embedded in a dense underground network of households, many of them Quaker, that provided support to runaways. On one occasion, "a negro man, named Peter, from Virginia," arrived at their door in "tattered" clothing "to ask for something to help him out of town." Though he was reluctant to say more than he had to, the Drinkers "had very little doubt of his being a runaway." On another, one of their dailies came to ask for their help when her sister and three small children arrived from Virginia and took refuge with her. The children's father was a free man, but they had heard that their master was planning to send them down to the Carolinas as "slaves for life," and so the mother and children made their escape; the Drinkers arranged for them to make their way out to Atsion, New Jersey, where Henry had friends and co-owned an ironworks. Despite Quaker protests, the international slave trade was still in operation, and Philadelphians got a glimpse of what that meant in practice when the U.S. *Ganges* captured a foreign schooner carrying "one hundred and eighteen black people without the least clothing" and brought them to Philadelphia in the summer of 1800. When they arrived at the quarantine station south of the city, a local newspaper asked "humane citizens" to send clothes over to the Health Office. Elizabeth put together a bundle of "good and suitable things for the poor naked creatures" and dispatched one of her black indentured servants to deliver it.[53]

Enslaved people were also arriving in Philadelphia as refugees from the bloody slave uprising in Saint-Domingue that erupted in 1791. The Drinkers heard about developments there from newspaper accounts and friends in the mercantile community who had business ties with the French colony.[54] Antislavery activist Warner Mifflin, a close friend of the Drinker family, compared the aspirations of Saint-Domingue's enslaved people to those of Americans in launching their own recent uprising against the British. Elizabeth was at best ambivalent about the American Revolution, which she had experienced mainly in terms of violence, cruelty, and what she saw as the needless suffering of her family, relatives, and friends. This doubtless colored her perspective on events in Saint-Domingue. Her comments about the uprising there focused almost entirely on the horrifying violence that it unleashed and the atrocities on all sides ("shocking doings," she wrote). Her recollection of Henry's imprisonment, exile, and illness during the War for Independence surely influenced her description of leading insurrectionary Toussaint Louverture's eventual death in prison, "without a friend to close his eyes, and without ever having been visited in his imprisonment by his wife and children." The Atlantic World was now in the grip of revolutions that trumpeted their dedication to liberation, equality, and love for humankind, but that seemed from Elizabeth's perspective to bring a tidal wave of cruelty and tragedy in their wake.[55]

Elizabeth watched, with evident fascination, as Philadelphia's black population became an increasingly visible part of the city's cultural fabric. When her son William returned home from attending Anthony Benezet's funeral in May 1784, he told her that "a great number of blacks" had come to pay their respects, this the only detail that she chose to include in her brief description of Benezet's funeral. In June 1797, she reported that twin processions of white and black Freemasons had paraded through the streets, adding that this was the first time she had heard of black Masons. A year later, she watched a black funeral procession pass by her home, "in different order from any I have ever before seen: six men went before the coffin, one with a book in his hand, they sang aloud psalms, I suppose, in a very loud and discordant voice: a large concourse followed." She thought they were Methodists but clearly saw the peculiarities of the spectacle in racial as much as denominational terms.[56]

Yet even as Elizabeth acknowledged "negroes" as a growing presence within her home city and in principle welcomed that they did so as free people, she had difficulty coming to terms with that social reality and its implications. She struggled with the notion that black residents of the city could and did act as independent agents. When yellow fever swept through the city in 1793, Elizabeth noted that "negroes" were prominent among those nursing the sick. A significant number of Philadelphians had become convinced—incorrectly, as it turned out—that blacks would not contract the disease. At first, she wrote that white officials had instructed them to help, though she then crossed out "are appointed" and replaced that passive phrase with the active "have offered," once she realized that they were volunteers and not conscripts. Elizabeth was clearly uncomfortable with any behavior on the part of "black people" that suggested a sense of entitlement or even a claim to respectability. She referred to African American servants who dressed up for social outings as "black gentry" and "black quality," her pen dripping with sarcasm. Elizabeth was not pleased when Richard Allen, whom she described as "a black man of consequence," had a broadsheet printed in which he criticized absent citizens who left behind cats or dogs which then "disturb[ed] the neighbors by their howlings." Elizabeth compared reading this announcement to a horse hearing an ass bray for the first time: "I have wondered a horse should be frightened at a creature so near his own species, but the noise is so singular, I am no longer surprised at it." A "black man," even "of consequence," might be "near [her] own species," but he and she were not the same. Elizabeth had little time for attempts by well-meaning Philadelphians to shed language that seemed to them inappropriate now that African Americans were, at least in theory, free and equal citizens. In 1803, she noted that "many" now refused to "call the black people negroes," thinking it "rather a harsh appellation." Yet she saw "no impropriety in it," as this was "a common name for them" and derived from the Latin word "niger," which meant "black." Nor could she reconcile herself to the alternatives that some of her neighbors were advocating: "Africans, Ethiopians indeed—but those here are neither."[57]

Not all white domestics wanted to live and work in a multiracial household. In 1804, the Drinkers' white servant Nancy Stewart quit, having been "in ill humor for some time past" with the three black servants currently living in the house. After she left, Elizabeth found out that Nancy had been angry because she thought Peter Woodward, one of the black domestics, "backward in waiting upon her." Nancy had not mentioned this previously to her mistress, perhaps because she thought she would get no sympathy. Elizabeth was aware that Nancy had refused to "eat with negroes" and she noted that they had not forced her to do so, but this latest revelation doubtless deepened Elizabeth's irritation with her employee: their servants were there to wait on the Drinkers, not each other. On one occasion when the Drinkers left Philadelphia to escape an epidemic and stayed with two of their married daughters and their families, there occurred "a rumpus in the kitchen among the servants," which Elizabeth explained in terms of there being "too many of them together of different sorts." Some of the discord may have resulted from several sets of servants combining under one roof, but Elizabeth's comment that "different sorts" of people were not getting on suggests that race may have been at least partly to blame for the row.[58]

Servants of mixed race occupied an especially ambiguous position in the Drinkers' multiracial domestic landscape. Men and women of mixed race tended not to work as full-time domestics but instead hired themselves out to employers as independent laborers, women often taking in laundry and men frequently working as waiters. Elizabeth noted that one such fellow, known to her only as "Stevens or Stevenson," was "well known to many families" in the city "as a very handy waiter" and performed that function at her daughter Ann's wedding. It is unclear whether mixed-race Philadelphians lived out by choice or because employers preferred it this way, perhaps uncomfortable with their liminal identity. (It is worth recalling that the Drinkers never allowed Sally Brant's baby into their Philadelphia residence.) Elizabeth usually distinguished between "yellow" or "mulatto" and "black" or "negro" people, sometimes even differentiating between a parent and child if their skin color differed, though all these servants shared in her mind a nonwhite identity.[59] Elizabeth's strong sense of commitment to worthy employees, even decades after they left her service, included mixed-race servants. Yet because the latter rarely lived in, there would not have been the same degree of intimacy that developed between the Drinkers and those servants who lived and slept in their home. Employers may have been more willing to accept black servants as cohabitants in their homes because there was a clearer and so more comfortable sense of racial difference.[60]

Nonetheless, Elizabeth relied on servants of whatever color for their expertise and appreciated their skills. "Negroes," she wrote, "are useful to us, when they behave well." She praised them as she did white servants when she thought they deserved it and could prove a loyal, supportive patron to them as to all her deserving dependents, including those who worked in the homes of her grown children. Patience Gibbs, a young black woman who worked for many years as an indentured servant in Ann Skyrin's household, became well acquainted with her mistress's parents and earned Elizabeth's respect. Many years later, Patience wrote that she would "never forget" Elizabeth or her sister: "they were always so kind to me." When her indenture ended and she left to live with her father, Patience paid the Drinkers a farewell visit before leaving the city. Her father, Absalom Gibbs, went with her, and he impressed Elizabeth as "a decent sensible negro man." Two years later, Patience returned and worked for the Skyrins again, this time as a free servant. Patience came first to Elizabeth's house, and the Drinkers had her driven out to Frankford, where the Skyrins were currently staying, so that she could meet with Ann. Patience saw the Drinkers regularly as the two families exchanged visits. On one occasion, she discussed with Elizabeth a lump on her neck that "a black doctor" had treated with "a caustic plaster." Elizabeth noted in her diary that the doctor had "shown much skill." When she heard that Susannah Swett, Henry's former mother-in-law, wanted the same physician to treat her, Elizabeth met with him on Swett's behalf. Both women clearly respected the doctor, whatever his skin color, and were eager to enlist his services.[61]

Less satisfactory was a black domestic named Richard Stevens, whom Elizabeth described as "a very lusty lazy fellow." Henry Drinker bought Stevens's indenture in early 1798 after his previous master tired of his behavior; he then passed him on to his son Henry Sandwith, who soon wrote to complain that "the negro" they had sent him was "intolerably lazy" and would "not do." That April, a constable found the young man drunk in a boat and arrested him. It turned out that he had absconded after a confrontation with his master. According to Richard, Henry Sandwith had been about to beat him with a stick "for drunkenness and laziness," but he had "wrenched the stick from his master's hand," and when Henry Sandwith left to get a warrant to put the fellow in jail, Richard ran away. Henry Sr. had the servant brought before a magistrate and sent to jail, but in a cell on his own to keep him away from "bad company." Henry Sandwith did not want the servant back following his release, and so his father sent Richard off to the Atsion ironworks. "Lazy as he is," wrote Elizabeth, "yet he will be kindly treated."[62]

The Drinkers were willing to use corporal discipline on white as well as black servants and even family members when the occasion seemed to call for it. Yet tellingly, of the six individuals whom Elizabeth mentioned as having been subjected to or threatened with corporal punishment, four were black men and two were white children, both girls; none of them was an adult white male. Three years before, eleven-year-old white servant Sally Dawson had run away to her father and stepmother's house, telling them that the Drinkers' adult son William had hit her. When the stepmother came around to tell the Drinkers that Sally was with them, William confirmed that he had struck her and that "she deserved much more than he gave her." Elizabeth was very fond of Sally and noted that until that point no one in the household had struck her, other than "a light slap on her cheek," though she "often deserved it," so the child was doubtless shocked. Yet Sally's stepmother did not seem to think the blow inappropriate and sent Sally back to the Drinkers "with a good scolding." A year later, Elizabeth recorded giving Sally her first whipping after she "behaved amiss." She hoped that this would "mend her." When Elizabeth's daughter Ann whipped her own daughter Eleanor for being "rather naughty," the grandmother admitted that doing so was "hard work" but "sometimes necessary." It mattered a great deal to Elizabeth whether the person administering corporal discipline was an employer or a family member and so, from her perspective, had the right to do so; she was outraged when a neighbor named Pantlif "beat and bruised" one of her own servants. Pantlif's dog had apparently attacked "black Tom," who responded by throwing a stone at the dog. In reprisal, Pantlif's wife "set their dog at him," and the animal bit Tom in several places before Pantlif himself beat Tom. There was undoubtedly a strong element of possessiveness in Elizabeth's response to a neighbor disciplining her servant, but she also saw Pantlif's response as excessive: she described him as "wicked" and his behavior toward Tom as "shameful." Elizabeth noted approvingly that Tom exercised his rights as a free man and lodged a formal complaint against Pantlif.[63]

A succession of African American children came to live in the Drinker household and grew up there as indentured servants. Elizabeth's comments about these youngsters resembled her diary entries about white children such as Sally Dawson: she took care of them, clearly cared about them, and did not hesitate to judge them based on whether or not they behaved well and worked hard or were lazy and troublesome. Consider the experience of three "little black boys" who came to live with the Drinkers for a trial period in the late fall of 1794. Their names were Scipio Drake, Peter Savage, and Peter Woodward. Eleven-year-old Scipio arrived first, in mid-October, and he proved to be the least satisfactory of the three. Scipio had already worked in several other households but ran away from each of them to his mother, who lived and worked in another Philadelphia household. His mother's master did not appreciate Scipio's repeated arrivals on his doorstep and put the boy in prison. It was from there that Henry Drinker had extracted him, apparently hoping that he could settle the lad, but Elizabeth thought Scipio "very sulky" and confided to her diary, "I can't say I like him." Scipio ran off the first chance he had, the day after his arrival, leaving behind in the yard some knives they had sent him outside to clean. His father, who also lived in the city, brought him back a few hours later and asked the Drinkers to give his son another chance. They duly fed the lad and sent him off to bed, but Elizabeth hoped that if he ran away again they would have done with him. Scipio did settle down over the coming days, but he turned out to have lice and so subjected the household to further inconvenience as they purged him and his clothes of the offending creatures. He also started a fire in their backyard two weeks after his arrival, which Elizabeth read as an accident due to his stupidity in throwing hot ashes behind the stable instead of burying them, though it may have been an expression of resentment and resistance against his servitude. Scipio remained with the Drinkers for just over a year, but Elizabeth gave no sign in her diary that she warmed to him. In December 1795, when she noted in her diary that her husband had "sold" the boy (again a striking choice of language, given that Scipio was formally free), she wasted no ink on regrets or indeed any comment about his departure.[64]

Peter Savage, "a negro boy, aged seven years," arrived from Virginia several weeks after Scipio, according to Elizabeth "weakly" but "otherwise well disposed." Peter did not attract Elizabeth's disapproval in the ways that Scipio did, but the Drinkers sent him away as well, a year later, to work in the household of Henry Sandwith. It had always been the plan to keep just one or at most two of the boys. Elizabeth hoped that Savage would prove "a good boy," though he was at present "but little worth." Over the coming years, she occasionally noted seeing him as the two families spent time at each other's homes, and the lad sometimes visited Henry and Elizabeth on his own account. He gradually transformed in Elizabeth's mind from "little Peter Savage" to "Peter Savage, HSD's boy," to Henry Sandwith's "man Peter Savage." In early 1807, she was shocked to hear that Peter had almost died while crossing a frozen river at night: he fell through a hole in the ice and could not get out. Fortunately, a boatman who lived nearby heard his cries and with the assistance of several other men in the vicinity rescued him. He was apparently lifeless when first pulled out of the river, and it was, Elizabeth wrote, "several days before he was restored to health . . . poor Peter, he was, as it were, dead."[65]

Of the three boys who had come to live with the Drinkers that fall, only Peter Woodward stayed with them until adulthood. He had arrived in a ship from the Chesapeake in poor condition, but once scrubbed, fed, and warmed, he recovered rapidly. On first viewing, Peter seemed to his new mistress "formidable" and "hard favored," but her impression of him quickly softened. Elizabeth was initially under the impression that he had no relatives in the city, but a few days after they took him in, his father, Anthony, whom he had not seen in eight years, came to the door for a visit, having heard that his son was newly arrived in the city. The boy went away with his father to see his mother, Alice, who was also in Philadelphia, and she brought him back after a weeklong visit. It was not until the end of March in 1796, almost sixteen months after his arrival, that Peter's parents formally bound their son to the Drinkers. Perhaps the Drinkers delayed until sure of the boy's reliability; perhaps the parents waited until confident that the Drinkers would take good care of their son. According to his indenture, Peter would serve the Drinkers until his twenty-first birthday. There had been some debate over how old he was: Warner Mifflin, who arranged for the Drinkers to take Peter, thought him eleven or twelve, but a relative said he was almost fourteen. The indenture described him as twelve, which maximized the time he would serve the Drinkers in exchange for the fifteen pounds they paid for his labor.[66]

Peter was now part of the Drinker family. The family's friend and physician Benjamin Rush treated him when he was sick and inoculated him against smallpox, along with Peter Savage. Elizabeth herself stayed up with him when he was sick; he was, after all, both a valuable asset and a child under her care. They sent both Peters to worship at "the Negro's Meeting," and Elizabeth arranged for a seamstress to spend several days at the house making clothes for "our black boys" (Elizabeth herself spent a day in the kitchen "cutting out undergarments for our blacks and whites").[67] Peter performed a wide range of chores. On one occasion, his master sent him out to their country estate to join the haymaking crew. On another, the lad helped to load goods into the hold of a vessel on the wharf. He carried one of Elizabeth's grandchildren back to her parents' home after a visit to North Front Street. He assisted in transporting the family's possessions back and forth between their house in the city and their country home. He was sent to help the Skyrins move house and the Downings gather apples at their country estate. He laid "stones at the back of the kitchen." Like the other servants, he served as a conduit for information both within the home and across the Drinkers' familial network: his employers sometimes sent him to the homes of relatives to inquire about their health, and on one occasion, he passed on to his master and mistress "disagreeable intelligence" about Sally Brant's less than maidenly "conduct."[68]

Yet even though Peter had proved himself as a helpful and versatile member of the household's workforce, his mistress was reluctant to trust the young man, even as he approached adulthood and the end of his indenture. Elizabeth made occasional comments over the years about what she saw as his carelessness (a common trait of servants, in her opinion): once the lad fell asleep in the kitchen sitting next to the stove and burned his eyelid; on another occasion, he fell ill after eating too many blackberries. She also thought him "very fond of idleness and fun." In a passage complaining about his and Sally Dawson's impertinence, she wrote that their domestics were "not what they ought to be by any means." By his late teens, Peter was eager to take over as the family's driver. This would take him farther afield from the Drinker home and so broaden his horizons; he would have to go out on his own to collect or deliver articles in the family's wagon and so have more independence; and the position may have carried more prestige than that of a regular servant. His mistress was not enthusiastic. Elizabeth acknowledged that the eighteen-year-old was "capable" but thought him "not so experienced and steady as I should like." Yet her husband eventually allowed him to take on the position. A few years later, the young man got into a fight with one of their neighbors, a hatter named Cake, who had been shoveling dirt against the Drinkers' fence in the back alley. The two combatants each took out a warrant against the other and ended up together at a local magistrate's house, where, as Elizabeth reported, "the matter was settled with small cost on either side." Her husband, she noted, had told the hatter that he should have come to him with any complaints about Peter's behavior. It would soon become clear just how protective the Drinkers' feelings toward him were, but along with that came an unwillingness to respect his autonomy as a free adult. Peter most likely still remained in their eyes the ragged, underfed child they had taken in a decade before.[69]

When Peter reached the end of his indenture, Elizabeth hoped that he would stay on under their wing, just as she had hoped Sally Dawson would do. True freedom, his mistress believed, depended on the ability to exercise that freedom responsibly, and when it came to "the lower sort," regardless of their skin color, she had her doubts. "Peter Woodward is this day a free man," she wrote, "if being twenty-one years and out of his time will make him so—no talk of parting yet, poor fellow, I sincerely wish him well." Yet Peter was now developing an independent life outside the Drinker home as he explored Philadelphia's black community. In January 1806, Elizabeth noted in her diary that he was out that evening at a party "of black beaux and misses." The young man had also asserted his spiritual autonomy, attending Methodist services as well as Quaker worship meetings, and he had other plans to exercise his independence. Just under a year after his indenture ended, he decided to go to sea and signed on with a trading firm that was sending a sloop, the *Rising Sun,* to Saint-Domingue. Peter may have caught the maritime bug from Pompey, a servant in the household of their daughter Mary: Pompey had left his master and mistress to go to sea in 1804 and then visited Peter after returning from his maiden voyage.[70]

Peter did not tell the Drinkers about his plan until he had already committed himself, a detail that Elizabeth noted in her diary. They did all they could to dissuade him, stressing the dangers involved: not only would the ship be heading out to sea in winter weather, but it might be seized and he "made a slave of, being black." Peter would be in particular danger as he approached Saint-Domingue because of the race war unleashed by the slave uprising there. One of their neighbors, a merchant named James Wood, told them that if the French got hold of Peter, they would almost certainly hang him. Elizabeth was unsure whether to share this information with Peter ("to tell him such a thought just now," she wrote, "as he seems determined, would be hard perhaps, yet I hardly know how to forbear"), but Elizabeth's daughter Sarah had no such inhibitions and passed the prediction on to Peter. Yet Peter was adamant. He was doing all he could to protect himself and had obtained a certificate affirming his U.S. citizenship. These protected American seamen from impressment if a foreign power captured their vessel; at least in theory, they also prevented captors from selling African American freemen into slavery. Elizabeth knew that Peter had "long wished to go to sea" but suspected that he was mostly interested in "novelty" and did not understand fully the dangers he faced. Her anxiety on Peter's behalf intensified when the ship he was to sail in "nearly filled with water and in measure sunk, owing to a hole . . . overlooked in a late repair." The Drinkers also worried about the corrupting influence of liquor and profanity on board ship, and Peter's master gave him a lecture on this subject before the young man took leave of them. He returned twice before the ship finally sailed, once for a meal and then to collect an umbrella he had decided to sell.[71]

Over the coming weeks, the Drinkers kept track of the ship's progress via newspaper announcements, and that April they received a letter from Peter, telling them that all was well. When the *Rising Sun* returned in July, Peter came to visit and told the Drinkers that he planned to remain in Philadelphia if he could find a good position but otherwise would "go to sea again." It is not clear from Elizabeth's diary if Peter was interested in returning to the Drinker household, but his former mistress evidently considered that as a possibility, noting however that the servant who was now working in Peter's place had proven quite satisfactory, so that she could not justify dismissing him. A few days later, she heard that Peter had found a place elsewhere in the city. Elizabeth was clearly still concerned about the young man's welfare, moral and otherwise. When he visited again that September, she lent him *The Cheap Repository,* a collection of religious tales and morally improving essays that she thought "well calculated for the use of those called the lower class of people," a good example, she would have thought, of why it made sense to teach servants such as Peter how to read. A few weeks later, she was disappointed to hear that Peter had married a young woman who was "by accounts not so good as she ought to be." Her diary entry blended disapproval with sympathy: "I am sorry for Peter," she wrote, but he was "a foolish blockhead." Elizabeth probably saw this latest misstep as evidence of Peter's inability to manage responsibly his own freedom: she may have believed that had Peter still been under their wing, and had he consulted with her or Henry first, the marriage might have been avoided.[72]

Whether Peter read the book she lent him, appreciated his former mistress's intentions, or knew what she thought about his marriage, we cannot know, but he and his relatives still saw the Drinkers as a source of support in times of trouble. In 1801, when Peter was still indentured, his father had come to ask for a winding sheet in which to bury his daughter, who had just "died of a consumption." Peter's mother died three years later in the almshouse, apparently "deranged for some time past." In March 1807, when Peter's father died, his new wife came to ask for decent clothes in which to bury him. Peter's brother visited the Drinkers to request medicine for his sore tongue. Jacob Downing, Elizabeth and Henry's son-in-law, hired Peter's twelve-year-old nephew as a servant; he was about the same age as Peter when he arrived to live with Elizabeth and Henry, though this little boy was a free laborer, not an indentured servant. In the late fall of 1807, Peter came to talk with Henry, whom Elizabeth still referred to as "his master," about taking a position at the Atsion ironworks, and Henry was happy to oblige. In one of Elizabeth's final diary entries, she noted the arrival of a letter from the ironworks manager describing Peter and his wife as "very serviceable and handy." Peter was once again within the Drinker family's sphere of influence and acquitting himself well. "I am pleased to hear it," she wrote.[73]

~

If Sally Dawson had survived her battle with yellow fever and gone on to become "serviceable and handy" as an adult employee, Elizabeth would have been as pleased by that happy ending as she was to read about Peter Woodward's settling comfortably into a life of service under her family's patronage.

Both of these young adults had arrived to live with the Drinkers as indentured children. One was white and the other black, yet their experiences in the household had been remarkably similar: they worked hard, were cared for and worried over as they grew into adulthood, and were appreciated yet never entirely trusted to exercise independent judgment as free adults. Once no longer bound to the Drinkers by their indentures, they were free to make their own mistakes, and the Drinkers understood that, but they did not welcome their servants' newfound freedom any more than Elizabeth welcomed in general the transformation in labor relations that she lived through and had to accommodate, at least to some degree.

Elizabeth had a deeply ingrained sense of the responsibility that went along with her position as a household mistress, and throughout her married life, she was generous in her support of domestics who met her standards of diligence, deference, and gratitude. Like other employers, she availed herself of the greater flexibility that went along with a system of wage labor. Yet she clearly hankered after a past, however real or imagined, in which the household had been a more stable structure, a tight-knit hierarchical family rather than a series of business arrangements lacking any sense of sustained commitment or deference on the part of employees. Even as she supported the abolition of slavery, Elizabeth resented assertions of independence and respectability by free blacks, just as she bristled when white servants behaved in ways that threatened the distinctions that she and her peers drew between "the lower class of people, as they are too justly called," and themselves. If Elizabeth's acceptance of political independence was reluctant and tinged with bitterness, so too was her acknowledgment of the greater autonomy that free laborers welcomed. Times had assuredly "much altered," but that did not mean that Elizabeth had to like it, and for the most part she did not.[74]

8 • "A Scene of Affliction and Grief"

In Which Elizabeth and Henry Drinker Face New Challenges to Their Family's Survival

Anxiety must have gnawed away at many families during the American Revolution, as fathers, brothers, and sons went off to fight, as armies burned homes and looted farm supplies, and as chilling reports spread far and wide about brutal sexual assaults carried out by soldiers from both sides as they passed through local communities. Vocal supporters of the Revolution must have worried about their likely fate if the British won the war, while families labeled as "disaffected" from the patriot cause had ample reason to worry as the revolutionary authorities railed against alleged enemies of the people. The Drinkers were among those who learned from harrowing experience during the War for Independence that they could not take their survival for granted. Nor could they and other Friends assume that all their brethren would stand firm in the day of trial: during those years, the Society of Friends fractured and then split as some Quakers abandoned their commitment to pacifism, took up arms against the British, and following their disownment joined together as Free Quakers.

Even once Americans began to reconcile, at least superficially, in the aftermath of the war, Quakers still felt endangered as they contemplated less obvious yet worrying threats to their integrity and survival. As Friends rebuilt their lives, they only partly reintegrated back into mainstream society as they reaffirmed their commitment to an inward-looking reform movement that had launched before the Revolution. They feared not only the hostility and distrust of non-Friends but also the corrupting influence of mainstream social values that might over time dilute Quaker values. They responded by forging a self-consciously separatist community in which constellations of Quaker families would socialize together and intermarry, protecting themselves as far as possible from what they saw as the materialism, vanity, and belligerence of the outside world. Friends had come to believe that they could ensure the purity and continuity of their faith only through a process of self-insulation, and the key to succeeding in that endeavor was their children.

Quakers knew well that because they could not rely on outsiders to embrace their faith or encourage membership in their church, they had to raise young people who would sustain that faith into the next generation. As a family friend of the Drinkers wrote in 1779, only "due care and oversight" would ensure that children grew up "in the nurture and admonition of the Lord." This friend hoped that Henry and Elizabeth's children would serve as "pillars for their dear parents to lean upon in their declining years," but he also and crucially trusted that they would become "stakes in Zion." Raising devout and loving children was as important for the larger Quaker community as for individual families. Yet that was no easy task, especially in a teeming seaport such as Philadelphia, where children and young adults would encounter in the course of everyday life behavior and attitudes very different from those their parents had taught them; they might also form relationships that drew them away from Quakerism. During the War for Independence, Quaker parents in Philadelphia must have worried that the romantic appeal of uniformed soldiers, along with the public celebration of military prowess, might seduce their children and challenge their own pacifist message, while the conspicuous consumption and merry-making that accompanied the British occupation of their city posed another kind of threat to Quaker values. When Henry declared that his children's welfare mattered to him "above all earthly or temporal considerations," he was defining parenthood as a primarily spiritual endeavor. Even during his exile, he tried as best he could to maintain a firm grip on his children's behavior. Except for attending public worship, he wanted them to stay "at home, retired from a corrupted world." Only then could he be sure that his beloved children would remain "preserved in true godliness, innocency, and purity." Yet what parents intended as loving protection might seem downright repressive to their offspring, and two of the Drinker children would in desperation devise an escape from "our father's mode of thinking."[1]

Once those children became young adults, anxiety focused on whom they would choose as husbands or wives and what impact those decisions would have, not only on their own personal happiness but also on the larger Quaker community. Toward the end of the colonial period, a growing number of young adults who had grown up in the Society married non-Friends, giving rise to fears that they might not raise their own children as Quakers. In the early 1760s, just as Henry and Elizabeth were starting a family, the Society of Friends committed to a much stricter enforcement of marriage regulations, hoping that the threat of expulsion from the Society would motivate young adult Friends to marry fellow believers. A few decades later, Henry became actively involved in clarifying those procedures. He and Elizabeth cared deeply that their sons and daughters become conscientious members of the Quaker community and expected them to marry within the faith in accordance with established protocols. They also hoped that their sons and daughters would find in their married lives the peaceable companionship idealized within Quaker teachings. Elizabeth took her maternal responsibilities very seriously, whether dealing with her own children or the indentured servants whom she guided from childhood into adulthood. Just as she had difficulty accepting that servants who had grown up under her care could now make responsible choices as free adults, so she was sometimes reluctant to trust her own sons and daughters to make wise decisions. Yet she and Henry found that they had much less influence than they would have liked over the future well-being of their offspring and, through them, the welfare of the Quaker community that meant so much to them both. Indeed, their children's marriages brought discord, scandal, and anxiety into their home and community.[2]

Friends saw themselves collectively as a family of committed believers, and so Quaker parents such as the Drinkers did not struggle in isolation. Their belief in spiritual equality led them to emphasize horizontal relationships that bound brethren together in the loving bonds of brotherhood and sisterhood, but they also depicted elders who led and inspired them, including Henry Drinker, as parental figures. The use of familial language to depict social, political, and religious relationships pervaded eighteenth-century transatlantic culture. Even as patriots engaged in ritual patricide, destroying paintings and statues of their formerly venerated father figure George III, they remained committed to the family as a potent metaphor for national identity. Citizens of the new republic celebrated the fraternal bonds that drew them together in defense of their liberties, revered President Washington as an enlightened father of the nation, and praised the role played by mothers in raising their children to become virtuous citizens. Americans cared deeply about familial bonds, whether literal or figurative. Yet Quakers had their own specific reasons for nurturing the family: their own holy nation faced many dangers, and they believed that unless they worked hard to maintain their integrity as a family of families, joined in devotion to their God, the Society of Friends could not hope to survive.

Whether Quakers would survive as a coherent spiritual community depended not just on the choices that individuals and couples made but also on the physical survival of its members. Here we encounter a particular challenge in trying to understand eighteenth-century anxieties. Sickness and death were commonplace, unpredictable, and all too often beyond human control in ways that we can barely imagine. Whereas modern Westerners tend to believe that they can cure most illnesses, or at least control the symptoms, eighteenth-century Americans had no such confidence. Most people knew from personal experience that any family could suddenly find itself in danger of losing loved ones or in mourning. Disease, mishap, and death were great equalizers. Affluent families such as the Drinkers could afford to summon expensive doctors when a member of the household fell ill, yet even prominent physicians could offer little more than hopeful guesswork. Well-heeled Philadelphians could purchase whatever medicines their doctors recommended and visit spa towns where immersion in healing springs and the drinking of mineral waters also promised relief (Elizabeth did so on several occasions), but few of these treatments worked. Far better to die in a comfortable bed than freezing cold in an alley, but affluent citizens had no more prospect of effective treatment than did homeless beggars. When epidemics swept through Philadelphia, the wealthy could leave and take shelter elsewhere, yet doing so provided no guarantee of immunity against infection or the panic that epidemics aroused. No one was ever entirely safe. As Elizabeth commented pithily, "Old people must die and young ones often do! How populous the grave!"[3]

Because the Society of Friends sustained itself through highly personalized networks of loving friendship, any individual illness, death, or disgrace struck a blow not only to immediate family and friends but also to the larger community. Consider the reaction when John Pemberton, a close friend of the Drinkers, died in 1795. Elizabeth's heart went out to his wife, who had lost her closest friend and companion. "Poor Hannah," she wrote. "I feel for her, she has lost, it may be truly said, one of the best of husbands." The Drinkers were also devastated: Elizabeth wrote that her entire family had "loved him well . . . my husband particularly." Yet the loss transcended these immediate ties. Pemberton had proven an inspiring leader within the Society of Friends, "a truly sympathizing brother." His passing was, Henry wrote, "deeply felt" by all those "brethren and sisters who knew that excellent man and his superior worth." Pemberton's gift had been unusually visible, but because Quakers depended so much on mutual support, every death within the community was both a personal and a collective loss. Though their faith taught them to face bereavement in a spirit of submission to God's will, such "steady dependence and confidence in the Almighty" was, as Elizabeth acknowledged, "hard, very hard, in many cases to effect." Indeed, she often described bereaved friends as "in trouble" as their depth of sorrow, however natural, expressed their failure to submit to whatever Providence had in store for them. Elizabeth dwelled repeatedly on the difficulty of accepting with due resignation the death of loved ones. "When sickness and grief visit a family who love one another," she wrote, "it must be by great exertion and the favor of the Lord that the survivors get the better of it."[4]

Elizabeth felt for any soul in pain, need, or distress ("those among us who do not sympathize," she wrote, "must be unfeeling indeed"), but the frequently precarious state of her own children's health most consumed her attention. Elizabeth was a devoted mother, and her anxiety on their behalf featured among the most common refrains in her diary. "Since I have been a mother," she wrote, "my children have been my chiefest care, both soul and body." Far from diminishing once they became adults, her concerns if anything increased as all but one of them married and so were no longer under her direct supervision. "If I could but give a peep at my four dear absent children," she fretted, "though it might perhaps distress me." As she acquired grandchildren, that anxiety extended to them. Her older son William remained at home unmarried, and even though his health proved extremely fragile, his mother wrote that "in some respects" she worried about him less because he was right there, "under the shadow of my wing." Her younger son, Henry Sandwith, moved away to live with his new wife on a farm some thirty miles from Philadelphia. Elizabeth lamented that she did not hear from them as often as she would have liked and worried that he traveled around the countryside "in all weathers." Though much more robust than William, he was not, she averred, "one of the invulnerables." Once her daughters established their own households in Philadelphia, messages passed daily back and forth between them, often describing the various ailments afflicting their loved ones. Elizabeth's relentless quest for information about her children's and grandchildren's health testified not only to their closeness as a family and the matriarch's desire to maintain even at a distance what she called her "jurisdiction" over their lives but also to the worry that such ailments provoked. It might be tempting to dismiss or trivialize diary entries such as these as the words of an overprotective mother, but that would be a mistake. News of a stomach cramp may seem mostly inconsequential to us, but in eighteenth-century Philadelphia, it could seem and sometimes was life threatening. Furthermore, for members of a community that already felt endangered and relied on interpersonal support over formal structure, illness and death struck at all community members and represented one more nail in a collective coffin.[5]

"Dead and Dying in Almost Every Direction"

Life in eighteenth-century Philadelphia presented many hazards. Fires spread with terrifying speed through congested neighborhoods and had no respect for property or privilege. Cries of "Fire!" often woke the Drinkers at night, drawing them out of bed to gather anxiously at a window or to join neighbors in the street as they exchanged rumors about where exactly the latest blaze had appeared and where it was heading; they knew only too well that a combination of fire and a brisk wind could prove deadly. On one occasion, Elizabeth and her husband were roused from sleep by a light "shining strongly into our chamber." It turned out that a chair maker's shop in a nearby alley had gone up in flames; several other buildings burned to the ground before neighbors could extinguish the blaze. Another fire at the home of a local printer took six lives, including the printer's wife and their three children, "a negro boy," and a maid. "Every human bosom," Elizabeth declared, "must be wrung with anguish at the recital of the shocking catastrophe." Once her children married, Elizabeth worried that the latest conflagration might endanger their homes. "When I hear the cry," she wrote, "my daughters come first in my mind, as is natural, and 'till I know where it is, I am uneasy."[6]

Simply walking or riding through the streets could prove dangerous as horses reared or bolted and carriages crashed. In 1799, Henry was lucky to walk away with only a swollen left wrist and a bruised thigh when a carriage he was riding in overturned; the other three passengers were "mercifully preserved from injury." Several years later, a similar accident left him with several dislocated bones in his right wrist.[7] Even bowel movements could prove fatal if the floorboards in outside privies gave way, plunging the occupant downward into a pit filled with urine and excrement. In the summer of 1791, a baker's wife survived such an accident only because the floor that went down with her provided some support; she remained there submerged up to her shoulders until someone found her. "How careful should every family be," declared Elizabeth on hearing of this narrow escape, "to examine those places that they are secure, to prevent these very terrible accidents which too often happen." Twelve years later, the Drinkers panicked when they could not find their little grandson Sammy, fearing that he might have fallen into the privy and drowned. William lowered a long piece of string with a candle tied at the end down into the pit, "but could not determine the matter." Much to everyone's relief, the little boy arrived soon afterward from playing down the street with other children. Not all such deaths were accidental: Elizabeth heard about a servant who had committed suicide by removing the privy seat and letting himself down into the pit one evening; the next morning, someone coming out to use the privy found him down there dead.[8]

Appalling though the prospect of death by fire or drowning in human excrement must have been, what aroused most fear among Philadelphians during this period was epidemic, especially the yellow fever that swept through the city in 1793 and then again in 1797, 1798, 1799, 1803, and 1805. City dwellers might contain fires if they acted quickly, and householders could be diligent about keeping their coaches and privies in good repair, but even medical experts disagreed as to what caused the yellow fever and how to fight it. The epidemic of 1793 struck a devastating blow to Philadelphia. The virus that caused yellow fever, transmitted by the bite of an infested mosquito, probably arrived that summer in ships from Saint-Domingue carrying thousands of refugees from the bloody revolution that raged there. The ghastly symptoms included yellowing eyes and skin due to liver failure (thus the disease's name), purple hemorrhages in the skin, fever and chills, intense pain in the head and stomach, internal hemorrhaging that produced black vomit, and comatose delirium, often followed by death. In truth, tuberculosis claimed more lives than yellow fever in the 1790s, and Americans also died in large numbers from respiratory and intestinal illnesses, smallpox, measles, diphtheria, whooping cough, and malaria. The yellow fever had visited Philadelphia on several occasions during the colonial period, wiping out a third of the city's population in 1699, but the last occurrence had taken place in 1762. Since then, improvements in sanitation and the water supply, stronger quarantine procedures, subsidized health care for poorer residents, and better diets had resulted in an overall healthier population and increased average life expectancy. Yet physicians now proved helpless against the dreaded fever. Its reappearance after three decades' absence shocked Philadelphians to their core. Several thousand people died that fall, between a third and a half of the city's residents fled into the surrounding countryside, and hundreds of children became orphans. Business ground to a halt, the city, state, and federal governments ceased to operate, the basic social fabric of the city unraveled, and the devastating impact of the epidemic undermined Philadelphia's bid to retain its status as capital of the United States.[9]

That fall, the city streets filled with carriages and wagons taking wealthier families and their servants out of Philadelphia to seek refuge in neighboring communities; the same streets conveyed death carts that bore away dozens of bodies each day for rapid burial. The poor were at greater risk because they could not afford to leave the city; overwork, overcrowding, and the persistence of insanitary living conditions, deficient diets, and inadequate health care would have accentuated this disparity. One contemporary account estimated that seven-eighths of those who died were poor. Yet all Philadelphians were vulnerable, and the entire city succumbed to frantic anxiety. Even Alexander Hamilton, secretary of the U.S. Treasury, contracted the disease along with his wife, Elizabeth, though they were lucky and both recovered. Newspapers published regular updates, including long lists of the dead; doctors argued about how best to combat the epidemic; and families watched anxiously for signs of infection in their neighborhoods, dreading that they and their loved ones might soon become the latest entries in the tally of death. Residents tried to protect themselves by chewing garlic, smoking cigars, burning gunpowder, and wearing tar-coated ropes around the neck, but no one knew for certain what would work, how long the epidemic would last, or how many lives it would end up taking. "We live in the midst of death," wrote twenty-two-year-old Isaac Heston ten days before he also succumbed to the virus. The impact was as much psychological as physical: "they have suffered so much," Martha Washington wrote, "that it cannot be got over soon by those that were in the city."[10]

The Drinkers were among those who could leave the city in times of danger and wait out the crisis until it was safe to return, and if they suspected that a member of the household had contracted the fever, they could summon respected physicians for advice and treatment, yet this did not guarantee them immunity from the deadly epidemic. Henry and Elizabeth were both well aware that the fever had first appeared in their neighborhood. Some believed it had arrived in a ship that lay at the wharf behind their store; others suspected that rotting fish, coffee, and other waste piled up alongside the river had turned putrid in the heat of the summer and so gestated the fatal disease. As a man of business, Henry bemoaned the epidemic's economic impact, but his main concern was the danger to his family as the fever "baffled the skill of our most eminent physicians" and "swept off several thousands." By late August, he wrote, people were "dead and dying in almost every direction." His language in these letters was much more dramatic and emotional than his customary prose style. The "raging disease" had "deranged" the city, he declared, and it was "deeply trying and awfully affecting" to witness "the present ravages of the gloomy agent." Both Henry and Elizabeth saw the devastation as a warning from God with a clear message for Philadelphians. The Almighty was responding, Henry opined, to "pride, wantonness, and a too general forgetfulness of that divine hand which for many years has so abundantly blessed and favored this land." Elizabeth noted that by midautumn even leading physician Benjamin Rush believed "the disorder was now past the art of man or medicine to cure, [so] that nothing but the power of the Almighty could stop it." She hoped that everyone would "endeavor for preparation and resignation." Those who survived should remember "with humble thankfulness" that God had spared them and commit to "amendment of life."[11]

In the meantime, Elizabeth recorded in grim detail the epidemic's progress. When the fever first struck in August 1793, she and most of her children had already left the city and were spending the summer in Germantown and Downingtown. Henry Sandwith rode back and forth between them and the city, where he was helping his father with business matters. Elizabeth became more and more alarmed as visitors from the city brought with them daily news of illness and death: what at first seemed merely "a sickly time" now appeared much more catastrophic. William and his father were suffering from what seemed to be "the influenza," and William went back to the city for several days so that he could consult with the family doctor. Henry's reluctance to leave Philadelphia and her sister's insistence on staying to look after him caused Elizabeth particular anxiety. "I am much distressed," she wrote, "that any of our family continues in town." One of their servants had fallen ill and was now at "some negro house where they have promised to take care of him." The Drinkers could only hope that it was not "the contagious fever," for his sake and theirs. A few weeks later, another of their servants turned up in Germantown "very pale and weak." He wanted to take refuge with them, but Elizabeth wrote that they "would have been as well pleased if he had gone elsewhere." Deciding whether to grant the sick servant's request would have been a difficult decision, but their landlord told them that he could not stay, so they had no choice but to send him off to relatives in New Jersey. Much to Elizabeth's relief, her husband and sister finally relented and joined her in Germantown at the end of August. Their neighborhood in the city, she wrote, was now "depopulated by deaths and flight." Houses were "shut up from one corner to the next," and most of those still in town hid themselves away, so that the streets were largely deserted.[12]

As Philadelphians who had fled to the countryside worried about those left behind, they drew on a constant stream of information that circulated via official announcements and newspaper reports, private correspondence, and gossip in streets and parlors. Elizabeth acknowledged that much of that information was unreliable, yet she became a voracious consumer of any and all reports about "the melancholy and distressed state of our poor city." She scoured published lists of the recently deceased for the names of friends and neighbors. She read about official measures taken in hope of containing the disease, such as marking the front doors of houses that contained fever patients so that their neighbors would know not to enter. She lamented the fraying of respect for the dead as fear and the sheer scale of mortality drove Philadelphians to put the dead in their coffins immediately instead of changing their clothes, cleaning their bodies, and laying them out according to time-honored custom. Coffins were now "kept ready in piles by the state house for poor people," and mass trenches awaited dying indigents in the paupers' burying ground; even respectable graveyards now had holes dug in advance so that people could bury the dead with all possible haste. She recorded a string of heartrending stories arising from the crisis, dwelling in particular on those left to die alone as fear of infection deprived them of the usual support given to the sick. These stories combined with other horrors to suggest a world in physical and moral collapse. That October, she read in the newspaper that a mob had seized the queen of France on her way to prison and "tore her in pieces." Meanwhile, a drought was prompting forecasts of meager crops and starvation. "Disorder, cruelty, and distress," she wrote, "has of late resounded in our ears from many quarters."[13]

Yet Elizabeth remained, as always, focused on her immediate domestic world and the terrifying possibility that one or more of her own family members might fall prey to the epidemic. Each time that the yellow fever revisited Philadelphia, Henry's reluctance to abandon his business affairs and join her outside the city became a source of contention between them. In August 1797, as the fever spread rapidly through their neighborhood, Henry tried to diffuse the tension between them through black humor, claiming in one letter that his and Mary's continuation in Philadelphia should not be a major concern as they were "pretty far advanced in years" and regardless of epidemic might not be long for this world. Whether or not Elizabeth managed a wry smile on reading this, her anxiety deepened on hearing that the governor had issued a proclamation quarantining all infected neighborhoods and declaring that those who fell sick, regardless of their social status, must remove from their homes to the hospital, surely the equivalent of a death sentence. Henry now assured his wife that he had packed all his important papers in a tea chest, so that he could depart quickly if it seemed necessary. "You are capable of thinking," she replied with grim resignation, "and I trust will do what is right." Only one servant, Sally Kidd, remained to help maintain the household, and she refused to stay at home, which put both herself and her employers in danger. When news arrived that her stepfather was ill and might have the dreaded fever, Mary told her that they wished to keep her on but could not do so if she insisted on visiting him. Sally then departed in a fit of pique, leaving Henry and Mary without any domestic assistance. Elizabeth now threatened to return home if the stubborn pair still refused to leave. Henry protested in turn that thieves were targeting empty houses and he did not want to leave their home unprotected; he was also consulting with others how best to distribute money allocated by the state assembly to relieve the sick and unemployed. Yet a few hours after writing these words, he and Mary finally decided to shut up the house and leave the city.[14]

With each successive wave of infection, the Drinkers had to decide what measures they would take to protect themselves. In 1803, their servant Sally Dawson fell prey to the fever and died a few days after her removal to the hospital. Elizabeth lurched back and forth between distress about Sally's condition and anxiety for her own family. She fretted that her husband had stood very close to men from the hospital who had come to take Sally away and took a paper from one of them to read its contents. She was also well aware that neighbors were shunning their house as a possible site of contagion and was duly grateful when a friend came to spend the evening. "It is kind," she wrote, "when others are afraid to come." In 1794, Elizabeth had suspected for a time that one of her own daughters had the deadly fever, and Sally Dawson's death in 1803 must have intensified that sense of endangerment, yet it was impossible to insulate oneself completely. When Elizabeth's doctor advised in September 1805 that she lose some blood, the man who came to carry out the procedure told her that he had used the same lancet to bleed many individuals suffering from the fever: "I did not altogether like it," she wrote. That fall, the family decided to stay put in Philadelphia and brave the latest wave of epidemic, but Elizabeth worried that her husband's dislike of "confinement" might endanger his life: she was convinced that the air became more infectious after dark and fretted when he and their servant Peter Woodward refused to stay at home in the evenings. Their houseguest John Tyler, on the other hand, was afraid to venture out into the streets at all and took to pacing in the backyard like a caged animal. On September 20, the family heard a coffin mounted on wheels rumble past their front door as it carried a neighbor's son to his burial. "We don't feel comfortable," Elizabeth confessed.[15]

"My Feelings Are Not to Be Expressed in Words"

Terrifying as these waves of epidemic must have been, they were but one of many ways in which illness could strike at loved ones. Though Elizabeth was by temperament inclined to anxiety, her fearful response to any signs of illness in her young children was hardly an overreaction, given the common occurrence of infant and child mortality, not least in her own family: four of her nine children died in infancy. Even after her children reached adulthood, their health remained a matter for constant concern, and in 1791, she and Henry almost lost the older of their two surviving sons when twenty-four-year-old William contracted tuberculosis. Billy, as he was known in the family, had been "drooping" for some time and had not left his bedchamber for several months during the previous winter, but after an extended convalescence, he departed in June 1791 on a monthlong excursion into the countryside. As the young man drove away in a newly purchased two-wheeler pulled by the family's old mare, his mother prayed that the trip would bring him better health, "the greatest blessing that mankind can enjoy in this world, next to a good conscience." The adventure began badly as Billy fell downstairs while visiting his two older sisters in Germantown. He was apparently wearing boots too big for him and the soles had become slippery after a walk in wet grass; he bruised his hip, and his little niece Eliza, whom he was carrying at the time, had some bruises on her face. Yet once he recovered from this initial setback, the trip seemed to have the desired effect.[16]

Things did not go so well that fall when Billy set off on another adventure, this time on horseback. According to his father, who described the shocking chain of events in letters to relatives and friends, William's doctors had again advised him to seek "moderate exercise and change of air." He intended to head north into New England, but the young man got no farther than Rye, some thirty miles beyond New York, where he came down with a fever and started to spit blood. He hired a chaise to bring him back to New York, where Henry and Hannah Haydock, family friends and fellow Quakers, took him in. Billy had apparently ruptured a blood vessel in his lung: he brought up two quarts of blood in three days, and the doctors thought him in grave danger. When news of Billy's condition reached Philadelphia, Henry and Elizabeth set off immediately for New York, their daughter Nancy and her husband, John, following a day later. Writing during a stop in New Jersey to his sister-in-law back home, Henry confessed that he found it "hard work to keep to a calm resigned state of mind." In a subsequent letter, he told Mary that her sister, "though greatly weighed down," was clinging to the possibility that Billy might have fallen into "a refreshing slumber." Elizabeth had asked Henry to communicate this "ray of hope," but they both wanted to prepare Mary, in effect a third parent to their children, for the possibility that they might not arrive in New York "before the solemn close." In a separate note, Elizabeth reminded her sister, and perhaps herself, that this eventuality would take Billy "past all affliction, grief, or pain."[17]

Elizabeth later acknowledged that she and Henry had "fully expected to have found my dear boy a corpse on our arrival." When Henry Haydock's son greeted them with the news that William was still alive and somewhat improved, Elizabeth was at first "incapable of taking in the full force of the words" and stood speechless outside the Haydocks' house "in a torpid state" until taken inside. William had stopped vomiting blood and had "fortified himself" as best he could in preparation for his parents' arrival. Blood occasionally reappeared in his phlegm over the coming days and he had a bad cough, but after a few weeks, he was able to start moving around his chamber and then the rest of the house, though still, in his mother's words, "amazingly weak." Henry, who returned to Philadelphia after spending almost a fortnight in New York, drew comfort from his son's gradual improvement and his "remarkably calm, quiet, and steady frame of mind." Yet Henry admitted that he was "a good deal shaken" by the crisis. Usually in command of every detail, he had accidentally left New York with the key of Elizabeth's trunk in which her clothes were packed.[18]

As the Drinkers braced themselves for a lengthy and precarious convalescence, they drew on the support of a large and loving community. Relatives, neighbors, and friends in New York and Philadelphia provided emotional reinforcement and recommended a range of treatments that they hoped would strengthen Billy and help to mend his ravaged lung. Henry was convinced that the bleeding had stopped because of "absorbent earth" provided by "a widow Gomez" in New York. The family's doctors back in Philadelphia recommended the application of blisters (irritants intended to produce a discharge of noxious fluids), though they disagreed as to whether these should be placed on William's sides or arms. Other friends urged the use of ethereal salt, tar water, St. John's wort, "Pyrmont Water" (a carbonated mineral water said to help in cases of debility), and stewed prunes. Yet another suggested a voyage to Europe, in large part because the sea itself was medicinal; he also recommended the healing power of music, in particular the pianoforte.[19]

Yet the couple's chief mainstay during this crisis seems to have been each other. For the second time in their marriage, Elizabeth and Henry endured a lengthy separation marked by extreme anxiety and the very real possibility of death: during Henry's exile in 1777, two of his fellow prisoners had died and his own survival had been far from certain; now their eldest son was in peril. As in their earlier wartime correspondence, their letters to each other during Elizabeth's two-month stay in New York contained a good deal of practical information, but they also dwelt at length on their own emotional and religious responses to the crisis. Elizabeth reported that her son was in spiritual as in other respects a model patient, having "resigned" himself to "the will of the Lord," and both parents tried to follow his example. They alternated between "hoping and doubting" in the possibility of Billy's survival, but whatever happened, Elizabeth wrote, they "must submit." Henry likewise aspired to "humble acquiescence," committing "to bow in reverent thankfulness" if his son survived and "to kiss the boot" if he died. He also hoped that they would draw strength from their memory of previous ordeals, which had so often ended in "unexpected deliverances." Elizabeth might have reminded him of her miscarriages and the death of their four infant children, but her husband clearly wanted to focus on the perils they had escaped: "We have indeed much to be thankful for," he declared. Yet lurking behind and breaking occasionally through these assertions was naked, raw fear: "What to say for thine and his comfort I hardly know," he declared when Billy had a relapse. "My feelings are not to be expressed in words."[20]

As before, Henry wrote that he traveled in "flights of the mind" to join his loved ones in New York, which gave him "a degree of gratification better to be felt than expressed." He informed his wife that he was going to adopt a "compact and mercantile mode" of letter writing and asked her to assume that each epistle contained messages of love from him, their immediate family members, and their friends, "whether expressed or not." Yet what he did write was powerful enough. One of his letters ended "with abundant love. Divide it, my dearest, and take to thyself a large share." He sometimes tried to lighten the tone of their exchanges with a jest. On November 18, he wrote to her twice in one day and pointed out in the second letter that if he added up the cost of materials, along with the value of his time, the debt might confound any "private or national fund." However, he added, the balance would always be in Elizabeth's favor, as his "obligations in various respects" to "the best of wives" were "so numerous, for thirty years past heaped up," that any attempt "to balance the account by trifling or visionary items trumped up in my favor" would be utterly futile. A little humor wrapped around a touching tribute to his wife as she sat at their son's bedside: Henry's prose style was much more eloquent than he claimed.[21]

Distressed as Henry was by his son's condition, he also worried that his wife might damage her own health by "undue exertions." He urged her to rely more on the Haydocks for assistance, and on several young Friends in the neighborhood who had offered to come and sit with William. Henry knew from their three decades together that Elizabeth's constitution, for all its apparent fragility, had "a degree of toughness" that had carried her through many ordeals and could still "bear a good deal of wear and tear." Yet he wanted his wife to escape her son's sick chamber as often as possible, noting that he could rely on her "good judgment in all matters . . . save in the most essential matter, the use of fresh air and exercise," a glimpse perhaps into his views on her frequent self-confinement at home in Philadelphia. Henry was also concerned about his sister-in-law, who apparently often dissolved into tears as she fretted about Billy's situation. Mary wanted to join her sister in New York, but Henry opposed her making such a journey in the late fall and "at her advanced time of life." He may also have thought he could not spare her at home. Mary agreed to remain in Philadelphia, where she busied herself making a pair of flannel sheets for William to use on his homeward journey. Ann stayed on in New York for a month, and then their youngest daughter, Mary, replaced her as Elizabeth's companion until William could travel. Henry Sandwith accompanied Mary and stayed for several days. Their father returned to New York on a few visits and told his wife that he would like to join her more often so that he could "clasp" her to his "bosom." However, with his characteristic mixture of affection and practicality, he would then cite his many responsibilities as a church elder and his preoccupation with business affairs. Indeed, Mary and Henry Sandwith had delayed their departure for New York because he needed his son's assistance.[22]

Billy's convalescence turned out to be lengthy and faltering. He returned to Philadelphia at the beginning of December, his father having rejoined the members of his family in New York to plan for the journey. It was a daunting prospect, given the patient's still frail condition and the possibility of foul weather at that time of year. Much to everyone's relief, the three-day journey went without a hitch: Billy reached home "shaken and wearied" but "in no way essentially injured."[23] He remained housebound for most of the winter and over the coming two years careened back and forth between periods of improvement and relapse. At the end of 1793, Elizabeth described him as "now, the many pull backs considered, as well as might be expected." The doctor had told them that if Billy survived to the end of his twenties, still a few years away, he might "still become a healthy man." Yet Henry wrote to a friend almost four years after the crisis that his son's condition remained fundamentally unchanged, "subject to much bodily weakness" and "affected by small variations in the weather." Billy would remain fragile for the rest of his life and his mother continued to worry if he showed the slightest sign of sickness. Henry took comfort in his conviction that William had endured these trials in an appropriate spirit of resignation. As for his family, they had "labored" to achieve that same state of mind, but as Henry acknowledged, "to be enabled to say in perfect resignation, 'Not my will but thine be done,' is indeed what very few arrive at."[24]

"When We Give Ourselves Away"

Quaker parents whose children survived into adulthood and enjoyed good health could sigh with relief and celebrate that they had raised a new generation of Friends. They doubtless hoped that their adult children would then marry, produce children of their own, and so ensure the future of their religious society. The latter, however, depended on whether their children grew up to become conscientious Friends, married fellow Quakers, and raised their offspring in the faith. Friends did not leave this to chance: those who could afford to do so sent their children to schools that provided an education imbued with Quaker principles; they also created an elaborate set of rules to guide young adults in their choice of spouses and to regulate their entry into marriage. In theory, couples who neglected to abide by these restrictions faced a range of sanctions that included expulsion from the Society of Friends. Yet in practice, many offenders before the 1760s met with lenient treatment: Monthly Meetings often pardoned those willing to express contrition and automatically admitted to full membership the offspring of mixed marriages. This may well have encouraged a marked increase in exogamous marriage during the 1740s and 1750s. After all, potential delinquents could be reasonably confident that local Meetings would forgive them just so long as they declared themselves penitent after the fact. During the 1750s, Monthly Meetings in Pennsylvania disowned only half of marriage offenders.[25]

Growing consternation about the trend toward mixed marriages and its potential consequences played a significant role in launching the reform movement that got under way within the Society of Friends in the 1760s, which included a much firmer stand against mixed and clandestine marriages. In 1762, the Yearly Meeting for Pennsylvania and New Jersey urged Monthly and Quarterly Meetings to disown marriage offenders swiftly instead of waiting patiently for indications of reform, as had formerly been the practice, and to readmit offenders who submitted acknowledgments only after thorough investigation to ensure that such confessions were heartfelt. Furthermore, Meetings should accept the children of mixed marriages as members only after confirming that they had received a religious education. Between that Yearly Meeting and 1776, roughly 11 percent of Pennsylvanian Quakers found themselves disowned because they had married non-Quakers or otherwise ignored marital regulations; the percentage of offenders who ended up disowned rose to over two-thirds. Following the War for Independence, Quakers reaffirmed their commitment to unity and discipline. Central to that endeavor was the formation in the 1790s of a high-profile committee to collate and refine the rules governing marriage, along with other aspects of Quaker life. Henry Drinker served on that committee.[26]

The rapid increase in disownments expressed a renewed determination among Quakers to promote and enforce endogamy, but it also showed that a growing number of young Friends were still determined, whatever the cost, to sidestep marital regulations and choose partners based on their own inclinations, regardless of their parents' wishes or religious background. That independent-minded attitude was entirely consistent with a broader trend in the late eighteenth century toward the assertion of greater personal freedom by young people as they entered adult relationships. Sexual experimentation before marriage was also on the rise, resulting in skyrocketing bridal pregnancy rates; many Americans worried that unscrupulous male lovers might seduce young women and then abandon them to single motherhood. Elizabeth and Henry had themselves belonged to a pioneering generation that laid much greater emphasis on romantic courtship. Now, as parents, they became involved in a clash between their own community's desire to reassert control over marital choices and a broader transformation that pointed in the opposite direction and had given rise to a nationwide debate over the navigation of courtship and marriage. One evening in March 1795, the Drinkers' son William, daughter Mary, and houseguest Samuel Preston debated after dinner "on the subjects of love, courtship, and marriage, but could not jump in judgment." A month later, Elizabeth described a wedding in the neighborhood as "expeditious doings," whether because the couple was already pregnant or because they had ignored marital procedures is unclear.[27]

Henry and Elizabeth clearly expected their children to become Quakers, marry Quakers, and raise children within the Quaker faith. Their five surviving children had grown up in a social environment that blended Quaker values with urban gentility. Most of the friends, acquaintances, and business associates who flowed in and out of their home were Friends; their father frequently hosted Quaker committee meetings at the Drinker home. The children attended worship regularly with their father and aunt, and in later years, they went on their own to meetings designed specifically for young adults. All five attended schools run by Quaker teachers, who held classes in their own homes or those of their pupils' parents. Boys and girls generally went through their elementary schooling together, but William and Henry Sandwith then went on to "man's school" when each reached the age of eight. The children also attended supplementary classes that focused on particular subjects: both boys took Latin; Ann and William took French. The girls continued to work with teachers on their writing but also learned more gender-specific skills: Ann and Sarah attended knitting classes; Ann also went to "drawing school." Quaker teachers would have imbued their classes with the precepts of their faith and eleven-year-old William received a lesson in the politicization of education as well as the limits of revolutionary commitment to liberty when patriots shut down his school in 1778 because the schoolmaster had refused to take the oath of allegiance, leaving William "at a loss for employment."[28]

Quaker parents who wanted to protect teenagers and young adults from undesirable influences and to prevent their forming close relationships with non-Quakers faced an uphill struggle, especially if they lived in a large and heterogeneous city such as Philadelphia. Elizabeth disapproved of young Quakers "going in companies to public houses" and was not pleased when her children occasionally joined such excursions. Nor did she approve of their visiting an ice cream parlor that opened in the neighborhood, as there was no knowing whom they would meet there. Yet parents could not entirely prevent young adults from making their own choices. When two of her children attended a party on New Year's Eve, she responded with reluctant resignation: " 'tis not the way I would wish my children to conclude the year . . . but we can't put old heads on young shoulders." In 1791, when Elizabeth's youngest daughter, Mary, joined her in New York to help take care of William, Henry was clearly worried about his daughter's potential exposure to undesirable influences as she explored a new city and made new acquaintances. He claimed that he had tried over the years not to be overly protective of his children and he hesitated to veto activities "which they might with safety and without endangering their innocence be indulged in." Henry assured his wife that he trusted her judgment and did not want "to restrict or limit more than true prudence dictates," but he worried that "too great a latitude" might be dangerous and was "deeply concerned" for his daughter's moral safety.[29]

The Drinker patriarch was equally concerned about his two sons. He considered both of them extremely impressionable and wished that they had encountered "none but profitable and instructive examples." Yet it was impossible to ensure "total separation from the spoiled boys and girls of this city" (or, lamented Henry, "the petulant humors" of their sisters), thus William's "follies and weaknesses," which often obscured "the goodness of his heart." As for Henry Sandwith, wrote his father, "[He] is a young man as honest as most of his age, but quickly catches the words and the manners of those he consorts with, which plainly show the truth of that saying, that 'evil communication corrupts good manners.'" In his late teens, Henry Sandwith went to live with the Lightfoot family in Reading, about fifty miles away from Philadelphia, so that he could learn surveying methods from Thomas Lightfoot. His hosts were fellow Quakers, and Henry Drinker could presumably trust them to keep an eye on their young charge. Yet even so, he wrote repeatedly urging his son to avoid "the snares and temptations which unguarded, inexperienced youth are abundantly exposed to," and that might lead them away from "innocence, purity, and godly simplicity." The stakes were high, as whether or not the children of Quakers committed to upholding their parents' faith would in turn determine if the Society of Friends survived as a distinct spiritual community. Parents could only hope that in major life decisions, especially the choice of husbands and wives, their offspring would cleave closely to the values they had tried to instill in them.[30]

None of the Drinker children actually abandoned the faith of their parents, but their behavior by no means always accorded with their parents' definition of appropriate Quaker conduct. Elizabeth and Henry were probably disappointed that William remained a lifelong bachelor, though neither left behind any comment to that effect. Their other son and three daughters did marry, all choosing fellow Quakers as their partners, and they had between them twenty-eight children, whom they raised in the faith. Yet their marriages were far from idyllic. Sarah married Jacob Downing in 1787 at the age of twenty-six. Downing was a flour merchant who would later become owner of the Atsion ironworks. By then the ironworks was in utter disarray owing to conflict between the previous co-owners, who included Henry Drinker. Elizabeth predicted that her son-in-law's purchase would prove "a troublesome bargain," and sure enough, Jacob's fraught business affairs soon became a topic of conversation at the Drinker home. Ann was twenty-seven in 1791 when she married another merchant, John Skyrin, who turned out to be a doubly problematic choice as his business began to suffer serious losses and their personal relationship became increasingly fraught. The Drinkers' youngest surviving child, Mary, was in her early twenties when she scandalized her parents and the local community in 1796 by eloping with Samuel Rhoads. This was especially mortifying because of Henry's involvement in the Philadelphia Meeting's review of marriage protocol, and Henry's response to the elopement would create an unusual degree of tension between himself and Elizabeth. Samuel was another merchant who did not prosper in his chosen calling; he would die in his mid-thirties on a voyage from Montevideo to Havana after having to sign his property over to creditors. Henry Sandwith decided to become a farmer, but he married Hannah Smith, the daughter of a merchant, and the world of commerce would steal him away in the final year of Elizabeth's life when he decided to leave his farm and family behind to travel as a merchant's agent. Henry Sr. had decided following the War for Independence not to revive his import and export business, but all four of these marriages embedded his family more deeply than ever in a network of trading connections at a time when merchants were going bankrupt by the wagonload. In 1787, William and his new brother-in-law, Jacob Downing, considered going into business together. Henry thought his son "steady" and his son-in-law "capable of conducting most branches [of business] reputably." He was confident that together they would "execute any concerns entrusted to them with fidelity and judgment." Yet Henry and Elizabeth knew from experience that trade was a perilous enterprise. That prospective partnership between Drinker and Downing never materialized, but each of their married children would face significant economic uncertainties.[31]

Henry and Elizabeth both voiced their belief that wedded life could provide great happiness, but they insisted that a couple had to be personally compatible and firmly committed to their faith if they were to cope with the trials that doubtless awaited them. When Sarah married Jacob in 1787, her father wrote of his "comfortable hope that they are equally and rightly yoked, both being of happy, easy disposition, and promise fair to be proper help mates to each other." It was his "earnest desire" that "they so abide near and under the humbling, sanctifying power of Truth as to be established therein and thereby be prepared and fortified to pass through the various cares and vicissitudes of this life." When Henry Sandwith married Hannah in 1794, Elizabeth inserted into her diary three poems to mark the occasion. The first of these recognized the challenges that her son would face and the need for God's support:

> If the Lord, in condescension,
> Deigns to hear a mother's prayer,
> He will attend this morning's meeting,

And be with my Harry there;
Great indeed's the undertaking!
When we give ourselves away,
But if He approve the action,
Blessed is the nuptial day.

The second poem wished the bride and bridegroom a long life together, "quite free from anxious cares, disturbing thoughts, [and] distressing fears." Elizabeth hoped that the young couple would live so as "to deserve an exemption" from anxiety and hardship. Yet the third acknowledged that however steady and virtuous her son and daughter-in-law might prove, they would nonetheless encounter testing times. When that happened, they would find peace of mind only through resignation in the face of affliction:

There is a lesson worthy notice,
Which requires our frequent care,
In every scene of life that's trying,
Learn to bear, and to forbear;
Youth too seldom mind this maxim,
But when arrived to riper years,
Experience shows it is effectual,
To alleviate cares and fears.

We do not know if any of Elizabeth's children read these poems, but the four who married would each encounter trials that their mother saw as calling for a spirit of resignation, on her part and theirs.[32]

"In a Proper Key"

Sarah and Ann married during periods when their mother was either not keeping a diary or writing entries that have not survived, but Elizabeth described Henry Sandwith's marriage in loving detail, characterizing his union as a model of conventionality that clearly delighted his parents. In order to become fully adult, Henry Sandwith had to acquire both an occupation and a wife. The young man had chosen to take up farming, and so, in the fall of 1793, his father purchased for him a 202-acre property out in Chester County that Henry Sandwith named North Bank. Whatever he told his parents at the time, Henry Sandwith would later confess to his brother William that his principal motive for settling in the countryside was to escape the repressive atmosphere that pervaded their home because of Henry Drinker's insistence that his family conform to the strict code of behavior urged by Quaker reformers. That reformist agenda, wrote Henry Sandwith, had "such an influence on our father's mode of thinking as to spread unhappiness throughout all our family." It also led their father "to discourage in his sons any method of improving their fortunes by entering into the world or their understandings by going abroad, lest they might become unquakered." Whether William, his sisters, or their mother would have agreed with the claim that Henry Drinker's imposition of a strict moral code had cast a shadow of "unhappiness" over the entire family, we have no way of knowing, but Henry Sandwith could not "bear the restraint." From his perspective, "removal into the country" was "more the effect of necessity than of choice." He admitted to his brother that "timidity" had prevented him "from ever expressing" to their father his true "sentiments" on this or indeed any other matter. Reluctant to defy Henry Drinker openly, he chose farming because he was confident that the patriarch "would not object" to a secluded, rural way of life: this was the only escape route he could pursue without "displeasing" his father, whom he clearly loved and did not wish to disappoint.[33]

At the time, Henry Sandwith seems to have kept his inner motives entirely to himself, and his decision surprised some of the young man's friends, who predicted he would soon regret abandoning city life to farm in the middle of nowhere. Henry Sandwith insisted that what they saw as "a romantic idea of rural pleasure and Arcadian felicity" would in fact bring him "good health and good spirits." He claimed that he could think of no other occupation that appealed to him and in which he was likely to achieve "any tolerable degree of excellence or even of mediocrity." One of his friends asked if he had in his sights "a beautiful all amiable partner," to which he replied rather unromantically that before finding himself a wife he needed to establish himself and a home in which to welcome her; he anticipated that such practical matters would require his full attention for some time. Yet his mother was already looking forward to that next decision. As her son set about making improvements to the farm, she hoped that Providence would "direct his steps in that, and another undertaking of greater consequence," which she assumed he would "ere long be thinking of."[34]

That turned out to be the case as her outwardly filial and well-regulated son settled on a thoroughly respectable young woman as his life companion and helpmate. Hannah Smith, the daughter of Friends James and Esther Smith, was born in Burlington, New Jersey. Her family had moved to Philadelphia in 1784 when Hannah was ten years old. James Smith was a merchant and well known to the Drinkers: many years before, he had served as Henry's apprentice (Elizabeth referred to him at the time as Jammy). Hannah's family pedigree was impressive: her paternal grandfather, John Smith, also a merchant, had served as treasurer of an insurance company known as the Philadelphia Contributionship, as secretary of the Philadelphia Hospital, and as a member of Pennsylvania's provincial assembly before relocating to New Jersey, where he had become a member of the Governor's Council. Hannah's paternal grandmother, Hannah (Logan) Smith, was a Quaker preacher and daughter of James Logan, who had made a fortune in trade as well as serving on the Governor's Council in Pennsylvania and as chief justice of that colony's Supreme Court. Hannah's parents had blotted their copybook in the eyes of the Quaker community when they married without following established procedures, but that had been over two decades ago, and her highly respectable lineage more than compensated for any fading memories of impropriety.

The Society of Friends required that young adults contemplating marriage submit their choice of partner for approval by their parents or guardians and at two successive Monthly Meetings. Following the first announcement and confirmation that the parents or guardians of both applicants approved of the match, Friends then appointed two men and two women to ascertain if each partner was free of prior commitments and if the candidates' behavior together was above reproach. At the second meeting, assuming that the inquisitors had brought to light no obstacle or impropriety, the couple would receive permission to proceed. The marriage itself was supposed to take place at a regular worship meeting. As usual, people would enter quietly and sit in silence. Someone might rise to say a few words of encouragement or exhortation, and then the couple would take each other by the hand, declare in turn that they took each other as husband or wife, and sign a certificate to ratify their commitment, which all those present at the ceremony also signed as witnesses. If a celebration took place afterward, the rules of conduct stipulated that there should be neither "immoderate feasting or drinking" nor any "unseemly, wanton, or rude" behavior that would bring scandal to the families concerned or the Society of Friends. Two men and two women appointed by the Monthly Meeting should attend the ceremony and celebration to ensure that everyone followed these requirements and returned to their homes "in seasonable time."[35]

Henry Sandwith proceeded to court and wed Hannah in complete conformity with these requirements. His mother's only reservation about the relationship seems to have been that Henry Sandwith made her "not a little uneasy" by staying out late at night when visiting his intended. Many years before, Elizabeth had expressed doubts about the propriety of her own Henry sitting with her till late in the evening when he was wooing her, but now she focused on her son's health and safety. "When young men go a courting," she wrote, "they should make their visits shorter, and not walk two miles in a dark night alone; the risk of meeting with mischievous persons, or of taking cold this season of the year, should have some weight with 'em." Elizabeth was out at Clearfield when Henry and Hannah formally requested permission to marry at the Monthly Meeting in October, and so she did not attend. She did, however, add her signature of support to the written application (which must have been taken out to Clearfield for that purpose), wrote "a few lines" to her prospective daughter-in-law the day before the Meeting, and then noted in her diary that the young couple had "performed well" after her sister, Mary, sent a report out to Clearfield. Their second appearance at Monthly Meeting also went smoothly, and Elizabeth now referred to Hannah as "the bride," commenting in one of her entries that surely people could refer to a young woman as such "with propriety" once she had "declared her intentions of marriage publicly." She clearly saw the young couple as all but married, though she would not have agreed with the time-honored popular assumption that betrothal rather than formal marriage marked the moment at which sexual intimacy became acceptable. Fortunately, at least from Elizabeth's perspective, none of her children seemed to act on that assumption; or at any rate, any such intimacies did not result in conception before marriage.[36]

The wedding was to take place that December, by which time Elizabeth was back in Philadelphia. A few days beforehand, her husband's clerk delivered invitations around town. Esther Smith had a badly swollen foot and so could not accompany her daughter to the ceremony, but the weather was temperate, and so Elizabeth, who had not attended public worship in a long time, felt able to brave the short journey to Market Street. The bridal couple traveled to and from the meetinghouse in a carriage, the bridesmaids following in another, but everyone else walked. William, though frail, had been determined to witness his brother's marriage and joined the assembly late that morning. About fifty people attended, and it was, as Elizabeth put it, "a favored time." Henry Sandwith and Hannah, who "spoke very distinctly and in a proper key," were "much commended for their conduct and behavior." At the celebration that followed, which took place at the home of Hannah's parents, the guests consumed "a very plentiful and elegant dinner well served" around three o'clock. Mary Sandwith left with William "towards evening, the latter much fatigued," but Elizabeth stayed for the supper at nine and remained until the party broke up at around ten, having "passed the day better than expected." She noted with satisfaction that "nothing" had "occurred to cause displeasure or uneasiness that I heard of, as sometimes does in large companies."[37]

The couple spent their wedding night at the Smith residence, but two days later Henry Sandwith invited his and Hannah's younger friends over to his own parents' home for a postnuptial celebration. Elizabeth wrote in her diary that although she and Henry were "not fond of such parties," they "could not deny so innocent a request." The guests arrived at five in the afternoon and feasted on "cakes, wine, coffee, tea, almonds, raisins, nuts, pears, apples, etc." Elizabeth conceded that the partiers behaved "inoffensively" (at least so far as she could tell, given that she took refuge in another part of the house), but she did complain that they "made rather too much noise." A few days later, the couple set off for Clearfield, where they would live until the house at North Bank was finished, hopefully the next summer. A week after that, Hannah's mother persuaded Elizabeth to ride out with her to visit their children. The youngest Drinker daughter, Mary, also visited with "several other lasses and lads," taking tea with the newlyweds one Sunday, though her mother approved neither of her going on First Day nor of their staying till after dark. A year later, when Henry and Hannah finally relocated to North Bank, Elizabeth confided to her diary how hard it was to part with "a beloved son," though she noted somewhat grudgingly that "it must be more so" for Esther Smith, forced "to part with a child-bearing daughter, perhaps equally beloved."[38]

Over the coming years, neither Henry Sandwith nor Hannah gave their parents any cause for serious grief or complaint until the death of two infants in 1798 and 1801, followed by a stunning revelation in the fall of 1802. Henry Sandwith was thinking of abandoning his farm and family to become a supercargo, or mercantile agent, traveling on voyages to East India. A year earlier, in May 1801, the young man had written a memorandum laying out his plan and reasons for pursuing it. He had not expected farming to make his fortune, and the acquisition of wealth had not been his goal, but now his growing family had made him reconsider his priorities. He should be looking to the future and thinking how best to increase the "bounty" provided by his father, not least to pay for his children's education. He also wanted to prove himself a worthy son, though he acknowledged that he had never felt explicit pressure to do so from his "highly regarded" father. He was unwilling to enter into "pecuniary speculations . . . which I do not understand and the termination of which I cannot foresee." Yet he had heard that young men were making considerable sums by serving as agents on trading voyages to the East Indies and China, also that many of these men had done well despite knowing little beforehand about "eastern merchandise," as was his case. He admitted that leaving his family behind would be difficult for him and that this plan would most likely dismay those who loved him, but a sense of duty to his father and his own family must supersede his "personal feelings" and "the feelings of others who are dear to me."[39]

Henry Sandwith was quite correct in predicting that this scheme would dismay members of his family. We do not know how his wife, Hannah, reacted to the news, but his parents were, to put it mildly, unsympathetic. When Henry Sandwith eventually plucked up the courage to send his father the memorandum he had written, long after he had started to look around for a position as supercargo, he wrote in a cover note that he hoped for his parents' "acquiescence," if not their "approbation." In their first face-to-face conversation on the subject, Henry Drinker made it clear to his son that he thought the plan "extravagant and unnecessary," but Henry Sandwith noted afterward that his father had treated him "with the utmost kindness" and he trusted that the older man would come around. Yet in a letter written several months later, Elizabeth Drinker reported that her husband still thought the plan "a ridiculous, foolish whim," and she evidently agreed. She could scarcely believe that Henry Sandwith was thinking of leaving behind "a young family of precious children, and parents in precarious health, to go nine thousand miles on a tempestuous sea . . . Art thou insane?" she enquired. Hannah's father, James Smith, was a good deal less blunt, but he doubted that working as a supercargo would prove as lucrative as his son-in-law believed and suggested to Henry Sandwith that trading in dry goods might yield more profit. If Smith was hoping to establish and maintain a united front with his son-in-law's parents, he was to be sorely disappointed. Smith visited the Drinkers at Front Street that fall and was shocked when Henry Drinker declared that he thought Hannah responsible for driving his son to this extremity, through "bad management . . . gadding abroad and neglecting her family affairs." Hannah's aggrieved father relayed this conversation to Henry Sandwith, who was in turn outraged. "It is a cruel mistake indeed," he declared, "and has destroyed all my tranquility."[40]

Ill feeling between Henry Sandwith and his parents as well as between the two sets of parents deepened over the coming months. At the end of one particularly tense week, Henry Sandwith wrote, "May I never pass such another week, striving to wear an aspect of serenity, with an horrid, dead, leaden weight at my heart, an ache in every bone, and my brain stung almost to madness." In December 1803, Henry Sandwith asked his sister Ann to pass on to their parents his "heartfelt contrition for having given them pain," but relations remained strained. Two months later, when he wrote his parents a letter in which he neglected to use approved "Quaker language" (which required that Friends address each other as "thee" instead of "you"), Elizabeth wrote back that she and his father felt insulted and disrespected. "Whatever language thou mayest think proper to use to other people, with whom thou art used to converse," she declared, "thy parents who have been always used to the contrary, ought to be clear of it from their children." Henry Sandwith noted in the margin of his mother's letter that he had intended no offense, but everyone was by this point on edge. His relationship with the Smith family also soured after he called his mother-in-law "a fool" in a heated moment and his offended parents-in-law stopped visiting North Bank, which must have been distressing to their daughter. Henry Sandwith delayed for several years before finally following through with his plan, but meanwhile his family back in Philadelphia fluctuated back and forth between strained silence and "a great deal of talk" on the subject. Neither his parents nor his siblings nor his aunt Mary approved of his "whim." His mother was worried for him and at the same time angry. "My heart aches for my son," she declared in her diary, "though I am displeased at him." In another entry she wrote, "Poor dear Henry, the latter would not perhaps thank me for my pity, I feel much for him nevertheless—I know he loves me, his love is not lost."[41]

"Mischief Going Forward"

Almost two years after Henry Sandwith's marriage to Hannah Smith and several years before he dropped his bombshell, the Drinker household and its reputation were rocked by their youngest daughter's marriage to Samuel Rhoads, which was as disorderly and scandalous as Henry Sandwith's had been well regulated and respectable. On August 8, 1796, Henry Drinker, his sister-in-law, and his son William returned from a short trip out of town. Elizabeth, who had stayed in Philadelphia with her twenty-two-year-old daughter Mary, was over at Rebecca Waln's house when she saw the family carriage pass by. She rushed home, delighted as always to have her loved ones returned to her safe and sound. Mary, known to her family as Molly, was not there, but Elizabeth thought nothing of it because the young woman had said she was going shopping with a friend. Later that afternoon, neighbor Robina Miller came to visit Henry on business, and once initial pleasantries had been exchanged the two retired from the parlor to his office. After dusk had fallen and the candles been lit, a young man arrived with an unsealed letter that he delivered into William's hand just as Henry and his guest were returning to the parlor. The letter was addressed to Henry and Elizabeth Drinker, so William handed it over to his mother. She opened the letter, curious as to who it could be from, saw the words "My Dear Parents" at the top of the page, then looked down to the bottom, and to her "unspeakable astonishment" saw that it was signed by Molly, but with the last name Rhoads instead of Drinker. "I exclaimed something," Elizabeth wrote later, "and no doubt my countenance showed my inward feelings." Robina Miller, observing Elizabeth's expression, said, "I see you have met with something afflicting," and had the good grace to withdraw. Once their guest had departed, Elizabeth shared with her husband, sister, and son the stunning news that the Drinkers' youngest daughter had eloped and married Samuel Rhoads.[42]

The young couple had disregarded Quaker regulations governing marriage in almost every respect. Given that Molly's own father had recently served on a committee charged with revising those regulations and had even hosted committees in their front parlor to go over the changes, this turn of events was especially embarrassing for the Drinkers. Molly's parents had not sanctioned the match, and indeed neither of them had "the least suspicion of anything of the kind occurring." We do not know if Samuel's widowed mother knew about the young couple's plans or, if so, whether she quietly approved, though this seems unlikely. The couple had not given their Monthly Meeting any opportunity to vet the match; they did not wed at a public meeting; and no official representatives of the Monthly Meeting were on hand to supervise any celebration afterward.[43]

Samuel Rhoads was twenty-two years old, the same age as Molly. His father, a Quaker merchant, had died twelve years before, leaving behind a widow and three small children. Sammy, as his friends and family called him, was now planning to follow in his father's footsteps (and those of Henry Drinker), but he was very young and offered no guarantee of success or financial stability. The two young people had courted the previous fall, but Molly's parents were under the impression that the courtship had ended at Henry's prompting. On November 10, 1795, Elizabeth had written in her diary, "Molly has orders to dismiss!" Three days later, Sammy had an interview with Molly's father that did not end well, at least for the young man. Elizabeth was "entirely ignorant" of that meeting (very unusually, she had been out almost the entire day), but

Sammy came to see her two days after that, perhaps hoping to win her support. Elizabeth did not record what she said to him, but she had written in a recent entry that she was "uneasy . . . on account of my dear MD," and she evidently shared her husband's perspective on the proposed union. "Matters are, I expect, concluded," she now wrote. "I sincerely wish we may do better." Elizabeth had herself hesitated to marry Henry, apparently because she thought she might do better. Despite her occasional frustrations over Henry's preoccupation with business, he had turned out to be a loving husband, economically successful, and a leading member of their religious society. However, at the time of their marriage, Henry had already established himself as a junior partner in a rising mercantile firm; Samuel's plans were so far no more than that, and he therefore presented a much greater risk.[44]

Elizabeth was unaware that Molly had even seen Sammy during the months before their elopement. She had witnessed Molly's defiant mood, noting in her diary that in mid-July "MD at dinner parle trop a son pere [literally, spoke too much at her father]!" She may have lapsed into French because she found her daughter's lack of deference so shocking. What she did not realize was that this outburst was a harbinger of much worse to come. Molly was in all likelihood seething with anger against her parents' disapproval of Sammy and may already have been planning to elope. It would emerge a few days after the clandestine marriage that the couple had decided to run away because they believed her father "would never consent." Henry was, not surprisingly, "much displeased and angry" when they first learned that Molly had eloped. Elizabeth wanted to know where her daughter was staying, but he "charged" his wife "not to stir in the affair by any means" and then stalked off to bed. Elizabeth sat up with her sister and William late into the night and when Mary eventually retired to her own bed Elizabeth spent the night in her son's room, "knowing I could not sleep and unwilling to disturb my husband." The next day, neither Elizabeth nor William ventured downstairs, both feeling unwell and perhaps preferring to keep out of Henry's way. Mary was out and about trying to ascertain who had attended the marriage, where it had taken place, and where the couple was lodging.[45]

Elizabeth's uncharacteristically detailed and colorful description of her daughter's elopement might have been lifted from one of the novels that she enjoyed reading. Eighteenth-century novels attracted a large readership on both sides of the Atlantic, but they were highly controversial, in large part because many of them dwelt in lurid detail on the dangers posed by seductive, unscrupulous rakes who seduced innocent young women and then abandoned them to unmarried pregnancy and social disgrace. Defenders of the genre insisted that such stories would prepare young women to resist such threats, but detractors worried that the romantic tone of these novels might captivate readers, who would then become even more vulnerable. Elizabeth claimed that she did not approve of romantic novels and would not encourage young people to indulge in "much of that business." Yet she acknowledged that in her youth she had enjoyed them, and now in the mid-1790s, even as she expressed disapproval, Elizabeth was herself returning to the genre. Molly seems to have shared her mother's enthusiasm: Elizabeth mentioned in one entry that her daughter had been reading *The Mysteries of Udolpho,* a popular romance by Ann Radcliffe, published in 1794. Some of the crises that these novels described arose because of disagreements between parents and children over the choice of a marriage partner. Authors warned that parents who frustrated the wishes of their children might drive them to extremes, and Molly may have learned from these novels that she had options other than deference to her parents. Now Elizabeth and Henry faced a very real elopement and the prospect of estrangement from their beloved daughter.[46]

Sister Mary returned with unwelcome news: gossip about the marriage was already spreading through the neighborhood. The young couple had married nearby in Chestnut Street at the home of Quaker Ann Pemberton, the groom's aunt. Pemberton's son Joseph had attended, but the rest of the family was out of town, and Ann later declared that she "knew nothing of the matter, or she would not have suffered a runaway marriage to have been performed in her house." A magistrate and Friend, Robert Wharton, had officiated at the ceremony and followed the standard Quaker format. Afterward the couple had left with several friends for the home of another Quaker just outside the city. The close involvement of Friends and the use of Quaker rubric at the ceremony provided Elizabeth with some consolation, but the Friends involved had betrayed the Drinkers and collaborated in the violation of Quaker regulations. Over the coming few days, Elizabeth and her sister pieced together various reports to compile a list of those who had been at the wedding, all of them Quakers. These accessories to elopement would have to brave Henry's displeasure, as well as that of other scandalized brethren. A neighbor told Elizabeth's sister that "a female friend" had stayed over in the Fisher home with Molly and Sammy on their wedding night, but she "was almost afraid to tell who." Mary, herself in a delicate position as she navigated between her sister's desire to know what had happened and her brother-in-law's anger, apparently declared, "I will not ask who it was, that I may not know if questioned."[47]

There was another consolation. Sammy Rhoads, though not the catch that Henry and Elizabeth had wanted for Molly, came from a Quaker family and was well thought of in the community. One family friend assured Henry "that Sammy was a lad of very good moral character, and that those who he had heard speak of the matter made light of it," though Henry apparently responded tartly, "So do not I." Another visitor told Mary (Elizabeth herself remained in seclusion) that he considered it "a very suitable match, Sam being a worthy young fellow." William told his mother that when he read in the letter that his sister had eloped with a Rhoads, that information lifted "a greater burden from his mind," adding hastily, "not that he had any other particular person in his thoughts." William was at least relieved that his sister had not fallen into the hands of a reprobate. Nonetheless, that Molly had resorted to clandestine marriage was a matter of amazement and mortification. "Little did I think," wrote Elizabeth, "that a daughter of mine would or could have taken such a step, and she always appeared to be one of the last girls that would have acted such a part—to leave her father's house, and go among strangers to be *married!*"[48]

Six days after the elopement, news reached the Drinker household that the married couple would return to Philadelphia the following day and stay for the time being with the groom's mother, Sarah Rhoads. "I am pleased to hear it," wrote Elizabeth, but Henry was far from pleased to discover that "busybodies" were spreading rumors about the elopement and Elizabeth wondered how Molly's siblings would react when they found out what had happened; Henry had evidently told his wife, sister-in-law, and William not to tell them. Henry Sandwith's wife, Hannah, was staying in town and when she heard the news went to see the new bride; she then visited at Front Street and reported that Molly "looked very poorly." For her part, Elizabeth "knew not what to do." Almost two weeks after their elopement, the newlyweds sent Henry and Elizabeth a note "expressive of their uneasiness at the pain they had caused," asking "to be taken into favor." Elizabeth made no mention of what, if anything, her husband said on reading this letter, but neither he nor Elizabeth sent any reply. In her diary, she responded bitterly: "I have undergone," she wrote, "a *pretty* large share of uneasiness." The next day William went quietly to visit his sister and did so again the following day, while his father and aunt were out at meeting.[49]

Elizabeth may perhaps have been relieved when Henry, still fuming, decided to leave town for several days to visit North Bank. She hoped that Molly and her new husband would take advantage of Henry's absence to pay her a visit, but they did not call, and Elizabeth felt yet more aggrieved on hearing that they were dining out elsewhere; her daughter had intimated that "she did not intend to go out anywhere till she was reconciled to us." Elizabeth did receive visits from her two other sons-in-law, who by now had heard the news: John Skyrin was "much agitated," Jacob Downing somewhat less so, though the following day he and his mother-in-law had a "painful" conversation. Mary now visited the newlyweds (though Henry had forbidden his wife to reach out to their daughter, he did not have the same authority over his sister-in-law), but her account of the visit gave Elizabeth "no consolation." Henry's mood did not improve following his brief absence, and almost three weeks after the elopement, Elizabeth had "un parlez avec HD, pas fort agreeable—comme quelque autres [a talk with HD, not very agreeable—like several others]." This was one of very few occasions on which Elizabeth acknowledged being at odds with her husband, making a painful situation even more so. Molly was "but rarely" mentioned in the house, "though much talked of abroad, and much thought of." The situation and its potential implications for the entire family weighed on Elizabeth's (and presumably Henry's) mind. "May I be enabled," she wrote, "to bear all that kind Providence thinks proper to suffer or permit."[50]

As the weeks passed by, Elizabeth had to rely on her sister and children for updates about her youngest daughter. She had not even left the house since Molly's elopement: unable to visit the young bride, she "thought it not right to go elsewhere." In early October, she noted resentfully that it was now almost two months since they had seen each other. "I know not why it is so," she wrote, "I am sure I wish it otherwise." Molly finally paid her mother a visit on October 9 while Henry was again out of town. Elizabeth was delighted and a week later came to a momentous decision: she defied Henry and went with William to see her daughter at Sarah Rhoads's house. Her husband had given "no reason . . . why I should not," and so, she declared, "I feel best pleased that I went." Elizabeth "heartily" wanted "an amicable meeting" to take place between father and daughter, but she did not tell her husband that she had disobeyed him, let alone propose that he visit Molly. Her other children continued to maneuver carefully around their father. Sarah and Ann visited their mother in company with Molly during meeting time, knowing that he would be out. When Molly's aunt asked her during one of these visits to stay for dinner, she refused because "she was afraid to see her father."[51]

The strain created by all this subterfuge compounded an already stressful state of affairs. Molly was unwell and her mother, who under normal circumstances would have been actively involved in caring for her, was "at a loss how to act on her account, she being from me, and things so out of joint." Elizabeth's distress was further deepened by vague reports about "mischief going forward" as Friends continued to gossip about the marriage and the community's likely response to the couple's violation of Quaker regulations. Whatever action the local Meeting decided to take, it was inevitable that at some point Molly and her father would have to meet. On November 1, Henry returned from meeting early because he was "disordered in his bowels." Molly was there on a visit and had not expected him back so soon. Overall, the unplanned meeting went well. According to Elizabeth, "he talked to her plainly, and at the same time kindly; she wiped her eyes and made a speech that I did not attend to, having feelings of my own at the time." Henry promised to call on Sammy's mother, and Elizabeth wrote that night that she hoped things were finally "getting in a fair train." Now that the long-dreaded first meeting between father and daughter had taken place, the parties involved could take other necessary steps toward reconciliation. Over the coming weeks, Molly and Sammy began to visit 110 North Front Street as a couple, supping there for the first time and gradually normalizing their relationship with Molly's parents and siblings. Henry visited the widow Rhoads as he had promised and asked her to keep an account of what she spent on hosting the young couple so that he could reimburse her.[52]

Yet even as the Drinkers reconciled themselves to the marriage, there remained the issue of the young couple's relationship with their larger faith community, which they had so blatantly disrespected. In January 1797, the Northern District Meeting to which Molly and Sammy both belonged launched a formal investigation into their clandestine marriage. A committee of two women and another of two men met with the bride and bridegroom separately, after which Molly and Sammy each prepared a written acknowledgment of their wrongdoing. Neither the Men's nor the Women's Meeting was satisfied with these statements, and new committees were appointed in late February to seek further clarification. The process dragged on into the spring as delegation after delegation visited to quiz the couple about their relationship. Though intensive investigations into irregular marriages were now standard practice, Elizabeth commented repeatedly and with increasing bitterness in her diary about "the many impertinent questions" to which her daughter was subjected. Elizabeth became convinced that the visiting inquisitors intended "to lengthen out the business" as long as possible and complained that such treatment was likely to alienate "innocent young women" instead of bringing them back into the fold.[53]

Elizabeth's use of the word "innocent" was significant and pointed. She did not recount in detail the questions asked of her daughter, but they apparently ranged far beyond the specific issue of her having married without her parents' permission or that of the Monthly Meeting. Those charged with the investigation most likely suspected that the couple was pregnant at the time of their marriage. One of the men appointed to engage with Sammy told Elizabeth "there was a great deal of out-of-doors talk" about the union, and she referred to the women visiting Molly as "curious impertinents," masquerading "under a show of religious duty." Elizabeth resented the suggestion that her daughter had flouted moral codes as well as procedural regulations. " 'Tis a pity," she wrote, "that a sensible, sincere, and delicate mind should be troubled by the evil insinuations of designing and unprincipled persons." Molly was in fact pregnant by the time the local Meeting launched its investigation, and it was doubtless not a coincidence that the Women's Meeting finally accepted her statement of contrition toward the end of May, by which point it was clear that the baby, as yet unborn, could not have been conceived before the marriage. Molly was, then, "innocent" in this respect, if not in others. " 'Tis well they have nothing worse against her," her mother declared, "though it is bad enough, but there are some who have endeavored to make more of it than it comes to." Not until November 1797 were Molly and Sammy formally reinstated, "sixteen months and upwards," Elizabeth noted, "since they were married."[54]

Henry's prominent status in the local Quaker community may have contributed to the intense scrutiny of Molly's clandestine marriage. According to Elizabeth, some of those who refused to accept Molly's initial acknowledgment of culpability said they were reluctant to take the young woman's assurances on faith, "lest it should look like partiality." A Friend visiting from South Carolina during the investigation told the Drinkers that when her daughter had married a young man without informing her Monthly Meeting first, "she thought it her duty to desire Friends to disown them," even though the bridegroom was a Friend, "as her husband was an elder and their stations high in the church." Elizabeth added, "for example's sake, I suppose." The visitor's words doubtless stung, though Elizabeth acknowledged that she seemed "kind-hearted" and "well-minded." In none of her own comments about the ongoing inquiry did Elizabeth mention Henry or his perspective on what must have been for him a mortifying situation. Had he stood aside silently while the investigation proceeded? Had he encouraged his fellow Quakers to pursue the matter with particular care, perhaps because he thought his daughter and son-in-law deserved such scrutiny, or because he did not want his family to appear in any way exempt from the surveillance of their community?

Elizabeth noted that her own sister had not attended Monthly Meeting as long as "the affair" was on the table, though why exactly she did not say. Elizabeth herself did not hesitate to be "partial" and was clearly outraged that the business dragged on for so long. When she heard that her daughter's acknowledgment was to be read out at the Monthly Meeting in November 1797, she not only stayed away herself but also sent a note over to Molly warning her: "Though it is no matter of scandal," she wrote, "she would not like to be present at the time." In fact, it was a matter of scandal, and Elizabeth knew well that such was the case.[55]

The illicit marriage cast a long shadow. Several years later, in 1801, Elizabeth feared that Friends currently making pastoral visits in her neighborhood might make unwelcome references to the elopement when they called on her, though in the event "nothing offensive occurred." Sammy, whom the Drinkers had rejected as a suitor for Molly's hand, seems to have kept his distance from them. Elizabeth complained that when Molly and her children were away in the country and Sammy remained in town on business, he rarely called on them, so that they had to send to Sarah Rhoads, with whom he stayed, for updates on their daughter's health and doings. For their part, Elizabeth and Henry were unwilling to reach out to him, especially as he seemed to think they had been in the wrong and so should court him: "he requires more attention than he chooses to pay," wrote Elizabeth, "and it don't suit us to run after him."[56]

The "Excruciating Trouble" of Childbirth

Once adult children were married, preferably in an orderly and respectable fashion, their parents waited anxiously for the young couples to embark on the dangerous enterprise of pregnancy and childbirth. This was, of course, not the only threat to a married woman's health. Each of the Drinker daughters faced serious illnesses and disability. Ann's eyes gave her much pain and anxiety over the years, while Sarah hurt her elbow falling from a horse in 1798 and ended up with a permanently dislocated bone; the doctor at first thought she had merely bruised the swollen joint and so did not attempt to reposition it. Sarah herself pointed out that this would have been more troublesome if she had to work for a living. Sarah had a reputation in the family for making the best of a difficult situation, and the disabled elbow doubtless had a greater impact on her day-to-day life than she wished to admit. Yet it paled into insignificance nine years later as Sarah died slowly and painfully of cancer, the only one of Henry and Elizabeth's adult children to die during their lifetime. Illnesses and accidents such as these were mostly unpredictable, but women faced a much more dependable threat in the form of serial pregnancy. Though none of the Drinker daughters died in childbirth, Elizabeth described their pregnancies as harrowing ordeals, and a botched delivery left her youngest daughter with lasting, at the time irreparable, aftereffects that caused her much pain and distress. All three daughters had fewer children than their mother, in line with a broad trend toward lower birthrates that resulted from deliberate choice on the part of women. Whereas Elizabeth had nine (four of whom died in infancy), Sarah had six (one of whom died in infancy), Ann had three (all of whom reached adulthood), and Mary had five (one of whom died in infancy, another in childhood, and yet another in his teens). Even so, the dangers associated with childbirth still figured prominently in their lives and perhaps in their decisions to limit the size of their families.[57]

Elizabeth dwelt frequently in her diary on the difficulties that she and her daughters experienced in delivery. Often "the child was ready for the birth," she wrote, "but there was not strength to bring forth," resulting in lengthy and grueling labor pains. These ordeals often ended only when the attending doctor "supplied the place of nature," administering drugs to stimulate birth or using forceps to extract the baby. Elizabeth thought that Sally and Molly had worse confinements than she had, and Nancy, though less so, had "very laborious times." Far from celebrating fecundity and childbirth, Elizabeth clearly saw this recurrent feature of a woman's life as more a curse than a blessing. When her daughter-in-law, Hannah, gave birth to twins in August 1804, Elizabeth noted that Hannah and Henry Sandwith now had six living children and had buried two, all within nine years and eight months of marriage. "Oh dear!" From Elizabeth's perspective, going through the agony and danger of childbirth every year or two was hardly a matter for rejoicing.[58]

Elizabeth experienced afresh the ordeal of giving birth as her own daughters and daughter-in-law went through the same ordeal. She identified closely with their distress, declaring on one occasion, "How often have I suffered labor pains in my mind for my daughter." She wrote a few years later, "Was I to have a daughter in this way every month for a year, I believe it would put an end to my existence! But we know not what we can pass through!" In 1799, as Sally approached her sixth delivery in "almost continual pain," Elizabeth noted that it was now thirty-eight years since she had herself given birth to Sally "in agonies" and predicted that this would be another "lingering labor." She tried to lighten her daughter's spirits by pointing out that because Sally was almost forty this might be her last child, "if she could suckle her baby for two years to come" and so hopefully prevent conception until the arrival of menopause. Although entries such as these focused on her own memory of pain as much as the present discomfort of her daughters, Elizabeth was clearly empathizing with them. That empathy extended also to her own mother. She noted that she had "never brought a child into the world without thinking how much my dear mother might have suffered with me," and the evening before her birthday in February 1800, Elizabeth lay awake "thinking of my mother's situation" as she began the ordeal of giving birth.[59]

The period during which Elizabeth's daughters were bearing children coincided with a significant and potentially lethal change in the management of childbirth. Most of the fatalities associated with delivery that Elizabeth noted in her diary fell within the last twenty years of her life, by which time wealthier Philadelphians were routinely using male doctors at deliveries instead of midwives. Doctors were more inclined to intervene in the birthing process, which could prove dangerous and even fatal if they were clumsy or if their unsterilized hands and instruments caused infection. Yet Elizabeth and her daughters eagerly embraced the new fashion and drew repeatedly on the services of William Shippen Jr., who by this time had become one of the most respected and capable obstetricians in the city. When Nancy had to rely on a midwife during one of her deliveries because the family was out at Frankford and there was no doctor within easy reach, Elizabeth worried that her daughter was "so far from proper help." They asked Shippen to attend at ten of their deliveries, and he was able to oblige at seven. Elizabeth noted with approval his supervision of several problematic deliveries, but Sally may have had a lucky escape at her last delivery when the baby became "wedged on or near the shear bone." Shippen could not "get at it to alter the position of its head," and so he went home to collect implements with which to extract the baby. These proved unnecessary, and Sally gave birth to "a fine boy," but afterward Shippen assured the Drinkers that he had been at the ready with the requisite tools. He clapped his hand against his coat pocket so that the instruments there rattled, resting completely unsanitized with whatever else was in the coat pocket.[60]

Molly was not so fortunate when Nicholas Way stood in for Shippen at the delivery of her first and stillborn child in 1797 (Shippen was attending on Molly's sister Sally, whose fifth baby was due at almost the same time). Dr. Way tore Molly's vagina, leaving her with a rectovaginal fistula, an opening between the rectum and vagina that resulted in the leaking of bowel contents through the vagina; this was at the time irreparable and would cause Mary serious problems for the rest of her life. The dead infant had been stuck in the birthing canal from eight in the morning till late in the afternoon. Elizabeth was much affected by the loss of this "very pretty well made boy" and the mother's suffering, especially as Molly might soon become pregnant again and so go through "the same excruciating trouble." Molly was "undoubtedly much hurt," and although the doctor assured them that all would be well, Elizabeth became increasingly worried, having heard about other "very disagreeable instances of the same kind." As the weeks and months passed by, Elizabeth noted repeatedly that Molly was "disordered . . . in her bowels." The bereaved mother was often unable to sleep at night because of the pain and remained permanently "afflicted in that way," though her mother noted admiringly that Molly maintained a "brave" demeanor and had "a wonderful knack of keeping up under indisposition."[61]

That stillborn baby was one of seven grandchildren to die in childbirth or infancy, four of these in Elizabeth's lifetime, and the anguish leaked through onto the pages of her diary. Henry Sandwith and Hannah's fourth child, James, born "very lusty" in March 1800, died the following year from a severe attack of what contemporaries called hives (a less specific term than it is today, referring not only to the skin disorder we call hives but also to inflammation of the bowels, laryngitis, and diphtheria). Henry and Elizabeth remained "in suspense" for several days as they waited for news of their grandson's condition. Hannah's father was present while the child was ailing and reported back to the Drinkers that "he never saw anyone in such extreme pain," though the little boy apparently suffered through the agony with a stoicism that Quakers would have seen as boding well for a spirit of resignation in later life, had he survived. Elizabeth wrote that it was "very trying to part with a dear child, just beginning to know and love you." She heard that her son had "attended him diligently" through his illness and that the child died in his father's arms. "My son feels much as a father," she wrote. Two days after they heard, Hannah's father came over to talk about their "dear little deceased grandson," the two families joined in grief.[62]

"A Crooked ~~Rib~~ Mate to Deal With"

As Quakers labored to create a tight-knit community of faith that would guide the next generation into a life of committed piety, parents worried not only about the survival of their children's children but also the domestic environment in which they grew up and its conformity to Quaker expectations.

This gave Henry and Elizabeth another source of anxiety to contend with: three of their grandchildren lived in a household that quite spectacularly failed to provide a model for the peaceable way of life to which Quakers aspired. No sooner had Henry and Elizabeth made peace with Molly's union and established some semblance of cordiality with her husband than Ann's marriage became a matter for serious concern and embarrassment as the Skyrin home exploded in episodes of drama that ricocheted through their neighborhood. Quakers laid great stress on the need for harmonious companionship within marriage, but this was assuredly not Ann's experience of wedlock. Her three daughters endured periods of utter mayhem at home as their parents and the household servants engaged in what amounted to domestic civil war.

Ann's husband, John Skyrin, had a volatile personality that was on full display in the aftermath of Molly's elopement, when Elizabeth had to manage not only her husband but also her son-in-law, the latter "much agitated" as his "pride and passion" bubbled over in response to the scandal. Whereas Henry often said so little that Elizabeth complained she had no idea what he was thinking or feeling, John Skyrin had a very different temperament, so that Elizabeth had to ask him not to "trouble" Ann "with everything that fretted him." He should, she counseled, "rule his will, and bear his own burdens." A series of business reversals in the early 1800s doubtless exacerbated the situation, his pride dashed and his future cast into doubt. "Poor Nancy," declared her mother, "she has a crooked ~~rib~~ mate to deal with." When Elizabeth wrote this entry, she initially described John Skyrin as a crooked rib, linking him to Eve, that catastrophic spouse from the pages of Genesis who disobeyed God's commandments, persuaded Adam to do likewise, and so caused their ejection from Eden. Just as Adam and Eve abandoned their innocent nakedness in favor of crude clothing to mask their sense of shame, so Elizabeth saw her own "innocent, worthy" daughter as having undergone physical transformation, which her mother doubtless blamed on the unhappiness of Ann's marriage, declaring, "I have rarely seen a beautiful woman so altered as she is." Elizabeth then drew back, however, and deleted "rib" in favor of "mate," a more gender-neutral word with much less negative baggage. Perhaps she felt uncomfortable comparing John Skyrin to a woman; or perhaps she thought she was going too far in associating him with a figure notorious for having cast a shadow over the entirety of human history. Yet even with the deletion, Elizabeth clearly saw John as primarily responsible for the marital problems that he and Nancy were experiencing.[63]

Those problems manifested most obviously, at least to outsiders, in the husband and wife's inability to manage their household staff. Elizabeth's most common reason for mentioning the Skyrins, other than describing her daughter and grandchildren's illnesses, was to comment on misbehavior by their servants and the utter ineffectuality of master and mistress in handling such situations. Elizabeth acknowledged that all households, including her own, faced challenges in dealing with increasingly assertive and unreliable domestics.[64] Yet Ann proved to be singularly inept in this regard and repeatedly found herself "perplexed" by the challenge of managing "saucy" servants. According to her mother, Nancy simply "could not keep order in the house—far from it." The chaos sometimes spilled out beyond the Skyrin home and drew neighbors into the maelstrom. One afternoon when Ann was away for a few hours, two of her black maidservants laid into "a negro man" who insulted them in Elfrith's Alley and gave him a good thrashing with a horsewhip, so that a crowd gathered to watch. Whether or not their response was justified, to have women under one's charge involved in an alley brawl was deeply embarrassing for any respectable family. On two occasions that Elizabeth noted, Ann called on her father to intervene because she could not cope with servants supposedly under her authority. It is striking that she turned to her father and not to her husband. John was sometimes away on business, but when he was at home and became involved, the situation tended to deteriorate even further because of tensions between husband and wife that their servants did not hesitate to exploit. "When man and woman do not live in unison," Elizabeth lamented, "what latitude it gives to servants," and so the servants ran amok.[65]

Tensions in the Skyrin home reached crisis point in October 1801. Elizabeth related the tawdry proceedings in her diary with a mixture of sympathy for her daughter and disapproval of everyone involved. The Skyrins were at this point living at 96 North Front Street, just seven doors away from Elizabeth and Henry. While Ann was visiting her parents one day, three Skyrin servants—described by Elizabeth as "bad girl Hen and new maid Fanny, and good for nothing black John"—went down into the cellar and helped themselves to rum from one of the hogsheads stored there. When Ann returned home, "black John" had disappeared, but Hen was still down in the cellar, presumably drunk. Ann "felt cowardly" and came back to her parents' house. Elizabeth returned with her along the street and stayed until her son-in-law came home that evening. When they could find neither "black John" nor "bad girl Hen," Ann's husband was "much displeased and made a rumpus," so she left the house with her youngest child and went back to 110 for a few hours, after which her parents advised her to go home. It was now around midnight. The two missing servants had reappeared and were in bed, but John Skyrin was still "in a passion," and so Ann fled the house for the third time that day, again seeking sanctuary with her parents, "which all things considered," Elizabeth reported in her diary, "I did not wonder at." By the time they all got to bed, it was close to three o'clock in the morning.[66]

Ann ended up staying with her parents for almost a month. A few days after her arrival, she went home briefly to fire Fanny, but that young woman was back at the Skyrins' house later the same month, visiting "bad boy John." Then the master of the house discovered that the same John had a key to their storeroom that Hen had told them was lost: he fired John and threw Hen out of the house in a rage. It turned out that "bad boy John" had taken with him a considerable quantity of tobacco that he stole from his master, though Elizabeth declared she was not in the least sorry for this loss because the Skyrins had now got rid of "a very bad servant." Hen meanwhile headed over to the home of Alice Wright, who had worked for the Drinkers as a washerwoman. "Nancy has had her troubles," Elizabeth wrote that evening, "and will continue, I fear, to have new ones." The next day Alice came over to tell them that Hen was threatening to leave in company with a married man. Hen was indentured to the Skyrins, and so her master threatened to get a warrant and put her in jail to prevent her from absconding, though Elizabeth doubted that he would follow through on his threat: "saying and doing are two things with him," she declared.[67]

The Drinkers had no way of knowing for sure if their daughter and son-in-law would reconcile or whether any such reconciliation would prove permanent. Pennsylvania had passed a divorce law in 1785, and growing numbers of Philadelphians availed themselves of that option; many others simply stopped living together and subsequently entered other relationships. The Quaker community did not approve of such proceedings, but Quaker codes of conduct had not prevented their youngest daughter from eloping. Even if the couple stayed together, Elizabeth and Henry must have worried about the atmosphere in which Ann's three daughters would grow up. They may well have had mixed feelings when, after three weeks of separation, John Skyrin wrote to his wife and began to visit her at the Drinkers' home, usually spending time with her upstairs rather than down in the parlor with other members of the family, who apparently found him difficult to stomach. (When Jacob Downing had dinner with him one day, Elizabeth expressed her "admiration" that he had done so.) John had now retrieved Hen, but was talking about "selling her," as Elizabeth put it (in fact, it was the remainder of her indenture that was up for sale, but Elizabeth and perhaps also her son-in-law made no distinction between that and selling Hen herself). Ann had been over to the house and "found things there in disorder." Her husband went ahead and sold the remainder of the time that Hen owed them to another family but, since there were no other servants in the house, delayed sending Hen to her new place of employment. John was evidently trying to persuade his wife to return home. Ann was "much at a loss how to act" and planned to stay with her parents for at least a while longer, but one morning John arrived and begged his wife to come home. Ann gave way and returned with him, though she went back and forth between the two homes several times before the day was over, perhaps in search of solace and advice as she grappled with the physical disarray and emotional wreckage over at her own house.[68]

~

Henry must have sighed in agreement when a friend who had heard about Molly's elopement wrote that it reminded him of a recent comment his own brother had made, "that he believed the most comfort parents had oft with their children was while they were rocking them in the cradle." A few years later, Elizabeth wrote in a similar vein. "Those who have children and love them," she declared, "especially married children, have many cares." Indeed, Elizabeth filled her diary with expressions of anxiety about her family's health and welfare. Even as she reached the end of her life, none of her children had found the settled, secure life she wished for them. "Maybe I may live," she sighed, "to see them all comfortably yet." Elizabeth recognized that her family was not uniquely afflicted and described sympathetically many "a scene of affliction and grief" unfolding in other homes, yet as she would have readily acknowledged, her attention focused on her own household. Henry's world was more expansive, but despite his frequent preoccupation with business and church matters, he clearly loved his children and became deeply distressed when all was not well with them. Ideally, Elizabeth wrote, they should be "truly thankful for the good we receive, and resigned to what is called the reverse," but this was all too often an elusive goal. Domestic woes were, moreover, never just domestic in their implications: because Quakers envisaged their embattled Society of Friends as a loving family of families, the fate of each individual family connected inextricably to the fate of the entire community. That placed a significant burden on parents as the ripples from their personal disappointments spread outward.[69]

As Elizabeth grew older and anticipated her departure from this world to the next, she hoped that she would at least leave her children safe from want or undue distress and reconciled to their lot. Though she recognized that "true happiness or unmixed felicity" was "inconsistent with humanity and not to be met with in this state of probation," she believed that her children were fortunate because they had each other, and if they could hold onto that, all would be well. One evening in the summer of 1802, now in her late sixties, Elizabeth penned in her diary the following benediction to her children: "May the Almighty in his fatherly kindness unite you one to another, so as to give you strength in your union, to be councilors and helps to each other." Those words and Elizabeth's description of her offspring as "entwined in my very heartstrings" reflected her sense of family as a tightly knit community of loving souls, a miniature of their larger religious society. Her immediate family had survived repeated threats to its physical survival and its integrity as a bastion of Quaker values. Whatever lay ahead, she was convinced that their devotion to each other and to their savior would carry them through. Little did she know what a nightmare the closing months of her life would turn out to be, and how deep a trial of her own capacity for resignation lay ahead as her family began to disintegrate before her eyes.[70]

9 • "To the Place of Fixedness"

In Which the Drinkers Reach the End of Their Journey

As Henry Drinker reached his seventieth birthday in March 1804, his wife, who was one year behind him, wrote that they were both feeling their age—"though not," she added, "so much as many of our age." The Drinkers had now reached that melancholic stage of life at which they had to watch old friends and neighbors pass away one by one. When news of Frederick Pigou's death arrived the following year, Henry was himself gravely ill; the two men had long been close friends, and so Henry's family delayed telling him until he had recovered somewhat and had the strength to deal with this blow. From the perspective of Quakers who had lived through many testing times, including the American Revolution, deceased friends left behind an unstable, violent, and often heartbreaking world for what Elizabeth called "the place of fixedness" where, wrote Henry, "all sorrows cease and all tears are wiped away." Those remaining would soon follow them, so this was not permanent loss but a temporary parting, with the prospect of reunion and final relief from what Elizabeth called repeatedly "a world of trouble." Yet even temporary separation was still a poignant experience. This confederacy of survivors had depended in times of trial on the close emotional ties that bound them in solidarity; now the members of that confederacy were disappearing one by one. "Thus our contemporaries move off, one after another," wrote Elizabeth. "How many of my old friends are gone before me."[1]

Both Henry and Elizabeth now saw their own deaths as an imminent prospect. When Henry's brother John died in 1800, Elizabeth was surprised to hear that he had been laid to rest beside her father, "the spot I expected to have occupied myself." She wrote that she had no objection, but she was clearly thinking about where her own remains would lie. In 1801, when a former neighbor died in her early sixties, Elizabeth noted that many died at "about that age." She had recently turned sixty-six. "The idea always strikes me with a kind of awe," she wrote the following year, "to think that I have lived another year and my dear family still with me—how long it will continue so, the Lord only knows!—may we be properly prepared for a separation!"[2]

As Elizabeth entered the final years of her life, she moved around less and less, yet she now spent much of her time traveling—back into her past. Elizabeth had always been careful to note the anniversaries of births, marriages, illnesses, the departure of loved ones on perilous journeys, and especially deaths, but now her relationship with the past intensified. She reread books that "revived old feelings" from when she and the friends of her youth, now mostly departed, had "read them in times of old, together, with pleasure." Even without those associations of past friendship, the simple act of rereading was "like meeting with an old acquaintance." She started going through old correspondence, including the letters written by Henry during his exile in Virginia and while she was looking after their convalescent son William in New York. Though time had not erased "recollections of that time," revisiting correspondence from the past "renewed old feelings." The death of Nathaniel Falconer in late 1806 reminded her of Henry's 1760 journey to England in a ship that Falconer had captained, and the death of Ann Warner Jr. a few months later took Elizabeth back to the four years that she and Mary had spent boarding with Ann's mother before Elizabeth's marriage: "one of my old acquaintances," she noted wistfully. Yet Elizabeth did not live exclusively in the past: she also looked forward with anxiety to a time when she would no longer be there to watch over her children. "I must soon leave them," she wrote fretfully, "May the Lord preserve them!"[3]

Elizabeth's experience of time had always been as much cyclical as linear. Though her diary marked the passing of months and years, her life also proceeded according to the seasons of the year that she witnessed through annual transformations in her garden and the migration back and forth of her family between the front and back parlors, embracing or fleeing the warmth of the sun. Reproductive cycles racked Elizabeth's body and then those of her daughters, ruling and threatening their lives. Yet Elizabeth's engagement with time now became even more multifaceted: at once calendrical, cyclical, retrospective, prospective, and at times almost suspended. As physical frailty left her increasingly housebound, she noted "a sameness in my way of living every day," so that she sometimes felt she had little to say when sitting down to write. "All days seem alike, or nearly so, to me," she declared in one entry. In

December 1806, Elizabeth sought to knit past, present, and future together when two of her granddaughters came to visit and she "gave each of them a picture worked between fifty and sixty years ago by my dear friend Nancy Swett," also their grandfather's first wife. The girls were delighted, and Elizabeth was doubtless gratified to see different strands of her life's journey entwined together.[4]

Despite Elizabeth's complaints about the sameness of her day-to-day existence, the present was far from uneventful for the Drinkers as they entered the nineteenth century. Neither would experience the "peaceable retreat from this transient scene" that they both hankered for in their final years. Henry continued to work hard as a Quaker elder and, more grudgingly, as he supervised the management of land investments from which he had tried but failed to extricate himself. Those investments remained a constant source of frustration and anxiety for him and for Elizabeth as she watched his health deteriorate. The family's assets were impressive, but because they now mostly took the form of landed property that proved difficult to liquidate, Henry was often cash-strapped, his financial situation persistently worrisome. Meanwhile, their immediate family faced crises and losses that proved a grievous trial to both husband and wife. In the volatile economic climate of the new republic, they could take nothing for granted, and all three of their sons-in-law had gone into trade, a way of life fraught with uncertainty. Ann's marriage had proven far from stable, and the Drinkers were well disposed to neither her husband nor Mary's. Then, in late 1806, Elizabeth's largely sedentary life of reminiscence and worried observation came to an abrupt end as she and Henry found themselves swept up in a nightmarish train of events that carried off two of their beloved children—the first through departure on the high seas, the second through a slow and painful death.[5]

"An Abyss of Perplexities"

Not the least of Elizabeth's worries was her husband. As Henry advanced from his sixties into his seventies, church and business affairs still consumed most of his time. "HD all day busy, busy, busy as usual," wrote his wife in October 1800. A year later she noted that he was staying at home more often in the evenings but that during the day he still spent much of his time out at meetings and when at home was often in the office writing. Henry complained in letters to friends that his time was still "swallowed up with various concerns . . . more so than is pleasant at this advanced stage." He was "now an old man" and "feeling a sensible decrease of strength," so these many demands on his time and energy increasingly took their toll. Henry served on a seemingly endless succession of Quaker committees. "There are certain duties," he wrote, "which we owe to the community at large," adding with a touch of resentment, "which seem to fall to the lot of some in a much greater degree than others." Many of these committees formed to address specific problems facing the local Quaker community, and some of the situations they had to deal with proved quite stressful. In 1795, Henry attended a number of meetings to consider the case of Rebecca Griscomb, a troubled and troublesome individual with a long list of grievances who repeatedly disrupted public worship and railed against leading Friends. Elizabeth noted in her diary entries that Griscomb often "had to be taken forcibly out of meeting" and that she repeatedly threatened Henry, whom she considered one of the "instigators" in a conspiracy that she believed to be working against her. On one occasion, another Friend had to remove her "gently" from Henry's office, where she had come to pay him "a visit of accusation." Henry took part in several attempts to persuade Griscomb that her behavior was inappropriate, and that September the Drinkers actually hosted an intervention in their parlor. Griscomb, however, persisted in her disorderly and decidedly unfriendly behavior, so that eventually the Northern District Meeting disowned her, though this did not end her verbal assaults on those she held responsible for her disownment, including Henry. Elizabeth clearly resented Griscomb's continued attacks on her husband, and he doubtless felt the same way; this must have been an unpleasant and exhausting ordeal.[6]

Even when he was not dealing with errant and obdurate Friends, the demands on Henry were daunting. Church meetings often dragged on for several hours, and he found them "spending to the body" as well as "wearing to the spirits." As early as 1791, Henry had complained to his wife that "long sittings" were proving an ordeal, and he sometimes returned home afterward with a backache as well as "pain in my head." The Yearly Meeting of Friends in Philadelphia, which lasted several days, was for Henry a relentless and grueling marathon. Not only did he attend numerous committee meetings and plenary sessions, but the Drinkers also hosted visiting delegates, so that when he came home there was no reprieve, and indeed some of the committees met at the Drinker residence. As the Yearly Meeting of April 1806 got under way, Elizabeth noted in one entry that Henry had been out twice that day to attend committees and "came home much worn down." Yet even when feeling sick or exhausted, Henry felt compelled to carry on, as many of his contemporaries either had died or were "in a declining way," leaving a void in leadership that he felt obliged to fill as best he could.[7]

Henry often received invitations to attend Meetings outside the city, and Friends throughout the region clearly expected him as a prominent elder to lend them his presence. A member of the Quarterly Meeting in Bucks County who had counted on Henry's attendance at a Meeting in 1791 was quite blunt in expressing his disappointment when Henry proved unable to be there and "wondered" at the failure of Philadelphian Friends to attend, "considering the number who have bright talents for usefulness." Yet these visits could prove tiring, especially for older Friends, and when Henry returned home he rarely had a chance to recuperate, as business matters that had accumulated during his absence demanded his attention. In 1796, he embarked on a three-week journey to attend the first Monthly Meeting at Cattawissa on the Susquehanna River, traveling "over a country for the most part very mountainous, rough, and stony." As Henry pointed out, he did this "old as I am and with less bodily qualification than formerly."[8]

Other Friends occasionally claimed that they did understand the many pressures weighing on Henry as church elder, land investor and promoter of Quaker settlement on the frontier, husband, father, and grandfather. Ruth Anna Rutter, a Quaker minister, gently berated him for not having written to her lately, but she recognized "the many cares and engagements" that occupied his time. She went on to reassure him that even though he doubtless had "much to combat with," Friends would revere him for his efforts: his "sun" would "go down with brightness," she wrote, "and nothing shall be permitted to eclipse the glory thereof." Yet Henry had no great desire for glory, and Rutter did nothing to lighten the pressure when she told him that he had been to her an "elder brother" and "truly a father in Israel." Another female Friend also described him as "a very dear friend and precious father," no doubt a touching tribute but also its own form of burden for an aging man who now needed to be cared for as much as to care for others. Henry himself assured another Friend that God would support those who devoted themselves to serving him and that their "earnest labors" would bring them closer to "the divine treasury," but he worried that his friend's "zeal in the best of causes" might prove more than his "weak frame" could bear. If Elizabeth saw this letter, she may well have sighed wistfully: if only her husband would take his own advice.[9]

Henry might have found his responsibilities as an elder more manageable had he been able to set aside at least some of his many business concerns. In

1792, he had written to a relative in Ireland, "It was pleasing to find thou had a view of so withdrawing from business as to be less enslaved thereby than heretofore and more at liberty, which at thy time of life and mine is much to be desired." Henry had similar aspirations but despite his best intentions remained embroiled in ventures that were time-consuming, stressful, and galling. At the end of 1804, his wife noted that he was still "much perplexed with respect to his outward affairs." He lamented repeatedly in letters to friends that far from ridding himself of the "numerous vexations and troubles" that resulted from his land investments and the ill-fated maple sugar project, he found himself "entangled in additional difficulties" that seemed to multiply with each passing year. As Henry began to recognize that he might not "continue here" much longer, so an edge of desperation surfaced occasionally in his correspondence as he tried to chip away at the many layers of hindrance, confusion, and controversy that stymied these ventures. Some of the problems he faced were beyond his control, but Henry was himself partly to blame. He was far too trusting, far too forbearing toward debtors who strung him along for decades on end, and all too often a bad judge of character. He also knew precious little about the agricultural world in which he had invested his family's resources.[10]

Henry's business troubles not only deprived him of the "peaceable retreat" he longed for but also endangered the financial security of his family. He possessed vast tracts of land, but these had proven persistently worrisome and difficult to sell. Henry had not needed to borrow in order to purchase these land lots, which was more than some other investors could say, but he did find himself strapped for cash and eventually forced into debt because many of those who owed him money could not or would not pay, including settlers who had bought land from him. The collection of debts owed to James and Drinker was still ongoing decades after the dissolution of that partnership, and most of the work involved in trying to sort out Abel James's estate now fell to Henry as the other trustees became "unfit . . . for business." Henry had still not reached terms with Samuel Preston for the dissolution of their partnership, and the Stockport estate had yet to produce any income that reached Henry, while the buildings constructed there at Henry's expense were "going to decay." David Sands had still not paid for the land he had agreed to purchase many years before, and Preston enraged Henry by claiming that he should receive part of any forthcoming payments, despite Henry's insistence that Preston owed him a considerable sum of money. Henry wrote that he was "heartily tired" of dealing with both Sands and Preston.[11]

As "a lover of peace," Henry was dismayed to find himself involved in a string of bitter disputes with debtors, some of whom had appealed successfully over the years to his compassion and his eagerness to avoid conflict. Henry had been an indulgent creditor and did all he could to avoid suing those in default, but now a shortage of liquid funds forced him to take decisive action. "I am advanced to old age," he wrote to one of them, "and cannot as an honest man indulge others at the expense of my own reputation. Unless the sum due from thee is speedily paid, thy bonds will be put in suit." Debt collection could prove a tawdry business. When land agent Ephraim Kirby died in 1804, owing him large sums of money, Henry had no choice but to scrabble about for information about Kirby's assets, including salaries still owed him as an agent to the Natchez Nation on behalf of the U.S. government and as a judge in the territory of New Orleans. Another protracted debt dispute with Friend Robert L. Bowne ended up in Quaker arbitration. The referees eventually sided with Henry, but only after protracted hearings during which the slippery behavior of Bowne and especially his father left Drinker and his wife dismayed and disgusted.[12]

Of all the debts that Henry had to chase after during the final decade of his life, "the most trying and distressing" turned out to be that owed him by the estate of Samuel Wallis, a surveyor and land speculator in Lycoming County. Over the years, Wallis had become overstretched and notorious for business ineptitude; many also suspected him of shady dealings. Yet Henry remained stubbornly loyal to Wallis: he continued to loan him money, provided security for other debts, and on several occasions put up bail to save him from imprisonment. Henry seems to have been convinced that all would come right in the end, despite mounting evidence to the contrary, and it was a rude awakening when he finally realized how seriously he had misread Wallis and the relatives who survived him. Henry was a major claimant against this dubious character's estate following his death in 1798, and he found the financial morass that Wallis left behind overwhelming. "Now it seems one entanglement after another is brought to light," he wrote in 1803. "Sufficient are they to discourage a man of common prudence from dipping further in such an abyss of perplexities." The estate's administrators proved evasive and argumentative, subjecting Henry to what he considered "cold neglect," "gross deceptions," and unseemly allegations that he was misrepresenting the debts owed him. As the years passed by without any resolution, Henry penned many letters expressing his outrage that after so many "services rendered and enormous advances made," he should be so "baffled and trifled with." The central issue for him became the family's "treachery and base ingratitude," in the face of which, he averred, "Christian coolness of temper may be difficult."[13]

These and many other outstanding debts forced Henry in turn to borrow considerable sums of money. He assumed that future land sales and eventual payments by those who owed him money would fund his own debt payments, but a drastic slowdown in land sales and the continued inability or refusal of many debtors to pay up left him in serious difficulty. What made this situation even more galling was that many of his debtors thought their delinquency entirely inconsequential: given his wealth, they reasoned, he could well afford to wait. "Thou entertains," he wrote to one of them, "the same mistaken notions with some others as to my thousands, as thou expresses it. True it is, I am possessed of considerable landed property, but I owe large sums and am pinched and distressed for want of cash to extinguish those debts." Eventually Henry had to pay off his own debts by handing over bonds and securities for debts owed him. He wrote apologetically to those who would find themselves in the hands of creditors a good deal less patient than he had been, but he now had to sacrifice those who owed him money in order to save himself. The Embargo Act of 1807 (which responded to violations of U.S. neutrality by Britain and France during the Napoleonic Wars by prohibiting foreign trade and so preventing American or foreign vessels from shipping goods abroad) made matters worse, as agricultural prices fell and farmers were often unable to sell their produce, leaving them without money for payment of debts. There were occasional glimmers of hope. In the summer of 1807, rumors reached him of lead deposits beneath the surface of one of his tracts, and this led to a flurry of correspondence in which Henry urged his agents to investigate the possibility, however remote, that the rumors might be true. They found no lead, and at the time of Henry's death, there was no relief in sight.[14]

However great Henry's aversion to conflict, there were additional battles that he had little choice but to fight. In 1804, the year of his seventieth birthday, a rancorous conflict erupted over the fate of the Atsion ironworks. This site, about twenty-seven miles away in New Jersey, had been developed by a fellow named Charles Read in partnership with two other men in the 1760s, but Read had landed in financial difficulties and in 1773 sold his shares to James and Drinker, who became majority owners. By 1804, Henry owned five-eighths of the venture; the heirs of his deceased brother John Drinker owned one-eighth; and the remaining quarter belonged to the heirs of Lawrence Saltar, one of the original partners, who had died in 1783. In March 1804, the Saltars took possession of the entire property by force and removed

Reynold Keen, the ironworks manager appointed by Henry. The Saltars claimed that the Drinkers were indebted to them and that therefore they were justified in appropriating articles produced there along with any profits from their sale. They would not even allow Keen to take a horse on which to ride back to Philadelphia. When Keen reached the city and reported what had happened, Henry and his nephews (who had inherited their father John's one-eighth share) were outraged: they believed that the Saltars owed them money, besides which Henry felt that he had been extremely generous over the years to the Saltar family. As in the case of the Wallis estate, he was at least as upset by their betrayal as by the potential financial loss. This was, as Elizabeth put it, "very ungrateful, all things considered."[15]

Over the ensuing spring and summer, Henry and his nephews worked hard to reinstall Keen, prevent the sale of goods from the ironworks by the Saltars, and disprove claims by the Saltars about Henry's behavior toward them, claims that he insisted were slanderous. So extreme was the "breach in confidence and harmony" that Henry could not imagine any further working relationship with them. He was in any case eager to withdraw from the iron business and determined to sell his shares, even if at a loss. That fall the Drinkers and Saltars went to court. The judges appointed referees to adjudicate, and that process then dragged on for many months. It was not until the following June that the ironworks was put up for sale. Jacob Downing, the Drinkers' son-in-law, bought the entire estate, by now ransacked and ramshackle. "A troublesome bargain," Elizabeth predicted. Yet this was not the end of Henry's involvement. He continued to hound debtors who owed money to him and the other previous owners. He received periodic updates as Jacob tried to revitalize the facility and watched approvingly as his son-in-law maintained the facility's reputation for "order and sobriety," with no liquor allowed on the premises. He also helped to secure reliable employees for the ironworks, including the Drinkers' former servant Peter Woodward.[16]

Alongside seemingly endless debt disputes and his struggle for control of the Atsion ironworks, Henry had to deal with the consequences of his rash though well-intentioned agreement to look after a succession of boys and girls sent to Philadelphia by trading partners in the Bay of Honduras. It was not unusual for parents to ask contacts across the Atlantic World to look out for their children when they sent them to be educated or to work as apprentices far from home. Merchants in the Caribbean often wanted their sons to be educated on the North American mainland, and the Quakers among them were especially eager for other Friends to keep a watchful eye over their offspring.

Henry earned a reputation for being diligent and trustworthy in caring for those under his wing, and so he ended up serving as guardian to ten children sent northward from the Bay of Honduras, but the youngsters caused him so much trouble that in 1801 he determined not to accept any more. As he told Thomas Potts, one of his correspondents down in the bay, even had these young people been models of good behavior, they needed "more watchful care than it is any way convenient for me to afford at my advanced time of life."[17]

Some of these charges turned out to be less than angelic, and Potts's own sons, Robert and James, proved particularly aggravating. The Drinkers received frequent complaints about "naughty boy" Robert, whom Elizabeth described in several entries as "in disgrace" and "under a cloud." Following their father's death in 1806, both brothers ended up in prison for debt. Their insistent and sometimes abusive requests for financial assistance, well in excess of the regular allowances allotted from their father's estate, shocked and embarrassed Henry. To make matters worse, the two young men were spending this money on loose living; Henry condemned Robert in particular for his "profligate" and "corrupt habits." Yet his frequent harangues had little effect, and he could only hope that suffering would eventually bring about "an amendment in principle and conduct." Other wards proved troublesome because they had aspirations beyond what Henry and his wife thought appropriate for their social rank. They returned one lad, John Lawless, to his mother before the end of his indenture because he was unhappy with the trade assigned him. "He knows not what is most proper for him," Elizabeth sniffed.[18]

Sometimes Henry found his duties as guardian much more gratifying, though becoming "friend and advisor" to children or young adults far from home and family could prove burdensome even when they turned out to be well behaved. One happy moment occurred in January 1803 when Henry received a visit from a young man called Charles Townsend who wished to marry one of his female wards, Priscilla Kirk; Townsend needed Henry's permission before he could "pay his addresses." The young man had a good reputation, and so Henry readily gave his consent, received an invitation to their wedding, and visited them after they were married. Another of Henry's charges, Ann Marie Hodskinson, turned out to be very satisfactory, "a good girl" who avoided "all improper company." Ann apparently liked the "orderly respectable family" he sent her to live with, and she paid frequent visits to the Drinkers' home, often dining or taking tea with them. However, when Ann's parents died, Henry had to find out what assets they had left behind and how to arrange for Ann to receive the estate, so that she would have something to depend on in times of need. "At my advanced age," Drinker wrote, "cares of this sort by no means suit me." Those who trusted Henry to take care of their children seem to have assumed that he and Elizabeth would cope regardless of their age and whatever else was happening in their lives. In August 1807, just as the Drinkers were in the midst of a crippling family crisis, one of Ann Hodskinson's siblings, Henry James Hodskinson, arrived without any prior notice from the Bay of Honduras. Another brother had sent him to attend school and assigned him to their care without even asking if this suited them. The unexpected additional burden dismayed Henry: "he thanks him not," was Elizabeth's terse comment. They nonetheless took the boy under their wing. He seemed to Elizabeth "quite an illiterate lad," but once he had acquired basic skills in handwriting and arithmetic, Henry sent him out to the Atsion ironworks as assistant to the store clerk. He trusted that the lad would prove "useful in his station."[19]

This particular young man would most likely not have had the requisite skills to assist Henry as he grappled with the steady flow of correspondence arising from his multifarious business concerns, even had Henry been willing to admit that he still needed full-time clerical assistance. In March 1805, he had dismissed his last remaining clerk, Paul Brown, and sent him to work for his son-in-law Samuel Rhoads. Brown had been working as his clerk for five years, but Henry felt that he did not have "sufficient employ for him at this time of life," and in any case, the young man wanted to learn about the shipping business. Yet there was still more work than Henry could cope with. The paperwork relating to his land investments that continually crossed his desk must have been tiring for old eyes and stressful in other ways. As he grew older, he found "the use of the pen more and more difficult, a tremor in my hand rendering it a greater task than formerly," and a carriage accident left him with several dislocated bones in the wrist he wrote with, which made putting pen to paper "tedious and difficult." Henry also sensed that his memory was failing him, though his grasp of detail was still impressive, and in the last few years of his life, illness sometimes prevented him from writing for weeks on end.[20]

Throughout these final years, William, now in his thirties, served as his father's right-hand man. Elizabeth wrote that her son was often "busy as a bee" writing letters, poring over maps or papers, and consulting with land agent Robert Rose. William was closely involved in negotiations over the Atsion ironworks and spent many days at the bank making detailed arrangements for the transfer of ownership. Yet he remained fragile following his struggle with tuberculosis, and his mother worried that he would "hurt himself much by such close application." Henry Sandwith provided additional assistance during his visits and made several journeys out to the backwoods on his father's behalf, but he was busy running his own farm at some distance from Philadelphia. John Skyrin, who had recently suffered serious business reversals, approached his father-in-law in 1807 about taking on "something in the agency way," as Elizabeth put it. He set off on the first of several trips to the backcountry that October and became an enthusiastic booster for the region. William mostly stuck close to home, fearful that any undue exertion from traveling long distances would lead to another health crisis.[21]

Though Henry was clearly worried about the state of his business concerns, both of his sons were convinced that he either did not realize or would not admit just how serious the situation was. Insisting on a candid discussion was difficult for sons who loved but also feared their father. Yet in May 1804, Henry Sandwith summoned up the courage to confront his father, albeit by letter, imploring him to "come forward and make an open and honorable exposure" of his financial embarrassment. He believed that his father could still "satisfy every claim," especially if he secured compensation for the land he had purchased from the state and could not sell because of the ongoing dispute with settlers from Connecticut, but he needed to act before things got worse. Henry Sandwith wrote that he, his siblings, their mother, and their aunt found it "most painful" to watch the patriarch weighed down by these concerns. He urged his father to "grant them his confidence," allowing his sons to become actively involved as trusted partners rather than as mere assistants, and to "repose himself on their affection." Henry, however, refused to acknowledge that the situation was as dire as his son claimed it to be, or to cede control over his business affairs. Just over a year later, in July 1805, Henry Sandwith wrote to his brother, declaring that William must now speak with their father "as peremptorily [his underlining] as respect and affection will permit. You have a right to speak without reserve," he wrote. "You have been a faithful slave to our father and spent the best part of your life and your health and your constitution in his service. Why then cannot you muster up resolution enough to speak plainly of those things which prey upon your spirits?" Henry Sandwith knew that William would quail at the prospect of such a confrontation and did his best to calm his brother's nerves. "There is no use in distressing oneself," he wrote, adding and then crossing out, "~~Keep cool and comfortable if possible. This I try to do, but indeed I have felt for a long time a horrid lump of lead in the inside of me that has almost deprived me of the~~

~~power of exertion.~~" Henry Sandwith now carried on his own shoulders the burden of his parents' disapproval over his plan to travel abroad, a weight of anxiety about their family's future security, and the fear that their father still inspired. Yet he must stand beside his brother, even if long distance from North Bank. He gave William permission to show their father his letter, if he showed no sign of relenting, and William noted at the bottom of the letter that he did read it aloud. Henry Drinker apparently listened "without comment."[22]

Whether through pride or lack of faith in his sons' abilities, Henry refused to surrender control over his affairs. "Old vessels do best in still waters where there is less strain," one of his correspondents had written back in 1796. Yet the waters that Henry continued to navigate were anything but calm. In a letter that he wrote in early 1807, he envisaged heaven as a place of relief, "where the wicked cease from troubling and the weary are at rest." Peace and quiet were now his ultimate fantasy. Meanwhile, even with William's assistance, he could no longer maintain a firm grip over all of the many matters under his purview. In the spring of 1801, one of the city's health officers cited him for leaving "a quantity of filth" on his property that was "very offensive to the neighborhood" and threatened "the health of the city." Henry had served many years before as one of the commissioners charged with cleaning up the city streets, and it is difficult to imagine such a fastidious, detail-oriented man allowing this situation to develop on his own premises unless distracted and overwhelmed. In entry after entry, Elizabeth worried about the relentless pace that Henry still maintained even when feeling ill. One stormy day in April 1801, she noted that he had spent part of the morning preparing accounts for presentation at a meeting but then had to turn back on his way there because he felt unwell, yet he went to another meeting that afternoon "notwithstanding." Henry was so reluctant to cancel engagements that when he did stay home this accentuated Elizabeth's anxiety, suggesting as it did that he must be feeling particularly unwell. According to his wife, Henry's state of health was generally quite good, though at times "precarious." The abdominal pains that had troubled him for many years occasionally reappeared, he sometimes had blood in his urine, and he took a regular dose of laudanum. The more general problem was that he was getting old and refused to slow down.[23]

In early 1805, Henry became seriously ill, much to the distress of his family and the larger community of Friends in Philadelphia, that miniature of a holy nation in which he had become a treasured father. There was one particularly "trying day" when all of their children gathered at the house and upward of twenty friends called, while many others sent messages. Elizabeth was exhausted from the strain of nursing both her husband and her own anxiety: "I am more and more uneasy," she admitted that evening, "but still I trust he will be restored." At this distance of time, we cannot discern with any confidence what Henry was suffering from: his initial symptoms included a head cold along with "disordered bowels," cramps in his legs, and hiccups (which seemed to have caused Elizabeth particular alarm); as time went on, he also experienced "tightness" and "oppression" in his chest. He may have had some variant of flu that developed into bronchitis. Elizabeth described in loving and fretful detail her husband's symptoms, the doctors' running commentary on his condition, and the array of treatments that he underwent. These included poultices, enemas, the application of "blisters" to cause a discharge of noxious fluids, injections of flaxseed or cinnamon tea with liquid laudanum and carbonate of lime added to the mix, the chewing of rhubarb as a laxative, and the injection of pills containing a mixture of soap and opium. On March 4, Henry became seventy-one years old and the doctors pronounced him "in a state of convalescence," but his symptoms were still severe and Elizabeth concluded that even if the doctors were right, his road to recovery would be slow. By mid-March, he was clearly on the mend ("a favor," she wrote, "for which we are, I trust, truly thankful"), yet this had been a blow. Elizabeth was accustomed to her husband being the stronger of the two, and when her seemingly indomitable sister also fell ill, the blanket of security that had swathed Elizabeth for many years began to disintegrate.[24]

Henry was determined to resume his normal routine with all possible speed, and he was soon back at work arranging for the future of the Atsion ironworks, often staying out until late in the evening. Negotiations with the Saltars overlapped with the Yearly Meeting, which would on its own have put a strain on Henry's stamina. Elizabeth herself no longer felt equal to the pressure and noted that the household was "backward getting ready" to receive guests as Henry's illness had "prevented cleaning house quite as it should be done." Elizabeth welcomed neither the disruption that accompanied the influx of lodgers during the Yearly Meeting nor the appropriation of their front parlor for some of the smaller committee meetings. "I expect the ensuing week will be more trying to me than to the hardest worker in our house," she wrote in an entry that may well have raised her servants' eyebrows. Yet her husband strode back into the fray with his customary determination. Over the coming few years, he occasionally gave his wife further scares. One morning in October 1806, he spat some blood, and though it did not continue long, Elizabeth was understandably unnerved: "how many painful occurrences take place to those of sensibility," she bemoaned that evening. Yet in general, she wrote at the close of that year, he seemed "in better health" than he had for some time. She noted with relief that the same was true of her sister.[25]

"The Lord Only Knows How Things May Terminate with Us"

Elizabeth herself was becoming frailer with each passing year. She continued to experience the headaches and stomach pains that had dogged her throughout much of her adult life, which she managed in part with doses of laudanum, which all members of the Drinker household used to reduce pain, and with pinches of snuff, which she took when she felt "unwell and uncomfortable." Over the decades, Elizabeth had endured several prolonged periods of debilitating illness, but now in addition she had to come to terms with the general infirmity that accompanied old age. "When a weakly person comes to be near three score and ten," she wrote in 1805, "they cannot lay out for much of what is called comfort in this world—if they can keep from a large share of bodily pain, 'tis all that some of us ought to look for." Physical discomfort was part of everyday life in a world without antibiotics, anesthetics, or effective cures for most ailments, but for elderly people suffering from permanent aches and pains, along with reduced resistance to infection, the medical profession's limitations had particularly grim implications. Elizabeth now noted repeatedly that feeling unwell was for her the norm: "I spent this day like many others, in pain at times," she wrote in one entry. She also complained that previously helpful remedies no longer had any effect. From December 1805, she refused to take medicine of any kind.[26]

A succession of illnesses during the last five years of Elizabeth's life punctuated and probably accelerated a general decline. In the spring of 1803, she was "taken" repeatedly with giddy spells, and that fall a bad cough and cold confined her for several weeks to her chamber. Throughout the winter that bridged 1804 and 1805, she barely left the house, and Henry's illness in early 1805 took a significant toll on her, physically and emotionally. In May 1805, when she went on her first long walk since the previous fall, she described herself as "very weak and tottering." There were days when "changing my clothes this morning was almost too much for me," and sometimes she felt "as weak as the kitten that is playing about my feet." Her condition remained frail but relatively stable until that October, when one morning she tried to get up and found she was "incapable." She had lost all bodily strength, felt mentally confused, and "nearly, if not quite, fainted away." For the next ten days, she wrote no diary entries and noted afterward that she had been "so weak as not to be able to walk to the easy chair without help." Her sister and son William were also unwell, so her daughters Ann and Mary moved in to nurse them all. "I know not what we should have done without them," Elizabeth declared. When she went to visit a neighbor in May 1806, it was the first time she had left the house in eight months. The ailing couple could no longer tolerate any unnecessary disruption, and one visible indication of their decline was delayed maintenance and decoration in the house, though in late 1806 they did have the parlor wallpaper replaced. "It was in very bad order," she wrote, "or it would not have been done, as we do as little of that kind of business as we can well avoid." The room also needed to be painted, but that would "be omitted at present." Their grandchildren, who had been welcome visitors in the 1790s, sometimes for weeks at a time, now had to be kept away when the couple felt unable to cope with their exuberant presence, and so, wrote Elizabeth, "I am deprived of the pleasure of my dear little grandchildren's company as much as I should like."[27]

Though Elizabeth did not enjoy having to remain in her chamber for long stretches, she was quite content to stay at home. Indeed, when feeling "in tolerable health" (which for her meant suffering through only minor or intermittent pain) she felt "as happy, and more so, at home than anywhere else." Elizabeth found Sundays "tedious" as she did not attend public worship and restricted herself to reading in observation of the Sabbath, but for the rest of the week she was "generally busied." Sometimes she would help or supervise in the kitchen: notations on the outside covers of her diaries for 1803 and 1805 show that she was involved in pickling walnuts, a process that stretched over several weeks. Yet Elizabeth spent much of her time in reading and needlework, occupations that she considered "proper" and "agreeable" for a genteel matron. She acknowledged occasionally that she had a great deal of free time, not least because her sister still supervised the running of the household, which left her at liberty to do "such work as I like best." Elizabeth had always enjoyed sewing and was clearly proud that she could still do this work. She noted in her diary the completion of "a Queen-stitch mat" for her daughter Mary, a pair of shoes for one granddaughter, cotton stockings for another, several pincushions, a pair of "fine yarn gloves" for her husband (the first men's gloves she had ever made), and "a large mat to cover a bowl of fruit" (finished "in my seventy-second year"). Whereas a woman who made her living from hard physical labor could find herself in serious trouble as she entered old age, unless she had children to support her, affluent women like

Elizabeth could carry on much longer with the activities that they characterized as work: neither supervision of employees nor needlework involved strenuous exertion.[28]

Elizabeth's eyes must have remained quite strong as she continued to read voraciously across an impressive range of literature that spanned history and biography, political treatises, religious and moral tracts, natural history and geography, travel narratives, medical volumes, children's literature, poetry, novels, newspapers (mostly those with a Federalist slant), and pamphlets on current political issues. "There are few books," she wrote, "in which you cannot find some good pickings, or something worth attending to, especially when wrote by men of sense and learning," though she added that some volumes "might have had all the usefulness comprised in one fourth of the size." From 1799 onward, she finished each volume of her diary with a list of the books she had read that year, along with brief editorial comments. (For 1804 these included "trash, sentimental nonsense," "very foolish," "middling," "pretty enough, though rather simple," "the only apology for this is the age it was wrote in," "sad subject, but very droll verses," and "very unfit for the pen of a reverend divine.") For Elizabeth the author's moral character was of paramount importance. She considered the controversial women's rights advocate Mary Wollstonecraft to be "a prodigious fine writer" and confessed that she "should be charmed by some of her pieces" if she had "never heard her character." Wollstonecraft's unmarried relationships and illegitimate daughter placed her well beyond the pale as far as Elizabeth was concerned.[29]

Important though these various activities were to Elizabeth, her principal occupation seems to have been worrying about her family. When she wrote in 1802 that her children were "as dear to me, seemingly, as my existence," adding, "I believe no wife or mother is more attached to her near relatives than myself," she was not overstating her devotion. Yet despite occasional expressions of approval and appreciation, most of that maternal feeling took the form of anxiety. Elizabeth constantly mulled over information arriving from the households of her married children, at the same time watching fretfully the comings and goings of her unmarried son and husband. Her diary entries recorded even the slightest hints of impending illness and the treatments she and other family members used to alleviate the symptoms. She also worried about her daughters' material security as she watched all three of her sons-in-law grapple with business difficulties. Elizabeth believed that her children's well-being in this world would depend ultimately on their loyalty to each other as siblings. It was her "sincere desire and prayer" that they be "united, kind, and affectionate to one another" (without, she added, "any slight or neglect" to their spouses). Until the older generation disappeared from the scene, they should also be "dutiful and kind" to their father, "now in the decline of life," and of course their aunt. She did not mention in this particular entry their duty toward herself, perhaps because she assumed she would die first. However, she noted elsewhere with a touch of melancholy and perhaps bitterness that she did not see her children as often as she could wish and came close to accusing them of negligence: "they don't consider that they will not have their mother long to visit," she wrote. "I don't like to tell them so, as I trust there is no love wanting." Elizabeth's children were in fact quite attentive, as her notations of their visits amply demonstrate, but they had lives and problems of their own to deal with.[30]

In truth, there was plenty in the Drinker children's lives to worry loving parents. Mary remained a semi-invalid because of the injuries she had sustained during a botched episiotomy in 1797, William's health continued to be fragile, and Ann had recurrent problems with her eyes that clearly frightened her. The crisis in Ann's marriage seemed to have passed, but her husband's business concerns floundered and in the summer of 1804, John Skyrin left on a trip to explore alternative opportunities that lasted almost a year. Elizabeth never suggested in her diary that Ann was distressed by John's absence or missed him, but her daughter was apparently "perplexed to know how to act" regarding her living arrangements since she had no idea when he would return. She spent part of the time in Frankford but more than seven months with her parents. A year later, Samuel Rhoads left on a business trip to Havana amid escalating attacks on U.S. ships by British and French vessels as the young republic found itself caught between these two rival powers. Samuel's absence on a lengthy ocean voyage in what his mother-in-law called "these stormy times" and the possibility that he might catch the yellow fever while in the Caribbean plunged his wife, Mary, into prolonged anxiety. Elizabeth tried to comfort her often-tearful daughter, but could only "wish and trust that all may end well." Samuel returned safely after an absence of just over three months, but his business affairs were also "rather deranged," and in June 1807, he and his family moved into his mother's house. "Oh dear!" was Elizabeth's response. "Molly will behave, I trust, with prudence." Meanwhile, Elizabeth worried that her other son-in-law, Jacob Downing, had made a mistake in purchasing the Atsion ironworks, and sure enough, Jacob revealed a year later that he was worried about his business concerns. "Maybe I may live to see them all comfortably yet," wrote Elizabeth fretfully. Henry made no mention of these various troubles in his correspondence, but when he wrote to a friend in 1804 that he hoped his children had settled to his satisfaction, adding that it was "a comfort to parents when that is the case," his own lack of comfort on that score may well have been on his mind.[31]

Elizabeth had watched her children go through a succession of illnesses, traumatic deliveries, marital tensions, and business problems, but she suffered in the last year of her life two devastating blows as she bade farewell to her younger son and lost her oldest daughter. Henry Sandwith had not abandoned his plan to give up his life as a farmer and travel abroad as a mercantile agent. He had first mentioned this as a possibility in the fall of 1802, and his parents had been appalled. Their opposition to the scheme in turn wounded Henry Sandwith, who became less and less communicative as time went on, though Elizabeth could tell that the final decision he had yet to make lay "heavy on his mind." He had initially planned to keep the farm that his father had bought for him and pass it on to his son, even if he was no longer running it himself, but in the summer of 1805, he made up his mind to put it on the market. "It hurts me," his mother wrote, "to hear of its being sold." She made no mention of Hannah's or their children's distress at having to leave the home in which they had lived for a decade. Relations between Henry Sandwith and his parents-in-law, already embittered, deteriorated further when James Smith turned down his request for financial assistance after the younger man found that the proceeds from the sale of his farm, following payment of debts, would not meet his family's needs. Relations with his own parents had settled into resentful silence, which must have been resounding in a family accustomed to regular communication. Elizabeth and Henry had to rely on information passed on by William and their sons-in-law, with whom Henry Sandwith was communicating more openly. Elizabeth now said "nothing to oppose him," but her son remained hurt by what she and his father had said when he first mentioned his plan. "With me he talks none relative to his intended absence," she wrote, "he thinks we injured him by our opposition some years ago."[32]

Henry Sandwith finally determined in the fall of 1806 to accept a position offered him by Thomas Pym Cope and John Thomas, trading partners and both related by marriage to the Drinkers.[33] That position would take him eastward in one of their ships to Calcutta in the British colony of India. He and his family had been living out at Atsion since selling the farm, but he now rented a house in Burlington, New Jersey, not Philadelphia, where his wife and children would live during his absence. Elizabeth was dismayed to learn that he would be sailing in the *Susquehanna,* "a new ship never before at sea," but held back from asking exactly when he was likely to leave. "Oh dear!" she wrote. "How many things to give pain to those who feel and think!" That November, her son set off to meet the *Susquehanna* at Baltimore; after sailing back to Philadelphia aboard the vessel, he then departed for Burlington to bid farewell to his family and returned two days later, accompanied by his eleven-year-old son William. Elizabeth busied herself making gingerbread for Henry Sandwith to take on his journey. Over the coming few days she saw little of him: he spent most of his time out and about, preparing for his departure and securing letters of introduction from the British consul in Philadelphia and the consul general for the Middle and Southern States of America. He agreed to let his son sail unaccompanied in the *Susquehanna* down to Newcastle, a port town on the Delaware, planning to follow him in a smaller boat and then to send him back, again unaccompanied. Elizabeth thought her grandson far too young to embark on such a journey alone, but no one consulted her, and the lad departed on November 18.[34]

The moment of departure finally arrived. Henry Sandwith informed his parents that he would be leaving early in the morning of November 20, and so Elizabeth asked their servant Rose to wake them at seven, but she failed to do so, and it was after eight when the couple came downstairs to find that their son had already left, without a word of farewell. Elizabeth was hurt afresh but told herself that their son must have intended to "save some painful moments." After breakfast, her husband went down to the wharf and could see the boat far in the distance, heading down to Newcastle. "May the Lord be with him," wrote Elizabeth that evening, "this has been a painful day to me." She made no mention of her husband's mood in the wake of their son's departure. A few days later, little William returned early in the morning and was in such a hurry to catch the boat to Burlington that he dashed into the pantry for some bread and butter and then rushed off without seeing anybody but the one servant already downstairs. The lad left behind a short letter from his father, written two days before, telling them that the *Susquehanna* would weigh anchor the following day (now yesterday). "I should have had many questions to ask him," Elizabeth wrote of her grandson that night, "and should have liked to keep him here twenty-four hours to have his linen washed, etc.—but he is gone." As well, she might have added.[35]

Over the coming weeks, Elizabeth fretted about her absent son, "floating, if living, on the wide ocean, the distance increasing daily." A few days after his departure, they received a second letter that Henry Sandwith had written just before the *Susquehanna* headed out to sea, but they did not hear from him again until four months later, when a letter arrived via a whaler who had met up with the *Susquehanna* at sea. In the meantime, they heard that the brother-in-law of Henry Sr.'s barber had died on his way back from Calcutta, apparently from "a disorder of the climate," which did nothing to reassure Elizabeth. When a third letter arrived from their son in March 1807, the Drinkers sent it on to his wife, who received it shortly before news arrived of her own mother's death. "How fluctuating and uncertain," wrote Elizabeth, "is everything in this transitory world." That spring she and her remaining son William dispatched letters in vessels sailing for Calcutta. In October 1807, they heard from Henry Sandwith again, when a letter written in May arrived, telling them he was in good health but did not know how long he would stay in Calcutta. A month later, Thomas Cope arrived at their door with news that the *Susquehanna* was sailing homeward but had left Calcutta later than the Drinkers had expected. Henry Sandwith was apparently still in good health. "To hear he is well," wrote Elizabeth, "is the chief matter at present." She would never see her son again: five days later, Elizabeth wrote her last diary entry, and she died on November 24.[36]

The departure of Henry Sandwith for India was a serious blow to his parents. He had helped his father with business matters when in town and had traveled into the backcountry on his behalf, so this was a practical loss as well as an emotional one. However, even as Elizabeth continued to worry about her younger son throughout 1807, that anxiety was soon overshadowed by a much more harrowing ordeal as she and Henry watched their oldest daughter, Sarah, die slowly and painfully from what her doctors and family believed to be scrofula, a form of tuberculosis affecting the lymph nodes of the neck. Sarah, known to the family as Sally, most likely died of lymphatic cancer, and if so, this was the second death from cancer that the family had to deal with that year. Susannah Swett, mother of Henry's first wife, succumbed in March 1807 after having an operation the previous July to remove from her face a tumor the size of "a very large garden bean," followed by a series of other grueling treatments that proved ineffective. Swett had lived with the Drinkers for over a year following her husband's death in 1775 and more recently from December 1799 to August 1801. Though she was now living elsewhere, her former son-in-law nonetheless paid for her medical care. The Drinkers visited the elderly woman and received regular reports of her decline. "I hope she does not feel as miserable as she looks," wrote Elizabeth a few weeks before Swett's death. Sally was already ill, and now her parents would have to watch in helpless distress as their daughter underwent her own excruciating death.[37]

Elizabeth had first admitted to serious anxiety about Sally at the end of 1806. On the last day of that year, she noted that all three of her daughters were "far from well." Ann's eyelids were once again inflamed, and Mary was in the final trimester of another difficult pregnancy, but their mother worried that Sarah might be "more poorly than we are aware of," and it turned out that she was right. In January, Mary gave birth to her fifth child and was "safe" after taking medicine "to ease after pains," but Elizabeth remained "very uneasy on account of Sally's throat and Nancy's eyelids." Sally had a persistent swelling in her neck and complained of "a gathering in her ear." She was "cupped" (a form of bleeding that involved placing a glass over an incision and then heating it to create a vacuum), and blisters were applied to her throat and face. The doctors at first told Elizabeth that her daughter's "disorder" was "very prevalent at present," not necessarily reassuring, but as the weeks wore on, it became clear that Sally's condition was much more than a throat infection making its rounds through the city.[38]

As winter passed into spring, the Drinkers called in several doctors to examine and treat their daughter. These included Benjamin Rush (Henry's preferred physician), Adam Kuhn (who had become Elizabeth's doctor of choice), and Philip Syng Physick (the surgeon who operated on Susannah Swett). William went over to his sister's house almost every day, bringing back detailed accounts of Sally's progress and the treatments she was undergoing. The doctors gave orders for repeated bleeding with leeches, which seemed to provide short-term relief, though she hated having this done. Elizabeth visited the Downing home whenever she had the strength to leave her own, and on one occasion in April, Sally visited her mother, who "spread a plaster for her face." According to Elizabeth, Sally was blessed with a cheerful disposition and coped with the pain "as well as anybody could," but the protracted ordeal increasingly wore her down. Doctor Kuhn assured Elizabeth in April that Sally's situation was "not dangerous," but Elizabeth wrote in entry after entry that her heart was "heavy" and her spirits "oppressed." In mid-May, the doctors made a seton-stitch in the back of Sally's neck: they ran a thread under the skin to form a loop that joined up outside and provided an opening to drain fluids. This procedure "hurt her more than she expected," wrote Elizabeth that night, though Sally struck her as "more cheerful this day than I have seen her for a long time past." Elizabeth dreaded the removal of the cord, which might well be "festering in the sore" and thus extremely painful to draw out: "dear creature," she wrote, "I think I could willingly bear it for her." Sally was understandably "much distressed" at the end of the month when the doctors applied another twenty leeches to her face in a two-hour ordeal and recommended a second seton-stitch.[39]

By early summer Elizabeth was visiting Sally almost every day, though she sometimes felt so weak herself that the short journey wore her down even before she had to deal with the emotional toll of seeing Sally in so much pain. Elizabeth clearly needed to be with her daughter and was horrified when the doctors advised Sally to leave for the seaside so that she could bathe in the ocean. Elizabeth doubted that Sally was strong enough to travel and knew that she herself could not do so. "I would much rather have her here at our house," she wrote, "where everything could, I trust, be done for her, the minutiae attended to, but I am opposed, more is the pity." Elizabeth now began to admit, at least in the privacy of her diary, that she feared her daughter might not recover, though she tried to persuade herself into an optimistic frame of mind: "who knows but it may please the Lord to raise our dear Sally again—women at her time of life sometimes go through many trying scenes." She had "many questions" for Dr. Kuhn but "had not courage to ask" when he came to visit. Elizabeth was herself unwell and Kuhn recommended she also undergo bleeding. "Days and nights of trial to me," she lamented.[40]

The Downings left for the seaside at the end of June after spending their last night in town at Elizabeth and Henry's house. John and Nancy Skyrin accompanied them to Long Branch, New Jersey, returning a few days later to reassure the Drinkers that Sally had "bore the journey with more strength than was looked for." Elizabeth knew that the boardinghouse where the Downing family had arranged to stay was a lively establishment and so "very unfit in my opinion for a person so much of an invalid as S.D. is." When in good health her daughter loved company, but this was no ordinary summer excursion, and so Elizabeth was dismayed to receive reports that "numerous and noisy" vacationers were arriving day by day. Immersion in cold seawater failed to improve Sally's condition. Jacob Downing wrote to inform his parents-in-law that his wife felt "rather worse than better" and wanted to return home. That the normally gregarious Sally was eager to leave a large crowd of pleasure-seekers spoke volumes as far as Elizabeth was concerned: "if she had been tolerably well, she would rather have stayed."[41]

The Drinkers must have been shocked when Jacob arrived back in Philadelphia at the end of July without his wife. Sally had decided to stay in Trenton, placing herself under the care of a local doctor who she hoped might be able to help her. This Dr. Belleville was apparently going to treat her face with a poultice made of hemlock bark, "which is poison," Elizabeth noted with anxiety in her diary that night, though Dr. Kuhn subsequently assured her that this was "quite proper and safe." Belleville thought Sally's situation "critical" but believed he could help her if only she could keep up her strength. He claimed to have "cured a woman that was much worse, who had five tumors as hard as bone." William visited Trenton a few days later and reported that his sister was "as comfortably situated as she could be among strangers," but Elizabeth was not pleased that Jacob had left his wife there alone and eventually informed him rather pointedly at the dinner table that it was ten days since he had done so. Jacob took the hint and headed off to visit his wife. He found her showing some signs of improvement and reported that Dr. Belleville was "cautiously optimistic," but Elizabeth had her doubts. "My dear Sally," she wrote, "how art thou in reality?" The distraught mother quoted scripture to herself as she struggled to maintain a spirit of resignation: "If that the hand of righteousness afflict thee, and who can plead against it, who can say, to power almighty, thou hast done enough!" A few days after Jacob's return, a letter from Sally arrived for him, saying that she felt no better and wished to come home, so he set off again. He brought her back to her parents' home on August 17, and there she would stay.[42]

Henry was meanwhile following up on a lead that he hoped might provide a promising treatment for his daughter. Rebecca Jones—a Quaker minister, schoolmistress, and family friend—mentioned to the Drinkers that during a recent visit to New York she had heard about a plant, the name of which she could not recall, that a physician there had recommended as a cure for "scrofulous complaints." Henry wrote in mid-August to their friend James Allinson in New York, asking if he would consult with the physician and if possible send them "a supply of said plant with directions how it is to be used." Allinson moved quickly and mailed the Drinkers a bundle of roots from the plant, instructing them to separate the sap from the pith by pounding the roots, and then to apply the sap in a dressing. A few weeks later, Henry wrote asking for another supply; he told Allinson that his daughter continued "in a very low way," but their own doctors recommended that she continue to use the root extract in hopes that it might have an impact. Henry also requested more detailed instructions as they were having difficulty extracting the sap and feared they might not be using the right technique; nor were they certain how much of the sap to apply and how often. What Henry did not say, perhaps because he could not admit as much to himself, let alone anyone else, was that time might be running out for his daughter.[43]

The weeks that followed Sally's return to her parents' home must have been emotionally devastating for everyone involved. A few days after her arrival, the invalid spent a few hours downstairs and went out into the garden, but watching her move around was itself distressing. " 'Tis hard to think of," her mother wrote that night, "but she cannot walk by herself." Within a short time, she could no longer come downstairs at all. Sally was often in extreme pain, and the doctor, unable to provide any material comfort, could only counsel patience. Ann and Mary were constantly in and out of the house, taking turns at helping their mother to nurse the invalid. In early September, Henry also fell ill and was confined to his chamber for several weeks, so they now had two patients to care for. "I cannot put down my feelings," Elizabeth wrote one evening. As the days passed by, relatives and neighbors visited to express their concern. Some of them stayed overnight and so unintentionally added to the strain bearing down on Elizabeth's shoulders. "It is a pleasure to see kind friends," she wrote, "but at this time every addition makes more to do." She became increasingly exhausted and by mid-September felt so weak that at times she was "ready to fall." William, who was trying to keep up with his father's business concerns as well as helping to care for both of the patients, seemed to his mother "almost over done." Though Elizabeth had not entirely given up hope, she feared that her absent son would never see his sister again. "This is a time of deep trial," she wrote. "The Lord only knows how things may terminate with us."[44]

As Henry showed signs of gradual improvement, Sally grew weaker by the day, eating nothing, paying little attention to anything taking place around her, and refusing to see those who called. This must have seemed particularly ominous to those who knew how sociable she had always been. "Without a change for the better ere long," Elizabeth wrote on September 22, "I fear she cannot hold out but a short time." That evening Sally was "so very low" that her husband and their three daughters "stayed all night." On September 24, William took the carriage to collect Mary, who had been confined at home by "unsettled" bowels for several days but insisted on coming to spend a few hours with her sister, even though her doctor had forbidden her to leave the house. Elizabeth had watched over her "beloved child" throughout the previous night, but she was so tired that one of Jacob's relatives took over the following night, so that Elizabeth could try to get some rest. Amid all of this, news arrived that one of their former servants had passed away: "she worked for us when a girl," Elizabeth wrote that night, "and we valued her."[45]

It was three days later when Elizabeth took up her pen again. "From the 24th to the 28th," she wrote, "I cannot recollect in any order." What followed was the most emotionally raw entry of her entire diary. "My beloved Sally," she wrote, "is in her grave since yesterday between twelve and one o'clock." Sally had died on September 25, a month from her forty-sixth birthday: "she was very quiet, did not appear in any pain, without any struggle, sigh, or groan—a great favor!" And yet: "Oh! What a loss! To a mother near seventy-two years of age—my first-born darling—my first, my third, my fifth, seventh, and ninth are in their graves—my second, fourth, sixth, and eighth are living, if Henry is yet spared to us." Elizabeth was referring to Henry Sandwith, but her husband, Henry, was still unwell and could not attend his daughter's funeral. William and Mary accompanied their mother in the procession that took Sally's remains from the house in Front Street to the Friends' burial ground and on "to the place of fixedness—to be seen no more in this world." Elizabeth's sister, who had been "very poorly" with the flu in late August but then recovered sufficiently to help nurse her niece and brother-in-law, had probably stayed at home to be with Henry. The Friend who spoke briefly at the graveside said that he had "a sense of the well-being of the deceased," and another who spoke at their house remarked that he saw in the expression of the departed "a sweet serenity" suggesting that same "well-being," in other words, her acceptance into heaven. This must have been a comfort to Elizabeth, who acknowledged that her daughter was "no high professor" of religion, though she believed Sally to have had "an uncorrupted heart." The many neighbors, friends, and relatives who had come to the house over the past few days would doubtless have added their own words of comfort, but Elizabeth saw very few of them. She was physically and emotionally shattered. Now, as another evening passed into night, her husband was asleep and "all things quiet, the other room evacuated—oh my heart!"[46]

Over the coming days and weeks, Elizabeth noted over and over how long it had been since her daughter's passing. "Our dear Sally has been the 52nd part of a year in the silent grave," she wrote a week after her death. She marked the first rainfall over the grave ("it cannot hurt her"), and when she had a bad pain in her back, she consoled herself with the thought that Sally had "escaped the pains of old age." Elizabeth did not speak at her daughter's funeral, as far as we can tell, but she did enter her own private testimonial into her diary, writing that during her life Sally had been "happy and contented," with "a good and kind husband, five dear children, and every conveniency her heart could wish." Now, she insisted, they had not "lost" but "parted with" her. As for the realm into which she had passed, Elizabeth could not be certain if she had been "accepted," but she could and did "hope and trust" that Sally was "at rest with her maker." If so, she wrote, " 'tis well . . . may it be my case when it pleases the Lord to call me hence."[47]

As illness and death racked their household, so too was the outer world roiled by political strife and warfare. The vicious and sometimes violent partisanship that tainted political life in the last decade of Elizabeth's life clearly dismayed her. Even worse was the "carnage" taking place on the other side of the Atlantic as European powers warred with each other. "Shocking doings!" she declared, using language reminiscent of her response to the violence and cruelty inflicted by both sides during the War for Independence. As the United States edged closer toward a second war with Great Britain, the thought of what might follow was "enough to make one sick at heart," even if there were no "other troubles" to contend with. "Will the world never be at peace?" she asked. Elizabeth hoped that this combination of "foreign and domestic trouble," surely a sign of God's anger, would awaken humankind to a recognition of its sinfulness. "We ought to be humble indeed," she declared.[48]

The family stumbled onward as best it could. Henry's health was improving, albeit very slowly; it was not until late October that he had the strength to attend a religious service. Elizabeth made no mention of her husband's emotional state following Sally's death, though just over a week afterward he wrote to one of his land agents that he had "passed through a deeply afflicting scene in the loss of a beloved and my eldest child . . . who departed I hope to a better country on the 25th of last month." William, who had relayed news about his sister's condition for months on end and then watched her edge hour by hour closer to death once she came home for the last time, was in a bad way. "To see his dear vivacious sister laid low has been a trial to him," Elizabeth wrote. Ann had stayed overnight for the last few days of Sally's ordeal and did the same for several days after the funeral, though she was also unwell. Mary was still suffering from "disordered" bowels; Elizabeth's sister had a bad cough. As for Elizabeth, she never really recovered from Sarah's illness and death. That October, she tripped and fell, bruising herself badly. She refused to take any medicine, as she had for almost two years, though she did rub her side with vinegar and salt. Elizabeth now preferred to put her trust elsewhere: "I am," she wrote, "in the hands of the Lord."[49]

Throughout the first half of November, Elizabeth pottered around the house and occasionally ventured into the garden, entertaining herself by watching spiders build webs across the boxwoods. Her bruises continued to hurt, and she wrote that she felt "far from well," though she devoted much less ink to her aches and pains during these final weeks than in many years past. She watched the comings and goings of her family and neighbors. She listened to John Skyrin talk about settlers in the backwoods. She recorded "news from Europe, not agreeable." She worried about her grandson Henry Drinker after hearing that he had swallowed some peach stones. She read approvingly a letter from the Atsion ironworks manager praising their former servant Peter Woodward, now an employee there along with his wife. And she rejoiced at the arrival of a letter from Henry Sandwith. In that letter, he told his family that he had received an invitation to attend the ceremonial burning of a widow alongside "the remains of her deceased husband." At first, he had been intrigued by the prospect of witnessing "so extraordinary a spectacle," but then he lost his nerve and so did not attend. His mother wrote that she had thought "that unnatural practice . . . at an end long ago," but "suppose[d] the poor creatures think they merit Heaven by the sacrifice." Henry Sandwith had no way of knowing that his sister would have died by the time this letter arrived or that his mother was nearing her own departure, but whether either of them would "merit Heaven" had been on Elizabeth's mind, and his anecdote must have seemed grimly apposite.[50]

A brief entry for November 18 described the weather, the departure of grandson William, who had arrived the day before and stayed overnight, her own son William's afternoon visit to the Downing home, and the news he brought back with him; granddaughter Elizabeth had the toothache. Elizabeth's diary ended with the words, "a clear moonlit night." Her obituary would note that she had kept a diary "nearly from the time of her marriage to the evening preceding her last illness." This must have been that evening. She died just under a week later on November 24 at the age of seventy-two.[51]

"Here We Have No Continuing City"

Henry had never dwelt at length on personal matters in his business correspondence, and that did not change now, but he had been a constant letter writer. Now, laid low by a combination of illness and grief, he was uncharacteristically silent throughout September, the month of Sally's death, then again through December and into early January, following the loss of his wife. Those silences were themselves eloquent. William wrote several letters on his father's behalf during December, describing him as unwell but making no mention of the two deaths that had just occurred. The two men may have decided together that he would hold back from revealing what had happened; if William made the decision on his own, perhaps because he could not bring himself to write about the double bereavement, Henry would surely have understood when he later saw copies of those letters what that silence on paper masked. William had been at his mother's side day by day for many years, sometimes cared for by her and increasingly caring for her, accompanying her out on walks when she felt well enough to leave the house, and conveying news between their home and that of his sisters. Her death left a massive hole in the young man's life.

Henry mentioned his double loss—"the sore affliction I have had to drink deeply of"—in only a handful of letters. In these he referred to Elizabeth as "a beloved companion" and "the mother of my children," while he described Sally as his eldest child and "the mother of diverse grandchildren." It is hardly surprising that Henry would have characterized both women in terms of their roles, alongside his own, as parents and grandparents. He had always been a loving, though at times intimidating, parent. Despite his daily preoccupation with business affairs throughout his marriage, a preoccupation that his wife occasionally complained about in the pages of her diary, Henry nonetheless thought of Elizabeth as his "beloved companion." In times of separation and crisis, their letters had reaffirmed that they were a devoted and mutually supportive couple, but now in bereavement Henry must have been especially aware of what he no longer had. Following his wife's death, Henry copied out a dozen entries from the last few years of her diary that captured Elizabeth's appreciation of nature, her religious faith, and her devotion to their children; others mentioned her ailing health, and he included some of the entries immediately following Sally's death. Just over a year later, when he heard about a friend's "final separation" from his wife, he penned a letter to console the grieving widower in his "painful . . . affliction": "my mind was dipped in sympathy with thee," he wrote . . . a telling choice of words, evoking their shared immersion in loss and grief.[52]

Elizabeth's husband survived her by nineteen months and two days. Because there is no diary to draw on for those months, we have to rely on fragments of information contained in letters and other sources to piece together the final phase of Henry's life. For several months following the loss of his wife and daughter, he remained ill and mostly confined to his bedchamber, from what exactly we do not know. By March 1808, he wrote that he could now "move about" but had by no means fully recovered. During his confinement, he lamented, "business had slept." William had done his best to keep up with correspondence and to represent his father's interests, but once Henry was well enough to review the situation, he concluded that he had been that winter "a great sufferer," in practical concerns as well as in his illness and double bereavement. The local Quaker community must also have felt the impact of Henry's absence during those months, though not everyone was sensitive to his situation. In April 1808, just months after the loss of Elizabeth and as he still struggled with the aftereffects of illness, one of Henry's neighbors urged him to become involved in an escalating controversy over the behavior of a local Friend. Though she claimed that she did not want "to add improperly" to his "burdens in a tender state of health," she insisted that "to fill up the measure of duty" was a necessary requirement for peace of mind and conscience. She therefore requested that he, "as one of our senior elders," give "sympathetic attention" to the situation. "Those who are appointed to the important station of caretakers of the ministry," she added, "may be strengthened at times in the discharge of duty by intimations from others." She was, in other words, berating Drinker, albeit gently, for neglecting his responsibilities. Perhaps she thought that delving into the controversy would distract Henry from his grief, but the tone of the letter was a good deal less sympathetic to the elderly widower's plight than might have been expected from a loving Friend.[53]

At the end of 1808, Henry informed his friend and land agent Robert Rose that the family at 110 North Front Street—now reduced to his son William, sister-in-law Mary, and himself—was "favored with health in a good degree." Yet advanced age and the physical frailty that came with it had confirmed for him "one truth, that here we have no continuing city." Now more than ever, in preparation for his departure, Henry wished to free himself from "the corroding cares of this life," but as he lamented in several letters that year, his time was still "crowded with various concerns," depriving him of the repose he had sought for many years. Eventually, though, the call came, so that debtors and deceivers could no longer trouble him, and our weary friend finally found rest. All we know about Henry Drinker's eventual passing from his home in Philadelphia to what his wife had called "the place of fixedness" comes from a passage in Benjamin Rush's commonplace book:

> June 26 [1809]: This evening died in the seventy-sixth year of his age my excellent friend and patient, Henry Drinker. . . . His life was peaceable and his death equally so. Dear friend Adieu!

Benjamin had perhaps attended Henry in his capacity as a trusted physician during his last few days, though whether he was present when his friend passed on is unclear. He did not mention if Henry had been sick or simply faded away, though his description of his death as "peaceable" suggests the latter. However shadowed by practical worries and personal tragedy his final years may have been, the moment of passing seems to have matched, finally, what he hoped to find in the world beyond.[54]

Epilogue

Henry Drinker was a practical as well as pious man and had hoped to leave behind the means to secure his children's future comfort. His estate was, at least on paper, quite grandiose. Yet much of it took the form of land that his heirs could not readily liquidate, in practice more a burden than an asset, and his two sons, William and Henry Sandwith, would devote the rest of their lives to managing their father's fraught land investments. Henry's will left specific sums of money to his surviving brothers, Joseph and Daniel, and to the heirs of his deceased brother, John. It divided the remainder of the estate, after payment of debts, into five equal portions. The first went to Henry's older son William and his heirs (of whom there were none, as he remained unmarried in Philadelphia until his death in 1821). The second went to his younger son Henry Sandwith, who died in 1824, and then his eight surviving heirs. Henry Drinker's surviving daughters, Ann and Mary, received the third and fourth portions, with the husband in each case explicitly denied access, the legacy held in trust for each daughter until death and then distributed equally among her surviving children. Henry evidently trusted neither John Skyrin nor Samuel Rhoads to protect these legacies. The fifth portion went in equal amounts to the five children of Henry's deceased daughter Sarah Downing. Henry acknowledged in his will that it was difficult to estimate how much the estate was actually worth, given the volatility of land prices, but if each of these fifths amounted to at least ten thousand dollars, his executors were to fulfill several philanthropic bequests. These were to the Philadelphia Friends' Public School, the Pennsylvania Hospital, the Philadelphia Dispensary, the Committee of the Yearly Meeting in Philadelphia responsible for "instructing and improving the Indian natives in a more civilized and comfortable mode of living," and the

Northern District Monthly Meeting, for the "use and relief" of Friends deemed "proper objects of help and assistance."[1]

The house that Henry and Elizabeth had lived in since 1771 and their furniture went up for sale in November 1809, five months after Henry's death, along with a two-horse carriage purchased in 1804 that the estate sale advertisement described as "little used." The family silverware went to Henry Sandwith, William, and Jacob Downing. Henry Sandwith received a coffee pot, tankard, teapot, and bowl; William got a small stand, sugar dish, cream pot, and tea strainer, as well as a soup spoon, a tablespoon, a marrow spoon, and fourteen teaspoons; to Jacob went a tankard, a porringer, a pepperbox, a mustard pot, six tablespoons, tea tongs, and a teaspoon. Mary Sandwith had her own collection, consisting of a teapot, a tankard, a porringer, saltcellars, a tea strainer, tea tongs, four tablespoons, six teaspoons, and a small stand. She and William deposited their silverware at the Bank of North America on November 10, 1809, "in a wooden box with a card nailed on the top" that named them as the owners. Aunt and nephew now left the home in which Mary had lived for almost forty years and William since he was four years old. They probably put these items in safekeeping because they did not yet know where they would settle. Other family members doubtless took mementoes away with them, but the bulk of the home in which Henry and Elizabeth had raised and protected their children was now broken up and scattered among other householders. Save for the memories of those who had lived or visited there, the Drinkers' domestic world evaporated.[2]

In the years that followed, neither Mary Sandwith nor William Drinker established an independent household. Mary owned several properties in the city, but she had spent her entire life living in homes that belonged to other people and evidently saw no need to break that pattern; she apparently moved in with one of her relatives or a friend in the city. Mary died in 1815, and her final will, written the year before, left the bulk of her considerable estate, which consisted of lots in and outside Philadelphia along with stocks in canal and turnpike companies, to William. He had moved frequently since his parents' death and continued to do so even after he settled as a lodger in the home of Ann Coffin, a widow who relocated repeatedly and took him with her. William died suddenly in 1821 without having made a will, the cause of death "apoplexy" (a cerebral hemorrhage or stroke). His youngest sister, Mary Rhoads, took on the executorship of his estate, which she divided among herself, her two surviving siblings, and the children of Sarah and Jacob Downing.[3]

Following his return from India, Henry Sandwith had relocated with his family from Burlington, New Jersey, to Philadelphia, where he remained until his death in 1824. No more adventures on the high seas for him, and William repeatedly paid the bills for his brother's children's schooling, which suggests that Henry Sandwith was short of money. At the time of his death, he was away from home, visiting one of his father's properties at Silver Lake in Susquehanna County. Henry Sandwith apparently committed suicide by cutting his throat with a razor. Samuel Rhoads died in 1810, having recently declared himself bankrupt; his widow, Mary, lived on in Philadelphia until her death in 1856. John Skyrin, whose mercantile ventures had long since collapsed, died around 1824, and five years later Ann moved out to Ohio with her two unmarried daughters, Elizabeth and Mary, joining her other daughter, Eleanor, who had married Joseph Drinker, grandson of Henry Drinker's brother John; Joseph was a clerk at the U.S. Bank in Cincinnati. Ann Skyrin died the following year. In 1843, a lengthy legal document divided the residue of Henry Drinker's estate among his surviving grandchildren. None of the Drinker children had become destitute, thanks in large part to the legacies they received from their parents and their support of one another, but this was a sorry end to their parents' hopes for them.[4]

Fortunately for us, Elizabeth and Henry's descendants preserved many of their writings. At first, this responsibility fell to William. Each time that he moved, he took with him "a great quantity of my father's old books and papers . . . also James and Drinker's books, and a great number of boxes containing their papers, and the Atsion books and papers." Eventually, William became "so weary" of arranging to have these records shifted from one residence to the next that when his landlady moved in 1817 and he relocated with her, he destroyed "a cartload of them." However, a large collection of family letters and documents, including Elizabeth's diary, did survive William's purge and passed from one generation to the next. In the 1880s, one of Elizabeth and Henry's great-grandsons, Henry Drinker Biddle, inherited a trunk in which family papers had been stored for many decades and made a study of its contents. He pasted many of the items into five large albums and published a volume of extracts from Elizabeth's diary in 1889; he also wrote a genealogical history of the Drinkers that he published in 1893. Another of Elizabeth and Henry's great-grandsons, Henry Sturgis Drinker, donated some of his ancestors' papers to the Historical Society of Pennsylvania in 1888. Whether those came from the same trunk that his cousin Henry Drinker Biddle had inherited is unclear; Elizabeth and Henry's descendants may have divided the family records at some point. Several decades later, in 1937, Cecil Drinker, one of Henry Sturgis Drinker's sons and a professor of physiology who became dean of the School of Public Health at Harvard, published another set of diary extracts that focused on illness and health care in Philadelphia. One of Cecil's brothers, a lawyer named Henry Sandwith Drinker, wrote a history of the Drinker family that he published privately in 1961. That same Drinker donated Elizabeth's diary to the Historical Society of Pennsylvania and the correspondence between Henry and Elizabeth during Henry's exile to Haverford College. In 1968, three years after Henry Sandwith Drinker's death, his daughter Ernesta Drinker Ballard, who led the Pennsylvania Horticultural Society for almost two decades, donated another large collection of papers to the Historical Society of Pennsylvania.[5]

We will never know how Henry and Elizabeth would have felt about the attention that modern historians have given to their lives and writings, but they would surely have been gratified to know that their neighbors and friends remembered them as exemplars of a genteel Quaker sensibility that blended religious principle with urbane sophistication. Their neighbor Ann Warder, not one to mince words, described Elizabeth as "a very sensible agreeable woman," Henry as "a fine man . . . blessed in his family," their daughters as "really fine accomplished women," and Mary Sandwith as "a kind creature." Benjamin Rush added to his record of Henry's death a brief personal tribute. He described his "excellent friend" as "a man of uncommon understanding, and great suavity and correctness of manners" who "possessed talents and judgment in business which would have qualified him for the office of a Secretary of State." Within the Society of Friends, he was "universally esteemed and beloved." The more formal obituary that appeared in *Poulson's American Daily Advertiser* a few days later noted that Henry had been "formerly a merchant in very extensive business and of great respectability." It went on to state that "benevolence, and beneficence (exercised without ostentation) marked his character as a Christian," while "urbanity and a great share of natural politeness distinguished him as a gentleman." He had "faithfully performed his duties in religious and civil society, gaining the esteem and confidence of those with whom he acted," and as "a public man" had been "much called upon." The obituary ended by declaring, "It is not an overstrained encomium to say that by those who had the best opportunity of knowing his worth he lived beloved and died lamented."[6]

Together these two tributes drew attention to several aspects of Henry's life: his considerable abilities as a merchant, his conscientiousness as a citizen and within the Society of Friends, his credentials as a gentleman, and of course his piety. That a prominent newspaper now praised him as a dutiful and esteemed "public man" was quite remarkable, given that during the War for Independence patriots had arrested and imprisoned him on suspicion of treason. That Philadelphians should remember him as an urbane gentleman would presumably have pleased Henry, just so long as this did not eclipse his reputation as a man of faith and moral integrity. Consistent with the spirit of the new republic, his obituary described him as having a "natural politeness" rather than the stilted manners that characterized Europe's effete aristocracy, and Henry does seem to have been relatively down-to-earth in dress and behavior, as befitted a Friend. Some of those who owed him money and other business associates with whom he became increasingly exasperated during the last two decades of his life would perhaps have penned a less generous estimation of his personality. He would doubtless have countered that posterity could explain, if not entirely forgive, any lapses in civility as a reaction to mistreatment: no man was so immaculate in spirit that he could always achieve complete resignation in the face of abuse and suffering. Neither Benjamin Rush nor the public obituary said anything about the ordeal that Henry had gone through during the War for Independence, erasing in effect the suspicions and horrors of that period. Nor did they mention the disappointments that he experienced as a man of business in his later years.

There was, furthermore, no reference to Henry's life as a family man or his love for Elizabeth, his children, and his grandchildren. In sharp contrast, the obituary that appeared a week after Elizabeth's death emphasized her roles as household mistress, wife, and parent. It declared that "her chief happiness consisted in the discharge of her domestic duties" and that "in every part of her conduct, she might be pointed out as an example of the affectionate wife and tender mother." Such distinctions between male and female obituaries were standard and might tempt a modern reader to conclude that men cared less about family life than did women. Yet we know from Henry's letters and his wife's diary that he was a devoted, albeit sometimes distracted, husband and a loving, though at times austere, father who took his children and grandchildren fishing and sleighing, who cared deeply about their spiritual welfare, and whom they loved dearly in return.

Elizabeth's obituary described her as having "possessed uncommon personal beauty, which the gentleness of her temper preserved, in a great degree, to the last." (There was no mention of Henry's physical appearance in his obituary.) The unnamed author acknowledged that she had "received an education much superior to what was common for young ladies in this country sixty years ago." Yet the emphasis throughout was on her "sweetness of disposition," her "propriety of conduct," and her religious faith, which was "firm" and yet "free from all bigotry of sentiment or narrowness of feeling." There was a brief and implicit reference to the trials the family had gone through when the author noted that Elizabeth had passed on her religious principles to her children "not only as a rock of salvation in another world, but as a harbor of refuge from the cares and afflictions of this." The final section described her "fondness for literature," a testament to her sophistication and good taste; it went on to note that she had "for many years amused herself" by keeping a diary. In that diary, the author claimed, there was "not to be found a single misrepresentation or illiberal observation; for her words flowed from her heart, and that was a source which was ever pure and serene." Some of Elizabeth's diary entries were, in fact, a good deal less generous in spirit than this eulogist claimed, though like her husband, Elizabeth would have defended her sharper remarks by arguing that she wrote them under considerable provocation.[7]

More misleading was the claim that Elizabeth's heart was "serene," for her diary testified to a journey characterized more by anxiety and fear than serenity. The obituary's ending was especially rose tinted: "In truth, to no one can be applied with more perfect propriety the inspired language of the scriptures, that 'Her ways were ways of pleasantness, and all her paths were peace.'" Whether one reads "her ways" as referring to the circumstances in which Elizabeth found herself or how she chose to live her life, the claim seems in either case highly dubious. Perhaps her outward persona hid the inner turmoil that comes across so clearly in some of the diary entries. According to the obituary, "her countenance was a perfect index of a mind whose feelings were all attuned to harmony," but perhaps that "countenance" was less "a perfect index" than a carefully maintained facade. Her diary told another story. "That state of tranquility, or equality of mind, which good or bad fortune, as it is called, can neither exalt nor depress, is hard to attain," she wrote a year before her death. "Sure I am, I have not arrived at it." Elizabeth would certainly have liked to live a peaceful life, but she and her family had endured a bloody, frightening civil war, and their home was by no means consistently the haven of tranquillity and peaceful companionship to which Quakers aspired. To a servant or a homeless beggar on the streets of Philadelphia, her life may well have seemed one of "pleasantness," yet in truth, many phases of her life were anything but that. Elizabeth described herself as "not of a very sanguine disposition, but apt to fear the worst, unless circumstances tend to the contrary." She wrote this as her eldest daughter was dying, but that was the latest of many ordeals Elizabeth had faced, and each left its mark. "This is a world of trouble," she wrote in 1803. "May we so live as to find peace in the next."[8]

~

The lengthy diary and vast correspondence that Elizabeth and Henry Drinker left behind them allow us to travel with them through a uniquely tumultuous period in American history. Their writings give us access to their interior as well as external lives and remind us that the fraught political issues of their era had personal, spiritual, and emotional ramifications that played out in private as well as public spaces. In some respects an unremarkable couple, Elizabeth and Henry lived through extraordinary times and became remarkable through their courage and resilience in the face of persecution and suffering. Economically privileged and yet in other ways extremely vulnerable, they had to steer their way through a series of political crises and a grueling war that placed Quakers in serious danger once patriots began to target them as enemies of the Revolution. In the aftermath of the War for Independence, both husband and wife had to adapt to a challenging new world. While Elizabeth battled with increasingly assertive servants who threatened the stability of her domestic kingdom, Henry had to navigate the economic uncertainties of the post-revolutionary period as he tried to reinvent himself as a visionary entrepreneur and secure his family's future. Unlike many of his contemporaries, he did not have to face bankruptcy, but his ventures brought him little reward, and he limped to his grave badly battered by the experience. Though respected by fellow Quakers and other Philadelphians during their lifetime, Henry and Elizabeth might easily have slipped into obscurity, mere footnotes in history. Yet their writings, preserved by their descendants and then by archivists in and around Philadelphia, have made this couple remarkable again as the words they penned so long ago bring back to life a period of profound change.

In some ways, Elizabeth and Henry traveled quite different journeys. The distinct roles, expectations, and opportunities assigned to men and women during that era ensured that they engaged with their world in different ways and to varying degrees. Though raised in a religious community that gave extraordinary voice and agency to women, Elizabeth became as the years went by less and less involved in the public aspects of Quaker faith, partly because of ill health and partly from personal choice, whereas Henry became and remained an active, respected elder in the Society of Friends. Yet during the war both Elizabeth and Henry faced unexpected disruptions of their previously quite conventional gender roles. Elizabeth had never been one to put herself forward in public, and at home, like most of her female contemporaries, she rarely questioned patriarchal authority; but she now found herself acting as temporary household head in a militarily occupied city and took part in a dangerous diplomatic mission to secure Henry's release. Elizabeth assumed these responsibilities with courage and determination, but she did not seek them out and, once Henry returned home, retreated into her more conventional life as household mistress. She gave no sign in the years that followed of wanting to become more active or vocal in the local Quaker community and for the most part seems to have viewed the roles she assumed during the war as onerous duties rather than welcome opportunities, forced on her by the exile of her beloved husband. Henry, meanwhile, underwent public humiliation and removal from the community in which he had become an influential figure; supplanted for several months in his own home by another man in British uniform, he was unable to protect his family as household head from the dangers posed by both sides in the conflict. Henry clearly resented his impotence in exile, though he tried at a distance to support his wife as she stepped into his shoes. Yet despite their different, sometimes difficult paths and their occasional disagreements, they mostly weathered the storm as a couple. They remained throughout their marriage united by a lasting love for one another, unwavering devotion to their children, and loyalty to the Society of Friends. Even when separated, even when their spheres of concern and action seemed distinct, they remained linked together by these three fundamental commitments and emotional truths.

Henry and Elizabeth experienced the multilayered transformations of that era as they played out on the national and international stage, in local communities, and in their own home. Along with political revolution came economic, social, and cultural changes that sometimes reinforced and at others clashed with one another. The Drinkers' observations about these changes as they unfolded around them show us in vivid and intimate detail how major historical events and trends affected people in their everyday lives. The spread of free wage labor destabilized households, offices, and workshops as it created a more independent-minded and assertive workforce, much to the dismay and disgust of masters and mistresses such as Henry and Elizabeth; it also created more flexibility for employers and so made workers more vulnerable to the whims of their masters and mistresses. Changing attitudes toward sex and marriage gave more autonomy to young adults and reduced the ability of parents to control or protect their children as they reached maturity. Meanwhile, the Society of Friends had launched a reform movement that pointed in quite the opposite direction, reaffirming parental and community control over young adults as they decided whom to marry. For Quakers such as the Drinkers, raising children in the midst of these competing forces proved a daunting challenge. Each of these transformations began during the late colonial period, but the Revolution put wind in their sails as servants and young people drew inspiration from the rhetoric of liberty, equality, and independence that reverberated through streets, parlors, and kitchens. The late eighteenth century can seem in retrospect a period of historic and largely positive achievement, as revolutionaries laid the foundations for much of what we claim as American modernity, yet for those who lived through those decades and faced multiple upheavals in their everyday lives, that experience often seemed more traumatic than triumphant.

That the Drinkers survived at all was in itself remarkable. Most obviously, Henry's arrest and exile as a suspected traitor could have ended differently. Both husband and wife gave thanks to Providence for bringing them through that time of trial, but they and their children had to endure many other testing times, including illnesses and accidents that no wealth or privilege could shield them from. Elizabeth knew well that she and their daughters faced the possibility of death each time they became pregnant; she and her husband mourned the loss of four infant children and several grandchildren; they also watched helplessly as two of their adult children went through protracted illness, one of them dying in agony. These intimate dramas can seem comparatively insignificant in the grand sweep of history, yet they consumed those involved and had profound implications for imperiled communities such as the Quakers whose very survival depended on the transmission of faith from one generation to the next. Instead of ending their lives in peaceable tranquillity, surrounded by children who had established successful and secure families of their own, Henry and Elizabeth died in the shadow of tragedy, disappointment, and anxiety for the future. "It requires fortitude, patience, and resignation to live in this world as we ought to do," wrote Elizabeth, though she then added, "If we can be fitted for the next, all will end well!" She and Henry always had one eye on the world to come and the peaceful repose it promised. In the meantime, they created for themselves and their children a haven of comfort and loving support that sustained them well enough through all that they had to endure. Yet Elizabeth was right: theirs had been "a world of trouble."[9]

Family Trees

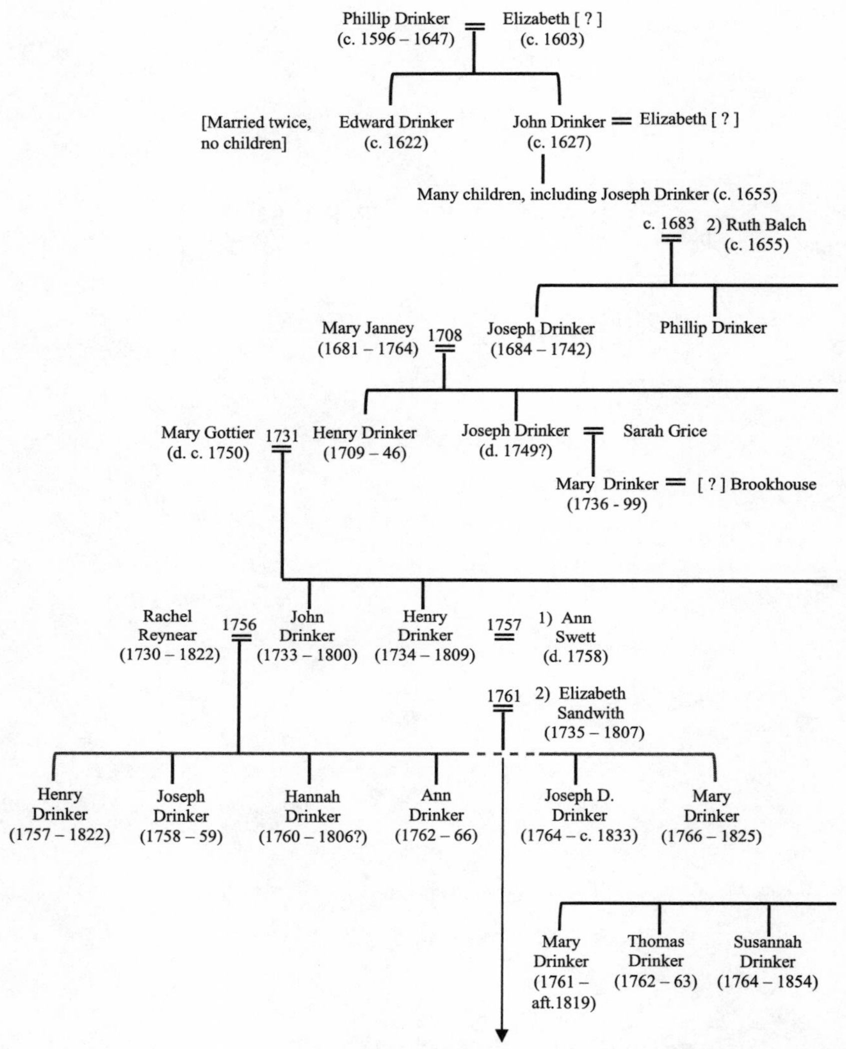
Phillip Drinker (c. 1596 – 1647)
Elizabeth [?] (c. 1603)
[Married twice, no children]
Edward Drinker (c. 1622)
John Drinker (c. 1627)
Elizabeth [?]
Many children, including Joseph Drinker (c. 1655)
c. 1683
2) Ruth Balch (c. 1655)
Joseph Drinker (1684 – 1742)
Phillip Drinker
Mary Janney (1681 – 1764)
1708
Mary Gottier (d. c. 1750)
1731
Henry Drinker (1709 – 46)
Joseph Drinker (d. 1749?)
Sarah Grice
Mary Drinker (1736 - 99)
[?] Brookhouse
Rachel Reynear (1730 – 1822)
1756
John Drinker (1733 – 1800)
Henry Drinker (1734 – 1809)
1757
1) Ann Swett (d. 1758)
1761
2) Elizabeth Sandwith (1735 – 1807)
Henry Drinker (1757 – 1822)
Joseph Drinker (1758 – 59)
Hannah Drinker (1760 – 1806?)
Ann Drinker (1762 – 66)
Joseph D. Drinker (1764 – c. 1833)
Mary Drinker (1766 – 1825)
Mary Drinker (1761 – aft.1819)
Thomas Drinker (1762 – 63)
Susannah Drinker (1764 – 1854)
See Henry and Elizabeth Drinker's Family Tree

Henry Drinker's Family Tree

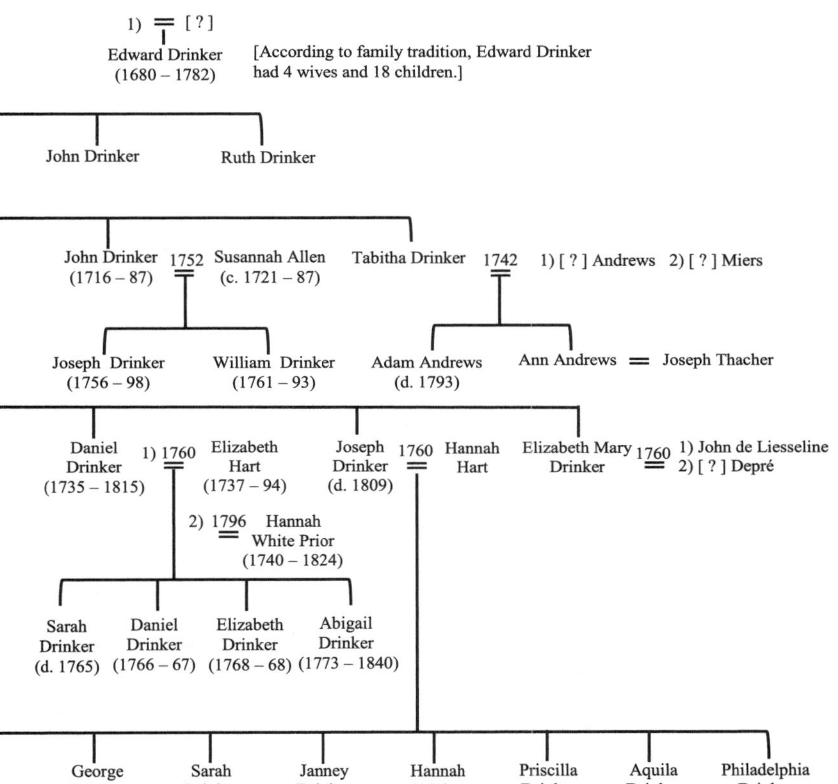

Elizabeth Drinker's Family Tree

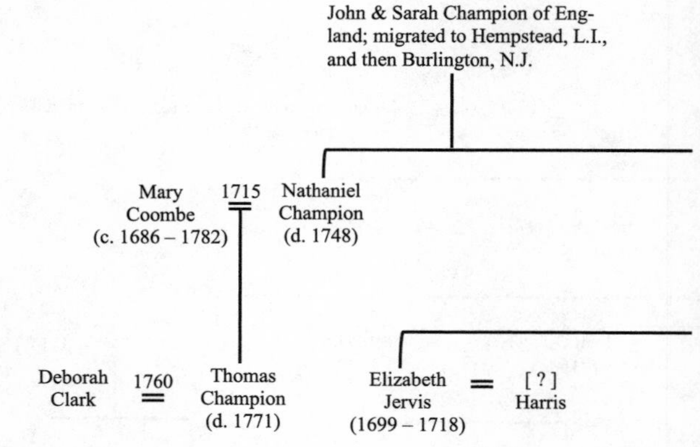

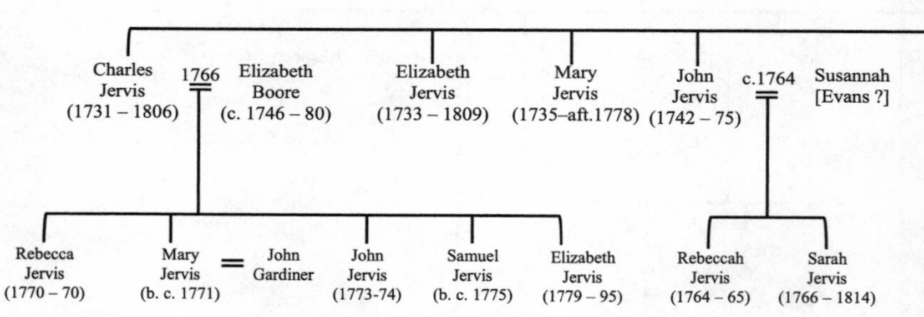

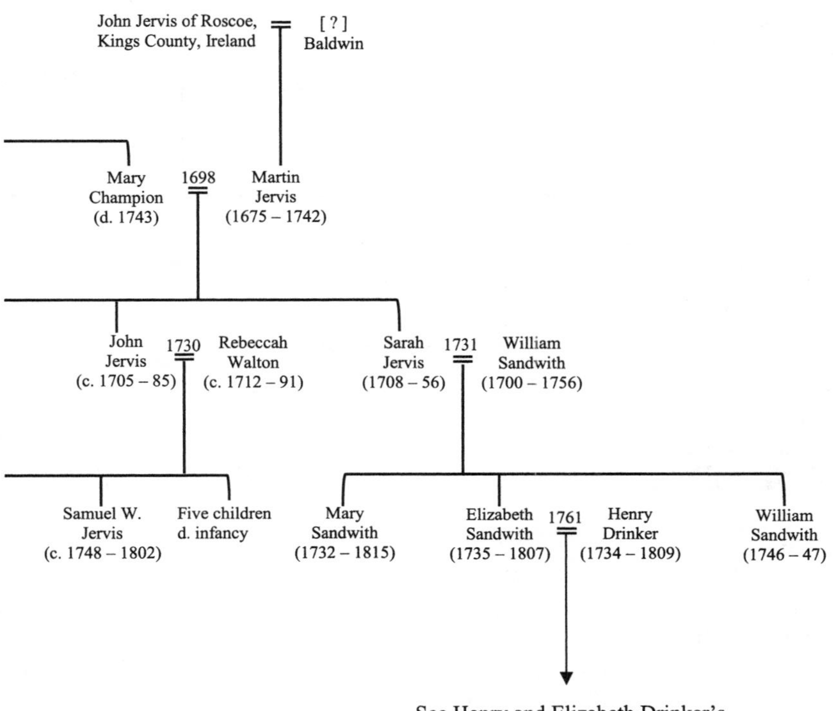

See Henry and Elizabeth Drinker's
Family Tree

Henry and Elizabeth Drinker's Children and Grandchildren

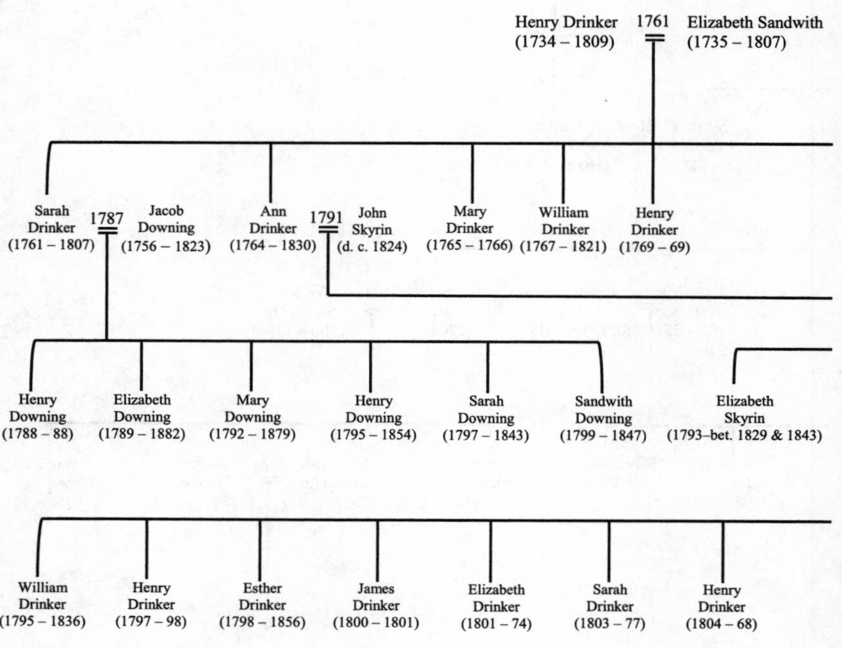

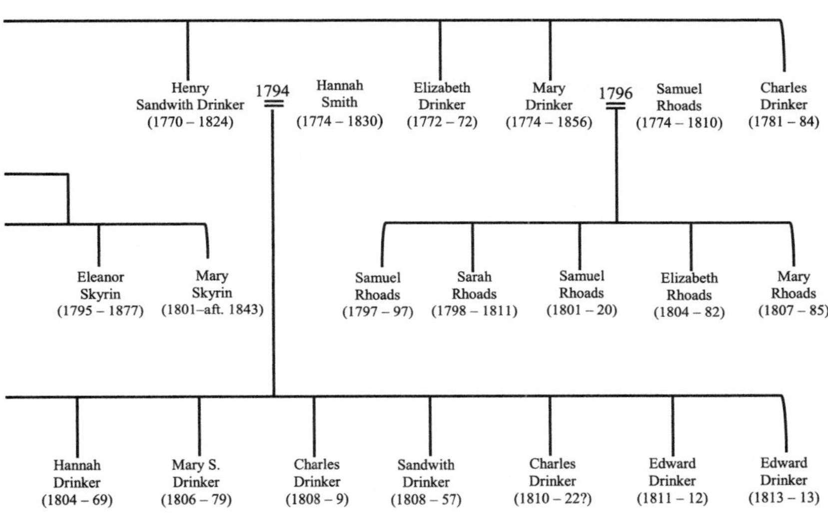
Henry
Sandwith Drinker
(1770 – 1824)
1794
Hannah
Smith
(1774 – 1830)
Elizabeth
Drinker
(1772 – 72)
Mary
Drinker
(1774 – 1856)
1796
Samuel
Rhoads
(1774 – 1810)
Charles
Drinker
(1781 – 84)
Eleanor
Skyrin
(1795 – 1877)
Mary
Skyrin
(1801–aft. 1843)
Samuel
Rhoads
(1797 – 97)
Sarah
Rhoads
(1798 – 1811)
Samuel
Rhoads
(1801 – 20)
Elizabeth
Rhoads
(1804 – 82)
Mary
Rhoads
(1807 – 85)
Hannah
Drinker
(1804 – 69)
Mary S.
Drinker
(1806 – 79)
Charles
Drinker
(1808 – 9)
Sandwith
Drinker
(1808 – 57)
Charles
Drinker
(1810 – 22?)
Edward
Drinker
(1811 – 12)
Edward
Drinker
(1813 – 13)

Chronology

1732 Birth of **Mary Sandwith** (parents Sarah [Jervis] and William Sandwith)

1734 Birth of **Henry Drinker** (parents Mary [Gottier] and Henry Drinker)

1735 Birth of **Elizabeth Sandwith** (parents Sarah [Jervis] and William Sandwith)

1761 Marriage of **Elizabeth Sandwith** and **Henry Drinker**

1761 Birth of **Sarah Drinker** (parents ED and HD)

1764 Birth of **Ann Drinker** (parents ED and HD)

1765 Birth of first **Mary Drinker** (parents ED and HD)

1766 Death of first **Mary Drinker**

1767 Birth of **William Drinker** (parents ED and HD)

1769 Birth and Death of **Henry Drinker** (parents ED and HD)

1770 Birth of **Henry Sandwith Drinker** (parents ED and HD)

1772 Birth and Death of **Elizabeth Drinker** (parents ED and HD)

1756–63 War with France

1765 Passage of Stamp Act

1766 Repeal of Stamp Act

1773 Passage of Tea Act, and **James and Drinker**'s commission from East India Company

1774 Birth of second **Mary Drinker** (parents ED and HD)

1781 Birth of **Charles Drinker** (parents ED and HD)

1784 Death of **Charles Drinker**

1787 Marriage of **Sarah Drinker** and **Jacob Downing**

1791 Marriage of **Ann Drinker** and **John Skyrin**

1794 Marriage of **Henry Sandwith Drinker** and **Hannah Smith**

1796 Marriage of **Mary Drinker** and **Samuel Rhoads**

1807 Death of **Sarah [Drinker] Downing**

1807 Death of **Elizabeth [Sandwith] Drinker**

1809 Death of **Henry Drinker**

1815 Death of **Mary Sandwith**

1821 Death of **William Drinker**

1824 Death of **Henry Sandwith Drinker**

1830 Death of **Ann [Drinker] Skyrin**

1856 Death of **Mary [Drinker] Rhoads**

1776 Declaration of Independence

September 1777–April 1778 **Henry Drinker**'s imprisonment and exile in Virginia

1783 Treaty of Paris

1787 Constitutional Convention

1789 Inauguration of President George Washington

1790 First maple sugar manufacturing season at Stockport

1792 Formation of Sugar Company and maple sugar manufacturing project at Union Farm

1795 Dissolution of Sugar Company and abandonment of maple sugar manufacturing project at Union Farm

1797 Inauguration of President John Adams

1801 Inauguration of President Thomas Jefferson

1809 Inauguration of President James Madison

Notes

Abbreviations

AJ	Abel James
APS	American Philosophical Society, Philadelphia
DED	*The Diary of Elizabeth Drinker,* edited by Elaine Forman Crane, 3 vols. (Boston: Northeastern University Press, 1991)
DSP	Drinker and Sandwith Papers, 6 vols., Historical Society of Pennsylvania, Philadelphia
ED	Elizabeth Drinker
FHL	Friends Historical Library, Swarthmore College, Swarthmore, Pa.
FL	Foreign Letters
HD	Henry Drinker
HSDP	Henry S. Drinker Papers, Historical Society of Pennsylvania, Philadelphia
HSP	Historical Society of Pennsylvania, Philadelphia
J&D	James and Drinker
JL	Journal
LB	Letter Book
LC	Library of Congress, Washington, D.C.
MS	Mary Sandwith
PH	*Pennsylvania History*
PMHB	*Pennsylvania Magazine of History and Biography*
QMR	Quaker Meeting Records at Quaker and Special Collections, Haverford College, and Friends Historical Library of Swarthmore College
QSC	Quaker and Special Collections, Haverford College, Haverford, Pa.

Introduction

1. *DED,* 228 (Sept. 9, 1777); Sarah Logan Fisher Diaries, Sept. 13, 1777, HSP; Thomas Gilpin [Jr.], *Exiles in Virginia: With Observations on the Conduct of the Society of Friends during the Revolutionary War* (Philadelphia: C. Sherman, 1848), 106, 133–34. For the names of the thirty men arrested and of the twenty sent into exile, ibid., 67, 148. The one non-Quaker sent into exile was Thomas Pike, a fencing and dancing instructor. Of the nineteen Quaker exiles, two had been disowned and so were not formally members of the Society: Elijah Brown, a financially embarrassed merchant, for not making sufficient effort to pay off his debts, and William Drewet Smith, a physician, for marrying a non-Quaker. Twenty-two men were originally on the list of those marked for exile, but Phineas Bond and Thomas Coombe were taken off the list before departure.

2. *DED,* 228–29 (Sept. 11, 1777); ED to HD, Sept. 16, 1777, Feb. 2, 1778, DSP, 3:6, 34.

3. See Jane E. Calvert, *Quaker Constitutionalism and the Political Thought of John Dickinson* (New York: Cambridge University Press, 2009), esp. part 1. For other studies of Quakers and the American Revolution, see Isaac Sharpless, *The Quakers in the Revolution* (1902; Honolulu: University Press of the Pacific, 2002); Arthur Mekeel, *The Relation of the Quakers to the American Revolution* (Washington, D.C.: University Press of America, 1970); Richard Bauman, *For the Reputation of Truth: Politics, Religion, and Conflict among the Pennsylvanian Quakers, 1750–1800* (Baltimore: Johns Hopkins University Press, 1971); and Sarah Crabtree, *Holy Nation: The Transatlantic Quaker Ministry in an Age of Revolution* (Chicago: University of Chicago Press, 2015).

4. For the Quaker movement in seventeenth-century England, see William C. Braithwaite, *The Beginnings of Quakerism* (London: Macmillan, 1923); Hugh Barbour, *The Quakers in Puritan England* (New Haven: Yale University Press, 1964); Christopher Hill, *The World Turned Upside Down: Radical Ideas during the English Revolution* (New York: Penguin, 1984); and H. Larry Ingle, *First among Friends: George Fox and the Creation of Quakerism* (Oxford: Oxford University Press, 1994). For the history of Quakerism in colonial North America, see Rufus M. Jones et al., *The Quakers in the American Colonies* (London: Macmillan, 1911); Allen C. Thomas, *A History of the Friends in America* (Philadelphia: John C. Winston, 1930); Frederick B. Tolles, *Quakers and the Atlantic Culture* (New York: Macmillan, 1960); James Bowden, *The History of the Society of Friends in America,* 2 vols. (New York: Arno Press, 1972); J. William Frost, *The Quaker Family in Colonial America: A Portrait of the Society of Friends* (New York: St. Martin's Press, 1973); Elbert Russell, *The History of Quakerism* (Richmond, Ind.: Friends United Press, 1979); Hugh Barbour and J. William Frost, *The Quakers* (New York: Greenwood Press, 1988); Barry Levy, *Quakers and the American Family: British Settlement in the Delaware Valley* (New York: Oxford University Press, 1988); Thomas D. Hamm, *Quakers in America* (New York: Columbia University Press, 2003); and a special forum on "Quakers and the Lived Politics of Early America," *William and Mary Quarterly,* 3rd ser., 74

(2017). For Quakers in Pennsylvania, see Frederick B. Tolles, *Meeting House and Counting House: The Quaker Merchants of Colonial Philadelphia, 1682–1763* (1948; New York: Norton, 1963); Gary B. Nash, *Quakers and Politics: Pennsylvania, 1681–1726* (Princeton, N.J.: Princeton University Press, 1968); Bauman, *Reputation of Truth;* Jack D. Marietta, *The Reformation of American Quakerism, 1748–1783* (Philadelphia: University of Pennsylvania Press, 1984); Sally Schwartz, *"A Mixed Multitude": The Struggle for Toleration in Colonial Pennsylvania* (New York: New York University Press, 1987); and John Smolenski, *Friends and Strangers: The Making of a Creole Culture in Colonial Pennsylvania* (Philadelphia: University of Pennsylvania Press, 2010).

5. *DED*, 594 (Sept. 16, 1794); ED wrote as militiamen set out for western Pennsylvania to suppress the so-called Whiskey Rebellion in 1794, but her comment was doubtless informed by her previous experience. For the statistics cited in this paragraph and a more detailed account of the violence and intimidation that accompanied the Revolution, see Holger Hoock, *Scars of Independence: America's Violent Birth* (New York: Crown, 2017), esp. 17; and Anne Ousterhout, "Controlling the Opposition in Pennsylvania during the Revolution," *PMHB* 105 (1981): 23. For scholarship on loyalists, see chap. 3, n63.

6. For an example of patriots using threats of tarring and feathering to further their ends, see Committee for Tarring and Feathering to the Delaware Pilots and Captain Ayres of the Ship Polly, Philadelphia broadside dated Nov. 27, 1773, Printed Ephemera Collection, portfolio 143, folder 31, LC. See also Benjamin H. Irvin, "Tar, Feathers, and the Enemies of American Liberties, 1768–1776," *New England Quarterly* 76 (2003): 197–238; and Frank W. C. Hersey, "Tar and Feathers: The Adventures of Captain John Malcolm," Colonial Society of Massachusetts Publications, *Transactions* 34 (1941): 429–73.

7. *DED*, 393 (Oct. 24, 1781); see also Diary of Anna Rawle, Oct. 25, 1781, Letters and Diaries of Rebecca Shoemaker and Her Daughters Anna and Margaret Rawle, HSP, 487–88 (typescript).

8. ED to HD, Dec. 27, 1777, Feb. 26, Mar. 23, 1778, DSP, 3:27, 36, 41; Gilpin, *Exiles in Virginia*, 133. For Quaker involvement in Pennsylvania politics, see esp. Alan Tully, *Forming American Politics: Ideals, Interests, and Institutions in Colonial New York and Pennsylvania* (Baltimore: Johns Hopkins University Press, 1994), esp. chap. 7; and Calvert, *Quaker Constitutionalism*, chaps. 3, 4.

9. See Marietta, *Reformation of American Quakerism.*

10. For the notion of Quaker nationhood, see Crabtree, *Holy Nation;* for the campaign to conflate Quakers with loyalists, see Jane E. Calvert, "Thomas Paine, Quakerism, and the Limits of Religious Liberty during the American Revolution," in Ian Shapiro and Jane E. Calvert, eds., *Selected Writings of Thomas Paine* (New Haven: Yale University Press, 2014), 602–29.

11. For changing attitudes toward sex, see Richard Godbeer, *Sexual Revolution in Early America* (Baltimore: Johns Hopkins University Press, 2002), chaps. 7–9; and

Clare A. Lyons, *Sex among the Rabble: An Intimate History of Gender and Power in the Age of Revolution, Philadelphia, 1730–1830* (Chapel Hill: University of North Carolina Press, 2006); for romantic courtship, chap. 1, n7; for Quaker reforms relating to marital procedure, Marietta, *Reformation of American Quakerism,* chap. 3; for labor relations in the eighteenth century, chap. 7, nn3,4. For the challenges faced by Quaker merchants living in major cities, see Benjamin L. Carp, " 'Fix'd Almost amongst Strangers': Charleston's Quaker Merchants and the Limits of Cosmopolitanism," *William and Mary Quarterly,* 3rd ser., 74 (2017): 77–108.

12. This is the first book-length study focused on the Drinkers. Scholars working on a wide range of topics have mined Elizabeth's diary, especially since the diary's publication in a deeply researched and deservedly admired edition by Elaine Forman Crane, yet no one has penned a biography of Elizabeth, let alone her husband. A handful of essays examine various aspects of Elizabeth's life and a few have discussed Henry's business activities, which also feature briefly in several books about trade and land investment, but historians have also given his voluminous correspondence much less attention than it deserves. This may be due in part to the unwieldy and by now fragile volumes in which most of those letters have survived, often in faded ink and transcribed by a succession of clerks, each with different handwriting. Elizabeth's diary can also seem daunting. Yet I hope that *World of Trouble* will be the first of several books written about the Drinkers. Some readers will doubtless be frustrated that I have not given more attention to topics that they find particularly interesting or significant, but the pages that follow do not aim to provide an all-encompassing reconstruction of Elizabeth's and Henry's lives. This remarkable couple has much more to tell us than can fit within the jacket of a single volume.

For the complete diary, see Elaine Forman Crane, ed., *The Diary of Elizabeth Drinker,* 3 vols. (Boston: Northeastern University Press, 1991). Two previous volumes contain extracts from the diary: Henry D. Biddle, ed., *Extracts from the Journal of Elizabeth Drinker* (Philadelphia: J. P. Lippincott, 1889); and Cecil K. Drinker, *Not So Long Ago: A Chronicle of Medicine and Doctors in Colonial Philadelphia* (New York: Oxford University Press, 1937). For genealogical information about the Drinkers, see Henry S. Drinker, *History of the Drinker Family* (Merion, Pa.: privately printed, 1961; copy at HSP). For editions of diaries by two other women who lived in Philadelphia during the revolutionary era, see Catherine La Courreye Blecki and Karin Wulf, eds., *Milcah Martha Moore's Book: A Commonplace Book from Revolutionary America* (University Park: Pennsylvania State University Press, 1997); and Susan E. Klepp and Karin Wulf, eds., *The Diary of Hannah Callender Sansom: Sense and Sensibility in the Age of the American Revolution* (Ithaca, N.Y.: Cornell University Press, 2010).

For essays about Elizabeth Drinker, see Kenneth A. Radbill, "The Ordeal of Elizabeth Drinker," *PH* 47 (1980): 147–72; Elaine F. Crane, "The World of Elizabeth Drinker," *PMHB* 107 (1983): 3–28; Sarah Blank Dine, "The Diary of Elizabeth Drinker: An American Legacy," *Documentary Editing* 9 (1987): 1–5; Susan Branson, "Elizabeth

Drinker: Quaker Values and Federalist Support in the 1790s," *PH* 68 (2001): 465–82; Sarah Blank Dine, "Diaries and Doctors: Elizabeth Drinker and Philadelphia Medical Practice, 1760–1810," *PH* 68 (2001): 413–34; Alison Duncan Hirsch, "Uncovering 'the Hidden History of Mestizo America' in Elizabeth Drinker's Diary: Interracial Relationships in Late-Eighteenth-Century Philadelphia," *PH* 68 (2001): 483–506; Debra M. O'Neal, "Elizabeth Drinker and Her 'Lone' Women: Domestic Service, Debilities, and (In)Dependence through the Eyes of a Philadelphia Gentlewoman," *PH* 68 (2001): 435–64; Wendy Lucas Castro, "'Being Separated from My Dearest Husband, in This Cruel Manner': Elizabeth Drinker and the Seven-Month Exile of Philadelphia Quakers," *Quaker History* 100 (2011): 40–63; and Desiree Henderson, "'The Impudent Fellow Came in Swaring': Constructing and Defending Quaker Community in Elizabeth Drinker's Diary," in Michele Lise Tarter and Catie Gill, eds., *New Critical Studies on Early Quaker Women, 1650–1800* (Oxford: Oxford University Press, 2018), 146–63. For Ph.D. and M.A. theses that focus partially or wholly on Elizabeth Drinker, see Linda Ringer, "Seven Women Diarists of Eighteenth-Century Philadelphia" (Ph.D. diss., Oklahoma State University, 1987); Susan Branson, "Politics and Gender: The Political Consciousness of Philadelphia Women in the 1790s" (Ph.D. diss., Northern Illinois University, 1992); Debra M. O'Neal, "Mistresses and Maids: The Transformation of Women's Domestic Labor and Household Relations in Late Eighteenth-Century Philadelphia" (Ph.D. diss., University of California, Riverside, 1994); and Stephanie N. Patterson Gilbert, "Childbearing Cycles and Family Limitation in an Eighteenth-Century Affluent Household: The Fertility Transition of Elizabeth Sandwith Drinker and Her Daughters" (M.A. thesis, Pennsylvania State University, Harrisburg, 2005).

For essays about Henry Drinker, see David W. Maxey, "The Union Farm: Henry Drinker's Experiment in Deriving Profit from Virtue," *PMHB* 107 (1983): 607–29; and David W. Maxey, "Of Castles in Stockport and Other Strictures: Samuel Preston's Contentious Agency for Henry Drinker," *PMHB* 110 (1986): 413–46.

This book joins several recent biographies of eighteenth-century Quakers, including Thomas P. Slaughter, *The Beautiful Soul of John Woolman, Apostle of Abolition* (New York: Hill and Wang, 2008); Maurice Jackson, *Let This Voice Be Heard: Anthony Benezet, Father of Atlantic Abolitionism* (Philadelphia: University of Pennsylvania Press, 2009); Geoffrey Plank, *John Woolman's Path to the Peaceable Kingdom: A Quaker in the British Empire* (Philadelphia: University of Pennsylvania Press, 2012); Gary B. Nash, *Warner Mifflin: Unflinching Quaker Abolitionist* (Philadelphia: University of Pennsylvania Press, 2017); and Marcus Rediker, *The Fearless Benjamin Lay: The Quaker Dwarf Who Became the First Revolutionary Abolitionist* (Boston: Beacon Press, 2017). However, none of these books tells the life of a Quaker woman or a Quaker couple; for a less recent but imaginative and thought-provoking study that does do so, see Cristine Levenduski, *Peculiar Power: A Quaker Woman Preacher in Eighteenth-Century America* (Washington, D.C.: Smithsonian Institution Press, 1996). For recent biographies of Early American women who were not Quakers, see Allan Greer, *Mohawk Saint:*

Catherine Tekakwitha and the Jesuits (New York: Oxford University Press, 2005); Jon F. Sensbach, *Rebecca's Revival: Creating Black Christianity in the Atlantic World* (Cambridge, Mass.: Harvard University Press, 2005); Marla R. Miller, *Betsy Ross and the Making of America* (New York: Henry Holt, 2010); Catherine A. Brekus, *Sarah Osborn's World: The Rise of Evangelical Christianity in Early America* (New Haven: Yale University Press, 2013); Ann M. Little, *The Many Captivities of Esther Wheelwright* (New Haven: Yale University Press, 2016); and Scott Paul Gordon, *The Letters of Mary Penry: A Single Moravian Woman in Early America* (University Park: Pennsylvania State University Press, 2018).

13. For examples of stricken responses to the death of loved ones, see Abigail Adams to Thomas Jefferson, May 20, 1804, in Lester J. Cappon, ed., *The Adams-Jefferson Papers* (New York: Simon and Schuster, 1971), 169; John Adams to Abigail Adams, Oct. 13, 1775, July 28, 1777, in Margaret A. Hogan and C. James Taylor, eds., *"My Dearest Friend": Letters of Abigail and John Adams* (Cambridge, Mass.: Harvard University Press, 2007), 81, 190; Martha Washington to Fanny Bassett Washington, Mar. 9, 1794, and to Tobias Lear, Mar. 30, 1796, in Joseph E. Fields, ed., *"Worthy Partner": The Papers of Martha Washington* (Westport, Conn.: Greenwood Press, 1994), 261, 291; and John G. Jackson to Molley Madison, Oct. 8, 1808, in David B. Mattern and Holly C. Shulman, ed., *Selected Letters of Molley Payne Madison* (Charlottesville: University of Virginia Press, 2003), 89. For studies of health care in the eighteenth century, see chap. 2, n29.

14. *DED*, 597, 2061 (Sept. 23, 1794, Aug. 1, 1807).

15. ED's diary, along with most of her surviving letters and the bulk of HD's correspondence, are on deposit at the HSP. Additional correspondence is on deposit at the FHL, QSC, and APS.

16. For example, though we know that ED and HD had nine children together, almost no information survives about the nature of their sexual relationship. Writing to a recently married friend, HD did refer jokingly in a 1775 letter to "the old doctrine of taking down wives in their wedding shoes," that is, establishing sexual control over a wife right at the start of a marriage, though he warned against "stretching the prerogative" too far. Whether HD understood his sexual relations with ED in this way is impossible to tell: their marriage was clearly framed in hierarchical terms, yet it was also loving and affectionate, which may equally have been reflected in their sexual relations; HD to Joseph Smith, Sept. 7, 1775, HSDP; and Elizabeth A. Foyster, *Manhood in Early Modern England: Honour, Sex, and Marriage* (London: Longman, 1999), 195.

We also know remarkably little about ED's relationship with her unmarried sister, Mary, who lived with the Drinkers throughout their marriage, though it is clear that HD and the five Drinker children were very fond of MS. ED's attitude seems at times to have been more ambivalent, though references to MS in her diary are for the most part more tantalizing than truly revealing.

17. That September, HD complained in a letter to Frederick Pigou that "government" had contributed to widespread and prolonged economic malaise that affected "all ranks of people" by allowing the "evil practice" of paying debts in depreciated currency, but he made no mention of the proposed restructuring of government that Federalists promised would address this and other economic problems. Indeed, the only comfort he drew was from the fine harvest that year in Pennsylvania, though this "favorable circumstance" would, he feared, "fall very short of affording full relief either to the country or the city trader." In December 1787, three days after Pennsylvania ratified the federal constitution, HD wrote that neither Britain nor France seemed prepared for war, whatever the tensions between them, a relief to "all lovers of peace." Yet he wrote not a word about dramatic events closer to home; HD to Frederick Pigou Jr., Sept. 3, 1787, and to Joseph Sandwith, Dec. 15, 1787, HD LB 1786–90.

18. *DED*, 106, 219, 1253 (Aug. 31, 1763, Sept. 13, 1776, Dec. 31, 1799); *Poulson's American Daily Advertiser*, Dec. 2, 1807; silhouettes at HSP.

19. *DED*, 612, 1252, 1885 (Oct. 28, 1794, Dec. 31, 1799, Dec. 13, 1805). For examples of Philadelphians sharing their journals, see *DED*, 58, 60, 510, 2085 (May 20, June 2, 1760, Sept. 27, 1793, Oct. 10, 1807). For ED's use of French, see also Henderson, "'Impudent Fellow,'" 156–57.

20. *DED*, 1253, 1274, 1688 (Dec. 31, 1799, Feb. 12, 1800, Sept. 29, 1803).

21. *DED*, 612 (Oct. 28, 1794). For the diary's recording and even creation of community, see Henderson, "'Impudent Fellow,'" esp. 161–63.

22. *DED*, 1243 (Dec. 2, 1799).

23. For two thoughtful essays about biography and microhistory, see Jill Lepore, "Historians Who Love Too Much: Reflections on Microhistory and Biography," *Journal of American History* 88 (2001): 129–44; and Richard D. Brown, "Microhistory and the Post-Modern Challenge," *Journal of the Early Republic* 23 (2003): 1–20.

24. *DED*, 1074, 2034 (Aug. 28, 1798, May 8, 1807); HD to Warner Mifflin, July 15, 1790, HD LB 1790–93; HD to ED, Oct. 23, 1791, DSP, 4:18. For AJ and HD's dealings with the sugar islands, see chap. 2. For scholarship on Quakers and slavery, see chap. 7, n7.

25. HD to George Bowne, Aug. 24, 1790, HD LB 1790–93; HD to Bowne, Jan. 21, 1795, HD LB 1793–96; HD to William Dillwyn, June 18, 1807, HD LB 1806–9.

26. *DED*, 795 (Apr. 22, 1796); Jan Lewis, "The Republican Wife: Virtue and Seduction in the Early Republic," *William and Mary Quarterly*, 3rd ser., 44 (1987): esp. 707, 712–13; Nancy Cott, *Public Vows: A History of Marriage and the Nation* (Cambridge, Mass.: Harvard University Press, 2000), esp. 17. For other marriages in which educated and informed women accommodated patriarchy, albeit sometimes reluctantly, see Sheila Skemp, *Judith Sargent Murray: A Brief Biography with Documents* (Boston: Bedford, 1998); Rosemarie Zagarri, *A Woman's Dilemma: Mercy Otis Warren and the American Revolution* (Wheeling, Ill.: Harlan Davidson, 1995); and G. J. Barker-Benfield, *Abigail and John Adams: The Americanization of Sensibility* (Chicago: University of Chicago Press, 2010). For scholarship on Quaker women, see chap. 5, n5.

Chapter 1. "A Cornerstone to My Love-Fabric"

1. By 1790, New York's population would in turn outstrip Philadelphia's. For the flooding on Water Street, see *DED,* 1289 (Apr. 6, 1800).

2. Indenture of HD to George James, DSP, 1:17; HD, Journal of a Voyage to England, Sept. 1, 1759, DSP, 1:22–26.

3. J&D to William Neate, Aug. 22, 1759, J&D LB 1759–62; Anthony Benezet to Jonas Thompson, Aug. 28, 1759, Miscellaneous Manuscripts Collection, FHL. For more on Benezet, see Maurice Jackson, *Let This Voice Be Heard: Anthony Benezet, Father of Atlantic Abolitionism* (Philadelphia: University of Pennsylvania Press, 2009).

4. Journal of a Voyage to England, Sept. 1, 1759; note by ED, n.d., DSP, 4:115.

5. Journal of a Voyage to England, Sept. 1–7, 1759; HD to Elizabeth Sandwith, Jan. 1, 1760, DSP, 2:42.

6. Journal of a Voyage to England, Sept. 14, 15, 18, 1759; HD to Elizabeth Sandwith, Jan. 1, 1760, DSP, 2:42.

7. HD to Elizabeth Sandwith, Dec. 11, 24, 1759, DSP, 1:27. This is not to suggest that love was absent from earlier courtships. Puritans, for example, laid great stress on love and sexual attraction as components of a healthy marriage, for which see Richard Godbeer, *Sexual Revolution in Early America* (Baltimore: Johns Hopkins University Press, 2002), chap. 2. Yet the eighteenth-century emphasis on romance and companionship as key to a successful marriage did represent a significant shift in tone. For the rise of romantic courtship, see Lawrence Stone, *The Family, Sex, and Marriage in England, 1500–1800* (London: Weidenfeld and Nicolson, 1977); Daniel Scott Smith, "Parental Power and Marriage Patterns: An Analysis of Historical Trends in Hingham, Massachusetts," *Journal of Marriage and the Family* 34 (1973): esp. 426; Ellen Rothman, *Hands and Hearts: A History of Courtship in America* (New York: Basic Books, 1984); John Gillis, *For Better, for Worse: British Marriages, 1600 to the Present* (New York: Oxford University Press, 1985); Karen Lystra, *Searching the Heart: Men, Women, and Romantic Love in Nineteenth-Century America* (New York: Oxford University Press, 1989); Martha Tomhave Blauvelt, "Making a Match in Nineteenth-Century New York: The Courtship Diary of Mary Guion," *New York History* 76 (1995): 153–72; Nicole Eustace, " 'The Cornerstone of a Copious Work': Love and Power in Eighteenth-Century Courtship," *Journal of Social History* 34 (2001): 517–46; and Ruth H. Bloch, "Changing Conceptions of Sexuality and Romance in Eighteenth-Century America," *William and Mary Quarterly,* 3rd ser., 60 (2003): 13–42. See also Alan Macfarlane's review essay in *History and Theory* 18 (1979): 103–26, for an example of the reservations that some British historians have expressed about Stone's thesis.

8. HD to MS, Jan. 3, 1760, DSP, 2:43.

9. *DED,* 83 (Dec. 9, 1760). A dramatic increase in sexual intimacy between courting couples during these years and widespread concern about premarital pregnancy gave older adults additional justification for involvement in the courtship process,

though there is no evidence to suggest that Henry and Elizabeth gave those around them any cause for anxiety on this account; see Godbeer, *Sexual Revolution,* chap. 7. Contemporaries often shared accounts of their travels with friends and relatives back home. When Samuel Samson Jr. returned from England in the spring of 1760, Elizabeth read parts of his travel journal and went to look at some of the "prospective views" that he had drawn or painted during his time abroad; *DED,* 56–58, 60 (May 7, 14, 20, June 3, 1760).

10. For an example of this sexual adventurism, see Louis B. Wright and Marion Tinling, eds., *William Byrd of Virginia: The London Diary (1717–1721) and Other Writings* (New York: Oxford University Press, 1958).

11. For cultural critiques of libertinism, including its association with a distinctly aristocratic sensibility, see Michael McKeon, *The Origins of the English Novel, 1600–1740* (Baltimore: Johns Hopkins University Press, 1987).

12. John Drinker to HD, n.d. 1759, DSP, 1:21; Journal of a Voyage to England, Sept. 1, 1759. For the ethos of companionate marriage, see Jan Lewis, "The Republican Wife: Virtue and Seduction in the Early Republic," *William and Mary Quarterly,* 3rd ser., 44 (1987): 689–721.

13. HD to Elizabeth Sandwith, Dec. 11, 24, 1759, DSP, 1:27.

14. HD to Elizabeth Sandwith, Jan. 1, 1760, DSP, 2:42; Sansom and Swett to HD, Jan. 22, 1760, Daniel Mildred to HD, Jan. 22, Nov. 23, 1760, and William Neate to HD, Feb. 4, 1760, HSDP. HD imagined in his journal a conversation between his partner, AJ, and other Friends attending the Yearly Meeting in Philadelphia. One of them avowed that HD's marriage was "not far from being fixed. At least our Monthly Meeting have guarded the wording [of] his certificate as if etc., etc." According to this, HD had already persuaded fellow Friends to prepare paperwork for his espousal in hope that Elizabeth would eventually agree to wed him. Journal of a Voyage to England, Sept. 29, 1759.

15. HD to Elizabeth Sandwith, Jan. 1, 1760, DSP, 2:42.

16. HD to Elizabeth Sandwith, Dec. 11, 24, 1759, DSP, 1:27. See also Eustace, "'Cornerstone of a Copious Work,'" esp. 518.

17. *DED,* 30, 51 (Sept. 1, 3, 1759, Mar. 21, 1760); Journal of a Voyage to England, Sept. 29, Oct. 11, 1769 (see also Oct. 6, 9, 14, 1769).

18. See Lisa Wilson, *Ye Heart of a Man: The Domestic Life of Men in Colonial New England* (New Haven: Yale University Press, 1999), chap. 2; and Kenneth A. Lockridge, *On the Sources of Patriarchal Rage: The Commonplace Books of William Byrd and Thomas Jefferson and the Gendering of Power in the Eighteenth Century* (New York: New York University Press, 1992).

19. Ann Swett to Elizabeth Sandwith, n.d., DSP, 2:23a, 24b.

20. Ann Swett to Elizabeth Sandwith, n.d., DSP, 2:22; Elizabeth Moode to Sandwith, Mar. 11, 1755 [original letter in French, translated by author], DSP, 2:32.

21. Elizabeth Moode to Elizabeth Sandwith, Feb. 14, 1760, DSP, 2:44.

22. Before the older Joseph's marriage with Ruth Balch (whose grandparents were founding settlers in Salem Town and on Cape Ann) in or around 1683, he had spent time working farther south in the region that became Pennsylvania in 1682. There he sired a son named Edward, almost certainly with a woman other than Ruth; that son was born in 1680 and died 102 years later, famous in Philadelphia for having reached such a prodigious age. ED mentioned in her diary that HD and their son William attended the burial of HD's great-uncle Edward; *DED*, 406 (Nov. 19, 1782).

23. The couple did not wed at a Quaker Meeting and Henry's parents had not consented to the match, but Henry and Mary clearly raised their children within the Quaker faith and Henry's father, Joseph, named him in his will, so that at some point a reconciliation must have taken place between parents and son. Joseph Drinker died in 1742, but Mary Janney Drinker lived on for another two decades: she died in 1764 at the age of eighty-three.

24. See Hannah Benner Roach, comp., "Taxables in the City of Philadelphia, 1756," *Pennsylvania Genealogical Magazine* 22 (1961): 3–41; and Gary B. Nash and Billy G. Smith, "Philadelphia Tax List 1756," *Magazine of Early American Datasets* (Philadelphia: McNeil Center for Early American Studies, http://repository.upenn.edu).

25. J&D to [?], May 15, 1756, J&D LB 1756–59; J&D to David Barclay and Sons, July 1, 1760, J&D LB 1759–62.

26. *DED*, 863 (Nov. 29, 1796); see also Benjamin Say, *A Short Compilation of the Extraordinary Life and Writings of Thomas Say* (Philadelphia, 1796), 10.

27. *DED*, 82, 85, 1055 (Nov. 28, Dec. 26, 1760, July 20, 1798). For the lives of single women in eighteenth-century Philadelphia, see Karin Wulf, *Not All Wives: Women of Colonial Philadelphia* (Ithaca, N.Y.: Cornell University Press, 2000).

28. *DED*, 34 (Sept. 26, 1759).

29. Elizabeth Moode to Elizabeth Sandwith, June 30, 1759, DSP, 2:38b.

30. *DED*, 62–66, 1290 (June 20–22, 24–30, July 2–4, 6, 7, 10, 13, 15–18, 1760, Apr. 10, 1800).

31. *DED*, 66–67, 77, 78, 81, 85 (July 19–28, Oct. 15, 22, Nov. 22, Dec. 22, 1760).

32. HD and ED to MS, Sept. 7, 1764, DSP, 2:56; *DED*, 1253 (Dec. 31, 1799). Susannah Swett, the mother of HD's first wife, came to live with the Drinkers for more than a year after her husband's death in 1775.

33. HD to MS, Jan. 3, 1760, DSP, 2:43.

34. *DED*, 72, 87–88 (Sept. 5, 1760, Jan. 6–12, 1761); HD to MS, Nov. 3, 1760, DSP, 2:46.

35. See esp. Jack D. Marietta, *The Reformation of American Quakerism, 1748–1783* (Philadelphia: University of Pennsylvania Press, 1984).

36. Elizabeth Moode to Elizabeth Sandwith, undated poem, and June 30, 1759, DSP, 2:31, 38b. See Cassandra A. Good, *Founding Friendships: Friendships between Men and Women in the Early American Republic* (New York: Oxford University Press, 2015); Richard Godbeer, *The Overflowing of Friendship: Love between Men and the Creation*

of the American Republic (Baltimore: Johns Hopkins University Press, 2009); Naomi Tadmor, *Family and Friends in Eighteenth-Century England* (New York: Cambridge University Press, 2001); Anya Jabour, *Marriage in the Early Republic: Elizabeth and William Wirt and the Companionate Ideal* (Baltimore: Johns Hopkins University Press, 1998); and Carroll Smith-Rosenberg, "The Female World of Love and Ritual: Relations between Women in Nineteenth-Century America," in *Disorderly Conduct: Visions of Gender in Victorian America* (New York: Knopf, 1985), 53–76.

37. Ann Swett to Elizabeth Sandwith, n.d., DSP, 2:24b; Elizabeth Moode to Sandwith, undated poems, DSP, 2:31, 41.

38. Elizabeth Moode to Elizabeth Sandwith, undated poem, and June 30, 1759, Feb. 14, 1760, DSP, 2:31, 38b, 44; *DED*, 1698 (Oct. 23, 1803).

39. *DED*, 44, 45 (Jan. 20, 27, 1760).

40. *DED*, 35 (Oct. 6, 1759).

41. ED mentioned the deaths of both these teachers in her diary; *DED*, 55, 422 (Apr. 28, 1760, May 4, 1784). ED's obituary described her education as "much superior to what was common for young ladies in this country sixty years ago"; *Poulson's American Daily Advertiser*, Dec. 2, 1807.

42. *DED*, 40, 47, 83 (Nov. 25, Dec. 4, 1759, Feb. 8, Dec. 9, 1760).

43. *DED*, 37, 47, 48, 62 (Nov. 1, 1759, Feb. 13, 20, 22, June 16, 1760). For gardens as a site for courtship, see Godbeer, *Overflowing of Friendship*, 44–45.

44. *DED*, 1–3 ("Work done in part of the Years: 1757, 1758, 1759, 1760"), 6, 27, 35 (Nov. 20, 1758, Aug. 6, Oct. 11, 1759). Many of ED's entries about excursions to local stores mentioned buying materials necessary for her needlework; e.g., *DED*, 10, 14, 25, 36, 38, 45 (Jan. 13, 16, Mar. 22, July 13, Oct. 20, Nov. 6, 1759, Jan. 26, 1760).

45. *DED*, 17, 20, 34–35, 37, 42, 45, 52, 54, 55, 57, 81 (Apr. 17, May 25, Oct. 5, 14, 26, Dec. 27, 1759, Jan. 22, Mar. 28, Apr. 15, 24, May 8, Nov. 20, 1760). For a detailed discussion of Quaker marital procedures, see chap. 8.

46. *DED*, 3, 12, 14, 18, 32, 35, 57, 61, 71, 83 (Oct. 8, 1758, Feb. 17, Mar. 15, Apr. 29, Sept. 17, Oct. 5, 1759, May 8, June 11, Aug. 28, Dec. 7, 1760). For birthing practices in the early republic, see Laurel Thatcher Ulrich, *A Midwife's Tale: The Life of Martha Ballard, Based on Her Diary, 1785–1812* (New York: Knopf, 1990), chap. 5.

47. *DED*, 10, 82 (Jan. 18, 1759, Dec. 6, 1760). In 1795, ED's twenty-one-year-old daughter Mary would stay up all night with her older sister, Ann, while she gave birth, but this was, as ED wrote, "a new scene to Molly"; *DED*, 728 (Sept. 12, 1795).

48. *DED*, 31–32, 33, 36, 39, 53, 55, 98, 1232, 1644, 1819 (Sept. 13, 18, Oct. 24, Nov. 13, 1759, Apr. 5, 22, 1760, Dec. 2, 11, 13, 15, 24, 1762, Oct. 31, 1799, Apr. 20, 1803, Mar. 23, 1805). See Sarah Blank Dine, "Inoculation, Patients, and Physicians: The Transformation of Medical Practice in Philadelphia, 1730–1810," *Transactions and Studies of the College of Physicians of Philadelphia*, 5th ser., 20 (1998): 67–93; and Peter Razzell, *The Conquest of Smallpox: The Impact of Inoculation on Smallpox Mortality in Eighteenth-*

Century Britain (Firle, U.K.: Caliban Books, 1977), 113–37. For more on ED's support of medical innovations, especially with regard to childbirth, see chap. 8.

49. It is unclear where HD was living at this time. He was apparently very close to his grandmother Mary Janney Drinker, but in a letter to Mary Sandwith he referred to a cold remedy given him by his "good landlady." It seems unlikely that he would have referred to his grandmother in this way. He may have been living with the family of AJ, in which case it would not have been odd for him to describe Rebecca James in this way. See HD to Mary Sandwith, Nov. 3, 1760, DSP, 2:46.

50. J&D to John Clitherall, Dec. 1, 1759, to William Neate, May 21, 1760, and to John Lindoe, Aug. 22, 1760, J&D LB 1759–62. George Dillwyn, who purchased products from the ironworks in which HD became a part owner for sale in his own store, described himself to HD in a 1782 letter as "a less profitable than affectionate customer," signing off as "thy sympathizing fellow traveler." However frustrating he may have been as a customer, the bond of spiritual affection was for him of paramount importance; George Dillwyn to HD, March 1, 1782, Balderston Family Papers, FHL. For mercantile networks, see Thomas M. Doerflinger, *A Vigorous Spirit of Enterprise: Merchants and Economic Development in Revolutionary Philadelphia* (Chapel Hill: University of North Carolina Press, 1986); Natasha Glaisyer, "Networking: Trade and Exchange in the Eighteenth-Century British Empire," *Historical Journal* 47 (2004): 451–76; and Jordan Landes, *London Quakers in the Trans-Atlantic World* (London: Palgrave Macmillan, 2015).

51. J&D to Pigou and Booth, Mar. 5, 1776, J&D FL 1772–85. See also Doerflinger, *Vigorous Spirit of Enterprise*, 58–62.

52. HD to John Pemberton, Dec. 10, 1782, May 29, 1783, Dec. 21, 1785, Dec. 11, 1787, May 24, 1788, DSP, 1:35, 37, 40, 41, 43; HD to Nicholas Waln, Apr. 17, 1784, Nicholas Waln Family Papers, 1783–1895, QSC.

53. John Drinker to HD, n.d. 1759, DSP, 1:21.

54. John Drinker, poem for HD, n.d., DSP, 6:1; *DED*, 82 (Nov. 28, 1760). Internal evidence indicates that John was himself a bachelor when writing; he married in 1756, so he probably wrote the poem in or before that year. For rising premarital pregnancy rates, see Godbeer, *Sexual Revolution*, chap. 7.

55. J&D to Edmund Jenney, Oct. 26, 1760, J&D LB 1759–62; *DED*, 84, 85, 87 (Dec. 19, 24, 26, 1760, Jan. 5, 1761).

56. *DED*, 88 (Jan. 9, 1761).

57. The official record of their union declared as follows: "Whereas Henry Drinker of the City of Philadelphia in the Province of Pennsylvania, merchant, son of Henry Drinker, late of the said city, deceased, and Elizabeth Sandwith of the same place, daughter of William Sandwith, late of Philadelphia aforesaid, deceased, having declared their intentions of marriage with each other before several Monthly Meetings of the people called Quakers at Philadelphia aforesaid, according to the good order used among them, and having consent of relations and friends concerned, their said

proposals of marriage were allowed of by the said Meeting. Now these are to certify whom it may concern that for their full accomplishing their said intentions this thirteenth day of the first month in the year of our Lord one thousand seven hundred and sixty-one, they, the said Henry Drinker and Elizabeth Sandwith, appeared in a public meeting of the said people at Philadelphia aforesaid, and the said Henry Drinker, taking the said Elizabeth Sandwith by the hand, did in a solemn manner openly declare that he took her, the said Elizabeth Sandwith, to be his wife, promising through the Lord's assistance to be unto her a loving and faithful husband until death should separate them. And then and there in the same assembly the said Elizabeth Sandwith did in like manner declare that she took him, the said Henry Drinker, to be her husband, promising through the Lord's assistance to be unto him a loving and faithful wife until death should separate them. And moreover, they, the said Henry Drinker and Elizabeth Sandwith (she according to the custom of marriage assuming the name of her husband), as a further confirmation thereof, did then and there to these presents set their hands. And we whose names are here under also subscribed, being present at the solemnization of the said marriage and subscription, have as witnesses thereunto set our hands the day and year above written." Marriage Certificate of Henry Drinker and Elizabeth Sandwith, Jan. 13, 1761, DSP, 6:7.

Chapter 2. "Tenderness, Care, and Anxiety" at Home and Abroad

1. Isaac Weld, *Travels through the States of North America . . .* (London, 1799), 6; Abraham Ritter, *Philadelphia and Her Merchants* (Philadelphia: published by author, 1860); Harry Kyriakodis, *Philadelphia's Lost Waterfront* (Charleston, S.C.: History Press, 2011), chap. 17.

2. *DED,* 360, 425, 499 (Sept. 26, 1779, July 20, 1784, Sept. 2, 1793); Ritter, *Philadelphia and Her Merchants,* 116–22; Cornelius William Stafford, *Philadelphia City Directory for 1801* (Philadelphia: William W. Stafford, 1801). According to HD's account book, he purchased this property in 1770 from the executors of Benjamin Shoemaker, whose death ED had noted in June 1767; HD JL 1776–91, 1; *DED,* 136 (June 29, 1767).

3. *DED,* 425, 1055 (July 20, 1784, July 20, 1798).

4. *DED,* 1957 (Aug. 21, 1806); see also 1935 (June 3, 1806).

5. HD to ED, July 2, 1771, DSP, 2:78a; Philadelphia Contributionship Insurance survey S01454, Nov. 6, 1770, Philadelphia Contributionship Digital Archives, http://www.philadelphiabuildings.org; advertisements for sale of 110 North Front Street, following HD's death, in *Poulson's American Daily Advertiser,* Nov. 15, 1809, and the *Democratic Press,* Nov. 13, 15, 1809.

6. *DED,* 498, 790, 832 (Aug. 30, 31, 1793, Apr. 10, Aug. 14, 1796).

7. For Sally Brant's pregnancy, see chap. 7. In the same year that the Drinkers purchased their home on Front Street, they also bought a much smaller house on Water Street that they rented out along with the wharf that came with the lot. In addition,

they owned a house in Strawberry Alley inherited by ED from her grandfather Martin Jervis, a stable in the Northern Liberties district of Philadelphia deeded to the Drinkers by AJ and his wife in 1774, another small lot in that same part of town purchased in 1771, a meadow lot on the Delaware River deeded by AJ and Rebecca James in the same year that they handed over the Northern Liberties lot, and more than five thousand acres of land in the colony of New York that HD and AJ bought together. In addition to Quarry Bank and Clearfield, they acquired two "plantations" in Kingtown, N.J. ("Retreat" and "Mount Carmel"), and another in Providence, Philadelphia County. HD also bought a sawmill and in 1773 became co-owner of the Atsion ironworks in New Jersey, having previously invested in another New Jersey ironworks venture at Brunswick in 1764. HD JL 1776–91, Jan. 19, 1776, July 13, 1784; "Fanny Saltar's Reminiscences of Colonial Days in Philadelphia," *PMHB* 40 (1916): 198; *DED*, 560, 565, 566 (May 24, June 14, 17, 1794). For a sketch of the Quarry Bank lot, see DSP, 1:57.

8. Philadelphia Yearly Meeting to Quarterly and Monthly Meetings, 7th month 17, 1737, QMR; Philadelphia Yearly Meeting Miscellaneous Papers, Epistles, QMR; Manuscript Discipline (Samuel Parson's copy), 1747, QMR; Philadelphia Monthly Meeting, Women's Minutes, 7th month 29, 1757, 2nd month 24, 1764, 5th month 30, 1766, QMR; *DED*, 799, 802, 1288, 1290, 1537 (May 3, 14, 1796, Apr. 4, 10, 1800, July 25, 1802); HD to Daniel Smith, July 5, 1763, HD LB 1762–86; Daniel Mildred to HD, Oct. 10, 1763, Mildred and Roberts to HD, Jan. 28, 1764, HSDP. See also Frederick B. Tolles, "Of the Best Sort but Plain," *American Quarterly* 11 (1959): 484–502; Emma Jones Lapsansky and Anne Verplank, eds., *Quaker Aesthetics: Reflections on a Quaker Ethic in American Design and Consumption, 1720–1920* (Philadelphia: University of Pennsylvania Press, 2002); Sarah Fatherly, *Gentlewomen and Learned Ladies: Women and Elite Formation in Eighteenth-Century Philadelphia* (Bethlehem, Pa.: Lehigh University Press, 2008), esp. chap. 2; and James Emmet Ryan, *Imaginary Friends: Representing Quakers in American Culture, 1650–1950* (Madison: University of Wisconsin Press, 2009), as well as Richard L. Bushman, *The Refinement of America: Persons, Houses, Cities* (New York: Knopf, 1992); and Catherine E. Kelly, *Republic of Taste: Art, Politics, and Everyday Life in Early America* (Philadelphia: University of Pennsylvania Press, 2016).

9. *DED*, 359, 696, 1411–13 (Sept. 14, 1779, Sept. 25, 1795, May 16, 19, 22, 1801), 1623 n10; see also Catherine Lynn, *Wallpaper in America: From the Seventeenth Century to World War I* (New York: Norton, 1980), 107–9, 154.

10. *DED*, 579, 1058–63 and n91, 1184, 1185, 1535, 1661, 1664 and n39, 1666, 1667, 1674, 1756, 1759, 1762, 1764–67, 1840–41, 1845, 1847, 1855, 1948, 1954–55, 1959, 2043, 2062 (Aug. 4, 1794, July 29–31, Aug. 2–4, 7, 1798, June 28, July 1, 1799, June 21, 1802, June 24, July 8, 14, 16, Aug. 10, 1803, July 16, Aug. 1, 20, Sept. 1, 4, 10, 17, 1804, June 17, 20, July 9, 13, Aug. 15, 1805, July 18, Aug. 7, 24, 1806, June 6, Aug. 7, 1807).

11. *DED*, 759–60, 886, 1080 (Dec. 12, 1795, Feb. 3, 1797, Sept. 8, 1798).

12. *DED*, 759, 808, 1342 (Dec. 12, 1795, May 31, 1796, Sept. 24, 1800).

13. HD to ED, June 20, 1762, Feb. 7, 1766, and ED to HD, n.d. and Aug. 15, 1770, DSP, 2:50, 62b, 74b, 76a; John O'Kely to HD, Mar. 3, 15, June 17, 1770, HSDP.

14. HD to ED, Sept. 3, 1762, and ED to HD, Feb. 3, 1766, Aug. 17, 1770, DSP, 2:49a, 63, 74a.

15. *DED,* 91, 92, 106, 116, 119, 120 (July 22, Aug. 4, 1762, Aug. 31, 1763, June 18, July 18, 19, 30, 1765).

16. ED to MS, July 13, 1771, DSP, 2:80a.

17. *DED,* 112–13, 153–56, 166–70, 183–84, 199–201 (Sept. 3–9, 1764, Sept. 10–22, 1770, Aug. 22–Sept. 5, 1771, Apr. 11–16, 1773, Apr. 27, May 7, June 10, 1774).

18. HD to ED, Jan. 26, 1766, DSP, 2:61; *DED,* 759, 1787 (Dec. 12, 1795, Dec. 27, 1804). For references in the diary to HD's negotiations over land sales, see *DED,* 548, 1010 (Mar. 12, 1794, Mar. 9, 1798). ED was also well aware of the land disputes in which her husband became embroiled, for which see chap. 6, and the bitter disagreements that arose over the Atsion ironworks, of which HD had become a co-owner, for which see chap. 9. On at least some occasions, HD did keep social and business conversations separate. ED mentioned in a 1796 entry that Robina Miller "came on business to HD" and that the two of them "adjourned" to the office where HD did most of his work at home. Their business done, they returned to the parlor; *DED,* 829 (Aug. 10, 1796).

19. "Diary of Ann Warder," Jan. 15, 1787, HSP; HD JL 1776–91, June 17, 1776; *DED,* 1797, 1895 (n.d., n.d.).

20. William Shippen Jr.'s ledger for 1775 through 1792 is in the Shippen Family Collection, LC (described in the catalog as Document Book); Shippen Jr.'s daybook for 1789 through 1791 is at the APS (described in the catalog as Recipe Book). See also Sarah Blank Dine, "Diaries and Doctors: Elizabeth Drinker and Philadelphia Medical Practice, 1760–1810," *PH* 68 (2001): 423–27.

21. *DED,* 198, 385–91, 893, 911, 919, 929, 1227 ("from March the 7 to April the 12," 1774, Apr. 5, 6, May 3, 4, 27, July 1, 18, 22, Aug. 9, Oct. 28, 1781, Feb. 25, 26, Apr. 26, May 17, June 14, 1797, Oct. 23, 1799).

22. For ED's miscarriages, see *DED,* 99, 139 (Feb. 6, 1763, May 26, 1768); she may have had another in May 1780: *DED,* 369 (May 20, 1780).

23. *DED,* 132, 420 (July 1, 2, 4, 1766, Mar. 13–17, 1784).

24. *DED,* 566, 593–95, 1245, 1432 (June 17, Sept. 16–18, 1794, Dec. 9, 1799, Aug. 4, 1801). Rebecca (Becky) James, the wife of HD's business partner, had four miscarriages that ED was aware of, and she also noted visiting two other neighbors, Mary Pleasants and Catherine Howell, soon after they miscarried; Catherine had been "very ill" afterward. Two of Becky's miscarriages and Catherine's occurred in 1763, the same year in which ED had her first miscarriage; *DED,* 99, 109, 117, 139, 360 (Mar. 24, Sept. 19, Dec. 3, 1763, July 1, 1765, June 3, 1768, Oct. 1, 1779).

25. Hannah Haydock to ED, Aug. 24, 1764, DSP, 2:55; HD to ED, Oct. 17, 1777, Jan. 25, 1778, DSP, 3:12, 32.

26. HD to Samuel Emlen, Sept. 20, 1766, HD LB 1762–86.

27. *DED*, 148, 332, 397–98, 415, 421, 437–38, 506, 650, 703, 778–79, 893, 1161, 1183, 1400, 1470, 1488, 1655, 1661, 1664, 1975 (Apr. 25, 1769, Oct. 19, 1778, Mar. 31, 1782, Sept. 19, 1783, Apr. 10, 1784, Aug. 1, 9, 1785, Sept. 16, 1793, Feb. 16, July 11, 1795, Feb. 23, 24, 1796, Feb. 25, 1797, Apr. 25, June 25, 1799, Apr. 10, Dec. 8, 1801, Jan. 26, 1802, June 5, 25, July 3, 1803, Oct. 24, 1806). For women's efforts to limit family size, see Susan E. Klepp, *Revolutionary Conceptions: Women, Fertility, and Family Limitation in America, 1760–1820* (Chapel Hill: University of North Carolina Press, 2009).

28. *DED*, 100, 104–6, 136–37, 139, 200 (June 20, Aug. 5, 23, 31, 1763, June 22–July 8, 1767, n.d., May 27, 1774); John O'Kely to HD, Nov. 4, 1770, HSDP; ED to Elizabeth Emlen, n.d., DSP, 2:65.

29. For eighteenth-century health care, see Richard Shyrock, *Medicine and Society in America, 1660–1860* (New York: New York University Press, 1960); David Freeman Hawke, *Benjamin Rush: Revolutionary Gadfly* (Indianapolis, Ind.: Bobbs-Merrill, 1971); Whitfield J. Bell Jr., *The Colonial Physician* (New York: Science History Publications, 1975); John Duffy, *The Healers: A History of American Medicine* (Urbana: University of Illinois Press, 1976); Laurel Thatcher Ulrich, *A Midwife's Tale: The Life of Martha Ballard, Based on Her Diary, 1785–1812* (New York: Knopf, 1990); Lamar Riley Murphy, *Enter the Physician: The Transformation of Domestic Medicine, 1760–1860* (Tuscaloosa: University of Alabama Press, 1991); Oscar Reiss, *Medicine in Colonial America* (Lanham, Md.: University Press of America, 2000); Rebecca J. Tannenbaum, *The Healer's Calling: Women and Medicine in Early New England* (Ithaca, N.Y.: Cornell University Press, 2002); Stanley Finger, *Doctor Franklin's Medicine* (Philadelphia: University of Pennsylvania Press, 2006); Elaine G. Breslaw, *Lotions, Potions, and Magic: Health Care in Early America* (New York: New York University Press, 2012); and Jeanne E. Abrams, *Revolutionary Medicine: The Founding Fathers and Mothers in Sickness and in Health* (New York: New York University Press, 2013).

30. *DED*, 12, 13 (Feb. 25, Mar. 1, 3, 5, 1759).

31. *DED*, 98, 99, 188, 345 (n.d., Feb. 6, 1763, Feb. 18, 1773, May 4–5, 1779); *Pennsylvania Gazette*, Dec. 2, 1762.

32. *DED*, 126, 127, 129 (Jan. 24, 25, Feb. 3, 17, 1766). See also Marylynn Salmon, "The Cultural Significance of Breastfeeding," *Journal of Social History* 28 (1994): 256; and Rebecca Larson, *Daughters of Light: Quaker Women Preaching and Prophesying in the Colonies and Abroad, 1700–1775* (Chapel Hill: University of North Carolina Press, 1999), 159.

33. For fatherhood in Early America, see esp. Lisa Wilson, *Ye Heart of a Man: The Domestic Life of Men in Colonial New England* (New Haven: Yale University Press, 1999), chap. 5; and Anne S. Lombard, *Making Manhood: Growing Up Male in Colonial New England* (Cambridge, Mass.: Harvard University Press, 2003), chap. 1.

34. *DED*, 111, 113, 162–64, 166, 170–72, 174, 178 (July 3, Oct. 23, 1764, July 13, 18, 22, 23, 28, Aug. 11, 19, Sept. 28, 29, Oct. 26, Nov. 17, 18, 21, Dec. 9, 1771, Feb. 1, July 20,

1772); HD to MS, Sept. 20, 1769, and ED to MS, July 13, 1771, DSP, 2:73a, 80a; HD to ED, Apr. 14, 1778, DSP, 3:52.

35. *DED*, 391 (Oct. 28, 1781); HD to MS, Nov. 10, 1776, and MS to ED, July 19, 1771, DSP, 2:80b, 85.

36. HD to ED, July 2, 1771, DSP, 2:78a; *DED*, 183, 197, 201–4, 210 (Apr. 9, Dec. 31, 1773, June 22, Aug. 12, 19, 20, 26, Oct. 6, 7, 1774, July 9, 1775).

37. Thomas P. Cope Diary ("My Mirror and Record of Events"), vol. 11, Mar. 17, 1851, QSC; HD to ED, Sept. 16, Oct. 14, Nov. 11, 1777, Jan. 25, 1778, DSP, 3:5, 11, 18, 32. See chap. 8 for tensions between the Drinkers and their children.

38. HD to ED, Sept. 20, 1777, DSP, 3:8. Nor was ED blind to what she saw as her children's less endearing characteristics. She informed HD in 1770 that Sally was "a chattering thing, whose tongue is always running, continually asking questions." The little girl was "much admired," but had "a pertness hanging round her," which their younger daughter Nancy was "entirely destitute of"; ED to HD, Aug. 28, 1770, DSP, 2:76b.

39. ED to HD, Feb. 3, 26, 1778, and HD to ED, Feb. 7, 1778, DSP, 3:36, 37.

40. HD JL 1776–91, Jan. 19, 1776.

41. J&D to John Clitherall, Sept. 3, 1762, J&D LB 1759–62; *Pennsylvania Gazette*, Oct. 1, 29, 1761, Jan. 10, 1765, Apr. 3, 1766. Bohea was a black oolong, Hyson a Chinese green tea.

42. J&D to William Pitt and George Hewm, Oct. 7, 1758, J&D LB 1756–59; J&D to Abraham and George White, Mar. 27, 1759, J&D LB 1759–62. Closer to home, J&D were eager to minimize the use of black labor, though for reasons that were far from humanitarian. In 1760, they wrote that they wished Pennsylvania "and indeed all the northern colonies" had fewer "negroes" because their presence encouraged white workers to think of physical labor as beneath their dignity: "wherever they are in great numbers, they bring labor into contempt with the whites, and as idleness follows, the consequent evils are beyond estimation"; J&D to William Fletcher and Co., Feb. 12, 1760, J&D LB 1759–62. See also Frank Griffith Dawson, "William Pitt's Settlement at Black River on the Mosquito Shore: A Challenge to Spain in Central America, 1732–87," *Hispanic American Historical Review* 63 (1983): 677–706; and David Eltis and David Richardson, *Atlas of the Transatlantic Slave Trade* (New Haven: Yale University Press, 2010). For more on the Drinkers' attitude toward slavery and people of color, see chap. 7.

43. HD to Joseph Sandwith, Nov. 27, 1762, HD LB 1762–86; J&D to Edward Spain, Aug. 4, 1774, HD FL 1772–85; *Pennsylvania Gazette*, July 31, 1760.

44. HD to Frederick Pigou Jr., Apr. 30, 1764, HD LB 1762–86.

45. James West, John Baynton, and J&D to Daniel Rees, Apr. 23, 1756, J&D LB 1756–59.

46. J&D to John Clitherall, July 27, 1756, and to [?], Sept. 4, 1756, J&D LB 1756–59; J&D to William Neate, Mar. 2, 1759, J&D LB 1759–62.

47. J&D to George Carr, Apr. 21, 1758, and to Daniel Rees, Apr. 21, 1758, J&D LB 1756–59. William Neate negotiated with the government in London on J&D's behalf to secure payment for use of the *Concord;* J&D to William Neate, Nov. 2, 1758, J&D LB 1756–59.

48. J&D to Edward Spain, June 23, 1758, to Nathaniel Falconer, June 24, 1758, and to Daniel Rees, Nov. 27, 1758, J&D LB 1756–59; J&D to Edmund Jenney, June 26, 1760, and to Rees, Aug. 14, 1760, J&D LB 1759–62.

49. J&D to John Clitherall, May 9, 1760, to Thomas and John Randle Phillips, July 25, 1761, and to David Barclay and Sons, Aug. 22, 1761, J&D LB 1759–62. Even as the war with France seemed to be winding down, so rumors began to circulate of war with Spain, which belatedly entered the fray as an ally of France in 1762. One of J&D's ships was on its way to Jamaica and now faced the possibility of attack by Spanish vessels if news of war reached the region; J&D to David and Thomas Beveridge, Apr. 5, 1762, J&D LB 1759–62.

Chapter 3. "Obliged to Wade through This Sea of Politics"

1. HD to Frederick Pigou Jr., Apr. 30, 1764, HD LB 1762–86.

2. J&D to David Barclay and Sons, Oct. 20, 1764, and to Neate, Pigou, and Booth, Nov. 6, 1764, J&D LB 1764–66.

3. Alan Tully, *Forming American Politics* (Baltimore: Johns Hopkins University Press, 1994), chap. 7; Jack D. Marietta, *The Reformation of American Quakerism, 1748–1783* (Philadelphia: University of Pennsylvania Press, 1984). Tully characterizes the blend of impulses that shaped Quaker political strategy as "civic Quakerism."

4. During the French and Indian War, J&D lobbied through their business associates in London for the Admiralty to have warships accompany and defend colonial trading vessels as they sailed southward to the Caribbean. Indeed, they went so far as to hope that British warships would "thin" the French privateers so that their own ships would be less vulnerable on arrival in the region. See J&D to David Barclay and Sons, May 19, 1762, and to [?], July 2, 1762, J&D LB 1759–62. This was consistent with the position taken by earlier Quakers that the state should protect its citizens even if those same citizens would not fight themselves for reasons of conscience. Even after many Friends committed themselves to a much more comprehensive version of their peace testimony, refusing to do anything that would support warfare, AJ was still willing to serve in 1755 and 1764 as a signer of paper money issued in part to fund military campaigns defending the colony, and in 1771, he endorsed currency intended to pay for fortifications that would defend Philadelphia. Yet he was firmly opposed to the violent tactics used by some protesters to further their cause in the 1760s and 1770s. Paper money became the focus of controversy repeatedly during the revolutionary period. Parliament's Currency Acts of 1751 and 1764 caused much anger among colonists by seeking to prevent the use of depreciated colonial currency to pay British merchants and other creditors. Quakers later came under attack for refusing to accept continental

currency, which they saw as intended primarily to support the War for Independence. Patriots accused some individuals of conniving to bring about the depreciation of continental currency and established an official exchange rate for the payment of debts in British sterling, threatening those who refused to comply.

5. Tully, *Forming American Politics*, chap. 7; Jane E. Calvert, *Quaker Constitutionalism and the Political Thought of John Dickinson* (New York: Cambridge University Press, 2009), chaps. 3, 4; Hermann Wellenreuther, "The Political Dilemma of the Quakers in Pennsylvania, 1681–1748," *PMHB* 94 (1970): 135–72.

6. For a detailed narrative of this crisis and its aftermath, see Kevin Kenny, *Peaceable Kingdom Lost: The Paxton Boys and the Destruction of William Penn's Holy Experiment* (New York: Oxford University Press, 2009).

7. "Declaration," in John R. Dunbar, ed., *The Paxton Papers* (The Hague: Martinus Nijhoff, 1957), 101, 104; *The Journals of Henry Melchior Muhlenberg*, trans. Theodore G. Tappert and John W. Toberstein, 3 vols. (Philadelphia: Muhlenberg 1942–58), 1:18–20.

8. For growing unrest and resentment among laborers and artisans in urban seaports, see Charles S. Olton, *Artisans for Independence: Philadelphia Mechanics and the American Revolution* (Syracuse, N.Y.: Syracuse University Press, 1975); Gary Nash, *The Urban Crucible: Social Change, Political Consciousness, and the Origins of the American Revolution* (Cambridge, Mass.: Harvard University Press, 1979); Steven Rosswurm, *Arms, Country, and Class: The Philadelphia Militia and the "Lower Sort" during the American Revolution* (New Brunswick, N.J.: Rutgers University Press, 1987); and Ronald Schultz, *The Republic of Labor: Philadelphia Artisans and the Politics of Class, 1720–1830* (New York: Oxford University Press, 1993).

9. HD to Frederick Pigou Jr., Apr. 30, 1764, HD LB 1762–86. See T. H. Breen, *The Marketplace of Revolution: How Consumer Politics Shaped American Independence* (New York: Oxford University Press, 2004).

10. Calvert, *Quaker Constitutionalism*; Sarah Crabtree, *Holy Nation: The Transatlantic Quaker Ministry in an Age of Revolution* (Chicago: University of Chicago Press, 2015).

11. William Tennent, "To the Ladies of South Carolina," *South Carolina Gazette*, Aug. 2, 1774; Caroline Gilman, ed., *Letters of Eliza Wilkinson* (New York: Samuel Colman, 1839), 17; Sarah Logan Fisher Diaries, Jan. 14, 1777, HSP. For this politicization and its limits, see Linda K. Kerber, *Women of the Republic: Intellect and Ideology in Revolutionary America* (Chapel Hill: University of North Carolina Press, 1980); Mary Beth Norton, *Liberty's Daughters: The Revolutionary Experience of American Women, 1750–1800* (Boston: Little, Brown, 1980); Joy Day Buel and Richard Buel Jr., *The Way of Duty: A Woman and Her Family in Revolutionary America* (New York: Norton, 1984); Ronald Hoffman and Peter J. Albert, eds., *Women in the Age of the American Revolution* (Charlottesville: University Press of Virginia, 1989); Judith Van Buskirk, "They Didn't Join the Band: Disaffected Women in Revolutionary Philadelphia," *PH* 62 (1995): 306–29; Rosemarie Zagarri, *A Woman's Dilemma: Mercy Otis Warren and the American Revolution* (New York: Harlan Davidson, 1995); Joan R. Gunderson, *To Be Useful to the World: Women in Revolutionary America, 1740–1790* (New York: Twayne, 1996); Sarah

Fatherly, *Gentlemen and Learned Ladies: Women and Elite Formation in Eighteenth-Century Philadelphia* (Bethlehem, Pa.: Lehigh University Press, 2008), chap. 5; Rosemarie Zagarri, *Revolutionary Backlash: Women and Politics in the Early American Republic* (Philadelphia: University of Pennsylvania Press, 2008); Sheila Skemp, *First Lady of Letters: Judith Sargent Murray and the Struggle for Female Independence* (Philadelphia: University of Pennsylvania Press, 2009); and Vivian Bruce Conger, "Reading Early American Women's Political Lives: The Revolutionary Performances of Deborah Read Franklin and Sally Franklin Bache," *Early American Studies* 16 (2018): 317–52.

12. J&D to Neate, Pigou, and Booth, Oct. 22, 1764, to John Wickham and Son, Nov. 3, Dec. 18, 1764, and to John Clitherall, Nov. 26, 1764, J&D LB 1764–66.

13. J&D to John Wickham and Son, Dec. 18, 1764, to Parvin and James, Jan. 8, 1765, to David Barclay and Sons, May 21, 1765, to Neate, Pigou, and Booth, June 19, 1765, and to John Dowell, July 18, 1765, J&D LB 1764–66.

14. J&D to John, Robert, Samuel, and Emanuel Elam, Nov. 28, 1765, to William Brown, Mar. 1, 1766, to Neate, Pigou, and Booth, May 28, 1766, and to David Barclay and Sons, June 7, 1766, J&D LB 1764–66.

15. J&D to David Barclay and Sons, Oct. 14, 1765; see also J&D to Thomas Callahan, Oct. 16, 1765, J&D LB 1764–66.

16. J&D to Parvin and James, Oct. 12, 1765, to Charles McDonnell, Nov. 7, 1765, to Moses Holstein, Oct. 31, 1765, and to Parvin and James, Oct. 30, Nov. 2, 1765, J&D LB 1764–66.

17. See, e.g., J&D to Robert Evans, Dec. 4, 1765, to Thomas Lawrie, Dec. 5, 1765, to Peter Tallman, Dec. 6, 1765, and to John Hutchins, Dec. 6, 1765, J&D LB 1764–66.

18. J&D to David Barclay and Sons, Oct. 14, 1765, J&D LB 1764–66.

19. J&D to Charles McDonnell, Nov. 7, 1765, and to David Barclay and Sons, Nov. 9, 1765, J&D LB 1764–66.

20. J&D to David Barclay and Sons, Oct. 14, 1765, to John, Robert, Samuel, and Emanuel Elam, Nov. 28, 1765, and to Devonshire and Reeve, Dec. 16, 1765, J&D LB 1764–66.

21. J&D to Jones and Shepard, Nov. 21, Dec. 3, 1765, and to Anthony Merry, Dec. 16, 1765, J&D LB 1764–66.

22. J&D to Jones and Shepard, Nov. 21, 1765, and to Charles McDonnell, Dec. 20, 1765, J&D LB 1764–66.

23. J&D to Parvin and James, Dec. 7, 27, 1765, to Captain Daniel Wilcocks, Dec. 28, 1765, and to Captain William Barnes, Dec. 27, 1765, J&D LB 1764–66.

24. J&D to John Bailey, Jan. 1, 1766, to Parvin and James, Feb. 8, 1766, to Lewis Teissier, Feb. 20, 1766, and to Charles McDonnell, Feb. 21, 1766, J&D LB 1764–66.

25. J&D to David Barclay and Sons, Mar. 3, 1766, to Stephen Skinner Esq., Mar. 10, 1766, to Parvin and James, Mar. 28, 1766, and to Jacob Shepard, Apr. 2, 1766, J&D LB 1764–66.

26. *DED,* 131 (May 19, 20, 1766).

27. J&D to William Geddis, Apr. 15, 1766, to Lewis Teissier, May 1, 1766, to Joseph Powell, May 14, 1766, to John Bayly, May 21, 1766, to William Freeman, May 28, 1766, and to Neate, Pigou, and Booth, May 28, 1766, J&D LB 1764–66; HD to Samuel Emlen Jr., Sept. 20, 1766, HD LB 1762–86.

28. J&D to Lancelot Cowper, Mar. 19, 1770, J&D LB 1769–72.

29. See, e.g., J&D to Robinson and Sandwith, May 6, 1769, and to Captain Peter Young, June 10, 1769, J&D LB 1769–72.

30. John Fothergill to James Pemberton, Sept. 9, 1768, Etting Collection, Pemberton Papers, HSP; List of Subscribers to Non-Importation Agreement, Feb. 6, Mar. 10, 1769, HSDP; "Letter from a Committee of Merchants in Philadelphia," *Pennsylvania Chronicle*, Aug. 28–Sept. 4, 1769.

31. J&D to John Clitherall, July 15, Aug. 23, 1769, and to George Smith, Sept. 18, 1769, J&D LB 1769–72.

32. John Masterson to HD, Mar. 13, 1770, HSDP.

33. HD to AJ, Dec. 9, Feb. 12, Apr. 29, 1770, transcribed in "Effects of the Non-Importation Agreement in Philadelphia, 1769–1770," *PMHB* 14 (1890): 41, 43; Meeting for Sufferings Held at Philadelphia for Pennsylvania and New Jersey to Our Friends and Brethren in These and the Adjacent Provinces, Sept. 1, 1769, Ferdinand J. Dreer Collection, HSP.

34. John O'Kely to HD, May 21, 28, 1770, HSDP. For references to ED's illness, see O'Kely to HD, Mar. 3, 15, June 17, 1770, HDSP; HD to AJ, May 16, 1770, transcribed in "Effects of the Non-Importation Agreement," 44.

35. HD to AJ, May 26, 1770, transcribed in "Effects of the Non-Importation Agreement," 45; J&D to Lancelot Cowper, July 17, Sept. 6, 15, 1770, and to James Read, Nov. 30, 1770, J&D LB 1769–72; William Neate to HD, Sept. 10, 1770, Correspondence Box 1741–92, HD Papers, HSP.

36. J&D to Pigou and Booth, Sept. 15, Nov. 5, 1770, and to Lancelot Cowper, Oct. 24, 1770, J&D LB 1769–72.

37. Frederick Pigou Jr. to Court of Directors of the United East India Company, June 1, 1773, Pigou and Booth to Honorable Committee of Warehouses, July 8, 1773, and to J&D, July 24, Aug. 4, 1773, Benjamin Booth to J&D, Aug. 4, Oct. 4, 1773, J&D to Pigou and Booth, Oct. 5, 1773, and Pigou to J&D, Nov. 3, 1773, HSDP; J&D to Pigou and Booth, Aug. 27, 1773, HD FL 1772–85.

38. Address of Diverse Freemen to the Mayor and Commonalty of Philadelphia, June 28, 1773, Dorothy Merriman Schall Papers, Box 18, Philadelphia Business folder, QSC; J&D to Pigou and Booth, Oct. 5, 1773, HD FL 1772–85; J&D to Pigou and Booth, Sept. 29, Oct. 3, 1773, J&D LB 1772–86; J&D to Pigou and Booth, Oct. 7, 14, 1773, HSDP; Pennsylvania Stamp Act and Non-Importation Resolutions Collection, 1765–1775, APS. See also Richard Alan Ryerson, *The Revolution Is Now Begun: The Radical Committees of Philadelphia, 1765–1776* (Philadelphia: University of Pennsylvania Press, 1978).

39. Report from "committee appointed to wait upon the gentlemen who, it is said, are named commissioners for the sale of the tea intended to be sent here by the India Company," Oct. 17, 1773, Pennsylvania Stamp Act and Non-Importation Resolutions Collection.

40. J&D, Open Letter to Citizens of Philadelphia, Oct. 22, 1773, and the Committee's Response, Oct. 23, 1773, Pennsylvania Stamp Act and Non-Importation Resolutions Collection.

41. J&D to Pigou and Booth, Oct. 26, 29, 1773, HSDP; Broadside, "To the Commissioners Appointed by the East India Company for the Sale of Tea in America," Pennsylvania Stamp Act and Non-Importation Resolutions Collection.

42. J&D to Pigou and Booth, Oct. 5, 7, 14, Nov. 6, 1773, and Pigou and Booth to J&D, Oct. 18, 1773, HSDP; J&D to Pigou and Booth, Nov. 20, 1773, HD FL 1772–85; J&D to Pigou and Booth, Nov. 18, 20, 1773, J&D LB 1772–86.

43. J&D to Pigou and Booth, Oct. 8, 1773, Pigou and Booth to J&D, Nov. 12, 1773, and HD to Pigou and Booth, Nov. 30, 1773, HSDP; Committee for Tarring and Feathering to the Delaware Pilots and Captain Ayres of the Ship Polly, Philadelphia broadside dated Nov. 27, 1773, Printed Ephemera Collection, portfolio 143, folder 31, LC; J&D to Pigou and Booth, Nov. 20, 30, 1773, HD FL 1772–85.

44. Public Notice to James and Drinker, Dec. 2, 1773, and James and Drinker to the Citizens of Philadelphia, Dec. 2, 1773, Pennsylvania Stamp Act and Non-Importation Resolutions Collection.

45. J&D to the citizens of Philadelphia, Dec. 2, 1773, Pennsylvania Stamp Act and Non-Importation Resolutions Collection; J&D to Pigou and Booth, Dec. 4, 1773, HSDP; J&D to Pigou and Booth, Jan. 1, 1774, HD FL 1772–85.

46. *DED,* 196 (Dec. 2, 1773).

47. J&D to Pigou and Booth, Dec. 7, 24, 28, 1773, HSDP; *DED,* 197 (Dec. 24, 25, 27, 1773).

48. J&D to Pigou and Booth, Oct. 29, Dec. 28, 31, 1773, and to Benjamin Booth, July 7, 1774, HSDP; J&D to Pigou and Booth, Jan. 1, 1774, HD FL 1772–85.

49. J&D to Pigou and Booth, June 11, 1774, HD FL 1772–85. Many years later, in the mid-1790s, HD would write to a friend that he had always "been biased in favor of the English nation" and still felt "a strong attachment to the people of that island." Yet that "bias" did not translate into unquestioning loyalty, let alone loyalism. He responded "with real pain" to the British government's high-handed behavior toward the United States in the 1790s (refusing to respect U.S. neutrality in the war between Britain and France, boarding U.S. ships and seizing their cargoes, maintaining forts in U.S. territory that it had promised to evacuate, and closing the West Indies to American ships), condemning those actions as "arbitrary, tyrannical, and unjust," just as he had condemned British policy in the pre-revolutionary years and refused to side with Britain in the ensuing war; HD to Enoch Edwards, July 17, 1794, HD LB 1793–96.

50. J&D to Pigou and Booth, May 14, June 11, Sept. 28, Nov. 15, 1774, HD FL 1772–85; J&D to Pigou and Booth, May 24, 31, Aug. 4, 9, 1774, and to Benjamin Booth, June n.d., 1774, J&D LB 1772–86; *DED*, 201 (June 22, 1774).

51. J&D to Pigou and Booth, June 29, 1774, HD FL 1772–85; J&D to Benjamin Booth, Sept. 10, 1774, HSDP; J&D to Booth, Sept. 24, 1774, and to Thomas Pearsall, Sept. 24, 1774, J&D LB 1772–86.

52. J&D to Benjamin Booth, Sept. 29, 1774, and to Pigou and Booth, Jan. 31, 1775, J&D LB 1772–86; J&D to Captain Edward Spain, Sept. 28, 1774, to Booth, Sept. 29, 1774, to Pigou and Booth, Jan. 31, 1775, and to Laugher and Hancox, Feb. 27, 1775, HD FL 1772–85; Lancelot Cowper to J&D, Jan. 6, 1775, HSDP.

53. J&D to Benjamin Booth, Oct. 8, 1774, and to Samuel Cornell, Oct. 11, 1774, J&D LB 1772–86; J&D to Baugh, Ames, and Company, Nov. 6, 1774, HD FL 1772–85; Minutes of Yearly Meeting for Pennsylvania and New Jersey, Sept. 26–Oct. 1, 1774, QMR.

54. *DED*, 199, 211 (May 3, 1774, Sept. 6, 1775).

55. J&D to Pigou and Booth, Sept. 28, Oct. 25, 1774, Jan. 18, 1775, and to Lancelot Cowper, Mar. 27, 1775, HD FL 1772–85; J&D to Pigou and Booth, Nov. 3, 1774, J&D LB 1772–86; *The Ancient Testimony and Principles of the People Called Quakers Renewed, With respect to the King and Government; and Touching the Commotions Now Prevailing in These and Other Parts of America* (Philadelphia, Jan. 20, 1776), 2–3.

56. Minutes of Yearly Meeting for Pennsylvania and New Jersey, Sept. 27–30, 1773, QMR; J&D to Robert and Nathan Hyde, Sept. 16, 1774, to Pigou and Booth, Sept. 28, Oct. 25, 1774, to Jones, Campbell, and Company, Nov. 26, 1774, and to Zachary Philip Fonnereau and Sons, Mar. 4, 1775, HD FL 1772–85; J&D to Thomas Pearsall, Jan. 12, 1775, J&D LB 1772–86.

57. J&D to James Arnice and George Lampriere, Apr. 29, 1775, and to Philip Winter and Company, June 1, 1775, HD FL 1772–85; see also letters to Thomas Durell, Apr. 29, 1775, to Philip Robin, Apr. 29, 1775, and to De Gruchy and Fiott, Apr. 29, 1775, HD FL 1772–85; William Duane, ed., *Passages from the Diary of Christopher Marshall* (Philadelphia, 1839–49), 24 (Apr. 29, 1775). According to Stephen Collins, another merchant writing in May 1775, a report was circulating that the captain of one of the ships due to leave for Newfoundland had declared that he would leave regardless of what his employer or "the people" said. In response, "three to four thousand of the inhabitants gathered round the home of the merchant in pursuit of the captain (who had got out of the way)." The merchant confirmed that he would hand over all the customs papers "and that the vessel should absolutely be stopped," which satisfied the crowd. This was almost certainly neither HD nor AJ, since ED's diary makes no mention of any such incident and it seems unlikely that she would have neglected to describe a demonstration outside her own home or that of the James family. Nonetheless, the two partners would have heard about the confrontation, another reminder of their own vulnerability; Stephen Collins to William Tudor, May 2, 1775, Stephen Collins Letterbook, LC.

58. J&D to William Freeman, May 8, 1775, and to Thomas Durell and Company, May 29, 1775, HD FL 1772–85; J&D to Pigou and Booth, June 15, 1775, to Jonathan Worth, June 22, 1775, to Lodowick Sprogell, June 26, 1775, and to James Inskeep, Aug. 2, 1775, J&D LB 1772–86.

59. J&D to Lancelot Cowper and Company, Aug. 26, 1775, to Hoare and Potts, Sept. 1, 1775, to Captain Edward Spain, Sept. 4, 1775, and to Frederick Pigou Jr., Sept. 5, 1775, HD FL 1772–85.

60. J&D to Captain John Harper, July 18, 1775, and to David Barron and Company, Aug. 2, 1775, J&D LB 1772–86; J&D to William Freeman, Sept. 5, 1775, HD FL 1772–85.

61. J&D to Alexander Donaldson, Aug. 10, 1775, J&D LB 1772–86; J&D to Captain George Sivret, May 27, 1775, to James Read, July 5, 1775, to Hornby and Hankinson, July 8, 1775, to Thomas Strettel, Aug. 31, 1775, and to Hoare and Potts, Sept. 1, 1775, HD FL 1772–85; *DED*, 211 (Oct. 14, 1775).

62. J&D to Laugher and Hancox, Feb. 27, 1775, and to Lancelot Cowper, Mar. 27, 1775, HD FL 1772–85.

63. Jane E. Calvert, "Thomas Paine, Quakerism, and the Limits of Religious Liberty during the American Revolution," in Ian Shapiro and Jane E. Calvert, eds., *Selected Writings of Thomas Paine* (New Haven: Yale University Press, 2014), 606. For Quakers' views on civic engagement and constitutional change, see Calvert, *Quaker Constitutionalism*. For studies of the loyalists, see Lorenzo Sabine, *The American Loyalists; or, Biographical Sketches of Adherents to the British Crown in the War of Revolution* (Boston: Charles C. Little and James Brown, 1847); William Nelson, *The American Tory* (Oxford: Oxford University Press, 1961); Wallace Brown, *The King's Friends: The Composition and Motives of the American Loyalist Claimants* (Providence, R.I.: Brown University Press, 1965); Wallace Brown, *The Good Americans: The Loyalists in the American Revolution* (New York: Morrow, 1969); Mary Beth Norton, *The British-Americans: The Loyalist Exiles in England, 1774–1789* (Boston: Little, Brown, 1972); Robert M. Calhoon, *The Loyalists in Revolutionary America, 1760–1781* (New York: Harcourt, Brace, Jovanovich, 1973); Bernard Bailyn, *The Ordeal of Thomas Hutchinson* (Cambridge, Mass.: Harvard University Press, 1974); Kenneth S. Lynn, *A Divided People* (Westport, Conn.: Greenwood Press, 1977); Robert M. Calhoon, Timothy M. Barnes, and George A. Rawlyk, eds., *Loyalists and Community in North America* (Westport, Conn.: Greenwood Press, 1994); Joseph S. Tiedemann, Eugene R. Fingerhut, and Robert W. Venables, eds., *The Other Loyalists: Ordinary People, Royalism, and the Revolution in the Middle Colonies, 1763–1787* (Albany: State University of New York Press, 2009); Maya Jasanoff, *Liberty's Exiles: American Loyalists in the Revolutionary World* (New York: Vintage, 2011); and Ruma Chopra, *Choosing Sides: Loyalists in Revolutionary America* (New York: Rowman and Littlefield, 2013).

64. *Ancient Testimony and Principles of the People Called Quakers*, 4.

65. Meeting for Sufferings Held at Philadelphia for Pennsylvania and New Jersey to Our Friends and Brethren in These and the Adjacent Provinces, Sept. 1, 1769, Ferdinand J. Dreer Collection, HSP; Philadelphia Yearly Meeting to Quarterly and Monthly

Meetings, Minutes of the Philadelphia Yearly Meeting, 1773, QMR; *Ancient Testimony and Principles of the People Called Quakers*, 1–3.

66. *Ancient Testimony and Principles of the People Called Quakers*, 4.

67. Minutes of Yearly Meeting for Pennsylvania and New Jersey, Sept. 25–30, 1775, QMR; *The Testimony of the People called Quakers, Given Forth by a Meeting of the Representatives of Said People, in Pennsylvania And New Jersey, Held at Philadelphia the Twenty-Fourth Day of the First Month, 1775* (Philadelphia, 1775); *The Address of the People Called Quakers to the Representatives of the Freemen of the Province of Pennsylvania, in General Assembly Met, October 26, 1775* (Philadelphia, 1775).

68. *A Declaration and An Information from Us the People of God Called Quakers* (London, 1660), 2, 5, 7; Rebecca Jones to John Pemberton, Sept. 16, 1784, Pemberton Papers, HSP; *Testimony of the People called Quakers; Address of the People Called Quakers; Ancient Testimony and Principles of the People Called Quakers*, 1. For an examination of the Quakers' sense of themselves as a distinct, holy people, see Crabtree, *Holy Nation*.

69. Ellis Sandoz, ed., *Political Sermons of the American Founding Era, 1730–1805*, 2nd ed. (Indianapolis, Ind.: Liberty Fund, 1998); Harry S. Stout, *The New England Soul: Preaching and Religious Culture in Colonial New England* (New York: Oxford University Press, 1986), chap. 14.

70. Philadelphia Yearly Meeting, *To Our Friends and Brethren in Religious Profession* (Philadelphia, Dec. 20, 1776); "Common Sense," in Shapiro and Calvert, eds., *Selected Writings of Paine*, 48, 50; "To the Honorable the Council of Safety of the State of Pennsylvania," ibid., 91. See also Calvert, "Thomas Paine, Quakerism, and the Limits of Religious Liberty," 602–29.

71. J&D to David and John Barclay, Jan. 2, 1775, to Lancelot Cowper, Feb. 23, 1775, and to Hornby and Hankinson, Feb. 25, 1775, HD FL 1772–85; J&D to Lodowick Sprogell, June 26, 1775, J&D LB 1772–86; Minutes of Yearly Meeting for Pennsylvania and New Jersey, Sept. 27–30, 1773, Sept. 26–Oct. 1, 1774, Sept. 25–30, 1775, QMR; William Penn, *To the Children of Light in This Generation* (London, 1678), reprinted as broadside, QSC; untitled poem, DSP, Box 6. The poem is in HD's handwriting; he may have composed it himself, or he may have copied it because he identified with its message.

72. *DED*, 214, 215 (Jan. 30, Feb. 9, 15, 1776); *Colonial Records of Pennsylvania*, 16 vols. (Harrisburg, Pa.: T. Fenn, 1831–53), 10:486–87; *Pennsylvania Journal*, Feb. 7, 1776.

73. J&D to Thomas Pearsall, Mar. 19, 1776, to Usher, Roe, and Company, May 7, 1776, to Pearsall, July 11, 1776, to John Vangerle, Oct. 7, 1776, and to James Inskeep, Oct. 9, 1776, J&D LB 1772–86; untitled poem, DSP, Box 6.

Chapter 4. "Cruelty and Oppression"

1. J&D to Benjamin Booth, May 14, 1776, J&D LB 1772–86; John Brinton to HD, Dec. 3, 1776, and Joseph Drinker to HD, Feb. 25, May 6, July 15, Dec. 1, 1776, Jan. 6, Feb. 9, May 18, 1777, HSDP.

2. "Diary of James Allen," *Pennsylvania Magazine of History* 9 (1885–86): 193; "Letters of Robert Proud," *PMHB* 34 (1910): 64; George Washington to John Lacey Jr., Mar. 20, 1778, in David R. Hoth, ed., *The Papers of George Washington,* Revolutionary War Series, vol. 14 (Charlottesville: University of Virginia Press, 2004), 238; John Lacey's orders quoted in Isaac Sharpless, *A History of Quaker Government in Pennsylvania,* vol. 2, *The Quakers in the Revolution* (Philadelphia: T. S. Leach, 1889), 183; Edward Rutledge to Robert R. Livingston, Oct. 2, 1776, in Paul H. Smith et al., eds., *Letters of Delegates to Congress,* 24 vols. (Washington, D.C.: LC, 1976–2000), 5:295. For more on the disownments, see Arthur J. Mekeel, *The Relation of the Quakers to the American Revolution* (Washington, D.C.: University Press of America, 1979), 131–33, 194–95, 199–201.

3. *DED,* 218, 230, 238, 262, 303, 308 (July 16, 1776, Sept. 13, 15, Oct. 1, 2, Dec. 9, 1777, Apr. 30, May 30, 1778); Sarah Logan Fisher Diaries, Dec. 27, 1776, Oct. 23, 1777, HSP. ED referred to Americans as "provincials," which might lead a patriot to conclude that she thought the colonies' rightful status was subordinate to Britain, though what she probably meant was that no one could justify overthrowing any government, British or otherwise. Quakers admitted that they were "friends of government," but this was because they believed governments to be God-ordained, so the overthrow of any regime constituted a rebellion against divine will and reenacted the rebellion of Satan. Fisher described the patriots as "influenced" by the "wicked spirit" of their "infernal master" the Devil, who "presided as general adviser and director of their assemblies"; Fisher Diaries, Aug. 13, 1777. For references to Americans as "provincials," see *DED,* 246 (Oct. 19, 1777); and Fisher Diaries, Jan. 24, Feb. 19, 1777; to "friends of government," see Fisher Diaries, Dec. 21, 1776, Apr. 25, 1777.

4. For previous accounts of HD's exile as experienced by ED, see Kenneth A. Radbill, "The Ordeal of Elizabeth Drinker," *PH* 47 (1980): 147–72; Judith Van Buskirk, "They Didn't Join the Band: Disaffected Women in Revolutionary Philadelphia," *PH* 62 (1995): 306–29; and Wendy Lucas Castro, " 'Being Separated from My Dearest Husband, in This Cruel Manner': Elizabeth Drinker and the Seven-Month Exile of Philadelphia Quakers," *Quaker History* 100 (2011): 40–63.

5. *DED,* 217 (May 8, June "2 or 3," 1776); *Pennsylvania Gazette,* May 8, 22, 1776.

6. *DED,* 218, 222, 225 (July 16, 1776, Jan. 25, June 5, 1777); Fisher Diaries, Jan. 4, 23, 1777.

7. Philadelphia Yearly Meeting, *To Our Friends and Brethren in Religious Profession* (Philadelphia, Dec. 20, 1776), 1–2; *Statutes at Large of Pennsylvania, 1682–1801,* 18 vols. (Philadelphia and Harrisburg, 1896–1901), 9:75–94; *DED,* 224 (Mar. 5, 8, 1777). See also Fisher Diaries, Mar. 5, 1777.

8. John Lansing to Richard Varick, Apr. 10, May 29, 1777, Richard Varick Papers, New-York Historical Society; *DED,* 225 (July 4, 1777); Fisher Diaries, July 4, 1777.

9. *Journals of the Continental Congress,* 34 vols. (Washington, D.C.: U.S. Government Printing Office, 1905–37), 8:678–79; *DED,* 226 (July 31, 1777).

10. *DED*, 226 (Aug. 14, 1777); Fisher Diaries, Aug. 2, 6, 10, 14, 15, 1777.

11. John Sullivan to John Hancock, Aug. 25, 1777, Otis G. Hammond, ed., *Letters and Papers of Major-General John Sullivan*, 3 vols. (Concord: New Hampshire Historical Society, 1930–39), 1:443–44; Resolution of Congress, Aug. 28, 1777, Quaker Miscellany, QSC; *Colonial Records of Pennsylvania*, 16 vols. (Harrisburg: T. Fenn, 1831–53), 11:283–84, 288–89. For the names of the thirty men arrested, see Thomas Gilpin, [Jr.], *Exiles in Virginia: With Observations on the Conduct of the Society of Friends during the Revolutionary War* (Philadelphia: C. Sherman, 1848), 67.

12. *DED*, 226–27 (Sept. 2, 3, 1777).

13. HD to "wife, sister, and children," Sept. 3, 1777, DSP, 3:1. The originals of HD's and ED's letters written during HD's imprisonment and exile are in the QSC; the HSP has a typescript of these letters filed as DSP, 3:1–53.

14. *DED*, 227 (Sept. 4, 5, 1777); Fisher Diaries, May 3, Sept. 2, 1777.

15. HD to ED, Sept. 4, 1777, and to "dear brother," Sept. 4, 1777, DSP, 3:1, 2.

16. Israel Pemberton, John Hunt, and Samuel Pleasants to the Supreme Executive Council of Pennsylvania, Sept. 4, 1777, and Petition to the President and Council of Pennsylvania, Sept. 5, 1777, Quaker Miscellany; "Address to the Inhabitants of Pennsylvania," in Gilpin, *Exiles in Virginia*, 88, 98; *DED*, 228 (Sept. 8, 1777).

17. *DED*, 227 (Sept. 6, 7, 1777); HD, "Memorandum Preparatory to My Banishment from My Habitation," DSP, 3: unnumbered item.

18. *DED*, 227–28 (Sept. 8, 9, 1777); Instructions to Caldwell and Nesbitt, Sept. 10, 1777, Quaker Miscellany.

19. *DED*, 228–29 (Sept. 10, 11, 1777); ED to HD, Sept. 16, 1777, DSP, 3:6; Fisher Diaries, Sept. 13, 1777; "Diary of Robert Morton," *PMHB* 1 (1877): 4–5. For the names of the twenty exiles, see Gilpin, *Exiles in Virginia*, 148.

20. HD to ED, Sept. 12, 1777, DSP, 3:3.

21. *DED*, 229, 231 (Sept. 12, 16, 1777).

22. *DED*, 230–35 (Sept. 14–16, 19, 22, 23, 25, 1777).

23. *DED*, 234, 235 (Sept. 23, 25, 26, 1777); Fisher Diaries, Sept. 26, 1777. For a detailed account of the British occupation of Philadelphia, see Aaron Sullivan, *The Disaffected: Britain's Occupation of Philadelphia during the American Revolution* (Philadelphia: University of Pennsylvania Press, 2019), unfortunately not yet available when this book went to press.

24. HD to ED, Sept. 13, 1777, DSP, 3:4; Gilpin, *Exiles in Virginia*, 136 (Sept. 14, 1777).

25. HD to his family, Sept. 16, 1777, and to ED, Sept. 18, 1777, DSP, 3:5, 7; Gilpin, *Exiles in Virginia*, 136.

26. HD to ED, Sept. 20, 1777, DSP, 3:8. For Zane, see Roger W. Moss Jr., "Isaac Zane Jr., a 'Quaker for the Times,'" *Virginia Magazine of History and Biography* 77 (1969): 291–306; and Gilpin, *Exiles in Virginia*, 136, 154. I am grateful to Norman E. Donoghue for alerting me to this article on Zane.

27. HD to ED, Oct. 12, 1777, DSP, 3:10; "Diary of Morton," 18–19.

28. HD to ED, Oct. 14, 17, 23, Nov. 6, 11, 1777, DSP, 3:11, 12, 13, 17, 18.

29. HD to ED, Nov. 20, 1777, DSP, 3:21, 22 (two versions of the same letter).

30. HD to ED, Dec. 13, 1777, DSP, 3:25; Fisher Diaries, Apr. 25, 1777; Canada Loyalist Claim Form of William Drewet Smith, 1784, American Loyalist Claims, 1776–1835, U.K. National Archives. I am grateful to Norman E. Donoghue for the last citation.

31. Gilpin, *Exiles in Virginia,* 185–93; HD to ED, Jan. 12, 1778, DSP, 3:30.

32. HD to ED, Jan. 12, 25, 26, 1778, DSP, 3:30, 32, 33.

33. HD to ED, Jan. 30, 1778, DSP, 3:35.

34. HD to ED, Nov. 1, 1777, DSP, 3:15.

35. *DED,* 236–38 (Sept. 27, 28, Oct. 1, 1777); Fisher Diaries, Jan. 3, 1777.

36. *DED,* 242, 247–48 (Oct. 11, 21, 23, 1777).

37. *DED,* 255–58 (Nov. 20–22, 24, 25, 1777); Maria Pemberton to James Pemberton, Nov. 24, 1777, Pemberton Family Papers, vol. 31, HSP; see also Fisher Diaries, Dec. 5, 1777.

38. *DED,* 245, 247, 256, 261 (Oct. 18, 20, Nov. 22, Dec. 6, 1777).

39. *DED,* 237, 238, 242–43, 250 (Sept. 29, Oct. 2, 12, Nov. 1, 1777).

40. *DED,* 247, 251, 257, 262–64, 285, 289 (Oct. 20, Nov. 5, 22, Dec. 9, 11, 14, 1777, Feb. 20, Mar. 11, 1778); Fisher Diaries, Dec. 26, 1777 (see also Nov. 1, 5, 1777).

41. *DED,* 237, 238, 247, 249–51, 260 (Sept. 29, Oct. 2, 21, 27, Nov. 1, 5, Dec. 2, 1777). See also "Diary of Morton," 20; Fisher Diaries, Nov. 1, 1777.

42. *DED,* 262–64, 269 (Dec. 7, 9, 11, 13–15, 22, 1777). See also Fisher Diaries, Mar. 25, 1778; "Diary of Morton," 8, 23; and *Pennsylvania Gazette,* Jan. 10, 1778.

43. *DED,* 240–42, 248 (Oct. 6, 8–11, 25, 1777).

44. *DED,* 253, 256 (Nov. 13, 21, 1777).

45. *DED,* 258–59 (Nov. 25, 1777).

46. *DED,* 259–61, 269 (Nov. 26, Dec. 1, 2, 4, 23, 1777).

47. *DED,* 273 (Jan. 4, 1778).

48. *DED,* 265, 266 (Dec. 15, 18, 1777).

49. *DED,* 266 (Dec. 19, 1777).

50. *DED,* 266 (Dec. 19, 1777).

51. *DED,* 267–68 (Dec. 20, 1777).

52. *DED,* 269–71 (Dec. 23, 27, 29, 1777).

53. *DED,* 271, 272, 276, 287 (Dec. 30, 1777, Jan. 1, 19, Feb. 27, 28, 1778).

54. *DED,* 271–74, 283, 284, 289, 290 (Dec. 31, 1777, Jan. 2, 5, 8, Feb. 14, 17, Mar. 14, 19, 1778).

55. *DED,* 276 (Jan. 20, 1778); Rebecca Franks to Anne (Harrison) Paca, Feb. 26, 1778, *PMHB* 16 (1892): 216–18; Fisher Diaries, Jan. 28, Mar. 15, 1778. See also Fred Lewis Pattee, "The British Theatre in Philadelphia in 1778," *American Literature* 6 (1935): 381–88; and Darlene Emmert Fisher, "Social Life in Philadelphia during the British Occupation," *PH* 37 (1970): 237–60.

56. ED to HD, Dec. 3, 31, 1777, Jan. 1, 1778, DSP, 3:23, 29.

57. HD to ED, Jan. 26, 30, 1778, DSP, 3:33, 35.

58. ED to HD, Jan. 25, Feb. 26, 1778, DSP, 3:31, 36.

Chapter 5. "Inward and Outward Trials"

1. Hannah Griffitts, "To My Worthy Banish'd Friends in Virginia" (1778), Hannah Griffitts Papers, Library Company of Philadelphia.

2. HD to Jonah Thompson, Feb. 14, 1778, Jonah Thompson Collection, 2:119, HSP; HD to his family, Sept. 16, 1777, and to ED, Nov. 20, Dec. 19, 1777, DSP, 3:5, 21 and 22 (two versions of same letter), 26.

3. HD to Jonah Thompson, Feb. 14, 1778, Thompson Collection, 2:119; HD to ED, Sept. 18, Nov. 2, 6, 20, Dec. 13, 19, 1777, DSP, 3:7, 17, 21, 22, 25, 26.

4. ED to HD, Dec. 18, 27, 1777, Feb. 26, 1778, DSP, 3:27, 36; HD to ED, Nov. 18, Dec. 13, 1777, Jan. 12, Feb. 7, 1778, DSP, 3:20, 25, 30, 37.

5. For local variations in the power that Women's Meetings had relative to Men's Meetings, see *DED,* 330n56. Scholars differ over the extent to which female Friends could overcome conventional gender restrictions. There is an enormous literature on Quaker women, but see especially Margaret Hope Bacon, *Mothers of Feminism: The Story of Quaker Women in America* (San Francisco: Harper and Row, 1986); Barry Levy, *Quakers and the American Family: British Settlement in the Delaware Valley* (New York: Oxford University Press, 1988), esp. chap. 6; Mary Maples Dunn, "Women of Light," in Carol Ruth Berkin and Mary Beth Norton, eds., *Women of America: A History* (Boston: Houghton Mifflin, 1979), 114–36; Mary Maples Dunn, "Saints and Sisters: Congregational and Quaker Women in the Early Colonial Period," in Janet Wilson James, ed., *Women in American Religion* (Philadelphia: University of Pennsylvania Press, 1980), 27–46; Jean Soderlund, "Women's Authority in Pennsylvania and New Jersey Quaker Meetings, 1680–1760," *William and Mary Quarterly,* 3rd ser., 44 (1987): 722–49; Mary Maples Dunn, "The Eighteenth Century: Latest Light on Women of Light," in Elizabeth Potts Brown and Susan Mosher Stuard, eds., *Witnesses for Change: Quaker Women over Three Centuries* (New Brunswick, N.J.: Rutgers University Press, 1989); Bonnelyn Young Kunze, *Margaret Fell and the Rise of Quakerism* (Stanford, Calif.: Stanford University Press, 1994); Phyllis Mack, *Visionary Women: Ecstatic Prophecy in Seventeenth-Century England* (Berkeley: University of California Press, 1995); Christine Levenduski, *A Peculiar Power: A Quaker Woman Preacher in Eighteenth-Century America* (Washington, D.C.: Smithsonian Institution Press, 1997); Rebecca Larson, *Daughters of Light: Quaker Women Preaching and Prophesying in the Colonies and Abroad, 1700–1775* (Chapel Hill: University of North Carolina Press, 2000); Elsa F. Glines, ed., *Undaunted Zeal: The Letters of Margaret Fell* (Richmond, Ind.: Friends United Press, 2003); Sally Bruyneel, *Margaret Fell and the End of Time: The Theology of the Mother of Quakerism* (Waco, Tex.: Baylor University Press, 2010); and Amanda

Herbert, "Companions in Preaching and Suffering: Itinerant Female Quakers in the Seventeenth- and Eighteenth-Century British Atlantic World," *Early American Studies* 9 (2011): 73–113.

6. *DED*, 275 (Jan. 11, 13, 14, 1778). See also Joy Day Buel and Richard Buel, *The Way of Duty: A Woman and Her Family in Revolutionary America* (New York: Norton, 1984).

7. ED to HD, Nov. 4, 5, 11, 1777, and HD to ED, Oct. 23, Nov. 20, 1777, Feb. 7, 1778, DSP, 3:13, 16, 19, 22, 37. The older children also wrote to their father: see, e.g., Ann Drinker's touching letter of Mar. 1, 1778, HSDP.

8. HD to his family, Sept. 16, 1777, and to ED, Sept. 20, Oct. 14, Nov. 11, 1777, Jan. 25, 26, 1778, DSP, 3:5, 8, 11, 18, 32, 33.

9. HD to ED, Sept. 18, Oct. 23, Nov. 2, 6, 11, 1777, and ED to HD, Oct. 4, 28, Nov. 5, 11, 1777, Feb. 26, 1778, DSP, 3:7, 13, 14, 16–19, 36.

10. ED to HD, Oct. 28, Dec. 3, 5, 1777, Jan. 25, Feb. 2, 1778, and HD to ED, Oct. 14, 1777, DSP, 3:11, 14, 23, 24, 31, 34; Hannah Pemberton to John Pemberton, Dec. 30, 1777, Pemberton Manuscripts, FHL.

11. *DED*, 232–33, 237–38, 243 (Sept. 21, 22, 30, Oct. 1, 2, 14, 1777); HD to ED, Oct. 14, 1777, DSP, 3:11.

12. HD to his family, Sept. 16, 1777, and to ED, Oct. 14, Nov. 1, 20, 1777, DSP, 3:5, 11, 15, 21, 22.

13. ED to HD, Oct. 28, Dec. 3, 8, 1777, Feb. 3, 1778, DSP, 3:14, 23, 24, 36; *DED*, 243, 260, 267 (Oct. 16, Dec. 2, 20, 1777).

14. HD to ED, Dec. 13, 1777, and ED to HD, Nov. 11, 17, Dec. 3, 18, 27, 1777, Feb. 26, 1778, DSP, 3:18, 19, 23, 25, 27, 36. The letters that Mary and Israel Pemberton wrote to each other, as well as those written by Hannah to John Pemberton, were similar in content to those between ED and HD: they shared news of their children and of events unfolding in Philadelphia, worried about the prisoners' clothing in winter weather, discussed the prospects for the exiles' release, deplored their treatment by the patriots, and struggled to accept the ultimate benevolence of God's will; see Pemberton Manuscripts.

15. HD to ED, Feb. 16, 1778, and ED to HD, Feb. 26, 1778, DSP, 3:36, 38.

16. HD to ED, Mar. 8, 1778, DSP, 3:40.

17. HD to ED, Jan. 30, Mar. 8, 1778, and ED to HD, Mar. 23, 27, 1778, DSP, 3:35, 40, 41; see also Sarah Logan Fisher Diaries, Mar. 20, 1778, HSP.

18. HD to ED, Mar. 24, 1778, DSP, 3:42.

19. HD to ED, Feb. 7, Mar. 31, 1778, DSP, 3:37, 43.

20. *DED*, 292 (Mar. 27, 1778); Thomas Wharton Sr. to Rachel Hunt, Mar. 6, 1778, Wharton Family Papers, HSP; ED to HD, Mar. 29, Apr. 3, 1778, DSP, 3:44.

21. *DED*, 280, 282 (Feb. 3, 7, 1778); Fisher Diaries, Jan. 28, 1778.

22. *DED*, 289, 291 (Mar. 14, 25, 1778).

23. *DED*, 293–94 (Mar. 28, 31, 1778).

24. *DED*, 292–95 (Mar. 27, 28, 31, Apr. 1, 2, 1778); Mary Pemberton to George Washington, Mar. 31, 1778, in Thomas Gilpin, [Jr.], *Exiles in Virginia: With Observations on the Conduct of the Society of Friends during the Revolutionary War* (Philadelphia: C. Sherman, 1848), 222.

25. *DED*, 295–97 (Apr. 3–5, 1778).

26. *DED*, 296–97 (Apr. 5, 1778).

27. *DED*, 297 (Apr. 6, 1778); George Washington to Thomas Wharton, Apr. 5, 1778, in Gilpin, *Exiles in Virginia*, 222–23. For Lee's return and his welcome at Washington's headquarters, see Elias Boudinot, *Journal or Historical Recollections of American Events during the Revolutionary War by Elias Boudinot* (Philadelphia: Frederick Bourquin, 1894), 78; and "Diary entry of Elijah Fisher for Sunday, Apr. 5, 1778," in Carlos E. Godfrey, *Commander-in-Chief's Guard: Revolutionary War* (Washington, D.C.: Stevenson-Smith, 1904), 275. I am grateful to Norman E. Donoghue for alerting me to the arrival of Lee on the same day as the Quaker embassy and the connections among Washington, Colonel George Gilpin, and the exiles, mentioned in the next paragraph below.

28. *DED*, 297 (Apr. 6, 1778); George Washington to Thomas Wharton, Apr. 6, 1778, in Gilpin, *Exiles in Virginia*, 223; Paul F. Boller Jr., "George Washington and the Quakers," *Bulletin of Friends Historical Association* 49 (1960): 67–83. Washington had additional personal reasons for viewing these four women and their mission with sympathy. Colonel George Gilpin, a good friend of Washington's and a member of his inner circle at the military headquarters, was the younger brother of exile Thomas Gilpin, who had just died in Winchester. Colonel Gilpin had secured leave to spend a month with his exiled brother and had subsequently lobbied both Congress and Pennsylvania's Executive Council on the exiles' behalf. Gilpin also married two of Martha Washington's cousins, Catherine Peters and then Jane Peters. Indeed, a member of the British high command claimed to have information that General Washington's wife lobbied successfully for the exiles' release. Whether or not this report was accurate, a good deal more than "humanity" alone motivated the Washingtons to receive the Quaker embassy sympathetically and write on their behalf. Gilpin, *Exiles in Virginia*, 202, 210; John W. Jordan, *Colonial and Revolutionary Families of Pennsylvania: Genealogical and Personal Memoirs*, 3 vols. (New York: Lewis, 1911), 1:608; Carl Baurmeister to Major-General von Jungkenn, May 10, 1778, in Carl Baurmeister, Bernhard A. Uhlendorf, and Edna Vosper, eds., "Letters of Major Baurmeister during the Philadelphia Campaign, 1777–1778," *PMHB* 60 (1936): 171.

29. *DED*, 297 (Apr. 6, 1778).

30. *DED*, 297–98 (Apr. 6–9, 1778); ED to Friends in Philadelphia, Apr. 10, 1778, DSP, 3:47.

31. ED to HD, Apr. 10, 11, 1778, DSP, 3:46, 51.

32. HD to ED, Apr. 11, 14, 1778, DSP, 3:50, 52.

33. *DED*, 298, 299 (Apr. 10, 14, 1778); Timothy Matlack to Samuel Allinson, Apr. 15, 1778, Allinson and Taylor Family Papers, QSC.

34. *DED*, 298–301 (Apr. 10, 11, 14, 20, 1778).

35. HD to ED, Apr. 16, 1778, DSP, 3:53.

36. ED to Mary Sandwith, Apr. 22, 23, 1778, DSP, 3:51; *DED*, 302 (Apr. 24, 25, 1778).

37. *DED*, 303 (Apr. 27–29, 1778).

38. *DED*, 303–4 (Apr. 29–30, 1778). Fisher made a similar remark in her diary, though her account of this entire ordeal was suffused throughout with spiritual commentary; Fisher Diaries, May 29, 1778.

39. *DED*, 304, 305 (Apr. 30, May 1, 4, 6, 9, 11, 1778).

40. *DED*, 367, 375, 379, 385, 387, 395, 399 (Apr. 10, Sept. 15, Nov. 17, 1780, Apr. 4–7, May 18, 1781, Jan. 16, May 19, 1782). HD estimated in 1776 that his share of the profits from J&D's operations between 1761 and 1776 (excluding "dubious and bad debts") was £20,566. By 1784, his "part of the stock in their hands" (again excluding "dubious and bad debts") had risen to £24,081, due in part to additional payments by those in debt to J&D; HD JL 1776–91, Jan. 19, 1776, July 13, 1784.

41. *DED*, 316, 317, 319, 367, 381, 397 (July 15, 22, Aug. 4, 1778, Apr. 1, 1780, Dec. 19, 1781, Mar. 28, 1782).

42. *DED*, 308, 310, 326, 363, 403–4 (May 27, June 9, Sept. 11–12, 1778, Nov. 30, 1779, Sept. 14, 16, 18, 1782); Jesse George to HD, June 16, 1778, HSDP.

43. HD to unnamed friend, Dec. 16, 1779, DSP, 3:58; *DED*, 344 (May 2, 1779).

44. *DED*, 354, 355, 359–60, 370 (June 15, 28, Sept. 14, 18, 1779, June 25, 1780).

45. *DED*, 306 (May 18, 1778); "Letters of Major Baurmeister during the Philadelphia Campaign, 1777–1778," *PMHB* 60 (1936): 178–80; Hannah Griffitts, "Meschianza; or, Answer to the Question, What Is It?," Griffitts Papers. For examples of advertisements posted by "Ladies Hair-Dressers from London," see *Pennsylvania Ledger*, Dec. 10, 1777, and *Royal Pennsylvania Gazette*, Mar. 24, 1778.

46. *DED*, 305–7 (May 14, 19, 20, 22–25, 1778).

47. *DED*, 308–10 (May 26, June 8, 9, 1778).

48. *DED*, 310, 337, 386, 392 (June 9, 14, Dec. 18, 1778, Apr. 27, Sept. n.d., 1781).

49. *DED*, 311, 312 (June 18, 19, 1778). Though Sarah Fisher had been critical of the British during their occupation of the city, especially for their "wanton destruction" of property, her "apprehensions of again coming under the arbitrary power of the Congress" were "very dreadful." When the changeover occurred, she wrote, "Judge, O any impartial person, what were my feelings at this time"; Fisher Diaries, June 8, 12, 18, 1778.

50. *DED*, 312–14 (June 19, 22, 24, 30, July 2, 4, 1778).

51. Fisher Diaries, Dec. 9, 1777; *DED*, 316, 318–20, 323 (July 14, Aug. 1, 11, 14, 25, 1778); Elias Hicks to HD, Oct. 13, 1779, Elias Hicks Manuscript Collection, FHL.

52. *DED*, 317, 321–22 (July 23, Aug. 20–24, 1778). Rebecca Shoemaker was later banished to New York; when she returned a year later by permission of the Executive Council, ED visited her in company with several other Friends; *DED*, 398 (Apr. 29, 1782). Shoemaker's husband left for England in 1783 but returned to the United States in 1786. After losing her home, Grace Galloway boarded with Quaker Deborah Morris

in comparative poverty. She never again saw her husband or daughter and died in 1782. She had hoped that the patriot authorities would let her keep the land she had inherited from her father, but that property was sequestrated until her husband died in 1803. He had sailed to England with their daughter Betsy in October 1778 and never returned; see Grace Galloway, *The Diary of Grace Growden Galloway*, ed. Raymond C. Werner (New York, 1971), esp. 51.

53. *DED*, 322, 327 (Aug. 24, Sept. 21, 1778).

54. *DED*, 314–16, 319–22 (July 6, 7, 12, 13, Aug. 2, 15, 16, 20, 21, 1778).

55. *DED*, 325, 326, 328–32 (Sept. 6, 13, 25, 26, 30, Oct. 2, 6, 17, 20, 1778). For an account of the Roberts trial, see David W. Maxey, *Treason on Trial in Revolutionary Pennsylvania: The Case of John Roberts, Miller* (Philadelphia: APS, 2011).

56. *DED*, 333–34, 337 (Oct. 28, Nov. 3–5, Dec. 19, 1778).

57. *DED*, 341, 342, 356, 357, 391 (Feb. 26, Mar. 30, July 23, 29, 1779, Aug. 10, 1781); Anne Ousterhout, "Controlling the Opposition in Pennsylvania during the Revolution," *PMHB* 105 (1981): 23. For Samuel Fisher's account of his trial and captivity, see "Journal of Samuel Rowland Fisher, 1779–1781," *PMHB* 41 (1917): 145–97, 274–333, 399–457.

58. *DED*, 348–50 (May 22, 24, 25, 1779).

59. *DED*, 351, 352, 357, 359 (May 28, 31, June 6, July 29, Aug. 30, 1779).

60. *DED*, 361–62 (Oct. 4–6, 10, 13, 1779).

61. *DED*, 383, 389 (Jan. 25, July 1, 1781).

62. *Pennsylvania Packet*, Aug. 12, 1780; *DED*, 376, 379–80, 382, 384 (Oct. 4, Nov. 23, 1780, Jan. 12, Mar. 11, 1781).

63. *DED*, 393 (Oct. 24, 1781); Diary of Anna Rawle, Oct. 25, 1781, Letters and Diaries of Rebecca Shoemaker and Her Daughters Anna and Margaret Rawle, 1780–86, Shoemaker Papers, HSP, 487–88 (typescript). Anna Rawle was stepdaughter of a well-known loyalist.

64. *DED*, 394 (Dec. 22, 1781).

65. HD to ED, May 6, 1779, DSP, 3:55; HD to John Pemberton, Dec. 10, 1782, DSP, 1:35.

66. *DED*, 340, 344 (Feb. 20, 21, 23, May 2, 1779).

67. *DED*, 364, 366, 399, 404–7 (Dec. 8, 1779, Feb. 7, 1780, May 8, Oct. 6, 22, Nov. 26, Dec. 3, 1782).

68. *DED*, 699, 938, 1050, 1424, 1530 (July 4, 1795, July 4, 1797, July 4, 1798, July 4, 1801, July 5, 1802). Judith Van Buskirk charts the journey of several women, including ED, toward "a certain kind of peace, however grudging, with their new rulers" in "They Didn't Join the Band: Disaffected Women in Revolutionary Philadelphia," *PH* 62 (1995): 306–29 (quotation 308).

69. *DED*, 2051–52 (July 3–4, 1807). For ED's views on post-revolutionary politics, see Susan Branson, "Elizabeth Drinker: Quaker Values and Federalist Support in the 1790s," *PH* 68 (2001): 465–82.

70. Theodore Thayer, *Israel Pemberton: King of the Quakers* (Philadelphia: Historical Society of Pennsylvania, 1943), 231–32; Hannah Griffitts, "Wrote on the Death of a Person Who Died of a Violent Nervous Disorder Occasioned by the Distress She Suffered in the Late Distracted Times," Griffitts Papers. For wartime losses recorded by the Meeting for Sufferings, see Arthur J. Meekel, *The Relation of the Quakers to the American Revolution* (Washington, D.C.: University Press of America, 1979), 202.

71. Diary of Anna Rawle, Oct. 26, 1781, and Rebecca Shoemaker to Samuel Shoemaker, Dec. 13, 1783, Letters and Diaries of Rebecca Shoemaker and Her Daughters Anna and Margaret Rawle, 489, 238 (typescript).

72. For a similar argument, see Van Buskirk, "They Didn't Join the Band," esp. 313, 322, 324. Ousterhout suggests that neighborly ties may have contributed to the patriots' lenient enforcement of harsh laws passed against "disaffected" Pennsylvanians during the War for Independence; "Controlling the Opposition," 33.

73. HD to Samuel Neale, July n.d., 1784, HD LB 1762–86; Elias Hicks to HD, July 28, 1782, June 3, 1783, Vaux Family Papers, QSC. Ironically, Hicks's teachings would become a major cause of the Hicksite-Orthodox split that occurred within Quakerism in the early nineteenth century.

74. HD was not alone in feeling this way; see Jack D. Marietta, "Wealth, War, and Religion: The Perfecting of Quaker Asceticism, 1740–1783," *Church History* 43 (1974): 239–41.

75. HD to John Pemberton, 29 May 1783, DSP, 1:37.

Chapter 6. "The Cause of Humanity, as Well as Our Interest"

1. HD to John Pemberton, May 29, 1783, DSP, 1:37.

2. *DED,* 413, 419 (Sept. 3, 1783, Feb. 8, 1784); HD to Frederick Pigou Jr., July 3, 29, 1784, HD LB 1762–86; see also Thomas M. Doerflinger, *A Vigorous Spirit of Enterprise: Merchants and Economic Development in Revolutionary Philadelphia* (Chapel Hill: University of North Carolina Press, 1986), 142n14. In addition to those who actually declared bankruptcy, other merchants who found themselves in trouble abandoned trade before they went under.

3. HD to Frederick Pigou Jr., July 3, 29, 1784, HD LB 1762–86; HD to John Pemberton, Dec. 11, 1787, DSP, 1:41; HD to Pigou, Mar. 29, Oct. 8, 1787, Feb. 16, 1788, HD LB 1786–90; *DED,* 421 (Apr. 10, 1784).

4. HD to Frederick Pigou Jr., July 3, 1784, HD LB 1762–86; HD to Samuel Preston, Dec. 7, 1787, and to Pigou, Feb. 16, 1788, HD LB 1786–90; HD to Pigou, May 22, 1790, HD LB 1790–93; HD to David Barclay, Jan. 4, 1794, HD LB 1793–96; AJ to George Bowne, Apr. 20, 1789, AJ LB 1785–90, HSP; Rebecca Shoemaker to Samuel Shoemaker, July 23, 1784, Letters and Diaries of Rebecca Shoemaker and Her Daughters Anna and Margaret Rawle, 1780–86, Shoemaker Papers, HSP, 289 (typescript); *DED,* 435 (June 30, 1785).

5. HD, John Drinker, and John Field to Frederick Pigou Jr., May 31, 1786, and HD to Pigou, Feb. 16, 1788, HD LB 1786–90; HD to John Pemberton, Dec. 11, 1787, DSP, 1:41. A committee appointed to deal with the situation met with AJ several times in 1785, and that November he presented a paper acknowledging that he had acted irresponsibly, but the Monthly Meeting nonetheless disowned him for engaging in commerce "beyond his ability to manage." He appealed to the Quarterly Meeting, which instructed the Monthly Meeting to continue working with him in hope of finding a way forward. A new committee appointed by the Monthly Meeting decided that the original disownment had been justified. The Philadelphia Yearly Meeting then stepped in and formed a joint committee consisting of representatives from the Monthly and Quarterly Meetings. In June 1790, committee members from the Quarterly Meeting took the view that AJ had adequately expressed contrition, but members from the Monthly Meeting still had their doubts, and so yet another committee was appointed to investigate whether he had said and done enough to merit his continuation as a Friend in good standing. When AJ died, still unreconciled to his Monthly Meeting, Friends abandoned further consideration of his case. Philadelphia Monthly Meeting for the Northern District, Apr. 5, 1785–Apr. 24, 1787, passim, Feb. 26, 1788–Nov. 9, 1790, passim, QMR; Philadelphia Quarterly Meeting, Feb. 5, 1787, QMR.

6. HD to Frederick Pigou Jr., Nov. 3, 1790, HD LB 1790–93; see also HD to George Bowne, Oct. 29, 1790, HD LB 1790–93; *Independent Gazette,* Nov. 6, 1790; *DED,* 672–73 (Apr. 19, 20, 1795).

7. Emily C. Blackman, *History of Susquehanna County, Pennsylvania* (Philadelphia: Claxton, Remsen, and Haffelfinger, 1873), 87. According to Drinker, his estate, after payment of all debts, was currently worth over £20,000; HD to Frederick Pigou Jr., Nov. 3, 1790, HD LB 1790–93. HD also occasionally took care of goods passing through Philadelphia on behalf of mercantile friends; see, e.g., HD to ED, Oct. 17, 1791, DSP, 4:8.

8. See Lance Banning, *The Jeffersonian Persuasion: Evolution of a Party Ideology* (Ithaca, N.Y.: Cornell University Press, 1978); Drew McCoy, *The Elusive Republic: Political Economy in Jeffersonian America* (Chapel Hill: University of North Carolina Press, 1980); Joyce Appleby, *Capitalism and a New Social Order: The Republican Vision of the 1790s* (New York: New York University Press, 1984); J. G. A. Pocock, *Virtue, Commerce, and History* (New York: Cambridge University Press, 1985); James T. Kloppenberg, "The Virtues of Liberalism," *Journal of American History* 74 (1987): 9–33; and Alan Houston, *Benjamin Franklin and the Politics of Improvement* (New Haven: Yale University Press, 2008).

9. HD served on the Philadelphia Yearly Meeting's Committee for the Civilization and Welfare of the Indian Natives, formed in 1795, which promoted diplomatic relations with Indian nations, sponsored missionary work in native communities, and donated agricultural equipment to Indian farmers. ED's diary contains many references to peace negotiations with Indian nations and to Indian representatives visiting

Philadelphia. On one occasion, the Drinkers invited "six Indians with their interpreter" to dinner; ED noted that they "behaved with great propriety"; *DED,* 1387 (Feb. 22, 1801). See also *DED,* 477, 622, 654, 749, 775, 807, 997, 1006, 1124, 1388, 1391–92, 1473, 1710, 1759, 1762 (Mar. 14, 1792, Nov. 30, 1794, Feb. 28, Nov. 7, 1795, Feb. 6, May 31, 1796, Jan. 20, Feb. 21, Dec. 30, 1798, Feb. 23, Mar. 7–8, Dec. 21, 1801, Dec. 7, 1803, Aug. 4, 18, 1804); Minutes of the Indian Committee, Philadelphia Yearly Meeting, QMR; and Rayner W. Kelsey, *Friends and the Indians* (Philadelphia: Associated Executive Committee of Friends on Indian Affairs, 1917), 89–110.

10. HD to John Canan, Oct. 15, 1795, HD LB 1793–96; Isaac Hicks to HD, Mar. 15, 1790, HD Correspondence, 1785–1840, QSC; for the certificate of election, see DSP, 1:48. ED left behind no diary entries that year other than for three weeks in July, so we have no record or comment from her on HD's election, which occurred on Apr. 14, 1789; nor do any of HD's letters allude to his election.

11. HD to Thomas Pearsall, Feb. 20, 1805, and to Jason Torrey, Sept. 2, 1805, HD LB 1802–6; *DED,* 992, 1061 (Jan. 1, Aug. 4, 1798); see also *DED,* 1005, 1559, 1563 (Feb. 19, 1798, Sept. 3, 9, 1802).

12. HD to Samuel Preston, June 14, 1792, HD LB 1790–93; HD to John Hilborn, Nov. 15, 1802, to John Tyler, Nov. 15, 1802, to Hilborn and Tyler, Dec. 8, 1802, to Augustine Smith, Dec. 1, 1802, to William Fisher, Feb. 27, Apr. 2, 1804, and to David Prouty Jr., Mar. 11, 1806, HD LB 1802–6.

13. HD to William Cooper, July 9, 1794, to Samuel Watkinson, June 4, 1795, to Frederick Pigou Jr., June 5, July 18, 1795, Jan. 14, 1796, and to John Craig Miller, June 9, 1796, HD LB 1793–96. Land speculators hoped that Europeans would be eager to buy tracts in North America, but military conflict in Europe toward the end of the eighteenth century diverted much of the capital that might otherwise have gone into transatlantic land investment, and those purchases that did take place often led to recrimination.

14. HD to Samuel Preston, Sept. 17, Oct. 19, 1792, HD LB 1790–93; HD to Preston, July 7, 1793, HD LB 1793–96.

15. HD to Samuel Preston, Oct. 29, 1796, HD LB 1793–96; HD to Preston, Apr. 28, 1804, Aug. 14, 1805, and to David Sands, Jan. 17, 31, 1806, HD LB 1802–6; Preston to HD, May 3, Sept. 23, 1805, HD, "Notes on Subjects [Extracts from Letters], 1789–1809," HSP. (For extracts from Preston's letter to HD about Sands, ibid., 421–73.) By this point, HD and Preston were themselves at loggerheads, for which see below. The three men agreed to let Robert Bowne, a New York merchant, mediate among them. The deed was dated Dec. 13, 1806, and recorded in Wayne County, Sept. 12, 1811 (Deed Book, vol. 3, 264).

16. HD to Samuel Preston, July 7, 1793, Nov. 1, 1794, HD LB 1793–96; Preston to HD, Aug. 6, 1795, HD, "Notes on Subjects [Extracts from Letters], 1789–1809"; HD to William Tate, Feb. 27, 1804, HD LB 1802–6. This preference for virtuous laborers had proved a challenge for Puritan leaders in seventeenth-century New England; see

Stephen Innes, *Creating the Commonwealth: The Economic Culture of Puritan New England* (New York: Norton, 1995), chap. 6; and Richard Godbeer, *Sexual Revolution in Early America* (Baltimore: Johns Hopkins University Press, 2002), 21–28.

17. HD to Samuel Preston, June 14, 1792, HD LB 1790–93; HD to Preston, May 9, June 11, Dec. 19, 1793, Aug. 13, Nov. 17, 1794, HD LB 1793–96.

18. HD to Samuel Preston, May 9, 1792, HD LB 1790–93; *DED,* 1961 (Sept. 1, 1806); Benjamin Franklin, *The Autobiography and Other Writings,* ed. Kenneth Silverman (New York: Penguin, 1986), 59–60, 69. ED was also a great believer in the redemptive power of good literature and lent a morally improving volume to one of their former servants, who may or may not have appreciated this gesture, for which see chap 7.

19. Samuel Preston to HD, June 20, July 7, Oct. 11, 1795, HD, "Notes on Subjects [Extracts from Letters], 1789–1809"; HD to Preston, Jan. 4, 1796, HD LB 1793–96; Minutes of Philadelphia Monthly Meeting, Jan. 27, Feb. 2, 1797, QMR.

20. HD to Samuel Preston, Sept. 1, 1795, HD LB 1793–96.

21. For Henry Sandwith's travels on his father's behalf, see "Extracts from HSD's Journal in the Beech Woods" (1788 and 1789), HD Papers, HSP; and HD to John Hilborn, Nov. 15, 1802, HD LB 1802–6. As HD wrote to one of his agents in 1802, "Though my son Henry might at times quit his farm and spend some time with you, yet that would subject him to no small inconvenience and at the same time not answer so good a purpose as my being constantly represented on the spot"; HD to John Tyler, Nov. 15, 1802, HD LB 1802–6.

22. HD to John Hilborn, Nov. 15, 1802, and to Samuel Preston, Feb. 23, 1803, HD LB 1802–6.

23. HD to Samuel Preston, June 23, 1803, and to David Sands, Jan. 31, 1806, HD LB 1802–6. See also "Extracts from the Journal of Samuel Preston, Surveyor, 1787," *PMHB* 22 (1898): 350–65.

24. HD to Samuel Preston, July 12, Dec. 7, 1791, May 23, 1792, HD LB 1790–93; HD to Preston, July 15, 1795, Jan. 4, 1796, HD LB 1793–96; HD to Preston, Apr. 16, 1800, HD LB 1796–1800; HD to Preston, Aug. 15, 1803, HD LB 1802–6.

25. Samuel Preston to HD, Nov. 24, 1789, HD, "Notes on Subjects [Extracts from Letters], 1789–1809"; HD to Preston, Nov. 15, Dec. 7, 1791, HD LB 1790–93; HD to Preston, June 22, 1793, HD LB 1793–96; HD to Preston, Nov. 11, 1797, HD LB 1796–1800; HD to Preston, Oct. 28, 1800, HD LB 1800–1802.

26. Samuel Preston, *A Charge Delivered to the Grand Jury of Wayne County* (Easton, Pa.: Samuel Longcope, 1800); *DED,* 530, 1307 (Nov. 24, 1793, June 11, 1800); HD to Preston, Apr. 16, 1800, HD LB 1796–1800; HD to Preston, Jan. 24, 1801, HD LB 1800–1802; HD to Preston, June 23, 1803, Jan. 13, July 17, 1804, HD LB 1802–6.

27. Samuel Preston to HD, Oct. 4, Nov. 14, 16, Dec. 6, 1805, Jan. 15, 28, 1806, HD, "Notes on Subjects [Extracts from Letters], 1789–1809"; HD to Preston, Oct. 23, Dec. 7, 1805, HD LB 1802–6; *DED,* 1879 (Nov. 22, 1805).

28. HD to Samuel Preston, Apr. 28, June 8, 1804, and to David Sands, Jan. 31, 1806, HD LB 1802–6; HD to Preston, Mar. 19, 1808, HD LB 1806–9.

29. Samuel Preston to HD, Jan. 31, 1802, Sept. 23, 1805, HD, "Notes on Subjects [Extracts from Letters], 1789–1809"; HD to Preston, Sept. 17, 1803, Apr. 28, June 8, 23, 1804, HD LB 1802–6; HD to Preston, Dec. 13, 1806, Oct. 13, 1807, HD LB 1806–9; *DED,* 2010, 2056 (Feb. 18, July 18, 1807); see also *DED,* 2012, 2013, 2015, 2052–55, 2057–59 (Feb. 26, 28, Mar. 6, July 6, 8–11, 13–14, 21–23, 28, 1807).

30. HD and Richard Wells to William Cooper, Jan. 26, 1789, HD LB 1786–90; Cooper to HD and Wells, Jan. 29, 1789, and to HD, June 2, 28, 1789, Correspondence Box 1741–1792, HD Papers, HSP; HD to Robert Morris, Aug. 17, 1789, HSDP. See also Alan Taylor, *William Cooper's Town: Power and Persuasion on the Frontier of the Early American Republic* (New York: Knopf, 1995), 118–19. For two older studies of frontier magnates, see Stephen Innes, *Labor in a New Land: Economy and Society in Seventeenth-Century Springfield* (Princeton, N.J.: Princeton University Press, 1983); and Alan Taylor, *Liberty Men and Great Proprietors: The Revolutionary Settlement on the Maine Frontier, 1760–1820* (Chapel Hill: University of North Carolina Press, 1990).

31. William Cooper to Benjamin Rush, Mar. 23, 1790, Benjamin Rush Correspondence, Rush Family Papers, Library Company of Philadelphia, 26:42; Samuel Stanton to HD, Aug. 22, 1794, and HD to Cooper, May 14, 1802, Correspondence Box 1793–1812, HD Papers, HSP; HD to Cooper, July 9, 1794, HD LB 1793–96; HD to Cooper, May 14, 1803, Apr. 21, 1804, HD LB 1802–6; Joshua Gilpin, "Journey to Bethlehem," *PMHB* 46 (1922): 134; see also Taylor, *William Cooper's Town,* 129.

32. William Cooper to HD, July 29, 1791, Correspondence Box 1741–1792; Cooper to HD, July 6, 1793, Correspondence Box 1793–1812; HD to Cooper, June 13, 1793, HD LB 1793–96. For the sums handed over to Letitia Woodruff, see HD JL 1791–98, 33, 78, 90, 114.

33. See, e.g., HD to William Cooper, Oct. 4, 1791, HD LB 1790–93. For more on the challenges of getting information from one place to another in Early America, see Katherine Grandjean, *American Passage: The Communication Frontier in Early New England* (Cambridge, Mass.: Harvard University Press, 2015).

34. HD to John Tyler, May 26, 1804, Dec. 27, 1805, and to Jason Torrey, May 31, 1804, July 1, 1805, HD LB 1802–6; HD to Torrey, June 8, 1807, HD LB 1806–9. For examples of HD's problems with contractors for road projects, see HD to John Hanna, June 21, 1803, to Adam Hoops, July 20, 1803, to Tyler, May 26, 1804, Dec. 27, 1805, and to Torrey, May 31, 1804, July 1, 1805, HD LB 1802–6.

35. HD to John Coolback, Jan. 19, 1804, to Stacy Potts, Jan. 17, 1805, and to Samuel Preston, Feb. 15, 1805, HD LB 1802–6; see also Phineas G. Goodrich, *History of Wayne County, Pennsylvania* (Honesdale, Pa.: Haines and Beardsley, 1880), 2–4. For Preston's involvement in this struggle, see *DED,* 1140, 1143, 1146, 1147, 1150, 1496, 1499, 1505, 1805 (Feb. 27, Mar. 9, 15, 16, 18–21, 31, Apr. 1, 1799, Feb. 25, Mar. 9, Apr. 4, 5, 1802, Feb. 7, 1805).

36. HD to Augustine Smith, Dec. 1, 1802, to Daniel Stroud, May 28, July 15, 1803, to William Ellis, Aug. 3, 1803, to William Tate, Feb. 27, 1804, and to William Best, Nov. 28, 1805, HD LB 1802–6.

37. See, e.g., HD to John Kinsey, May 9, June 11, 17, July 2, 1793, July 22, Dec. 9, 24, 1794, and to Samuel Preston, June 22, 1793, HD LB 1793–96.

38. HD to Samuel Preston, June 4, 1796, HD LB 1793–96; HD to Elisha Tracy, Dec. 30, 1802, HD LB 1802–6.

39. HD to Elisha Tracy, Dec. 30, 1802, to Ebenezer Bowman, Jan. 10, 1803, to John Hilborn and John Tyler, Mar. 2, 14, Apr. 26, 1803, to Tyler, Mar. 18, 1803, to Hilborn, Apr. 4, 1803, to Bowman, May 7, 1803, and to Robert Rose, Sept. 19, 1803, HD LB 1802–6; *DED*, 1136, 1646 (Feb. 12, 1799, Apr. 26, 1803).

40. HD to John Tyler, Jan. 13, 1803, to Samuel Law, Feb. 17, 1803, to John Hilborn and Tyler, Mar. 31, 1803, to John Bunting, May 10, 1803, and to Ebenezer Bowman, June 7, 1803, HD LB 1802–6; *DED*, 1648 (May 7, 1803); Albert Henry Hinds, *History and Genealogy of the Hinds Family* (Portland, Me.: Thurston Print, 1899), 40–41.

41. HD to William Ellis, May 30, 1803, to James Chapman, June 2, 1803, to Stacy Potts, June 2, 1803, to John Hilborn and John Tyler, June 7, 1803, and to Robert Rose, Sept. 17, 1803, HD LB 1802–6; HD to Rose, Aug. 18, 1806, HD LB 1806–9. For the committee meetings mentioned by ED, see *DED*, 1460, 1507, 1510, 1523, 1592, 1593, 1618, 1630, 1631, 1634, 1637, 1649, 1652, 1654, 1656, 1658, 1660, 1667, 1680, 1685, 1699, 1702–4, 1710, 1713–15, 1723, 1725, 1727, 1737, 1742, 1744, 1745, 1762, 1781, 1797, 1799, 1802, 1805, 1824, 1833, 1853, 1855, 1874, 1896, 1903, 1906, 1907, 1937, 1982, 2001 (Oct. 29, 1801, Apr. 15, 22, June 9, 11, Nov. 19, 25, 1802, Jan. 18, Feb. 25, Mar. 2, 15, 25, May 10, 20, 27, 30, June 8, 13, 15, 21, July 15, Sept. 2, 19, Oct. 24, 25, Nov. 2, 4, 9, 10, 12, Dec. 7, 15, 20, 22, 1803, Jan. 6, 19, Feb. 8, Apr. 10, May 8, 17, 21, 24, Aug. 22, Nov. 21, 1804, Jan. 1, 8, 25, Feb. 8, Apr. 11, May 20, Aug. 5, 15, Oct. 30, 1805, Jan. 3, Feb. 4, 14, 19, June 11, Nov. 22, 1806, Jan. 13, 1807).

42. *DED*, 1694 (Oct. 11, 1803); for visitors from the backcountry and conversations about the Connecticut claims, *DED*, 1136, 1284, 1629, 1724, 1779, 1785, 1800, 1821, 1971, 1983, 1985 (Feb. 12, 1799, Mar. 22, 1800, Feb. 23, 1803, Jan. 20, Nov. 11, Dec. 18, 1804, Jan. 15, Mar. 30, 1805, Oct. 7, Nov. 24, Dec. 1, 1806); for resolution of the court case defending the Intrusion Act of 1795, *DED*, 1613 (Jan. 1, 1803); for the Wayne County courthouse controversy, *DED*, 1140, 1143, 1146, 1147, 1150, 1496, 1499, 1505, 1805 (Feb. 27, Mar. 9, 15, 16, 18–21, 31, Apr. 1, 1799, Feb. 25, Mar. 9, Apr. 4, 5, 1802, Feb. 7, 1805); for the obstacles agents faced surveying the land, *DED*, 1646 (Apr. 26, 1803); for violence against Bartlett Hinds, *DED*, 1648 (May 7, 1803). For ED's awareness of the Union Farm project, discussed below, see *DED*, 536, 555, 748, 939 (Dec. 30, 1793, Apr. 30, 1794, Nov. 4, 1795, July 7, 1797).

43. *DED*, 1714 (Dec. 19, 1803); HD to Ebenezer Bowman, Nov. 15, 1803, to James Harris, Jan. 5, 1804, to Samuel Law, Mar. 21, 1804, to John Ewing, Apr. 9, 1804, and to Robert Rose, July 24, Aug. 7, 14, 1804, HD LB 1802–6.

44. HD to Samuel Law, Oct. 4, 1803, to Jason Torrey, Oct. 19, Nov. 8, 1804, Sept. 2, 1805, and to Samuel Preston, Aug. 14, 1805, HD LB 1802–6; HD to Thomas Eddy, May 10, 1809, HD LB 1806–9; Benjamin Rush to HD, Aug. 13, 1801, HSDP.

45. George W. Corner, ed., *The Autobiography of Benjamin Rush: His "Travels through Life" Together with His Commonplace Book for 1789–1813* (Princeton, N.J.: Princeton University Press, 1948), 177.

46. *Federal Gazette,* Apr. 12, 1790. Maple sugar promoters argued that the production of cane sugar in the West Indies was inefficient and expensive, especially if one took into account the initial cost of buying slaves and the money spent by imperial powers in defending the sugar islands; *National Gazette,* Dec. 5, 1791.

47. *Pennsylvania Gazette,* Sept. 9, 1789; *Pennsylvania Mercury,* Sept. 10, 1789; *Federal Gazette,* June 12, Aug. 26, 27, 31, 1790. For the impact of Saint-Domingue's revolution on sugar availability and prices, see *Dunlap's American Daily Advertiser,* Feb. 25, 1792; and HD to William Cooper, Oct. 4, 1791, HD LB 1790–93.

48. *Federal Gazette,* Aug. 31, Sept. 9, 1790; *Pennsylvania Mercury,* May 16, 1789; *National Gazette,* Dec. 5, 1791; Benjamin Rush, *Account of the Sugar Maple Tree of the United States* (Philadelphia, 1792), 13–14.

49. *General Advertiser,* Aug. 19, 1791; *Federal Gazette,* Aug. 27, 31, 1790; *Pennsylvania Mercury,* June 22, 1790; *Federal Gazette,* Mar. 15, Aug. 26, 1790.

50. *National Gazette,* Dec. 5, 1791; *Federal Gazette,* Feb. 18, Apr. 16, 1792; *National Gazette,* Mar. 19, May 3, 1792; *Pennsylvania Gazette,* Apr. 11, 1792; HD to William Cooper, Mar. 29, 1792, HD LB 1790–93.

51. Rush, *Account of the Sugar Maple Tree,* 9–12. Rush framed his paper as a letter to Thomas Jefferson, who apparently used "no other sugar in his family than that which is obtained from the sugar maple tree." For more on maple sugar boosters and their writings, see Mark Sturges, "'Bleed On, Blest Tree!': Maple Sugar Georgics in the Early American Republic," *Early American Studies* 16 (2018): 353–80.

52. William Cooper to HD, Nov. 24, 1789, Correspondence Box 1741–1792. HD did worry that maple sugar manufacturers might decide at some point to produce rum instead from the sap, but Arthur Noble, an Irish investor who experimented with maple sugar, reassured HD during a visit to Philadelphia that he thought it was overall "more advantageous to make sugar"; HD to Samuel Preston, Apr. 29, 1791, HD LB 1790–93.

53. HD to Robert Morris, Aug. 17, 1789, HSDP; Corner, *Autobiography of Benjamin Rush,* 177. Tench Coxe's *View of the United States of America* (1794) included a chapter on maple sugar and its economic potential.

54. William Cooper to HD, Dec. 3, 1789, Correspondence Box 1741–1792. HD's store in Philadelphia was currently advertising the availability of sugar kettles, for which see *Pennsylvania Gazette,* Aug. 5, 19, 26, 1789.

55. HD to Robert Morris, Aug. 17, 1789, and Morris to HD, Aug. 23, 1789, HSDP; William Cooper to HD, May 22, July 21, 1790, Correspondence Box 1741–1792; "To

The Public," *Albany Gazette,* July 22, 1790, reprinted in *Federal Gazette, Pennsylvania Mercury,* and *Universal Advertiser,* Aug. 3, 1790.

56. HD to Robert Morris, June 16, July 5, 1790, to Benjamin Wilson, Sept. 1, 1790, to George Bowne, Sept. 3, 1790, and to George Joy, Jan. 24, May 14, 1791, HD LB 1790–93; George Washington to HD, June 18, 1790, DSP, 3:79.

57. Edward Pennington to HD, Sept. 21, Oct. 27, 1790, Correspondence Box 1741–1792; HD to William Cooper, Jan. 15, Feb. 7, Mar. 16, 1791, HD LB 1790–93; HD JL 1776–1791, Oct. 25, 1790; *Federal Gazette,* Aug. 31, 1790.

58. *Pennsylvania Packet,* Aug. 24, 1789; HD to Robert Morris, June 16, July 5, 1790, HD LB 1790–93; *Remarks on the Manufacturing of Maple Sugar, with Directions for Its Future Improvement, Collected by a Society of Gentlemen in Philadelphia and Published for the General Information and Benefit of the Citizens of the United States* (Philadelphia, 1790).

59. HD to William Cooper, Jan. 15, 1791, and to George Joy, Jan. 24, 1791, HD LB 1790–93; Tench Coxe to Benjamin Rush, n.d., Benjamin Rush Correspondence, 27:54. I am grateful to Alec Dun for his persuasive argument, based on internal evidence, that Coxe wrote this undated letter in late 1790 or early 1791.

60. John Lincklaen, a Dutchman who was investigating the potential for maple sugar manufacturing in the region, visited Stockport and spent some time with Samuel Preston in late 1791. Lincklaen wrote that he learned little from his host, perhaps because Preston was playing his cards close to his chest, but perhaps because he did not actually have much knowledge to impart. See John Lincklaen, *Travels in the Years 1791 and 1792 in Pennsylvania, New York, and Vermont,* ed. and trans. Helen Lincklaen Fairchild (New York: G. P. Putnam's Sons, 1897), 48–50.

61. HD to John Hilborn, Jan. 26, 1791, and to William Cooper, Mar. 16, Apr. 14, May 6, 1791, HD LB 1790–93; Cooper to HD, Apr. 2, 9, May 14, 1791, Correspondence Box 1741–1792. Cooper had tried to recruit Hilborn, who declined partly on grounds of ill health but also because he was considering a land development scheme of his own in partnership with his brothers. HD then offered to negotiate on Cooper's behalf with a sugar boiler recommended by Edward Pennington, but this fellow also turned out to be unwell and so unable to make the journey into the interior; HD to Cooper, Dec. 25, 1790, Feb. 7, 8, 1791, HD LB 1790–93.

62. HD to George Joy, May 14, Dec. 20, 1791, HD LB 1790–93; see also Corner, *Autobiography of Benjamin Rush,* 194.

63. HD to Samuel Preston, Nov. 15, 1791, and to William Cooper, Mar. 29, 1792, HD LB 1790–93; *Federal Gazette,* Aug. 18, 1791; *Dunlap's American Daily Advertiser,* Aug. 19, 1791; Cooper to Benjamin Rush, Apr. 8, 1791, Benjamin Rush Correspondence, 21:60.

64. William Cooper to HD, Apr. 21, May 3, 1792, Correspondence Box 1741–1792; HD JL 1791–98, Apr. 16, Oct. 18, Nov. 2, 1791; HD to Cooper, June 23, 1792, HD LB 1790–93; see also HD to Cooper, Aug. 6, Nov. 29, 1793, Oct. 21, 1794, HD LB 1793–96.

65. HD to William Cooper, Mar. 16, 1791, to Samuel Preston, June 30, Aug. 9, Sept. 8, 17, 1792, and to John Kinsey, Sept. 14, 19, 1792, HD LB 1790–93.

66. John Watson to HD, Feb. 9, 1793, HSDP; HD to John Kinsey, Apr. 17, May 9, 1793, and to Samuel Preston, June 20, 1793, HD LB 1790–93; HD to Preston, July 2, 7, 1793, HD LB 1793–96.

67. HD to John Kinsey, Dec. 18, 1793, Jan. 8, Feb. 15, Mar. 28, July 22, Nov. 4, 25, Dec. 9, 1794, Jan. 9, 1795, and to Samuel Preston, July 22, Nov. 1, 1794, HD LB 1793–96; *DED,* 567, 572 (June 19, July 7, 1794).

68. HD to Joseph Leaper, June 27, 1794, to Samuel Preston, Oct. 8, 1794, and to John Kinsey, Jan. 9, 1795, HD LB 1793–96. A rival venture funded by Dutch investors also proved unsuccessful and was dismantled in November 1794; Paul Demund Evans, *The Holland Land Company* (Buffalo, N.Y.: Buffalo Historical Society, 1924), 14–15, 63–66.

69. HD to John Kinsey, Apr. 18, 1795, to Thomas Wright, Mar. 27, 1795, and to Samuel Preston, July 15, Sept. 1, Nov. 11, 20, 1795, HD LB 1793–96; HD to Jason Torrey, Sept. 18, 1806, HD LB 1806–9; "Society for Promoting the Manufacture of Sugar from Sugar Maple Trees, 1795," Society Miscellaneous Collection, Box 7B ("Philadelphia Miscell. 1697–1915"), folder 17, HSP; *Pennsylvania Session Laws,* Act of Mar. 30, 1833 (no. 65), 110–11; Alfred Mathews, *History of Wayne, Pike, and Monroe Counties, Pennsylvania* (Philadelphia: R. T. Peck, 1886), 631.

70. HD to John Pemberton, May 29, 1783, DSP, 1:37; HD to George Rome, Oct. 19, 1787, HD LB 1786–90; *DED,* 1066, 1618 (Aug. 14, 1798, Jan. 17, 1803); HD to William Cooper, June 13, 1793, HD LB 1793–96; HD to Jason Torrey, Nov. 14, 1808, HD LB 1806–9; HD to Thomas Scattergood, Nov. 12, 1796, Scattergood Family Papers, QSC.

71. HD to William Cox Ellis, Feb. 15, 1808, HD LB 1806–9.

72. HD to John Pemberton, May 20, 1788, DSP, 1:42.

Chapter 7. "Times Are Much Changed, and Maids Are Become Mistresses"

1. *DED,* 998–99, 1127 (Jan. 29, 1798, Jan. 3, 1799). Cassimere was a closely woven wool fabric.

2. *DED,* 1149–52, 1159, 1239, 1320 (Mar. 27, 31, Apr. 4, 22, Nov. 18, 1799, July 21, 1800).

3. William Priest, *Travels in the United States of America . . .* (London: J. Johnson, 1802), 24; Benjamin Rush, *Essays Literary, Moral, and Philosophical* (Philadelphia, 1798), 121; *DED,* 233, 243, 254, 337, 1013 (Sept. 22, Oct. 13, Nov. 18, 1777, Dec. 18, 1778, Mar. 15, 1798). For more on the friction between householders and domestics, see Karie Diethorn, *Domestic Servants in Philadelphia, 1780–1830* (Philadelphia: Independence National Park, 1986), part 1; Stuart Blumin, *The Emergence of the Middle Class: Social Experience in the American City, 1760–1900* (New York: Cambridge University

Press, 1989), esp. 39; and Debra M. O'Neal, "Mistresses and Maids: The Transformation of Women's Domestic Labor and Household Relations in Late Eighteenth-Century Philadelphia" (Ph.D. diss., University of California, Riverside, 1994).

4. See Cheesman A. Herrick, *White Servitude in Pennsylvania* (1926; New York: Negro Universities Press, 1969); Abbot Emerson Smith, *Colonists in Bondage: White Servitude and Convict Labor in America, 1607–1776* (Chapel Hill: University of North Carolina Press, 1947); David W. Galenson, *White Servitude in Colonial America: An Economic Analysis* (Cambridge: Cambridge University Press, 1981); and esp. Sharon V. Salinger, *"To Serve Well and Faithfully": Labor and Indentured Servants in Pennsylvania, 1682–1800* (New York: Cambridge University Press, 1987), 134–35.

5. Rush, *Essays,* 122; *The Works of George Fox,* 11 vols. (Philadelphia: M. T. C. Gould, 1831), 8:24; Sarah Logan Fisher Diaries, 1776–95, Dec. 20, 1786, HSP. In 1775, around two-thirds of the indentured population in Philadelphia were minors; Diethorn, *Domestic Servants in Philadelphia,* 26.

6. *Moreau de St. Méry's American Journey,* ed. and trans. Kenneth Roberts and Anna M. Roberts (Garden City, N.Y.: Doubleday, 1947), 285, 297–98; see also Robert C. Smith, ed., "A Portuguese Naturalist in Philadelphia, 1799," *PMHB* 78 (1954): 80; Richard Godbeer, *Sexual Revolution in Early America* (Baltimore: Johns Hopkins University Press, 2002), chap. 9; and Clare A. Lyons, *Sex among the Rabble: An Intimate History of Gender and Power in the Age of Revolution, Philadelphia, 1730–1830* (Chapel Hill: University of North Carolina Press, 2006).

7. For the history of slavery in Philadelphia and the city's emergence as a haven for free blacks and runaways, see Gary B. Nash, "Forging Freedom: The Emancipation Experience in Northern Seaport Cities, 1775–1820," in *Slavery and Freedom in the Age of the American Revolution,* ed. Ira Berlin and Ronald Hoffman (Charlottesville: University Press of Virginia, 1983), 3–48; Gary B. Nash, *Forging Freedom: The Formation of Philadelphia's Black Community, 1720–1840* (Cambridge, Mass.: Harvard University Press, 1988); Gary B. Nash and Jean R. Soderlund, *Freedom by Degrees: Emancipation in Pennsylvania and Its Aftermath* (New York: Oxford University Press, 1991); Erika Armstrong Dunbar, *A Fragile Freedom: African American Women and Emancipation in the Antebellum City* (New Haven: Yale University Press, 2008); and Michael Dickinson, "Surviving Slavery: Oppression and Social Rebirth in the Urban British Atlantic, 1680–1807" (Ph.D. diss., University of Delaware, 2017). For Quakers and slavery, see Jean Soderlund, *Quakers and Slavery: A Divided Spirit* (Princeton, N.J.: Princeton University Press, 1985); Ryan P. Jordan, *Slavery and the Meetinghouse: The Quakers and the Abolitionist Dilemma, 1820–1865* (Bloomington: Indiana University Press, 2007); Thomas P. Slaughter, *The Beautiful Soul of John Woolman, Apostle of Abolition* (New York: Hill and Wang, 2008); Maurice Jackson, *Let This Voice Be Heard: Anthony Benezet, Father of Atlantic Abolitionism* (Philadelphia: University of Pennsylvania Press, 2009); Michael J. Crawford, *The Having of Negroes Is Become a Burden: The Quaker Struggle to Free Slaves in Revolutionary North Carolina* (Gainesville: University Press of

Florida, 2010); Brycchan Carey, *From Peace to Freedom: Quaker Rhetoric and the Birth of American Antislavery, 1657–1761* (New Haven: Yale University Press, 2012); Geoffrey Plank, *John Woolman's Path to the Peaceable Kingdom: A Quaker in the British Empire* (Philadelphia: University of Pennsylvania Press, 2012); Julie L. Holcomb, *Moral Commerce: Quakers and the Transatlantic Boycott of the Slave Labor Economy* (Ithaca, N.Y.: Cornell University Press, 2016); Gary B. Nash, *Warner Mifflin: Unflinching Quaker Abolitionist* (Philadelphia: University of Pennsylvania Press, 2017); and Marcus Rediker, *The Fearless Benjamin Lay: The Quaker Dwarf Who Became the First Revolutionary Abolitionist* (Boston: Beacon Press, 2017).

8. *DED*, 543, 657, 983, 1015, 1018 (Jan. 30, 1794, Mar. 11, 1795, Nov. 30, 1797, Mar. 23, Apr. 2, 1798). Joseph Drinker, HD's brother, wrote an essay advocating full admission for blacks and circulated it among Friends in 1795; see Thomas E. Drake, "Joseph Drinker's Pleas for Admission of Colored People to the Society of Friends, 1795," *Journal of Negro History* 32 (1947): 110–12; and Nash, *Forging Freedom*, 180. For Warner Mifflin's work as an antislavery activist, see Nash, *Warner Mifflin*. For correspondence between Warner Mifflin and HD about the placement of black children in Philadelphia households, see Warner Mifflin to HD, Jan. 21, 1795, Apr. 1, June 16, 1798, HD Correspondence, 1785–1840, QSC. Quakers such as HD sometimes found it difficult to disassociate entirely from the slave system. When HD and Isaac Hicks found that they had been named as executors for the estate of a merchant based in the Bay of Honduras (now known as Belize), the two men agreed that they should, on principle, leave any matters relating to "slaves and black people" to the other four executors who lived there. Yet separating out the handling of enslaved people from other components of the estate was entirely artificial and served only to salve HD's and his friend's consciences; HD to Isaac Hicks, Jan. 3, 1807, HD LB 1806–9.

9. On one occasion, ED mentioned that their son Henry Sandwith was copying letters because his father currently had no clerk. One young fellow had just been dismissed "as not capable for HD's business," while another, Isaac Child, who was "capable but very unsteady," had disappeared yet again on one of his drinking binges; *DED*, 1144 (Mar. 13, 1799); for Isaac Child, *DED*, 1131, 1132, 1136, 1139, 1146, 1151, 1156 (Jan. 19, 22, Feb. 11, 25, Mar. 16, Apr. 2, 3, 15, 1799).

10. *DED*, 1055, 1616 (July 20, 1798, Jan. 11, 1803).

11. *DED*, 326, 811 (Sept. 10, 1778, June 10, 1796). For more on servants' duties, see Diethorn, *Domestic Servants in Philadelphia*, part 2. For the number of domestic staff employed in several Philadelphia households at this time, ibid., app. A.

12. See Ryan K. Smith, *Robert Morris's Folly: The Architectural and Financial Failures of an American Founder* (New Haven: Yale University Press, 2014), esp. 81, 134; and Robert C. Alberts, *The Golden Voyage: The Life and Times of William Bingham, 1752–1804* (Boston: Houghton Mifflin, 1969), esp. 163–64. The Drinkers did need to have at least one servant on hand who could cook competently and at times had difficulty finding someone with the appropriate skills; see *DED*, 1748, 1753, 1766, 1776, 1934, 1941 (June

6, July 2, Sept. 8, Oct. 29, 1804, May 30, June 26, 1806). ED was very pleased when indentured servant Sally Dawson turned out to be "a handy cook" so that she could help to prepare meals alongside her other household tasks; *DED,* 981 (Nov. 21, 1797).

13. See Laurel Thatcher Ulrich, *Good Wives: Image and Reality in the Lives of Women in Northern New England, 1650–1750* (New York: Knopf, 1982).

14. *DED,* 580, 1475 (Aug. 8, 1794, May 28, 1802). For the rising importance of ironing, see Annegret S. Ogden, *The Great American Housewife: From Helpmate to Wage Earner, 1776–1986* (Westport, Conn.: Greenwood Press, 1986), 22. The diaries and journals of other Philadelphian household mistresses such as Sarah Fisher, Deborah Logan, Nancy Shippen, and Ann Warder also contain references to working in the kitchen alongside servants. ED seems to have been more sensitive about her menfolk performing tasks that she thought appropriate for servants; see *DED,* 748, 1662 (Nov. 4, 1795, June 27, 1803).

15. *DED,* 765 (Dec. 29, 1795); Hester Chapone, *Letters on the Improvement of the Mind* (Philadelphia, 1786), 99, 100, 102; Elizabeth Griffith, *Letters Addressed to Young Married Women* (Philadelphia, 1796), no. 7, pp. 55–56; Ethel Armes, ed., *Nancy Shippen: Her Journal Book* (1935; New York, 1968), 220–21; Fisher Diaries, Sept. 27, 1788, Apr. 9, 1795. Before ED's marriage, she and her sister regularly shut themselves away to go over their account books; see, e.g., *DED,* 62–64, 68, 70 (June 18, 25, July 4, 31, Aug. 18, 1760). Once married, ED made little mention of such matters in her diary entries, but she did note down separately on the covers of several diary volumes calculations relating to the cost of clothing and other household expenses; see *DED,* 158–59, 185–87, 1612, 1797 (n.d.). She also kept a detailed inventory of expenditures in a memorandum book, from which HD copied extracts into his own account book; see HD JL 1776–91, June 17, 1776.

16. Bernard L. Herman, *Town House: Architecture and Material Life in the Early American City, 1780–1830* (Chapel Hill: University of North Carolina Press, 2005), chap. 4; Chapone, *Letters on the Improvement of the Mind,* 99, 100. But when ED went to stay with relatives or friends, she often shared a room with one or more of her servants. A sermon published in 1800 on the subject of "domestic happiness" advised that household mistresses should avoid "foolish familiarity" that would "confound all distinction of rank," and Nancy Shippen noted the importance of not allowing daughters to "converse with servants." Yet regular conversation and a degree of familiarity were inevitable. See Joseph Buckminster, *Domestic Happiness: A Sermon* (Portsmouth, N.H., 1800), 10–11; and Armes, *Shippen,* 148.

17. *DED,* 653, 1387, 1417, 1426, 1441, 1454, 1457–58, 1460, 1506, 1507, 1845 (Feb. 24, 1795, Feb. 19, June 5, July 15, Aug. 31, Oct. 9, 20, 28, 1801, Apr. 9, 11, 13, 1802, July 7, 1805).

18. On one occasion ED mentioned that she and HD had differed over whether to keep a problematic servant, and on another she questioned HD's decision to promote a servant to the position of driver; both cases are discussed below.

19. *DED,* 765, 810, 848, 1456, 1941 (Dec. 29, 1795, June 9, Oct. 1, 1796, Oct. 14, 1801, June 26, 1806). Several former employees returned to ask the Drinkers for recommendations; see *DED,* 1684, 1754, 1856, 1991, 2007 (Sept. 14, 1803, July 6, 1804, Aug. 20, 1805, Dec. 21, 1806, Feb. 5, 1807).

20. *DED,* 781, 788–89, 793–94, 807, 1285, 1289, 1456, 1511, 1517–19, 1588, 1590, 1904, 1911, 2008, 2030, 2065, 2083 (Mar. 8, Apr. 6, 18, May 30, 1796, Mar. 25, Apr. 9, 1800, Oct. 17, 1801, Apr. 28, May 21, 22, 26, Nov. 5, 14, 1802, Feb. 6, Mar. 11, 1806, Feb. 8, Apr. 25, Aug. 15, Oct. 4, 1807); HD to ED, Apr. 17, 1796, DSP, 4:76.

21. *DED,* 678 (May 6, 1795); Simon Gratz, "Some Material for a Biography of Mrs. Elizabeth Fergusson, née Graeme," *PMHB* 39 (1915): 387.

22. *DED,* 603, 667, 672–73 (Oct. 7, 1794, Apr. 8, 19, 1795); see below for references to the baby's skin color.

23. *DED,* 580, 581, 584, 599 (Aug. 8–11, 20, Sept. 27, 1794). The Haines household also had to deal with the embarrassment of an indentured servant giving birth to an illegitimate child: "Aunt is anxious to get a place for it somewhere in the country, within a few miles, as they can't think of keeping it in the house" (Hannah Marshall Haines to Sarah H. Young, July 17, 1809, Wyck Association Collection, APS).

24. *DED,* 584, 600, 603 (Aug. 19, Sept. 30, Oct. 7, 1794).

25. *DED,* 586–88, 603, 613, 615–18 (Aug. 28, 29, Sept. 3, Oct. 9, 31, Nov. 7, 8, 11, 13, 1794).

26. *DED,* 623, 624, 627, 632, 635 (Dec. 2, 6, 13, 23, 27, 1794).

27. *DED,* 632 (Dec. 23, 1794).

28. *DED,* 603, 649, 652, 655, 705 (Oct. 8, 1794, Feb. 14, 21, Mar. 3, July 14, 1795). For another occasion on which HD resorted to physical violence, whipping a servant who "had got in liquor and left the horses in the road," see *DED,* 958 (Aug. 31, 1797).

29. *DED,* 667, 672–73 (Apr. 8, 19, 1795); see also Godbeer, *Sexual Revolution,* chap. 8.

30. *DED,* 642, 669, 679, 681, 697, 698, 700, 704–5 (Jan. 21, Apr. 11, May 9, 15, June 29, July 2, 5, 14, 1795).

31. *DED,* 673, 745, 763, 791, 808, 824 (Apr. 19, 23, Oct. 25, Dec. 19, 1795, Apr. 11, 12, June 2, July 23, 1796).

32. *DED,* 995, 1024, 1120, 1141, 1945, 2022 (Jan. 12, Apr. 18, Dec. 15, 1798, Mar. 1, 1799, July 8, 1806, Apr. 1, 1807). When Sally's sister had died in September 1795, HD had agreed then also to authorize her burial in the Friends' burial ground, though as ED pointed out in her diary, the family had "no claim to such indulgence"; *DED,* 734 (Sept. 28, 1795).

33. *DED,* 396, 1143 (Feb. 21, 1782, Mar. 8, 1799). Maria Johnson, "a negro" whom ED hired in June 1806, also hoped that domestic employment would provide a solution to her plight. When ED became suspicious that Maria was pregnant (or, as she put it, "in a way that will not suit"), she asked her "point-blank," and Maria admitted that this was the case. She explained that her husband had died shortly after siring the child and

that she had traveled from New Jersey in search of work. When asked why she did not stay with her kinfolk, Maria replied that she needed money and that relatives would not "pay her wages." ED asked if her family had treated her well, and when Maria admitted they had, her mistress declared, "Then go back to them and live without wages till thou art up again." The next day, the Drinkers put Maria on a boat that would take her back to New Jersey; *DED*, 1941, 1949, 1950 (June 26, July 21–23, 1806).

34. *DED*, 366, 816, 833, 995, 1029, 1030, 1249, 1264, 1756 (Feb. 10, 1780, June 23, Aug. 17, 1796, Jan. 14, May 4–6, 1798, Dec. 24, 1799, Jan. 6, 1800, July 17, 1804).

35. *DED*, 1239, 1287, 1401, 1485 (Nov. 18, 1799, Mar. 31, 1800, Apr. 16, 1801, Jan. 8, 1802); for an example of a mother bringing her child to work, see *DED*, 1939 (June 21, 1806).

36. *DED*, 952, 1047, 1050, 1059, 1061–62, 1066, 1517, 1647, 1649, 1656, 1658 (Aug. 15, 1797, June 26, July 3, 31, Aug. 4, 14, 1798, May 18, 1802, May 4, 9, June 8, 13, 1803).

37. *DED*, 1473, 1631, 1632 (Dec. 20, 1801, Mar. 4, 7, 1803).

38. *DED*, 1470, 1473, 1633, 1650, 1676, 1686 (Dec. 10, 20, 1801, Mar. 12, May 13, Aug. 14, Sept. 22, 1803); *Moreau de St. Méry's American Journey*, 285, 297–98.

39. *DED*, 773–74 (Jan. 20, 1796). Though such acts of generosity were generally contingent upon the servant's deference and good behavior, on one occasion ED gave assistance even to a woman, now married and pregnant, who as a girl had proved "so very naught" as a servant that they had "parted with her." Her present needs eclipsed her former behavior; *DED*, 773 (Jan. 26, 1796).

40. *DED*, 430, 431, 624, 634, 1059, 1278 (Nov. 22, Dec. 10, 1784, Dec. 6, 26, 1794, July 29, 1798, Feb. 24, 1800). The Drinkers also hosted temporarily a number of minors who arrived in the city as refugees from slavery until they moved on to other households.

41. *DED*, 533, 535, 634, 662, 670, 682, 694, 772, 796, 816, 821, 860, 981, 995, 1057, 1090, 1546 (Dec. 5, 20, 1793, Dec. 26, 1794, Mar. 27, Apr. 14, May 20, June 22, 1795, Jan. 21, Apr. 26, June 24, July 9, Nov. 14, 1796, Nov. 21, 1797, Jan. 14, July 26, Sept. 30, 1798, Aug. 10, 1802).

42. *DED*, 1687–89 (Sept. 28, 29, 1803).

43. *DED*, 1689–91, 1712 (Sept. 30–Oct. 3, Dec. 12, 1803); HD to Robert Rose, Oct. 4, 1803, and to Samuel Law, Oct. 4, 1803, HD LB 1802–6.

44. *DED*, 677–78 (May 5, 6, 1795).

45. *DED*, 679–80, 682, 692, 748 (May 9, 10, 18, June 15, Nov. 4, 1795); for James Denning's departure, *DED*, 770 (Jan. 11, 1796).

46. *DED*, 879, 881, 891–93, 1202 (Jan. 11, 19, Feb. 21, 24, 25, 1797, Aug. 24, 1799); see also Coroner's Inquisition, Chester County, Dec. 18, 1796, and Chester County Quarter Sessions Docket E, February Term 1797, 9, Quarter Session Papers, both in Chester County Archives, West Chester, Pa. William Benemann suggests that the deceased young man might have made sexual advances toward Denning, who then beat him to death either in outrage or because he had similar feelings but panicked;

William Benemann, *Male-Male Intimacy in Early America: Beyond Romantic Friendship* (New York: Haworth Press, 2006), 207–11. There is not a shred of evidence to support this reading.

47. For Benjamin Oliver, *DED*, 1556 (Aug. 31, 1802); for Mary Brookhouse, *DED*, 412, 891, 947, 955, 981, 1175, 1195, 1203, 1227, 1230, 1233–35, 1238 (July 26, 1783, Feb. 22, July 31, Aug. 21, Nov. 21, 1797, June 4, Aug. 2, 24, Oct. 23, 28, Nov. 5, 9, 10, 16, 1799); for Alice Wright, *DED*, 1622, 1623, 1629, 1630 (Feb. 2, 4, 23, 25, 26, 1803).

48. *DED*, 853, 863, 898, 902, 912, 952, 1233, 1234 (Oct. 17, Nov. 30, 1796, Mar. 13, Apr. 28, Aug. 12, 1797, Nov. 2, 6, 1799); Daily Occurrence Docket, May 18, 1790, Guardians of the Poor, Philadelphia City Archives. Many of the women who gained admittance to the poorhouse had been servants in affluent families but were now reduced to poverty by illness or old age; see Billy G. Smith, *The "Lower Sort": Philadelphia's Laboring People, 1750–1800* (Ithaca: Cornell University Press, 1990), 170–71; and O'Neal, "Mistresses and Maids," 242–46. Commendations could make all the difference in ensuring that an applicant gained admittance, and former employers could bestow this favor without assuming actual responsibility for the indigent's care. A few years earlier, the Drinkers' neighbor Jacob Hiltzheimer had escorted one of his ex-servants, Margaret Yankin, to the poorhouse after a lame arm and bad health made it impossible for her to support herself; Jacob Hiltzheimer, Diary, Oct. 19, 1795, APS.

49. For example, *DED*, 528 (Nov. 19, 1793). See also Susan E. Klepp, "Philadelphia in Transition: A Demographic History of the City and Its Occupational Groups, 1720–1830" (Ph.D. diss., University of Pennsylvania, 1980); Lisa Wilson, *Life after Death: Widows in Pennsylvania, 1750–1800* (Philadelphia: Temple University Press, 1992); and Carole Shammas, "The Female Social Structure of Philadelphia in 1775," *PMHB* 107 (1983): 69–83.

50. *DED*, 1925, 1928, 1929, 1977 (May 2, 12, 13, Nov. 1, 1806). The Philadelphia County census for 1810 includes a household head in Southwark named Anna Duffey who had two men living under her roof. Perhaps these were lodgers, and perhaps she had finally succeeded in her venture (Pennsylvania Census for 1810, HSP).

51. *DED*, 1354, 1389, 1615, 1673 (Nov. 15, 1800, Feb. 28, 1801, Jan. 6, Aug. 4, 5, 1803); Daily Occurrence Docket, Apr. 8, May 12, 1807, Almshouse Admissions and Discharges, Apr. 5, June 13, 1811, Guardians of the Poor, Philadelphia City Archives. For more discussion of single older domestics working in Philadelphia, see Debra M. O'Neal, "Elizabeth Drinker and Her 'Lone' Women: Domestic Service, Debilities, and (In)Dependence through the Eyes of a Philadelphia Gentlewoman," *PH* 68 (2001): 435–64.

52. *DED*, 1192, 2086 (July 22, 1799, Oct. 12, 1807).

53. *DED*, 1327, 1502, 1525–26, 1527, 1725 (Aug. 5, 1800, Mar. 24, June 21, 25, 1802, Jan. 21, 1804).

54. Augustine Jones, a young sailor and merchant who sailed back and forth between Philadelphia and Port-au-Prince, corresponded with HD and visited the Drinker home on a number of occasions. Their conversations must have included discussion

of the uprising and its implications. For references to Jones and his visits to Front Street, see *DED*, 367, 666, 668, 670, 675, 709, 747, 782, 784, 821, 823, 825, 868, 895, 1051 (Feb. 16, 1780, Apr. 5, 9, 15, 30, July 24, Nov. 2, 1795, Mar. 14, 22, July 11, 18, 27, Dec. 18, 1796, Mar. 2, 1797, July 7, 1798).

55. *DED*, 471, 582–83, 1489, 1497, 1601–2, 1659 (Sept. 21, 1791, Aug. 15, 1794, Jan. 26, Mar. 5, Dec. 24, 1802, June 17, 1803). See also Gary Nash, "Reverberations of Haiti in the American North: Black Saint Dominguans in Philadelphia," *PH* 65, special issue: "Explorations in Early American Culture" (1998): 44–73; Ashli White, *Encountering Revolution: Haiti and the Making of the Early Republic* (Baltimore: Johns Hopkins University Press, 2010); Janet Polasky, *Revolutions without Borders: The Call to Liberty in the Atlantic World* (New Haven: Yale University Press, 2015); and James Alexander Dun, *Dangerous Neighbors: Making the Haitian Revolution in Early America* (Philadelphia: University of Pennsylvania Press, 2016).

56. *DED*, 422, 935, 1043 (May 5, 1784, June 24, 1797, June 10, 1798). For more information about the first black Freemason lodges in the United States, see *DED*, 935n96.

57. *DED*, 502, 998–99, 1074, 1703 (Sept. 8, 1793, Jan. 29, 30, Aug. 28, 1798, Nov. 8, 1803).

58. *DED*, 1097, 1763 (Oct. 13, 1798, Aug. 24, 1804).

59. *DED*, 1036 (May 22, 1798). ED referred to Lydia Williams as "a yellow woman" and her daughter Judia as a "black child." In 1800, when William Merritt came to visit in hope of placing his little daughter, five-year-old Becky, ED described him as "mulatto" and his daughter as "black"; *DED*, 828, 1288, 1292 (Aug. 6, 1796, Apr. 2, 20, 1800); see also *DED*, 1773 (Oct. 13, 1804). On the other hand, though ED usually referred to her mixed-race washerwoman Alice Wright as "yellow," in one entry she grouped her with other women working for her and her daughter Ann as "negroes"; *DED*, 1239 (Nov. 18, 1799).

60. An exception to this pattern was Thomas Batt, a "yellow man" who replaced their sick driver for a few months in 1796 and lived in; *DED*, 781 (Mar. 8, 1796).

61. *DED*, 674, 1239, 1385, 1661, 1662, 1741, 1744, 1755, 1993 (Apr. 28, 1795, Nov. 18, 1799, Feb. 10, 11, 1801, June 23, 24, 27, 1803, May 1, 17, July 11, 1804, Dec. 30, 1806); Patience Gibbs to Elizabeth Skyrin, Apr. 15, 1807, DSP, 5:26.

62. *DED*, 995, 1020, 1022, 1024 (Jan. 12, Apr. 9, 15, 19, 1798).

63. Several weeks later, the dog bit another neighbor's "negro boy" in the thigh, inflicting a more serious wound than Tom had suffered. That neighbor had the dog shot. *DED*, 399–401, 682, 811, 1495 (May 23, 24, July 11, 1782, May 19, 20, 1795, June 12, 1796, Feb. 20, 1802); see also *DED*, 1516 (May 13, 1802). In addition to the instances of corporal discipline mentioned in this and the preceding paragraph, see *DED*, 652, 958 (Feb. 21, 1795, Aug. 31, 1797); for another incident that may or may not count as corporal punishment, see *DED*, 1879 (Nov. 21, 1805).

64. *DED*, 606–7, 612, 615, 758 (Oct. 18, 19, 28, Nov. 7, 1794, Dec. 7, 1795).

65. *DED*, 620, 624, 758, 1662, 1888, 1974, 2012 (Nov. 22, Dec. 6, 7, 9, 1795, June 29, 1803, Dec. 26, 1805, Oct. 18, 1806, Feb. 27, 1807).

66. *DED*, 624, 625, 629, 786 (Dec. 6, 10, 15, 1794, Mar. 30, 1796).

67. *DED*, 668, 669, 673, 680, 712, 726, 729, 737, 752, 775 (Apr. 10, 11, 13, 14, 22, May 10, Aug. 4, Sept. 9, 15, Oct. 4, Nov. 16, 1795, Feb. 2, 1796). African Americans did not generally attend regular Quaker worship meetings; see Henry J. Cadbury, "Negro Membership in the Society of Friends," *Journal of Negro History* 21 (1936): 152–53.

68. *DED*, 691, 730, 745, 755, 936, 974, 1531, 1577, 1593 (June 14, Sept. 17, Oct. 25, Nov. 26, 1795, June 26, Oct. 25, 1797, July 11, Oct. 7–9, Nov. 23, 1802).

69. *DED*, 876, 1531–32, 1546, 1590, 1879 (Jan. 2, 1797, July 12, 13, Aug. 10, Nov. 14, 1802, Nov. 21, 1805).

70. *DED*, 1749, 1766, 1818, 1895, 1897 (June 12, Sept. 8, 1804, Mar. 20, 1805, Jan. 1, 8, 1806). For Peter's attendance at Methodist services, see *DED*, 1760, 1762, 1768 (Aug. 5, 19, Sept. 23, 1804).

71. *DED*, 1897, 1898, 1093–5 (Jan. 8, 11, 14, Feb. 5, 6, 8, 9, 1806).

72. *DED*, 1923, 1947, 1949, 1961, 1967 (Apr. 24, July 15, 19, Sept. 1, 23, 1806). See *DED*, 823 (July 20, 1796), for ED's description of *The Cheap Repository*.

73. *DED*, 1400, 1784, 2015, 2032, 2042, 2091, 2095 (Apr. 11, 1801, Dec. 11, 1804, Mar. 7, May 2, June 4, Oct. 31, Nov. 17, 1807).

74. *DED*, 836–37 (Aug. 26, 1796).

Chapter 8. "A Scene of Affliction and Grief"

1. Elias Hicks to HD, Oct. 5, 1779, Elias Hicks Manuscript Collection, FHL; HD to his family, Sept. 16, 1777, DSP, 3:5; HD to Thomas Scattergood, May 16, 1796, Scattergood Family Papers, QSC; *DED*, 1537 (July 25, 1802); Henry S. Drinker to William Drinker, July 5, 1802, Cope Family Papers, HSP.

2. For increasingly rigorous marital regulation within the Society of Friends, see Jack D. Marietta, *The Reform of American Quakerism, 1748–1783* (Philadelphia: University of Pennsylvania Press, 1984), 61–67; Barry Levy, *Quakers and the American Family: British Settlement in the Delaware Valley* (New York: Oxford University Press, 1988), 71–75, 132–33; and J. William Frost, *The Quaker Family in Colonial America* (New York: St. Martin's Press, 1973), chaps. 8, 9.

3. *DED*, 1332 (Aug. 20, 1800).

4. *DED*, 473, 636, 677 (Sept. 28, 1791, Dec. 31, 1794, May 6, 1795); HD to John William Gerar de Brahm, June 30, Oct. 17, 1795, HD LB 1793–96.

5. *DED*, 663, 731, 1188, 1537, 1668 (Mar. 28, Sept. 21, 1795, July 9, 1799, July 25, 1802, July 17, 1803).

6. *DED*, 748–49, 857, 884–85, 889 (Nov. 5, 1795, Nov. 1, 1796, Jan. 27–28, Feb. 13, 1797).

7. *DED*, 1198 (Aug. 12, 1799); HD to William Dillwyn, July 4, 1806, HD LB 1806–9. See also *DED*, 645, 708, 1406 (Jan. 31, July 22, 1795, May 1, 1801).

8. *DED*, 463, 1058, 1663 (July 20, 1791, July 28, 1798, July 2, 1803).

9. Estimates of how many died during the 1793 epidemic vary, but it seems likely that more than five thousand perished, or around a tenth of the city's population; Susan E. Klepp, "'How Many Precious Souls Are Fled?': The Magnitude of the 1793 Yellow Fever Epidemic," in J. Worth Estes and Billy G. Smith, eds., A *Melancholy Scene of Devastation: The Public Response to the 1793 Philadelphia Yellow Fever Epidemic* (Canton, Mass.: College of Physicians of Philadelphia and Library Company of Philadelphia, 1997), 163–82; Tom W. Smith, "The Dawn of the Urban-Industrial Age: The Social Structure of Philadelphia, 1790–1830" (Ph.D. diss., University of Chicago, 1980), 90–91. See also John Harvey Powell, *Bring Out Your Dead: The Great Plague of Yellow Fever in Philadelphia in 1793* (Philadelphia: University of Pennsylvania Press, 1949); Simon Finger, *The Contagious City: The Politics of Public Health in Early Philadelphia* (Ithaca, N.Y.: Cornell University Press, 2012), chap. 8; and Billy G. Smith, *Ship of Death: A Voyage That Changed the Atlantic World* (New Haven: Yale University Press, 2013).

10. Mathew Carey, *A Short Account of the Malignant Fever Lately Prevalent in Philadelphia* (Philadelphia: Mathew Carey, 1793), 74; Edwin B. Bronner, ed., "Letter from a Yellow Fever Victim: Philadelphia, 1793," *PMHB* 86 (1962): 205–7; Martha Washington to Fanny Bassett, Jan. 14, 1794, in Joseph E. Fields, ed., *"Worthy Partner": The Papers of Martha Washington* (Westport, Conn.: Greenwood Press, 1994), 254. Relatives and friends outside the city often had no way of knowing who had died until long afterward. "How often have I been afraid to hear from Philadelphia," wrote William Cooper that December, "lest my best friend Henry Drinker or some of his family should have fallen"; Cooper to HD, Dec. 16, 1793, Correspondence Box 1741–92, HD Papers, HSP. See also Isaac Robinson to HD, May 11, 1799, Vaux Family Papers, QSC.

11. *DED*, 495, 515, 516, 586 (Aug. 23, Oct. 9, 10, 1793, Aug. 26, 1794); HD to Enoch Edwards, Sept. 28, 1793, to James Harris, Oct. 24, 1793, to Richard Lawrence, Nov. 15, 1793, to John Kinsey, Nov. 23, 1793, and to Frederick Pigou Jr., Nov. 27, 1793, HD LB 1793–96.

12. *DED*, 494–98, 500, 504, 517 (Aug. 16, 19, 23, 26–28, 30–31, Sept. 3, 11, Oct. 12, 1793).

13. *DED*, 496, 501, 503, 510, 517–18 (Aug. 26, Sept. 6, 10, 27, Oct. 13–14, 1793). For examples of these personal tragedies, see *DED*, 500, 503–6 (Sept. 4, 9, 11, 16, 1793).

14. *DED*, 949–52, 955–57 (Aug. 6–9, 21, 24, 26–27, 1797); HD to ED, Aug. 25, 28, 30, Sept. 2, 7, 8, 11, 1797, DSP, 4:84, 86–90, 93–94; ED to HD, Aug. 28, Sept. 9, 12, 1797, DSP, 4:85, 92, 95; *Claypoole's American Daily Advertiser*, Aug 24, 1797.

15. *DED*, 1208, 1689, 1691–92, 1862, 1863, 1865, 1866 (Sept. 7, 1799, Sept. 30, Oct. 4, 1803, Sept. 6, 8, 10, 16, 19, 20, 1805). For ED's suspicion that her daughter Ann might have had the yellow fever in 1794, see *DED*, 608, 633, 658 (Oct. 21, 22, Dec. 24, 1794, Mar. 15, 1795).

16. *DED,* 456, 457, 464, 537 (June 17, 21, 24, 1791, Dec. 31, 1793).

17. HD to MS, Oct. 5, 1791, DSP, 3:80; ED and HD to MS, and ED to MS, Oct. 5, 1791, DSP, 4:3; HD to MS and his children, Oct. 7, 1791, DSP, 4:4.

18. *DED,* 471, 474, 537–38 (Sept. 20, Oct. 4, 1791, Dec. 31, 1793); HD to MS, Oct. 9, 1791, and to ED, Oct. 17, 1791, DSP, 4:5, 8; HD to Samuel Preston, Oct. 17, 1791, HD LB 1790–93.

19. HD to MS and his children, Oct. 9, 1791, DSP, 4:5; HD to ED, Oct. 17, 20, 27, Nov. 6, 1791, DSP, 4:8, 14, 25, 38; Benjamin Rush to HD, Nov. 10, 1791, DSP, 1:49; HD to John William Gerar de Brahm, June 30, 1795, HD LB 1793–96; Joshua Edwards to HD, Jan. 18, 1793, HSDP.

20. HD to Frederick Pigou Jr., Oct. 18, Dec. 1, 1791, HD LB 1790–93; ED to HD, Oct. 18, 21, 1791, DSP, 4:9, 15; HD to ED, Oct. 21, 23, Nov. 6, 1791, DSP, 4:17, 18, 39.

21. HD to ED, Oct. 18, 19, 21, Nov. 8, 18, 1791, DSP, 4:10, 12, 16, 42, 56.

22. HD to ED, Oct. 17, 19, 21, 23, 27, Nov. 1, 6, 10, 1791, DSP, 4:8, 12, 16, 18, 26, 31, 38, 45.

23. *DED,* 538 (Dec. 31, 1793); HD to ED, Nov. 23, 1791, and to MS, Nov. 29, 1791, DSP, 4:61, 64; HD to Joshua Edwards, Dec. 13, 1791, HD LB, 1790–93.

24. *DED,* 538 (Dec. 31, 1793); HD to Samuel Preston, Dec. 7, 1791, HD LB 1790–93; HD to John William Gerar de Brahm, June 30, 1795, HD LB 1793–96.

25. Marietta, *Reformation of American Quakerism,* 62–65.

26. Ibid., 65–67. The committee's efforts were duly approved and published as *Rules of Discipline and Christian Advices of the Yearly Meeting of Friends for Philadelphia and New Jersey* (Philadelphia: Samuel Sansom, 1797).

27. *DED,* 662, 670 (Mar. 27, Apr. 16, 1795). For this transformation in sexual mores, see Richard Godbeer, *Sexual Revolution in Early America* (Baltimore: Johns Hopkins University Press, 2002), chaps. 7–9.

28. *DED,* 115, 198, 202, 204, 208, 246, 323, 341, 368, 405, 410 (Apr. 8, 1765, Mar. 1, July 20, Sept. 7, 1774, May 3, 1775, Oct. 20, 1777, Aug. 25, 1778, Mar. 4, 15, 1779, Apr. 24, 1780, Nov. 4, 1782, Apr. 13, 1783).

29. HD to ED, Nov. 13, 1791, DSP, 4:48; *DED,* 636, 676–77, 1839 (Dec. 31, 1794, May 5, 1795, June 15, 1805). The Drinkers and their children disagreed about a range of issues that the parents saw as morally significant, but once the children reached adulthood, there were limits to parental control. HD disapproved of portraiture and refused to change his position even when assured that other "genteel Quakers" had done so. Yet both of their sons sat for Henry Elouis and James Sharples; William then commissioned Sharples to draw profiles of his sisters. When ED noted that her children played at cards and dominoes in her home, she shifted into French, apparently from embarrassment, and she did the same when recording her suspicion that Molly had been to the theater; *DED,* 799, 828, 1053, 1105, 1235, 1236, 1375, 1408, 1411 (May 2, Aug. 6, 1796, July 15, Nov. 2, 1798, Nov. 9, 11, 1799, Jan. 6, May 6, 15, 1801).

30. Undated sketch by HD of his children, DSP, 2:85; HD to Henry S. Drinker, April 24, July 25, 1787, Cope Family Papers.

31. *DED*, 1845, 1990 (July 8, 1805, Dec. 19, 1806); HD to Hoare and Potts, Aug. 11, 1787, and to Robinson and Sandwith, Sept. 5, 1787, HD LB 1786–90. For more on the dispute over the Atsion ironworks, see chap. 9.

32. HD to Joseph Sandwith, Dec. 15, 1787, HD LB 1786–90; *DED*, 626–27 (Dec. 11, 12, 1794).

33. Henry S. Drinker to William Drinker, July 5, 1802, Cope Family Papers.

34. Henry S. Drinker to Richard Thomas, Oct. 8, 1793, DSP, 4:67; *DED*, 525, 539 (Nov. 6, Dec. 31, 1793); for the acreage of Henry Sandwith's farm, see HSP 1:101.

35. *Rules of Discipline and Christian Advices*, 64–71.

36. *DED*, 584, 612–13, 621–22 (Aug. 19, Oct. 28–31, Nov. 28, 1794).

37. *DED*, 626 (Dec. 11, 1794).

38. *DED*, 627–28, 629, 632, 635, 758 (Dec. 13, 15, 23, 29, 1794, Dec. 9, 1795).

39. Note by Henry S. Drinker, May 1801, DSP, 1:69.

40. Henry S. Drinker to HD, June 17, 1802, and to James Smith, Oct. 17, 1802, Smith to Henry S. Drinker, Nov. 15, 1802, and Henry S. Drinker to James Smith Jr., Nov. 19, 1802, Cope Family Papers; ED to Henry S. Drinker, Oct. 21, 1802, Cope Evans Family Papers, QSC.

41. Henry S. Drinker to Sarah Smith, Mar. 21, 1803, and to Ann Skyrin, Dec. 5, 1803, ED to Henry S. Drinker, Feb. 12, 1804, Esther Smith to Hannah Drinker, Mar. 15, 1805, and James Smith to Hannah Drinker, Mar. 15, 1805, Cope Family Papers; *DED*, 1594, 1595, 1599 (Nov. 27, Dec. 2, 15, 1802). For Henry Sandwith's actual departure and its emotional impact on his mother, see chap. 9.

42. *DED*, 829 (Aug. 10, 1796).

43. For HD's involvement in the committee revising Philadelphia's Rules of Discipline, see *DED*, 640, 651, 678 (Jan. 13, Feb. 20, May 7, 1795).

44. *DED*, 750–52 (Nov. 9, 10, 12, 15, 1795). For references to Mary and Samuel spending time together in the weeks preceding this earlier crisis, see *DED*, 744, 747, 750 (Oct. 21, Nov. 1, 8, 1795). Mary had "received a broad hint . . . from her father" after going out with Sammy Rhoads and Sally Zane in August 1795; ED did not specify what this "hint" was about, but HD may already have been warning against any intimacy with the young man; see *DED*, 716 (Aug. 13, 1795).

45. *DED*, 823, 829–30 (July 19, Aug. 10, 1796).

46. *DED*, 663–64, 694, 769 (Mar. 30, June 20, 1795, Jan. 7, 1796). For the seduction and abandonment genre, see Cathy N. Davidson, *Revolution and the Word: The Rise of the Novel in America* (New York: Oxford University Press, 1986); Godbeer, *Sexual Revolution*, chap. 8; and Rodney Hessinger, *Seduced, Abandoned, and Reborn: Visions of Youth in Middle-Class America, 1780–1850* (Philadelphia: University of Pennsylvania Press, 2005).

47. *DED*, 830–31 (Aug. 10, 11, 1796).

48. *DED*, 829–31 (Aug. 10, 11, 1796).

49. *DED*, 832–35 (Aug. 13, 14, 16–18, 21–23, 1796).

50. *DED*, 835–36, 838–39 (Aug. 24–26, 29–31, 1796).

51. *DED*, 850, 852 (Oct. 8, 9, 15, 1796).

52. *DED*, 854, 856–58 (Oct. 21, 30, Nov. 1, 4, 1796). Sally Rhoads was already purchasing furniture and other items that the couple would need when they left to set up a household of their own. ED and HD thought it would be tactless "to take the business out of her hands," so they agreed to her supervising these preparations if they could then foot the bill. When the time came for the young couple to move into their new home, ED sent along additional items but acknowledged, perhaps with a hint of condescension, that Rhoads had "showed her taste and judgment in furnishing a house." See *DED*, 883, 888, 905 (Jan. 24, Feb. 7, Apr. 6, 1797). For the purchases made by Sally Rhoads and the Drinkers, see DSP, 1:60, 61, 62.

53. *DED*, 882, 891, 901, 911 (Jan. 24, Feb. 21, Mar. 24, Apr. 25, 1797).

54. *DED*, 835, 902, 906, 909, 911, 921, 979 (Aug. 23, 1796, Mar. 28, Apr. 12, 20, 25, May 23, Nov. 11, 1797). See also Philadelphia Monthly Meeting Northern District Records, QMR: Men's Minutes, 1795–1804, 116, 124, 131, 151, 164; Women's Minutes, 1796–1811, 17, 18–19, 32.

55. *DED*, 913, 921, 979 (May 1, 23, Nov. 11, 1797). ED also stayed away, but that was not unusual.

56. *DED*, 1173, 1342, 1395 (May 28, 1799, Sept. 23, 1800, Mar. 25, 1801).

57. *DED*, 1091, 1100, 1102, 1123 (Oct. 2, 22, 25, Dec. 25, 1798). See also Susan E. Klepp, *Revolutionary Conceptions: Women, Fertility, and Family Limitation in America, 1760–1820* (Chapel Hill: University of North Carolina Press, 2009).

58. *DED*, 931–32, 1452, 1761 (June 17, 1797, Oct. 7, 1801, Aug. 13, 1804). ED's involvement in childbirth as an older woman focused almost exclusively on her daughters. She rarely assisted neighbors during their deliveries, at least in part because of her own precarious health and lengthy periods of confinement at home. For an exception, see *DED*, 415 (Oct. 1, 1783). ED also visited newborn children and their mothers less frequently than most of the women she knew. She was, she wrote, not "desirous" for such visits and so did not look out "for the business," though she did sometimes pay visits of condolence when deliveries ended in tragedy; *DED*, 1216 (Sept. 27, 1799).

59. *DED*, 1087, 1227, 1279, 1452–53 (Sept. 24, 1798, Oct. 23, 1799, Feb. 27, 1800, Oct. 7, 1801).

60. *DED*, 666–67, 931, 1228, 1436–37, 1452 (Apr. 6, 1795, June 17, 1797, Oct. 23–24, 1799, Aug. n.d., Oct. 7, 1801); William Shippen Jr., Document Book, Shippen Family Collection, LC, and Recipe Book, APS.

61. *DED*, 929–30 and n85, 941, 985, 1000–1001, 1011, 1012, 1130, 1195 (June 14–15, July 12, Dec. 10, 1797, Feb. 6–7, Mar. 10, 13, 1798, Jan. 15, Aug. 3, 1799).

62. *DED*, 1286, 1461–62 (Mar. 28, 1800, Nov. 1–5, 1801); see also *DED*, 993 (Jan. 5, 6, 1798).

63. *DED*, 835, 1454 (Aug. 24, 1796, Oct. 9, 1801).

64. Sally and Jacob Downing also had problems with their servants, especially a fellow named Harry, for whom see *DED*, 1574, 1640, 1644–46, 1734, 1761 (Sept. 30, 1802, Apr. 6, 21, 26, 1803, Mar. 22, Aug. 15, 1804). See also chap. 7.

65. *DED*, 1315, 1454, 1506, 1541 (July 5, 1800, Oct. 9, 1801, Apr. 9, Aug. 4, 1802). For the two occasions mentioned by ED when Ann asked her father to intervene, see 653, 1507 (Feb. 24, 1795, Apr. 11, 1802).

66. *DED*, 1453 (Oct. 8, 1454). For more on Hen, see *DED*, 1118, 1315, 1387, 1416, 1417, 1426, 1435 (Dec. 8, 1798, July 5, 1800, Feb. 14, June 3, 5, July 15, Aug. 14, 1801).

67. *DED*, 1455, 1457, 1460 (Oct. 12, 20, 28, 29, 1801).

68. *DED*, 1458, 1460–63 (Oct. 23, 27–29, 31, Nov. 1–7, 1801). For divorce and informal separation in post-revolutionary Philadelphia, see Godbeer, *Sexual Revolution*, chap. 9 (esp. 308–11).

69. Warner Mifflin to HD, Sept. 4, 1796, HD Correspondence, 1785–1840, QSC; *DED*, 473, 609, 1622 (Sept. 28, 1791, Oct. 22, 1794, Feb. 1, 1803).

70. *DED*, 669, 1537 (Apr. 11, 1795, July 25, 1802).

Chapter 9. “To the Place of Fixedness”

1. *DED*, 1682, 1731, 1744, 1806, 1828, 2080 (Sept. 7, 1803, Mar. 4, May 20, 1804, Feb. 11, Apr. 25, 1805, Sept. 28, 1807); HD to John William Gerar de Brahm, June 30, 1795, HD LB 1793–96.

2. *DED*, 1324, 1396, 1603 (July 29, 1800, Mar. 27, 1801, Dec. 31, 1802).

3. *DED*, 1698, 1857, 1897–99, 1978–79, 2014 (Oct. 23, 1803, Aug. 22, 1805, Jan. 8, 15, 18, Nov. 8, 1806, Mar. 3, 1807).

4. *DED*, 1231, 1376, 1679, 1697, 1885, 1990 (Oct. 29, 1799, Jan. 8, 1801, Aug. 28, Oct. 21, 1803, Dec. 13, 1805, Dec. 16, 18, 1806).

5. HD to Samuel Preston, Sept. 1, 1795, HD LB 1793–96.

6. *DED*, 1347, 1476 (Oct. 13, 1800, Dec. 31, 1801); HD to Samuel Preston, Nov. 25, 1794, and to Frederick Pigou Jr., Jan. 14, 1796, HD LB 1793–96; HD to James Morris, Mar. 17, 1803, and to Pigou, Apr. 13, 1803, HD LB 1802–6. For Rebecca Griscomb, see *DED*, 712, 726, 731–32, 735, 740, 743, 745, 747, 754, 759, 761, 764 (Aug. 3, Sept. 8, 22, 29, Oct. 13, 20, 27, Nov. 2, 24, Dec. 9, 14, 22, 1795). The Northern District disowned Rebecca Griscomb on Nov. 24, 1795; see Philadelphia Monthly Meeting Northern District Records, QMR: Women's Minutes, 1791–96, 155, 235–36, 243, 249, and Minutes, Misc. Papers, 1795; see also Marla R. Miller, *Betsy Ross and the Making of America* (New York: Henry Holt, 2010), 289–95.

7. *DED*, 1777–78, 1921 (Nov. 5, 1804, Apr. 18, 1806); HD to Samuel Preston, Sept. 1, 1795, HD LB 1793–96; HD to ED, Oct. 26, 1791, DSP, 4:23; HD to William Dillwyn, July 4, 1806, HD LB 1806–9.

8. George Churchman to HD, June 3, 1791, HD Correspondence, Miscellaneous Manuscripts Collection, FHL; HD to Thomas Scattergood, May 16, 1796, Scattergood Family Papers, QSC.

9. Ruth Anna Rutter to HD, July 1, 1797, HD Correspondence, Miscellaneous Manuscripts Collection; Hannah Yarnall to HD, June 19, 1798, HD Correspondence, 1785–1840, QSC; HD to Thomas Scattergood, Dec. 24, 1794, Scattergood Family Papers.

10. HD to Joseph Sandwith, Apr. 26, 1792, HD LB 1790–93; HD to Daniel Smith, June 24, 1806, and to Robert McClure, Jan. 22, 1808, HD LB 1806–9; *DED*, 1789 (Dec. 31, 1804).

11. HD to Frederick Pigou Jr., Dec. 13, 1802, HD LB 1802–6; HD to Robert Bowne, Dec. 22, 1806, and to Samuel Preston, Mar. 19, 1808, HD LB 1806–9.

12. HD to Francis Semple, May 16, 1804, HD LB 1802–6; HD to John Richards, May 24, 1806, HD LB 1806–9; see also HD to William Alexander, Aug. 18, 1804, to Samuel Law, Apr. 2, 1805, and to Edward James, May 24, 1805, HD LB 1802–6. For Kirby, HD to Samuel Law, Jan. 16, Apr. 2, 1805, to William Parker, Jan. 17, 1805, and to Benjamin Tallmadge, Apr. 6, 1805, HD LB 1802–6; for Bowne, HD to Isaac Hicks, Feb. 10, 14, 18, Apr. 18, June 18, 1804, HD LB 1802–6; *DED*, 1728 (Feb. 15, 1804).

13. HD to administrators for Samuel Wallis, June 1, 1802, HD LB 1800–1802; HD to Daniel Smith, Mar. 1, May 3, Aug. 31, Sept. 14, Oct. 12, 1803, HD LB 1802–6; HD to Charles Huston, May 29, 1806, to Daniel Smith, Apr. 13, 1807, and to John Boyd, Aug. 6, 1807, HD LB 1806–9; see also Norman B. Wilkinson, "Land Policy and Speculation in Pennsylvania, 1779–1800" (Ph.D. diss., University of Pennsylvania, 1958), 92–104.

14. HD to Augustine Smith, Feb. 28, 1806, HD LB 1802–6; see also HD to Samuel Preston, Dec. 18, 1794, HD LB 1793–96; to Ephraim Kirby, June 25, 1803, and to Samuel Law, Nov. 3, 1803, HD LB 1802–6; HD to Law, Dec. 26, 1808, Jan. 16, 1809, HD LB 1806–9. For the rumors about lead, see HD to John Tyler, July 20, 1807, HD LB 1806–9.

15. *DED*, 1732–34 (Mar. 14, 15, 21, 22, 1804).

16. HD to Hicks, Jenkins, and Co., June 7, 14, July 20, 27, 1804, to Richard Stockton, Sept. 5, 1804, to Thomas Eddy, Sept. 17, 1804 (quotation), Feb. 7, 1805, and to Blackwell and McFarlane, Nov. 16, 1804, Aug. 22, 1805, HD LB 1802–6; HD to Jonathan Hunn, Oct. 29, 1807, HD LB 1806–9; *DED*, 1756, 1765–69, 1776–78, 1781, 1784, 1785, 1798, 1818, 1822–25, 1828–31, 1840–41, 1845, 1964, 1975, 1976 (July 18, Sept. 4–8, 10, 11, 14, 19, 21, 22, 25–27, 29, Oct. 29, Nov. 2, 3, 10, 22, Dec. 14, 17, 1804, Jan. 3–5, Mar. 20, 22, Apr. 3–6, 8, 11–13, 15, 24, 25, 30, May 2, 3, 7, 8, June 20, July 8, 1805, Sept. 10, Oct. 24, 26, 1806).

17. HD to Thomas Potts, Mar. 14, 1801, HD LB 1800–1802.

18. HD to Isaac Hicks, Apr. 6, 1807, to Hinks, Jenkins, and Co., Apr. 4, May 2, 1807, May 19, June 23, 28, Aug. 10, 1808, to James Potts, Feb. 24, June 15, 1808, and to Robert Potts, Sept. 20, 1806, Jan. 7, Mar. 5, 1807, Feb. 29, May 4, 1808, May 3, 1809, HD LB 1806–9; *DED*, 1724, 1725 (Jan. 13, 15, 23, 1803). For references to John Lawless, see *DED*, 1728, 1767, 1769 (Feb. 10, 11, Sept. 21, 29, 1804); see also *DED*, 768n5.

19. For Townsend and Kirk, *DED,* 1620–21, 1695, 1704 (Jan. 27, Oct. 13, Nov. 14, 1803); for Hodskinson, *DED,* 1682, 1909 (Sept. 9, 1803, Feb. 25, 1806); HD to Marshall Bennett and James Hyde, Apr. 27, 1807, May 17, 1809, and to Ann Marie Hodskinson, Nov. 9, 1808, HD LB 1806–9; for Henry James, *DED,* 2069, 2084, 2086, 2091 (Aug. 26, Oct. 5, 6, 12, 31, 1807); HD to James McIntire, Apr. 20, 1808, HD LB 1806–9.

20. DED, 1819 (Mar. 25, 1805); HD to Thomas Scattergood, May 16, 1796, Scattergood Family Papers; HD to William Dillwyn, July 4, 1806, to Charles Huston, May 25, 1807, and to Samuel Law, July 16, 1808, HD LB 1806–9.

21. *DED,* 1771, 1782, 1799, 1823, 1826, 1850, 1868, 1869, 1872–73, 1953, 1985, 1987, 2082, 2084, 2094 (Oct. 7, Nov. 26, 28, 1804, Jan. 11, Apr. 6, 16, July 25, Oct. 1, 3, 22, 23, 1805, Aug. 1, Dec. 2, 4, 5, 1806, Oct. 2, 8, Nov. 10, 1807); HD to John Tyler, Jan. 20, 1808, HD LB 1806–9. HD's letters from the last two years of his life were sprinkled with references to Henry Sandwith's and John Skyrin's expeditions on his behalf. William did go on one short business trip in 1805, and another the following year; he ventured farther afield in August 1807, returning twelve days later; *DED,* 1836, 1985, 1987, 2060, 2064 (June 3, 5, 1805, Dec. 2, 4, 5, 1806, July 30, 31, Aug. 11, 1807).

22. Henry S. Drinker to HD, May 1, 1804, and to William Drinker, July 19, 1805, Cope Family Papers, HSP.

23. David Sands to HD, July 18, 1796, HD Correspondence, 1785–1840; William Allen to HD, May 25, 1801, HSDP; HD to Mercy Ellis, Jan. 26, 1807, HD LB 1806–9; *DED,* 1403, 1603, 1680 (Apr. 22, 1801, Dec. 31, 1802, Sept. 1, 1803).

24. *DED,* 1807–17 passim (Feb. 20–Mar. 18, 1805).

25. *DED,* 1824, 1829–31, 1921, 1974, 1994 (Apr. 11, 30, May 2, 3, 7, 8, 1805, Apr. 18, Oct. 18, December 31, 1806).

26. *DED,* 1835, 1872, 1885, 1992, 2089 (May 28, Oct. 20, Dec. 11, 13, 1805, Dec. 25, 1806, Oct. 24, 1807).

27. *DED,* 1652–54, 1659, 1705, 1717, 1835, 1845, 1846, 1870–71, 1875, 1883–85, 1888, 1925, 1973 (May 18, 21, 23, 25, 26, June 17, Nov. 18, 19, Dec. 31, 1803, May 28, July 7, 10, Oct. 6, 16, Nov. 1, 2, Dec. 6, 8, 11–13, 26, 1805, May 6, Oct. 17, 1806).

28. *DED,* 1274, 1483, 1502, 1777, 1831, 1899, 1901, 1921, 2002, 2014 (Feb. 12, 1800, Jan. 1, Mar. 26, 27, 1802, Nov. 1, 1804, May 8, 1805, Jan. 18, 24, Apr. 19, 1806, Jan. 18, Mar. 5, 1807); for the notations on the outside covers of her diaries about pickling walnuts, *DED,* 1612, 1797 (n.d.).

29. *DED,* 1254, 1478, 1790, 1791, 1793, 1796 (Mar. 6, 1799, Mar. 26, 1801, Feb. 6, Apr. 6, 24, May 2, July 18, Oct. 16, Dec. 30, 1804). In the 1790s, she had sometimes been a little defensive about the amount of time she could now spend reading. "Though I seldom make mention of any other employment," she wrote in 1795, "yet I believe I may say, without vanity, that I was never an indolent person, or remarkably bookish, though more so for five or six years past than at any other time since I was married, having more leisure. When my children were young, I seldom read a volume"; *DED,*

683–84 (May 22, 1795). Early the following year, she mentioned the knitting and needlework she had done "to show that I have not spent the day reading"; *DED*, 780 (Feb. 29, 1796).

30. *DED*, 1537, 1595, 1929–30 (July 25, Dec. 2, 1802, May 15, 1806). ED's sensitivity about visits from her children was not new. In the summer of 1791, she spent several weeks in Germantown and noted resentfully that Henry Sandwith, who had stayed in Philadelphia, made little effort to visit her there. One evening that July, she sat in her landlady's parlor "busy thinking and mending stockings for my son Henry, who has not thought it worth his while to come to see me, though I have been here near two weeks"; *DED*, 464 (July 23, 1791).

31. *DED*, 1679 (Aug. 29, 1803); for Ann and John Skyrin, *DED*, 1726, 1756, 1757, 1759, 1828–29, 1831–33 (Jan. 26, 27, July 17, 21, Aug. 2, 3, 1804, Apr. 25, 27, 29, May 6, 15–17, 1805); for Samuel and Mary Rhoads, *DED*, 1961, 1964, 1967, 1970, 1972, 1975, 1983, 1984, 1988, 1990, 2036, 2047 (Sept. 1, 10, 23, Oct. 3, 13, 23, Nov. 24, 26, 27, Dec. 8, 19, 1806, May 16, June 20, 1807); for Jacob Downing, *DED*, 1990 (Dec. 19, 1806); HD to William Fisher, Apr. 2, 1804, HD LB 1802–6.

32. *DED*, 1622, 1631, 1635, 1672, 1724, 1730, 1751, 1783, 1787, 1834, 1837, 1857, 1972 (Feb. 1, Mar. 4, 17, Aug. 1, 2, 1803, Jan. 13, Mar. 2, June 24, Dec. 6, 26, 1804, May 23, June 8, Aug. 22, 1805, Oct. 11, 1806).

33. Cope had married Mary Drinker, daughter of HD's brother John; Thomas had married Hannah Drinker, another daughter of the same John Drinker.

34. *DED*, 1902, 1964, 1973–75, 1977, 1979–81 (Feb. 1, Sept. 10, Oct. 15, 18, 25, Nov. 3, 10–18, 1806); Phineas Bond [British consul general for the Middle and Southern States of America], Introduction for Henry S. Drinker, Philadelphia, Nov. 18, 1806, and Dill M. Erkine [British consul in Philadelphia] to Lord Minto [HM's governor general, Calcutta], Nov. 19, 1806, DSP, 5:19.

35. *DED*, 1981–83 (Nov. 19–23, 1806).

36. *DED*, 1984, 1986, 1991, 1992, 2020, 2027, 2028, 2033, 2087, 2090–91, 2095 (Nov. 26, Dec. 2, 22, 24, 1806, Mar. 24, 26, Apr. 16, 19, May 7, Oct. 15, 30, Nov. 13, 1807); Henry S. Drinker to HD, May 3, 1807, DSP, 5:29.

37. *DED*, 1244, 1437, 1951, 1993, 2009, 2013, 2021 (Dec. 4, 1799, Aug. 20, 1801, July 24, Dec. 31, 1806, Feb. 12, Mar. 1, 27, 1807); Sarah Blank Dine, "Diaries and Doctors: Elizabeth Drinker and Philadelphia Medical Practice, 1760–1810," *PH* 68 (2001): 429–30.

38. *DED*, 1994, 2003, 2009, 2011, 2012 (Dec. 31, 1806, Jan. 19, Feb. 13, 17, 23, 26, 1807).

39. *DED*, 2023, 2025, 2029, 2030, 2032, 2037, 2040 (Apr. 2, 9, 10, 22, 25, May 1, 18, 19, 30, 1807).

40. *DED*, 2045–49 (June 13, 16, 20, 23, 25, 26, 1807).

41. *DED*, 2051, 2055, 2058, 2059 (July 3, 12, 14, 24, 25, 1807).

42. *DED*, 2059–63, 2065, 2066 (July 27, 29, 30, Aug. 3, 5, 6, 8, 9, 14, 17, 1807).

43. HD to James Allinson, Aug. 11, 21, Sept. 1, 1807, HD LB 1806–9.

44. *DED,* 2067, 2069, 2071–73, 2076 (Aug. 19, 20, 25, 26, Sept. 3, 4, 7, 16, 1807).

45. *DED,* 2079–80 (Sept. 22–24, 1807).

46. *DED,* 2080–81 (Sept. 28, 1807). For MS, see *DED,* 2067, 2068, 2070, 2075 (Aug. 20, 25, 30, Sept. 13, 1807). That ED made so little mention of MS's illness and help during those weeks indicates where her emotional priorities lay.

47. *DED,* 2081, 2083, 2085, 2087 (Sept. 29, Oct. 4, 9, 15, 1807).

48. *DED,* 1905, 1906, 2029, 2035, 2039, 2052 (Feb. 12, 13, 1806, Apr. 21, May 12, 27, July 6, 1807).

49. HD to John Canan, Oct. 2, 1807, HD LB 1806–9; *DED,* 2081, 2085, 2088, 2089, 2091 (Sept. 29, Oct. 10, 20, 24, 25, Nov. 1, 1807).

50. *DED,* 2091–94, 2096 (Nov. 2, 7, 10, 17, 1807).

51. *DED,* 2096 (Nov. 18, 1807); *Poulson's American Daily Advertiser,* Dec. 2, 1807.

52. HD to John Tyler, Jan. 11, 1808, to Samuel A. Law, Jan. 25, 1808, to William Henry Pigou, May 9, 1808, and to Thomas Brown, Feb. 4, 1809, HD LB 1806–9; "Extracts from E.D.'s Diary," DSP, 5:45. HD inserted a comment of his own, shown here in italics, after one of the entries: "15th 11th month [1806]. This is the middle of the 11th month, half gone. What may be the situation of our family this day twelve month the Lord only knows! May we deserve his favor." [*E.D. was taken ill in the evening of the 18th of the 11th month 1807, one year and three days after writing the above.*]

53. HD to John Allen, Mar. 2, 1808, HD LB 1806–9; Ann Mifflin to HD, Apr. [?], 1808, HSDP.

54. HD to Hicks, Jenkins, and Co., Apr. 9, 1808, to Samuel Law, Sept. 3, 1808, and to Robert Rose, Dec. 12, 1808, HD LB 1806–9; *DED,* 2080 (Sept. 28, 1807); Benjamin Rush, Commonplace Book, 1792–1813, APS, published in George W. Corner, ed., *The Autobiography of Benjamin Rush: His "Travels through Life" Together with His Commonplace Book for 1789–1813* (Princeton, N.J.: Princeton University Press, 1948), 316.

Epilogue

1. Will of Henry Drinker, Mar. 28, 1808, DSP, 1:110.

2. Estate of Henry Drinker, 1809: List of Plate, DSP, 5:55, and Plate Belonging to Mary Sandwith and William Drinker Sent to Bank of North America, Nov. 10, 1809, DSP, 5:56.

3. Summary of MS's three wills, DSP, 5:67; for William's payment of rent to Ann Coffin, DSP, 5:91, 99, 107; for the cause of William's death, Philadelphia Monthly Meeting Minutes: Grave Books, 1814–23, QMR; for the distribution of William's estate, DSP, 1:127, 128.

4. For William's payment of bills for the schooling of Henry Sandwith's children, see DSP, 5:82; for Henry Sandwith's suicide, see James P. Parke, "Records of Births, Marriages, and Deaths of Many Acquaintances of James P. Parke," HSP; for the eventual

division of HD's estate, see DSP, 5:110–23. Relative Thomas P. Cope claimed that both William and Henry Sandwith committed suicide, but this appears to have been untrue. Though Cope did not hold the three Drinker daughters responsible for their husbands' financial problems, he did comment: none of them was "remarkable for being a frugal housewife"; Thomas P. Cope Diary ("My Mirror and Record of Events"), vol. 11, Mar. 17, 1851, QSC.

5. For William's destruction of family papers, see DSP, 5:90. Henry Drinker Biddle, *Extracts from the Diary of Elizabeth Drinker, from 1759 to 1807, A.D.* (Philadelphia: J. B. Lippincott, 1889); Henry Drinker Biddle, *The Drinker Family in America* (Philadelphia: J. B. Lippincott, 1893); Cecil K. Drinker, *Not So Long Ago: A Chronicle of Medicine and Doctors in Colonial Philadelphia* (New York: Oxford University Press, 1937); Henry S. Drinker, *History of the Drinker Family* (published privately, 1961). I am grateful to Cary Hutto for her assistance in tracking down accession information.

6. Journal of Ann Warder, Jan. 15, 1787, Ann Head Warder Papers, HSP; Benjamin Rush, Commonplace Book, 1792–1813, APS, published in George W. Corner, ed., *The Autobiography of Benjamin Rush: His "Travels through Life" Together with His Commonplace Book for 1789–1813* (Princeton, N.J.: Princeton University Press, 1948), 316; *Poulson's American Daily Advertiser*, June 29, 1809.

7. *Poulson's American Daily Advertiser*, Dec. 2, 1807.

8. *DED*, 1682, 1984, 2061 (Sept. 7, 1803, Nov. 26, 1806, Aug. 1, 1807).

9. *DED*, 589, 1526 (Sept. 4, 1794, June 22, 1802).

Index

Unless otherwise stated, familial relationships in parentheses are to Henry and Elizabeth Drinker.